Graphical Presentation of the Forecasting Process (continued)

Phase 3: Evaluation

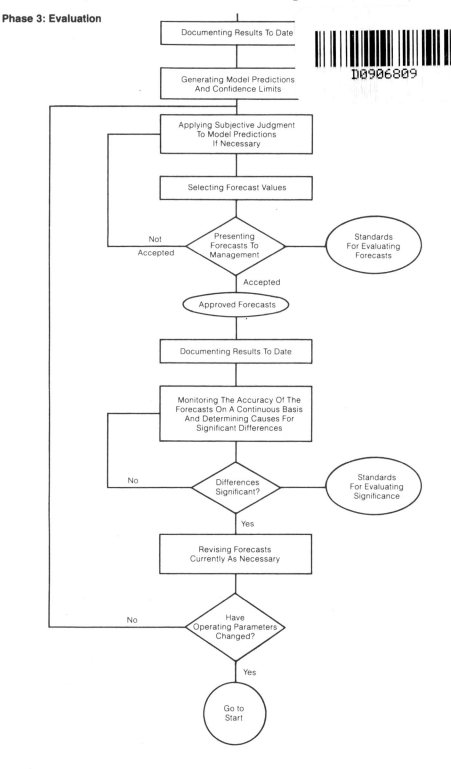

D0906809

The Modern Forecaster

The
Modern
Forecaster:

The Forecasting Process Through Data Analysis

Hans Levenbach
James P. Cleary

LIFETIME LEARNING PUBLICATIONS
Belmont, California

A division of Wadsworth, Inc.

London, Singapore, Sydney, Toronto, Mexico City

Designer: Richard Kharibian
Composition: Graphic Typesetting Service

Printed in the United States of America

1 2 3 4 5 6 7 8 9 10———87 86 85 84

Library of Congress Cataloging in Publication Data

Levenbach, Hans.
   The modern forecaster.

   Adaptation of: The beginning forecaster / Hans Levenbach, James P. Cleary. ©1981. The professional forecaster / James P. Cleary, Hans Levenbach. ©1982.
   Bibliography: p.
   Includes index.
   1. Economic forecasting.   2. Business forecasting.
3. Forecasting.   I. Cleary, James P.   II. Levenbach, Hans. Beginning forecaster.   III. Cleary, James P. Professional forecaster.   IV. Title.

HB3730.L413   1984   338.5'442   84–889
ISBN 0-534-03361-X

Contents

"An optimist is someone who believes the future is uncertain."

Edward Teller

Preface

Purpose of This Book

The Modern Forecaster is designed as a one-term course in beginning forecasting methods. It is suitable for courses offered in programs in Management Science or Quantitative Methods departments, in departments of Economics, Industrial Engineering, or Operations Research, as well as in corresponding one-term continuing education courses.

Our aim is to prepare a student for the real-world of business forecasting through a unified and practical presentation of the subject. To this end *The Modern Forecaster* reflects the most modern methods used by forecasters in leading American corporations. The principal unifying element of this book is the presentation of *forecasting as a process,* rather than as a series of disconnected techniques. A further unifying element is our constant emphasis on *data analysis.* The exercises, examples, and workshops included in this work are also consistent with our goal of preparing the reader for the immediate practice of forecasting in the world of work.

While *The Modern Forecaster* is an adaptation of our earlier books, *The Beginning Forecaster* and *The Professional Forecaster,* it has evolved primarily from our lectures at Columbia University and Stevens Institute of Technology. *The Modern Forecaster* differs from the earlier works in several significant respects, the most important of which is its orientation to a classroom environment and its reflection of our experience with students in management sciences, industrial engineering, and business.

Features

The Modern Forecaster features, in particular, the following elements:

- Establishment of a *process* for effective forecasting. Specific methods and techniques are presented within the context of the overall process.

- Selection of the forecasting and analytical techniques most appropriate for any given problem. The methods discussed are the ones that have proved to be most useful and reliable to us as practicing forecasters.

- Preliminary *analysis of data* before attempting to build models. Computer-generated graphic displays enable you to see in one picture what you might otherwise have to glean from a stack of computer printouts.

- Refocusing the attention of practitioners away from the *mechanistic execution of computer programs* and towards a greater understanding of data and the processes generating data.

- Use of *robust/resistant methods* in addition to traditional methods to ensure that a few bad data values do not seriously distort the conclusions that are reached. Experience with a wide variety of practical applications has convinced us that data rarely perform well enough for the direct application of traditional modeling assumptions. The robust/resistant methods produce results that are less subject to the distortions caused by a few outlying data values. By comparing traditional and robust results, the practitioner is in a better position to decide which results are most appropriate for the problem at hand.

In addition, this volume shows how the results from the traditionally diverse fields of time series and econometric modeling can be combined into a decisive forecast, which can be presented authoritatively and credibly.

Examples are used wherever possible throughout the book. They are predominantly drawn from the experience of the authors in the telecommunications business on the assumption that the characteristics of the data are what are important, and not whether or not the data are telephone-related. Other data sets from nontele communications sources have also been used where appropriate to make certain points or illustrate a particular technique. These data sets are listed in Appendix B.

Problems are provided at the end of Parts 1, 2, 3, and 5 to complement chapter material. They serve to reinforce the concepts and technical details of the forecasting methodologies described in the text. These problems can be assigned for students to complete on an individual basis.

Computer packages are widely available to perform a whole range of forecasting functions in a cost-effective and timely fashion. The twelve *Computer Workshops* in this text are designed to help the student understand the steps in developing a forecast. These Workshops will be completed by small teams (3–4 students) as a joint project on a microprocessor or via timesharing on a mainframe computer. The Workshops can be completed using the data from Appendix 3 or data selected from your own sources. By completing them in sequence, students will have sufficient material from each Workshop for a case presentation. Workshop 12 provides a format for a model-building case presentation.

Coverage

Our experience suggests that, in practice, the failure of many forecasting efforts begins with flaws in the quality and handling of data rather than in the lack of modeling sophistication. Thus our objective has been to place greater emphasis on data-analytic methodology (much of it intuitive and graphical) as a key to improved forecasting.

A number of forecasting methods useful to students of forecasting are not covered in great detail in this text. The omitted methods are typically used when data are scarce or nonexistent. As an example, the whole area known as technological forecasting, which requires a grounding in probabilistic (in contrast to statistical) concepts, is not treated. Likewise, new-product forecasting, for which data are unavailable, also falls within this category. Since this book deals with exploratory data analysis along with confirmatory modeling, we have emphasized techniques for which a reasonable amount of data are available or can be collected.

Organization

The Modern Forecaster is divided into five parts. The first part comprises four chapters that introduce the forecasting process. In Part 2, three chapters deal with exploratory data analysis and the importance of graphical techniques of displaying and summarizing data. In Part 3, seven chapters deal with smoothing and regression techniques useful for short-term forecasting applications. The first of these seven chapters, Chapter 8, treats forecasting with classical exponential smoothing models. Chapter 9 deals with seasonal adjustment and provides a subjective method for projecting a cyclical (or business cycle) component into the near future. Chapters 10 and 11 deal with regression methods for developing functional relationships between one or more variables (such methods are basic to all quantitative forecasting applications) and the uses and interrelationships of these methods. Chapter 12 focuses on the often-neglected subject of residual analysis for testing modeling assumptions. Chapter 13 treats serial correlation correction procedures. Chapter 14 describes the use of confidence limits for forecast tracking and evaluation.

Part 4 contains six chapters on the econometric approach to forecasting. This part begins with an introduction to econometric methods (Chapter 15), then discusses demand analysis as a forecasting process (Chapter 16), treats estimation of demand elasticities (Chapter 17), and deals with the uses of dummies and lagged variables (Chapter 18). Additional specification issues are discussed in Chapter 19 and the section closes with the pooling of cross-sectional and time series data (Chapter 20).

Part 5 contains six chapters on time series modeling that use the Box-Jenkins methodology. The identification, estimation, and diagnostic checking of the ARIMA class of univariate time series models are covered extensively in Chapters 21–25. Chapter 26 presents some expanded examples of these techniques.

The last part of the book is a single chapter (Chapter 27), which summarizes management principles on which the forecasting process is based.

Acknowledgments

The authors would like to express their appreciation and indebtedness to the late Sir Ronald A. Fisher, F.R.S., Cambridge, and to Hafner Publishing Co. for permission to reprint Table IV from their book, *Statistical Methods For Research Workers;* to Professor E. S. Pearson and the *Biometrika* trustees for permission to reproduce the materials in Appendix A, Tables 1, 3, and 4; and to Professors J. Durbin and G. S. Watson for the values in Appendix A, Table 5.

Hans Levenbach
James P. Cleary

The Modern Forecaster

Part 1

Thinking About Forecasting

CHAPTER 1

Why Is Forecasting a Process?

As you begin to read this book, you may find it helpful to keep the following in mind:

- A grasp of mathematical and statistical knowledge, while necessary for the forecaster, will not in itself ensure successful forecasting.
- For the best results, apply such knowledge within a sound framework—a forecasting process.
- Following a sound process, which describes the sequence of activities to be followed, can reduce chances of inadvertently overlooking a key step.
- Omission of a key step, whether deliberate or inadvertent, can jeopardize a forecaster's credibility, and credibility is a forecaster's livelihood.

This chapter describes

- What a forecasting process is.
- Why it is a necessary approach in the forecasting profession.
- How, when, and by whom forecasting is done.

FORECASTING DEFINED

Probably the simplest definition of forecasting is that it is a process which has as its objective the prediction of future events or conditions. More precisely, forecasting attempts to predict change. If future events represented only a readily quantifiable change from historical events, future events or conditions could be predicted through quantitative projections of historical trends into the future. Methodologies that are used to describe historical events with mathematical equations (or a model) for the purpose of predicting future events are classified as quantitative projection techniques. However, there is much more to forecasting than projecting past trends.

Experience and intuitive reasoning quickly reveal that future events or conditions are not solely a function of historical trends. Even familiar abstractions such as trend, cycle, and seasonality, while extremely useful to business forecasters, cannot be completely relied upon when it comes to predicting future events. In the commercial world, goods and services are bought by individuals for innumerable reasons. Therefore, business forecasting must include other ingredients to complement quantitative projection techniques.

A forecast is not an end product but rather an input to the decision-making process. A forecast is a prediction of what will happen under an assumed set of circumstances. Often, a forecast is a prediction of future values of one or more variables under "business as usual" conditions. In planning activities, this is often referred to as the status quo, or, the "base case." Forecasts are also required for a variety of "what if" situations and for the formulation of business plans to alter base case projections that have proved unsatisfactory.

Learning from Actual Examples of Forecasting

As a unifying thread throughout this book, we shall frequently examine practical forecasting problems drawn from our experience in forecasting for the telephone industry. Where appropriate, we shall also use time series (data about changes through time) from other sources, to illustrate forecasting methods and to compare or contrast results.

The forecasting problems we shall borrow from telephone-industry experience arise from the requirement for accurate one- and two-year-ahead forecasts of revenues, products, and services. Specifically, throughout the book we shall develop forecasts of revenues to be derived from toll calls made by business customers.

The telecommunications industry involves a number of considerations common to many forecasting applications (Figure 1.1). For example, the overall state of the economy, as measured by nonfarm employment, is known to influence the demand

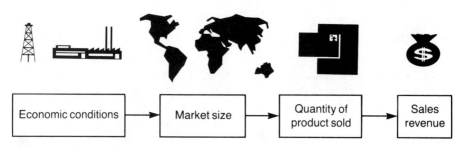

Figure 1.1 A generic forecasting problem.

for business telephone service. For other industries, different measures of economic activity, such as interest rates, industrial production, the unemployment rate, Gross National Product, volume of imports versus exports, inflation rates, or other variables, may have special significance in determining the size of some market at a designated time.

The market that generates telephone toll revenues may be viewed, in part, as the number of business telephones from which calls can be made (Figure 1.2). Toll messages (calls) may be viewed as the quantity of service rendered (or product sold). There is not a one-to-one correspondence between revenues and messages because additional factors, such as the distance between the parties, time of day, duration of calls, and whether or not an operator is needed, allow for variation in the revenue per message.

The revenue-quantity relationship in the most general sense is similar to what would be encountered in forecasting revenues from passenger-miles of transportation, mortgage commitments from housing starts, and revenues from barrels of crude oil after refining. In each instance, the revenue depends on the mix of the products sold. However, for financial planning purposes, very accurate total revenue forecasts can be derived without the necessity of forecasting every product or product combination and multiplying that by the sales price.

In this book we shall analyze and forecast variables by emphasizing basic forecasting techniques. We shall begin the analysis with classical approaches and follow them with robust/resistant solutions (those which safeguard against unusual values and departures from assumptions) to the same problems. More advanced techniques, including the ARIMA method (Autoregressive-Integrated-Moving Average, or Box-Jenkins) and econometric modeling with multiple variables and equations, will be applied as well.

Forecasting as a Process

The process of forecasting is not an exact science but is more like an art form. As with any worthwhile art form, the forecasting process is definitive and systematic,

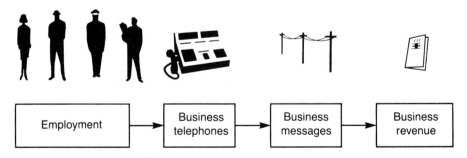

Figure 1.2 A telecommunications forecasting problem.

and is supported by a set of special tools and techniques that are dependent upon human judgment and intuition.

For example, business forecasting generally attempts to predict future customer demand for a company's goods and services. Once forecasting needs are identified, a data-gathering network capable of continuously providing pertinent information about market conditions must be established. The data that have been gathered are then placed into some form of data base for easy analysis. Data gathering and analysis precede and also follow the production of the forecast.

The starting point for the forecasting process is to identify all the things that will be needed to put a forecast together. These are inputs: typical inputs might be

- Finding sources of data about the item to be forecast.
- Obtaining information about external conditions—that is, about those factors in the environment influencing a forecast.
- Determining the needs of the user of the forecast.
- Gathering the human and financial resources required to produce a forecast.
- Listing projection techniques.

These are not only inputs to the forecasting process but also inputs to the judgment that is applied throughout the process.

The forecasting process also requires knowledge about the outputs of the process:

- Formatting the output of the final product.
- Presenting the forecast to the forecast users.
- Evaluating the forecast on an ongoing basis.

The forecast user will generally specify the format of the forecast output and consult with the forecaster about the kinds of analyses and/or variables that should be considered.

The end product of the forecasting process is clearly the forecast itself. A forecast should not be considered as being permanent or never changing. The dynamic nature of any market (customer demands for goods and services) dictates that the forecasting process be reviewable and repeatable at some future time. Since the value of any forecast is based on the degree to which it can provide information to a decision-making process, the view of a market and its demands on a company within that marketplace (as expressed in terms of a forecast) must be current to be useful.

The process by which forecasting is done is emphasized for several reasons. First, of primary importance to anyone who makes a forecast is that better forecasts will result if the proper process has been meticulously followed.

Second, a structured method for forecasting leads to a better understanding of the factors that influence demand for a product or service. The forecaster who has a good handle on demographic, economic, political, land-use, competition, and pricing considerations will develop expertise in making or evaluating forecasts for these considerations and relating them to the demand for a company's services.

A third reason for emphasizing the process of forecasting is that it focuses attention on selecting the right methodology for a given forecast. For example, one goal is to be certain not to use short-range methods for long-range forecasts. Instead of focusing first on the numbers they hope will result from a forecast, forecast managers and users should decide which method is likely to produce the most accurate forecast.

WHAT ARE FORECASTING MODELS?

A forecasting model is a job aid for forecasters: it attempts to create a simplified representation of reality. The forecaster tries to include those factors which are critical and exclude those which are not. This process of stripping away the non-essential and concentrating on the essential is the essence of modeling in the forecasting profession.

Although simplified, models permit the forecaster to estimate the effects of important future events or trends. In the telecommunications industry, for example, there are thousands of reasons why subscribers want their telephones connected or disconnected, or place calls over the switching network. It is beyond the scope of the forecaster to deal with all these reasons. Therefore, a forecaster attempts to distill these many influences into a limited number of the most pertinent factors.

As an example, consider a forecasting model for telephone demand in Detroit, Michigan; the model might look like Figure 1.3. This model assumes that the automobile industry creates jobs for people who then buy homes or rent apartments and want telecommunications services. The telephone forecaster's job, for instance, is to determine the relationships between employment levels, household growth, land use, and telephone demand.

Models are usually designed by using mathematical equations to represent the real situation being analyzed. Such an equation might take the form

$$\text{Telephone demand} = b_0 + b_1 \text{ (Number of employees)} + b_2 \text{ (Number of housing starts)},$$

where b_0, b_1, and b_2 are coefficients determined from data. Models such as these simplify the analysis of some problems, but, of course, sacrifice the ability to account for all the factors that cause people to behave as they do. Notice that the model summarized in the equation does not include information on the prices of other goods and services. There is a trade-off between simplicity and completeness in every model-building effort.

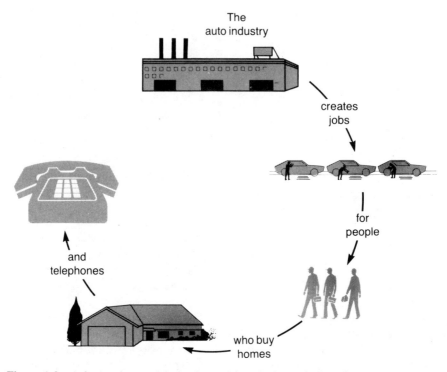

Figure 1.3   A forecasting model: the demand for telephones in Detroit.

Just as the forecasting process is tangible and structured, so are modeling or projection techniques. They perform the same task regardless of the data they use: while some of the inputs to the forecasting process are dependent upon the nature of the given situation, projection techniques are not. For this reason, the forecaster must exercise sound judgment in selecting and using the projection techniques for any given forecast. Through a systematic process of elimination, the forecaster can identify those projection techniques which will provide the greatest assistance in the development of the forecast output.

HOW TO DEVELOP A FORECAST

The process for developing a specific forecast consists of seven basic steps:

1. Set down basic facts about past trends and forecasts.
2. Determine causes of changes in past demand trends.
3. Determine causes of differences between previous forecasts and actual behavior.

4. Determine factors likely to affect future demand.

5. Make the forecast for some future period and provide the user with a measure of its accuracy and reliability.

6. Follow up on the accuracy of the forecast continually and determine the reasons for significant differences from the forecast.

7. Revise forecasts when necessary.

For anything which is to be forecast, there is a "start" point for the first forecast made of that product, but there is no "end" point until either the product no longer exists in its original form or there is no longer a need to forecast it. The first forecast utilizes all of the steps of the forecasting process. All following forecasts are revisions or extensions in time of the original forecast.

WHO MAKES THE FORECAST?

In this book, we assume that the forecaster and the person in need of a forecast are different people. This distinction is, of course, not a necessity, but rather a recognition that businesses tend to specialize their functions. Professional forecasting requires the development of unique knowledge and skills to support the planning function. This has resulted in the significant growth of lucrative forecasting and consulting firms in the past decade.

Role of the Forecaster

The forecaster is an advisor. The completed forecast must meet the requirements of the user in terms of timeliness, format, perhaps methodology, and presentation. In the forecaster–problem-solver partnership, the problem-solver is knowledgeable about the environment surrounding the problem and variables that should probably be considered. The forecaster is knowledgeable about the forecasting process and specific forecasting methods most appropriate for the problem. In large businesses, the volume and complexity of required forecasts is usually sufficient to support full-time forecasting staffs.

How Planners Use Forecasts

The diversity of business activities today has created work for a variety of planners—each with a special set of problems. The problems may be viewed in terms of a business's function and a time period for that function.

Executive managers are concerned with current performance but even more concerned with future direction—what is called strategic planning. In which markets should the business operate over the next five to ten years? An executive manager must identify and analyze key trends and forces that may affect the formulation and execution of strategies, including economic trends, technological developments, political climates, market environments, and assessment of potential competitors. In addition to strategic planning, executive managers are concerned with financial planning, for which they need short-term (one to three months), medium-term (up to two years), and long-term (greater than two years) forecasts.

Marketing managers are concerned with short- and long-term forecasts of demand for products and services. Forecasting methods suited to products and services have existed for some time. In forecasting a new product, these methods are applicable if analogous products exist or if careful market trials can be conducted. The demand for the product can then be related to the economic or demographic characteristics of the people in the market areas. These relationships can then be used to predict the product's acceptance in other areas having their own economic and demographic characteristics.

For *planners of competitive strategies,* forecasting techniques can be used to forecast the total market—for example, total gasoline consumption, passenger-miles of traffic between cities, automobile purchases by size (sedan, compact, subcompacts), computer storage requirements, or other such variables. Given the total market, each firm within it will then estimate its market share on the basis of product differences, price, advertising, quality of service, market coverage (including the size of a sales force), geography, and other factors specific to the market for the product or service. In many cases, market share is also estimated by using quantitative models.

Production and inventory control managers are generally concerned with short-term forecasts. In inventory control, exponential smoothing models find extensive application. (This technique is like a weighted moving average, in which the most current data are given the greatest weight.) For extremely complex inventory systems, these models provide forecasts which are closely monitored for deviations between estimated and actual inventories. Sometimes minor deviations can be modeled and used to alter future predictions. Large deviations are "flagged" as exceptions, for scrutiny and reevaluation of the model generating the forecasts.

✓ SUMMARY

- Forecasting is a structured process which produces a specific output, namely advice about the future. The steps of the forecasting process are independent of the item to be forecast and the input parameters.

- The purpose of the forecasting process is to identify and evaluate systematically all factors which are most likely to affect the course of future events and to produce a realistic view of the future. Since the future is not "completely predictable," the systematic structure of the forecasting process establishes the foundation on which the most important ingredient (human judgment and intuition) is based.

- This chapter has emphasized the need to think of forecasting as a process. A properly trained forecaster is one who does the right things in the correct sequence.

The next chapter will present detailed steps in the forecasting process. This will be followed by discussions that can help you improve your data analysis capabilities, build and evaluate quantitative models, and improve your management of these analytical functions and the forecasts they will lead to.

USEFUL READING

The books and articles listed at the end of each of the following chapters are those cited within the text; they are described in the Bibliography at the back of the book.

CHAPTER 2

How to Start
Making a Forecast

This chapter deals with the first two stages of the forecasting process:

- Defining the parameters that will govern the forecast.
- Making first choices of alternative projection techniques.

The considerations help the forecaster answer the question:

- Can cost-effective forecasts be provided to assist planners or managers in making their decisions?

The specific operations that must be performed in these and other stages of the forecasting process are diagrammed in a flowchart in the front of this book. Each chapter will highlight those flowchart operations relevant to that chapter, thus emphasizing the iterative nature of the forecasting process.

DEFINING PARAMETERS

Suppose that you are in charge of making the forecast that was used as an example in Chapter 1—a toll revenue forecast for telephone company use during the next two years. How do you begin to plan your work?

Defining User Needs, Forecastable Items, and the Forecaster's Resources

First, a forecaster will want to identify forecast users and their information needs. For example, the toll revenue forecast is needed to determine the expected net income and return on investment for a "base case" (described in Chapter 1). You would want to be certain too that you had an understanding of what products or services should be measured in your forecast.

Next, a forecaster's own practical needs must be recognized; if they are overlooked, the quality of the forecast will be diminished. So you would want to consider

- The forecaster's time.
- Clerical time.
- Expense dollars for computer operations.
- Transportation for field visits.

Identifying Factors Likely to Affect Changes in Demand

A forecaster also needs information about the economic environment in which a business operates: what factors have caused the demand for a product or service in the past and are likely to affect the demand in the future? For example, in the marketing environment, demand for a product may need to be forecast along with a measure of the effect a change in price of a product or service will have on the demand for it. Or the forecaster may need to consider demographic, economic, and land-use factors. In particular, factors such as income, market potential, and habit are usually an integral part of a formal demand theory.

- *Income* measures a consumer's ability to pay for a company's goods or services. The price of its goods or services and the prices of its competitors' are certainly important.

- The *market potential* represents the total market for products or services of the type being forecast. This might be the number of households or business telephones.

- Finally, *habit* is crucial because innovation and change create new products and services, thus causing people's tastes and habits to change; these changes must be monitored. For example, the introduction of air transportation caused people to change travel habits; the impact on the railroad industry was tremendous.

The beginning forecaster can develop a simple demand theory without building complex models. For example, the forecaster may be required to project the sales of a product or service per household. A total sales forecast can be obtained by multiplying the forecast of this ratio by an independent forecast of the number of households. In this way, an important relationship can be modeled that uses relatively simple forecasting methods. This gives a first approximation which may provide valuable and timely information to decision makers.

In addition to these demand factors, supply considerations may also need to be taken into account. In forecasting basic telephone services, it is important to recognize that a corporate charter requires a telephone company to serve customer demand. Its management does not have the option of meeting only a part of the demand. In other industries, where this isn't so, the interaction of demand and supply must be evaluated by the forecaster and the forecast user before arriving at the final forecast.

A Car-buying Analogy

At first glance, the first two stages of the forecasting process as depicted in the Flowchart may appear somewhat complex, so an analogy of buying a new car may help simplify its analysis.

The first stage in defining a car buyer's problem (definition of the item) is seemingly straightforward—a new car. It may later turn out that other alternatives (used car, public transportation) provide more appropriate solutions to the real problem; the potential car buyer doesn't overlook this possibility but wants to do some preliminary checking to see if the assumption that a car is needed will hold up.

Therefore the potential buyer defines the car's users and their requirements. In this example the users are family members, and their needs will be determined as part of the forecasting process. The needs primarily relate to the use to which the car will be put: the car might be needed for commuting, for family chores, for vacation trips, or for teenager transportation. The intended use will strongly influence the selection of the type of car to be purchased.

Potential constraints also need to be considered: these include family size and the family's financial limitations (including money for a down payment, the availability of financing, the cost of insurance, and maintenance and operating costs). To help in a basic understanding of these things, the potential buyer might read publications relating to new car quality, consult books, talk to friends for advice about their experiences, and go to several dealers to discuss prices and terms of sale. This leads to a listing of alternative solutions.

The problem-definition stage concludes with a determination of the costs versus the benefits of alternative solutions. What this modest forecast will have taught the potential car buyer is to look for solutions in which benefits exceed costs. But has the car buyer been sufficiently accurate in measuring costs and benefits? There are, after all, numerous alternative ways of generating any forecast.

ANALYSIS OF DATA SOURCES

Since all forecasting methods require data, the forecaster proceeds to analyze the availability of data from sources both external (outside a business or industry) and internal (within the company or its industry). For example, one potential source of internal data is corporate books, which normally contain a rich history of revenues, expenses, capital expenditures, product sales, prices, and marketing expenses.

The availability of external data is improving rapidly. Most of the required demographic data (age, race, sex, households, and so forth), forecasts of economic indicators, and related variables can be obtained from the data banks of computer firms, and from industry and government publications. A partial listing of data sources for marketing and social sciences is given in Armstrong (1978, pp. 448–51). Intriligator (1978, pp. 72–73), and Sullivan and Claycombe (1977, pp. 12–14) summarize some useful external data sources. Another overall reference for data sources at the national and international levels is the *Statistical Yearbook*, published annually by the United Nations.

CHOOSING ALTERNATIVE PROJECTION TECHNIQUES

The commonly used projection techniques can be classified as being either qualitative or quantitative.

Qualitative Techniques

The qualitative techniques provide the framework within which quantitative techniques (including forms of quantitative analyses, such as decision trees and linear programming) are brought to bear on a particular problem. The objective of qualitative techniques is to bring together in a logical, unbiased, and systematic way all information and judgments which relate to the factors of interest. These techniques use human judgment and rating schemes to turn qualitative information into quantitative estimates. Qualitative techniques are most commonly used in forecasting something about which the amount, type, and quality of historical data are limited.

Common qualitative techniques include the Delphi method, market research (focus groups), panel of consensus, visionary forecast, and historical analogies (Armstrong, 1978). Treatments of these subjects may be found in Makridakis and Wheelwright (1978), Sullivan and Claycombe (1977), and Wheelwright and Makridakis (1980).

Table 3.1 (p. 27) compares the properties of a number of qualitative and quantitative forecasting and analysis techniques. A brief description of some of these qualitative techniques follows.

Delphi Method   The point of the *Delphi method* is to obtain the consensus of a panel of experts about a given problem or issue. The method attempts to avoid the possible negative aspects associated with group dynamics (e.g., suppression of minority opinions, domination by strong individuals who may be incorrect, unwillingness to change public positions, and bandwagon effects). Therefore, instead of bringing these experts together in a debating forum, the Delphi method relies on the distribution of questionnaires to the experts with an admonishment not to discuss the problem among themselves. They may not know who the other members of the panel are and they are not provided with individual opinions or estimates.

The initial questionnaire may be used to state the problem and to obtain preliminary estimates and reasons or assumptions behind them. The responses are then summarized and fed back to the panel. Members with widely differing estimates are asked to review the responses and, if appropriate, revise their estimates. Through several iterations it may be possible to refine the differences between experts to a usable range of opinion. However, there is no attempt to force an expert to accept the majority opinion. If such an expert feels strongly about another position and can articulate it persuasively, the method will provide a range of opinion which may be desirable in conditions of high uncertainty.

Criticisms of the Delphi method include questions about panel members' true level of expertise, the clarity (or outright vagueness) of questionnaires, and the reliability of forecasts.

Market Research   *Market research* is often conducted to determine market potential, market share, desirable or unfavorable product attributes, responses to changes in price or terms and conditions, customer preferences, and key factors that customers consider important in deciding between a variety of purchase or lease products from alternative vendors.

In the early stages of a market research project, the objectives may be fairly well defined but the nature of the specific questions to be asked may be less well defined. Often small focus groups (three to ten people) of potential respondents, randomly selected, are brought together to discuss the questions. The session is directed by a moderator. By asking specific questions, and directing the discussion, it is possible for the moderator to determine whether the respondents understand the questions, whether or not they believe other issues are important (leading to additional questions), and whether or not it would be worthwhile to continue the project through questionnaire development, testing, surveying (telephone, mail), collecting, summarizing and analyzing the data, and developing recommendations. Market research studies may be used to identify the characteristics of existing users (income, age, product's life cycle position, nature of business, number of establishments, etc). It may then be possible to estimate market potentials by gathering similar data about customers or potential customers. An example of this approach using regression models is illustrated in Chapter 16; variables were selected based upon previous market research studies combined with available data sources.

Panel Consensus   Perhaps the most widely practiced qualitative technique, a *panel consensus* can be as simple as having managers sit around a conference table and decide collectively on the forecast for a product or service. Bringing executives from various business disciplines together increases the amount of relevant information available to the decision makers. A further advantage of the approach is the speed with which forecasts can be obtained, particularly in the absence of complete historical or market data. This advantage may be offset by the lack of accountability for the forecast.

The typical problems of group dynamics will also become apparent here and will be compounded by the relative rank of the executives. Unfortunately, the person with the best insight may not carry sufficient weight to sway the whole group decision.

Visionary Technological Forecasts Using Curve Fitting   A variety of techniques attempt to predict future *technological trends*. Often a set of "S" curves are constructed from data representing factors such as speed, efficiency, horsepower, and density, to predict the characteristics of the next generation of technological products. For example, the capacity of a memory chip to store a given number of bits of information can be plotted over time (often using logarithmic scales). By extrapolating the curve, the forecaster in effect predicts the next breakthrough. Similarly, the constant dollar cost per chip can be plotted and extrapolated. Since there are relatively few data values for most items being forecast, significant judgment is required and assumptions must be developed and evaluated. There are physical and theoretical limits to certain factors such as speed not exceeding the speed of light or efficiency not exceeding a certain value.

Another branch of study involves *morphological research*. Briefly, this technique involves identifying all possible parameters that may be part of the solution to a problem. A (multidimensional) box is created showing all possible combinations of parameters. Each possibility is then individually evaluated. By determining the number of parameters by which the proposed technology differs from present technology, one can evaluate which breakthroughs are most likely to occur.

Historical Analogue   History may be a reasonable guide in situations such as the introduction of a new product. The introduction of color television into households could be related to the earlier introduction of black and white television; perhaps the type of growth curve is comparable here. Depletion of natural resources may be viewed similarly. Wood burning was replaced by coal which was replaced by oil. As oil resources are depleted, and nuclear power continues to face problems, coal and solar technologies are once again being considered as serious energy alternatives.

Historical analogues may also be useful in the shorter term when a new product replaces and improves upon its predecessor. For example, each new generation of computers can be evaluated in price/performance terms relative to the existing market. The introduction or replacement rate can be hypothesized by comparing the current improvement in price/performance with previous new product introductions given their rate of price/performance improvement.

Role Playing   One of the potential drawbacks of using Delphi or panel consensus methods for business forecasting is that the competitor is frequently not adequately represented. In a *role playing* scenario, however, several members are assigned the role of the competitor. They are responsible for developing information about the competitor and for creating competitor strategies and reaction plans. In a simulated forecasting session, assumptions developed by the "home" team are challenged by the "competition." The separation of roles may allow for a greater range of possibilities to be explored and more realistic assumptions to be developed than would otherwise occur.

Decision Trees   *Decision trees* are used to help decide upon a course of action from a set of alternative actions that could be taken, based on selected criteria such as maximization of expected revenues or minimization of expected costs. The technique is based on probability theory. In most cases, however, the probability assessments are subjective in nature and cannot be tested for validity. Decision trees are frequently used in making pricing and product planning decisions and for developing hedging policies to protect against future currency changes in international financing arrangements.

Consider a situation in which a firm is deciding how to respond to a published request for bids for 1000 units of a non-standard product. The firm's managers believe there is a 30% chance of winning the contract with a bid of $1,000 per unit and a 70% chance of losing the contract to a competitor. A win would result in $1 million in revenue (1,000 units $\times$ $1,000/unit). At a price of $750 per unit the probability of a win is expected to be 60%. A win of $750 would result in $750,000 in revenue. If the decision is made to go with a bid of $1,000/unit, the expected value is equal to the probability of a win multiplied (.3) by the revenue ($1M) and the probability of loss (.7) multiplied by the revenue ($0) or $300,000. Similarly, for a $750 bid the expected value is (.6) ($750K) + (.4) ($0) or $450,000. If the managers' expected probabilities are correct, a lower bid would yield more revenue. Figure 2.1 illustrates a decision tree for this example. The profit margin for alternative B is less than for A but the probability of winning the bid is substantially increased. If a firm had little available capacity a $1,000 bid might be appropriate. If they win the bid, the job will be very profitable. If they lose the bid they still have plenty of business. A firm with a smaller backlog of orders on hand may be more interested in keeping the volumes up to help maintain revenues and operating efficiencies.

System Dynamic Modeling   Another branch of modeling involves building simulation models that replicate how systems operate and how decisions are made. In a business environment, the management would model the flows of orders, materials, finished goods, revenues, and subsystems would be developed for functional areas such as marketing/selling, pricing, installation/maintenance, research, product development and manufacturing. The information and operational feedback systems

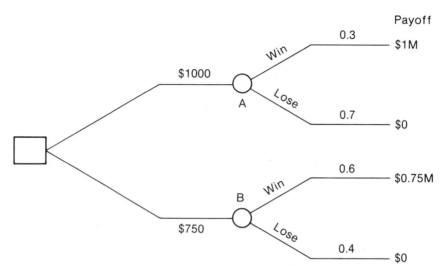

Figure 2.1   A decision flow-diagram.

would be modeled. The objective might be to evaluate alternative policies to determine the combination of policies and strategies that result in growth in assets employed and profitability.

The equations that describe the system are not based on correlation studies; rather, they are descriptive in nature. For example, the number of sales people this month equals the number last month plus new hires minus losses. Equations would then be developed describing how hires and losses are determined. If an individual salesperson can sell a given amount of product, the desired sales force equals the desired total sales divided by the quota per salesperson. Hires are initiated when the actual sales force size falls below the desired level.

In a similar manner a set of equations is developed that represents the behavior of the system or business. Parameters are established and the model is exercised using a simulation language incorporated in computer software. A properly developed model should be able to simulate past behavior and provide insights into strategies that can improve the performance of the system.

Quantitative Techniques

If appropriate and sufficient data are available, then quantitative projection techniques can be employed. Such quantitative techniques can be further classified into two more categories, statistical and deterministic.

- *Statistical (stochastic) techniques* focus entirely on patterns, pattern changes, and disturbances caused by random influences. This book treats some of these including summary statistics (Chapter 7), moving averages and exponential smoothing (Chapter 8), time series decomposition (Chapter 9), and regression models and trend projections (Chapter 11). The ARIMA models and other sophisticated time series techniques are taken up in Part 5.

- *Deterministic (causal) techniques* incorporate the identification and explicit determination of relationships between the factor to be forecast and other influencing factors. These include anticipation surveys, input-output models, econometric models, and leading indicators (Chambers et al., 1974; Wheelwright and Makridakis, 1980). Leading indicators are discussed in this book in Chapter 9, in connection with cycle forecasting. Econometric techniques are taken up in Part 4.

Within the listings of statistical projection techniques, there are essentially two approaches. The first approach is best illustrated by the *time series decomposition* technique. The primary assumption on which this methodology is based is that the data can be decomposed into several unobservable components such as trend, seasonality, cycle, and irregularity, and that the components can then be analyzed and projected into the future on an individual basis. The forecast is then merely the combination of the projections for the components.

A second approach is associated with the *Box-Jenkins* and *econometric time series modeling* methodologies. Their theoretical foundations are grounded primarily in statistical concepts and do not assume that the data are represented by the superposition of separate components. Rather, the data have an overall representation in which the components are not separately identifiable or specified.

There is often a further distinction made between time series and econometric methods: although they have strong similarities in their mathematical representation, they differ vastly in their estimation methodologies.

Time Series and Econometrics

A *time series* is a set of chronologically ordered points of raw data, such as the revenue received, by month, for several years. An assumption often made in the time series approach is that the factors that caused demand in the past will persist into the future.

Time series analysis can help to identify and explain any regularly recurring or systematic variation in the data owing to *seasonality*.

- Sales forecasters typically deal with monthly seasonality. This is usually related to weather and human customs.

- Economic forecasters more often deal with quarterly time series.

Time series analysis also helps to identify *trends* in the data and the growth rates of these trends.

- By trend is meant the basic tendency of a measured variable to grow or decline over a long time period. For many consumer products, the prime determinant of trend is growth in numbers of households.

Finally, time series analysis can help to identify and explain *cyclical patterns* that repeat in the data roughly every two, three, or more years.

- A cycle is usually irregular in depth and duration and tends to correspond to changes in economic expansions and contractions. It is commonly referred to as the "business cycle."

The concepts of trend, seasonality, and cycle are abstractions of reality. In Chapter 9 it will be seen how these concepts can be effectively used to make a "turning-point analysis and forecast."

The econometric approach may be viewed as a "cause-effect" approach. Its purpose is to identify the factors responsible for demand. The econometric models of the U.S. economy, for example, are very sophisticated and represent one extreme of econometric modeling. These models are built to depict the essential quantitative relationships that determine output, income, employment, and prices.

It is general practice in econometric modeling to remove only the seasonal influence in the data prior to modeling. The trend and cyclical movements in the data should be explicable by using economic and demographic theory. The Detroit model, discussed in Chapter 1, is an example of how an econometric system is used in the telecommunications industry. The growth in revenues might be analyzed, projected, and related to business telephones in service, a measure that is related to the level of employment. It is not necessarily assumed that the factors that caused demand in the past will persist in the future. Rather, the factors believed to cause demand are identified and forecast separately.

PRELIMINARY SELECTION CRITERIA

After generating a list of alternative projection techniques, it is often possible to reject some of these techniques immediately. Some of the considerations that go into such a preliminary selection include

- The time horizon of the forecasts.

- The accuracy requirements.

- The level of detail in the forecasts.

- The quantity of forecasts required.

Other considerations include the willingness of users to accept given techniques and approaches and the ease with which the methods or forecasts match their planning processes. The specific strategy for completing the preliminary selection is the subject of Chapter 3.

Time Horizon

A *time horizon* refers to the period of time into the future for which forecasts are required. The periods are generally short-term (one to three months), medium-term (three months to two years), and long-term (more than two years). Wheelwright and Makridakis (1980) also refer to the immediate term (less than one month). The business revenue forecasting example requires both short- and medium-term forecasts.

Accuracy Requirements

The *accuracy requirements* that a forecaster must deal with are normally related to the cost of forecast error. In an inventory control problem in which the inventory consists of numerous relatively inexpensive parts that are readily available (let us say boxes and mailing labels), the accuracy requirement will be less than for an inventory of very expensive parts with long lead times between order placement and delivery (for example, airplane engines and airplane fuselages). In the latter case, the production line could be affected adversely and sales could be lost to competitors if the inventory is not adequate. Alternatively, too great an inventory will cause a manufacturer to have unnecessarily high carrying charges, which might result in the need to raise prices to maintain profitability.

Each situation determines its own accuracy requirements. It is not uncommon for the forecast user to expect accuracy levels that realistically cannot be achieved. It is up to the forecaster, as advisor, to state what can be done. The user may well have to establish contingency plans to deal with the potential imprecision in the forecast. An objective accuracy level for the telephone revenue forecast example used in this book is less than 1.5 percent for monthly forecasts, less than 1.0 percent for annual forecasts, and less than 2.0 percent for two-year-ahead forecasts.

Levels of Detail and Quantities of Forecasts

Methods or forecasts that are appropriate for large-scale demand may not provide satisfactory results if applied to an individual product. For example, the projected total of automobile sales for all manufacturers may be related to certain large-scale economic variables such as real income or Gross National Product. This relationship may not be adequate to help an individual manufacturer (a custom car maker, for example) to determine its share of the market; much less does it enable the manufacturer to determine future sales for a given model.

Related to the level of detail is the quantity of forecasts that may be required of the forecaster. As the forecast process moves from executive management to production-line management, the quantity of required forecasts usually grows in a nonlinear manner. These could number in the thousands. A forecaster generally lacks resources to devote the full range of modeling techniques to that many forecasts. Instead, simple, more mechanical procedures must be applied. Checks for reasonableness must then be established to make sure that the total of the parts is in reasonable agreement with more sophisticated forecasts based on large-scale demand levels.

SUMMARY

Problem definition begins with

- A statement of the problem in specific terms.
- A demand theory stating what causes demand.
- A listing and preliminary evaluation of alternative solutions.

Problem definition is a critical phase of any project. It is necessary in this stage to define what is to be done and to establish the criteria for successful completion of the project or forecast.

- It is essential to agree on the required outputs, time, and money to be devoted to solving a problem, the resources that will be made available, the time when an answer is required and, in view of the above, the level of accuracy that may be achievable.
- Data analysis, forecasting, and model-building steps should only begin after these kinds of agreements are reached.

If the prospects for reasonably accurate forecasts are good, the forecaster proceeds to the next phase of the process.

USEFUL READING

ARMSTRONG, J. S. (1978). *Long-Range Forecasting: From Crystal Ball to Computer*. New York, NY: John Wiley and Sons.

CHAMBERS, J. C., S. K. MULLICK, and D. D. SMITH (1974). *An Executive's Guide to Forecasting*. New York, NY: John Wiley and Sons.

INTRILIGATOR, M. D. (1978). *Econometric Models, Techniques, and Applications*. Englewood Cliffs, NJ: Prentice-Hall.

MAKRIDAKIS, S., and S. C. WHEELWRIGHT (1978). *Forecasting Methods and Applications*. New York, NY: John Wiley and Sons.

SULLIVAN, W. G., and W. W. CLAYCOMBE (1977). *Fundamentals of Forecasting*. Reston, VA: Reston Publishing Co.

WHEELWRIGHT, S. C., and S. MAKRIDAKIS (1980). *Forecasting Methods for Management*, 3rd ed. New York, NY: John Wiley and Sons.

CHAPTER 3

Is There a Best Technique to Use?

This chapter describes the factors that must be considered before deciding on the most appropriate projection technique to solve a forecasting problem (see the Flowchart). These factors can be classified in terms of

- Characteristics of the data.

- Minimum data requirements.

- Time period to be forecast.

- Accuracy desired.

- Applicability.

- Computer and related costs.

SELECTING ALTERNATIVE PROJECTION TECHNIQUES

Suppose that you have made some basic determinations about the direction your forecast should take. Now you need to take a closer look at projection techniques. To select projection techniques properly, the forecaster must have

- An understanding of the nature of the forecasting problem.

- An understanding of the nature of the data under investigation.

- A listing of all potentially useful projection techniques, including information regarding their capabilities and limitations.

- Some predetermined criteria on which the selection decision can be made.

We explained how to make first approximations of some of these things in Chapter 2. The forecaster now must take the process a step further through data gathering, data preparation, and preliminary data analysis. The forecaster reviews literature and discusses similar problems with other forecasters to assess successes and failures of alternative approaches. Staff or company colleagues may be available for consultation; otherwise, industry associations, minutes of professional association meetings, and discussions with organizations such as the Conference Board (a nonprofit business research organization—see Conference Board, 1978) and government agencies may be helpful. If the scope of the project is large and requires extensive and ongoing consultations, consulting firms might be contacted for assistance. After conducting this initial research, the forecaster and the user are in a good position to select the most appropriate approach to solving the forecasting problems. Through the following discussions, imagine that you must select projection techniques for a telecommunications forecast of the kind introduced in Chapter 1; this will be considered as an illustrative example. First, however, notice what is compared in Table 3.1.

The first decision criteria shown at the left in Table 3.1 relate to the characteristics and amount of data. Beneath these are four selection criteria that relate to the inherent characteristics of various techniques in terms of

- The capability of handling the time horizon.
- Accuracy.
- Applicability.
- Computer costs.

These four parameters differ from the first two since they are influenced more by the requirements, resources, and objectives of the project than by the nature of the data. Let's examine each criterion in the table.

Data Characteristics

The pattern of data that can be recognized and handled is assessed in this part of the table. In the telecommunications example, the revenue series can be characterized in two ways: Figure 3.1 shows it to be markedly trending (having a tendency to grow or decline over time), while Figure 3.2 shows that the annual changes in revenue are highly cyclical. These two versions of the revenue series show how the nature of the data is critical in the selection of appropriate projection techniques.

A major factor influencing the selection of projection techniques relates specifically to the variable for which the forecast is being developed: namely, identification and understanding of historical patterns of data. If trend, cyclical, seasonal, or irregular patterns can be recognized, then techniques which are capable of handling those patterns can be readily selected. Questions to be asked include:

- Were there any data collection or input errors which could distort the analysis? (These might be evident as data gaps, discontinuities, or "oddball" data values.)

Table 3.1 Comparison of analysis and forecasting techniques.

	Qualitative					Quantitative — Statistical								Quantitative — Deterministic		
	Delphi method	Market research	Panel consensus	Visionary forecast	Historical analogue	Summary statistics	Moving average	Exponential smoothing	ARIMA (Box-Jenkins)	TCSI decomposition (Shiskin X-11)	Trend projections	Regression model	Econometric model	Anticipation survey, Intention-to-buy	Input-output model	Leading indicator
Pattern of data that can be recognized and handled — Horizontal	Not applicable					X	X	X	X	X	X	X	X	X	X	X
Trend	Not applicable					X	X	X	X	X	X	X	X	X	X	X
Seasonal	Not applicable					X	X	X	X	X		X	X			
Cyclical	Not applicable					X			X	X		X	X			
Minimum data requirements	Not applicable					5 Points	5 - 10 Points	3 Points	3 yrs. by mo.	5 yrs. by mo.	5 Points	4 yrs. by mo.	4 yrs. by mo.	2 yrs. by mo.	> 1000	5 yrs. by mo.
Time horizon for which method is most appropriate — Short term (0 - 3 mos.)	X	X	X	X	X	X	X	X	X	X		X	X	X		X
Medium term (3 mos. - 2 yrs.)	X	X	X	X	X	X	X	X	X	X	X	X	X	X	X	X
Long term (2 yrs. or more)	X	X	X	X	X				X		X	X	X		X	
Accuracy (scale of 0 to 10: 0 smallest 10 highest) — Predicting patterns	5	5	5	5	5	2	2	3	2	7	4	8	2	2	2	2
Predicting turning points	4	6	3	2	3	NA	2	2	6	8	1	5	7	8	0	5
Applicability (scale of 0 to 10: 0 smallest 10 highest) — Time required to obtain forecast	4	8	4	3	5	1	1	1	7	5	4	6	9	5	10	3
Ease of understanding and interpreting the results	8	9	8	8	9	10	9	7	5	7	8	8	4	10	3	10
Computer costs (scale of 0 to 10: 0 smallest 10 highest) — Development	Not applicable					0	1	1	8	6	3	5	8	NA	10	4
Storage requirements	Not applicable					4	1	1	7	8	6	7	9	NA	10	2
Running	Not applicable					1	1	1	9	7	3	6	8	NA	10	NA

Note: This table is a subjective adaptation of material presented in Chambers, Mullick, and Smith (1974, pp. 63–70) and Wheelwright and Makridakis (1980, pp. 292–93).

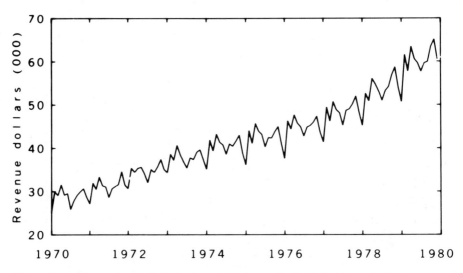

Figure 3.1   Time series plot of telephone toll revenue for the telecommunications forecasting problem.

- Are the data smooth or irregular?

The purpose of the foregoing analysis is to determine the true starting point for the forecast itself—i.e., the specific method or model to use. Not all projection techniques are appropriate for all forecasting situations. For instance, if the data are relatively stable, a simple exponential smoothing approach may be quite adequate. Other exponential smoothing models are appropriate for trending and seasonal data: the same model is not applicable in all cases. Notice, for example, that the simple exponential smoothing model can handle nontrending, nonseasonal data. Brown's linear exponential smoothing model is appropriate for data with linear trend. The Holt-Winters seasonal exponential smoothing model is appropriate for series that exhibit seasonal patterns.

As the forecast horizon increases, the cyclical pattern of the data may become a significant feature of the overall trend. In these cases, the need to relate the variable to be forecast to economic, market, and competition factors increases, since simple trend projections may no longer be appropriate.

Minimum Data Requirements

In the telecommunications example, ten years of monthly data are available and the full time period is considered appropriate for forecasting future revenues. The full range of statistical methods may be considered, based on the amount of available data.

The selection of a given technique assumes that the patterns of the time series

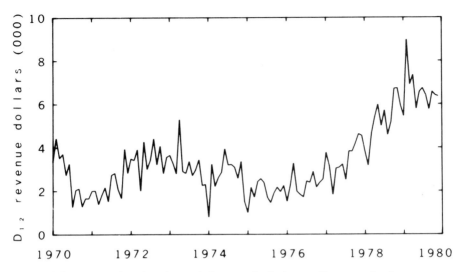

Figure 3.2   Time series plot of annual changes of telephone toll revenue for the telecommunications forecasting problem.

are such that the forecaster can make certain judgments as to what portion, if any, of the historical data are representative of patterns that will most likely occur throughout the forecast period. Thus the amount of relevant historical data and the patterns of that relevant data serve to reduce the number of projection techniques that can be considered useful. An extensive list of potentially useful projection techniques and their uses will be presented shortly.

Time Horizon

The time horizon for a forecast has a direct bearing on the selection of forecasting methods. In general, the longer the time horizon, the greater the reliance on qualitative methods.

For the short and medium terms, a variety of quantitative methods can be applied. As the horizon increases, however, a number of these techniques become less applicable. For instance, moving averages and exponential smoothing, and univariate ARIMA time series models are poor predictors of turning points; beyond two years into the future their use is not recommended. However, econometric and transfer function models may be more useful here. Regression models are appropriate for the short, medium, *and* long terms. Summary statistics, moving averages, trend–cycle–seasonal–irregular (TCSI) decomposition, and trend projections are quantitative techniques that are appropriate for the short and medium time horizons. The more complex Box-Jenkins (ARIMA) and econometric techniques are also appropriate. Input-output (I-O) models are not appropriate for short-term forecasting since they are usually based on cross-sectional data that are not very current.

Table 3.1 compares the various projection techniques on a scale of zero to ten for the next three selection criteria: accuracy, applicability, and costs. The scaling represents a subjective evaluation in which a score of zero represents the low end of the range and a score of ten represents the high end of the range. The material is adapted from similar tables in Chambers et al. (1974, pp. 63–70) and Wheelwright and Makridakis (1980, pp. 292–93).

Accuracy

The objective in the telephone revenue-forecasting example is to provide very accurate short-term and medium-term forecasts (up to two years). However, even two-year-ahead forecasts require great accuracy. Since a business cycle is approximately three to four years in duration, we shall assume that a turning point is expected in the second year but not the first.

Accuracy is relative: you will have whatever precision can be attained through the application of the various projection techniques. If it becomes apparent that the projection technique you plan to use will not meet your original precision objectives, the "go–no go" decision must be reevaluated. Assuming these objectives are attainable, then further assessment of relative precision will require you to examine your selection of data and their compatibility with the specific projection techniques you have chosen for the forecast.

For instance, experience has shown that the technically sophisticated ARIMA (Box-Jenkins) class of time series models can provide very accurate short-term forecasts. For a long-range forecast (say for a six-year plan), the forecaster will also want to make use of regression or econometric models. In the short term, the inertia or momentum of existing consumer behavior often resists sudden, dramatic change. Over a six-year period, however, customers can find new suppliers, and their needs may change as their suppliers change. Therefore, in the long term it is essential to relate the item being forecast to its "drivers" (as explanatory factors are called).

The accuracy of regression (or econometric) models during volatile forecast periods depends to some extent on the accuracy with which explanatory factors can be predicted. While these models can also be used in the short term, they are costlier and more complex than simpler ARIMA models, and they are seldom more accurate. This is particularly true when economic or market conditions are stable.

For forecasts between the medium and long terms, simple trend, regression, and econometric models are used increasingly. Certain trend projection techniques are relatively inexpensive to apply, but the forecasts they produce are often not as accurate as those resulting from econometric methods.

When sufficient data exist and the need for accuracy is great, as when predicting company revenues, the use of both ARIMA and regression (or econometric) models is recommended. Then the generally superior short-term forecasting abilities of ARIMA models balance with the econometric models, which are superior in relating the item to be forecast to economic conditions, price changes, competitive activities, and other explanatory variables.

When both ARIMA and econometric models yield similar forecasts, the analyst can be reasonably certain that the forecast is consistent with assumptions made about the future and has a good chance of being accurate. When the forecasts produced by two or more methods are significantly different, take this as a warning to exercise greater care: careful judgment will be more critical if you must decide to accept one or the other of these, or perhaps some combination of different methods producing different forecasts. It is also important to advise the people who have asked you to make the forecast that the risks associated with such forecasts are greater than when different methods produce consistent forecasts.

The methods that have the highest expected prediction accuracy for one-year-ahead forecasts (assuming no turning point) are the ARIMA and econometric models. Other methods suitable for one-year-ahead forecasts are regression models, time series decomposition, trend projection, and exponential smoothing, all described in this book.

For predicting turning points and—therefore—forecasts two years ahead, time series decomposition, econometric models, ARIMA models, and multiple regression models are suitable methods.

Applicability

Applicability of projection techniques is generally something a forecaster bases on experience with time series, techniques, the forecasting process, and cost. Forecasts are frequently needed in a relatively short time; exponential smoothing, trend projection, regression models, and time series decomposition methods have an advantage in this regard.

Ultimately a forecast will be presented to management executives for approval; ease of understanding and interpreting the results is therefore an important consideration. Regression models, trend projections, time series decomposition, and exponential smoothing models all rate highly on this criterion.

Computer and Related Costs

Computer costs are rapidly becoming an insignificant part of technique selection, and in recent years the proliferation of computer packages has lessened the need for forecasters to develop software. Moreover, machine charges for different system configurations (large mainframe, minicomputer, or microprocessor) and different computer services (in-house versus vendor) are hard to compare. Since desk-top computers (microprocessors) are certainly becoming commonplace for many forecasting organizations, other criteria will likely overshadow computer cost considerations in the future.

While computer costs are decreasing, certain labor-intensive costs associated with forecast development and implementation cannot be ignored. Start-up costs for developing forecasts for new products and services, analysis, and modeling work tend to escalate, especially when the experience level of the forecasting staff is low. The maintenance of a complex forecasting system, on the other hand, is relatively less costly provided adequate programming documentation and standards are kept current.

For computing costs some of the major considerations include:

- Processing costs.
- Connect-time and data storage costs.
- Supplementary charges for use of software packages and data base retrievals.
- Maintenance and support charges.
- Special hardware needs, such as terminals, cathode-ray tube devices, and plotters.
- Minimum charges (a consideration that can increase costs of small jobs).

ROLE OF JUDGMENT

As part of the final selection, each technique must be rated by the forecaster in terms of its general reliability and applicability to the problem at hand, its relative value in terms of effectiveness as compared to other appropriate techniques, and its relative performance (accuracy) level.

Now that selection criteria have been established, the forecaster can proceed to reduce the list of potentially useful projection techniques even further. An understanding of data and of operating conditions are the forecaster's primary inputs now. This knowledge must, however, be supplemented by a thorough knowledge of the techniques themselves. To see why this is so, let's look again at the telecommunications application.

Figures 3.1 and 3.2 depict a telecommunications revenue series as well as the changes in revenue over the same period in the prior year. Figure 3.1 is dominated by trend and Figure 3.2 is dominated by cycle. What projection techniques should be used in planning a forecast of these data?

Bear in mind first that a greater number of techniques are appropriate for the time horizon one year ahead than are appropriate for two-year-ahead forecasts. As one approaches forecasts two or more years ahead, the moving average, exponential smoothing, Box-Jenkins, and time series decomposition methods become less applicable.

Also apparent is that a greater number of techniques handle trending data than handle cyclical data. If we assume a turning point will occur in the second year, the moving average, exponential smoothing, and trend projection techniques are no longer applicable.

In terms of expected forecast accuracy for the one-year-ahead forecasts, the

ARIMA, econometric, regression, and time series decomposition approaches look most promising. With a turning point in the second year, the time series decomposition, econometric, and regression models look most promising.

If we consider time constraint and the desire to present an easily understood method, regression and time series decomposition approaches appear promising, followed by trend projection and exponential smoothing for the one-year-ahead forecasts.

The time series decomposition and linear regression methods appear most promising for the two-year-ahead forecasts.

Different conclusions might result, however, under the following circumstances:

- Shorter time horizons are involved.

- Computer costs are important.

- Accuracy requirements are less stringent.

- Time is not a constraint.

- Ease of understanding and explaining forecast methods is not important.

A LIFE-CYCLE PERSPECTIVE

Figure 3.3 provides broad recommendations of forecasting methods related to a *product's life cycle* (Chambers et al., 1974). The life cycle begins with the decisions and actions taken before the product is introduced. The techniques used to forecast a product's future at this stage include the Delphi method, market research related

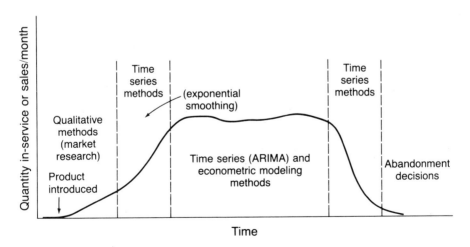

Figure 3.3   The life cycle of a product.

to the characteristics of the market and consumers' willingness to pay, panel consensus, visionary forecasts, historical analogues, decision trees, and other methods that can be applied with little or no historical data about the product. These techniques are presented in Wheelwright and Makridakis (1980), Makridakis and Wheelwright (1982).

Product introduction begins the next phase of the product life cycle. Quite often supply limitations, pipeline backups, and lack of customer awareness result in only a gradual buildup of the quantity of products sold. At this time, qualitative and market-research estimates may be refined.

The next stage in the life of a successful product is *rapid growth*. The product fills a need not otherwise met in the marketplace, or its price-performance characteristics are superior to its competitors, and it is adopted rapidly—faster, in fact, than would be accounted for by average growth in market or economic conditions.

At this stage, to project the product's future, time series methods become applicable. For less than thirty months of data, exponential smoothing techniques may be tried. For thirty or more months of data, ARIMA models can be built. When forty or more months of data are available, research shows that ARIMA models are superior to exponential smoothing models in terms of forecasting performance (see, for example, Geurts and Ibrahim, 1975; Granger and Newbold, 1977; Groff, 1973; Makridakis and Hibon, 1979; Newbold and Granger, 1974; and Reid, 1971).

As the product enters a *mature stage,* with three and preferably four or more years of data available on sales, prices, economic factors, market size, and so forth, econometric modeling techniques can be applied. These techniques offer an explanatory capability the time series methods lack. Whether or not this is an important consideration depends on the circumstances that have created the need for the forecast; in the mature phase a product is frequently modified, or its price may be adjusted, to maintain its competitiveness.

As new technology or other competitive products with superior price-performance characteristics also enter the market, demand for the "mature" product drops. The *fall-off* is greater than can be attributed to economic or market size considerations. Once again, time series methods may be more responsive in projecting the rapid decline of the product's sales.

In the final stage of the life cycle, the product is about to be abandoned. It is no longer profitable and its past history may not help in determining when it will be withdrawn. Financial considerations, or plans to introduce customers to a new product, will determine the product's fate.

A MULTI-METHOD APPROACH

Projection techniques are used during the forecasting process to describe the historical behavior of a time series in a simplistic, mathematical way and then, using that same mathematical model, to predict the future characteristics of the data. To describe the complexities of reality in terms of simplified models, clearly no single model can be considered universally adaptable to any given forecasting situation. The assumptions and theories on which the projection techniques are based limit their appropriateness and reliability.

The forecaster should be careful to avoid using techniques where the data characteristics do not match the assumptions of the method. Thus a basic principle is to utilize more than one projection technique. By observing this principle during the actual development of a forecast, the forecaster can be reasonably sure of avoiding biases which are inherent in any one projection technique or its use.

The purpose of using more than one technique is to ensure that the forecasting approach will be as flexible as possible and that the forecaster's judgment (which is so critical to the forecasting process) is not overly dependent upon one particular projection technique. It is not uncommon to see forecasters develop a preference for one forecasting technique over another, and then to use that technique almost exclusively even in a new situation. Such a preference can be easily established because of the highly specialized nature of some of the techniques.

Some forecasters always use the most statistically sophisticated techniques that can be found. In many cases, this tendency can greatly reduce the effectiveness of the forecasting process because some of the more sophisticated techniques are unresponsive to drastic pattern changes in the time series. The degree of forecast precision for the projection techniques is not necessarily a direct function of the degree of sophistication.

We recommend that two or more projection techniques be used to describe the historical behavior of the data and to predict this for the future. In essence, one is able to evaluate alternative views of the future. It is also necessary to provide a risk level associated with each alternative. A comparison can be made of the alternative views of the future and hence increase the chances that the selected forecast level is reasonable.

SUMMARY

To summarize the techniques selection process, the forecaster must

- Perform a general analysis on the time series.
- Perform a screening procedure that reduces the list of all available projection techniques to a list of those projection techniques that are capable of handling the data in question.
- Perform a detailed examination of the techniques that are still considered appropriate.
- Make the final selection of two or more techniques that are considered to be the most appropriate for the given situation.

Table 3.1 provides guidance on the relative abilities of a number of forecasting methods to handle the patterns in the data, the minimum amount of data required, the time horizon, accuracy, applicability, and costs.

- Careful analysis of the data in terms of the qualities shown in the table will indicate if the characteristics of the data match the requirements (assumptions) of the forecasting methods.

- A multi-method approach is recommended since the use of a single technique is neither the desirable nor practically attainable objective of the technique selection process.

USEFUL READING

CHAMBERS, J. C., S. K. MULLICK, and D. D. SMITH (1974). *An Executive's Guide to Forecasting*. New York, NY: John Wiley and Sons.

CONFERENCE BOARD (1978). *Sales Forecasting*. New York, NY: The Conference Board.

GEURTS, M. D., and I. B. IBRAHIM (1975). Comparing the Box-Jenkins Approach with the Exponentially Smoothed Forecasting Model Application to Hawaii Tourists. *Journal of Marketing Research* 12, 182–88.

GRANGER, C. W. J., and P. NEWBOLD (1977). *Forecasting Economic Time Series*. New York, NY: Academic Press.

GROFF, G. K. (1973). Empirical Comparison of Models for Short-Range Forecasting. *Management Science* 20, 22–31.

MAKRIDAKIS, S., and M. HIBON (1979). Accuracy of Forecasting: An Empirical Investigation. *Journal of the Royal Statistical Society* A 142, 97–145.

MAKRIDAKIS, S., and S. C. WHEELWRIGHT, editors (1982). *Handbook of Forecasting— A Manager's Guide*. New York, NY: John Wiley and Sons.

NEWBOLD, P., and C. W. J. GRANGER (1974). Experience with Forecasting Univariate Time Series and the Combination of Forecasts. *Journal of the Royal Statistical Society* A 137, 131–46.

REID, D. J. (1971). Forecasting in Action: A Comparison of Forecasting Techniques in Economic Time Series. *Proceedings, Joint Conference of the Operations Research Society*, Long-Range Planning and Forecasting.

WHEELWRIGHT, S. C., and S. MAKRIDAKIS (1980). *Forecasting Methods for Management*, 3rd ed. New York, NY: John Wiley and Sons.

CHAPTER 4

Do the Forecasting Assumptions Hold Up to Scrutiny?

This chapter deals with the final phase of the forecasting process:

- Evaluating the alternatives.
- Determining the reliability of the forecasts.
- Recommending the forecast values. This involves:
- Selecting the final forecast values.
- Packaging and presenting the forecast for approval.

Once one or more forecasting techniques have been selected, the forecaster uses the computer to estimate the model parameters and to assess the reasonableness of the model (see the Flowchart). It should be evident that the model-building process has similarities to general problem solving in other disciplines.

PARAMETER ESTIMATION

After narrowing down the possible alternatives, the forecaster must determine the parameters of a forecasting model. These parameters may be ratios such as housing units per acre or market penetration rates. Similarly, the potential car buyer doublechecks the parameters that make a certain car seem right, including the specific model, color, engine size, and extras such as power steering, power brakes, and a stereo radio.

Model parameters may also be coefficients estimated statistically from data by computer. Computer time sharing provides immediate access to, flexibility, and breadth of potentially useful forecasting techniques.

VERIFYING REASONABLENESS

Next, the car buyer attempts to validate the manufacturer's claims concerning ease of parking, comfort, noise level, braking, and acceleration. This is done by taking a road test. Forecasters also validate models through diagnostic checking. There are a number of analytical tools available (e.g., residual analysis and forecast tests) to determine if it is possible to improve on an initial model. These tools will, of course, be presented throughout the book.

As a result of the road test, the car buyer may decide to try a different make, model, or engine. The forecaster might decide to add new data, try a different method, or replace one time series such as the reciprocal of an unemployment rate with another series such as total employment in a revenue model.

The diagnostic checking stage usually means a number of iterations around a program loop. New variables can be considered, transformations of variables can be made to improve the models, and some techniques should be rejected at this stage because of their

- Inability to provide statistically significant results.
- Inability to achieve the desired objectives of accuracy.

In evaluating alternatives, the forecaster will find patterns or characteristics of the models that will influence the final selection of the models for use. For example, which techniques are more accurate in predicting turning points? In predicting stable periods? Which techniques have the best overall accuracy in the forecast test mode? Do some techniques tend to overpredict or underpredict in given situations? Are the short-term predictions of one model better than another? Do you actually need long-term predictions? Do the coefficients of one model seem more reasonable than those of another either in sign or magnitude?

DOCUMENTING RESULTS TO DATE

A vital part of forecasting is the documentation of the work at various stages of the process. The chore of documentation can be minimized by advance planning and continuous record keeping. The forecaster's documentation is as essential as the proof that a car has been serviced in compliance with a warranty would be for someone wanting to buy or sell a used car. The forecaster must write down the specific steps taken and the assumptions made. Only then can the forecaster and the manager have a meaningful analysis of results when the actual data are compared.

If work has been documented, it will be possible to specify a reason or set of reasons for the forecast's differing from actual accomplishments. The reasons would go a long way toward helping the manager evaluate the forecaster's performance.

Moreover, without documentation it will not be possible to learn from past experiences. Without documented methods and assumptions, it is not possible to determine where some problem lies.

From a manager's viewpoint, documentation also simplifies staff turnover problems. If the original forecaster is unavailable, a new forecaster will not have to reconstruct a forecast from scratch. A model or case study will exist and a body of information will be available for use.

The users of the forecast will also appreciate the additional documentation. Instead of simply having a set of numbers, they will have the kind of information they need to assist them in making decisions about their area of responsibility.

GENERATING MODEL PREDICTIONS AND CONFIDENCE LIMITS

The forecaster now reaches the stage where actual forecasts are produced, tested, and approved. This effort begins with a generation of predictions from the models that have survived the selection process.

In addition, the forecaster provides estimates of the reliability of the forecast in terms of limits at specified levels of confidence. Alternatively, reliability can be expressed as the likely percent (amount of) deviation between a forecast and actual performance. For example, suppose that new car purchases for the year are forecast to be 10 million plus or minus 700,000 at about a 90 percent confidence level. Another way of stating this might be that in a particular forecasting model, average annual deviation (absolute value) between what is forecast and actual new car sales is 7 percent.

One way forecasters can test the validity of their models is to work backward through a time series, generating predictions from the models over prior time periods for which the actual results are known. In this way it is possible to monitor the performance of the models and determine the likely forecast accuracy.

Table 4.1 illustrates how a forecaster could summarize forecast errors in a model with actual data from 1964 through 1979. A prediction from the model for 1975 is generated. Actual data through 1974 show that the prediction is 8.7 percent greater than the 1975 actual value. An additional year of actuals is then added to the model and 1976 is predicted. This time the prediction is only 1.2 percent greater than the actual.

This process can be continued and some average performance can be calculated. In this hypothetical example, the average absolute one-year-ahead forecast error for five periods is 4.3 percent. It might be useful to consider the median absolute percent error (here 3.8 percent) as well, to ensure that a very large miss one year doesn't unduly distort the average value. With this model, the forecaster might expect the one-year-ahead prediction to be within 4 percent of the actual value, on the average.

Table 4.1 Summary of one-year-ahead forecast errors from a hypothetical model with data from 1964 through 1979.

Historical fit	Percent error
1964–1974	− 8.7
1965–1975	− 1.2
1966–1976	+ 5.7
1967–1977	+ 3.8
1968–1978	− 2.3
Average absolute percent error =	4.3
Median absolute percent error =	3.8

Note: Percent error = 100 (Actual − Forecast) / Actual.

At this point, monitoring procedures can be established to determine the accuracy of the forecast. Likewise, the owner monitors a car's performance after purchase. Since the "forecast" the car buyer was attempting to make was whether a car would fulfill all projected contingencies, monitoring that forecast would entail measuring how family members use the car, its mileage, its maintenance costs, and so on: the buyer would also monitor factors such as changed public transit availability or cost, since those entered into the original definition of a car-buying forecast.

The forecaster does the same thing. Assumptions and results are continuously monitored.

RECOMMENDING THE FORECAST NUMBERS

The final steps of the process entail relating predictions from various models to the final forecast. The forecaster has several decisions to make. The forecaster recognizes that the various models are abstractions from the real world. The future will never be exactly like the past. The predictions from the models must be viewed as job aids in making a subjective judgment about the future.

Role of Judgment

Judgment plays an important role in the final determination of the forecast values and, later on, in the determination of when a forecast should be revised. Analogously, once the car buyer has purchased the car, subjective judgment comes into play if the car buyer realizes that the purchase was not a good decision. For example, during "verification" and "confidence" checks, suppose that the car buyer discovers a flaw so great that the dealer agrees either to repair the car or to exchange it for a slightly different model: the buyer needs to exercise judgment not called for in the original forecast in order to reconcile expectations and reality.

In an actual forecasting situation, it may become apparent that the actuals have exceeded the estimates for the last three months. Experience may suggest that a model's predictions be modified upwards by a given amount to account for the current deviation and the forecaster's expectation of whether or not that pattern will continue.

Subjective judgment in forecasting should be based on all available information, including changes in company policy, changes in economic conditions, contacts with customers, and government policy considerations. This judgment is a real measure of the skill and experience of the forecaster. For this reason data and processes are only as good as the person interpreting them. This judgment operates on many inputs to reach a final forecast.

Judgment is, by far, the most crucial element when trying to predict the future. Informed judgment is what ties the forecasting process and the projection techniques into a cohesive effort that is capable of producing realistic predictions of future events or conditions.

Informed judgment is an essential ingredient of

- The selection of the forecasting approach.
- The selection of data sources.
- The selection of the data collection methodology.
- The selection of analysis and projection techniques.
- The use of analysis and projection techniques during the forecasting process.
- The identification of influencing market and company factors which are likely to affect the future of the item to be forecast.
- The determination of how those factors will affect the item in terms of the direction, magnitude (amount or rate), timing, and duration of the expected impact.
- The selection of the forecast presentation methodology.

Informed judgment, therefore, plays a significant role in minimizing the uncertainty associated with forecasting. Automatic processes, models, or statistical formulas are sometimes used in computing future demand from a set of key factors. However, no such approach is likely to reduce the reliance upon sound judgment substantially. Judgment must be based on a comprehensive analysis of market activities and a thorough evaluation of basic assumptions and influencing factors.

Statistical approaches can provide a framework of information around which analytical skills and judgment can be applied in order to arrive at and support a sound forecast. To quote from Butler et al. (1974, p. 7):

In actual application of the scientific approaches, judgment plays, and will undoubtedly always play, an important role. . . . The users of econometric models have come to realize that their models can only be relied upon to provide a first approximation—a set of consistent forecasts which then must be "massaged" with intuition and good judgment to take into account those influences on economic activity for which history is a poor guide.

The limitations of a purely statistical approach should be kept clearly in mind. Statistics, like all tools, may be valuable for one job but of little use for another. An analysis of patterns is basic to forecasting and a number of different statistical procedures may be employed to make this analysis more meaningful. However, the human element is required to understand the differences between what was expected in the past and what actually occurred, and to predict the likely course of future events.

Selecting Forecast Values

Since future events and conditions cannot be predicted consistently with complete accuracy, the end product of the forecasting process can best be described as giving advice. In most cases, that advice is provided in the form of a single "best bet" figure which represents either the data value at some specific time or the cumulative value of a series of data points at the end of a specific period of time.

The "best bet" figure can be illustrated best with the median of a hypothetical frequency distribution. There is an even chance that the future outcome will fall above or below that median. Its primary weakness, however, is that the planning and decision-making processes assume that the forecast precisely describes the future, when in fact it cannot perform such a feat.

Decision making involves the assessment and acceptance of risk. Therefore, forecasters can assist decision makers by providing forecast levels and associated probability statements that indicate the chance of each of those levels being exceeded. This does not mean that the forecaster takes a "shotgun approach" to predicting the future by incorporating the extreme alternatives at either end of the range. It simply means that the forecaster should provide the "best bet" figure, and state the associated risk levels on each side of the "best bet." If a view of the future is presented in this format, the decision maker has much more information on which to assess the risk associated with decisions.

The probabilities associated with the alternative views of the future are, of course, highly subjective. In the physical sciences, probabilities are developed through some form of scientific sampling process over a long period of time. Such is not the case when it comes to quantifying the probabilities of future events or conditions in the business world. A multitude of influencing factors can enter into the picture after the forecast is made and thereby completely change the course of future events.

The principle of using more than one projection technique can again provide substance to the forecasting process by giving a certain degree of objectivity in the development of risk levels. It is clear, therefore, that the projection techniques play an important role in the decisions on the forecast level which is ultimately produced.

Forecast Presentation and Approval

Normally, it is necessary to obtain user acceptance and higher management approval of a forecast. When a car buyer presents his or her selected car to friends and family, the buyer tries to convince them that the car is a beauty and that its cost doesn't exceed what had been planned for. Besides, won't the neighbors be jealous? The buyer hopes to receive approval, especially since the relatives agreed to help in financing the purchase.

The forecaster must also present a forecast for approval. With pride of authorship, the forecaster thinks it is a beauty and is worth what it cost to produce. The managers will approve, hopefully, but never with much enthusiasm. After all, if things go wrong, it is your forecast!

The Forecast Package

After the forecast has been developed, it must then be documented and communicated to people who need the information. The purpose of the forecast package is to communicate the forecast to others and, at the same time, provide credibility to the forecast in the form of supporting documentation. Such a package should include

- The forecast.
- A display of the forecast which analytically relates it to the past data (through graphical and/or tabular display of the historical data and the forecast on the same page).
- Appropriate documentation of the rationale and assumptions regarding external and company factors which are likely to influence the item under study during the forecast period.
- Appropriate documentation on the approach that was used to make the forecast and on the projection techniques used during the forecasting process.
- A delineation of specific potential decision points related to risk levels and the significance of particular assumptions.

The value of a forecast is a function of its usefulness to decision makers in the face of future uncertainty. Therefore, the forecaster's job is not completed by merely developing the forecast. The product must also be sold to the decision maker. The supporting documentation should emphasize the quality of

- The process.

- The inputs used during the process.
- The judgment that was applied throughout the process.

SUMMARY

The forecaster has now reached the end of the forecasting process.

- After selecting the forecasting methods for study, the forecaster evaluates each method. This process is called diagnostic checking and often results in modifications of the initial models until acceptable models are obtained.
- A variety of test statistics and graphical analyses are reviewed to decide when the model is acceptable.

After passing these tests, predictions are generated from the models.

- Informed judgment, important throughout the process, is used to select the forecast values from among the possible candidates.
- Estimates are made of the precision of the forecast and a presentation is made to gain acceptance of the forecast.
- The forecasts are monitored to ensure their continuing relevance and forecast changes are proposed when necessary.

USEFUL READING

BUTLER, W. F., R. A. KAVESH, and R. B. PLATT, eds. (1974). *Methods and Techniques of Business Forecasting*. Englewood Cliffs, NJ: Prentice-Hall.

PROBLEMS

Thinking About Forecasting

1. The future path of interest rates is important to (1) investment managers of pension funds, trusts, and other accounts; (2) real-estate development companies, mortgage bankers and management companies; and (3) non-financial corporations in every major sector of the economy.

   a. Discuss how the forecaster must take into account both individual industry conditions, such as housing, and the specific needs of the investment decision maker.

   b. How are interest rates related to the demand for "money" as measured by, say, M1, the currency outside of banks and checkable deposits.

    c. In terms of the "generic" forecasting problem in Figure 1.1, describe the elements involved in forecasting interest rates. What are the markets?

2. Assume that a forecaster is attempting to analyze national industry sales of cross-country skis. Suggest several factors that are clearly related to ski sales, and discuss the rationale as to how these factors could be used to forecast ski sales.

3. An aircraft-engine company with multinational sales is making a forecast for jet-engine sales.

    a. Set up a set of economic, political and technological assumptions the company forecaster should consider in order to prepare the study.

    b. List the types of supply and demand data the forecasting group might be interested in using.

    c. Suggest a number of economic indicators that may be relevant in the study for correlation analysis.

    d. Without using formal statistical calculations, how could you most effectively display such correlations graphically?

4. Forecasting is an integral part of the planning process. A firm's sales forecast for the oncoming year is pessimistic, suggesting a 10 percent decline from the current year. Management reviews these data and decides that two courses of action are possible: (1) prepare for the expected decline in sales; and (2) attempt to offset the expected decline in sales. Discuss the steps required for each course of action.

5. In the car-buying analogy, buying a new car is likened to the selection of appropriate forecasting techniques. For this problem, make a list of desirable and undesirable product features that would characterize a new automobile (positives: seat belts, driver trunk release, etc.). For each feature assign a score (0–5, low–high) on how you would rate each one in a buying decision.

6. Many economic indicators have been successfully used to determine the current or future state of industry. For the following factors describe which type of decision maker/forecast user would be most interested in a given factor and how important each factor will be in the ultimate decision-making process.

Factor/Indicator	Decision Maker
New business formation	Capital banker
Manufacturing orders	R&D management— Capital goods market
Dow Jones index	Pension Fund manager
Housing starts	Manufacture of refrigerators

Building contracts	Marketing Sales Management—Wholesaler-Building supplies
Average hours worked	Production management

7. Consider a projection technique for a new product that is based on a projection of sales per month (10 percent per month). Assume limited sales data as given in the table below.

Month	Actual Sales (Cumulative)	Forecasted Percent	Year-end Projection
1	100	8.33	1,200
2	140	16.16	866
3	230	25.00	920
4	282	33.32	846
5	360	41.65	864

(Forecasted percent assumes $\frac{1}{12}$ of total yearly sales are made each month. What are some of the deficiencies of this method? Consider the viewpoint of customers and sales people in different geographical regions, store preferences, and seasonality.

8. Cash flow forecasting requires information about the level of cash flowing into a firm per month. Using the Detroit model, describe the "flow" of future cash in terms of variables whose levels are already known at the time the forecast is made.

9. An important distinction made among types of forecasting models concerns whether they are causal or non-causal (causal models are those that have as their basis a set of causal relationships). For the following forecasting situations provide your reasons for choosing to adopt a causal or non-causal modeling approach.

    a. chart analysis in the stock exchange

    b. sales of produce in supermarkets

    c. acceptability of a new product in the market

    d. demand for an existing product or service

Part 2

Learning from Looking at Data

CHAPTER 5

Why Stress Data Analysis?

Analysis of data is basic to the forecasting process. Analysis is essential for

- Summarizing and exposing detail in time series data so that the forecaster can effectively select a good starting model.

- Comparing a number of traditional and innovative analytical tools to increase one's understanding of "good" data. "Good" data are data that are typical or representative of the problem being studied. Such data are accurate in terms of reporting accuracy and also have been adjusted, where necessary, to eliminate unrepresentative or extreme values.

COMPONENTS OF A TIME SERIES

It is commonly assumed in practice that the total variation in a time series is composed of several basic *unobservable* components: a long-term trend plus a cyclical part, a seasonal factor, and an irregular or random term (Figure 5.1). In any given time series, one or more of these components may predominate.

In Chapter 2 we defined a trend as a prevailing tendency or inclination with time. When the term "trend" is applied to a straight line, it is often referred to as "slope." A trend may fall or rise and can have a more complicated pattern than a straight line: the Federal Reserve Board index of industrial production, depicted in Figure 5.2, is a good example of a time series that is predominantly trending upward. Trending data are often modeled with exponential smoothing models (Chapter 8) and regression methods (Chapter 11).

Figure 5.3 depicts a time series strongly dominated by seasonal effects—namely, monthly changes in telephone connections and disconnections. The seasonality results from the installation of telephones coincident with school openings and removal of telephones coincident with school closings each year. Thus, the seasonal peaks

49

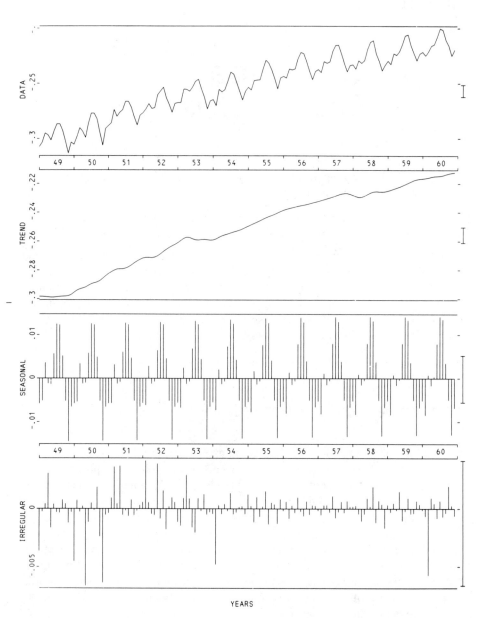

Figure 5.1   A time series decomposition into trend-and-cycle, seasonal, and irregular variation parts.

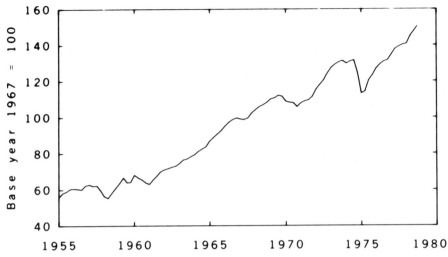

Source: Board of Governors of the Federal Reserve System.

Figure 5.2 Time plot of the FRB index of industrial production.

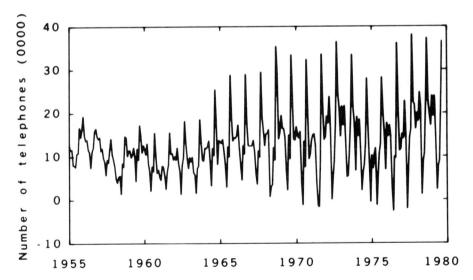

Figure 5.3 Time plot of monthly gain in a main telephone series.

and troughs appear with regularity each year. The trend in the net gain in telephones is related to the growth in households and the increasing use of telephones by former nonusers. Thus both trend and seasonal effects are superimposed on each other, as well as some residual effects which are not readily discernible from the raw data. Seasonal decomposition is the subject of Chapter 9.

The definition of cycle in forecasting is somewhat specialized in that the duration and amplitude of the cycle are not constant. This characteristic is what makes cycle forecasting so difficult. Although a business cycle is evident in so many economic series, its quantification is one of the most elusive in time series analysis (Chapter 9). In practice, trend and cycle are sometimes considered as a single pattern, known as the trend-cycle.

Other time series data are not strongly dominated by seasonal and trend effects, such as the University of Michigan Survey Research Center's index of consumer sentiment shown in Figure 5.4. In this case, the dominant pattern is a cycle corresponding to contractions and expansions in the economy. (Compare Figure 5.4 with the index of industrial production and housing starts in Figures 5.2 and 5.8, respectively.) Of course, a large irregular pattern is present in this series because there are many unknown factors that significantly affect the behavior of consumers and their outlook for the future.

The *irregular* is the catch-all category for all patterns that cannot be associated with trend, cycle, or seasonal effects. Except for some cyclical variation, the plot of the consumer sentiment index does not suggest any systematic variation that can be readily classified.

Irregulars are nontypical observations which may be caused by unusual or rare events, errors of transcription, administrative decisions, and random variation. The irregulars most often create the greatest difficulty for the forecaster since they are generally unexplainable. A thorough understanding of the source and accuracy of the data is required to recognize the true importance of irregularity.

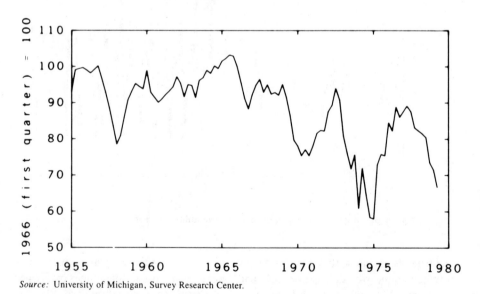

Source: University of Michigan, Survey Research Center.

Figure 5.4 Time plot of the University of Michigan Survey Research Center's index of consumer confidence (quarterly).

An example of an irregular—an unusual or rare event arising in a time series—is depicted in Figure 5.5, which shows a monthly record of telephone installations for the Montreal area from 1958 through 1968. Although dominated by trend and seasonality, the September 1967 figure is greatly reduced because of the influence of Montreal's World's Fair (Expo '67). Residential telephone installations normally accompany a turnover of apartment leases during September in Montreal, Canada. However, a large number of apartments were held for visitors to Expo that year. The dotted line depicts what might have happened under normal conditions in the absence of this "unusual" event.

Another example—this one is of a transcription error—is shown in Figure 5.6, which shows a series of monthly telephone message volumes. The general upward trend is quite evident and the unusual value in 1973 is due to a keypunch error.

Figure 5.7 shows an example in which an administrative decision influenced a time series. The series represents the number of "main" telephones (telephones for which separate numbers are issued) in service in a specific telephone exchange. The saturation (or "filling-up") of a neighboring exchange for a period in 1976 necessitated a transfer of new service requests from that exchange to the one depicted in the figure. This distorted the natural growth pattern. Any modeling effort based on these data must be preceded by an adjustment to account for this unusual event.

The components of a time series need not occur simultaneously and with equal strength. For example, many time series do not exhibit seasonality, while others, such as the weather, are not affected by the business cycle.

The purpose of analyzing time series data is to *expose* and *identify* these components. If appropriate, it is also desirable to correct, adjust, and transform data

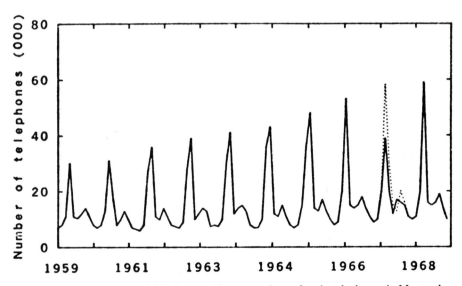

Figure 5.5   Impact of Expo '67 on monthly connections of main telephones in Montreal, Canada.

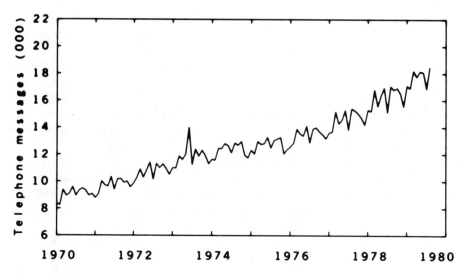

Figure 5.6   Time plot of a monthly telephone toll message series with a transcription error in 1973.

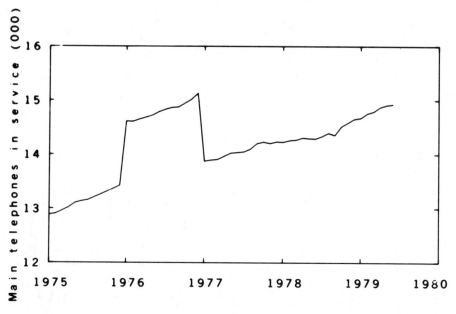

Figure 5.7   Time plot of main telephones in service in a telephone exchange.

prior to the modeling process. Exposing key components increases understanding of the data-generating process, in practice, and thus improves the likelihood of successfully predicting these patterns in the forecast period.

JUDGING THE QUALITY OF DATA

The analysis of data for forecasting purposes requires a careful consideration of the quality of data sources. A model or technique based on historical data will be no better than the quality of its source. There are several criteria that can be applied to data to determine appropriateness for modeling. The first of these is

- Accuracy: Proper care must be taken that the required data are collected from a reliable source with proper attention given to accuracy.

Survey data exemplify the need to ensure accurate data: survey data are collected by government and private agencies from questionnaires and interviews to determine future plans of consumers and businesses. The quarterly index of consumer sentiment, shown in Figure 5.4, is the result of an analysis made by the Survey Research Center at the University of Michigan. These data have certain limitations because they reflect only the respondent's anticipation (what they expect others to do) or expectations (what they themselves plan to do), not firm commitments. Nevertheless, such information may be regarded as a valuable aid to economic forecasting either directly or as an indication of the state of consumer confidence concerning the economic outlook.

Another criterion of appropriateness of data is

- Conformity: The data must adequately represent the phenomenon for which it is being used. If the data purport to represent economic activity, the data should show upswings and downswings in accordance with past historical business cycle fluctuations. Data that are too smooth or too erratic may not adequately reflect the patterns desired for modeling.

The Federal Reserve Board (FRB) index of industrial production for the United States, depicted in Figure 5.2, is an example of a cyclical *indicator of the economy*. It is evident that the time series variation is consistent with historical economic expansions and recessions. The FRB index measures changes in the physical volume or quantity of output of manufacturers, minerals suppliers, and electric and gas utilities. The index does not cover production on farms, in the construction industry, in transportation, or in various trade and service industries. Since the index of industrial production was first produced by the FRB in 1920, it has been revised from time to time to take account of the growing complexity of the economy, the availability of more data, improvement in statistical processing techniques, and refinements in methods of analysis.

Still another criterion is

- Timeliness: It takes time to collect data. Data collected, summarized, and published on a timely basis will be of greatest value to the forecaster. Often preliminary data are available first, so that the time delay before the data are declared "official" may become a significant factor.

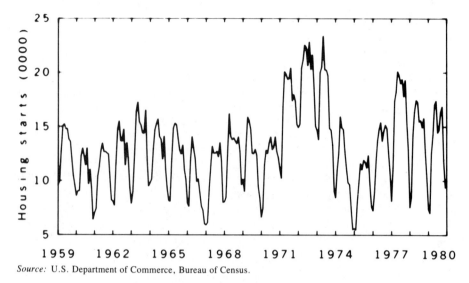

Source: U.S. Department of Commerce, Bureau of Census.

Figure 5.8   Time plot of monthly housing starts in the United States.

Demographic data may fall in this category for many users. The monthly housing starts shown in Figure 5.8 are demographic data reported by contractors and builders for use by government and private industry. Such *external data* are, of course, subject to adjustment because of data collection delays and reporting inaccuracies.

A final criterion is

- Consistency: Data must be consistent throughout the period of their use. When definitions change, adjustments need to be made in order to retain logical consistency in historical patterns.

The monthly increase in telephone gain, depicted in Figure 5.3, is an example of data that would be made available to telephone company forecasters. Such data, called *internal data,* are obtained from corporate books or from other company records made available to a forecaster's organization. Their definitions may vary because of changes in the structure of the company organization, accounting procedures, or product and service definitions. As part of the forecasting process, throughout this book various kinds of internal data will be related to economic indicators, survey data, and external data in a number of forecasting examples and case studies.

UNDERSTANDING DATA

With "good" data in hand, a forecaster can start the important task of exploratory data analysis. *Exploratory data analysis* means looking at data, absorbing what the data are suggesting, and using various summarizations and display methods to gain insight into the process generating the data. It is only a first step and not the whole story.

Exploratory data analysis is like detective work (Erickson and Nosanchuk, 1977; Hartwig and Dearing, 1979; Hoaglin et al., 1983; McNeil, 1977; Tukey, 1977 and Velleman and Hoaglin, 1981). It requires tools and understanding. Without an important tool such as fingerprint powder, a detective cannot find fingerprints. Without an understanding of where criminals will place their fingers, no fingerprints can be found. Exploratory data analysis uncovers indicators that are generally quantitative in nature; some are accidental, some are misleading. A planned forecasting and modeling effort that does not include provisions for exploratory data analysis often misses the most interesting and important results.

Simple summarization procedures provide a useful initial step in any modeling process. Many macroeconomic variables, such as the U.S. Gross National Product (GNP), employment, and industrial production are dominated by a strong trend. This pattern can be quantified in many cases by fitting a simple curve, such as a straight line, through the data. Certain sales data show strong peaks and troughs within the years, corresponding to a seasonal pattern. When seasonality is removed from these data, the secondary effects become apparent and may be important.

Inspection of time series data often indicates strong trend patterns. The fitting of trend lines is a simple and convenient way of exposing detail in data. A useful way of presenting the FRB index shown in Figure 5.2 is to compare it to some trend line, such as an exponential or straight trend line. This type of analysis brings out sharply the cyclical movements of the FRB index, and it also shows how the current level of output compares with the level that would have been achieved had the industrial sector followed its historical growth rate.

Although this may not be the best or final trend line for the data, the straight line is a simple summarization tool. In order to assess the value of this simple procedure, the deviations (data minus trend line) of the FRB data from the fitted straight line are depicted in Figure 5.9. It is evident that elimination of "trend" in the data now highlights the cyclical patterns corresponding to economic expansions and contractions.

LOOKING AT RESIDUALS

By considering the deviations from a fit, known as *residuals,* it is possible to expose other characteristics of the data without being distracted by the dominant trend. In the previous example based on FRB data, the residuals show a cyclical pattern which can be related to economic contractions and expansions. The recession in 1974–1975 is very dramatically shown by its plunge below the trend level. Also, the steady recovery to more normal growth is apparent in the last three years.

Implicit in this simple analysis is a model, characterized by the linear trend. However, the analysis is preliminary in that its summaries are based on a simple model that exposes residuals for more detailed analysis and possibly further mod-

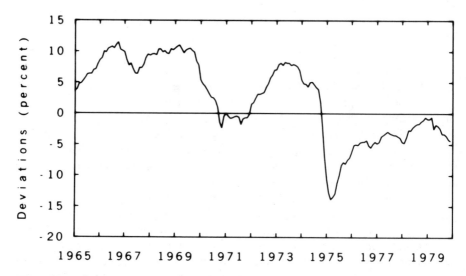

Figure 5.9 Time plot of the deviations of the FRB index of industrial production from a straight line trend.

eling at a later stage. This process is typical of the *iterative* procedure one follows in summarizing and exposing data.

During residual analysis, it may become apparent that certain individual observations or small sequences of them are in some sense extreme. Such unusual values, called *outliers,* can severely impact on the results of an analysis. Outliers are not expected to recur or to influence the data in the same way again, so that their effect should be negated by replacing them with more "typical" values.

This is particularly true when the objective is to use statistical forecasting techniques to extrapolate past results into the future. For example, the extremely severe snowstorms of 1977 and 1978 prohibited many people from getting to work. As a result, residential telephones were used more often and revenues increased significantly as people called their offices to say they would not be in, called friends and relatives to determine if they were safe, and so forth. For forecasting purposes, it is necessary to adjust downwards the 1977 and 1978 revenues to more typical revenues so as not to overstate the expected revenues in 1979.

On the other hand, if one is attempting to build a model to explain past results, one should think long and hard before adjusting past data. These may be useful in understanding how extreme or unusual events affect the process of generating data. If one wanted to know the impact of severe weather on telephoning habits, the 1977–1978 data provide excellent indications and as such should not be adjusted.

A residual analysis can be an effective procedure for isolating outliers. Among the unusual events that create outliers in business data, the most commonly occurring are related to weather, strikes, or changes in the observance of holidays. These events have predictable effects, so appropriate adjustments can generally be made.

More often, the reasons for unusual values are unknown and must be investigated. Even with the assistance of statistical methods, extensive subjective judgment is often required in selecting replacement values.

Residual analysis in the context of regression modeling is treated in Chapter 12.

SUMMARY

Data analysis is important in the preanalysis and diagnostic checking (residual analysis) stages of model building.

- It is also a lone-standing process that has significant value outside the realm of model building, too—that is, in the evaluation and interpretation of data.

- Data analysis should be performed to improve your understanding of what the data are trying to tell you.

- It can also be applied effectively in presenting the results of a study to management.

In terms of statistical methodology, much data analysis is informal. Like the modeling process

- Data analysis is open-ended and iterative in nature.

- The steps you may take will not always be clearly defined.

- The nature of the process will depend on what information is revealed to you at various stages.

At any given stage various possibilities may arise, some of which will need to be separately explored. To the beginner, such a process may seem inefficient and interminable; but in practice, a reasonable course will often become apparent, especially with experience.

USEFUL READING

ERICKSON, B. H., and T. A. NOSANCHUK (1977). *Understanding Data*. Toronto, Canada: McGraw-Hill-Ryerson Ltd.

HARTWIG, F., and B. E. DEARING (1979). *Exploratory Data Analysis*. Sage University Paper on Quantitative Applications in the Social Sciences, 07-016. Beverly Hills, CA: Sage Publications.

HOAGLIN, D. C., F. MOSTELLER, and J. W. TUKEY editors, (1983). *Understanding Robust and Exploratory Data Analysis*. New York, NY: John Wiley and Sons.

McNEIL, D. R. (1977). *Interactive Data Analysis*. New York, NY: John Wiley and Sons.

TUKEY, J. W. (1977). *Exploratory Data Analysis*. Reading, MA: Addison-Wesley Publishing Co.

VELLEMAN, P. F., and D. C. HOAGLIN (1981). *Applications, Basics, and Computing of Exploratory Data Analysis*. Boston, MA: Duxbury Press.

CHAPTER 6

The Importance
of Graphical Displays
# of Data

Forecasters will understand their data better if they also understand that data can be displayed in a variety of ways.

- Not only does it help to display raw data, results of an analysis of the data can also be shown graphically.

- Analyses, such as seasonally adjusted data, differenced or smoothed data, transformed data (e.g., logarithms and square roots), fitted values, and residuals, can all be generated effectively as "cheap-and-dirty" plots on high-speed printers and terminals; higher quality output is produced by CRT (cathode-ray tube) devices; highest quality output is produced with microfilm or penplotters.

Most of the visuals shown in this book were generated by computer graphics on microfilm by using the GR-Z graphics software package (Becker and Chambers, 1977).

GRAPHICAL DISPLAYS

Graphical forms of data displays are often easier to interpret than tabular forms of the same data. It is easier for the human eye and brain to extract a piece of information from a graph than a table. Graphical displays are flexible in their ability to reveal alternative structures present in data or to see relationships among variables. A wise choice in the scale of a graphical display can also make the difference between seeing something important in the data or missing it altogether. For example, rates of growth and changing rates of growth are easier to interpret from charts with a logarithmic scale than an arithmetic scale.

61

Some useful tools for displaying data include time plots, scatter diagrams, stem-and-leaf diagrams, histograms, and box plots. The latter two are discussed in Chapter 7.

The most commonly used graphical representations of time series data include the time plot and scatter diagram.

Time Plots

A *time plot* is simply a graph in which the data values are arranged sequentially in time. Since the values in a time series are arranged sequentially in time, the corresponding values must be plotted at equally spaced time intervals. These time intervals may be days, weeks, months, quarters, or years. A number of time plots were displayed in Chapter 5.

Another use of time plots arises when a time series is reexpressed in another form. When analyzing trending data, the percent changes (annually or quarterly) of a time series can be considered as a new time series. For example, Figure 6.1 shows a plot of the seasonally adjusted GNP in billions of 1972 dollars for some recent years. Figure 6.2 shows the annualized percent changes from previous quarters. Clearly, trend is essentially removed in the latter graph and attention is focused on the GNP growth rate, a comprehensive measure of the vitality of the economy.

The GNP is the most important and widely used indicator of the nation's economic health. It measures the market value of all the goods and services produced

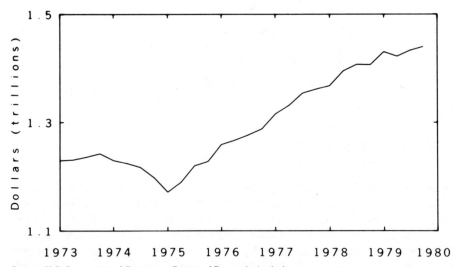

Source: U.S. Department of Commerce, Bureau of Economic Analysis.

Figure 6.1   Time plot of U.S. Gross National Product; seasonally adjusted (quarterly) in 1972 constant dollars.

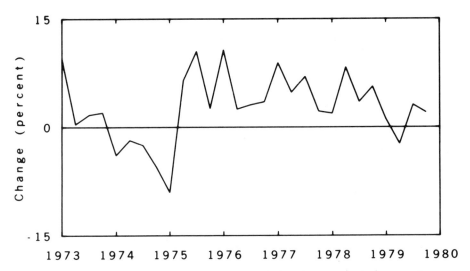

Figure 6.2   Time plot of the percent change from the previous quarter in the annual rates for GNP.

in the economy. Estimates of GNP are released quarterly by the U.S. Department of Commerce and are expressed in terms of seasonally adjusted annual rates. Because inflation distorts the validity of current-dollar data as a measure of "real" economic activity, GNP is also published in constant-dollar (1972) terms. All these forms of the GNP can be viewed as time series and displayed as time plots.

Scatter Diagrams

When the points of one variable are paired with corresponding values of a related variable, a linear or nonlinear relationship between the variables can be depicted in a *scatter diagram*. One variable is plotted on a horizontal ordered-number scale and the other variable is plotted on a vertical ordered-number scale. Such a plot is a valuable tool for studying the relationship among two or more sets of variables.

As a prelude to regression analysis (finding the line that best fits the points of the scatter diagram), an analyst may search for variables that are related to one another in a linear or functional manner: if an independent variable has been plotted against a variable that is dependent on it, the variables will have a functional (linear) relationship. As part of modeling, scatter diagrams can suggest if certain relationships among variables may be assumed linear on the basis of physical, economic, or even intuitive hypotheses. After regression, scatter diagrams play a role in the graphical analysis of residual series to help verify if assumptions are reasonable, and if, moreover, a proposed statistical model will give acceptable answers (i.e., will have a good fit to the data).

In our telecommunications example, consider the problem of forecasting telephone toll revenues from toll message volumes. In general, the amount of revenue would depend on the number of messages, the duration of the calls, and the rates charged for the calls. Toll message data were shown in Figure 5.6 of Chapter 5; toll revenues corresponding to these message volumes were shown as a time plot in Figure 3.1. Notice the similarity of the trend and seasonal patterns in the time plots. These two time series will be analyzed and modeled in detail throughout the book.

For example, for each toll revenue value you can associate a corresponding toll message value. In this case, it would simply mean associating the January 1976 toll revenue value with the January 1976 toll message value and so forth. These data are plotted in Figure 6.3 as a scatter diagram, in which the revenues are represented on the vertical axis and the message volumes are represented on the horizontal axis. The scatter diagram suggests that, *on the average,* toll revenues increase as toll message volumes increase. However, for a given number of toll messages, the toll revenue data have a good deal of *variability* depending on distance, operator assistance, time of day, duration of call, and possibly other factors.

A tight scatter is apparent, as may be expected. However, it is also apparent from the time plots that both series have similar seasonal patterns. If this were not the case, the diagram might appear much less smooth. Alternatively, a scatter diagram can also be plotted between toll revenues and toll message volumes that have been adjusted for seasonal variation. Such a scatter diagram would appear even smoother because small seasonal differences have been removed.

It is sometimes necessary to relate trend-cycle patterns in two series that have

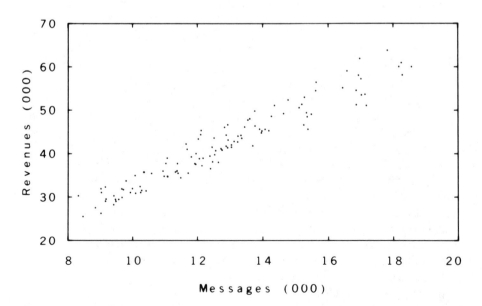

Figure 6.3 Scatter diagram of telephone toll revenue and message volumes.

different seasonal patterns, such as data about the increase in the number of main telephones and housing starts. For example, Figure 6.4 shows a scatter diagram between monthly main-telephone gain and U.S. housing starts. The broad scatter suggests a weak relationship between the variables. In fact, such broadly dispersed scatter diagrams are not likely to give rise to good forecasting models.

Any relationship between the trend characteristics of the main-telephone gain and housing starts is obscured by the differences in their seasonal characteristics. Here, it would be useful to remove seasonal influences first in both series before plotting a scatter diagram, by taking "differences of order twelve" on both time series (to be covered later in this Chapter). This will reduce or even remove the seasonal influence in the relationship. The resulting scatter diagram (Figure 6.5) between the "differenced" series shows a much clearer linear pattern, which is likely to produce better modeling results and possibly more accurate forecasts. A comparison of the forecasts resulting from these two ways of relating quarterly main gain to quarterly housing starts is provided as a problem in Part 3.

Stem-and-Leaf Displays

A *stem-and-leaf display* is a simple device for depicting frequencies as well as actual values in a single diagram. Table 6.1 shows the stem-and-leaf display for a simplified data set consisting of some travel time data (to be discussed in detail in the next chapter). The data themselves are not important for the moment.

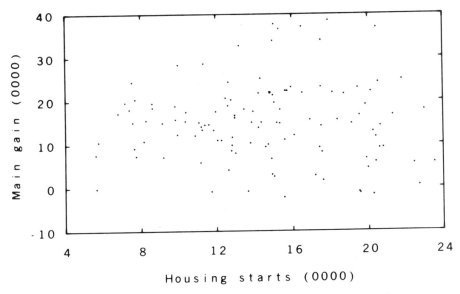

Figure 6.4 Scatter diagram between monthly main-telephone gain and housing starts.

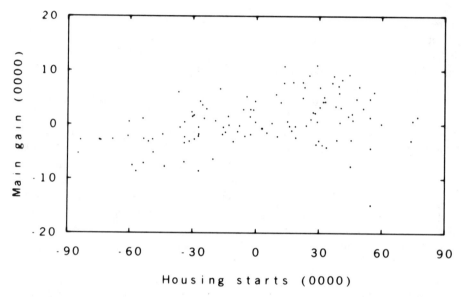

Figure 6.5   Scatter diagram between monthly main-telephone gain and housing starts—differenced data.

The "stem" is a vertical column: its unit divisions are multiples of ten. The "leaves" are horizontal rows of numbers; each of the numbers in a "leaf" represents a unit within the corresponding "tens" category, i.e., the first number is 3. By entering each number in this manner and ordering the numbers, one gets a visual impression of the distribution of the data, and, as well, an ordering of the data.

Table 6.1   A stem-and-leaf display of travel-time data.

Tens digit	Unit digit	Number of orders
0	33444566666777888999	20
1	000000111111223344678	21
2	012337	6
3	02	2
4	0	1
5		0
6		0
7		0
8		0
9		0
		(Total: 50)

Frequent values stand out (e.g., 10, 11) as well as atypical values and absences. For example, there are no values in the 33–39 range. Notice that the "leaves" have been ordered. The right-hand column provides a count that is useful as a check to see that all values are entered. A cumulative count will also turn out to be useful in the quick calculation of certain statistics, such as the interquantile difference (discussed later).

When the data are concentrated, as these are, it is often desirable to split each tens unit of the stem into two ranges (0 to 4 and 5 to 9). This is illustrated in Table 6.2. The absence of data in the 35–39 range becomes more apparent. Additional information can be added by the use of symbols to identify various qualities of data that may be helpful in understanding differences in data. For example, a circle might be used to indicate whether a travel-time value represented the first trip of the day (which usually takes longer than others because it begins at the service company's garage).

Stem-and-leaf displays are useful in that they

- Show inherent groupings.

- Show unsymmetric trailing off, going farther in one direction than another.

- Highlight unexpected popular or unpopular values.

- Show "about where" the values are centered.

- Show "about how widely" the values are spread.

Table 6.2 A stem-and-leaf display with split stem.

Range	Unit digit	Number of orders
0–4	33444	5
5–9	566666777888999	15
10–14	000000111111223344	18
15–19	678	3
20–24	01233	5
25–29	7	1
30–34	02	2
35–39		0
40–44	0	1
45–49		0
		(Total: 50)

$$\text{Median} = \frac{25\text{th} + 26\text{th observations}}{2} = \frac{10 + 10}{2} = 10$$

Choosing the number of lines L for a stem-and-leaf display is analogous to determining the number of intervals or the interval width for a histogram. A useful formula for the maximum L when n is below 100 data values is

$$L = 2\sqrt{n}$$

while for n greater than 100 the formula

$$L = [10 \log_{10} n]$$

is recommended (Hoaglin et al., 1983). The notation $[x]$ represents the largest integer not exceeding x. For the example that has $n = 50$, we have $2\sqrt{50} = 14.1$ and $[10 \log_{10} 50] = 16.9$. Thus a 10-line stem-and-leaf display for the travel-time data seems satisfactory.

PREPARING DATA FOR MODELING

Removing Trend/Seasonality by Differencing

It has been noted that differencing is required to

- Put time series on a comparable basis for cross-correlation studies and regression modeling.
- Render time series stationary prior to time series modeling.

Differencing is obtained by subtracting a lagged version of itself from the original time series, Y_t. For example, a first difference or *difference of order 1* of the time series Y_t results in a new time series Z_t defined by

$$Z_t = Y_t - Y_{t-1}.$$

Similarly, a *difference of order 4* (or fourth-*order* difference) is given by

$$Z_t = Y_t - Y_{t-4}.$$

Here, Z_t is the difference between a value of the time series and the value of the series four periods earlier. For quarterly data, this represents a year-over-year change.

The most commonly used differencing operation for monthly data is the *difference of order 12* (or twelfth-*order* difference):

$$Z_t = Y_t - Y_{t-12}.$$

Again, this is a year-over-year change for monthly data.

Since year-over-year changes should be essentially free of seasonal patterns, the differences of orders 4 and 12 are used to change seasonal time series to new time series that are free of seasonality. Notice that this operation is not the same as a seasonal *adjustment* or the *removal* of seasonality from a series. A differenced series does not have the same scale as the original series.

Another point worth noting is that a fourth-*order* (or twelfth-*order*) difference is *not* the same as a "fourth" (or "twelfth") difference. A "fourth difference" is a first difference repeated four times; that is, let

$$Z_t = Y_t - Y_{t-1},$$

which is a *first difference*. The *second difference* is the first difference of Z_t; that is,

$$
\begin{aligned}
Z^{(2)}{}_t &= Z_t - Z_{t-1} \\
&= (Y_t - Y_{t-1}) - (Y_{t-1} - Y_{t-2}) \\
&= Y_t - 2Y_{t-1} + Y_{t-2}.
\end{aligned}
$$

To carry this out two more times, let $Z_t^{(3)} = Z_t^{(2)} - Z_{t-1}^{(2)}$, and $Z_t^{(4)} = Z_t^{(3)} - Z_{t-1}^{(3)}$; then the "fourth difference" turns out to be

$$Z_t^{(4)} = Y_t - 4Y_{t-1} + 6Y_{t-2} - 4Y_{t-3} - Y_{t-4}.$$

This is clearly not the same as the fourth-*order* difference.

$$Z_t = Y_t - Y_{t-4}.$$

Autocorrelations and Correlograms

Data sequences one or more time periods apart are often statistically related. This effect is known as *serial correlation* or *autocorrelation* and plays a significant role in the analysis of many types of time series and forecast modeling applications.

When stock prices, sales volumes, population counts, and other data are measured or observed sequentially in time, the data may contain information about important sequential relationships that you should extract or quantify. An objective of autocorrelation analysis is to develop tools for describing the association or mutual dependence between values of the same time series at different time periods. A useful graphical tool for displaying these autocorrelations is the *correlogram*. Patterns in a correlogram can be used to analyze corresponding patterns in the data, such as seasonality, and help in the specification of time series and econometric models. Correlograms can be interpreted in terms of autocorrelation coefficients.

Given n discrete values of a time series $\{y_t; t = 1, \ldots, n\}$, a commonly used formula for the *first sample autocorrelation coefficient* (r_1) is

$$r_1 = \frac{\sum\limits_{t=1}^{n-1}(y_t - \bar{y})(y_{t+1} - \bar{y})}{\sum\limits_{t=1}^{n}(y_t - \bar{y})^2},$$

where $\bar{y}$ is the average (arithmetic mean) of the n values of the time series. The subscript in observation y_t denotes the "time" t; thus, y_{t-1} is the observation one period earlier.

In a similar fashion the formula for the *sample autocorrelation coefficient* (r_k) between observations a distance k *periods apart* is given by

$$r_k = \frac{\sum\limits_{t=1}^{n-k}(y_t - \bar{y})(y_{t+k} - \bar{y})}{\sum\limits_{t=1}^{n}(y_t - \bar{y})^2} \qquad k = 1, 2, \ldots$$

There are a number of closely related ways in which the sample autocorrelation coefficient at lag k is calculated. The differences are usually minor and have only theoretical value.

Table 6.3 shows a numerical example of the calculations involved in obtaining the first two sample autocorrelations of a simple trending series.

The interpretation of a correlogram is an art and requires substantial experience. Some common correlograms arise for time series with the following characteristics:

- Pure randomness.
- Low-order serial correlation.
- Trend.
- Alternating and rapidly changing fluctuations.
- Seasonality.

A *random time series* is one in which there is no time dependence between data values any number of time periods apart. Thus the autocorrelations would be zero at all lags, except at lag 0. At lag 0, the series is perfectly related to itself and has the maximum value 1. For a sampled random series, a correlogram will depict sample estimates of correlations of the data. Hence the correlogram shown in Figure 6.6 would be unity at lag 0 (shown by the column of pluses at the far left) and be very close to zero for all nonzero values k of the lag (there are forty of these plotted on the abscissa in the figure).

Table 6.3 An illustrative example of the calculation of sample autocorrelations.

Time period	Data y_t	$y_t - \bar{y}$	$(y_t - \bar{y})^2$	y_{t-1}	$(y_{t-1} - \bar{y})$	$(y_t - \bar{y})(y_{t-1} - \bar{y})$
1	0	-6	36	NA*	NA	NA
2	2	-4	16	0	-6	24
3	3	-3	9	2	-4	12
4	4	-2	4	3	-3	6
5	6	0	0	4	-2	0
6	7	1	1	6	0	0
7	8	2	4	7	1	2
8	9	3	9	8	2	6
9	10	4	16	9	3	12
10	11	5	25	10	4	20
Sum:	60	0	120			82

$\bar{y} = 60/10 = 6$;

$r_0 = 1$ (always);

$r_1 = 82/120 = 0.68 =$ First autocorrelation coefficient;

$r_2 = 50/120 = 0.42 =$ Second autocorrelation coefficient.

*NA = No data available.

A random series appears to have no systematic pattern that can be exploited for forecasting. It should be noted that a "random" series is not necessarily "normally" distributed (see Chapter 7 for a discussion on how data are "distributed").

Many time series, even after a certain amount of "differencing," exhibit short-term correlations (or "memory") in their pattern. Thus autocorrelation at shorter lags is greater than autocorrelation at longer lags. For a time series having this low-order dependence, a correlogram would show a decaying pattern. Figure 6.7 shows a correlogram of telephone toll revenue data. In this case, the strong trend in the data induces a "memory" pattern, and the correlogram corroborates this. Thus a correlogram can help identify structure in data; the pattern is not unique to the individual time series, however.

Other time series have a tendency to show periodicities in a fairly regular way. This means that correlograms for these series will also show this periodicity. A seasonal series like the main-telephone gain is a very special kind of periodic series in which the highs and lows correspond to a seasonal pattern. It is interesting to notice that correlograms of seasonal data will have their very own seasonality pattern: notice the high autocorrelation at lag 12 and at multiples of 12 for the main-telephone-gain data displayed in Figure 6.8.

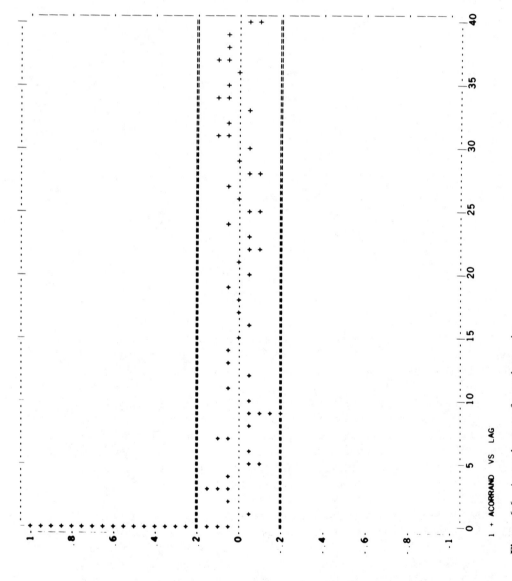

Figure 6.6   A correlogram of a random series.

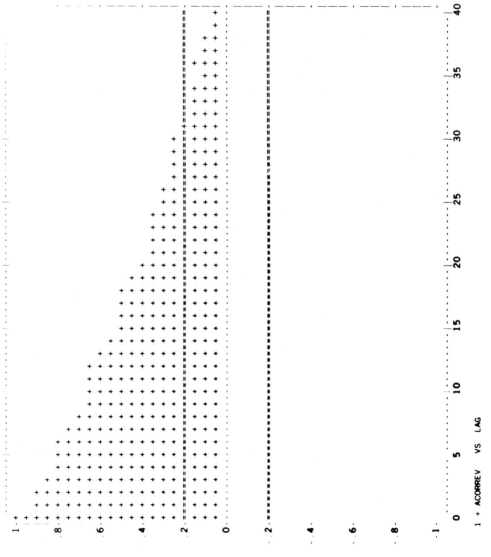

Figure 6.7 A correlogram of monthly toll revenue data.

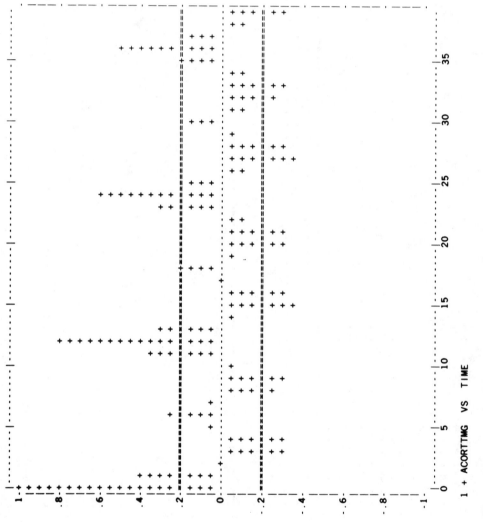

Figure 6.8 A correlogram for the monthly main-telephone-gain data.

Correlograms and their interpretations play a major role in ARIMA time series modeling. They are also used in the analysis of residuals from regression models. As part of the diagnostic checking process, an analyst either confirms or rejects the hypothesis that the residuals are randomly distributed.

SOFTWARE CONSIDERATIONS

All statistical computer packages and many desk-top computers nowadays contain some capability for displaying and summarizing data graphically. In your planning, you should make certain they can generate time plots and scatter diagrams on a printer plotter. Fewer software systems can provide output to selected high quality graphics devices, however, and this limitation should be considered carefully.

Among widely available statistical software packages, time plots and bivariate (scatter) plots are available through the P6D program in the University of California Biomedical Computer Programs (BMDP) (Dixon and Brown, 1979), the subprogram SCATTERGRAM in the Statistical Package for the Social Sciences (SPSS) (Nie et al., 1975), the PLOT PROC subprogram in the Statistical Analysis Sysstem (SAS) (SAS Institute, 1982), in STATLIB/ISX (Levenback et al., 1983), or in MINITAB (Ryan et al., 1976). IN SAS the PLOT option in PROC UNIVARIATE produces a stem-and-leaf plot (or a vertical bar chart) as part of the output and PROC AUTOREG provides a way to calculate autocorrelations.

McNeil (1977, Chapter 3, Section 7) discusses computer algorithms (using APL functions and FORTRAN subroutines) for "line and scat," which can be used for time plots and scatter plots, respectively. In Chapter 1, Section 7 he gives a program listing for the stem-and-leaf plot in APL and FORTRAN. BASIC and FORTRAN programs for stem-and-leaf plots are also given in Velleman and Hoaglin (1981).

In addition, many time series analysis and forecasting tools are available in the statistical and econometric software systems of a large number of commercial time-sharing firms. Through these service bureaus forecasters can often obtain access to software packages other than BMDP, SAS, or SPSS, such as Interactive Data Analysis (IDA) (Ling and Roberts, 1980), Minitab (Ryan, Joiner, and Ryan, 1976), SCSS (Nie et al., 1980), and SIBYL/RUNNER (Makridakis and Wheelwright, 1978).

SUMMARY

Effective graphical displays and summaries that help forecasters understand their data include

- Time plots that provide a visual indication of the predominant characteristics of a time series—trend-cycle, seasonal, and/or irregular.

- Scatter diagrams that are useful for studying relationships among variables and are widely applied in regression analysis.

- Stem-and-leaf displays that show groupings of data values, distribution or spread of the data, and unsymmetric trailing off at the low or high end. Central tendency, missing values, and unusual values can also be identified with this display. The display is particularly useful for examining residuals when a model is fit to a set of data.

- Autocorrelograms that show the strength of the relationship between data values separated by one or more periods. Seasonality can be identified with such plots, but they are more frequently used in the analysis of residuals from regression models. In this instance, the analyst looks for the absence of autocorrelation, i.e., a random pattern.

This chapter has stressed the importance of graphical tools for all aspects of the model building phases—exploratory as well as confirmatory. Additional uses for graphical displays will become evident in subsequent chapters.

USEFUL READING

BECKER, R. A., and J. M. CHAMBERS (1977). GR-Z: A System of Graphical Subroutines for Data Analysis. *Proceedings of Computer Science and Statistics, Tenth Annual Symposium on the Interface*. National Bureau of Standards Special Publication 503, 409–15.

DIXON, W. J., and M. B. BROWN (1979). *BMDP-79 Biomedical Computer Programs P-Series*. Los Angeles, CA: University of California Press.

HOAGLIN, D. C., F. MOSTELLER, and J. W. TUKEY, editors (1983). *Understanding Robust and Exploratory Data Analysis*. New York, NY: John Wiley and Sons.

LEVENBACH, H., W. M. BRELSFORD, and J. P. CLEARY (1983). *A STATLIB Primer.* Belmont, CA: Lifetime Learning Publications.

LING, R. F., and H. V. ROBERTS (1980). *User's Manual for IDA*. Palo Alto, CA: The Scientific Press.

McNEIL, D. R. (1977). *Interactive Data Analysis*. New York, NY: John Wiley and Sons.

MAKRIDAKIS, S., and S. C. WHEELWRIGHT (1978). *Interactive Forecasting—Univariate and Multivariate Methods*. San Francisco, CA: Holden-Day.

NIE, N. H., C. H. HALL, M. N. FRANKLIN, J. G. JENKINS, K. J. SOURS, M. J. NORUSIS, and V. BEADLE (1980). *SCSS: A User's Guide to the SCSS Conversational System*. New York, NY: McGraw-Hill Book Co.

NIE, N. H., C. H. HALL, J. G. JENKINS, K. STEINBRENNER, and D. H. BENT (1975). *SPSS: Statistical Package for the Social Sciences*, 2nd ed. New York, NY: McGraw-Hill Book Co.

RYAN, T. A., B. L. JOINER, and B. F. RYAN (1976). *Minitab Student Handbook*. North Scituate, MA: Duxbury Press.

SAS Institute (1982). *SAS User's Guide: Statistics*. Raleigh, NC: SAS Institute, Inc.

VELLEMAN, P. F., and D. C. HOAGLIN (1981). *Applications, Basics, and Computing of Exploratory Data Analysis*. Boston, MA: Duxbury Press.

CHAPTER 7

Summarizing
Batches of Data

The previous chapter discussed data displays, which reveal a great deal about patterns in data. This chapter deals with the analysis of the distribution of data, which is an important analytical step often overlooked in forecasting. It is important to recognize that:

- Summaries are required to quantify information about the shape or distribution of data.

- Summarizing data is part of the data analysis process. Assuming that an arithmetic mean is representative of a "typical" value may not be appropriate when the data have outliers (unusual data values).

- Assuming inappropriate distributions for data can result in misleading tests of significance. Hypothesis testing assumes that data are "normally" distributed, for example, and this may not be the case in reality.

TABULATING FREQUENCIES

Suppose that an analyst has been asked to determine the meaning of a set of numbers dealing with the travel time between a central garage and customers' locations for fifty service orders (visits) (Table 7.1). The following questions are to be answered:

- Where are most of the data values concentrated?
- What fluctuations are present in the data?
- Are there any extreme or unusual data values—values that don't seem to fit?
- Can the overall behavior of the data be described?

It is clear that the data displayed in Table 7.1 are not very enlightening. The analyst decides to condense the raw data by placing it into *cells* or *classes*. These

Table 7.1   Travel times (in minutes) from a garage to customers' locations for fifty service orders.

11, 23, 11, 8, 11, 10, 9, 6, 7, 8
23, 7, 32, 10, 12, 7, 14, 10, 6, 11
9, 10, 11, 10, 40, 13, 5, 9, 6, 27
14, 21, 11, 6, 17, 4, 30, 10, 6, 3
4, 4, 16, 22, 20, 3, 13, 8, 18, 12

cells can be either numerical or attributive (e.g., designated as either a "business" or "residence" service order) in nature. The first count and display of the data are shown in Table 7.2. The relative percent that each class is of the total number of orders suggests that between 9 to 11 minutes is the typical or most frequent travel time. Most of the observations are clustered within 3–14 minutes. The one observation between 39–41 minutes looks very unusual, and all values beyond 26 minutes look suspect because they are so far from the apparent average. Perhaps there were extenuating circumstances that caused these travel times to be so great. But how does the analyst determine if some of the data are truly "unusual"?

Relative Frequency Distributions

The procedure for counting the number of occurrences of a given characteristic in a grouping of data gives rise to frequencies. These frequencies, when considered as

Table 7.2   A frequency distribution for the fifty service-order travel times shown in Table 7.1.

Interval (in minutes)	Number of service orders		Relative percent of orders
3–5	ЦНↃ I	6	12
6–8	ЦНↃ ЦНↃ I	11	22
9–11	ЦНↃ ЦНↃ ЦНↃ	15	30
12–14	ЦНↃ I	6	12
15–17	I I	2	4
18–20	I I	2	4
21–23	I I I I	4	8
24–26			
27–29	I	1	2
30–32	I I	2	4
33–35			
36–38			
39–41	I	1	2
	(Total: 50)		

fractions, can be displayed as a *relative frequency distribution*. Table 7.2 is an example of a relative frequency distribution.

A grouping interval needs to be selected before tallying the data. The grouping interval will depend on the range of variation, the number of data values, and the palatability of the display to the user.

In Table 7.2 the intervals have a width of two minutes. An interval of one minute rather than two would result in a long table without providing added information. These groupings should be uniquely defined so that there is no ambiguity into which cell a given tally goes.

The relative frequencies are then determined by counting the number of data values in a cell divided by total number of data values recorded.

In the first cell, for example, there are six orders out of fifty giving a relative frequency of 12 percent. This information is then appropriately summarized as a relative frequency distribution in the last column.

Table 7.3 is another relative frequency distribution, but it has an additional column—the cumulative percent of orders. Once the 21–23-minute interval is reached, 92 percent of the observations have been counted. This reinforces the suspect nature of the remaining observations.

Several points need to be considered in establishing class intervals. The units should be meaningful. It should be decided first whether the number or attribute class is most appropriate. Also, the amount of data as well as the range of values of interest should be considered. If the data are integer-valued, the class intervals should not be fractional.

Many analysts use what is called "the 10/15/20 rule" for guidance in selecting the size of class intervals. The total range of data (maximum value minus minimum value) is computed first, and the result is then divided by 10, 15, and 20. For a small

Table 7.3 The cumulative frequency distribution of the service-order travel times.

Interval (in minutes)	Number of orders	Cumulative number of orders	Cumulative percent of orders
3–5	6	6	12
6–8	11	17	34
9–11	15	32	64
12–14	6	38	76
15–17	2	40	80
18–20	2	42	84
21–23	4	46	92
24–26		46	92
27–29	1	47	94
30–32	2	49	98
33–35		49	98
36–38		49	98
39–41	1	50	100

group of data (50 or so), a class interval in the range resulting after division by 10–15 is preferred; for a large group of data, take a class interval resulting from division by 15–20. Select the minimum value as the initial lowest class boundary. Add other classes according to whichever interval formula you have used. An example of this procedure is shown in Table 7.4.

The resulting graph of the frequency distribution can take the form of a *histogram,* as is shown in Figure 7.1. In a histogram, data are plotted as bars rather than as a single graph-line. Figure 7.1 shows that there are a very few long travel times (above 25 minutes) and that the times around the median (10 minutes) are the most typical. The distribution is said to have a "tail" skewed to the right. However, the shape of the histogram can be sensitive to the choice of class intervals. Figure 7.2 demonstrates the fact that it is often desirable to select several class intervals to be certain that the results are reasonable. (For the service order example, fractional intervals make little sense since the data are composed entirely of whole numbers.)

A relative frequency distribution can be turned into a *cumulative frequency distribution* when one is interested in quantities such as the proportion of items below (or above) a given standard value. Another situation requiring a cumulative frequency distribution arises when investigating whether a distribution follows some particular mathematical form. This will be touched on again in the section on quantile-quantile plots.

The Normal Distribution

The primary reason many analysts construct histograms is to compare them with a normal ("bellshaped") probability distribution. The normal distribution, which is deeply rooted in all statistical theory, looks symmetrical and is completely specified by two parameters (μ, σ); it is tabulated in Appendix A, Table 1.

Table 7.4   An illustration of the 10/15/20 rule.

- Compute range = Maximum value − Minimum value:
    Range = 40 − 3 = 37.
- Compute range divided by 10, 15, and 20:
    Range/10 = 3.7; Range/15 = 2.47; Range/20 = 1.85.
    Class length of 3 will yield between 10 and 15 classes.
- Select initial lower class bound not more than minimum value:
    Initial lower class bound = 3.
- Increment this bound by length of class interval to obtain subsequent lower class bounds:
    (3 − 5, 6 − 8, 9 − 11, . . .
- Upper class bound is highest possible value that is less than the subsequent lower class bound:
    . . . 33 − 35, 36 − 38, 39 − 41).

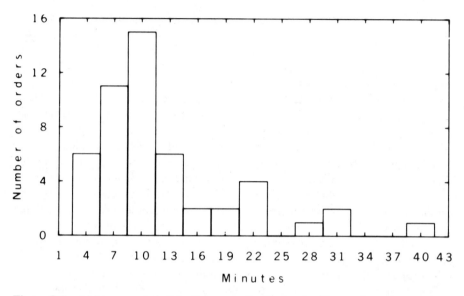

Figure 7.1   A histogram plot of the frequency distribution for fifty service-order travel times.

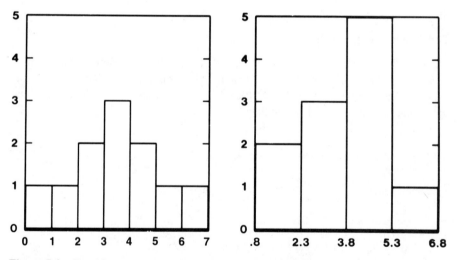

Figure 7.2   Two histograms using the same data but different class intervals.

In general, probability distributions are used to make statements about the probability that a certain portion of the data or that a statistic falls within a specified range. For a normal distribution with mean μ and standard deviation σ, the interval $(\mu - 1.64\sigma, \mu + 1.64\sigma)$ contains 90 percent of the distribution. Similarly, there is about a 68 percent probability that a random observation from a normal distribution will be between plus and minus one standard deviation (σ) of the mean (μ).

The use of confidence limits about the fitted values in regression theory is derived from the normal distribution. This subject is treated in Chapter 14.

DISPLAYING SUMMARY MEASUREMENTS

While time plots and scatter diagrams are useful for revealing overall patterns, it is often desirable to condense some features of the data into a few meaningful numbers. These summary measures are called *statistics*.

While statistics can be used for many purposes, they are commonly used for:

- Simply describing some aspect of the data that needs to be highlighted for a particular application, such as measures of central tendency or dispersion.
- Summarizing salient features of a frequency distribution, such as its percentiles.
- Comparing two or more frequency distributions.
- Confirmatory analysis, such as hypothesis testing.

There are a number of familiar ways, as described in elementary statistics texts, for summarizing data with statistics. The histogram has already been introduced. There are a number of other techniques that have sprung up in recent years as a result of the increased flexibility of computers in handling, analyzing, and displaying data. Much of this "new look" can be attributed to Tukey (1977). Other elementary books that emphasize exploratory data analysis include Chambers et. al. (1983), Erickson and Nosanchuk (1977), Hartwig and Dearing (1976), McNeil (1977), and Velleman and Hoaglin (1981).

Central Tendency

The *location,* or central tendency, of a group of data is the center of the data when arranged in order of size of the measure. One measure of location or central tendency is the median. Other commonly used measures of location are the mode, the arithmetic (sample) mean or average, and the midmean. The reason no single measure of location is always the best is that each provides its own perspective and insights, and in practical situations outliers or unusual data values can seriously distort the representativeness of certain statistics.

As an example, consider the following set of numbers:

$$\{1.1, 1.6, 4.7, 2.1, 3.1, 32.7, 5.8, 2.6, 4.8, 1.9, 3.7, 2.6\}.$$

The arithmetic mean is 5.56, and the median is 2.85. It is noteworthy that the mean, which is theoretically the "best" statistic for estimating central tendency for normally distributed data, has been severely distorted by the outlying value 32.7. The mean of the data, excluding the outlier, is 3.1, and appears much more representative.

One simple way to make the arithmetic mean less sensitive to extreme outliers is first to delete or "trim" a proportion of the data from each end and then calculate the arithmetic mean of the remaining numbers. Such a statistic is called a *trimmed mean*. The midmean, for example, is a 25-percent trimmed mean since 25 percent of the data values are trimmed from each end (i.e., the mean is taken of the values between the 25th and 75th percentiles). This will be discussed later in this Chapter. A thorough treatment of measures of location and their properties under varying realistic assumptions of distribution may be found in Andrews et al. (1972).

Dispersion

Besides measures of location for a frequency distribution, certain measures of *scale* or dispersion are useful. Some commonly used measures are range, standard deviation, and modifications of these. The range is simply the difference between the largest and smallest value in the data set.

The (sample) standard deviation is the most commonly used measure of dispersion, though, like the mean, it can be misleading when there are outliers. The standard deviation is the square root of the (sample) variance that has the formula

$$\sum_{i=1}^{n}(y_i - \bar{y})^2/(n - 1),$$

where $y_1, y_2, \ldots, y_n$ are the n data values and

$$\bar{y} = \sum_{i=1}^{n}y_i/n$$

is the sample mean. Historically, its popularity is due primarily to its theoretical advantages in formal statistical theory.

Other measures of dispersion include the *MAD statistic* (MAD stands for median of the absolute deviations from the median of the data), the sample variance of a truncated sample, and the *interquartile difference* (IQD), which is the difference between the 75th and 25th percentiles. The 25th percentile is $(n + 1)/4 = 13/4 = 3.25$; i.e., between the third and fourth smallest value. The 75th percentile is $3(n + 1)/4 = 9.75$; i.e., between the ninth and tenth value in the ranked data.

The calculation of a MAD is illustrated in Table 7.5. The "data" there are the same numbers used earlier to explain "median" and "arithmetic mean." The MAD is calculated by first ranking the data from smallest to largest (Column 2) and picking the median [it is $(2.6 + 3.1)/2 = 2.85$, since there is an even number of data values]. Absolute deviations from the median are calculated next (Column 3), and the result is reranked (Column 4). The midvalue of the latter set of numbers is the

Table 7.5 Calculation of the median absolute deviation
from the median (MAD).

Data (n)	Data, ranked	Deviations from the median	Absolute deviations from the median, ranked
1.1	1.1	−1.75	0.25
1.6	1.6	−1.25	0.25
4.7	1.9	−0.95	0.25
2.1	2.1	−0.75	0.75
3.1	2.6	−0.25	0.85
32.7	2.6 ⎤ Median	−0.25	0.95 ⎤ MAD = 1.1
5.8	3.1 ⎦	0.25	1.25 ⎦
2.6	3.7	0.85	1.75
4.8	4.7	1.85	1.85
1.9	4.8	1.95	1.95
3.7	5.8	2.95	2.95
2.6	32.7	29.85	29.85

First quartile = 1/4 (n + 1) = 13/4 = 3.25.

Median = (2.6 + 3.1)/2 = 2.85.

Midmean = (2.1 + 2.6 + 2.6 + 3.1 + 3.7 + 4.7)/6 = 3.13.

Third quartile = 3/4 (n + 1) = 39/4 = 9.75.

MAD [it is (0.95 + 1.25)/2 = 1.1]. For practical use the MAD and IQD are scaled by dividing by 0.6745 and 1.35, respectively. For normally distributed data this scaling makes these measures good approximations of the theoretical standard deviation (σ) if the number of observations is large.

The conventional sample mean and standard deviation do not offer much protection against outliers. Statistics based on the median or the mean of truncated data appear to be much more "resistant" to outliers. A statistic is said to be *resistant* if a change in a small fraction of the data will not produce a large distortion of a total calculated value—i.e., it is resistant to "weird" or unusual values. The arithmetic mean is clearly not resistant since its value can be changed by arbitrarily increasing only one of its terms. The median, on the other hand, is quite resistant. Later we will deal more thoroughly with techniques for ensuring against unusual values.

In the data we used for these examples—the twelve numbers with the single outlier—the standard deviation is 8.6, the MAD is 1.1, and the interquartile range is 2.75. For normally distributed data, the standard deviation can be approximated by dividing the MAD by 0.6745 (= 1.63) or by dividing the IQD by 1.35 (= 2.04). The mean plus three standard deviations is 31.35 [5.55 + (3)(8.6) = 31.35], which almost encompasses the outlier of 32.7. This is because the calculation of the standard deviation gives equal weight to all observations. However, if one considers the median plus three times 1.63 (= 7.74), then 32.7 is clearly very far away from the bulk of the data.

The Box Plot

A frequency distribution can be described by its percentiles. The pth percentile is the value which exceeds p percent of the data. In particular, the median is the 50th percentile; i.e., it is the value which exceeds 50 percent of the data. For example, the stem-and-leaf display described in Chapter 6 shows that the median of the travel-time data is 10 minutes. The distribution does not have a symmetrical shape, so it becomes essential to summarize the distribution with more than one percentile.

While percentiles can be used to summarize a frequency distribution, it is often desirable to describe a distribution with the smallest set of numbers possible. Rather than simply write down a sequence of such numbers, there is a graphical device, called the *box plot,* which is a five-number summary of a distribution (McGill et al., 1978, and Tukey, 1977). A box plot concisely depicts the median, the upper and lower quartiles, and the two extremes of any group of data. The upper and lower quartiles are respectively the 75th and 25th percentiles.

A box plot for the travel-time data previously discussed is shown in Figure 7.3. Fifty percent of the data values are tightly grouped (these are depicted with the box, which includes all data falling between the 25th and 75th percentiles; these quartiles are also called hinges). The upper tail appears longer than the lower tail. The median value is slightly lower than the midrange of the box. The upper extreme value appears to be an outlier since it is so far away from the bulk of the data. Since there may be

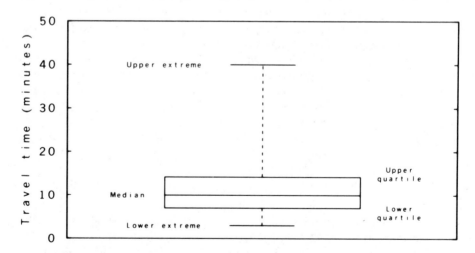

Figure 7.3   The box plot of the service-order travel-time data.

data values along the "whisker" (the vertical line), this conclusion needs to be confirmed with additional analyses. This plot gives a surprising amount of information for such a simple display.

The simple box plot summarizes the distribution in terms of five quantities. In addition, the distance between the quartiles is the interquartile range, a measure of dispersion. A missing link in this plot is the number of data values in the distribution, which impacts on the reliability of the estimate of the median. To indicate sample size, a *notched box plot* can be drawn in which the depth of the notch can be made proportional to the square root of the sample size (McGill et al., 1978).

Figure 7.4 shows a notched box plot for the annual variation in the twelve monthly values for the main-telephone-gain data across nine years. The changes in level as well as the variation of the data within years are summarized in a single display. Evidently, the difference between the high and low values within a year is increasing over time. Moreover, while the median values reflect the cyclical pattern of the economy (the 1970 and 1975 recessions), the range spanned by the inter-quartile range of the monthly values (the height of the box) varies considerably over time. These kinds of information can provide the forecaster with some insights about the nature of variation in data.

The single comprehensive box plot may not be enough by itself, however. One weakness is its inability to identify or discern data from two different populations. Figure 7.5 shows box plots for the travel times for three categories of service orders. It shows that there are really two distributions, one from the subset of nonkey telephone orders and the other from the orders for key telephone sets (a "key"

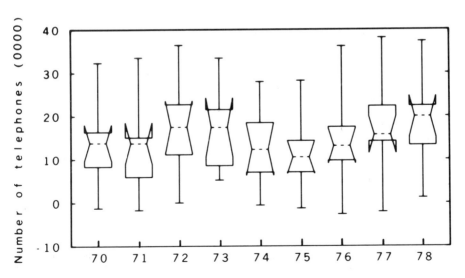

Figure 7.4 A notched box plot showing the annual variation in the twelve monthly values for the main-telephone-gain data.

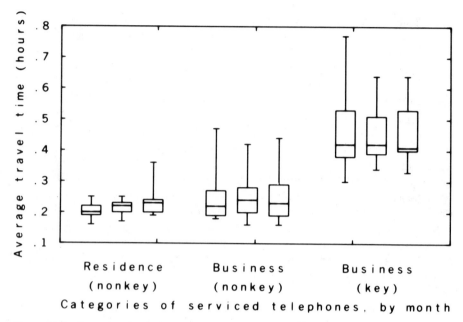

Figure 7.5   Box plots for the travel times for three categories of service orders.

telephone set is one linked to a multiple set of telephone numbers). The difference in the type of work that is required to service "key" and "nonkey" orders results in two separate distributions. A single box plot would clearly mask these differences.

The box plot can also be used to identify potential outliers. In the terminology of Tukey (1977), a "step" is defined as 1.5 times the interquartile range (height of the box). Inner fences are values one step above the top and one step below the bottom of the box. Outer fences are values two steps above and below the box. A value outside an inner fence can be an outlier, but a value outside an outer fence is much more likely to be one.

The Quantile-Quantile Plot

The Q-Q (quantile-quantile) plot is useful for determining if two data sets have the same probability distribution. The quantiles (percentiles) of one distribution are plotted against the quantiles of the second distribution. If two data sets have the same probability distribution, the Q-Q plot will be linear.

For example, the quantiles of an empirical data set can be compared to the quantiles of the standard normal distribution ($\mu = 0$, $\sigma = 1$) to test for normality. Each value corresponds to a quantile which can be compared to the same quantiles of the normal curve.

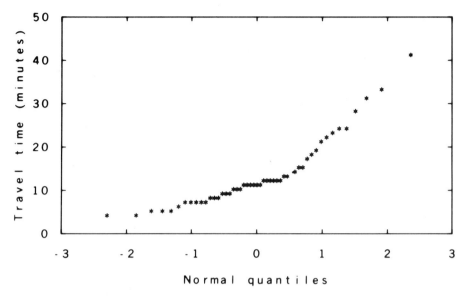

Figure 7.6   A quantile-quantile (Q-Q) plot for the service-order travel-time data.

A Q-Q plot for the travel-time data we have been using in this chapter is shown in Figure 7.6. This plot shows an upper tail in the empirical distribution that is much longer than that of the normal distribution. The tails of many data sets are longer than those of the normal distribution, but generally by a lesser amount than in this example.

INSURING AGAINST UNUSUAL VALUES

Statistical estimation is built upon a mathematical theory that is seldom realized exactly in forecasting practice. For estimating location and scale of data, for example, the arithmetic mean and sample variance can be shown to be "best" (i.e., have optimal properties) if the data are a random sample from the normal distribution. Likewise, correlation and least squares regression generally assume a normal distribution. Least squares techniques are not only "not best," however, but can be horribly misleading when the data deviate from the normality assumption. Because of this, it is important to have estimation procedures that will be "robust" against data that would otherwise be distortive.

The need for a nontraditional approach to estimation is motivated by two facts. The first is that a forecaster never has an accurate knowledge of the true underlying distribution of the data. Second, even slight deviations from a strict parametric model can give rise to poor statistical performance for classical (associated with the method of least squares) estimation techniques. Estimators that are less sensitive to these factors are often referred to as being *robust* (Box, 1953). In particular, it is well known that outliers can distort certain estimators; a robust procedure must produce estimates that are not seriously affected by the presence of a few outliers. Thus, some robust estimators are designed to be *resistant* to unusual data values—they give less weight to observations which stray from the bulk of the data.

The use of robust methods is illustrated by Mallows (1979), who describes several analyses of large data sets (more than 1000 observations) in which robustness considerations have proved relevant.

ROBUST ESTIMATES OF LOCATION

Consider an example of the effect one bad observation can have on the arithmetic mean of a group of numbers. The set of numbers {3, 4, 4, 5, 6, 6, 6, 7, 9, 10} has a mean of 6.0. But adding one observation, say 50, changes the mean to 10.0. The latter clearly does not represent the location or "center" of the bulk of the data. Depending on the use of the application, a forecaster should be cautious in using statistical measures blindly, since however well known they may be, some are possibly not well behaved.

The Trimmed Mean

Although the arithmetic mean is a classical estimator of location with a great deal of tradition, it is often accepted uncritically by the practitioner. The above example illustrates a bad quality of the arithmetic mean, namely that one outlier can have an undue effect on the arithmetic mean and even pull an estimate of the bulk of data away from its representative value. An alternative estimator of location is the α-*trimmed mean*. Recall that a trimmed mean is calculated by deleting or "trimming" a proportion of the ordered data from each end and then calculating the arithmetic mean of the remaining numbers. The deletion of points is based on their order, but the deleted points are not necessarily extreme values.

The procedure for calculating the α-trimmed mean can be defined as follows. Let $y_{(i)}$ equal the ith *ordered* observation. We will need to define $a = [\alpha n]$, where n is the number of observations and α denotes the trimming proportion; notice that the brackets [ ] represent the "greatest integer" function—i.e., the greatest integer equal to or less than the given number. Thus, if you trim 50 percent from each end of an ordered array of data, you will end up with the median.

The trimmed mean is equal to the sum of the untrimmed values divided by h, where $h = n - 2a$. Thus, the α-trimmed mean $m(\alpha)$ is defined by

$$m(\alpha) = \frac{1}{h} \sum_{i=a+1}^{n-a} y_{(i)}.$$

When using the arithmetic mean, the standard deviation is used to find an estimate of sample variability, and the standard deviation divided by $\sqrt{n}$ is an estimate of the standard error of the mean. The standard error of the trimmed mean, denoted by $s[m(\alpha)]$, can be approximated by

$$s[m(\alpha)] = [SS(\alpha)/h(h-1)]^{1/2},$$

where $SS(\alpha)$ is the sum of squares defined by

$$SS(\alpha) = \sum_{i=1}^{n} [w_i - m(\alpha)]^2.$$

The *Winsorized values* of $y_{(i)}$, denoted by w_i, are defined by

$$w_i = \begin{cases} y_{(a+1)} & i = 1, \ldots, a \\ y_{(i)} & i = a+1, \ldots, n-a \\ y_{(n-a)} & i = n-a+1, \ldots, n. \end{cases}$$

Notice that the trimmed values are replaced with the $(a + 1)$th value at the low end and the $(n - a)$th value at the high end.

Furthermore, Monte Carlo studies have shown that

$$[m(\alpha) - \theta]/s[m(\alpha)]$$

has an approximate t-distribution with $(h - 1)$ degrees of freedom. Here, θ is the location parameter for a symmetric distribution. Therefore, assuming an underlying symmetric distribution, a confidence interval for θ can be given by

$$m(\alpha) - t_{h-1}(\alpha/2)s[m(\alpha)] < \theta < m(\alpha) + t_{h-1}(\alpha/2)s[m(\alpha)],$$

where $t_{h-1}(\alpha/2)$ is the $100(1 - \alpha)$ percent significance level for a Student t-distribution on $h - 1$ degrees of freedom. Thus with 95 percent confidence ($\alpha = 0.05$), θ will lie between $m(\alpha) \pm t_{h-1}(0.025)s[m(\alpha)]$.

Notice that the underlying assumption of a symmetric distribution is less restrictive than the assumption of normality used in classical statistics. Estimates for the asymptotic (large sample) variance of the α-trimmed mean of asymmetric distributions have also been studied by Andrews et al. (1972).

M-Estimators

A method has been developed which will "automatically" reduce the effect of outliers by giving them a reduced weight when computing the "average" value of the data. This estimator, often called the *M-estimator,* is the "maximum likelihood estimate" (a good statistical property to assess) for the location parameter of a heavy-tailed distribution, defined by Huber (1964). Basically, the Huber distribution behaves like a normal distribution in the middle range and like an exponential distribution in the tails. Thus the bulk of the data appears normally distributed, while there is a greater chance of having extreme observations in the sample.

The steps necessary to compute the Huber *M*-estimator are:

1. Compute an initial (very "robust") estimate for θ, say $\hat{\theta}$ = median, and calculate the residuals from this estimate.

2. Estimate a scale statistic s by using MAD/0.6745 where MAD (median absolute deviation) is the median of

$$|y_i - \hat{\theta}|, \qquad i = 1, 2, \ldots, n.$$

3. Compute weights W_i^2, using residuals and the scale estimate s:

$$W_i^2 = \begin{cases} 1 & \text{if } |y_i - \hat{\theta}| \leq Ks \\ Ks/|y_i - \hat{\theta}| & \text{if } |y_i - \hat{\theta}| > Ks, \end{cases}$$

where a constant K is chosen that will obtain a desirable level of efficiency: a reasonable set of values are 1.0, 1.5, and 2.0. As K becomes smaller, more points receive a weight of less than 1 (Figure 7.7). The value of K depends on what percentage of the data are outliers or how much "efficiency" (see Chapter 10) you want to give up if the data are normally distributed.

4. Obtain a new estimate from

$$\hat{\theta} = \frac{\sum\limits_{i=1}^{n} W_i^2 y_i}{\sum\limits_{i=1}^{n} W_i^2}.$$

5. Repeat steps 2 through 4 until convergence.

It has been shown (Huber, 1973) that the asymptotic (large sample) variance of the Huber *M*-estimator can be estimated by

$$V(\hat{\theta}) = \frac{1}{(n^*)^2} \sum\limits_{i=1}^{n} W_i^4 (y_i - \hat{\theta})^2,$$

where n^* is defined as the number of observations with $W_i = 1$.

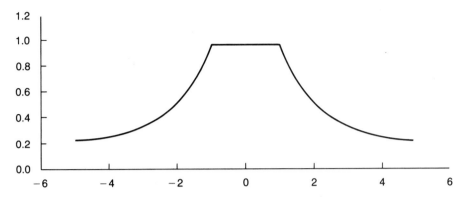

Figure 7.7 The Huber weight function.

A Numerical Example

To get some insight into the mechanics of calculating a robust estimate of location, it may be valuable to work out an example based on a small set of (ordered) data:

$$\{-67, -48, 6, 8, 14, 16, 23, 24, 28, 29, 41, 49, 56, 60, 75\}.$$

The first step in data analysis should be to investigate the data graphically. Reviewing the data, you would observe the extremely low values, -67 and -48. The next step might be to prepare a quantile-quantile (Q-Q) plot (Figure 7.8). If the data are normally distributed, they should lie along a straight line. The plot demonstrates that the two smallest data values are indeed extreme, indicating that the normality assumption may not be valid.

The Q-Q plot can also be used to get a "quick-and-dirty" robust estimate of the (μ, σ) parameters of the normal distribution. By "eyeballing" a straight line through the *bulk* of the points on the Q-Q plot, you can determine that the Y-intercept at $X = 0$ and the slope of the line correspond to estimates of $\hat{\mu}$ and $\hat{\sigma}$, respectively. On the other hand, the ordinary least squares estimates, calculated from the data, are $\hat{\mu} = 20.93$ and $\hat{\sigma} = 37.74$, which could be used to superimpose a straight line with intercept 20.93 and slope 37.74 on the Q-Q plot. As can be seen from Figure 7.8, the straight line determined from the least squares estimates doesn't represent the bulk of the data on the Q-Q plot.

Table 7.6 shows the calculations of the α-trimmed mean and *its* standard error for these data when 25 percent of the data are "trimmed." For $\alpha = 0.25$ and $n = 15$, the largest integer value of $(0.25 \times 15 = 3.75)$ is 3, and therefore three values are trimmed from each end.

Column 1 shows the ordered raw data. In Column 2, the Winsorized values of the ordered data are listed. The first three data values are replaced by the value of

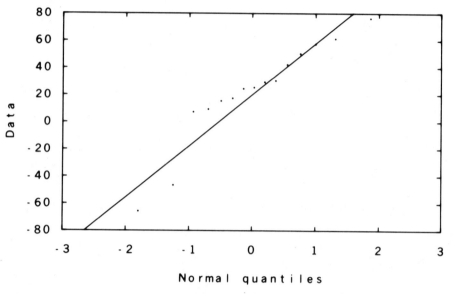

Figure 7.8   A quantile-quantile (Q-Q) plot for a small data set.

the fourth observation (the smallest untrimmed observation), and the last three values are replaced by the value of the twelfth observation (the largest untrimmed observation). The trimmed mean is the average of the fourth through the twelfth values and is $232/9 = 25.78$. Column 3 is the deviation between the Winsorized values and the trimmed mean. Column 4 is the square of Column 3 and is summed for use in the standard error calculation. The standard error of this trimmed mean is the square root of the sum of the squares of Column 3 divided by $(h)(h - 1)$: $(3913.45/72)^{1/2} = 7.37$.

Tables 7.7 and 7.8 show the calculations for the Huber M-estimator of location and its corresponding standard error for the raw data shown in Column 1 of Table 7.6 is the ordered raw data. The median of the data is 24. Column 2 is the idfference between the raw data and the median. The median absolute deviation is 17; it is the median of the absolute value of this column (the eighth largest absolute value of Column 2). An approximate unbiased scale statistic is the MAD/0.6745 = 25.2. The divisor 0.6745 is used because then MAD/0.6745 will be approximately equal to the standard deviation σ of a norma! distribution if the number of observations is large and if the data are actually a random sample from a normal distribution with variance σ^2.

By using $K = 2$ for observations whose absolute residuals are greater than two standard errors, deviations in Column 2 in excess of $Ks = (2)(25.2) = 50.4$ are downweighted. Therefore, observations 1, 2, and 15 receive less than full weight. Column 3 contains the weights $[W_{i_1}^2 = 50.4/|y_i - \text{median}|]$ for those values beyond Ks. A weighted mean is calculated by taking the product of corresponding entries in Columns 1 and 3 and summing over the 15 products $(= 357.38)$, then dividing

Table 7.6   The α-trimmed mean and its standard error for the 15 numbers. The trimming parameter is $\alpha = 0.25$.

(1) $y_{(i)}$	(2) w_i	(3) $(w_i - \hat{\theta})$	(4) $(w_i - \hat{\theta})^2$
-67	8	-17.78	316.13
-48	8	-17.78	316.13
6	8	-17.78	316.13
8	8	-17.78	316.13
14	14	-11.78	138.77
16	16	-9.78	95.65
23	23	-2.78	7.73
24	24	-1.78	3.17
28	28	2.22	4.93
29	29	3.22	10.37
41	41	15.22	231.67
49	49	23.22	539.17
56	49	23.22	539.17
60	49	23.22	539.17
75	49	23.22	539.17
Total:			3913.45

$\alpha = 0.25; n = 15$

$a = (0.25)(15) = 3.75(\text{integer } 3); h = n - 2(3) = 9$

$\hat{\theta} = m(0.25) = 1/9 \sum\limits_{i=4}^{12} y_{(i)} = 25.78$

$s[m(0.25)] = [3913.45/9(8)]^{1/2} = 7.37$

this by the sum of Column 3 ($= 14.24$). In Table 16.3, this calculation gives $\hat{\theta}_1 = 25.13$ for this first iteration. A second iteration provides a refined estimate of $\hat{\theta}_2 = 25.17$. Thus two iterations appear sufficient for convergence.

The standard error of this estimate is obtained by multiplying the square of the weights (Column 5 of Table 7.7) by the square of the deviations between the data and the location estimate $\hat{\theta}_2$, dividing by the square of the number of observations receiving full weight, and taking the square root of the resulting number. This calculation is shown in Table 7.8.

The results for the mean, the 0.25-trimmed mean (also called the midmean), and the Huber M-estimator are:

	Mean	Midmean	M-estimator
$\hat{\theta}$:	20.93	25.78	25.17
$V(\hat{\theta})$:	9.74	7.37	8.28

Table 7.7 Calculations of the Huber M-estimator of location, when $K = 2$ and $\hat\theta_0 = $ median $(y_i) = 24$.

(1) $y_{(i)}$	(2) $y_{(i)} - \hat\theta_0$	(3) W_{i1}^2	(4) $y_{(i)} - \hat\theta_1$	(5) W_{i2}^2
−67	−91	50.4/91	−92.13	50.8/92.13
−48	−72	50.4/72	−73.13	50.8/73.13
6	−18	1	−19.13	1
8	−16	1	−17.13	1
14	−10	1	−11.13	1
16	−8	1	−9.13	1
23	−1	1	−2.13	1
24	0	1	−1.13	1
28	4	1	2.87	1
29	5	1	3.87	1
41	17	1	15.87	1
49	25	1	23.87	1
56	32	1	30.87	1
60	36	1	34.87	1
75	51	50.4/51	49.87	1

Table 7.8 Calculations for the Huber M-estimator of the standard error, when $K = 2$ and $\hat\theta_0 = 24$ (median).

Iteration 0: $\qquad\qquad \hat\theta_0 = $ Median $= 24$.

Iteration 1:

$$s = \frac{\text{MAD}}{0.6745} = \frac{17}{0.6745} = 25.20;$$

$$Ks = 50.40;$$

$$\hat\theta_1 = \frac{\Sigma W_i^2 y_i}{\Sigma W_i^2} = \frac{357.38}{14.24} = 25.13.$$

Iteration 2:

$$s = \frac{\text{MAD}}{0.6745} = \frac{17.13}{0.6745} = 25.40;$$

$$Ks = 50.8;$$

$$\hat\theta_2 = \frac{\Sigma W_i^2 y_i}{\Sigma W_i^2} = \frac{358.72}{14.25} = 25.17;$$

$$V(\hat\theta) = \left[\frac{\Sigma W_i^4 (y_i - \hat\theta_2)^2}{(n^*)^2} \right]^{1/2} = \left[\frac{\Sigma W_i^4 (y_i - 25.17)^2}{(13)^2} \right]^{1/2} = 8.28,$$

where $n^* = $ number of observations receiving full weight.

Notice that $V(\hat{\theta})$ is the estimated standard deviation of the location *estimator* and not of the *sample*.

It is clear that the arithmetic mean is very sensitive to outliers or distant observations. Both the trimmed mean and Huber M-estimator provide estimates that are less sensitive to the extreme values. The standard error of the M-estimator is somewhat smaller than that for the mean. However, the standard error for the midmean is significantly less. This is somewhat expected since computations for the midmean begin by trimming and Winsorizing 40 percent of the data, the 40 percent being the most extreme values (three from each end), whereas these points still have some effect (but less than least squares) on the Huber M-estimator since their associated weight is not zero.

The Huber M-estimator is used again in Chapter 11 to downweight extreme observations so that they do not unduly distort the regression relationship determined by the bulk of the data.

SOFTWARE CONSIDERATIONS

Frequency tabulations are widely available in a number of statistical software packages, such as Program P2D in BMDP (Dixon and Brown, 1979), MINITAB (Ryan et al., 1976), PROC FREQ in SAS (SAS Institute, 1982), subprogram FREQUENCIES in SPSS (Nie et al., 1975) and STPAK in ISX/STATLIB (Levenbach et al., 1983). The P2D program in BMDP prints out a simple printer-plot version of the box plot. In SAS the PLOT option causes PROC UNIVARIATE to produce a box plot as part of the output. The BMDP program P5D prints a normal or half-normal probability plot of the data. The PROC RANK in SAS can be used to construct normal probability plots. A normal probability plot is also produced in SAS through the PLOT option in PROC UNIVARIATE. McNeil (1977, Chapter 1, Section 7) provides APL functions and FORTRAN subroutines for programming the box plot. Velleman and Hoaglin (1981) provide BASIC and FORTRAN programs for histograms and box plots.

The programs BMDP7D and BMDP2D (Dixon and Brown, 1979) calculate three robust estimates of location, including the Winsorized and trimmed mean. The program BMDP7D calculates robust confidence intervals and prints double asterisks (**) after the estimate of the mean with the shortest confidence interval length—i.e., after the most precise estimate of the mean. A single asterisk (*) is printed after the interval which is the next shortest. See also a software discussion by Afifi and Azen (1979, Section 2.7) for robust estimators, and McNeil (1977) and Velleman and Hoaglin (1981) for portable FORTRAN and BASIC programs for robust smoothers.

SUMMARY

In this chapter, the key points about tabulating frequencies are that:

- Summaries are necessary to quantify information inherent in the "shape" or distribution of data.
- Frequency distributions can be calculated and plotted to show what percentage each interval is of the total number of data.
- Cumulative frequencies or percentiles can be used to determine if a given data set follows a normal probability distribution.

Several measures are useful for summarizing distributions. These include:

- Statistics used to describe central tendency such as the mean, median, and trimmed mean.
- Measures of dispersion, such as the standard deviation, median absolute deviation, and range.
- The box plot, which is a convenient way of visually displaying a five-number summary of a distribution.
- The quantile-quantile plot, which is frequently used to determine if a data set, especially residuals from a regression model, follows a normal distribution. If it does, hypothesis testing can be carried out or confidence limits can be constructed.

The summarizing measurements discussed in this chapter provide important insights into understanding the shape of data—one of the early steps in model building or analysis. This may necessitate adjustments of the data so that a particular forecasting or analytical technique can be applied.

When data suggest nonnormal distributions with possible outliers, robust/resistant methods should also be considered:

- Robust methods are a way of dealing with estimation and modeling problems in the presence of outliers and nonnormality. Trimmed means and M-estimates are two examples of robust procedures.

- Robust procedures are recommended as complements to the usual (least squares) procedures (Hogg, 1979). When they are in essential agreement, they should be reported together. When substantial differences exist in the two analyses, the data should be examined more thoroughly for outliers or bad data values. Even if you use robust techniques, you should still plot the data for a thorough examination of it.

USEFUL READING

AFIFI, A. A., and S. P. AZEN (1979). *Statistical Analysis—A Computer Oriented Approach*, 2nd ed. New York, NY: Academic Press.

ANDREWS, D. F., P. J. BICKEL, F. R. HAMPEL, P. J. HUBER, W. H. ROGERS, and J. W. TUKEY (1972). *Robust Estimates of Location: Survey and Advances*. Princeton, NJ: Princeton University Press.

BOX, G. E. P. (1953). Non-Normality and Tests on Variances. *Biometrika* 40, 318–35.

DIXON, W. J., and M. B. BROWN (1979). *BMDP-79 Biomedical Computer Programs P-Series*. Los Angeles, CA: University of California Press.

ERICKSON, B. H., and T. A. NOSANCHUK (1977). *Understanding Data*. Toronto, Canada: McGraw-Hill-Ryerson Ltd.

HARTWIG, F., and B. E. DEARING (1979). *Exploratory Data Analysis*. Sage University Paper on Quantitative Applications in the Social Sciences, 07-016, Beverly Hills, CA: Sage Publications.

HOGG, R. V. (1979). Statistical Robustness: One View of Its Use in Applications Today. *The American Statistician* 33, 108–15.

HUBER, P. J. (1964). Robust Estimation of a Location Parameter. *Annals of Mathematical Statistics* 35, 73–101.

HUBER, P. J. (1973). Robust Regression: Asymptotics, Conjectures, and Monte Carlo. *Annals of Statistics* 1, 799–821.

LEVENBACH, H., W. M. BRELSFORD, and J. P. CLEARY (1983). *A STATLIB Primer*. Belmont, CA: Lifetime Learning Publications.

MALLOWS, C. L. (1979). Robust Methods–Some Examples of Their Use. *The American Statistician* 33, 179–84.

McGILL, R. J., J. W. TUKEY, and W. A. LARSEN (1978). Variations of Box Plots. *The American Statistician* 32, 12–16.

McNEIL, D. R. (1977). *Interactive Data Analysis*. New York, NY: John Wiley and Sons.

NIE, N. H., C. H. HALL, J. G. JENKINS, K. STEINBRENNER, and D. H. BENT (1975). *SPSS: Statistical Package for the Social Sciences*, 2nd ed. New York, NY: McGraw-Hill Book Co.

RYAN, T. A., B. L. JOINER, and B. F. RYAN (1976). *Minitab Student Handbook*. Boston, MA: Duxbury Press.

SAS Institute (1982). *SAS User's Guide: Statistics*. Cary, NC: SAS Institute.

TUKEY, J. W. (1977). *Exploratory Data Analysis*. Reading, MA: Addison-Wesley Publishing Co.

VELLEMAN, P. F., and D. C. HOAGLIN (1981). *Applications, Basics, and Computing for Exploratory Data Analysis*. North Scituate, MA: Duxbury Press.

PROBLEMS

Looking at Data

1. For the following 12-point data set {1.1, 1.6, 4.7, 2.1, 3.1, 32.7, 5.8, 2.6, 4.8, 1.9, 3.7, 2.6}:

    a. Determine a suitable stem-and-leaf display.

    b. Calculate a 15-percent trimmed mean (or trimean) and compare with the median. What does the trimean tell us about the symmetry of the data?

    c. Find the 75th (upper quartile) and 25th (lower quartile) percentiles, and calculate the interquartile range (IQR). Also determine the extreme values for the data.

    d. Along with the median, construct a box-plot using the 5-number summary.

    e. Define $QL - 1.5\,IQR$ and $QL + 1.5\,IQR$ as the "outlier cutoffs," where QL and QU denote the lower and upper quartiles respectively and IQR is the "interquartile range." Data values that are larger than $QU + 1.5\,IQR$ are called "outliers" and should receive special attention. Determine the outlier(s).

    f. Calculate the standard error for the 15-percent trimmed mean.

    g. Calculate a Huber M-estimator of location using $K = 1.5$ for 2 iterations, and summarize. Compare your result with the mean and trimmed mean.

2. Using the 15-point data set {−67, −48, 6, 8, 14, 16, 23, 24, 28, 29, 41, 49, 56, 60, 75}, calculate the values as in Exercise 1a–g.

3. Compare results for Exercises 1 and 2. How well do the trimean, median, and mean agree amongst themselves for the two data sets?

4. For the nonfarm employment data (NFRM) in Appendix B, plot and interpret the data as a quarterly and annual time series. By inspection:

    a. Contrast the trend pattern.

    b. What is the nature of the seasonal variation?

    c. How does the cyclical variation manifest itself?

5. For the quarterly nonfarm employment data, make a stem-and-leaf diagram and determine:

    a. Several measures of location (mean, median, and midmean).

    b. Several measures of scale (standard deviation and UMAD). Do these measures suggest the presence of unusual data values? Which measures would you recommend that a forecaster use in this case?

c. A box plot; in what range do the middle 50% of the data lie?

d. A normal Q-Q plot; is it reasonable to assume a normal distribution? If so, what would be your estimate for the mean and variance? How does this compare with your answers to (a) and (b)?

6. Take two subsets of 15 sequential values from the quarterly nonfarm employment data in Appendix B. Compute the autocorrelations and graph the sample autocorrelogram. Contrast the results.

7. Repeat questions 5 and 6 for the quarterly housing starts data (HOUS) in Appendix B.

8. Repeat questions 5 and 6 for the quarterly Federal Reserve Board index (FRB) in Appendix B.

9. Repeat questions 5 and 6 for the quarterly index of consumer sentiment (MOOD) in Appendix B.

10. Repeat questions 5 and 6 for the quarterly U.S. money supply (M1) data in Appendix B.

11. Make a normal Q-Q plot for the 30 values of quarterly nonfarm employment data in Exercise 6. Comment on the plot and contrast your answer with the results from question 5(d).

12. Select 50 values from a table of random numbers (or generate some pseudo-random data on a computer) and make a normal Q-Q plot. What does a normal Q-Q plot of data from a uniform distribution look like?

13. For the monthly revenue data (REV) in Appendix B, show the monthly variation as 12 box plots. Interpret your results in terms of information about a trend-cycle, seasonality, and irregularity.

14. Repeat question 13 for the cube root of the monthly revenue data (REV). Contrast your results. Interpret the normal Q-Q plot generated on normal probability paper or with a computer program.

15. Repeat question 13 for the monthly message volumes (MSG). How would you characterize the differences between the REV and MSG time series?

16. Repeat question 13 for the square roots of the monthly message volumes (MSG). Contrast your results with the untransformed MSG series in question 15. Generate and interpret the normal Q-Q plot.

17. Take two subsets of 30 sequential values from the quarterly main gain data in Appendix B. Compute the autocorrelations and graph the sample correlogram. Contrast the results.

LEARNING BY COMPUTER

The computer is a marvelous adjunct to the learning process. Computer packages are widely available to perform a whole range of forecasting functions in a cost-effective and timely fashion. These programs help the forecaster to do the following: enter data into the computer efficiently; display graphs of data patterns; examine relationships among variables to be forecast; summarize modeling results; chart output for presentation; document assumptions and modeling rationale; and save and store forecasts.

These next 12 computer-based workshops are designed to help the student understand the steps in developing a forecast. These workshops shall be completed by small teams (3–4 students) as a joint project on a microprocessor or via time-sharing on a mainframe computer.

Each workshop can be completed using the data from Appendix 3 or data selected from your own sources. The workshops cover most of the techniques discussed in the text. By completing them in sequence, students will have sufficient material from each workshop for a case presentation. Workshop 12 at the end of Chapter 27 provides a format for a model building case presentation.

COMPUTER WORKSHOPS

General Workshop Instructions

Spend at least half an hour reading each workshop and planning your procedures and methods before logging on to the terminal.

Be sure to have readily available the detailed commands necessary to generate the procedures of your workshop.

Emphasis in all workshops should be placed on understanding and interpreting the characteristics of the data you select. You should be more concerned with the reasoning behind your analysis than with developing the "best" model.

For the final case presentation (Workshop 12), you are to explain the characteristics of your data and the methodology of your analysis. The presentation should also be appropriate for the audience: for a technical audience, you can emphasize the theoretical and statistical rationale of your methodology; for a management audience, you should emphasize intuitive and logical reasoning when presenting your model (e.g., graphs, charts and tables, not statistical jargon).

Workshop 1—Data Display for Time Series

- Review the time series available for study in the data summary (see Appendix B). Make sure you understand what each series represents before proceeding.

- As part of your data analysis, examine the printout of each series and also the plots of each series against time.

- Select a series for your dependent variable and several other appropriate series as potential independent variables. Be sure to make all series consistent as far as their being quarterly or monthly data.

- Change a monthly series into a quarterly series, plot it against time, and review the detrended series.

- Examine these graphs for trend/seasonal characteristics. This important data analysis step will serve as a basis in subsequent workshops.

Important Note: Save all pertinent output because your data analysis will recur through your case problems.

Workshop 2—Basic Time Series Analysis

- Refer to the time plots executed in Workshop 1. From these graphs, determine if a series has any seasonal, trend, cyclic, or irregular variation.

- Plot a correlogram for each series, and confirm some of the data characteristics shown in previous plots.

- If trend and/or seasonality are present in the series, attempt to eliminate these by differencing. Determine the effectiveness of differencing by plotting the differenced data against time. Also plot the correlogram of the differenced data. Have trend and seasonality been removed to your satisfaction?

- Generate a correlation matrix for the detrended and deseasonalized series. Examine this matrix and consider changing any of the independent variables you selected in Workshop 1.

- Produce scatter diagrams of the dependent variable with each independent variable for the detrended and deseasonalized series. Examine each scatter plot and perform appropriate transformations (log, exp, etc.) if necessary. Plot your results. Have the transformations improved the relationship?

- Review the scatter plots, box plots, and time plots. Consider what effect, if any, potential outliers may have on your model-building process. Can you think of any procedures to take account of and/or adjust for these outliers?

Part 3

Developing
Plausible Forecasts

CHAPTER 8

Forecasting with Exponential Smoothing Models

An effective forecasting technique must provide a theoretical framework: it must be able to describe the variability in the forecast data and supply a methodology for parameter estimation. Exponential smoothing models provide such a framework and are dealt with in this chapter; these are specific statistical forecasting techniques that

- Are widely used in the areas of sales, inventory, and production management as well as in quality control, process control, financial planning, and marketing planning.

- Are based on the mathematical projection of past patterns into the future, accomplished by using forecasting equations that are simple to update and require a relatively small number of calculations.

- Are analytically "naïve," but are of great practical value.

- Are especially suitable for use with desk-top computers, since they require little data storage.

- Are suitable for applications in which there are large numbers of time series, since few calculations are needed.

WHAT IS SMOOTHING?

Most often *smoothing* refers to a procedure of taking weighted sums of data in order to "smooth out" very short term irregularities. To forecasters, smoothed data reveal information about secular trends (those of long duration) and economic cycles which need to be understood and projected by means of a set of assumptions about the **107** future. Smoothed data are required in econometric modeling in order to have meaningful estimates of changes for many time series. A very appealing aspect of the use of smoothed data is that these can be interpreted easily. A plot of a smoothed employment series or of a smoothed industrial production series readily communicates information about the health of the economy, and percent changes based on smoothed data are understandable by lay persons and corporate managers. Percentages based on unadjusted series, on the other hand, often behave too erratically to be practically meaningful.

The smoothing of data and their subsequent decomposition into components or their expression in the form of an econometric model assists an analyst in understanding the real economic world. If the analyst finds a variation between unadjusted and smoothed data that is of particular importance, this can then be explained in quantitative (statistical) or theoretical terms; if variations are less important, through smoothing they can be removed, since they are irrelevant for the purposes of a given analysis. In macroeconomics, the seasonal component is often removed and the notions of "trend-cycle" and "turning point" come about from analyzing a smoothed version of the resulting data.

However, unadjusted data and smoothed data may at times indicate movement in opposite directions, because of a technical feature in the smoothing method. As you gain experience you will learn to be aware of these anomalies so that their meaning can be properly interpreted and adequately communicated to forecast users. It is also worth noting that certain time series models known as ARIMA models do not require smoothed data as inputs and yet can produce excellent forecasting results.

Smoothing with Moving Averages

In order to create a smoothed time series in which the effect of seasonality and the impact of an irregular component has been reduced, you can often subject a time series to some type of *moving average* operation. In doing so, realize that too much smoothing will cause a delayed or even unnoticed change in direction in the data. Therefore, you must use discretion and match the degree of smoothing with each particular application.

The most common moving-average smoother is the *unweighted moving average,* in which each value of the data carries the same weight in the smoothing calculation. For n values of a time series $y_1, \ldots, y_n$, the three-term moving average z_t has the formula

$$z_t = \frac{1}{3} \sum_{i=0}^{2} y_{t-i} \qquad (t = 3, \ldots, n).$$

In general, the p-term moving average is written as

$$z_t = \frac{1}{p} \sum_{i=0}^{p-1} y_{t-i} \qquad (t = p, \ldots, n).$$

There are even more general ways in which a moving average can be expressed. In connection with most seasonal adjustment procedures, the *weighted moving average* plays a significant role. A (*p*-term) weighted moving avereage has the formula

$$z_t = \sum_{i=0}^{p-1} a_i y_{t-i} \qquad (t = p, \ldots, n),$$

where

$$\sum_{i=0}^{p-1} a_i = 1.$$

The *a*'s are known as weights and ultimately they sum to unity. Should the weights be positive and not sum to unity, however, then the weighted moving average must be divided by the sum of the weights (see Table 8.1 for an example of a weighted average). Thus, for the ordinary (*p*-term) moving average, the *a*'s are all equal to $1/p$.

In discussions of ARIMA time series models, the term "moving average" occurs in a different context with a somewhat different meaning. The moving average operation discussed here is a smoothing operation.

Two major difficulties arise in considering moving averages as a smoothing procedure:

- Isolated outlying values may cause undue distortion of the smoothed series.

- Cyclical peaks and troughs are rarely followed smoothly by the procedure.

A smoothing technique based on *moving* ("running") *medians,* on the other hand, overcomes these shortcomings quite well (Mosteller and Tukey, 1977, p. 52 ff; Tukey, 1977, p. 210). Similar smoothing techniques are used in the SABL computer program, the Bell Laboratories seasonal adjustment procedure, which is treated in Chapter 19 of *The Beginning Forecaster*.

Table 8.1 An example of a weighted-average calculation.

Observation	Weight	Observation × Weight
1.14	0.96	1.0944
0.00	1.00	0.0000
1.24	0.95	1.1780
2.08	0.86	1.7888
2.18	0.85	1.8530
Total:	4.62	5.9142

$$\text{Weighted average} = \frac{5.9142}{4.62} = 1.28$$

Single Exponential Smoothing

The exponential smoothing operation, in its simplest form, is expressed by

$$S_{t+1} = \alpha y_t + (1 - \alpha)S_t;$$

the forecast S_{t+1} is expressed in terms of the *smoothing constant* α times a historical value y_t in the current period of the data plus $(1 - \alpha)$ times S_t, the forecast of one period ago. The parameter α lies between 0 and 1, and can be estimated from past data or simply guessed at (as will be explained later).

By rewriting S_{t+1} in another way as

$$S_{t+1} = S_t + \alpha(y_t - S_t),$$

it can be seen that single exponential smoothing is a procedure in which the forecast for the next period equals the forecast for the prior period adjusted by an amount that is proportional to the most recent forecast error

$$e_t = y_t - S_t.$$

This illustrates the simplest form of control whereby the current forecast error is used to modify the forecast for the next period.

The name "exponential smoothing" comes from the fact that S_t can be expressed as a *weighted average* with exponentially decreasing weights. To see how this is so, substitute the expression for S_t and S_{t-1}, namely,

$$S_t = \alpha y_{t-1} + (1 - \alpha)S_{t-1}$$

and

$$S_{t-1} = \alpha y_{t-2} + (1 - \alpha)S_{t-2},$$

in the original expression for S_{t+1}. Thus

$$\begin{aligned} S_{t+1} &= \alpha y_t + (1 - \alpha)[\alpha y_{t-1} + (1 - \alpha)S_{t-1}] \\ &= \alpha y_t + \alpha(1 - \alpha)y_{t-1} + \alpha(1 - \alpha)^2 y_{t-2} + (1 - \alpha)^3 S_{t-2}. \end{aligned}$$

Successive substitutions for S_{t-k}, where $k = 2, 3, \ldots, t$, yields

$$S_t = \alpha \sum_{k=0}^{t-1} (1 - \alpha)^k y_{t-k} + (1 - \alpha)^t S_0 \qquad (0 < \alpha < 1),$$

when S_0 is an initial estimate of the smoothed value.

The initial estimate S_0 of the smoothed value can be estimated from historical data by using a simple average of the most recent observations. Without historical data, a subjective estimate must be made. In order for the model to be responsive to changes, a larger value of α can be used in the first few periods to allow for a rapid adjustment.

The weights sum to unity and hence the term "average." Since the weights decrease geometrically with increasing k, the most recent values of y_t are given the greatest weight. All the previous values of y_t are included in the expression for S_t. Since α is less than unity, the values of y_t most distant in the past will have the smallest weights associated with them.

The smoothing constant α must be determined judgmentally, depending on the sensitivity of response required by the model. The smaller the value of α, the slower the response. Larger values of α cause increasingly quicker reactions in the smoothed (forecast) value. This may or may not be advantageous since forecast changes may be the result of real changes in the data or random fluctuations. High values of α are appropriate for smooth data but will cause excessive forecast changes for volatile data. It is often recommended that α should lie between 0.01 and 0.30 (Montgomery and Johnson, 1976).

Comparing Exponential Smoothing with Moving Averages

The responsiveness of an exponential smoothing can be compared with that of a moving average. A moving average forecast M_t for time t averaged over n periods is given by

$$M_t = \frac{1}{n} \sum_{i=t-n}^{t-1} y_i.$$

The technique of forecasting one step ahead with moving averages is represented by

$$M_{t+1} = \frac{1}{n} \sum_{i=t-n+1}^{t} y_i$$

$$= \frac{y_t - y_{t-n}}{n} + M_t.$$

The moving average forecast M_{t+1} is given by the preceding moving average forecast M_t plus an adjustment (the average growth over the period n),

$$(y_t - y_{t-n})/n,$$

which generally becomes smaller for larger n. Thus the smoothing effect increases with larger n.

By approximating y_{t-n} by the smoothed value M_t, the expression for M_{t+1} can be made to look like a single exponential smoothing model:

$$M_{t+1} = \frac{1}{n} y_t + (1 - \frac{1}{n}) M_t,$$

where $\alpha = 1/n$ is the smoothing parameter.

To develop the comparison of exponential smoothing and a moving average further, it may be useful to calculate the "average age" of the data in the two methods. For an n-period moving average, the average age is

$$\frac{1}{n} \sum_{k=0}^{n-1} k = (n - 1)/2,$$

and for exponential smoothing, this is

$$\alpha \sum_{k=0}^{\infty} (1 - \alpha)^k k = (1 - \alpha)/\alpha.$$

Thus an exponential smoothing model that has the same average age as the n-period moving average would have a smoothing constant given by $\alpha = 2/(n + 1)$. It can be shown that the same result can be obtained by equating the variances of S_t and M_t (Montgomery and Johnson, 1976).

You can see that exponential smoothing is closely related to moving average methods. Like moving averages, single exponential smoothing models are not responsive enough to sudden changes in slope or level. While single exponential smoothing gives greater weight to the more recent observations, the subjective or *ad hoc* determination of the appropriate value of the weights is still a basic limitation of this method. On the positive side, the simplicity and low computation cost for many series have made single exponential smoothing an attractive, widely applied technique.

An Application of Single Exponential Smoothing

In Chapter 7 we made use of data about service-order travel times. In this chapter let us use those data to illustrate a single exponential smoothing model. The data represent the times it takes an installer or repair person to travel from a service-center garage to customers' locations. The data are erratic and contain possible outliers.

Several values of α were tried (0.5, 0.3, 0.2, 0.1, 0.05, 0.025). Recall that we indicated earlier that low values of α are generally better for volatile series. A criterion for selecting α is the minimization of the *mean square error* (MSE). Minimizing the mean square error is a technique for examining the accuracy of forecasts. The MSE is calculated by first squaring the forecast errors (actual value minus forecast) and then taking their average value. In this example, the MSE was minimized with $\alpha = 0.025$, though this does not represent the smallest value of α that could have been used. Figure 8.1 shows a plot of the actual and fitted travel-time values with $\alpha = 0.025$.

It is instructive to compare the effect of varying values for α for the travel time data. Using a starting value of $S_0 = 11$, Figure 8.2 shows a plot of the data along

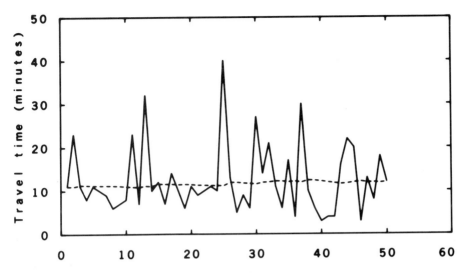

Figure 8.1 Time plot of actual and smoothed values from a single exponential smoothing model ($\alpha = 0.025$) for travel-time data. (Actual data are plotted with solid line; fitted values are plotted with a dashed line.)

with the forecasts using α of 0.025, 0.14, and 0.30. Notice that as α increases, the forecasts are more volatile since a smoothed value is adjusted by α times the forecast error that occurred in the preceding period.

Table 8.2 shows the forecasts with values of alpha of 0.025, 0.14, and 0.30. Thus the tenth value (9.93) in the $\alpha = 0.14$ column was obtained by taking the preceding forecast (10.41) and adding to that 0.14 (7.00 − 10.41).

The mean-squared error (MSE) and median absolute deviation (MAD) are commonly used as accuracy criteria in order to assess which alpha produces the "best" forecasts. Table 8.3 shows the results for the first fifteen values of the travel time data with alpha of 0.025, 0.14, and 0.30. On the basis of these two measures, it can be concluded that the best forecasts are produced with $\alpha = 0.025$, since the MSE and MAD have smaller values than with the other two alpha values. When all the fifty data values are used, the lowest MSE = 63.44 and the MAD = 3.3 for $\alpha = 0.025$. Thus the same conclusion is reached using all of the data in this case.

Other numerical examples of exponential smoothing may be found in Bowerman and O'Connell (1979, Section 3-3), Makridakis and Wheelwright (1978, Section 3-3), Montgomery and Johnson (1976), and Wheelwright and Makridakis (1980, Chapter 4).

Exponential smoothing was first introduced by Holt (1957) and popularized by Brown (1959, 1963). Winters (1960) introduced the seasonal exponential smoothing model. Other contributors include Trigg and Leach (1967) and Harrison (1965), who developed harmonic smoothing models.

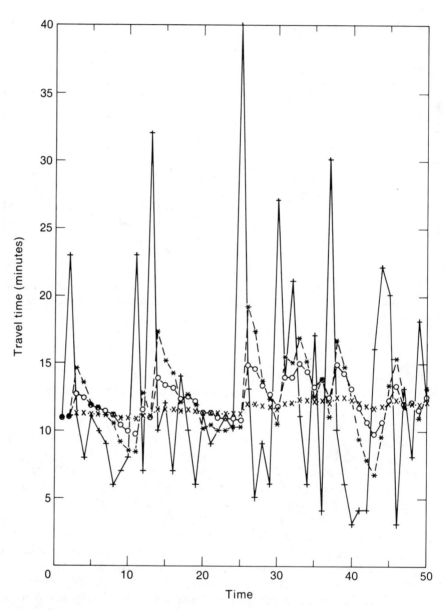

Figure 8.2   Time plot of actual (solid line) and smoothed values from single exponential smoothing for travel time data (x is $\alpha = 0.025$; o is $\alpha = 0.14$; * is $\alpha = 0.30$).

Table 8.2 Single exponential smoothing forecasts for the travel time data.

Observation	Data	α 0.025	0.14	0.30
1	11.00	11.00	11.00	11.00
2	23.00	11.00	11.00	11.00
3	11.00	11.30	12.68	14.60
4	8.00	11.29	12.44	13.52
5	11.00	11.21	11.82	11.86
6	10.00	11.20	11.71	11.60
7	9.00	11.17	11.47	11.12
8	6.00	11.12	11.12	10.49
9	7.00	10.99	10.41	9.14
10	8.00	10.89	9.93	8.50
11	23.00	10.82	9.66	8.35
12	7.00	11.12	11.53	12.74
13	32.00	11.02	10.89	11.02
14	10.00	11.55	13.85	17.31
15	12.00	11.51	13.31	15.12
16	7.00	11.52	13.13	14.18
17	14.00	11.41	12.27	12.03
18	10.00	11.47	12.51	12.62
19	6.00	11.43	12.16	11.83
20	11.00	11.30	11.30	10.08
21	9.00	11.29	11.26	10.36
22	10.00	11.23	10.94	9.95
23	11.00	11.20	10.81	9.97
24	10.00	11.20	10.83	10.28
25	40.00	11.17	10.72	10.19
26	13.00	11.89	14.82	19.14
27	5.00	11.92	14.56	17.29
28	9.00	11.74	13.22	13.61
29	6.00	11.68	12.63	12.22
30	27.00	11.53	11.70	10.36
31	14.00	11.92	13.85	15.35
32	21.00	11.97	13.87	14.94
33	11.00	12.20	14.87	16.76
34	6.00	12.17	14.32	15.03
35	17.00	12.01	13.16	12.32
36	4.00	12.14	13.70	13.73
37	30.00	11.93	12.34	10.81
38	10.00	12.39	14.81	16.57
39	6.00	12.33	14.14	14.60
40	3.00	12.17	13.00	12.02
41	4.00	11.94	11.60	9.31
42	4.00	11.74	10.54	7.72
43	16.00	11.55	9.62	6.60
44	22.00	11.66	10.51	9.42
45	20.00	11.92	12.12	13.20
46	3.00	12.12	13.22	15.24
47	13.00	11.89	11.79	11.57
48	8.00	11.92	11.96	12.00
49	18.00	11.82	11.41	10.80
50	12.00	11.98	12.33	12.96

Table 8.3 Comparison of Forecasting Errors for Single
Exponential Smoothing of Travel Time Data

Observation		$\alpha = 0.025$		$\alpha = 0.14$		$\alpha = 0.30$	
		Forecast	Error	Forecast	Error	Forecast	Error
1	11	11.00	0.	11.00	0.	11.00	0.
2	23	11.00	12.00	11.00	12.00	11.00	12.00
3	11	11.30	−0.30	12.68	−1.68	14.60	−3.60
4	8	11.29	−3.29	12.44	−4.44	13.52	−5.52
5	11	11.21	−0.21	11.82	−0.82	11.86	−0.86
6	10	11.20	−1.20	11.71	−1.71	11.60	−1.60
7	9	11.17	−2.17	11.47	−2.47	11.12	−2.12
8	6	11.12	−5.12	11.12	−5.12	10.49	−4.49
9	7	10.99	−3.99	10.41	−3.41	9.14	−2.14
10	8	10.89	−2.89	9.93	−1.93	8.50	−0.50
11	23	10.82	12.18	9.66	13.34	8.35	14.65
12	7	11.12	−4.12	11.53	−4.53	12.74	−5.74
13	32	11.02	20.98	10.89	21.11	11.02	20.98
14	10	11.55	−1.55	13.85	−3.85	17.31	−7.31
15	12	10.51	1.49	13.31	−1.31	15.12	3.12
MSE			54.8		58.5		64.7
MAD			5.30		5.54		5.76

EXPONENTIAL SMOOTHING FOR TRENDING DATA

The single-exponential smoothing technique just described is best suited for historical data that can be regarded as *stationary* or having essentially a horizontal pattern. When dealing with trend or even seasonal patterns, it becomes necessary to introduce *higher-order exponential smoothing*.

Double Exponential Smoothing

A *second-order* or *double* exponential smoothing is appropriate when a time series is expected to change linearly with time according to the model

$$y_{t+l} = \beta_{0,t} + l\beta_{1,t} + \varepsilon_t,$$

where y_{t+l} is the forecast l-periods ahead, and ε_t is the error term with zero mean and constant variance. The basic idea behind double exponential smoothing is to apply single exponential smoothing first to the original data. For a time series with a trend pattern, the smoothed series tends to lag or fall below the trend. Next, the exponential smoothing is applied again, but this time to the smoothed series. This results in

$$S_t^{[2]} = \alpha S_t + (1 - \alpha)S_{t-1}^{[2]},$$

where the notation $S_t^{[2]}$ implies the second-order smoothing step. An estimate of trend can be made by taking the difference between the single exponential smoothing statistic S_t and the double exponential smoothing statistic $S_t^{[2]}$. Thus the intercept is estimated by

$$\hat{\beta}_{0,t} = S_t + (S_t - S_t^{[2]})$$
$$= 2S_t - S_t^{[2]}.$$

The slope is estimated by

$$\hat{\beta}_{1,t} = \frac{\alpha}{1 - \alpha} (S_t - S_t^{[2]}).$$

To forecast l-periods ahead by using double exponential smoothing, the following forecasting equation is used:

$$y_{t+l} = \hat{\beta}_{0,t} + l\hat{\beta}_{1,t}$$
$$= (2 + \frac{\alpha l}{1 - \alpha})S_t - (1 + \frac{\alpha l}{1 - \alpha})S_t^{[2]}.$$

As with single exponential smoothing, the initial smoothed statistics S_0 and now $S_0^{[2]}$ need to be determined. With historical data available, a straight line regression can be used to obtain estimates $\hat{\beta}_{0,0}$ and $\hat{\beta}_{1,0}$; otherwise they have to be estimated subjectively. Then

$$S_0 = \hat{\beta}_{0,0} - (\frac{1 - \alpha}{\alpha})\hat{\beta}_{1,0},$$

and

$$S_0^{[2]} = \hat{\beta}_{0,0} - 2(\frac{1 - \alpha}{\alpha})\hat{\beta}_{1,0}.$$

A seasonally adjusted version of the logarithms of airline data from Box and Jenkins (1976, Series G) shows a trending pattern for which the use of a double exponential smoothing model seems appropriate. For those data, Brown's (1963) linear exponential smoothing model with $\alpha = 0.5$ resulted in zero mean percent error or bias, a mean square error of 10.4, and a mean absolute error of 0.4 percent.

Triple Exponential Smoothing

Higher-order (more than double) smoothing procedures arise when a higher-order polynomial is assumed as the trend model. Thus, for quadratic models, it is appropriate to use *triple* exponential smoothing. The quadratic or triple smoothing model produces forecasts that either increase or decrease in a quadratic manner according to

$$y_{t+l} = \beta_{0,t} + l\beta_{1,t} + \tfrac{1}{2}l^2\beta_{2,t} + \epsilon_t,$$

A third smooth is performed by using

$$S_t^{[3]} = \alpha S_t^{[2]} + (1 - \alpha)S_{t-1}^{[3]},$$

and the following equations are used to estimate the coefficients:

$$\hat{\beta}_{0,t} = 3S_t - 3S_t^{[2]} + S_t^{[3]};$$

$$\hat{\beta}_{1,t} = \frac{\alpha}{2(1 - \alpha)^2}[(6 - 5\alpha)S_t - 2(5 - 4\alpha)S_t^{[2]} + (4 - 3\alpha)S_t^{[3]}];$$

and

$$\hat{\beta}_{2,t} = \frac{\alpha^2}{(1 - \alpha)^2}S_t - 2S_t^{[2]} + S_t^{[3]}.$$

The initial conditions are

$$S_0 = \hat{\beta}_{0,0} - \frac{(1 - \alpha)}{\alpha}\hat{\beta}_{1,0} + \frac{(1 - \alpha)(2 - \alpha)\hat{\beta}_{2,0}}{2\alpha^2},$$

$$S_0^{[2]} = \hat{\beta}_{0,0} - \frac{2(1 - \alpha)}{\alpha}\hat{\beta}_{1,0} + \frac{2(1 - \alpha)(3 - 2\alpha)\hat{\beta}_{2,0}}{2\alpha^2},$$

and

$$S_0^{[3]} = \hat{\beta}_{0,0} - \frac{3(1 - \alpha)}{\alpha}\hat{\beta}_{1,0} + \frac{3(1 - \alpha)(4 - 3\alpha)\hat{\beta}_{2,0}}{2\alpha^2}.$$

Since the toll message volumes are strongly trending, it is of interest to compare the effect of single, double, and triple exponential smoothing on these data. Using ten years of monthly values and the MSE criterion, an optimium value of $\alpha = 0.065$ was obtained for double exponential smoothing for these data. Figure 8.3 shows a plot of the most recent four years of the data long with the single, double, and triple exponential smoothing forecasts with $\alpha = 0.065$. Notice that the single exponential smoothing forecasts lag significantly behind the trend.

Higher-order procedures are also treated in Montgomery and Johnson (1976) and Makridakis and Wheelwright (1978, Chapter 3). Bowerman and O'Connell (1979, Chapter 5) have a detailed example worked out for forecasting loan requests from a univeristy credit union. Since the computational complexities increase with higher orders, smoothing techniques of a higher order than double exponential may not be very practical.

Another two-parameter linear-exponential trend model was proposed by Holt (1957); Brown's (1963) model is generally preferred, however, since it requires that fewer parameters be estimated. Generally, α lies in the 0.1 to 0.2 range.

APPLICATION TO THE TELECOMMUNICATIONS EXAMPLE

Figures 8.4–8.7 display plots of the original (unadjusted) and seasonally adjusted time series, together with their predictions, for the telecommunications example introduced in Chapter 1 and used throughout the book as an illustrative data set. The computer program used selects the single, double, or triple exponential smoothing model on the basis of the minimum mean absolute deviation between the predictions and actual values.

The seasonal components in the four original series are relatively small. However, the seasonality is sufficient to cause the computer program to select optimum models in each of which the unadjusted time series is smoothed to one lesser degree than the seasonally adjusted data is (e.g., single versus double). Consequently, the mean absolute deviation for seasonally adjusted data in each model is significantly less than the deviation for the original series in each model. Table 8.4 summarizes the results of the model. Based on these results, for forecasting one might prefer to base the exponential smoothing models on seasonally adjusted data. Because the magnitude of the smoothing parameter is smaller in all models based on seasonally adjusted data, forecasts from these models will be less volatile than those based on unadjusted data.

There are at least two other approaches that can be tried as alternative ways of lessening seasonal patterns in data. The first approach is to use exponential smoothing models on year-over-year growth (the difference between the current period and one year ago). Differencing may remove linear trend as well, however, and produce a series with pronounced cyclical patterns which are rather difficult to forecast. The second approach is a somewhat complex seasonal exponential smoothing model due to Winters (1960). This model has an additional parameter that smooths the seasonal pattern. The approach is complex, however, in that it requires a trial-and-error method for selecting the three smoothing parameters (for randomness, trend, and seasonality).

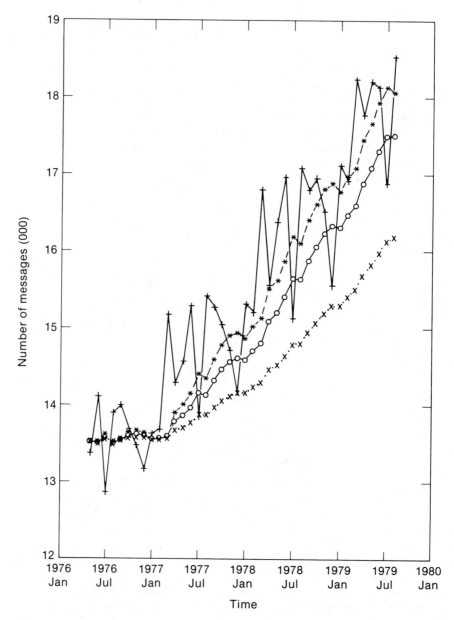

Figure 8.3   Time plot of actual (solid line) toll message volumes and single (x), double (o), and triple (*) exponential smoothing forecasts.

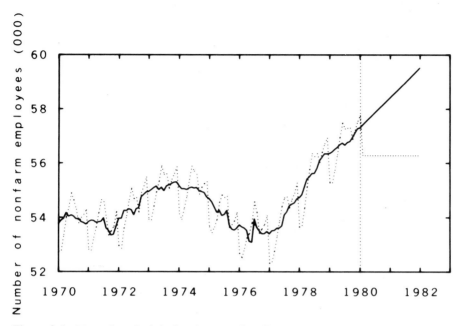

Figure 8.4   Time plot of original and seasonally adjusted nonfarm employment data shown with "best" exponential smoothing model.

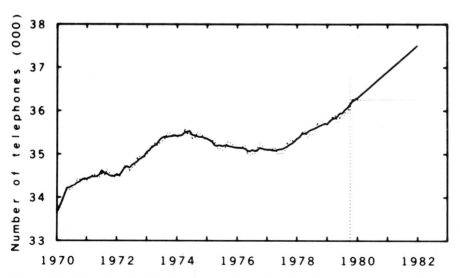

Figure 8.5   Time plot of original and seasonally adjusted business telephones data shown with "best" exponential smoothing model.

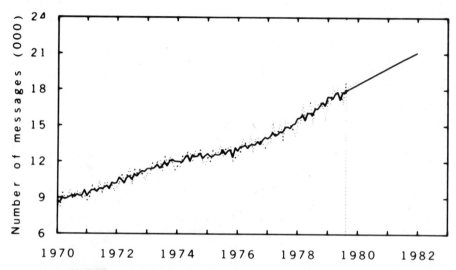

Figure 8.6 Time plot of original and seasonally adjusted toll-message data shown with "best" exponential smoothing model.

BE WARY OF "AUTOMATIC" FORECASTING METHODS AND SOFTWARE PROGRAMS

Computer programs for exponential smoothing are relatively simple to implement. Consequently, they are widely available in most time series packages. In fact, Sul-

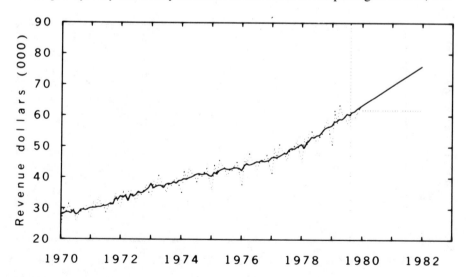

Figure 8.7 Time plot of original and seasonally adjusted toll-revenue data shown with "best" exponential smoothing model.

Table 8.4 Comparison of exponential smoothing models for unadjusted (U) and seasonally adjusted (SA) series, showing mean absolute deviation (MAD) and the estimate of α ($\hat{\alpha}$).

Time series	Model type			
	Unadjusted (U)		Seasonally adjusted (SA)	
	MAD	$\hat{\alpha}$	MAD	$\hat{\alpha}$
Employment	Single 470	0.95	Double 143	0.60
Telephones	Single 63	0.95	Double 26	0.60
Messages	Double 288	0.20	Triple 117	0.15
Revenues	Single 481	0.40	Double 103	0.20

livan and Claycombe (1977) provide a listing of an exponential smoothing program. Some exponential smoothing programs have built-in parameter-selection algorithms. This may work well when the data have low variability and are otherwise well behaved. However, the forecaster should always plot the data, fitted values, and forecasts to make certain that the "automatic" models do a reasonable job.

Figures 8.8 and 8.9 illustrate two examples of products in which potentially serious problems could result from blind acceptance of computer-selected forecasts, methods, and parameter estimates.

Product A—let us say it was a new kind of computer system—existed in the marketplace for a number of years; Figure 8.8 shows a plot of the quantity of the product used since 1977. In 1978 a new product (B) was introduced which had improved price-performance characteristics. The new product was promoted in late 1978 and started to take a share of the market away from Product A. Figure 8.10 shows three exponential smoothing forecasts (single, double, and triple) for product A that were generated automatically by computer-selected parameter estimates.

The computer program selected the quadratic (triple exponential) model as the best model because it minimized the mean absolute deviation. A characteristic of the quadratic smoothing model is that it tends to produce either rapidly rising or rapidly falling forecasts. In this case a sharp drop in demand for Product A (in terms of leased systems in service) predicted by the quadratic model could not be justified by the product manager. After all, even though the new product might be superior to the old, the cost of changing from the old to the new (cost of removal and installation) made wholesale replacements seem noneconomical for people who used Product A. What the computer program could not know is that the new product would be more economical for handling growth or new service requirements (that is, would be used by people who did not use Product A). Therefore, the linear

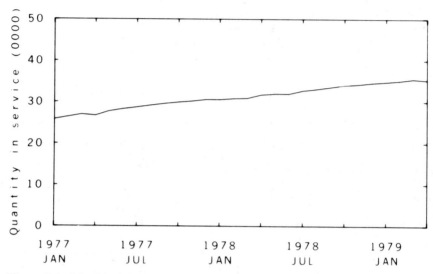

Figure 8.8   Monthly time plot of Product A from January 1977 to April 1979.

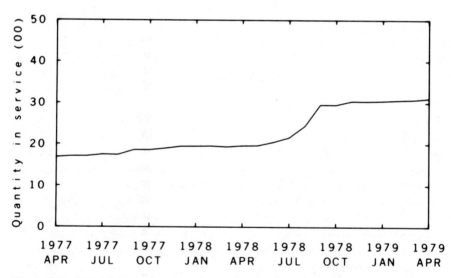

Figure 8.9   Monthly time plot of Product C from April 1977–June 1979.

smoothing model forecasts were selected for Product A by the forecaster, and the computer program's choice of a quadratic model was overridden.

A more dramatic depiction of the potential problems with automatic computer-selected models is illustrated for Product C. In this example, six curve-fitting models

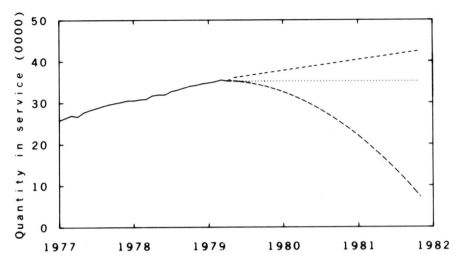

Figure 8.10   Single (middle), double (upper), and triple (lower), exponential smoothing forecasts for Product A.

were fitted to the data (linear, exponential, geometric, and three forms of the hyperbolic function). In the computer program used for this example, the computer program automatically selects the model with the highest R-squared statistic (the R-squared statistic is used as a measure of goodness-of-fit in regression, as is discussed in Chapter 11.

In this example the sharp increase in demand for 1978 caused the computer program to select one of the hyperbolic models: $[\hat{Y} = 1/(0.000667 - 0.000013 \cdot \text{Time})]$. The forecast profile of this model is shown in Figure 8.11. The peak forecast (April 1981) is almost 150,000 units larger than the quantity in service in 1979. The following month the forecast goes negative by a huge amount.

Figure 8.12 shows the forecasts from three exponential smoothing models for Product C. While the single smoothing model had the lowest mean absolute deviation (71, versus 79 for double and 129 for triple), the double exponential smoothing model forecasts were selected by the forecaster on the assumption that the market was not yet saturated.

The product forecasts for "Product A," "Product B," and "Product C" were taken from actual forecast situations for which data were limited and simple trending approaches were sought. The historical data for both series are somewhat erratic and highlight the problems that may exist in the mechanistic execution of computer programs. When the primary objective of a model is to generate forecasts, basing model selection on the maximum value for the R-squared statistic is highly questionable and cannot be recommended.

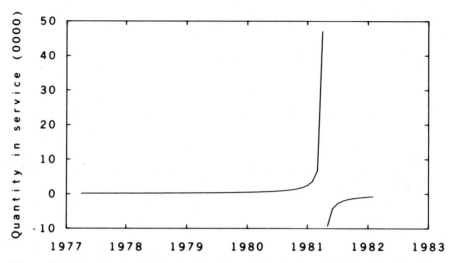

Figure 8.11   Forecast profile for the "best" model for Product C selected by an automatic curve-fitting program.

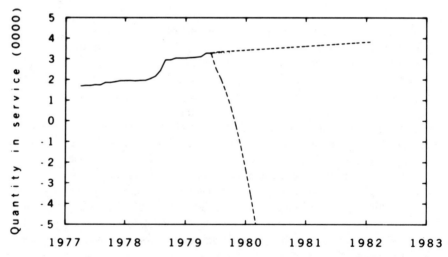

Figure 8.12   Single (middle), double (upper), and triple (lower) exponential smoothing forecasts for Product C. Single and double forecasts are virtually identical here.

SUMMARY

Exponential smoothing models have valuable characteristics that make them useful in practice:

- They are relatively simple, naïve forecasting methods.
- They can be applied with relatively little historical data and can be useful for short-term forecasting.
- The single, double, and triple exponential smoothing models are appropriate for horizontal, linear, and quadratic time series, respectively. Their forecasts should, however, be evaluated in the economic context or market that is expected to exist.

Other significant considerations include these:

- Since the models are incapable of providing this input, the forecaster's judgment plays a primary role. Never accept a model's prediction without plotting history and forecast on the same graph, for reasonableness.
- Whenever possible, the sum of the partial forecasts should be compared to the forecast of an appropriate aggregated variable. In product demand forecasting, for example, an independently derived total sales or revenue forecast can serve this purpose. Such a check of reasonableness is even more valuable when additional forecasting methods can be applied at the aggregated level.

For time series with significant seasonality, the series can be seasonally adjusted before modeling, or other methods, such as a seasonal exponential smoothing model, or—better yet—ARIMA time series modeling should be attempted.

USEFUL READING

BOWERMAN, B. L., and R. T. O'CONNELL (1979). *Time Series and Forecasting*. North Scituate, MA: Duxbury Press.

BOX, G. E. P., and G. M. JENKINS (1976). *Time Series Analysis—Forecasting and Control*. Rev. ed. San Francisco, CA: Holden-Day.

BROWN, R. G. (1959). *Statistical Forecasting for Inventory Control*. New York, NY: McGraw-Hill Book Co.

BROWN, R. G. (1963). *Smoothing, Forecasting and Prediction of Discrete Time Series*. Englewood Cliffs, NJ: Prentice-Hall.

HARRISON, P. J. (1965). Short-Term Sales Forecasting. *Applied Statistics* 14, 102–39.

HOLT, C. C. (1957). *Forecasting Seasonals and Trends by Exponentially Weighted Moving Averages*. Pittsburgh, PA: Carnegie Institute of Technology.

MAKRIDAKIS, S., and S. C. WHEELWRIGHT (1978). *Forecasting Methods and Applications*. New York, NY: John Wiley and Sons.

MONTGOMERY, D. C., and L. A. JOHNSON (1976). *Forecasting and Time Series Analysis*. New York, NY: McGraw-Hill Book Co.

MOSTELLER, F., and J. W. TUKEY (1977). *Data Analysis and Regression*. Reading, MA: Addison-Wesley Publishing Co.

SULLIVAN, W. G., and W. W. CLAYCOMBE (1977). *Fundamentals of Forecasting*. Reston, VA: Reston Publishing Company.

TRIGG, D. W., and A. G. LEACH (1967). Exponential Smoothing with Adaptive Response Rate. *Operational Research Quarterly* 18, 53–59.

TUKEY, J. W. (1977). *Exploratory Data Analysis*. Reading, MA: Addison-Wesley Publishing Co.

WHEELWRIGHT, S. C., and S. MAKRIDAKIS (1980). *Forecasting Methods for Management*, 3rd ed. New York, NY: John Wiley and Sons.

WINTERS, P. R. (1960). Forecasting Sales by Exponentially Weighted Moving Averages. *Management Science* 6, 324–42.

CHAPTER **9**

Seasonal Adjustment and Cycle Forecasting

Seasonally adjusted data and measures of seasonal variation have been used for over fifty years in the analysis of business and financial developments.

- In its simplest form, seasonality refers to regular periodic fluctuations which recur every year with about the same timing and intensity.

- Most procedures for seasonal analysis involve smoothing to eliminate unwanted irregular variation from patterns that are meaningful to the analyst.

The analysis of economic indicators is an important part of many forecasting activities:

- Forecasts of the levels of key economic indicators are often incorporated in quantitative models.

- Correlation studies are commonly made to assess the relative impact of expansions and contractions in the economy.

- Plots of economic indicators and their forecasts are frequently part of a presentation package for demand forecasts of business products.

Many national economic indicators are monitored on an ongoing basis by industry and government analysts.

USES OF SEASONAL ADJUSTMENT

There are generally three distinct uses of seasonal adjustment:

- The historical adjustment of all available past data.

129

- The current adjustment of each new observation.

- The predicted seasonal factors for future adjustment.

Many economic series show seasonal variation. For example, income from a farm in the United States may rise steadily each year from early spring until fall and then drop sharply. In this case, the main use of seasonal adjustment procedures is to remove such fluctuations to expose an underlying trend-cycle.

Many industries have to deal with seasonal fluctuations. To make decisions about price and inventory policy, and the commitment of capital expenditures, the business community wants to know whether changes in business activity over a given period of time were larger or smaller than normal seasonal changes. It is important to know whether a recession has reached bottom, for example, or whether there is any pattern in the duration, amplitude, or slope of business cycle expansions or contractions.

The methods of seasonal analysis considered in this chapter are based on smoothing procedures, since the object of the procedure is to measure usual or average seasonal movements. There are a wide variety of factors that influence economic data, so it is often difficult to determine the extent to which seasonal influences dominate changes in a time series. However, most methods are based on the assumption that seasonal fluctuations can be measured and separated from underlying trend and irregular fluctuations.

In general, seasonal adjustment procedures can be categorized as either additive or multiplicative procedures. If the magnitude of the seasonal increase or decrease is assumed to be essentially constant and independent of the level of the times series, an *additive model* is used:

Data = Trend-cycle + Seasonal + Irregular.

On the other hand, when the magnitude of the seasonal increase or decrease is assumed to be proportional to the level of the time series, a *multiplicative model* is used:

Data = Trend-cycle · Seasonal factor · Irregular factor.

Even in this circumstance an additive model could be used if you transform the original time series. If you take logarithms, this will tend to "stabilize" the magnitude of the seasonal pattern and allow you to use the additive model on the transformed series.

One desirable feature of a good seasonal adjustment procedure is to end up with a seasonal component that does not change over time. The choice between an additive or multiplicative model may be important here.

There are also methods that make simultaneous additive and multiplicative adjustments. Since all methods have their limitations, the practitioner needs to be aware of the advantages and disadvantages of seasonal adjustment procedures in the context of the particular application.

To illustrate how a forecaster could use seasonal factors, consider the simplified example that follows. Table 9.1 shows three rows of numbers. The first row shows the actual demand for a product during a given year. The second row shows seasonal factors that were developed, based on historical data and projected for the same year. The third row shows the seasonally adjusted data under an assumed additive model:

Data − Seasonal factor = Trend-cycle + Irregular.

In this example the actual values decline from January through May. The seasonal factors indicate that the first three months are generally strong, April has no significant seasonality, and May is generally weak. After adjusting for the seasonal effect, it can be seen that the adjusted demand grows after February. This might be a result of an economic recovery that is not apparent in the observed (first-row) values.

In Table 9.2, the same actuals are used, but a different seasonal pattern is assumed. After adjusting for the seasonal effect, the data show a flat demand pattern. In Table 9.3, the same actuals are used, but the seasonal factors have been distorted. We shall assume that the distortions are a result of severe outlies in the prior year's actuals—that is, the seasonal factors in Table 9.2 are "correct," but the method used to derive the seasonal factors in Table 9.3 has incorrectly handled outliers in the prior year. These distorted factors have then been projected into the current year. The result has been to alter the April and May seasonal factors. In this case it appears

Table 9.1   Using seasonal factors to adjust a set of data.

		Time			
Description	JAN	FEB	MAR	APR	MAY
1. Actual data	2000	1900	1700	1300	1100
2. Seasonal factors	1000	900	600	0	− 400
3. Seasonally adjusted data (1 − 2)	1000	1000	1100	1300	1500

Table 9.2   Using a different set of seasonal factors to adjust the data.

		Time			
Description	JAN	FEB	MAR	APR	MAY
1. Actual data	2000	1900	1700	1300	1100
2. Seasonal factors	500	400	200	− 200	− 400
3. Seasonally adjusted data (1 − 2)	1500	1500	1500	1500	1500

Table 9.3 Using seasonal factors that have been impacted by outliers in the prior year's data.

		Time				
Description		JAN	FEB	MAR	APR	MAY
1. Actual data		2000	1900	1700	1300	1100
2. Seasonal factors		500	400	200	0	−100
3. Seasonally adjusted data $(1-2)$		1500	1500	1500	1300	1200

that demand is falling off when it really is not. In *The Beginning Forecaster* a comparison of traditional and resistant seasonal adjustment methods, it will be shown how this problem can be avoided by using "resistant" methods.

The examples in Tables 9.1–9.3 show how the forecaster can use seasonal factors to:

- Identify turning points that are not apparent in the raw data.

- Adjust seasonality out of the data so that forecasting techniques that cannot handle seasonally unadjusted data—e.g., simple exponential smoothing models—can be applied to the seasonally adjusted data.

Table 9.3 also highlights the importance of assuring oneself that the seasonal factors are appropriate. Otherwise, incorrect conclusions can be drawn because of incorrect seasonal adjustment.

RATIO-TO-MOVING-AVERAGE METHOD

In the 1920's and early 1930's, the Federal Reserve Board and the National Bureau of Economic Research were heavily involved in the smoothing of economic time series. In 1922, Frederick R. Macauley of the National Bureau of Economic Research developed the ratio-to-moving-average method in a study done at the request of the Federal Reserve Board (Macauley, 1930).

The first step in the method is to obtain an estimate of the trend and cyclical factors by use of a p-month moving average, where p is the length of the seasonal period. This moving average is divided into the raw data to yield a series of "seasonal-irregular" ratios—symbolically, $(TC \cdot S \cdot I)/TC = S \cdot I$, where TC = trend-cycle, S = seasonal, and I = irregular. Smoothing these ratios for a given month over a number of years produces an estimate of the seasonal adjustment factor. The irregular factor is assumed to cancel out in the smoothing process.

Final seasonally adjusted data are obtained by dividing each monthly data value by the seasonal adjustment factor for the corresponding month. This corresponds to a multiplicative seasonal adjustment procedure. An additive procedure can be developed in an analogous manner. This simplicity of calculation was a necessity in the early days of seasonal adjustment procedures.

BUREAU OF CENSUS SEASONAL ADJUSTMENT

In 1954 the Bureau of the Census developed a software package known as Method I for decomposing time series (Shiskin et al., 1967). The first Census program contained refinements to the ratio-to-moving-average method. Subsequent variants included moving seasonal-adjustment factors and smoother and more flexible trend-cycle curves. Adjustments for variations in the number of working days and variable holidays (such as Easter) were included in the most recent version of the program, known as the *X-11 variant*. A brief description of the Census Method II seasonal adjustment procedure is given in an appendix in Kallek (1978).

X-11 Program

The X-11 program is a very widely used and accepted way to deseasonalize data. Literally thousands of economic and demographic time series reported by federal agencies for public use have been seasonally adjusted by these programs. There are separate programs to deal with monthly and quarterly data.

The basic goal of the X-11 program is to estimate seasonal factors from seasonal data. Then one can remove the seasonal component and produce an adjusted series which will most clearly show the trend-cycle and irregular variations. The basic strategy of the program is to remove the influence of extreme values so as to reveal the underlying movement in the data in a better way. The basic tactic is the use of iteration to achieve refinement.

The assumptions underlying the X-11 program are that a time series is composed of seasonal, trend-cycle, trading day, and irregular components. There are two versions of this program available—additive and multiplicative.

In the *multiplicative* version, the time series Y (the subscript t can be suppressed for convenience) is assumed to be a product of a seasonal factor S, trend-cycle TC, trading day (the number of active working or business days) D, and irregular component I:

$$Y = TC \cdot S \cdot D \cdot I.$$

The trading day adjustment is treated as a separate component since it consists of variations attributable to the composition of the calendar. The irregular component includes effects such as strikes, wars, floods, and other unusual events.

An alternative *additive* formulation is that the original time series is a summation of these components, in the form

$$Y = TC + S + D + I.$$

Generally speaking, the multiplicative model produces the best seasonal factors for most series. However, it will not work for series that have negative values and for series that are highly volatile; the additive model is more appropriate for these.

There are three major computational runs with the X-11 program. Run 1 produces a series of "B-tables," which are considered preliminary. Run 2 results in "C-tables," which are semifinal, and Run 3 results in final "D-tables" and subsequent analytical tables.

The program makes the following sequence of computations:

- The trend-cycle.
- The seasonal-irregular ratios.
- Replacement of extreme irregular ratios.
- Seasonal factors.
- Seasonally adjusted series.

Since a seasonally adjusted series consists of trend-cycle and irregular components, it is sometimes desirable to remove the irregular component and look at trend-cycle alone. This can be done by smoothing operations. The X-11 program creates two different series—the MCD series and Henderson curves.

The MCD stands for *Months for Cyclical Dominance,* which indicates the minimum period over which the average absolute change can be attributed to cyclical change rather than unexplained fluctuations. It is an unweighted moving average of, at most, six months. The irregular component is divided by the trend-cycle. The number of months that must be added together before that ratio is less than one becomes the "months for cyclical dominance." If the months for cyclical dominance exceed six, then six months is used as the maximum term in the smoothing.

The reason for using the MCD series is to have *current* values. Using a smoothing operation in which more than six terms are needed would introduce a significant lag in the data and many months would be lost at both ends of the data. Clearly the MCD series is particularly important when the most current data are of interest. Table F-2 of the X-11 program contains the MCD series.

A Henderson curve is a 9-, 13-, or 26-term weighted moving average; this is particularly useful for series with strong cyclical patterns. In the Henderson calculations, an attempt is made to overcome the lag introduced by long-term moving-average operations, by applying different weights to the varying months. Estimates are also made of what the last $(n - 1)/2$ months would be if future data were available, since with any centered moving average the end values are lost.

To determine the reasonableness of the estimates of the current months, an analyst compares the MCD curve with the Henderson curve. If the MCD curve moves in a different direction than the Henderson curve, the Henderson estimates for the last $(n - 1)/2$ months should not be used, or at least the estimates should be modified to conform to the most recent actual data. Table D-12 of the X-11 program contains data for Henderson curves.

Why Use the X-11 Program?

There are times when seasonally adjusted data may be the only data readily available. For instance, computerized data banks are available commercially which contain a wide variety of seasonally adjusted economic data. It often makes sense to use these commercially available sources, rather than to adjust many of these series yourself.

The methods of seasonal adjustment in the X-11 program isolate the seasonal and irregular factors, leaving a composite trend and cycle component in the form of a long-term (Spencer or Henderson) weighted moving average. An MCD (Months for Cyclical Dominance) moving average is a short-term alternative for this trend-cycle component.

It is also advisable to compare forecasting results that are obtained from seasonally adjusted data with those from unadjusted series (Plosser, 1979). The adjusted series still contain trend-cycle components that need to be modeled.

A recent development in the time series literature combines the ARIMA modeling approach with the X-11 seasonal adjustment procedure to produce future seasonal factors (Dagum, 1976). The technique shows considerable promise and is being tested extensively (Dagum, 1978).

Business Cycle Forecasting—a Subjective Approach

An approach that may be used to forecast cyclical series is based on and extends the time series decomposition methodology presented before. The approach should be considered qualitative or subjective even though it may involve statistical and regression techniques.

Time series models for the decomposition of a series into trend-cycle (T-C) seasonal (S) and irregular (I) components are as follows:

Data = Trend-cycle + Seasonal + Irregular
Data = Trend-cycle • Seasonal factor • Irregular factor

It is possible to make projections for the future by forecasting each of the components separately and then recombining or synthesizing the forecasts of the component parts.

First, forecasters often make a further decomposition of trend-cycle into trend and cycle components, which are separately projected. It is important to recognize that this approach does not deal with the causes of the variation in time series data. Rather, the effects of the many factors influencing the data (e.g., population growth and migration, interest rates, savings, liquidity, government policy, international economic conditions, etc.) are grouped by four factors: long-term trend, seasonal variation, cyclical variation, and irregular variation. These factors are then combined in a multiplicative or additive model.

Seasonal factors can be developed by using smoothed twelve-month moving averages to estimate a trend-cycle. Trend-cycle values are divided into the data to obtain seasonal-irregular indices

$$\frac{\text{T-C} \cdot \text{S} \cdot \text{I}}{\text{T-C}} = \text{S} \cdot \text{I}.$$

These indices are smoothed to obtain the seasonal factors. The seasonal factors themselves may be projected into the future using the X-11 methodology by adding one-half of the difference between the last two years' seasonal factors to the seasonal factor for the most recent year.

The irregular component is assumed to be random. For purposes of projection, it is set equal to 1.0 in the case of a multiplicative model or 0.0 in the case of an additive model.

The trend-cycle variation is decomposed into trend and cycle components by postulating a mechanism for generating long-term trend values. Perhaps the simplest trend equation is that of a straight line fit to the T-C values such that the sum of the vertical deviations about the line sum equal zero. In the following chapter the method of least squares regression is presented and this method is frequently used to estimate trend values.

Figures 9.1 and 9.2 illustrate the fitting of linear, quadratic, or exponential trend lines to T-C values. Since formal methods for fitting curves to data will be presented later, let us assume that the trend lines were fitted visually. The figures also show

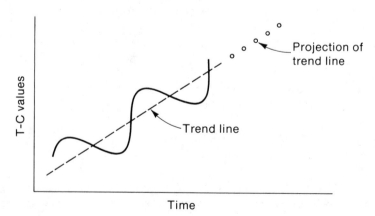

Figure 9.1   Fitting a trend line to T-C values.

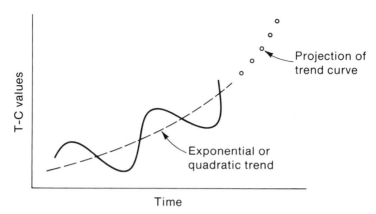

Figure 9.2   Fitting a trend curve to T-C values.

the extrapolation of the trend lines to obtain forecasts of the trend component for future periods. Over the historical period the trend values are subtracted from T-C to yield cyclical values.

Figure 9.3 illustrates the cyclical component, together with measures of duration (peak-to-peak, peak-to-trough, trough-to-peak and trough-to-trough).

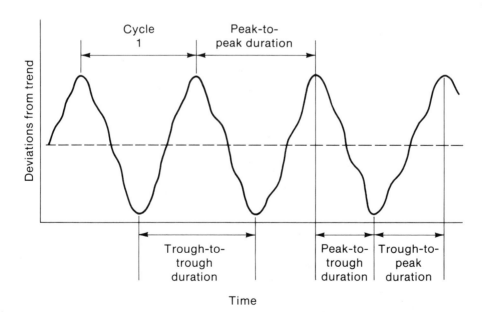

Figure 9.3   Calculating historical deviations.

Table 9.3 summarizes the durations for each cycle and the average duration of each measure. Figure 9.4 superimposes each peak on top of one another (a similar figure can be developed for each trough). The slopes represent the rate of expansion to the peak or contraction from the peak.

Figure 9.5 illustrates the projection of the cyclical component based on the information gathered over the historical period. In the absence of any specific information or confidence in the information regarding future economic conditions, three forecast scenarios are presented. The most likely forecast uses the average recovery duration over the historical period and a typical rate and magnitude of recovery. The optimistic scenario uses a shorter recovery, and a more rapid rate and magnitude of recovery. The pessimistic scenario uses a longer recovery period, a slower rate of recovery, and a lesser magnitude of recovery.

With current economic or market factors in hand, and comparing these with those from previous periods, the forecaster can readily decide whether a typical, rapid, or slower expansion appears probable. The decision on the forecast of the cyclical component is a highly subjective one. Thus, this approach is considered to

Table 9.3 Hypothetical Historical Durations—in Quarters

Cycle	Peak-To-Peak	Peak-To-Trough	Trough-To-Peak	Trough-To-Trough
1	16	4	12	15
2	14	5	9	15
3	18	5	11	19
Avg	16	5	10	15

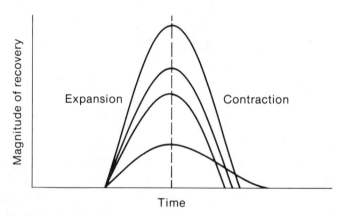

Figure 9.4 Superimposing cyclical peaks.

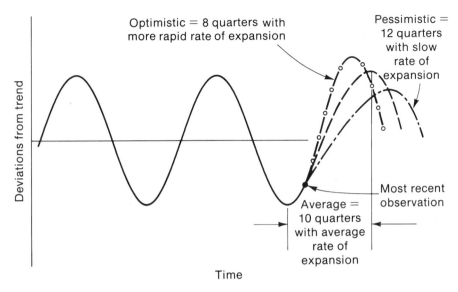

Figure 9.5   Projecting the cycle using historical durations.

be qualitative or subjective. The judgment applied is based on historical pattern analysis which can only be an imperfect guide to predicting future cycles. Nevertheless, the forecast obtained by adding (or multiplying) the four components can be a useful starting point. This forecast can be compared to forecasts generated by other quantitative methods (e.g. exponential smoothing, regression models, econometric methods, ARIMA models) to help the forecaster make the final subjective decision in the selection of the forecast values for future periods.

CYCLE ANALYSIS OF ECONOMIC INDICATORS

The selection of the duration, rate, and magnitude of recovery or contraction can be influenced by a knowledge of current economic conditions. The analysis of economic indicators is an important part of many forecasting activities:

- Forecasts of the levels of key economic indicators are often incorporated in quantitative models.

- Correlation studies are commonly made to assess the relative impact of expansions and contractions in the economy.

- Plots of economic indicators and their forecasts are frequently part of a presentation package for demand forecasts of business products.

- Many national economic indicators are monitored on an ongoing basis by industry and government analysts.

ORIGIN OF ECONOMIC INDICATORS

The origin of economic indicators dates back to the sharp business recession of 1937–1938. At that time an effort was initiated by the National Bureau of Economic Research (NBER) to devise a system that would signal the end of a recession.

Since quantitative analyses of the national economy were just beginning to receive attention within government circles, a considerable amount of data, assembled by the NBER since the 1920's, were analyzed to gain a better understanding of business cycles. These data, which included monthly, quarterly, and annual series on prices, employment, and production, resulted in a collection of twenty-one promising series that were selected on the basis of past performance and future promise as reliable indicators of business revival. Over the years this effort was greatly expanded to other public and private agencies (Shiskin and Moore, 1967; Moore and Shiskin, 1972).

A number of series, such as employment, indexes of consumer and wholesale prices, and manufacturers' orders, are published in the nation's newspapers. As indicators of the nation's economic health, they are followed very closely by professional economists and the business community at large, especially during periods of change in business activity.

LEADING, COINCIDENT, AND LAGGING INDICATORS

For convenience of interpretation, *economic indicators* have been classified into three groups—leading, coincident, and lagging (Sobek, 1973). *Leading indicators* are those that provide advance warning of probable changes in economic activity. *Coincident indicators* are those that reflect the current performance of the economy. *Lagging indicators* are those that confirm changes previously signaled.

Coincident indicators provide a measure of current economic activity. They are the most familiar and include Gross National Product, industrial production, personal income, retail sales, and employment (see Figure 9.6).

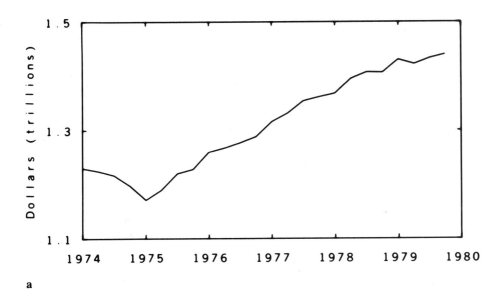

a

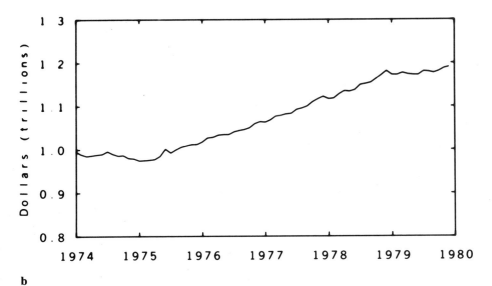

b

Source: U.S. Department of Commerce, Bureau of Economic Analysis for (a) and (b); U.S. Department of Commerce, Bureau of Census for (c); U.S. Department of Labor, Bureau of Labor Statistics for (d).

Figure 9.6   Time plots of several coincident indicators of the U.S. economy: (a) Gross National Product, (b) personal income, (c) retail sales, and (d) employment.

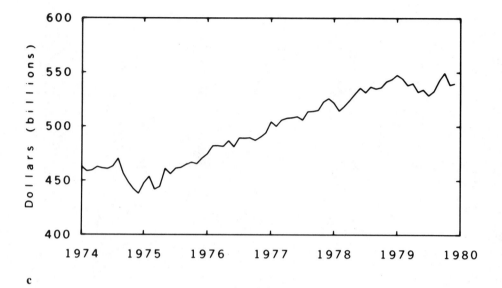

c

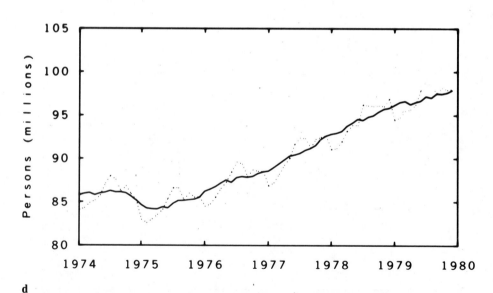

d

Figure 9.6 Time plots of several coincident indicators of the U.S. economy: (a) Gross National Product, (b) personal income, (c) retail sales, and (d) employment.

Use of Indicators

It would be very useful to forecasters and planners to have some advance warning of an impending change in the nation's economy. While coincident indicators are used to indicate whether the economy is currently experiencing expansion, contraction, recession, or inflation, leading indicators help forecasters to assess short-term trends in the coincident indicators. In addition, leading indicators help planners and policy makers anticipate adverse effects on the economy and examine the feasibility of corrective steps. Among the leading indicators, housing starts, new orders for durable goods, construction contracts, formation of new business enterprises, hiring rates, and average length of workweek are the most commonly quoted.

Housing starts, a key leading indicator plotted in Figure 9.7, tend to lead fluctuations in overall economic activity. The data are used throughout the text as an explanatory variable related to main telephone gain. The main reason that housing starts are a leading economic indicator (typically leading peaks in the business cycle by a year and troughs by six months) is that starts are very sensitive to fluctuations in interest rates. When interest rates rise substantially—as they generally do near the peak of an expansion—savings deposited with mortgage lenders tend to be diverted to other users of funds. Meanwhile, rising mortgage rates and stricter lending conditions curtail the demand for home loans. Thus homebuilding is squeezed from both sides—supply and demand—when interest rates rise.

A useful set of indicators for revealing and explaining the economy's broad cyclical movements includes manufacturers' shipments and orders (Figure 9.8). These are comprehensive indicators of industrial activity, an especially important sector because it is the economy's most volatile component, dropping four to five times as much as the total output during business recessions.

Shipments are an indicator of current economic activity, measuring the dollar value of products sold by all manufacturing establishments. Orders, on the other

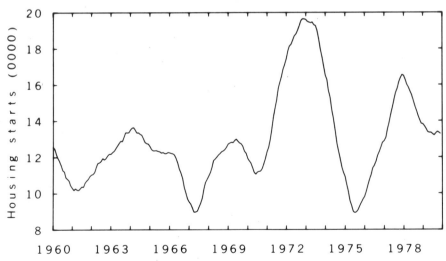

Source: U.S. Department of Commerce, Bureau of Census.

Figure 9.7 Time plot of a twelve-month moving average of the housing starts (new private housing units started).

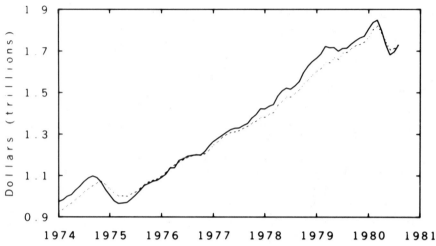

Source: U.S. Department of Commerce, Bureau of Census.

Figure 9.8   Time plot of manufacturers' shipments (dotted) and orders (solid).

hand, are a valuable leading indicator. They measure the dollar value of new orders—net of order cancellations—received by all manufacturers. The two series are distorted by inflation, since there is no relevant price index to convert it to real terms. It is the difference between shipments and orders, which shows what is happening to the backlog of unfilled orders, that gives insight into the degree of sustainability of current national output.

Lagging indicators usually follow, rather than lead, the fluctuations in the coincident indicators. Examples of lagging indicators are labor cost per unit of output (Figure 9.9), long-term unemployment, and the yield on mortgage loans.

Composite Indicators

In an attempt to reduce the number of series that must be reviewed, and at the same time not to lose a great deal of information, analysts have developed *composite indicators*. These series provide single measures of complicated economic activities that experience common fluctuations. The procedure involved includes "amplitude-adjustment" in which the month-to-month percent change of each series in the composite is standardized so that all series are expressed in comparable units. The average month-to-month change, without regard to sign, is 1.0. Each individual series is weighted by the score it receives from the scoring plan. The composite index is amplitude-adjusted so that its average month-to-month percent change is 1.0.

If an index shows an increase of 2.0 in a month, it is rising twice as fast as its average rate of change in the past. If an index increases by 0.5, it is rising only half

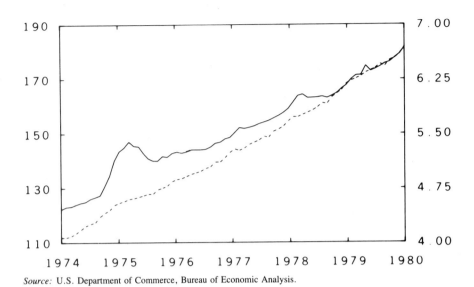

Source: U.S. Department of Commerce, Bureau of Economic Analysis.

Figure 9.9   Time plots of unit labor costs (solid) and hourly earnings (dotted).

as fast as its historical rate of increase. Composite indicators have been developed for the leading, coincident, and lagging series.

In order to have a more comprehensive coverage of the economy, the U.S. Commerce Department publishes *composite indexes* of leading and coincident indicators. These indicators are a weighted combination of individual indicators; for example, employment and real income are two components in the *index of coincident indicators*.

One problem with interpreting the index of leading indicators is that its month-to-month changes can be erratic. For example, the index dropped sharply in April 1980, only to recover partly during the summer, thus muddying any message about a future downturn. However, comparing movements of the index over a longer span helps to bring out the underlying cyclical movements. For example, Figure 9.10 shows the percent change in the current level of the leading index from the average level of the preceding twelve months. On that basis, the leading indicators have declined (i.e., fallen below zero) before every one of the five recessions since 1950. The two recessions during the 1970's are depicted by shaded areas.

Reverse Trend Adjustment of the Leading Indicators

Economists have been concerned about two aspects of the leading indicators:

- The lead at the business cycle peak is much longer than the lead at the trough.

- Leading indicators do not have the long-term trend that the economy as measured by coincident indicators has.

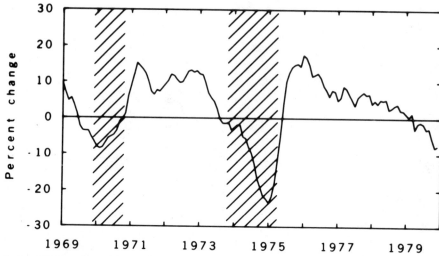

Source: U.S. Department of Commerce, Bureau of Economic Analysis.

Figure 9.10 Time plot of a composite index of leading indicators; it shows the percent change in the current level of the leading index from the average level of the preceding twelve months.

Since the objective of forecasting is to predict current levels rather than detrended levels, the *reverse trend adjustment* procedure adds a trend to the leading indicators (rather than removing the trend from the coincident indicators). First, however, it is necessary to eliminate whatever trend already exists in the leading indicators. Then the trend of the coincident indicators (based on full cycles) is added to the detrended leading indicators.

The effect of reverse trend adjustment is to shorten the lead time at business cycle peaks and increase the lead time at troughs. It also tends to reduce the number of false signals of recession that are evident when the unadjusted index turns down but a recession does not occur. Because reverse trend adjustment helps to reduce the lead time at peaks and increase the lead time at troughs, this makes the two lead times more equal. This will lessen the reaction time at the peak, however. Even with reverse trend adjustment, the lead at the peaks is about one or two months longer, on the average, than the lead at the troughs.

In forecasting with regression models, the generally *different* lead times must be reckoned with before regression models are used. Since regression models do not offer you the chance to vary lead/lag times in the explanatory variables at different periods in the cycle, the indicators will tend to average the impact of the lesser lead or lag at either the peak or the trough. It is possible to have one model in which the indicator has as its lead time the appropriate lead for a peak and a second model that has as its lead time the appropriate lead for a trough. Then, either the first or second model is used to generate forecasts, depending upon the state of the business cycle.

Sources of Indicators

The U.S. Department of Commerce publishes a monthly booklet called *Business Conditions Digest,* which contains current data for many different indicators. The charts and graphs cover the National Income and Product accounts series, cyclical indicators, series on anticipations and intentions, analytical measures, and international comparisons. The series are usually seasonally adjusted and the NBER (National Board of Economic Research) *reference dates* for recessions and expansions are shown. It is apparent from the plots that business contractions are generally shorter than business expansions. The average peacetime cycle is slightly less than four years. Another useful reference to data sources, their description, and their use in business cycle forecasting is Silk and Curley (1970).

SELECTING INDICATORS

Specified criteria have been applied by the NBER to hundreds of economic series from which a list of indicators could be selected. These criteria include *economic significance, statistical adequacy, historical conformity* to business cycles, *consistency of lead or lag, smoothness* of the data, and *timeliness* of the data. A score can be given for each of six criteria, and those series with the highest scores can then be retained. The scoring is subjective in many aspects.

Economic Significance

Some aspects of criteria of *economic significance* have already been discussed—that is, the role a given economic process has in theories that purport to explain how business cycles come about or how they may be controlled or modified.

A consideration in indicator selection and scoring is the *breadth of coverage.* A "broad" indicator covers all corporate activity, total consumption, or investment. A "narrow" indicator relates to a single industry or to minor components of the "broad" series.

A broad economic indicator may continue to perform well even if some components deteriorate because of technological developments, changes in customer tastes, or rapid growth or decline of single products or industries. Therefore, a "broad" indicator receives a higher score than a "narrow" indicator.

Statistical Adequacy

The characteristics you should consider in evaluating the *statistical adequacy* of a series include a *good reporting system* and *good coverage;* that is, the data should cover the entire period they represent, benchmarks should be available, and there should be a full account of survey methods, coverage, and data adjustments.

A *good reporting system* is one based on primary rather than indirect sources or estimates. Some important series, such as the index of industrial production, the index of net business formation, and Gross National Product, are based largely on indirect sources. Employment and retail sales are based on direct reporting from primary sources.

Good coverage means that if sampling is required, it should be a probability sample with stated measurement error regarding sample statistics.

Moreover, coverage means, for example, that monthly data should include all days and not be a figure based on one day or week. Also, the availability of benchmarks is important as a check on the accuracy of data. For example, the U.S. Census provides a benchmark for estimates of population.

Conformity to Business Cycles

The National Bureau of Economic Research developed an initial index to measure how well the variations in a series *conformed to business cycle* variations. A series that rose through every business expansion and declined during every contraction received an index score of 100. This particular index did not include extra cycles, such as occurred in 1966–1967, which are not classified as recession troughs. The index did not indicate whether the lack of conformity occurred early in the data or later; and it did not take into account the amplitude of the cycles. The scoring system subsequently developed by Shiskin and Moore (1967) takes these considerations into account.

Consistency of Timing

A number of considerations govern scoring a series on the basis of *consistency of timing*. The first is the consistency of lead or lag time relative to cycle peak or trough. The second is the variability about the average lead or lag time. A third consideration is the difference in lead time for a peak compared to the lead time for a trough. Finally, has there been any recent departure from historical relationships?

Leading indicators have a median lead time of two or more months. Lagging indicators have a median lag of two or more months. Coincident indicators have a median timing of -1, 0, or $+1$ months. Occasionally, median leads of $+2$ months are possible when the lead or lag is not constant over many cycles.

Smoothness and Timeliness

The factors that are weighed in arriving at a score for *smoothness* and *timeliness* include prompt availability of data and their smoothness. It is easier to identify changes in direction in a smooth series than in an irregular series. Generally speaking, because of irregularity of data, comparisons over spans greater than one month must usually be made to detect cyclical changes. Smoothing of some irregular series may result in some delay but may still provide a longer lead time than for other series which are less irregular but have shorter lead times.

Generally speaking, leading indicators are the most erratic; lagging indicators are the smoothest. Coincident indicators have the shortest publication lag and the highest conformity scores. For example, corporate profits after taxes received an average score of 68 in the NBER index. This indicator also received fairly high scores for economic significance, statistical adequacy, conformity, and timing. However, it received a score of 60 for smoothness, because it is irregular, and only 25 for timeliness, because it is a quarterly series subject to slow reporting.

CYCLE FORECASTING USING ECONOMIC INDICATORS

This section describes cycle or turning-point analysis using economic indicators to help determine the timing of the turning point, and the rate, duration, and magnitude of the cyclical component.

A Ten-Step Procedure for Making a Turning-Point Analysis

Here is an algorithm that will guide you through this procedure:

1. Plot the time series.

2. Remove seasonality (seasonal adjustment, differencing).

3. If necessary, remove irregularity with a low-order moving average.

4. Fit a trend line to the series in Step 3 and plot deviations from trend. This is the cycle. If necessary, transform the time series so that a trend line is appropriate (i.e., no cupshaped patterns should occur).

5. Follow Steps 1–4 for other national, regional, local, or industry series for comparison of cycle patterns.

6(a). If there is a historic relationship in the cycle patterns:

   - Obtain forecasts of the other variable.

   - Plot these forecasts in terms of deviations from trend.

   - Forecast the cycle for your series based on the cycle forecast of the economic variable. Take leading or lagging relationships into account.

(b). If there is no historical relationship, develop the cycle forecast based on a pattern analysis in which you have considered:

- Peak-to-trough or trough-to-peak historical durations (months, quarters).
- Peak-to-peak or trough-to-trough durations.
- Magnitudes (amplitudes) of peaks or troughs (amount, percent).
- Slopes of peaks or troughs (speed of recovery, decline).
- Anticipated future cyclical patterns based on economic, market, or industry information.

7. Project the trend line of Step 4 and add to it the cycle forecast from Step 6 to obtain trend-cycle forecasts.

8. To reintroduce seasonality (if desired), add the forecasts of the seasonal factors.

9. If appropriate, retransform the series (e.g., exponentiate, raise to a power) to the original scale in Step 7 or 8 if a transformation was taken in Step 4 or 2.

10. Plot the history and forecast together for reasonableness.

Preparing a Cycle Forecast for Revenues

Let's examine results of the ten-step procedure. Figure 9.11 is a plot of the revenue series (Step 1). Figure 9.12 is a plot of the seasonally adjusted series (Step 2) for

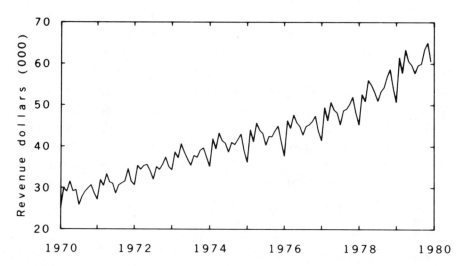

Figure 9.11 Time plot of the original telephone toll-revenue series. The data are not seasonally adjusted.

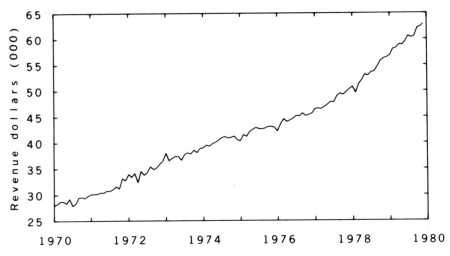

Figure 9.12   Time plot of the seasonally adjusted telephone toll-revenue series.

which the SABL procedure (*The Beginning Forecaster,* Chapter 19) was used. Next, a three-month moving average of the seasonally adjusted series was performed (Step 3). This smoothed the irregular component and resulted in a smoother cycle pattern in the later stages of analysis.

Figure 9.13 shows a trend line fitted to the data from Step 3 (Step 4). The deviations from trend in Figure 9.14 show a cupshaped pattern indicating the need to transform the series. (The peak-to-trough reference dates for the 1970–1971 and 1974–1975 recessions, as determined by the National Bureau of Economic Research, are shown as shaded areas in this and subsequent figures.) A logarithmic transformation was then taken of the smoothed series, and a straight-line trend-line was fitted; the deviations from trend are shown as a cycle in Figure 9.15.

Similar steps were followed for an economic series (nonfarm employment), and the deviations from trend are shown in Figure 9.16 (Step 5). From the shading in Figure 9.16, it can be seen that employment in the region for which the forecast is being made peaks at approximately the same time as it does in the rest of the nation but reaches bottom a year or more after the national economy has bottomed.

A comparison of the regional employment cycle with the revenue cycle shows similar patterns—especially since 1973. A forecast of the employment series was obtained and is shown (in terms of deviation from trend) by the dotted line in Figure 9.17. With this prediction as a starting point, three scenarios were developed for the revenue cycle (optimistic, most likely, pessimistic), and these are shown in Figure 9.18. The most likely scenario approximates the relationship that existed between the two series in the past. The optimistic scenario shows a somewhat shallower decline and a more rapid recovery. The pessimistic scenario projects a much sharper decline and more gradual recovery that is more similar to the 1976–1979 period. Because of the steadily worsening economic news in the first quarter 1980,

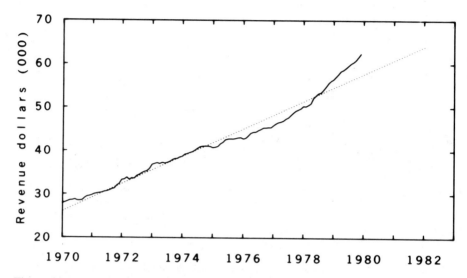

Figure 9.13   Three-month moving average of the seasonally adjusted revenue series fitted with a straight line.

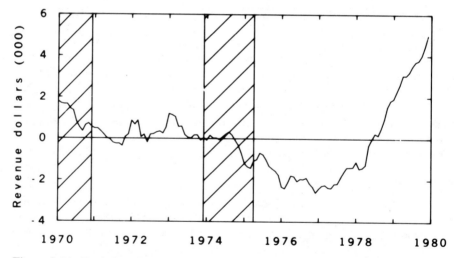

Figure 9.14   Deviations from trend suggesting a need for a transformation.

the pessimistic scenario is a more probable alternative forecast than the optimistic forecast.

Figure 9.19 shows a plot of history and forecast in terms of a smoothed seasonally adjusted series. The trend line was extrapolated, the cycle forecast was

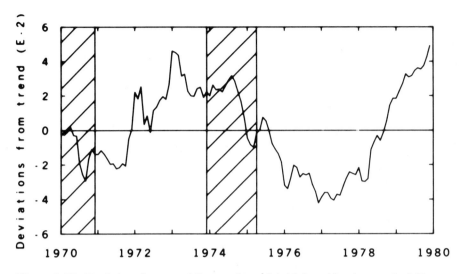

Figure 9.15 Deviations from trend for transformed (with logarithms), smoothed (three-month moving average), and seasonally adjusted (SABL) revenue data.

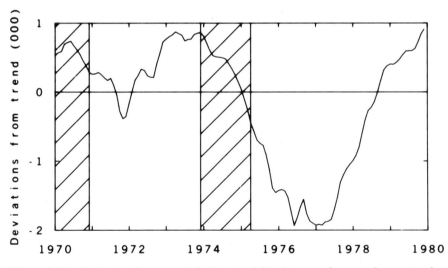

Figure 9.16 Deviations from a straight line trend fitted to a nonfarm employment series.

added, and the result was exponentiated and plotted as the dotted line. If desired, seasonality could be reintroduced by adding the historical and projected seasonal factors. The irregular component has been smoothed over the historical period and is projected to be zero over the forecast period.

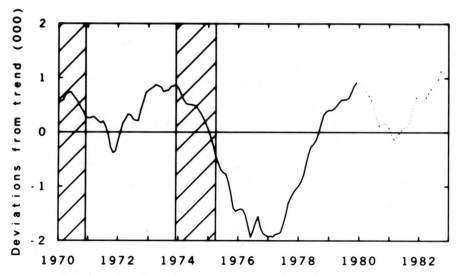

Figure 9.17   Historical and forecast deviations from trend for a nonfarm employment
series.

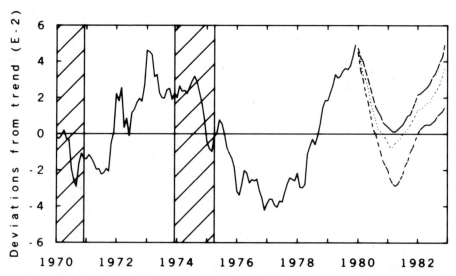

Figure 9.18   Three forecast scenarios for the revenue series are shown below: optimistic
(uppermost), pessimistic (lowest), and most likely (intermediate).

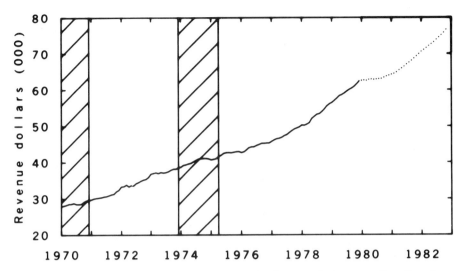

Figure 9.19 Historical time plot and a forecast for the smoothed, seasonally adjusted revenue series. The forecast is shown as a dotted line.

Alternative Approaches to Turning-Point Forecasts

Strong arguments against the use of seasonally adjusted data for econometric regression models have been made (Jenkins, 1979). The objections are related, in part, to the fact that you cannot be quite sure what the statistical properties of the residuals are after you have subjected the series to a seasonal adjustment procedure. This has an impact on the inferences that can be drawn—specifically for confidence limits about the forecast (Chapter 14). In the cycle forecasting approach, illustrated in the previous telephone revenues example, the subjective nature of the forecast and the intentional omission of confidence levels recognize that this is a *highly subjective* approach.

However, an alternative to modeling seasonally adjusted data is modeling appropriately differenced data. Figure 9.20 shows a cyclical pattern in which the deviation from the trend line is measured in differences of order 12. One can also take differences of economic data, compare patterns of deviations from trend of the two series, and develop cycle forecasts. The last step is to "undifference" the series by adding the predicted differences to the appropriate actual (and later predicted) values of the revenue series.

Despite the subjective nature of the turning-point forecast, it is intuitively appealing to upper-level managers, a consideration that cannot be dismissed. Even if this approach is not used to establish the forecast values, it is an effective way of presenting the forecast to higher management. In this instance, the deviations from trend are calculated instead of subjectively projected.

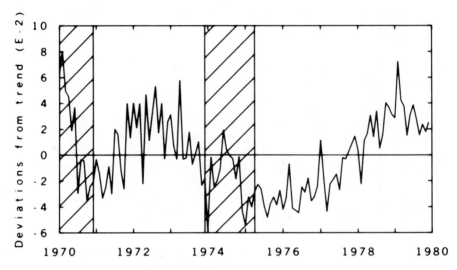

Figure 9.20   Deviations from a straight line trend of the differences of order 12 for the monthly revenue series.

SUMMARY

Seasonal adjustment is a useful procedure that helps identify turning points in the economy or the demand for products and services. Knowledge of the seasonal pattern also helps in planning employee workloads and inventory levels.

If you can remove seasonality from a time series, you can apply a number of forecasting techniques that otherwise would not handle seasonal data to these seasonally adjusted data—e.g., the simpler exponential smoothing techniques discussed in Chapter 8.

The Bureau of Census X-11 seasonal adjustment program is widely used to deseasonalize data in government and business.

- The program is capable of mass-processing data and producing detailed analyses of seasonal factors, and trend-cycle and irregular variations.

- It can be run in an additive or multiplicative form for quarterly or monthly data.

Qualitative approaches to obtaining cycle forecasts are based on the decomposition of a time series into trend, cyclical, seasonal, and irregular components. The components are individually analyzed, forecasted, and recombined to develop a forecast for the time series under study. We have seen first how a cycle forecast was obtained by identifying and projecting the historical patterns of an individual time series. Next, economic indicators were discussed. Finally, a cycle forecast was made using the predicted cycle values of the economic indicator to obtain predicted cycle values for the time series being forecast.

USEFUL READING

BOX, G. E. P., and G. M. JENKINS (1976). *Time Series Analysis—Forecasting and Control*, rev. ed. San Francisco, CA: Holden-Day.

DAGUM, E. B. (1976). Seasonal Factor Forecasts from ARIMA Models. *Proceedings of the International Statistical Institute, 40th Session, Warsaw, 1975*. Warsaw: International Statistical Institute, 206–19.

DAGUM, E. B. (1978). Modeling, Forecasting, and Seasonally Adjusting Economic Time Series with the X-11 ARIMA Method. *The Statistician* 27, 203–16.

JENKINS, G. M. (1979). *Practical Experiences with Modeling and Forecasting Time Series*. Jersey, Channel Islands: GJ&P (Overseas) Ltd.

KALLEK, S. (1978). An Overview of the Objectives and Framework of Seasonal Adjustment, in *Seasonal Analysis of Economic Time Series*, A. Zellner, ed. Washington, DC: U.S. Government Printing Office.

MACAULEY, F. R. (1930). *The Smoothing of Time Series*. Cambridge, MA: National Bureau of Economic Research.

MOORE, G. H., and J. SHISKIN (1972). *Early Warning Signals for the Economy in Statistics*. J. M. Tanur et al., eds. San Francisco, CA: Holden-Day.

PLOSSER, C. I. (1979). Short-Term Forecasting and Seasonal Adjustment. *Journal of the American Statistical Association* 74, 15–24.

SHISKIN, J., A. H. YOUNG, and J. C. MUSGRAVE (1967). *The X-11 Variant of Census Method II Seasonal Adjustment Program*. Technical Paper No. 15, U.S. Department of Commerce, Bureau of the Census. Washington, DC: U.S. Government Printing Office.

SHISKIN, J., and G. H. MOORE (1967). *Indicators of Business Expansions and Contractions*. Cambridge, MA: National Bureau of Economic Research.

PROBLEMS

The use of moving averages to calculate seasonal factors in the initial phases of the Bureau of the Census seasonal adjustment program can be illustrated with the following exercise. A multiplicative model is assumed.

1. For the observations in Column (1) of the following table, calculate centered twelve-month moving averages. Since there are an even number of months in the average, the first smoothed average is shown between June and July.

2. Smooth Column (2) using a two-month moving average. The first value appears opposite July. This value represents the trend-cycle component.

3. Calculate seasonal-irregular ratios by dividing Column (1) by Column (3). Note that ratios are not available for the first six and last six observations.

4. With more data a seasonal index for each month would be calculated by averaging the S $\times$ I values for each individual month (all January's, February's, etc.). The seasonal factors for a year should sum to 12.0. Ratio the factors in Column (4) so that the sum is 12.0.

5. Treatment of extreme irregular values is not part of this exercise, but is part of the Census method.

Year	Month	(1) Observations T-C $\times$ S $\times$ I	(2) 12 MMA of (1)	(3) 2 MMA of (2) = T-C	(4) S $\times$ I = (1)/(3)	(5) Ratio to Total = 12.0 For 1 Year
1	Jan	100				
	Feb	90				
	Mar	95				
	Apr	100				
	May	105				
	Jun	110				
			106.7			
	Jul	105		107.8		
	Aug	105				
	Sept	110				
	Oct	115				
	Nov	120				
	Dec	125				
2	Jan	125				
	Feb	110				
	Mar	115				
	Apr	115				
	May	120				
	Jun	125				
	Jul	110				
	Aug	110				
	Sept	120				
	Oct	130				
	Nov	130				
	Dec	135				

CHAPTER 10

Developing Functional Relationships

This chapter considers why a forecaster might want to consider building regression models, which are the most widely known and frequently used tools for forecasting and econometric analysis. These models can:

- Provide superior forecasts (once again, the accuracy of the forecasts of the independent variables is crucial).

- Provide forecast users with a model that is encompassing and appealing, since more than one variable is taken into account.

- Be constructed with an approach whereby one independent variable is chosen to explain the trend in the dependent variable and one or more other variables are chosen to explain the deviations about the trend.

A FORECASTING PROBLEM

Consider a telecommunications forecasting program in which the goal is to provide accurate forecasts of demand volumes in general, and main telephone gain in particular. Telecommunications companies find these forecasts are very important factors in determining construction (investment) programs, departmental budgets, and the size of installation and repair forces.

The Variable To Be Forecast

A *main telephone* is defined as a telephone that is connected directly with a central office (location of a telephone switching machine), whether the telephone is on an individual or party line. Only one telephone for each customer on each line is considered a main telephone.

Main telephone gain (or, more simply, main gain) is a highly seasonal time series in which about 81 percent of the total variation in the monthly series is attributable to seasonality (Figure 10.1). For modeling purposes, a seasonality can be removed by an appropriate seasonal adjustment program, or, by taking differences. To minimize calendar and other irregular variation, *quarterly* data were used in this analysis; differences of order 4 were taken to make the series stationary and free of seasonal variation. The differenced data showed a pronounced cyclical pattern in which the peaks and valleys generally corresponded to the business cycle (Figure 10.2).

Main gain represents the growth of main telephones in service and can be viewed as a difference of order 1 of main telephones in service. A difference of order 4 of main gain is then equivalent to a difference of order 1 followed by a difference of order 4 of main telephones in service. (Adjustment of in-service counts to compensate for errors in processing and transcription are ignored here.)

It is reasonable to assume that quarterly main gain could be forecast on the basis of a housing-starts time series (information that construction of a housing unit has begun), since main gain lags housing starts by about two quarters. Linear regression models can be used to describe a relationship between a variable of interest and one or more related variables that are assumed to have a bearing on the forecasting problem.

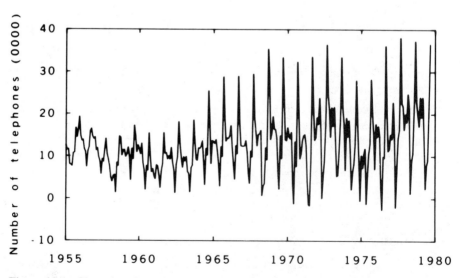

Figure 10.1   Time plot of a monthly gain in a main telephone series.

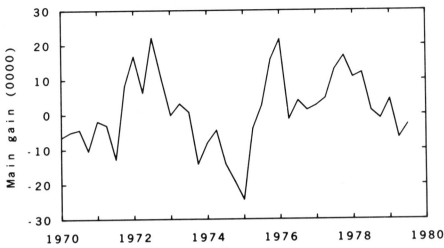

Source: Board of Governors of the Federal Reserve System.

Figure 10.2   Time plot of the differences of order 4 of the quarterly main gain, showing variation due to the business cycle. This time series is denoted as GAIN.

WHAT IS A REGRESSION MODEL?

In Chapter 6 we introduced the scatter diagram as a means of graphically displaying an underlying relationship between two variables, X and Y. For example, in relating monthly telephone-toll revenues to toll messages, Figure 10.3 shows a very narrow cluster of points lying along a line with positive slope. This suggests a tight relationship between revenues and messages, perhaps described by a simple curve. A more complicated situation arises if one considers the relationship between quarterly main telephone gain and housing starts as depicted in Figure 10.4. Here it would be more difficult to suggest a simple forecasting relationship, because of the wider dispersion of points.

The statistical technique of quantifying such relationships among variables is known as *regression analysis*. Such relationships can be used to predict one variable, called the *dependent variable*, from knowledge of other related variables known as *independent variables*.

The term "regression" has a rather curious origin in studies by Sir Francis Galton (1822–1911) of inheritance in biology. His studies showed that while tall (or short) fathers had tall (or short) sons, the sons were on the average not as tall (or as short) as their fathers. Thus Galton observed that the *average* height of the sons tended to move toward the *average* height of the overall population of fathers, rather than toward reproducing the height of the parents. This "regression" toward the mean is widely observed in other examples as well, and the term has therefore found general acceptance.

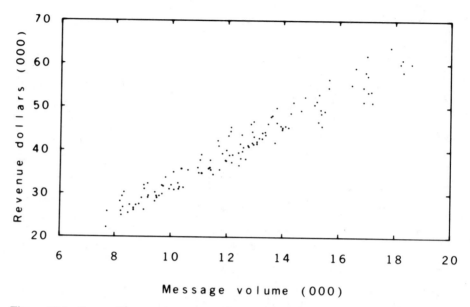

Figure 10.3 Scatter diagram of monthly telephone toll-revenue and message volumes (January 1969–December 1978).

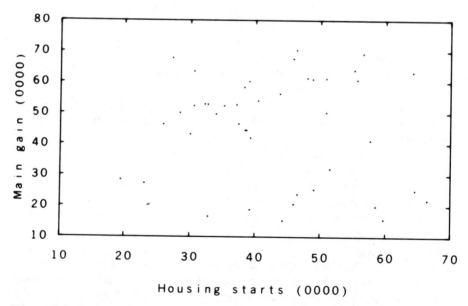

Figure 10.4 Scatter diagram of quarterly telephone gain and housing starts (first quarter 1969–third quarter 1978).

The Regression Curve

A *regression curve* (in a two-variable case) is defined as that curve which goes through the *mean value* of Y (the dependent variable) for each *fixed value* of X (the independent variable). If data are plentiful, a curve passing through the bulk of the data would represent the regression curve. The data are such that there is no functional relationship describing exactly one variable Y as a function of X. For a given value of the independent variable X, there is a *distribution* of values of Y. This relationship may be approximated by determining the *average* (or median) value of Y for small intervals of values of X.

In most practical situations, there are not enough observations to "even pretend that the resulting curve has the shape of the regression curve that would arise if we had unlimited data" (Mosteller and Tukey, 1977, p. 266). Instead, the observations result in an approximation. With only limited data, a shape for the regression curve (linear, quadratic, exponential) is assumed and the curve is fitted to the data by using a statistical method such as the *method of least squares*. This method will be explained shortly.

A Simple Linear Model

In the telecommunications example, let's assume that a simple linear relationship exists between the toll message and revenue volumes. Suppose you wish to predict the toll revenues from the toll messages. A sample of revenue and message volumes could be collected from a billing record and plotted as a scatter diagram, in which the dependent variable (revenue) is put on the vertical axis and the independent variable (message) on the horizontal axis. Figure 10.3 is a scatter diagram for the monthly volume of toll revenues and messages in our telecommunications example.

The scatter diagram shows that, *on average*, revenues increase with increasing message volumes (and vice versa), though for a given volume of messages there is a good deal of *variability* in revenues. This simple model is only partially descriptive in that it does not take into account other factors, such as time of day, duration of call, and distance.

Since regression analysis seeks an algebraic relationship between a dependent variable Y and one or more independent variables, the appropriate algebraic model describes the average value for Y given a specific value of X:

$$\text{Model} = \text{Average } Y, \qquad \text{when } Y = f(X).$$

If it were true that revenues change the same amount for each additional message, then the data would lie along a straight line. In practice, this may be approximately true, the difference being ascribed to *random errors:*

$$\text{Data} = \text{Average } Y + \text{Random errors.}$$

The slope β of this straight line would represent the *rate of change* in revenue with increasing message volume. The intercept α (revenue at "zero" message volume) would not be a meaningful quantity in this case. Thus

Model = Average revenue = $\alpha + \beta \cdot$ Messages.

Since a "zero" message volume in this example is not meaningful, the practitioner must be cautioned that the intercept α cannot always be interpreted physically. Thus the regression model, as described by an equation, is only *locally* correct in the sense that it describes a meaningful relationship *within the range* of values of the data that are reasonable.

However, there is considerable variability in revenue for a given volume of messages, so that one assumption in the linear regression model is that for any value of X, the value of Y is scattered around an *average value*. This average value is an unknown quantity which is often denoted by the Greek letter mu (μ) with a subscript $Y(X)$:

$$\mu_{Y(X)} = \alpha + \beta X.$$

The intercept α and slope β are known as the *regression coefficients*. The model is *linear* in X. Both α and β are unknown parameters to be estimated from the data. As a standard statistical convention, it is useful to designate unknown parameters in models by Greek letters, to distinguish them from the corresponding estimates made from the data.

The observed values of Y will not necessarily lie on a straight line in the XY plane but will differ from it by some random error ε:

Data = $\alpha + \beta \cdot$ Messages + Errors.

Thus the *simple linear regression model* is expressed by

$$Y = \mu_{Y(X)} + \varepsilon$$
$$= \alpha + \beta X + \varepsilon,$$

where the average (expected) value of ε is zero.

THE METHOD OF LEAST SQUARES

In a particular application of the model, the forecaster has data which are assumed to have arisen as a realization of the hypothetical model. The next step is to come up with a rational procedure for estimating the parameters in the model from a given set of data:

Data = Model + Errors.

There are a number of estimation techniques in the statistical literature, of which the method of *ordinary least squares* is the most common and easiest for mathematical analyses. This is not to say that other techniques have little merit. In fact, weighted least-squares techniques of several kinds are finding increased applications in the practical world, in particular, in robust regression (Mosteller and Tukey, 1977).

The Least-Squares Assumption

Consider now a reasonable criterion for estimating α and β from data. The method of *ordinary least squares* (OLS) determines values of α and β (since these will be estimated from data, we will replace α and β with Latin letters a and b) so that the sum of the squared *vertical deviations* (residuals) between the data and the fitted line,

Residuals = Data − Fit,

is less than the sum of the squared *vertical deviations* from any other straight line that could be fitted through the data:

Minimum of $\Sigma(\text{Data} - \text{Fit})^2$.

A "vertical deviation" is the vertical distance from an observed point to the line. Each deviation in the sample is squared and the least-squares line is defined to be the straight line that makes the sum of these squared deviations a minimum:

Data = $a + bX$ + Residuals.

Figure 10.5 (a) illustrates the regression relationship between two variables, Y and X. The arithmetic mean of the observed values of Y is denoted by $\bar{y}$. The vertical dashed lines represent the total deviations of each value y from the mean value $\bar{y}$. Part (b) in Figure 10.5 shows a linear least-squares regression line fitted to the observed points.

The *total variation* can be expressed in terms of (1) the *variation explained by the regression* and (2) a residual portion called the *unexplained variation*. Figure 10.6 (a) shows the explained variation, which is expressed by the vertical distance between any fitted (predicted) value and the mean or $\hat{y}_i - \bar{y}$. The circumflex ($\hat{\ }$) over the y is used to represent fitted values determined by a model. Thus, it is also

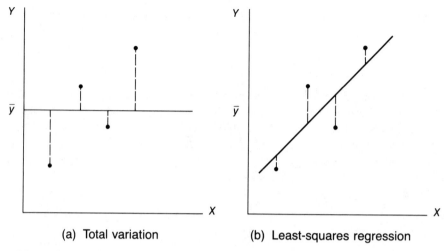

(a) Total variation   (b) Least-squares regression

Figure 10.5   The total variation of Y and the least-squares regression between Y and X.

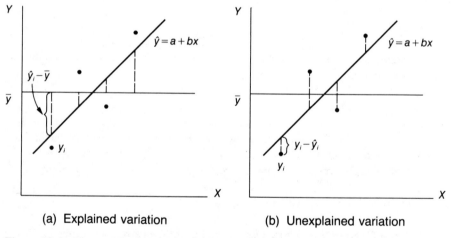

(a) Explained variation   (b) Unexplained variation

Figure 10.6   The explained and unexplained variation in least-squares regression.

customary to write $a = \hat{\alpha}$ and $b = \hat{\beta}$. Figure 10.6 (b) shows the unexplained or residual variation—the vertical distance between the observed values and the predicted values $(y_i - \hat{y}_i)$.

An Algebraic Derivation

The following is an elementary algebraic derivation of the coefficients in a simple linear regression model. It is instructive in that it illustrates the nature of the calculation involved in estimating a and b. We make temporary use of capital letters to stand for mean values: the expression $\Sigma D_i^2 = \Sigma(Y_i - a - bX_i)^2$ can be minimized and the minimizing solution will define a and b. Consider the data pairs (Y_i, X_i) for $(i = 1, \ldots, n)$. Let $y_i = Y_i - \bar{Y}$ and $x_i = X_i - \bar{X}$, where $\bar{Y} = \frac{1}{n}\Sigma Y_i$ and $\bar{X} = \frac{1}{n}\Sigma X_i$. The symbol Σ denotes the summation over n values. Then

$$
\begin{aligned}
\Sigma D_i^2 &= \Sigma[(y_i + \bar{Y}) - a - b(x_i + \bar{X})]^2 \\
&= \Sigma[(y_i - bx_i) + (\bar{Y} - a - b\bar{X})]^2 \\
&= \Sigma (y_i - bx_i)^2 + 2(\bar{Y} - a - b\bar{X})\Sigma y_i \\
&\quad - 2b(\bar{Y} - a - b\bar{X})\Sigma x_i + n(\bar{Y} - a - b\bar{X})^2 \\
&= \Sigma(y_i - bx_i)^2 + n(\bar{Y} - a - b\bar{X})^2,
\end{aligned}
$$

since

$$
\Sigma x_i = \Sigma(X_i - \bar{X}) = 0 = \Sigma y_i = \Sigma(Y_i - \bar{Y}).
$$

For any value of b, ΣD_i^2 will be minimized by a choice of a when the choice is such as to make the term $n(\bar{Y} - a - b\bar{X})^2$ zero. Hence $a = \bar{Y} - b\bar{X}$. With this choice of a, all terms of ΣD_i^2 except $\Sigma(y_i - bx_i)^2$ vanish, and

$$
\begin{aligned}
\Sigma D_i^2 &= \Sigma(y_i - bx_i)^2 \\
&= \Sigma y_i^2 - 2b\Sigma x_i y_i + b^2\Sigma x_i^2 \\
&= \Sigma y_i^2 + b^2\Sigma x_i^2 - 2b\Sigma x_i y_i.
\end{aligned}
$$

By completing the square for $(y_i - bx_i)$, this becomes

$$
\begin{aligned}
\Sigma D_i^2 = \Sigma y_i^2 &+ \left\{ \left[b\left(\Sigma x_i^2\right)^{1/2}\right]^2 - 2\left[b\left(\Sigma x_i^2\right)^{1/2}\right]\left[\frac{\Sigma x_i y_i}{(\Sigma x_i^2)^{1/2}}\right] + \right. \\
&\left. \left[\frac{\Sigma x_i y_i}{(\Sigma x_i^2)^{1/2}}\right]^2 \right\} - \left[\frac{\Sigma x_i y_i}{(\Sigma x_i^2)^{1/2}}\right]^2 \\
= \Sigma y_i^2 &+ \left[b\left(\Sigma x_i^2\right)^{1/2} - \frac{\Sigma x_i y_i}{(\Sigma x_i^2)^{1/2}}\right]^2 - \left[\frac{\Sigma x_i y_i}{(\Sigma x_i^2)^{1/2}}\right]^2 .
\end{aligned}
$$

Since b appears only in the middle squared term, ΣD_i^2 will be minimized by the choice of b when this term vanishes, or

$$b = (\Sigma x_i y_i)/\Sigma x_i^2.$$

Table 10.1 shows the calculations of a and b for a small set of data.

NORMAL REGRESSION ASSUMPTIONS

Next, you will want to know if the individual parameter estimates are *statistically significant* (e.g., significantly different from zero). This requires additional assumptions concerning the error term in the regression model. If it can be reasonably assumed that errors are normally distributed, then an extensive theory is applicable. Most statistics books containing chapters on statistical inference cover this area quite well (see, for example, Draper and Smith, 1981).

The normal assumption states that in a random sample of n outcomes y_1, $y_2, \ldots, y_n$ of Y, the corresponding error terms $\varepsilon_1, \varepsilon_2, \ldots, \varepsilon_n$ arise independently from a common normal distribution (also called Gaussian) with mean 0 and variance σ^2. In short, the *normal linear regression model* can be expressed by

$$Y_i = \mu_{Y_i} + \varepsilon_i, \qquad \text{where } \varepsilon_i \sim N(0, \sigma^2).$$

Table 10.1   Example illustrating the calculation of a and b in a simple linear regression equation.

	X	Y	$y_i = (Y_i - \bar{Y})$	$x_i = (X_i - \bar{X})$	$y_i \cdot x_i$	x_i^2
	1	3	-5	-2	10	4
	2	5	-3	-1	3	1
	3	7	-1	0	0	0
	4	14	6	1	6	1
	5	11	3	2	6	4
Sum:	15	40			25	10
Average:	$\bar{X} = 3$	$\bar{Y} = 8$				

$$b = \frac{\Sigma(x_i y_i)}{\Sigma x_i^2} = \frac{25}{10} = 2.5;$$

$$a = \bar{Y} - b\bar{X} = 8 - 2.5(3) = 0.5;$$

Regression equation: $Y = 0.5 + 2.5X$.

The normality assumption is widely used among forecasters primarily for the following reasons:

- Observed data are often represented reasonably well by a normal distribution. This can be verified by the use of empirical frequency distributions or various normal probability plotting techniques.

- When data are not normally distributed, it is theoretically possible to find a transformation of the data that renders the distribution normal. While this may not always be practical, sometimes a very simple transformation (such as taking the logarithm or square root of the data) results in residuals that appear approximately normal.

- Practice dictates a choice between what *can* be done and *should* be done. In the absence of anything better, normality usually implies what *can* be done.

- Fortunately, the normality assumption permits you to apply a very extensive (though not always realistic), often simple, and quite elegant set of statistical tests of significance to a multitude of forecasting problems.

COMPARING ESTIMATION TECHNIQUES

In selecting a reasonable estimator, one goal is to be able to test how the estimates differ from the true (unknown) parameters of the regression line. One set of criteria for choosing the estimates is that they possess certain theoretical properties. Among those, *unbiasedness, efficiency, consistency,* and *minimum mean-squared error* are the most often mentioned in discussions about comparative estimation techniques. While these concepts may have limited direct consequences on forecasting, they are nevertheless of great theoretical value and the practitioner does well to have a familiarity with them.

Strictly speaking, *unbiasedness, consistency,* and *asymptotic efficiency* are properties of estimators of a (real-valued) parameter. You may occasionally run into an unbiased test, a consistent estimator of a vector-valued parameter, or an asymptotically efficient ranking procedure, but they are really generalizations of the same concept when the estimation of a real-valued parameter is involved. Therefore, we will discuss only the basic forms of these concepts.

An Estimator Is a Random Variable

A typical estimation procedure goes as follows. First, you obtain data from a random experiment. Then you construct a model that relates the data to the physical quantities of interests (parameters) through an error structure. From this model, you can apply some theory to obtain the estimators. These estimators will be expressed as some function of the original raw data. The important point is that the estimators are themselves random variables. Therefore, each estimator should have a probability distribution. The shape of the distribution of an estimator (where it is centered, how it is concentrated, and so on) essentially will tell you everything about this estimator. In a way, unbiasedness, consistency, and asymptotic efficiency can be viewed as a technical way of describing the desirable shapes of the distributions of estimators.

Unbiasedness

In Figure 10.7, $f(x;\theta)$ describes the density function of an estimator δ of the unknown parameter θ. If you place a wedge along the x-axis, you can see that, at some point, the wedge will "balance" the density function. This balancing point is the expected value of the estimator δ, denoted by $E(\delta)$. An estimator δ is an *unbiased* estimator of θ if this balancing point *happens to be* θ; in symbols, $E(\delta) = \theta$.

Unbiasedness is a very restrictive property to require of an estimator. It is a convenient property to have if it comes naturally in the theory. For example, the least-squares criterion in regression leads to unbiased estimators.

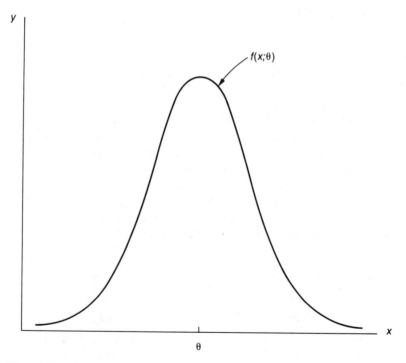

Figure 10.7   Unbiasedness of an estimator.

Consistency

As more and more observations are accumulated, the estimators should become better and better. Consistency is merely a formal statement of this property. Let δ_n denote the estimator of θ based on n observations. Figure 10.8 shows the distribution $f_n(x;\theta)$ of δ_n for $n = 10$ and $n = 100$. If, as $n \to \infty$, $\delta_n \to \theta$ (in some formally defined way), then δ_n is said to be a *consistent* estimator of θ. In Figure 10.8, this means $f_{100}(x;\theta)$ is much narrower than $f_{10}(x;\theta)$; it is a lot easier to have a typical δ_{100} close to θ than to have a typical δ_{10} close to θ.

Asymptotic Efficiency

If the density $f_n(x;\theta)$ of δ_n becomes narrower as n increases, then δ_n is likely to be consistent. Some other estimator, say d_n, of θ may have the same property, however. How does one compare δ_n and d_n? Let $g_n(x;\theta)$ denote the density of d_n. If, for large values of n at least, $f_n(x;\theta)$ is always narrower than $g_n(x;\theta)$, then δ_n is likely to be

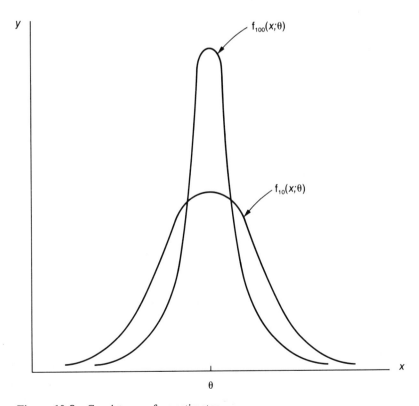

Figure 10.8   Consistency of an estimator.

closer to θ than d_n. When this is so, δ_n is said to be *asymptotically* (this means as $n \to \infty$) more *efficient* than d_n. If an estimator δ_n beats or ties every other d_n in this sense, δ_n is said to be an asymptotically efficient estimator of θ. Since the spread of $f_n(x;\theta)$ is usually measured by $\text{Var}(\delta_n)$, δ_n is said to be *asymptotically efficient* if

$$\frac{\text{Var}(\delta_n)}{\text{Var}(d_n)} \leq 1$$

for all other d_n and all large values of n.

In summary, an estimate or statistic is *unbiased* if its expected value is equal to the true value. An unbiased estimate is *efficient* if its variance is smaller than the variance of any other estimate. An estimate is *consistent* if it comes close in some sense to the true value of the parameter as the sample size becomes arbitrarily large.

Robustness of Efficiency

There are a variety of instances where observed data do not satisfy the normality assumption:

- When data arise from discrete measurements (such as stock prices quoted to the nearest $\frac{1}{8}$) or are based on counts. Then, their range of values cannot be every number between plus and minus infinity (by "infinity" is meant an arbitrary large number).

- When data distributions are skewed or have a greater proportion of extreme values (heavier tail) than a normal population.

In such cases a statistic such as the arithmetic mean can give misleading results. In addition, confidence intervals for the mean may be stated too conservatively. What is desired, in practice, are procedures that are robust against nonnormal tails in the data distribution, in the sense that they give rise to estimates that are much better than those based on normality. When normality cannot be achieved, robust regression may offer some protection against drawing incorrect inferences about the model.

There appear to be many meanings to the word "robustness" in modern statistical literature (Hoaglin et al., 1983). In the context of estimation, *robustness of efficiency* means that parameter estimates are highly efficient not only under idealized (usually normal) conditions but also under a wide class of nonstandard circumstances. The Princeton Robustness Study (Andrews et al., 1972) was an early effort to analyze systematically this concept for estimates of location. Estimates that have robust efficiency are often very resistant to outliers. This can be a very valuable consideration, since real-life data are frequently non-normal and possess hard-to-detect outlying observations.

IMPORTANT DISTRIBUTION RESULTS

References are made throughout this book to statistical significance tests based on the normal, Student's, chi-squared, and F-probability distributions. The following results point to why certain probability distributions result for significance tests arising from the normality assumption in regression errors.

1. If $Z_1, Z_2, \ldots, Z_n$ are normally and independently distributed random variables with mean μ_i and variance σ_i^2, then the sum $Z = \Sigma k_i Z_i$ (where the k_i are constants) is also distributed normally with mean $\Sigma k_i \mu_i$ and variance $\Sigma k_i^2 \sigma_i^2$.

2. If $Z_1, Z_2, \ldots, Z_n$ are normally and independently distributed "normalized" variables with mean equal to zero and variance equal to one, then the ΣZ_i^2 follows a chi-squared distribution with n degrees of freedom.

3. If S_1, S_2 are independently distributed random variables each following a chi-squared distribution with k_1 and k_2 degrees of freedom respectively, then

$$F = \frac{S_1/k_1}{S_2/k_2}$$

   has an F-distribution with (k_1, k_2) degrees of freedom.

Certain significance tests for summary statistics and those derived from normal regression theory utilize the above results. They may be found in any text on mathematical statistics or statistical inference, such as Draper and Smith (1981).

SUMMARY

The discussion in this chapter will give you most of the theoretical underpinnings required for applying regression theory to forecasting problems. It is worth noting that:

- Linear regression theory is basic to forecasting.

- Regression models can be used to describe a relationship between the variable to be forecast and one (or more) related variable(s).

- The method of least squares for parameter estimation, together with normality assumptions, provides the classical statistical formulas from which many forecasting techniques are derived.

In choosing from among estimation techniques, a variety of theoretical criteria are often taken into account. The ordinary least-squares estimators in normal regression theory can be shown to have the following characteristics:

- An estimator is unbiased if its expected value is the unknown parameter.

- Consistency is the property of an estimator whereby the distribution of the estimator becomes narrower as the sample size increases.

- An estimator is efficient if its variance is less than the variance of any other estimator.

USEFUL READING

ANDREWS, D. F., P. J. BICKEL, F. R. HAMPEL, P. J. HUBER, W. H. ROGERS, and J. W. TUKEY (1972). *Robust Estimates of Location: Survey and Advances*. Princeton, NJ: Princeton University Press.

DRAPER, N. R., and H. SMITH (1981). *Applied Regression Analysis*. 2nd ed. New York, NY: John Wiley and Sons.

HOAGLIN, D. C., F. MOSTELLER, and J. W. TUKEY, editors (1983). *Understanding Robust and Exploratory Data Analysis*. New York, NY: John Wiley and Sons.

MOSTELLER, F., and J. W. TUKEY (1977). *Data Analysis and Regression*. Reading, MA: Addison-Wesley Publishing Co.

CHAPTER **11**

Building Regression Models

Linear regression models can be used to

- Predict a dependent variable from one or more (related) independent variables.

- Describe a functional relationship among regressor variables in which the estimated coefficients provide an econometric interpretation.

- Develop plans for policy evaluation where the model serves to express various policy alternatives.

This chapter provides the statistical background necessary for building, interpreting, and evaluating linear regression models. The material is basic to most of the forecasting techniques used in practice.

MULTIPLE LINEAR REGRESSION

In the multiple linear regression model, the *regression function* $\mu_{Y(X)}$ takes the form

$$\mu_{Y(X)} = \beta_0 + \beta_1 X_1 + \cdots + \beta_k X_k ,$$

where $X_1, \ldots, X_k$ are k *independent variables* and $\beta_0, \ldots, \beta_k$ are called *regression coefficients*. This model arises when the variation in the dependent variable Y is assumed to be affected by changes in more than one independent variable. Thus the *average value* of Y can be made to depend on $X_1, \ldots, X_k$. The dependence on X is henceforth suppressed in the notation; let $\mu_{Y(X)} = \mu_Y$. In this case, one speaks of a *multiple regression* of Y on $X_1, \ldots, X_k$.

Standard Assumptions

Conventional *normal regression* theory is based on the following assumptions:

- The mean μ_Y of Y is *linear in the β's;* that is,

$$\mu_Y = \beta_0 + \beta_1 X_1 + \cdots + \beta_k X_k,$$

- where β_0, β_1, . . . , β_k are called the regression coefficients.
- The variance of Y has the same value, σ^2, for all values of X_1, . . . , X_k.
- Y is normally distributed.

Consider a sample (or time series values y_t, $t = 1$, . . . , n) in matrix form:

$$
\begin{array}{ccccc}
y_1 & x_{11} & x_{12} & \cdots & x_{1k} \\
y_2 & x_{21} & x_{22} & \cdots & x_{2k} \\
y_3 & x_{31} & x_{32} & \cdots & x_{3k} \\
\cdot & \cdot & \cdot & & \cdot \\
\cdot & \cdot & \cdot & & \cdot \\
\cdot & \cdot & \cdot & & \cdot \\
y_n & x_{n1} & x_{n2} & \cdots & x_{nk}
\end{array}
$$

The n independent values $(y_1, \ldots, y_n)$ of Y, observed together with the values of the corresponding independent variables, are used to estimate the regression coefficients β_0, β_1, . . . , β_k, and the error variance σ^2.

Multiple linear regression may be used to fit a polynomial function:

$$\mu_Y = \beta_0 + \beta_1 X + \beta_2 X^2 + , \cdots + \beta_k X^k.$$

By letting $X_1 = X$, $X_2 = X^2$, . . . , $X_k = X^k$, you obtain the original formulation. Often X is used to represent a time scale (weeks, months, or years). It is worth emphasizing that the regressors may be any functional form; there need only be linearity in the parameters.

Other functional forms for the regression function include

$$\beta_1 \sin(\alpha t) + \beta_2 \cos(\alpha t),$$

or

$$\beta_1 \exp(\alpha_1 t) + \beta_2 \exp(\alpha_2 t).$$

The formal theory of normal multiple linear regression is very extensive and is dealt with in great detail in general statistics texts. Only the interpretation of those aspects of the theory relevant to forecasting problems is treated in this chapter.

General theoretical developments of this important topic are found in Draper and Smith (1981), Rao (1973), Searle (1971), and Seber (1977).

First, summary statistics for simple linear regression models are discussed. These statistics included the t statistic, F statistic, Durbin-Watson or DW statistic, the R-squared statistic, and correlation coefficients. Next, the F and R-squared statistics are generalized to be applicable for models with multiple regressors. Additional statistics, the $\overline{R}$-squared and the "incremental" F statistics, are introduced for the first time, since they only have meaning in the context of multiple linear regression models.

The Printout

In Chapter 10 a scatter diagram of monthly telephone toll revenues against the number of toll messages generating those revenues was shown. Figure 11.1 is a STATLIB printout which shows the summary statistics from a simple linear regression model relating toll revenues as a function of toll messages. Whether it may be appropriate to transform the data first (such as with logarithms or the Box-Cox transformation) is not considered at this point. Let's examine some details of Figure 11.1.

The SAMPLE SIZE ($= 128$) refers to the *number of observations* used in the regression. In this case, the regression was performed over 128 months from January 1969 through August 1979. For a weighted regression, the SUM OF WEIGHTS may be less than the sample size, since outliers may receive less than their full weight (e.g., weight $= 0.5$ versus 1.0 for nonextreme observations). For ordinary least-squares regression, the SUM OF WEIGHTS equals the SAMPLE SIZE.

The ESTIMATED STD DEV ($= 2.37$), also called the *standard error of the estimate,* is a measure of the variability about the fitted regression function. Since this statistic is related to the magnitude of the unexplained variation, a desired objective is to find a model that has the lowest estimated standard deviation of the residuals.

One note of caution is that the ESTIMATED STD DEV can only be used to compare models when the dependent variable is of the *same form.* For example, the standard deviation of the residuals of a model built on the sales of a product cannot be directly compared to the same statistic for a model built on the logarithms of the sales of the product. The latter statistic will have a different interpretation because of the transformation.

The R-SQUARED statistic ($= 0.94$), also called the *coefficient of determination,* is the percent of the total variation about the mean value of Y that is explainable by performing a linear regression on X. In this case, 94 percent of the revenue variation about the mean is explained by the message data. This is known as a measure of the *goodness-of-fit* of the regression.

On the printout shown in Figure 11.1, the variable 0 represents the constant in the linear equation. The COEFFICIENT of this constant is $-1.8873D + 00$, which

```
SAMPLE SIZE        . . . . . .   128
SUM OF WEIGHTS     . . . . . .   1.2800D+02
ESTIMATED STD DEV    . . . . .   2.3683D+00
R SQUARED          . . . . . .   0.9409
```

VARIABLE	COEFFICIENT	ESTD STD DEV	T
0	-1.8873D+00	9.5882D-01	-1.9684
2 MSG	3.4244D+00	7.6449D-02	44.7940

1 REV ....   DEPENDENT VARIABLE

ANALYSIS OF VARIANCE

SOURCE	DF	SS	MS	F
REGRESSION	1	1.1254D+04	1.1254D+04	2006.499
ERROR	126	7.0670D+02	5.6087D+00	
TOTAL	127	1.1961D+04		

Figure 11.1 Regression output for a simple linear regression model relating telephone toll revenues (REV) as a function of toll messages (MSG).

means that the estimated intercept is -1.89. The variable 2 (MSG) is the independent variable. Its coefficient is $3.4244D + 00$, which means that the regression coefficient is 3.42. The variable 1 (REV) is the dependent variable.

The column headed by ESTD STD DEV represents the estimated standard deviation of the regression coefficients. With rounding, $9.5882D - 01$ means 0.96 ($D - 01 = 10^{-1}$) and $7.6449D - 02$ means 0.08 ($D - 02 = 10^{-2}$). The ratio of coefficients to estimated standard deviations produces the t-statistics in the "T" column. These statistics are shown in parentheses beneath the corresponding coefficient estimates in the following equation:

$$REV = -1.89 + 3.42MSG$$
$$(-1.97)\quad(44.8)$$

where "REV" is revenues and "MSG" is messages.

The R-Squared Statistic

The R-squared statistic is derived from the analysis of variance (ANOVA) part of Figure 11.1. It has the following derivation: The "sum of squares about the mean"

(TOTAL SS) can be expressed as the sum of two other terms, namely, the "sum of squares about regression" (unexplained variation—the ERROR SS entry in the table) and the "sum of squares due to regression" (explained variation—the REGRES-SION SS entry). Here regression is used in the sense of the fitted equation.

The *sum of squares about the mean* is

$$\Sigma(y_i - \bar{y})^2 = \Sigma[(y_i - \hat{y}_i) + (\hat{y}_i - \bar{y})]^2$$
$$= \Sigma(y_i - \hat{y}_i)^2 + 2\Sigma(y_i - \hat{y}_i)(\hat{y}_i - \bar{y}) + \Sigma(\hat{y}_i - \bar{y})^2.$$

It is illustrative to demonstrate the decomposition for a simple linear regression. The middle term equals zero, since

$$\Sigma(y_i - \hat{y}_i)(\hat{y}_i - \bar{y}) = \Sigma[y_i - \bar{y} - b(x_i - \bar{x})][b(x_i - \bar{x})]$$
$$= b\Sigma y_i(x_i - \bar{x}) - b^2\Sigma(x_i - \bar{x})^2$$
$$= b\Sigma b(x_i - \bar{x})^2 - b^2\Sigma(x_i - \bar{x})^2$$
$$= 0.$$

Hence

$\Sigma(y_i - \bar{y})^2$		$\Sigma(y_i - \hat{y}_i)^2$		$\Sigma(\hat{y}_i - \bar{y})^2$
[TOTAL SS on $(n-1)$ degrees of freedom]	$=$	[ERROR SS on $(n-2)$ degrees of freedom]	$+$	[REGRESSION SS on 1 degree of freedom]

Then

$$R^2 = \frac{\text{Explained variation}}{\text{Total variation}}$$
$$= (\text{TOTAL SS} - \text{ERROR SS})/\text{TOTAL SS}.$$

In the case of *simple* linear regression, the relationship between R-squared and the square of the sample product moment correlation coefficient (a measure of association) is quite simple; they are the same. However, for multiple linear regression there is more than one correlation coefficient, so one doesn't know what to compare R-squared with.

It is not necessarily true that a high R-squared statistic implies that you have a good model. On the other hand, you would expect "good" models to have a reasonably high value for R-squared. Notice that R-squared can never be negative or exceed unity.

The *t*-Statistic

A *t*-statistic measures the statistical significance of the regression coefficient for an independent variable. The *t*-ratio follows a *Student's t-distribution* that looks very similar to the bellshaped normal distribution (Figure 11.2). However, a *t*-distribution is shorter and fatter, and its variance $[= \nu/(\nu - 2)]$ is larger than that of the standard normal distribution ($= 1$). For each positive integer ν, called the degrees of freedom, there corresponds a different *t*-distribution.

   With $n < 30$, the observed *t*-value should be greater than approximately 2.0 in absolute value for significance at the 95 percent level (Appendix A, Table 2). When this is the case, you can reject the null hypothesis that the regression coefficient is zero. A statistically significant value not equal to zero is said to exist for the coefficient. Thus, in Figure 11.1, both observed *t*-values in the "T" column are regarded as significant. This cannot be interpreted as proof of a cause-and-effect relationship between the dependent and independent variables, however. For example, each variable may be related to a third (possibly causally linked) factor and only coincidentally related to each other.

The *F*-Statistic

The analysis of variance (ANOVA) table in the lower part of Figure 11.1 emphasizes a comparison of the average sum-of-squared deviations explained by the regression with the unexplained sum-of-squared deviations. This comparison forms the basis for the *F*-test:

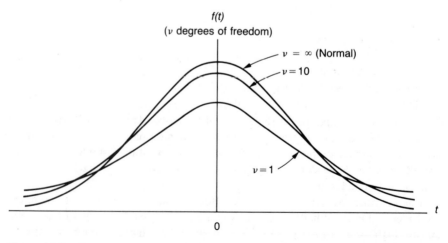

Figure 11.2 Comparison of two *t*-distributions with a standard normal distribution ($\nu = 20$).

$$F = \frac{\text{Mean square due to regression}}{\text{Mean square of errors}} = \frac{\text{MS REGRESSION entry in table}}{\text{MS ERROR entry in table}}$$
$$= 11{,}254/5.61 = 2006.$$

where

$$\text{MS REGRESSION} = \frac{\text{Sum of squares due to regression}}{\text{Degrees of freedom in regression}}$$
$$= \Sigma(\hat{y}_i - \bar{y}_i)^2/(m - 1)$$
$$= 11{,}254/1,$$

and

$$\text{MS ERROR} = \frac{\text{Sum of squares of errors}}{\text{Degrees of freedom in errors}}$$
$$= \Sigma(y_i - \hat{y}_i)^2/(n - m)$$
$$= 706.70/126 = 5.61.$$

Here m = number of coefficients in the model, including the constant. All sums are from 1 to n.

For a simple linear regression, $m = 2$, and

$$F = \frac{\Sigma(\hat{y}_i - \bar{y})^2/1}{\Sigma(y_i - \hat{y}_i)^2/(n - 2)}.$$

If there is no relationship between Y and X, then $\hat{y} = \bar{y}$ and F equals zero.

The calculated F-statistic is compared to the tabular value (Appendix A, Table 4) for the appropriate degrees of freedom. For a simple linear regression, $F = t^2$, and a value of F greater than approximately 4.0 indicates significance at the 5 percent significance level. For a multiple linear regression, one must use the F-table to determine if the overall regression is significant.

The rationale for the F-test is that if there is a relationship between the dependent and independent variables, the variation of the estimated values from the observed values will be less than the variation between the estimated values and the mean value of Y; i.e., the F-ratio will be significantly different from 1.0.

The D-W Statistic

In time series forecasting, it is not unusual to be in violation of normal regression assumptions because of *autocorrelated errors;* hence, it is important to be able to test for their presence. The Durbin-Watson (abbreviated as D-W) statistic, due to

Durbin and Watson (1950, 1951), is the traditional statistic used to test for auto-correlation (*first-order only!*). The ordinary correlogram is usually more informative in assessing the nature of autocorrelation.

The D-W statistic d has the formula

$$d = \sum_{t=2}^{n} (\hat{\varepsilon}_t - \hat{\varepsilon}_{t-1})^2 \bigg/ \sum_{t=2}^{n} \hat{\varepsilon}_t^2.$$

If time series residuals $\{\hat{\varepsilon}_t, t = 1, \ldots, n\}$ are positively correlated, the absolute value of $\hat{\varepsilon}_t - \hat{\varepsilon}_{t-1}$ will tend to be small relative to the absolute value of $\hat{\varepsilon}_t$. If the residuals are negatively correlated, the absolute value of $\hat{\varepsilon}_t - \hat{\varepsilon}_{t-1}$ will tend to be large relative to the absolute value of $\hat{\varepsilon}_t$. Therefore d will tend to be small (near 1.0) for positively correlated residuals, large (near 4.0) for negatively correlated residuals, and approximately equal to 2.0 for random residuals.

The sampling distribution of d depends on the values of the independent variable x_t in the sample. Therefore, the test is only able to provide upper (d_u) and lower (d_l) limits for significance testing (Appendix A, Table 5). One either accepts the null hypothesis of zero autocorrelation or rejects it in favor of *first-order* autocorrelation. If $d < d_l$, the zero correlation hypothesis is rejected in favor of *first-order* positive autocorrelation. If $d_l < d < d_u$, the test is inconclusive. If $d > 4 - d_l$, the zero autocorrelation hypothesis is rejected in favor of *first-order* negative autocorrelation.

It can be shown that d is closely tied to the first autocorrelation coefficient r_1 of the correlogram of the residuals. In fact, $d \simeq 2(1 - r_1)$. Thus, with the use of the computer, it is just as simple to plot the correlogram of the residuals of the model and assess the overall autocorrelation structure. The patterns of the correlogram will be discussed extensively in connection with the identification of ARIMA models in Part 5.

In models in which the residuals are autocorrelated, two main consequences of using ordinary least squares (OLS) are:

- Sampling variances of the regression coefficients are underestimated and invalid.

- Forecasts have variances that are too large.

In OLS estimation, the calculated acceptance regions or confidence intervals are narrower than they should be for a specified level of significance. This leads to a false conclusion that the parameter estimates are more precise than they actually are. There will be a tendency to accept a variable as significant when it is not, and this may result in a misspecified model.

There are several approaches to try to reduce the effects of autocorrelation:

- Model the first differences or the year-over-year percent changes of the time series.

- Transform the data, basing this on the assumed nature of the autocorrelated structure.

- Include an autoregressive term (the value one period back) in a multiple linear regression model.
- Build an ARIMA model on the residuals of the regression model.

These approaches require some advanced techniques to be covered in Part 5.

A MEASURE OF ASSOCIATION

At times you may not be interested in making a forecast of a dependent variable from a forecast of an independent variable. Rather, you may be interested in simply obtaining a measure of association or correlation between two variables.

Interchanging X and Y

It is not uncommon for beginning forecasters to think that the regression of X on Y and the regression of Y on X should give equivalent inferences about the relationships between X and Y, and Y and X. For example, the regression analysis for the telephone revenue-message data shows that the toll revenue Y and the toll messages X have a linear relationship estimated by the equation

$$\hat{Y} = a_1 + b_1 X$$
$$= -1.89 + 3.42X.$$

By interchanging the dependent and independent variables, and looking at the intercept and slope estimates from the least-squares fit in Figure 11.3, you can see that the regression equation for toll messages X against toll revenues Y becomes

$$\hat{X} = a_2 + b_2 Y$$
$$= 1.24 + 0.27Y.$$

The slope $b_1 = 3.42$ for the revenue equation ($\hat{Y}$) is not equal to the reciprocal of the slope $b_2 = 0.27$ for the message equation ($\hat{X}$), but why?

The reason why these two regressions give different results is that the line obtained by minimizing the sum-of-squared *vertical* deviations is different from the line derived by minimizing the sum-of-squared *horizontal* deviations (Figure 11.4). This property of least squares is often misunderstood by practitioners, and this misunderstanding can lead to the misuse of regression equations.

When the variables X and Y are nearly independent, b_1 and b_2 are very small and the two regression lines are almost at right angles. On the other hand, when they are so closely related that the one can be taken to determine the other absolutely, the

```
SAMPLE SIZE    . . . . . . . .    128
SUM OF WEIGHTS . . . . . . .    1.2800D+02
ESTIMATED STD DEV    . . . . .    6.7084D-01
R SQUARED    . . . . . . . . .    0.9409


VARIABLE          COEFFICIENT        ESTD STD DEV          T

0                 1.2417D+00         2.5258D-01         4.9163
2 REV . . . .     2.7476D-01         6.1340D-03        44.7940

1 MSG . . . .    DEPENDENT VARIABLE


ANALYSIS OF VARIANCE

    SOURCE          DF         SS               MS              F

    REGRESSION       1      9.0297D+02      9.0297D+02    2006.499
    ERROR          126      5.6703D+01      4.5002D-01

    TOTAL          127      9.5967D+02
```

Figure 11.3 Regression output for a (unrealistic) simple linear regression model relating toll messages (MSG) as a function of toll revenues (REV).

two regression lines coincide. In this case $b_1 = 1/b_2$. From this observation arises the notion of *linear correlation*.

The measure of the strength of the relationship between X and Y would seem to depend on the *angle* between the two regression lines. The most common measure of the strength of the relationship is the *sample product moment correlation coefficient*:

$$r = \frac{\sum_{i=1}^{n} (y_i - \bar{y})(x_i - \bar{x})}{\left[\sum_{i=1}^{n} (y_i - \bar{y})^2 \sum_{i=1}^{n} (x_i - \bar{x})^2\right]^{1/2}}.$$

Since $r^2 = b_1 b_2$, it can be seen that $r = 0$ when there is no association, and $r^2 = 1$ when one variable determines the other. The coefficient r ranges from -1 to $+1$. It is clear from the formula that r is the same no matter which variable is used to predict the other.

When two series have a strong positive correlation, the scatter diagram has a scatter of points along a line of positive slope. A negative correlation shows up as a scatter of points along a line with negative slope.

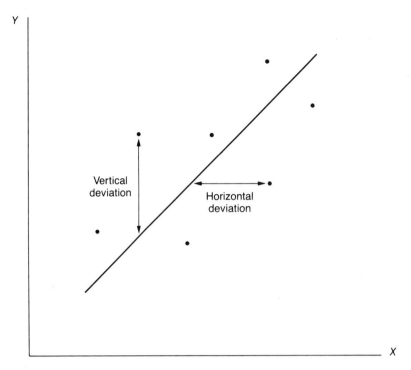

Figure 11.4   Vertical versus horizontal deviations in ordinary least-squares regression.

The Correlation Matrix

The *correlation matrix* gives a representation of the degree of correlation when there is more than one variable. This matrix is an array of all sample correlation coefficients between pairs of variables. Table 11.1 shows a correlation matrix for the toll revenues (REV), toll messages (MSG), business telephones (BMT), and nonfarm employment (NFRM) in the telecommunications forecasting example that has been used throughout this book.

The diagonal of a correlation matrix consists of ones, since each variable is perfectly correlated with itself. The variables are numbered 1 through 4, and each appears in a row and a column. The intersection of a row and a column is the correlation coefficient relating the row variable to the column variable. For example, the coefficient of correlation between toll revenues and toll messages is high (= 0.96). The business telephones have a positive correlation with toll messages (= 0.77) and a low correlation with nonfarm employment (= 0.015). The negative but very small correlations of the employment data with revenues and messages is not intuitively satisfying; however, their smallness suggests that this is probably not significant.

Table 11.1   Correlation matrix for the four time series in the telecommunications example. REV = toll revenues, MSG = toll messages, BMT = business telephones, and NFRM = nonfarm employment.

	1	2	3	4
1 REV	1.000			
2 MSG	0.963	1.000		
3 BMT	0.765	0.772	1.000	
4 NFRM	−0.128	−0.105	0.015	1.000

FITTING MULTIPLE REGRESSION MODELS

Goodness of Fit

In general, a measure of the effectiveness of the regression fit can be obtained by calculating the *multiple correlation coefficient R,* or its square, which is given by

$$R^2 = \frac{\text{Regression sum of squares}}{\text{Total sum of squares}}$$
$$= (T - Q) / T,$$

where $T = \Sigma (y - \bar{y})^2$ is the total variation, and $Q = \Sigma(y - \hat{y})^2$ represents the unexplained variation.

Hence R^2 is the proportion of the variation of Y that has been explained by including particular independent variables. It is also commonly referred to as the *coefficient of determination.*

To compare models with a different number of independent variables, the *corrected R^2, adjusted for degrees of freedom,* is used. This is given by

$$\bar{R}^2 = 1 - \left\{ \frac{(n - 1)(1 - R^2)}{n - k - 1} \right\},$$

where k = number of independent variables.

Unlike R^2, $\bar{R}^2$ can decrease when a variable is added. In fact, for $k \geq 1$, $R^2 \geq \bar{R}^2$ and, moreover, $\bar{R}^2$ can be negative.

An overall test of significance of the regression can be carried out by calculating the F statistic:

$$F = \frac{(T - Q)/\text{Regression degrees of freedom}}{Q/\text{Residual degrees of freedom}},$$

$$= \frac{\text{Regression sum of squares/Regression degrees of freedom}}{\text{Residual sum of squares/Residual degrees of freedom}}$$

$$= \frac{\text{Mean square due to regression}}{\text{Mean square due to error}}.$$

An examination of the F table (Appendix A, Table 4) shows that, for most practical problems, an observed value of approximately 4 or more probably points to *statistical significance* for the appropriate degrees of freedom, provided the normality assumptions are valid.

In general, if the F statistic is significantly greater than unity, it indicates that the data do not support the null hypothesis of zero values for the regression coefficients. Then one is inclined to accept the alternative hypothesis that there is a regression relationship with at least one of the $\beta_1, \beta_2, \ldots, \beta_k$ different from zero.

Significance of Regression Coefficients

You may test if a specific independent variable X_i is necessary, by using the t test on the estimated regression coefficient b_i. A nonsignificant t value implies that, given the effects of all other independent variables, X_i does not explain a significant amount of additional variability in Y. Cases can occur in which each regression coefficient b_i is not significant, and yet the regression as a whole is significant, as indicated by an F test. Hence, in multiple linear regression, an F test should always be performed.

In addition to summary statistics and significance tests, it is important also to consider

- The forecasts given by the model for future periods. Are they reasonable?

- The comparison of forecasts with actuals. Is the accuracy level acceptable?

- The residual pattern over the fitted and forecast periods. Does it appear to be random?

- Confidence limits for the residuals and their cumulative sum over the forecast period. These are useful for monitoring the forecasts as actual results become available. Patterns of overforecasts, underforecasting, or of too many values falling outside the limits suggest that the model needs to be reevaluated. This subject will be treated in detail in Chapter 12.

An Incremental F Test

It is often important to test to see if the inclusion of an additional variable significantly improves the fit of a linear regression model. For example, you may want to examine to see if the inclusion of the FRB Index of Industrial Production in a model relating main gain to housing starts results in a significant reduction in the sum of squares due to errors.

In multiple linear regression problems, the significance of the regression coefficient cannot, in general, be tested with t tests on a one-by-one basis. This is so because individual regression coefficients are correlated among themselves and the t ratios are not independently distributed with a Student's t distribution. It is then necessary to perform an incremental F test.

The numerator of this F statistic, $F*$, is the change in the sum of squares due to error in the old model minus the sum of squares due to error in the new model, divided by the difference in error degrees of freedom. The foregoing quantity is divided by the mean square error of the new model:

$$F* = \frac{[(\text{Residual SS}_{\text{old}} - \text{Residual SS}_{\text{new}})/(\text{df}_{\text{old}} - \text{df}_{\text{new}})]}{\text{Residual SS}_{\text{new}}/\text{df}_{\text{new}}}$$

When only one variable is added to the model at a time, the incremental F test is equivalent to a t test. If the t statistic for the new variable is significant, so is the incremental F statistic. However, when several variables are added at a time, the group of variables may be significant even though one or more t statistics may appear insignificant. For example, econometrics indicator variables are frequently used to account for seasonal variation. In this case, while one or more of the variables appear insignificant, the seasonal variation is described by the presence of *all* the indicator variables. The incremental F test will indicate whether the added variables as a *group* are statistically significant.

EVALUATING REGRESSION MODELS

The adequacy of model assumptions can be examined through a variety of methods, mostly graphical, involving the analysis of residuals. This topic is treated in Chapter 13. Graphical methods also play a role in assessing

- How individual data values affect the estimation of least squares estimates of regression coefficients.
- How the selection of independent variables impacts the fitting process.

Regression Pitfalls

There are a variety of regression pitfalls that you should be aware of and that must be avoided if possible. These pitfalls include trend collinearity, overfitting, extrapolation, outliers, nonnormal distributions, multicollinearity, and invalid assumptions regarding the model errors (e.g., independence, constant variance, and, usually, normality).

When the dependent and independent variables are time series, there are many special pitfalls to be avoided. Suppose that you are interested in forecasting the cyclical variation in one series on the basis of predictions of a related cyclical time series, such as revenues and employment.

In a simple or multiple linear regression model, a very high value of the R-squared statistic may result from what is known as *collinearity*. This often occurs when both series have very strong trends. It is quite possible that the trends are highly correlated but that the cyclical patterns are not. The dissimilarities in cycle may be masked by the strong trends.

Similarly, when a regression model is performed on raw time series, it is not clear just what information will result. If both series have rising trend and corresponding strong seasonality, the regression will very likely show a very high R-squared statistic. Alternatively, if there is a strong underlying relationship between variables but their seasonal patterns differ, the regression may appear insignificant.

As a rule, data should be adjusted for those possible sources of variation in which one is not interested in order to study the relationships with respect to those forces whose effects are of primary interest.

In the case of a telephone revenue–message relationship, seasonality is not of primary interest, so you can use seasonally adjusted data. A high correlation now means that there is a strong trend–cyclical correlation. In order to determine whether there is strong cyclical relationship, the appropriate procedure is to fit trend lines and correlate residuals from the fitted values.

Overfitting

Another source of danger in regression is overfitting. This occurs when too many independent variables are used to attempt to explain the variation in the dependent variable. Overfitting may also arise when there are not enough data points. If the number of independent variables is "close to" the number of observations, a "good fit" to the observations may be obtained, but the coefficient and variance estimates will be poor. This results often in very bad estimates for new observations.

Extrapolation

In forecasting applications, regression models are frequently used for purposes of extrapolation; that is, for extending the relationship to a future period of time for which data are not available. A relationship that is established over a historical time span and a given range of independent and dependent variables may not necessarily be valid in the future. Thus extreme caution must be exercised in using correlation analysis to predict future behavior among variables. There may be no choice in some cases, but the forecaster should recognize the risks involved.

Outliers

Outliers are another well-known source of difficulty in correlation analysis. A single outlier can have a significant impact on a correlation coefficient. Figure 11.5 shows a scatter diagram of sixty values from a simulated sample, from a bivariate normal distribution with theoretical correlation coefficient $\rho = 0.9$. One point was moved

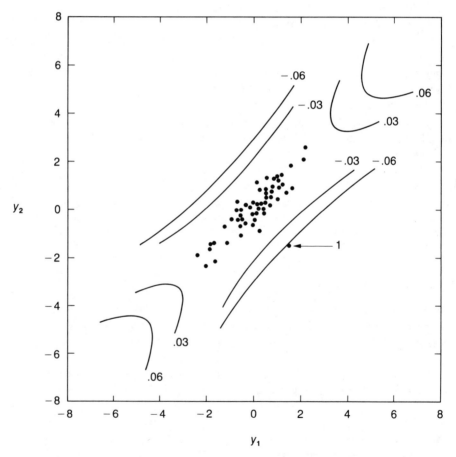

Figure 11.5 Scatter plot with influence function contours for a sample of bivariate normal data with the added outlier ($n = 60$, $\rho = 0.9$, $r = 0.836$).

to become an outlier. The empirical correlation coefficient is now calculated to be 0.84. The figure shows that, except for this single point, the scatter is quite linear, and in fact, with this outlier removed, the estimated correlation coefficient is 0.9 (Devlin, et al., 1975). Robust methods offer some protection in these instances as well as others in which there is nonnormality in the error distribution.

Multicollinearity

Multicollinearity arises when the independent variables in a regression model are highly correlated. Models with more than about five independent variables often contain regressors that are highly mutually correlated. In such cases, it may be profitable to seek linear combinations of these variables as regressors, thereby reducing the dimension of the problem. See, for example, Belsley, et al. (1980); Draper and Smith (1981); and Chatterjee and Price (1977, Chapter 7). See Chapter 19 for additional approaches for identifying and treating this problem.

The standard assumptions discussed in the beginning of this chapter regarding errors (independence, constant variance, and normality) and the additivity of the model need to be evaluated. If, for a particular set of data, one or more of these assumptions fail, it may help to transform the data. Tests for invalid assumptions are discussed in Chapter 12.

Regression and correlation analysis are only tools and cannot replace thoughtful and thorough data analysis on the part of the forecaster.

Choosing among Regression Models

In some applications, the forecaster may be faced with a relatively large set of independent variables that, on theoretical or statistical grounds, should be considered of value in explaining a dependent variable. In such situations, it is clearly impossible to develop a meaningful regression relationship by incorporating all the variables of interest. It is necessary to reduce the set of independent variables for the regression without jeopardizing the usefulness of the model. Generally, interpretation of the coefficients is secondary to the need to explain variability with an overall model.

The set of independent variables for the models fall into three groups:

- Those that for theoretical reasons should be included.

- Those that are likely to be of benefit, such as proxy and "dummy" variables. Dummy variables are categorical in nature (yes–no, on–off, war–peace, . . .) and generally take on the values of 0 or 1.

- Others that may have desirable intuitive or statistical properties.

Given a class of models and model assumptions, the next step is to establish rules for accepting or rejecting variables. Generally, it is desirable to estimate lack of fit by an estimate of the expected sum of squared deviations of the fitted values from the true values. Then, a good procedure would be one that minimized the lack of fit. For a linear regression model with a constant error variance of σ^2, the ideal quantity to minimize is

$$\sum_{i=1}^{n} \text{Var}(\hat{y}_i),$$

which is σ^2 times (the number of independent variables). The variance σ^2 can be estimated as

$$s^2 = \frac{1}{n-k} \sum_{i=1}^{n} (y_i - \hat{y}_i)^2,$$

where k is the number of independent variables and n is the number of observations.

There are other criteria available for choosing k. These include Mallows's C_p, Anscombe's $s^2/(n-k)$ (as modified by Tukey), and Allen's PRESS (standing for "PREdiction Sum of Squares"). These criteria, which are discussed in greater detail in Draper and Smith (1981), Chatterjee and Price (1977, Chapter 9), and Mosteller and Tukey (1977, Chapter 15), should be applied with care; they can serve as a useful guide in making a sensible choice of k.

There are a variety of algorithms in use among regression practitioners for selecting subsets of independent variables (Draper and Smith, 1981; Mosteller and Tukey, 1977). Most of these approaches, while widely used, suffer from a number of theoretical and practical difficulties. Among these are methods using all possible regressions, backward elimination, forward selection, and stepwise regression.

When a method makes use of *all possible regressions,* the method utilizes all possible regressions for k variables. While everything is covered, the method can be expensive, time consuming, and usually unwarranted.

Backward elimination begins with all variables in the model. A partial F test is used to calculate the contribution of each variable. The variable with the lowest F value is removed, and the process is repeated until all variables have F values greater than a preselected value. With this technique, results for the full model are available, and the procedure is cheaper than the all-possible-regressions procedure.

The *forward selection* procedure starts by selecting a variable that best explains the variation in the dependent variable, by using the partial correlation coefficient. By using the residuals, a second variable is found that best explains the remaining variation in the dependent variable. The model is then reestimated with the new variable included. The calculations and selection procedure are repeated until no remaining variable has a partial correlation larger than a preselected value. While this procedure is economical and leads to a continuous improvement in the model, it ignores the possible reduction in importance of earlier variables.

The *stepwise technique* is similar to forward selection. At each step, however, the previously selected variables are examined with a partial F test to determine if any are not now contributing significantly. This method takes into account possible relationships between independent variables but requires more selection criteria. There are also weighted and resistant fitting variations to the stepwise method; however, these approaches should never be used without examining numerical and graphical outputs, such as the residual distributions and outliers, and reviewing regression coefficients at each step for possible changes in magnitudes and signs.

REGRESSION BY STAGES

One approach for identifying variables that should be included in a model is to build a regression model in stages. Using Tukey's notation (Mosteller and Tukey, 1977) for convenience, let $Y_{.1}$ denote the residuals after fitting a model with X_1 only. Instead of plotting the residuals $Y_{.1}$ against a new variable X_2, you can first regress X_2 on X_1 and denote with $X_{2.1}$ the residuals of X_2 that result after fitting X_1. Then $X_{2.1}$ represents the *additional* information in X_2 that is not already captured by X_1.

Now you can plot $Y_{.1}$ against $X_{2.1}$, and this will show if X_2 has a strong apparent dependence with Y, given that X_1 is already in the model. In other words, this plot will show the relationship between the unexplained variation in Y and the additional information in X_2. In the case where X_1 and X_2 are highly correlated with Y and with each other, the plot of $Y_{.1}$ versus $X_{2.1}$ will show little correlation, since X_2 adds little, given that X_1 is in the model.

Next, X_3 is regressed on X_1 and X_2; the residuals that result are denoted by $X_{3.12}$. At the next stage, the residuals of the model containing both X_1 and X_2 (thus, $Y_{.12}$) are plotted against $X_{3.12}$. Those variables that show high dependence are included in the model and those with little dependence are reserved for future use.

In general, let $X_{i.\text{REST}}$ denote the residuals of X_i on the rest of the independent variables. By regressing Y on $X_{i.\text{REST}}$, the same regression coefficient will result for X_i that results from the regression of Y on all the X's. The remaining regression coefficients are, of course, different. By displaying $Y_{.\text{REST}}$ (the fit of Y on *all* X_i) against each $X_{i.\text{REST}}$, it is possible to see the impact of each variable and, in some cases, the impact of individual points on the estimate of the regression coefficient.

In order to examine how to combine or compare coefficients in different regressions, Tukey uses the "minvar modification" of the fitted coefficient b_i, denoted by $b_{i.\text{REST}}$. For each i, $b_{i.\text{REST}}$ is that linear combination of fitted regression coefficients, including unity times the ith coefficient b_i, which has minimum estimated variance. These coefficients can be compared with the estimated variance of b_i itself. As a set of ratios, they may point to a useful combination of independent variables and to important dependencies among estimated regression coefficients (Mosteller and Tukey, 1977, section 13H).

The regression-by-stages approach is illustrated in the following example. For the purposes of the present discussion, a regression relationship will be sought between the percent extension development in residences (extension telephones in households divided by main telephones in households) by geographic area, by income adjusted for the cost of living, by the percent of white-collar employees, and by the percent of households owning more than one automobile.

In a purely exploratory approach, you might consider all possible combinations of the independent variables and the dependent variable. In this example, interest lies in the relationship of the dependent variable to income, employment, and automobile ownership. Therefore, the first step is to display the frequency distributions or box plots of the variables, and the second step is to generate scatter diagrams between the percent extension development and the independent variables. The frequency distribution of "percent of development" is plotted in Figure 11.6

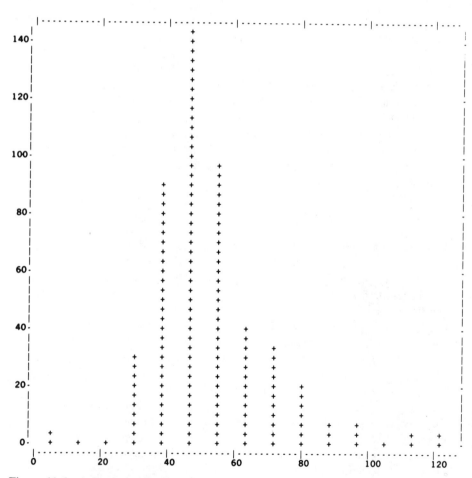

Figure 11.6   A frequency distribution of the percent of extension development, showing a long tail in the distribution at the high end.

and shows a long tail at the high end. At the low end are apparent observations showing 0–4-percent extension development. In actuality, these are transcription errors, which need to be removed prior to modeling. Since these small percentages are not totally unrealistic, they could remain undetected in an actual modeling procedure, and they have been left in as "undetected" outliers for this example; the impact of these outliers on the OLS parameter estimates will thus be partially assessable.

The scatter diagram between residence extension development and income in Figure 11.7 shows an essentially linear relationship, with most of the observations clustered below \$20,000 income. There is some indication of increasing variability with increasing income, and so a square root transformation of the dependent variable was taken in an attempt to obtain constant variance, and to "bring in" the high-leverage points in the upper righthand corner of the plot.

A scatter diagram of the square roots of extension development versus income showed some improvement in variance, but the points corresponding to very high income appeared to have bent downward, suggesting some nonlinearity.

Plotting the logarithms of the income variable (X_1) against the square roots of percent development appeared to exhibit the most promising relationship in terms of linearity, constancy of variance, and reduction in high-leverage points. A regression was performed and a plot of residuals $Y_{.1}$ against predictions was made. No obvious problems were apparent, and this was confirmed by the near straight-line configuration in a Q-Q plot of the residuals versus the normal quantiles.

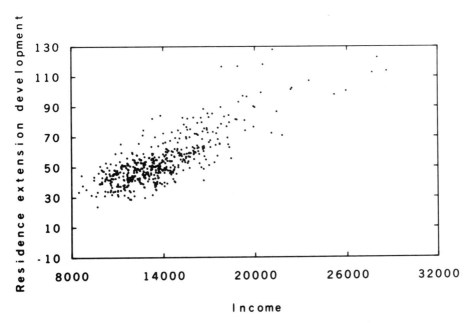

Figure 11.7 A scatter diagram between residence extension development and income.

The next variable that was entered in the regression was the percent of white-collar employment (X_2). This variable was regressed on X_1; then the residuals $Y_{.1}$ were plotted against the residuals $X_{2.1}$ (Figure 11.8). This plot shows the incremental explanatory power of X_2, given that X_1 is in the model. There is a slight linear positive relationship, with considerable variability. This variable was added into the model, the regression was performed, and the residuals showed no further problems.

The percent of households owning more than one automobile (X_3) was then regressed on X_1 and X_2. Plotting the residuals $Y_{.12}$ against the residuals $X_{3.12}$ showed a slight positive relationship, with even greater variability. Given that X_1 and X_2 are already in the model, X_3 provides relatively little additional information.

The final model included all three variables; a Q-Q plot (Figure 11.9) of the residuals depicts a linear pattern. (In Chapter 12, OLS and robust regression will be used to estimate a model for this example, and the results with the three outliers will be compared for the two estimation procedures).

Table 11.2 sumarizes the model results. R^2 increases and MSE (mean squared error) decreases as X_2 and X_3 are added to the model. All parameters are significantly different from zero (t test), and the F statistic is significant in all cases. The model for white-collar employment (X_2) shows significant correlation ($R^2 = 0.62$ percent) with income (X_1). The percent of households with more than one automobile (X_3) correlates less well ($R^2 = 0.54$) with income and employment. In this example, the first variable X_1 explains a large percent of the variation in Y. The addition of X_2 and X_3 raises R^2 from 0.61 to 0.69 and results in a 19-percent reduction in mean squared error.

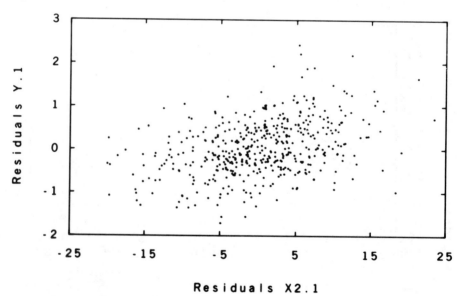

Figure 11.8 A plot of residuals $Y_{.1}$ against residuals $X_{2.1}$.

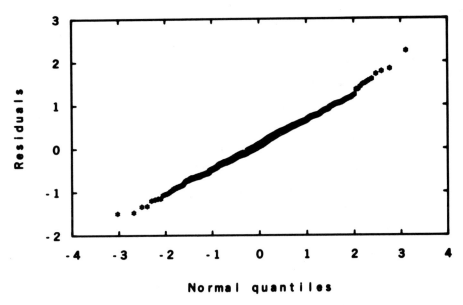

Figure 11.9   A normal Q-Q plot of the residuals in the full model.

Table 11.2   A summary of results from the final model.

Residuals included in model*	R^2	MSE	X_1	X_2	X_3
				t-statistic	
$Y_{.1}$	0.61	0.42	27.3	—	—
$Y_{.12}$	0.67	0.36	11.0	9.2	—
$Y_{.123}$	0.69	0.34	7.5	8.6	4.9
$X_{2.1}$	0.62	54.1	27.6	—	—
$X_{3.12}$	0.54	59.2	11.9	3.0	—

Final model

$$Y = -13.33 + 1.93(\log X_1) + 0.032(X_2) + 17(X_3)$$
$$[5.9] \qquad [7.5] \qquad\qquad [8.6] \qquad\quad [4.9]$$

*Y = Percent residence extension development
X_1 = Income
X_2 = Percent white collar employment
X_3 = Percent households with more than one auto

Note: All F statistics are significant at the 5-percent level.

MULTIPLE REGRESSION CHECKLIST

_____ Is the relationship between the variables linear?

_____ Have linearizing transformations been tried?

_____ What is the correlation structure among the independent variables?

_____ Have seasonal and/or trend influences been identified and removed?

_____ Have outliers been identified and replaced when appropriate?

_____ Do the residuals from the model appear to be random?

_____ Are any changes in the variance apparent (is there heteroscedasticity)?

_____ Are there any other unusual patterns in the residuals, such as cycles, or cupshaped or trending patterns?

_____ Have F tests for overall significance been reviewed?

_____ Do the t statistics indicate any unusual relationships or problem variables?

_____ Can the coefficients be appropriately interpreted?

_____ Have forecast tests been made?

SUMMARY

This chapter has explained

- The multiple linear regression model and its assumptions.

- The interpretation of basic summary statistics.

- An overview of common pitfalls to be avoided in building multiple linear regression models. Detailed discussions of the pitfalls are presented in the appropriate chapters.

- An overview of regression models that automatically select subsets of independent variables. Exercise caution when using automated variable selection programs.

- Modeling assumptions implicit in formulating a forecasting model, including robustness considerations.

- The importance of the availability of relevant and appropriate independent variables for both the historical and future time periods.

- The importance of the interpretation of the results in the light of the assumptions.

USEFUL READING

BELSLEY, D. A., E. KUH, and R. E. WELSCH (1980). *Regression Diagnostics*. New York, NY: John Wiley and Sons.

CHATTERJEE, S., and B. PRICE (1977). *Regression Analysis by Example*. New York, NY: John Wiley and Sons.

DEVLIN, S., R. GNANADESIKAN, and J. R. KETTENRING (1975). Robust Estimation and Outlier Detection with Correlation Coefficients. *Biometrika* 62, 531–45.

DRAPER, N. R., and H. SMITH (1981). *Applied Regression Analysis,* 2nd ed. New York, NY: John Wiley and Sons.

MOSTELLER, F., and J. W. TUKEY (1977). *Data Analysis and Regression*. Reading, MA: Addison-Wesley.

RAO, C. R. (1973). *Linear Statistical Inference and Its Applications*. New York, NY: John Wiley and Sons.

SEARLE, S. R. (1977). *Linear Models*. New York, NY: John Wiley and Sons.

SEBER, G. F. (1977). *Linear Regression Analysis*. New York, NY: John Wiley and Sons.

CHAPTER 12

Testing Modeling Assumptions

Residual analysis is a process designed to reveal departures from the assumptions of a regression model, such as independence, constant variance, and normality. In this process, we try to determine what the "unexplained" variable might tell about the adequacy of the model. Quite often, transformations of variables or inclusion of new variables are suggested by residual plots. This chapter will:

- Summarize the basics of residual analysis.
- Provide new graphical aids (e.g., partial residual plots) appropriate for multiple linear regression models.
- Suggest a sequence of procedures to follow to improve the efficiency of the residual analysis process for multiple linear regression models.

ANALYZING REGRESSION RESIDUALS

Residual analysis in regression modeling is a process designed to reveal departures from model assumptions about the error distribution, such as normality, independence, and constant variance. Since statistical significance of parameters and confidence limits depend on the validity of assumptions about the error distribution, residual analysis is, perhaps, the single most valuable *diagnostic tool* for evaluating regression models. Fortunately, much of the residual analysis can be carried out effectively by using graphical techniques.

Basic Residual Patterns

Five basic types of patterns are frequently seen in residual plots:

- No visible pattern.

- Cyclical pattern (positively autocorrelated residuals).
- Nonlinear relationships.
- Increasing dispersion.
- Linear trend.

A residual plot which has no visible pattern (Figure 12.1) provides no evidence against the assumption that the errors in the model are independent, have zero mean, and show constant variance. A plot in which no pattern is visible is consistent with the basic assumptions about *randomness* in a regression model. Tests will be discussed that indicate whether the randomness assumption can be supported by the data.

A Run Test for Randomness

Some tests indicative of randomness (or lack thereof) in residuals include tests based on first differences, runs of signs, and rank correlation. The *first-differences test* assumes that if there is nonrandomness in the form of trend, the number of positive first differences (also called differences of order 1) would be large for a residual series with an upward trend and small for a residual series with a downward trend.

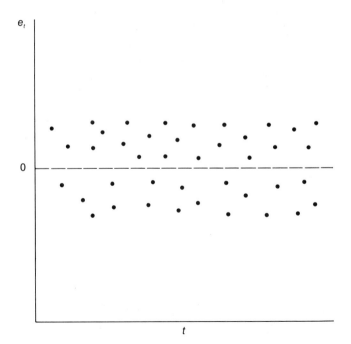

Figure 12.1   No pattern is visible in this residual plot.

The *runs-of-signs test* is a simple way to test for randomness by counting runs (Roberts, 1974). A run is a string of pluses ($+$) or minuses ($-$) that accumulates when a plus ($+$) value is assigned to an observation larger than the average value of the data and a minus ($-$) value is assigned to a value less than the average.

In counting these runs, let the number of consecutive runs of pluses be denoted by r and let n denote the number of data values in the sample. Then the average number of runs over all possible sequences of runs is

$$\frac{2r(n - r)}{n} + 1.$$

A measure of the expected dispersion of runs among different sequences that could have occurred is the standard error given by

$$\left[\frac{2r(n - r)[2r(n - r) - n]}{n^2(n - 1)} \right]^{1/2}.$$

Thus, if the observed number of runs is within two standard errors of the expected (average) number of runs, then there is little evidence that the series is not random. The runs measure is a measure of conformity of data to a model specification of randomness. It is often observed, for example, that changes in many stock prices behave essentially like a random series.

When signs-run counting is applied to residuals, one expects that the number of consecutive positive or negative residuals will be neither small nor large for a random residual series. A straight line trend with positive slope will have a run of negative signs followed by a run of positive signs. A wildly fluctuating series, on the other hand, will exhibit too many sign changes.

In the *rank correlation test,* residuals are ranked in order depending on size and then correlated with a straight line trend. The distribution of the test statistic is difficult to determine, so approximate tests based on the Student *t*-distribution are used. Details of these tests and similar ones may be found in Walsh (1962, Chapter 5).

Nonrandom Patterns

If a pattern can be discerned in a residual plot, then these patterns exemplify a violation of one or more assumptions about randomness in a regression model. The identification of such patterns and some remedies will be discussed first.

The *cyclical pattern* (Figure 12.2) is often evident when fitting linear models to time series data. For example, economic booms and recessions in the business cycle become apparent in a residual plot. In the special case of time series, it makes sense to connect residuals sequentially in time to expose underlying cyclical patterns. This

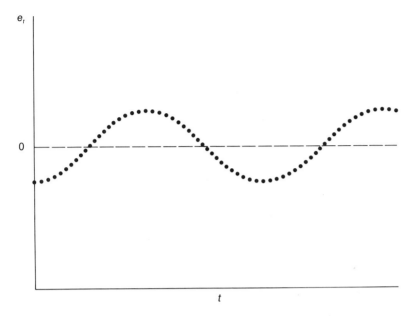

Figure 12.2   A cyclical pattern can be seen in a residual time series plot.

procedure will highlight autocorrelation in residuals. The Durbin-Watson test (Chapter 11) allows one to test for first-order autocorrelation.

When strong autocorrelation exists in the residuals, the ordinary least squares (OLS) method *understates* the variances of the regression coefficients as well as the variance of the residuals. Modeling year-over-year growth or percent changes of the variables often reduces the problem of autocorrelation considerably.

Another reason for the appearance of nonrandom patterns is that a linear model is being fit to an inherently nonlinear phenomenon. For instance, a plot of sales of a new product may show a rate of growth that is faster than linear growth. Likewise, the income tax rate on individual earnings has a nonlinear relationship with earnings. When you attempt to fit such nonlinear relationships with a linear model, the residuals will often appear to have a *cup shape* or inverted cup shape (Figure 12.3).

It often happens that the residuals for a nonlinear relationship may not look cupshaped over the entire regression period. However, if you were to make forecasts from the straight line model, the forecast errors might show *increasing dispersion* (Figure 12.4). If it did not become apparent that the data were nonlinear from analyzing residuals over the entire regression period, the pattern of over- or under-forecasting would certainly exhibit nonlinearity over a long enough period.

It is important to distinguish between nonlinear growth in trend and nonlinear variations as a result of a short-term cycle. In the first case, the nonlinear relationship between two variables will continue in the same direction over a long time. In the

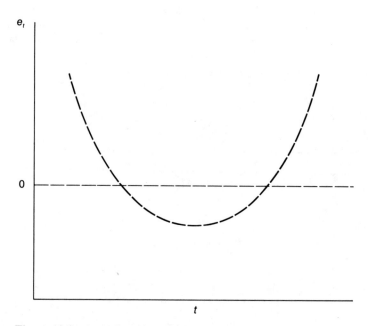

Figure 12.3   A cupshaped residual pattern.

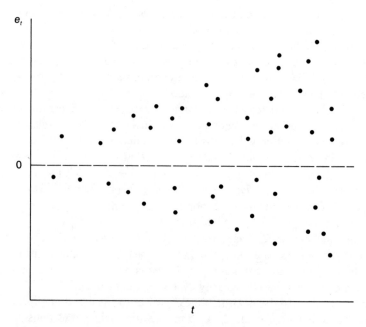

Figure 12.4   Increasing dispersion of forecast errors.

case of a short-term cycle, the nonlinear relationship will change direction at the peaks and troughs of each cycle.

Finally, a trend, up or down, may be apparent in the residuals (Figure 12.5). This pattern is also the result of a nonlinear relationship between the variables.

TRANSFORMING DATA IN ORDER TO FIT ASSUMPTIONS

Transformations of data are often required to realize regression assumptions. Assumptions that form a basis for selecting an appropriate transformation include:

- The approximate *normality* of the error distribution in a model.
- The constancy or *uniformity of the variability* in the errors.
- The applicability of *linear* forms for regression or time series (ARIMA) models.

Box-Cox Transformation

A useful family of transformations on a (positive) variable Y are the power transformations devised by Box and Cox (1964):

$$W = (Y^\lambda - 1)/\lambda \qquad \text{for } \lambda \neq 0,$$
$$= \ln Y \qquad \text{for } \lambda = 0.$$

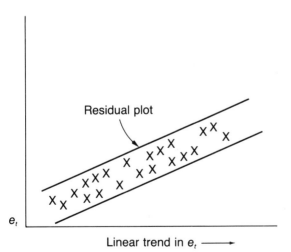

Figure 12.5   A linear trend in the residuals.

The parameter λ is estimated from the data, usually by the method of maximum likelihood. This procedure involves several steps:

- A value of λ is selected from within a reasonable range bracketing zero, say $(-2,2)$. A convenient set of values for γ is $\{\pm 2, \pm 1\frac{1}{2}, \pm 1, \pm \frac{2}{3}, \pm \frac{1}{2}, \pm \frac{1}{3}, \pm \frac{1}{4}, 0\}$.

- For the chosen λ, evaluate the likelihood

$$L_{max}(\lambda) = \frac{-n}{2} \ln \hat{\sigma}^2(\lambda) + (\lambda - 1) \sum_{i=1}^{n} \ln Y_i$$

$$= \frac{-n}{2} \ln (\text{Residual SS}/n) + (\lambda - 1) \sum_{i=1}^{n} \ln Y_i,$$

  where n is the total number of observations, and SS denotes "sum of squares."

- Plot $L_{max}(\lambda)$ against λ over the selected range and draw a smooth curve through the points. Figure 12.6 shows a plot of $L_{max}(\lambda)$ for the revenue series in a telecommunications forecasting problem used throughout this book for illustrative purposes.

- The value of λ that maximized $L_{max}(\lambda)$ is the *maximum likelihood estimate* λ of λ. Table 12.1 shows the maximum likelihood estimates of the four series in the telecommunications example.

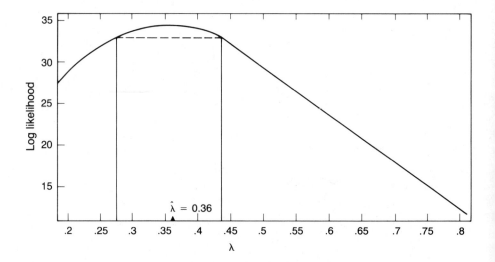

Figure 12.6   Plot of the logarithms of the likelihood function $L_{max}(\lambda)$ versus λ for the Toll revenue series. Associated 95-percent confidence limits for the maximum are shown.

Table 12.1   Estimate of λ in the Box-Cox transformation
for the telecommunciations example.

Series (Code)	$\hat{\lambda}$	Transformation close to
Toll revenues (REV)	0.36	Cube root ($\lambda = 0.33$)
Toll messages (MSG)	0.43	Square root ($\lambda = 0.50$)
Business telephones (BMT)	0.57	Square root ($\lambda = 0.50$)
Nonfarm employment (NFRM)	0.93	No transformation ($\lambda = 1.0$)

- For applications, round the maximum likelihood estimate $\hat{\lambda}$ to the nearest value that makes practical sense. This should have a minor impact on the results, especially if the likelihood function is relatively flat (as it is in many cases).

- Determine an approximate $100 (1 - \alpha)$-percent confidence interval for λ from the inequality

$$L_{\max}(\hat{\lambda}) - L_{\max}(\lambda) \leq \tfrac{1}{2}\chi_1^2(1 - \alpha),$$

  where $\chi_1^2(1 - \alpha)$ is the percentage point of the χ^2 distribution with one degree of freedom, which leaves an area of α in the upper tail of the distribution (Appendix A, Table 3).

- The confidence interval can be drawn on the plot of $L_{\max}(\lambda)$ against λ by drawing a horizontal line at the level

$$L_{\max}(\hat{\lambda}) - \tfrac{1}{2}\chi_1^2(1 - \alpha)$$

of the vertical scale. The two values of λ at which this cuts the curve are the end points of the approximate confidence interval. Figure 12.6 also shows the 95-percent confidence interval for λ for the revenue data (REV).

TRANSFORMING DATA TO IMPROVE RESIDUAL PATTERNS

In forecasting applications there are many time series that appear to grow exponentially with time. If these series are regressed against time, a pattern of increasing dispersion generally results, particularly in a comparison of forecasted values with actual data. The toll revenue and message series in the telecommunications example are two such examples.

Logarithmic Transformation

Over the regression period, for an exponential time series, the residuals from a fitted straight line will appear to have a cupshaped pattern (Figure 12.3); after fitting a straight line, the actual values would fall above the line in the beginning and end part and would be below the line in the middle part of the regression period. The appropriate technique for improving the fit is to take a logarithmic transformation of the data. Further, substantiation that taking logarithms is the correct course will come from considering year-over-year percent changes: if the percent growth values lie in a relatively small band, near-exponential growth of the data is suggested.

A plot of the fitted (with a straight line) and actual logarithms of the toll revenue series (Figure 12.7) demonstrates that the transformation is appropriate. The residuals (Figure 12.8) are no longer cupshaped and appear more *symmetrically* distributed. There is some evidence of a short-term cycle, but the residuals are more random than those of the straight line model.

On a rare occasion, the residuals from a straight-line regression of a log-transformed series may also show a cupshaped pattern. In this case it may be necessary to perform a logarithmic transformation on the log-transformed series, that is, a log-log transformation. Care must be exercised in these situations since forecasts based on such transformations will grow very rapidly and likely will appear unrealistic.

Another situation where a logarithmic (or power) transformation may be appropriate occurs when data show increasing dispersion. Figure 12.9 shows data of mobile telephone units, by state, against the number of cars for each state for a recent year. It is natural to assume that numbers of mobile telephones increase with

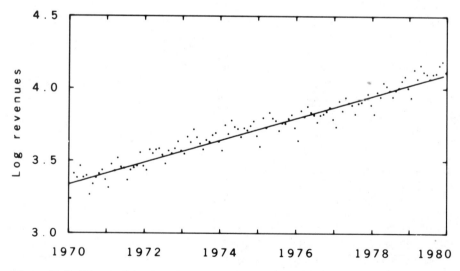

Figure 12.7 Historical fit of the logarithms of the telephone toll revenues with a straight-line regression model.

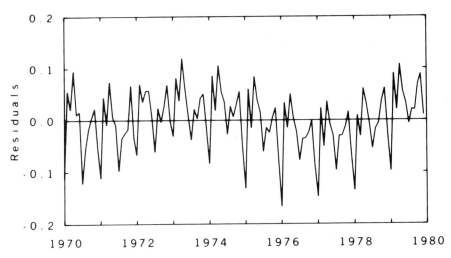

Figure 12.8   Residuals from the straight-line regression model for telephone toll revenues in Figure 12.7.

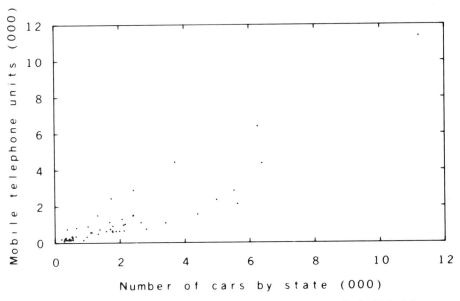

Figure 12.9   Mobile telephone units versus number of cars by state in the United States.

increasing numbers of cars. However, it is also apparent that the data show increasing variability with increasing numbers of cars.

Without examining residuals, a linear regression analysis could be performed with satisfactory statistical results (in terms of R^2, F, and t statistics). However, the resulting residual pattern (Figure 12.10) demonstrates that faulty inference could be derived from the model. It is noteworthy that there is increasing dispersion in the residuals. California is a large residual; one might expect a large number of mobile telephone units, but the model suggests that the state has an unusually large number of mobile phones for California's total number of vehicles. The model is clearly inappropriate because of this large dispersion (indicative of nonconstant variance) in the residuals. A logarithmic transformation of the data results in equally satisfactory statistical results; but a linear regression in the logarithmic domain clearly gives a superior pattern of residuals (Figure 12.11).

Moreover, the inferences that can be made about the mobile telephone market in the different states change substantially when a log transformation is made. First of all, the residuals no longer display an unusual pattern. California no longer represents an unusual situation. Rather, Nevada and West Virginia are now the closest to being viewed outliers in this regression. This observation is in fact consistent with the per capita income of the two states and the differences in the number of mobile phones relative to the number of cars.

Square-Root Transformation

A second transformation that may be appropriately applied to data representing "counts" of items is the square-root transformation. One reason is that the square-root transformation has a *variance-stabilizing* property; i.e., variability remains constant with size.

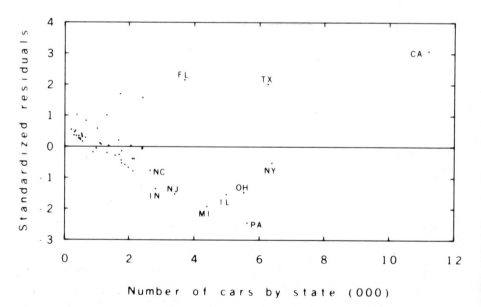

Figure 12.10   Mobile telephone unit data: residuals after regression, showing increasing dispersion.

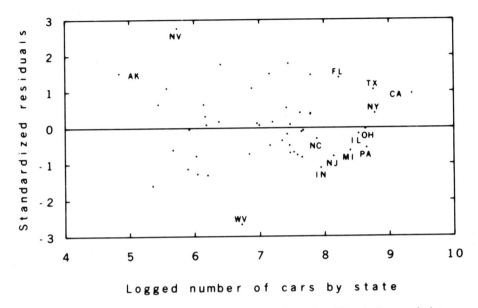

Figure 12.11   Residuals after regression for log-transformed mobile telephone unit data.

In other situations it may be known that data behave essentially in a quadratic manner because the data describe a physical process. For example, Figure 12.12 shows a scatter diagram relating stopping distance for a car to the car's speed (Ezekiel and Fox, 1959). This plot is clearly nonlinear. Although a simple linear regression

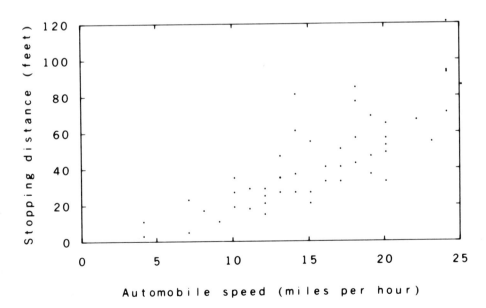

Figure 12.12   A scatter diagram showing stopping distance versus automobile speed.

would produce acceptable summary statistics for these data, an examination of the residuals shows a distinctly nonlinear pattern (Figure 12.13). The square-root transformation of the dependent variable produced equally satisfactory summary results for the regression, and the residual pattern clearly shows a significant improvement (Figure 12.14). The residuals appear random and symmetrical with no unusual patterns or outliers.

GRAPHICAL AIDS

In addition to the visual examination of residual plots for nonrandomness, nonlinearities, and outliers, other graphical aids include the histogram, stem-and-leaf display, box plot, and quantile-quantile (Q-Q) plot (Chapters 6 and 7).

Figure 12.15 shows box plots of the residuals for each of the two models for business telephones. The independent variables in the two regressions are nonfarm employment and nonfarm employment less manufacturing employment. The box plots of the residuals appear nonsymmetrical, with a somewhat longer tail for positive residuals.

A quantile-quantile plot (quantiles of the residuals of the model versus the quantiles of a normal probability curve) is shown for comparison in Figure 12.16.

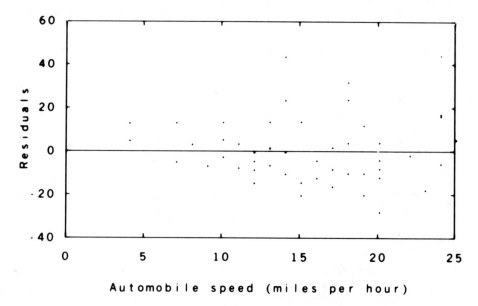

Figure 12.13 For the data in Figure 12.12, the residuals after regression show a nonlinear pattern.

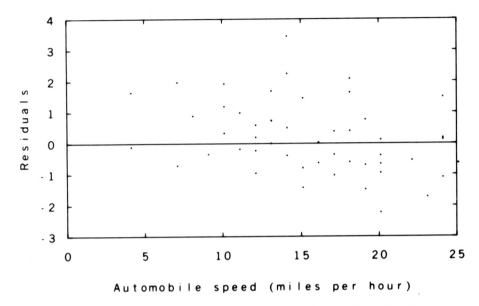

Figure 12.14 For the data in Figure 12.12, the residuals after transformation of the dependent variable (stopping distance).

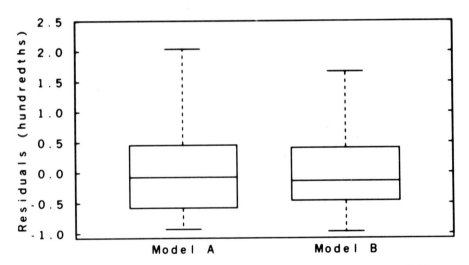

Figure 12.15 Box plot of residuals for the business telephone data of Figure 15.14; differences in variability and potential outliers among these are highlighted.

This plot is linear except for some large residuals. The cause of the large residuals is related to the 1975 economic downturn and corresponding high unemployment levels. Since the presence of just one outlier can change the OLS parameter estimates and the R-squared statistic significantly, certain observations could be deleted or

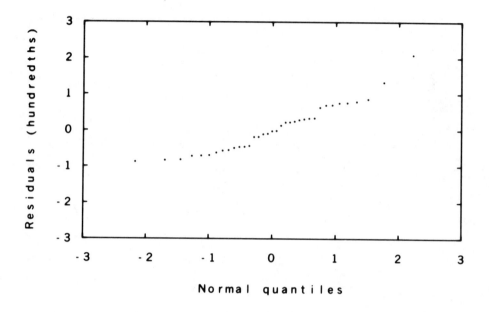

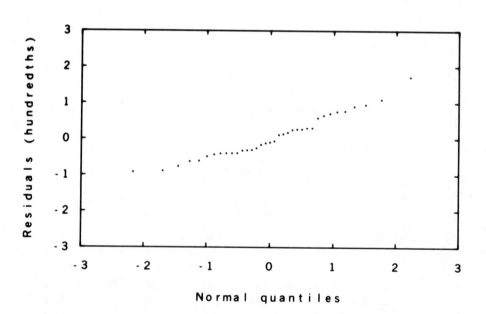

Figure 12.16 Q-Q plot of residuals for the business telephone data.

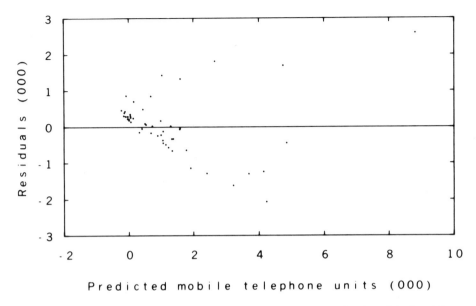

Figure 12.17 A plot of the residuals versus the predicted values for the original mobile phone unit data in Figure 12.9.

adjusted. The use of *robust regression* as a tool complementary to OLS should also be considered.

A plot of the residuals versus the predicted values, such as is shown for the mobile phone data in Figure 12.17, is often helpful in deciding if a transformation of the dependent variable is appropriate. For example, the plot shows increasing dispersion with increasing values of the dependent variable; a logarithmic or square-root transformation of the dependent variable may help. The model can then be reestimated, and the plot of the residuals versus the predicted values (Figure 12.18) will then show a uniform or constant variability about the zero line.

Figure 12.19 further supports the appropriateness of taking transformations for the mobile phone unit data described earlier. The Q-Q plots represent the distribution of the residuals from the models for the original and log-transformed data, respectively. Evidently, the transformed model appears to be closest to the normality assumption since its Q-Q plot is the straightest.

The residuals of a model can also be plotted against the independent variable to

- Detect outliers.

- Assess nonhomogeneity of variance.

- Determine if a transformation is required.

This graphical technique is particularly useful in the early stages of modeling.

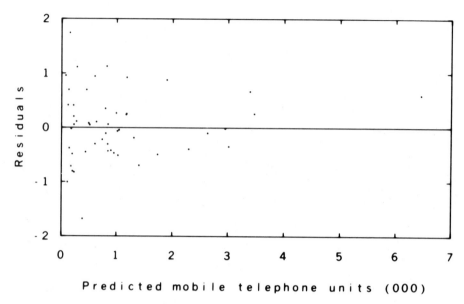

Figure 12.18 A plot of the residuals versus the predicted values for the log-transformed mobile phone unit data in Figure 12.10.

Using Partial Residual Plots

Larsen and McCleary (1972) have shown that plots of *partial residuals* can be very informative in regression analysis. The partial residual plot allows you to determine each independent variable's ability to "explain" the dependent variable uniquely, given that all the other independent variables are already in the model. It also lets you assess the importance of the nonlinearity of a particular variable, and helps in precise selection of the appropriate transformation.

In the case of a very close fit, the partial residual plot might mask nonlinearities and outliers. Also, if the independent variables are highly correlated with each other (an undesirable condition in OLS estimation), the partial residual plot loses, to some extent, its ability to explain the impact of each independent variable on the dependent variable.

Partial residuals are obtained in the following manner. First, the complete model is fitted, including the independent variable X_i. The usual residuals (Data − Fit) are then calculated. The value $\hat{\beta}_i X_i$ is added to the usual residuals. Consequently,

$$\text{Partial residual} = \text{Data} - \sum_{j \neq i} \hat{\beta}_j X_j \ .$$

Since the parameters have been estimated by considering all the independent variables, there is no bias in their estimates owing to a missing variable. The partial

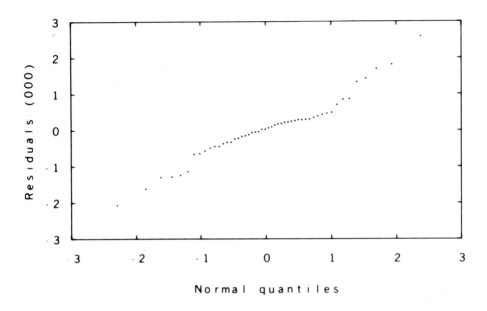

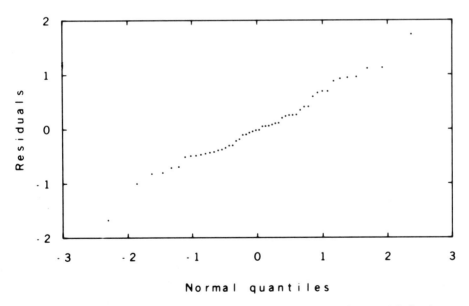

Figure 12.19   Q-Q plots of the mobile unit residuals; comparison of the models for the original and transformed data shows slight improvement (less curvature) in the tail area of the distribution of the residuals.

residual plot for an independent variable now includes the usual residuals plus any contribution provided by the variable X_i.

The plots of the partial residuals against each of the independent variables identify those variables that have the largest apparent dependence. These variables are retained in the model. Those with only slight dependence are candidates for elimination or replacement.

Figure 12.20 shows a plot of the usual residuals against the independent variable X_1. No violations of the model are apparent, and there seems to be little correlation with X_1. The partial residual plot depicted in Figure 12.21 shows a slight positive correlation with X_1, given that X_2, X_3, X_4, and X_5 are in the model.

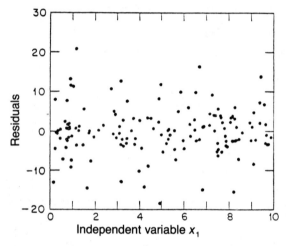

Figure 12.20 A plot of usual residuals against the independent variable X_1.

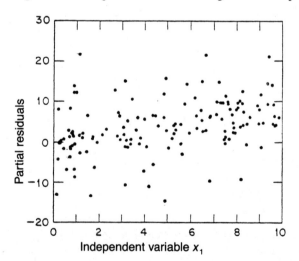

Figure 12.21 The partial residual plot shows slight positive correlation with X_1, given that X_2 through X_5 are accounted for in the model.

A plot of the usual residuals against X_2 will show increasing variability for this variable, and little correlation. The partial residual plot in Figure 12.22 shows a definite negative correlation between X_2 and Y. It also shows increasing variance, but of a lesser amount. It is often the case that the original plots of Y against X_i show little or nothing about the relationship of X_i and Y, given that all the other variables are in the model $(Y|X_1, X_2, \ldots, X_{i-1}, X_{i+1}, \ldots, X_k)$. The partial residual plot tells much more.

Figure 12.23 plots the usual residuals against X_3. This suggests the need for a quadratic term in the model. The partial residual plot in Figure 12.24 suggests that

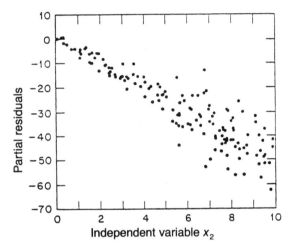

Figure 12.22 The partial residual plot shows negative correlation of X_2 with the dependent variable.

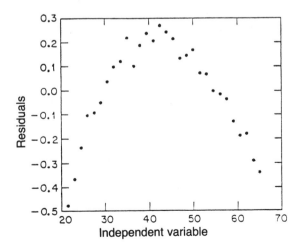

Figure 12.23 Plot of usual residuals against X_3.

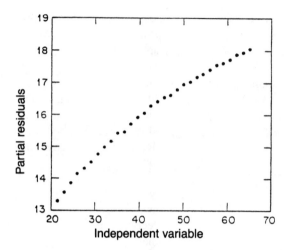

Figure 12.24 The partial residual plot against X_3 suggests a transformation is required.

a logarithmic term rather than a quadratic term will give better results, and this would require a transformation.

In What Sequence Should Residuals Be Analyzed?

How should the forecaster sort out all these different ways of analyzing residuals? First, the summary statistics (F, t, incremental F, and R-squared statistics) should be reviewed. If the model passes these tests, residual analysis can begin. A recommended sequence of residual analysis begins with a plot of the residuals against the predicted values of the dependent variable. This plot is reviewed for constancy of variance among residuals. Patterns of increasing dispersion, with increasing magnitude, as mentioned earlier, suggest that logarithmic or square root transformations of the dependent variable should be made as a first attempt. The model is then reestimated to accomplish this, and the residuals are plotted once again against predicted values.

Once a satisfactory transformation of the dependent variable has been obtained, if one is indeed required, partial residual plots against each independent variable can be generated. At this time

- Delete variables with little correlation. Reestimate the model.

- Transform independent variables that exhibit nonlinear relationships (one at a time). After each transformation, reestimate the model and generate a new set of partial residual plots.

- Progress to additional analyses if all plots show linear and significant (not horizontal) relationships.

For time series models, plot the residuals and the autocorrelogram of the residuals. Test for serially correlated residuals. Additional variables for consideration may be suggested by the plots. The techniques discussed in Chapter 13 may be required if the serial correlation problem remains.

The next step is to generate quantile-quantile plots of the residuals versus the quantiles of a standard normal distribution. This will highlight potential outliers (review each end carefully) and indicate if there are departures from normally distributed residuals. Outliers should be investigated and replaced, if replacement is appropriate. Transformations of the dependent variable may be required. Alternatively, robust regression may be appropriate if normally distributed residuals cannot be obtained.

While linear regression models based on nonlinearly related data may appear to give acceptable summary statistics, the inferences drawn from such models can be erroneous and misleading. Residual analysis is an effective tool for graphically demonstrating departures from model assumptions. When looking at regression residuals, keep in mind that

- A residual plot of constant variance with no visible pattern is consistent with the basic assumptions of the linear least-squares regression model. If the residuals are also normally distributed, a variety of significance tests can be performed. Also, the run test can be applied to test for nonrandomness.

- A residual pattern of increasing dispersion may suggest the need to transform one or more variables. The logarithmic and square-root transformations are the most commonly used to solve this problem. A plot of the residuals versus the dependent variable also highlights the need for transformations.

- The normal quantile-quantile (Q-Q) plot is a convenient way to decide if the residuals are normally distributed. Also, outliers are readily detected at one or the other end of the plot.

USEFUL READING

EZEKIEL, M., and K. A. FOX (1959). *Methods of Correlation and Regression Analysis*. New York, NY: John Wiley and Sons.

LARSEN, W. A., and S. J. McCLEARY (1972). The Use of Partial Residual Plots in Regression Analysis. *Technometrics* 14, 781–90.

ROBERTS, H. V. (1974). *Conversational Statistics*. Hewlett-Packard University Business Series. Palo Alto, CA: The Scientific Press.

WALSH, J. E. (1962). *Handbook of Nonparametric Statistics*. Princeton, NJ: Van Nostrand Co.

CHAPTER 13

Dealing with Serial Correlation

This chapter discusses the identification and avoidance of serial (auto) correlation in residuals. The underlying assumptions to be considered are that

- Ordinary least-squares estimation is based on model errors that are uncorrelated.

- Normality implies that model errors are pairwise independent; this may be unrealistic in practice.

Some additional ways of dealing with this problem for time series data are explored in later chapters on ARIMA modeling.

IDENTIFYING SERIAL CORRELATION

In forecasting applications serial correlation may arise because of an incorrect specification of the *form* of the relationship for the variables. Serial correlation manifests itself, in forecasting, in a pattern of prolonged overforecasting or underforecasting, period after period, into the future. We will refer to serial correlation when dealing with residuals or data and will associate autocorrelation with specifications of error in a model.

First-Order Serial Correlation

To begin to think about the occurrence of autocorrelation in forecasting models, consider

$$Y_t = \beta X_t + \varepsilon_t.$$

where ε_t depends on the value of itself one period ago—that is,

$$\varepsilon_t = \rho\varepsilon_{t-1} + \upsilon_t, \qquad \text{when } \upsilon_t \sim N(0,\sigma^2),$$

and υ_t is a normally distributed error term with a mean of zero and a variance of σ^2.

It can be shown that if the true parameter $\rho = 0.8$, the sampling variance of $\hat{\beta}$ will be more than four times the estimated variance given by the ordinary least-squares solution (Johnston, 1972, Chapter 8). Since the estimated variance is understated, a t test could falsely lead to the conclusion that the parameter is significantly different from zero.

Two main consequences of using OLS analysis in models in which the errors are autocorrelated are:

- Sampling variances of the regression coefficients are underestimated and invalid.

- Forecasts have variances that are too large.

When OLS is used for estimation, the calculated acceptance regions or confidence intervals will be narrower than they should be for a specified level of significance. This leads to a false conclusion that estimates of parameters are more precise than they actually are. There will be a tendency to accept a variable as significant when it is not, and this may result in a misspecified model.

The Durbin-Watson Statistic

Because of the serious problems created by autocorrelated errors, it is important to be able to test for their presence. The Durbin-Watson statistic is commonly used to test for *first-order* serial correlation in residuals (Durbin and Watson, 1950, 1951). The ordinary correlogram can also be used as a graphical tool for detecting the presence of first- or higher-order serial correlation.

The Durbin-Watson statistic is calculated from the residuals e_t in a model, and it has the formula

$$d = \frac{\sum\limits_{t=2}^{n} (e_t - e_{t-1})^2}{\sum\limits_{t=1}^{n} e_t^2}.$$

If the residuals $\{e_t, t=1, \ldots, n\}$ are positively correlated, the absolute value of $e_t - e_{t-1}$ will tend to be small relative to the absolute value of e_t. If the residuals are negatively correlated, the absolute value of $e_t - e_{t-1}$ will be large relative to the absolute value of e_t. Therefore d will tend to be small (near 1.0) for positively correlated residuals, large (near 4.0) for negatively correlated residuals, and approximately equal to 2.0 for random residuals.

The sampling distribution of d depends on the values of the independent variable X_t in the sample. Therefore, the test is only able to provide upper (d_u) and lower (d_l) limits for significance testing. One either accepts the null hypothesis of zero autocorrelation or rejects it in favor of first-order positive autocorrelation. If $d<d_l$, the zero autocorrelation hypothesis is rejected in favor of first-order positive auto-correlation. If $d_l<d<d_u$, the test is inconclusive. If $d>4-d_l$, the zero-autocorrelation hypothesis is rejected in favor of first-order negative autocorrelation (see Appendix A, Table 5).

With the advancements that have been made in computer processing, it is often simpler to plot the correlogram of the residuals of a model and to determine any serial correlation patterns (directly discussed under the identification of ARIMA models). Both the Durbin-Watson statistic and the correlogram are *inappropriate if lagged dependent variables* are used as explanatory variables, however.

The Durbin *h* Statistic

The h statistic can be used to test for serially correlated residuals when a lagged dependent variable appears as an independent variable in a model (Johnston, 1972, Chapter 8). The h statistic is defined by

$$h = r \{n/(1 - n \, \hat{V} \, (b_1))\}^{1/2} \qquad \text{for} \qquad n\hat{V} \, (b_1) < 1,$$

where $r \simeq 1 - 0.5d$ and $\hat{V}(b_1) = $ estimated variance of b_1 (the coefficient of Y_{t-1}).

The h statistic is a large $(n>30)$ sample statistic used to test for serially correlated residuals in a model. This statistic is tested as a standard normal deviate, and if $h > 1.645$, one rejects the hypothesis that the residuals have zero serial correlation (at the 5-percent level). Since only the estimated variance of b_1 is required to compute h, it does not matter how many independent variables or higher-order lagged dependent variables are included in the model.

ADJUSTING FOR SERIAL CORRELATION

There are several approaches that can be tried to eliminate the problem of serial correlation. These include:

- Modeling the first differences or the percent changes year-over-year in the time series.

- Perform a transformation on the data; the transformation should be based on the assumed nature of the autocorrelated error structure.
- Include an autoregressive term (last period's actual) in the model.
- Build an ARIMA model of the residuals of the regression model.

Taking First Differences

Modeling first differences of the data may solve a serial correlation problem. Let the assumed model be

$$Y_t = \beta_0 + \beta_1 X_t + \varepsilon_t,$$

where the errors are autocorrelated as follows (i.e., $\rho = 1$),

$$\varepsilon_t = \varepsilon_{t-1} + v_t,$$

and where v_t is a random error term that is not correlated with ε_t. Replacing $t-1$ for t in the model gives

$$Y_{t-1} = \beta_0 + \beta_1 X_{t-1} + \varepsilon_{t-1}.$$

Subtraction yields

$$Y_t - Y_{t-1} = \beta_1 (X_t - X_{t-1}) + (\varepsilon_t - \varepsilon_{t-1}).$$

Since $\varepsilon_t - \varepsilon_{t-1} = v_t$, this gives the result

$$Y_t - Y_{t-1} = \beta_1(X_t - X_{t-1}) + v_t.$$

If the errors in the original model were autocorrelated, modeling first differences of the variables would eliminate this restricted form of autocorrelation. By definition, the $\{v_t\}$ are assumed to be independent, identically distributed random variables.

It is often the case that the presence of serial correlation is so great that it becomes obvious from an analysis of the autocorrelogram of the residuals or the residual plot. An example of this problem is illustrated in a model relating growth in business telephones to nonfarm employment. A scatter plot (Figure 13.1) shows a strong relationship, since both nonfarm employment and sales of business telephones are increasing. In this case, both variables increase with time. The residuals of a regression between these variables will be serially correlated. Dummy variables were included in the model to account for seasonality. The regression model explained over 84 percent of the variation in the business telephone data; but the residual plot in Figure 13.2 shows that the residuals are serially correlated. From the correlogram of the residuals in Figure 13.3, a first-order autoregressive pattern is evident.

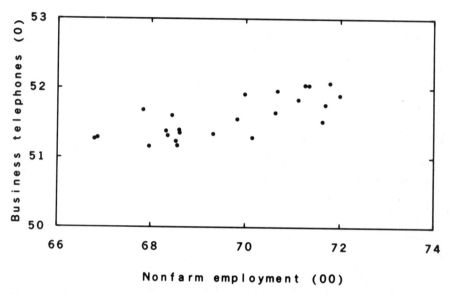

Figure 13.1   A scatter plot of business telephones against nonfarm employment.

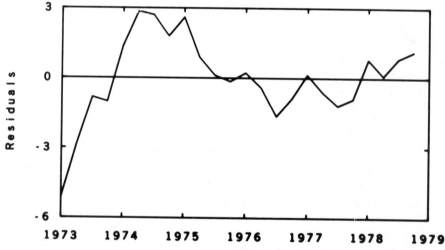

Figure 13.2   Residuals that result from regressing business telephones against nonfarm employment.

A regression between the first differences of the variables has an R-squared value of only 0.41. However, this is because the *changes* in the variables, which are very small relative to the level of the original series, are being modeled. The residuals of this model, shown in Figure 13.4, appear less cyclical. The correlogram of the residuals showed some first-order serial correlation, but of a lesser magnitude than that in Figure 13.3.

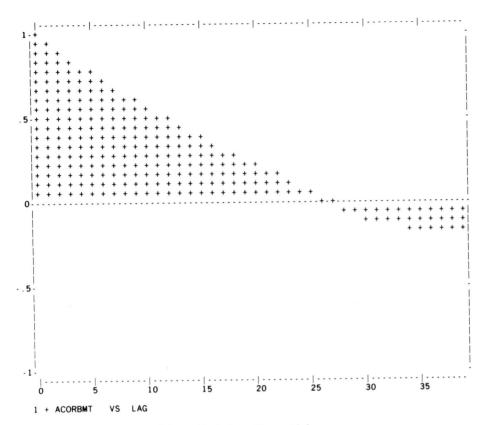

Figure 13.3   Correlogram of the residuals from Figure 13.2.

A First-Order Autoregressive Structure

In a slightly more general situation, it may be possible to assume an autoregressive structure in the error term. Then, by using the appropriate transformation, the transformed model will have uncorrelated errors, and established procedures can be used for analysis. However, this approach requires knowledge of the autoregressive error structure, which may not be realistic in practice.

Consider, for example, a model for a stationary ($|\rho| < 1$) error term given by

$$\varepsilon_t = \rho \varepsilon_{t-1} + v_t,$$

in a linear regression model

$$Y_t = \beta_0 + \beta_1 X_t + \varepsilon_t.$$

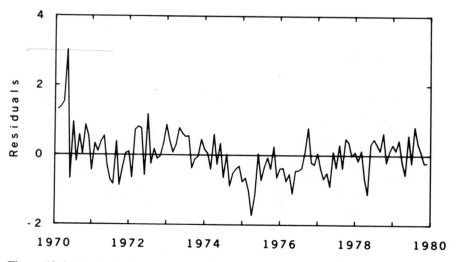

Figure 13.4   Residuals that show less of a cyclical pattern than those in Figure 13.2.

The data are first transformed by the operator $(1 - \rho B)$, where B is the backshift operator, so that

$$BY_t = Y_{t-1}, \quad B^k Y_t = Y_{t-k}.$$

This gives the generalized difference equation

$$(1 - \rho B) Y_t = \beta_0(1 - \rho) + \beta_1(1 - \rho B)X_t + (1 - \rho B)\varepsilon_t.$$

Thus

$$Y_t^* = \beta_0^* + \beta_1 X_t^* + \upsilon_t,$$

where

$$\beta_0^* = \beta_0(1 - \rho),$$

$$Y_t^* = Y_t - \rho Y_{t-1},$$

and

$$X_t^* = X_t - \rho X_{t-1},$$

and where all υ_t are independent, identically distributed errors. Notice that the parameter ρ has to be known for this procedure to work. An *estimate* of ρ could come from a correlogram of the residuals of the model. Care must also be taken with Y_1 and X_1, since their previous values are unavailable. The appropriate transformation for these values are $Y_1^* = (1-\rho^2)^{1/2}Y_1$ and $X_1^* = (1-\rho^2)^{1/2}X_1$.

The Hildreth-Lu Procedure

In the case of first-order autocorrelation, the Hildreth-Lu procedure provides a method of solving for ρ by using a nonlinear maximum-likelihood method due to Hildreth and Lu (1960). The equations are difficult to solve, and the solution is often easier if ρ is varied over the range from minus one to plus one. The best value can be selected from a procedure where ρ is the value that minimizes the sum of squared residuals.

Consider a differencing operation $(1-\rho B)$ on the model

$$Y_t = \beta_0 + \beta_1 X_t + \varepsilon_t.$$

This gives

$$(1-\rho B)Y_t = (1-\rho B)(\beta_0 + \beta_1 X_t + \varepsilon_t).$$

Equivalently,

$$Y_t - \rho Y_{t-1} = \beta_0(1-\rho) + \beta_1(X_t - \rho X_{t-1}) + (\varepsilon_t - \rho\varepsilon_{t-1}).$$

Then, by rewriting,

$$\varepsilon_t - \rho\varepsilon_{t-1} = (Y_t - \rho Y_{t-1}) - \beta_0(1-\rho) - \beta(X_t - \rho X_{t-1}).$$

Then solve for the minimum sum of squared errors, $\Sigma v_t^2 = \Sigma(\varepsilon_t - \rho\varepsilon_{t-1})^2$, using different values of ρ.

The Cochrane-Orcutt Procedure

Another procedure to estimate ρ in the presence of first-order autocorrelation was proposed by Cochrane and Orcutt (1949). This iterative procedure produces successive estimates of ρ until the difference between successive estimates becomes insignificant.

The initial estimate of ρ is derived from the residuals by

$$\hat\rho = \frac{\displaystyle\sum_{t=2}^{n} e_t e_{t-1}}{\displaystyle\sum_{t=2}^{n} e_{t-1}^2}.$$

The value $\hat{\rho}$ is substituted into the model

$$Y_t - \hat{\rho} Y_{t-1} = \beta_0(1 - \hat{\rho}) + \beta_1(X_t - \hat{\rho}X_{t-1}) + v_t,$$

and the transformed equation is solved by using OLS. A second estimate of ρ is made in the same manner:

$$\hat{\hat{\rho}} = \frac{\displaystyle\sum_{t=2}^{n} \hat{v}_t\hat{v}_{t=1}}{\displaystyle\sum_{t=2}^{n} \hat{v}_{t-1}^2},$$

where the $\hat{v}_t$'s are the residuals from the OLS fit.

The estimate $\hat{\hat{\rho}}$ is compared to the first estimate $\hat{\rho}$. If these two values are reasonably close, the second estimate is used. If not, another iteration is made.

The Cochrane-Orcutt procedure can also be used to obtain an initial estimate of ρ for use in the Hildreth-Lu procedure. This can minimize the range of ρ that needs to be searched. The Cochrane-Orcutt procedure cannot be used if there are lagged dependent variables in the model.

It should also be noted that the error term in the model can have a more general autoregressive structure. This complicates the problem, because it is now necessary to transform the model with a "generalized difference" of the form

$$(1 - \rho_1 B - \rho_2 B^2 - \cdots - \rho_k B^k).$$

If you feel that the model warrants more general error structures, we recommend that you consider the modeling approach discussed in Part V.

The previous model was estimated by using the Cochrane-Orcutt (C-O) auto-correlation routine. The final iteration yielded $\hat{\rho} = 0.56$. The residual plot appeared to be random and the correlogram of the residuals showed no significant autocorrelations.

Table 13.1 summarizes the statistics from the alternative models. The coefficient of employment in the C-O procedure is 0.032, which is almost identical to the value obtained from the OLS regression performed with the original series. The t statistics for the OLS and C-O models both suggest that β is significantly different from zero; but the value of the t statistic is less in the C-O procedure, as one would expect.

The model with the first differences of the series has a $\hat{\beta} = 0.024$, approximately one standard error less than what the C-O procedure estimates it should be. The C-O model, particularly with regard to serially correlated residuals, is the preferred model.

A Main Gain Model

In Chapter 5 of *The Professional Forecaster*, it was shown that the residuals of the main telephone gain model (as a function of housing starts, the FRBI series, and

Table 13.1 Summary of statistics in models for business main telephones (BMT) as a function of the nonfarm employment series.

Regression model using	R^2	$\hat{\beta}$ (Employment)	t statistic	$\hat{\rho}$	Durbin-Watson	Estimated standard deviation
BMT	0.84	0.033	10.6	—	0.52	1.77
First differences in BMT	0.41	0.024	3.1	1.00	1.01	1.19
Cochrane-Orcutt adjustment	0.79	0.032	8.7	0.56	1.39	1.12

the dummy variables used to account for labor strikes) were also autocorrelated. This model was estimated by using the Cochrane-Orcutt (C-O) and Hildreth-Lu (H-L) procedures, and the results are summarized in Table 13.2.

The H-L procedure results in a slightly lower standard deviation for the residuals than the C-O procedure does, indicating that $\hat{\rho}$ is closer to 0.40 than to 0.32.

It is interesting to note that the lost demand attributable to the 1971 strike (D_2) is lessened from $-225,270$ (as the OLS regression estimates it to be) to $-148,140$ (the H-L estimate). The coefficient of the housing starts variable shows a decline from 568.5 (OLS) to 493.5 (H-L). The standard error of the housing starts variable increases from 80.6 (OLS) to 106.9 (H-L) when the serial correlation in the residuals is corrected.

Table 13.2 Comparison of serial adjustment corrections in a model for main telephone gain (t statistics are shown in brackets below the coefficient estimates).

Parameter	Regression model		
	OLS	Cochrane-Orcutt	Hildreth-Lu
R^2	0.65	0.59	0.57
$\hat{\beta}_1$ (HOUS)	568.5 (7.05)	511.9 (5.17)	493.5 (4.62)
$\hat{\beta}_2$ (DFRB)	13,185 (6.32)	13,040 (5.91)	12,940 (5.78)
$\hat{\beta}_3$ (D_1)	$-246,720$ (-4.17)	$-237,490$ (-4.54)	$-235,740$ (-4.64)
$\hat{\beta}_4$ (D_2)	$-225,270$ (-3.81)	$-160,290$ (-3.08)	$-148,140$ (-2.93)
$\hat{\rho}$	—	0.32	0.40
Durbin-Watson	1.33	1.92	2.08
Estimated standard deviation	57,890	54,160	54,100

variable shows a decline from 568.5 (OLS) to 493.5 (H-L). The standard error of the housing starts variable increases from 80.6 (OLS) to 106.9 (H-L) when the serial correlation in the residuals is corrected.

SERIAL-CORRELATION CHECKLIST

_____ Are the residuals of any equation serially correlated?

_____ If serial correlation is present, have you tried:
  - Modeling first differences?
  - Including an autoregressive term?
  - An ARIMA model for the residuals of the initial model?
  - The Hildreth-Lu or Cochrane-Orcutt procedures for first-order autocorrelation?

_____ If a lagged dependent variable is included in the model, has the h statistic been calculated to test the zero autocorrelation hypothesis?

SUMMARY

The presence of serial correlation is a frequent problem in econometric modeling applications. Some techniques to deal with this include:

  - The use of autoregressive terms in the model.

  - Modeling first (or generalized) differences of the variables.

  - Making adjustments based on the Hildreth-Lu or Cochrane-Orcutt procedures.

USEFUL READING

COCHRANE, D., and G. N. ORCUTT (1949). Application of Least Squares to Relationships Containing Autocorrelated Error Terms. *Journal of the American Statistical Association* 44, 32–61.

DURBIN, J., and G. S. WATSON (1950). Testing for Serial Correlation in Least Squares Regression: I. *Biometrika* 37, 409–28.

DURBIN, J., and G. S. WATSON (1951). Testing for Serial Correlation in Least Squares Regression: II. *Biometrika* 38, 159–78.

HILDRETH, G., and J. Y. LU (1960). *Demand Relations with Autocorrelated Disturbances.* Lansing, MI: Michigan State University, Agricultural Experiment Station, Technical Bulletin 276.

JOHNSTON, J. (1972). *Econometric Methods,* 2nd ed., New York, NY: McGraw-Hill.

CHAPTER 14

Using Confidence Intervals for Forecast Tracking

This chapter deals with quantifying the uncertainty inherent in values predicted from a regression model. This is useful to:

- Provide the forecast user with an estimate of the accuracy of the forecast.

- Help in selecting the models for use. All other considerations equal, the forecaster places greater reliance on models that predict values with the least uncertainty.

- Track the forecasts against the actual values to determine if it is necessary to revise the forecast.

The main emphasis in this chapter is on the *accuracy* of the forecast and of estimated coefficients for simple linear regression models. "Accuracy" is, of course, not absolute but is measured in terms of limits or ranges within which a value is considered reasonably accurate.

HOW SHOULD CONFIDENCE INTERVALS BE CALCULATED?

As we have stated before, in the modeling process, a forecaster needs to identify an appropriate model for the data and then estimate the parameters of the model. The parameter estimation is made by using the sample data that are available, but since a "true" model cannot be known, all the forecaster can do is obtain a fitted model.

Let's assume the true model is a straight line as depicted in Figure 14.1 by a dashed line. A fitted model is shown as a solid line. The objective is to determine the slope and intercept of the hypothetical line, given that the probability distribution

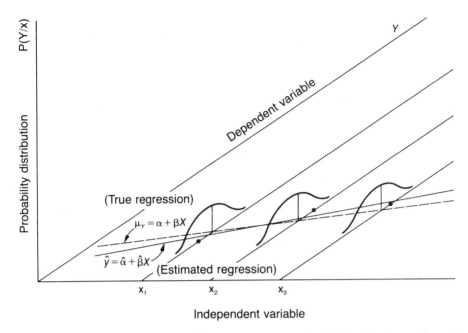

Figure 14.1 True and fitted regression models with error distributions for given values of the independent variable.

of errors in the assumed model does not make it possible to estimate the parameters precisely. Recognizing that there will always be random errors in the observations, it is important to provide a measure of the *precision* of the parameter estimates and of the *reliability* of the fitted coefficients in the regression equation.

The three questions to be answered are:

- How *precise* will the estimate of a model coefficient be?

- What is the confidence interval for the fitted equation *within* the observed range of the independent variable *X?*

- What is the confidence interval for a *new* observation that was not part of the data used to fit the equation?

Prediction Variances

In order to develop confidence limits on coefficients and model projections, it is necessary to derive expressions for the variances of these quantities (see, for example, Draper and Smith, 1981, and Wallis and Roberts, 1966, Chapter 17). A subsequent analysis of prediction errors in terms of the appropriate confidence intervals provides a *diagnostic function,* which is an important part of the *forecast monitoring* process.

For a *simple* linear regression model, the theoretical forecast equation (for a given $X = x_0$) is given by

$$\mu_{Y_0} = \alpha + \beta(x_0 - \bar{x}).$$

Here it should be noted that the independent variable X is expressed as the deviation of x_0 from $\bar{x}$. Thus $\hat{\mu}_{Y_0} = a + b(x_0 - \bar{x})$ is the estimated regression line for a given x_0. In repeated samples of size n from the same population, the values of a and b would be subject to random variation; the variances of a and b are, respectively,

$$\text{Var}(a) = \sigma^2/n \qquad \text{and} \qquad \text{Var}(b) = \sigma^2/\Sigma(x_i - \bar{x})^2,$$

where σ^2 is the variance of the error distribution in the model, which is assumed to be normal, in short, $N(0, \sigma^2)$.

Since a and b are uncorrelated, the variance of $\hat{\mu}_{Y_0}$ is

$$\text{Var}(\hat{\mu}_{Y_0}) = \sigma^2 \left[\frac{1}{n} + \frac{(x_0 - \bar{x})^2}{\Sigma(x_i - \bar{x})^2} \right].$$

The value x_0 to be used in $(x_0 - \bar{x})^2$ is the particular value at which the standard deviation

$$\sigma_{\hat{y}_0} = [\text{Var}(\hat{\mu}_{y_0})]^{1/2}$$

is sought. Note that $\sigma_{\hat{y}_0}$ is smallest for $x_0 = \bar{x}$.

In addition to calculating a prediction variance for the average $\hat{\mu}_Y$, it is also of interest to derive an expression for the prediction variance of a *new* observation y at x_0, a value of a variable which is independent of the observations used to estimate the model parameters. The variance of the difference between a *new* observation y_0 and the computed value $\hat{y}_0$ for the corresponding value of x_0 is

$$\sigma^2_{(y - \hat{y}_0)} = \sigma^2 \left[1 + \frac{1}{n} + \frac{(x_0 - \bar{x})^2}{\Sigma(x_i - \bar{x})^2} \right].$$

This will be larger than $\sigma_{\hat{y}_0}$ since it takes into account the variation of Y about μ_Y as well as the variation associated with the unknown coefficients.

The prediction variances can be calculated once the *standard error of estimate* σ is given. This is conventionally estimated by

$$\hat{\sigma} = \left[\sum_{i=1}^{n} (y_i - \hat{y}_i)^2/(n - 2) \right]^{1/2}.$$

and is often denoted by $s_{y \cdot x}$, the sample estimate of the standard error of estimate.

In the telephone revenue-message example in Chapter 11, it is of interest to compare $s_{y \cdot x}$ with s_y, the standard deviation of the revenues when messages are disregarded. Since $s_y = 9700$ for this example, the standard deviation is reduced from 9700 for revenues irrespective of messages to 2370 for revenues at a given message volume. This is a 76 percent reduction and suggests that toll messages help a great deal in explaining toll revenues.

By using $s_{y \cdot x}$ for $\hat{\sigma}$, the estimated standard deviation for the fitted forecast equation at any point $X = x_0$ becomes

$$\hat{\sigma}_{\hat{y}} = s_{y \cdot x} \left[\frac{1}{n} + \frac{(x_0 - \bar{x})^2}{\Sigma(x_i - \bar{x})^2} \right]^{1/2}$$

and that of a new observation is

$$\hat{\sigma}_{(y - \hat{y})} = s_{y \cdot x} \left[1 + \frac{1}{n} + \frac{(x_0 - \bar{x})^2}{\Sigma(x_i - \bar{x})^2} \right]^{1/2}.$$

These estimates are used to construct confidence intervals, which is the subject of the next section.

Confidence Limits and Intervals

Three types of confidence intervals (for the normal simple linear regression model) are considered:

- Confidence interval for the slope of the regression line.
- Confidence interval for the fitted equation.
- Confidence interval for a new observation.

If repeated samples are taken from the same normal population and corresponding regression coefficients are calculated for the regression line, what would result would be varying values of a and b. The pattern of variability would also follow a normal distribution with mean values equal to the corresponding parameter value α and β. The respective standard deviations are estimated by

$$\hat{\sigma}_a = \hat{\sigma}/n \qquad \text{and} \qquad \hat{\sigma}_b = \hat{\sigma} \Big/ [\Sigma(x_i - \bar{x})^2]^{1/2},$$

where $\hat{\sigma}$ is the standard error of estimate, as before.

Observe that $\hat{\sigma}_b$ is smaller

- The smaller the variability of Y for fixed values of X.
- The larger the sample size.
- The larger the dispersion of the independent variable.

A *confidence interval* provides a statement about the level of confidence that can be placed on an interval of values about a forecast (or coefficient) in order to be sure that the true value is within that range. For example, a 95 percent confidence interval would be the range in which the forecaster is 95 percent certain that the true value of the regression coefficient will be found.

A similar procedure can be applied to the fitted equation or a new observation. Given values of α and β in the regression equation and a value of X (say x_0) in that equation, how confident can the forecaster be that the true value μ_{Y_0} will be close to $\hat{\mu}_{Y_0}$? A confidence interval for a new observation takes the form

Lower limit $<$ New observation $<$ Upper limit

within which the forecaster can be, say, 95 percent sure that the new observation will lie.

The general form of a confidence interval based solely on the information provided by the data is

Point estimate $\pm$ (t-value)(Estimate of standard error of point estimate).

A *100(1 $-$ α) percent confidence interval for the slope b* is, for instance,

$$b \pm t_{n-2}(\alpha/2)\hat{\sigma}_b,$$

where $t_{n-2}(\alpha)$ refers to the $(1 - \alpha)$-percentile of the Student t-distribution on $(n - 2)$ degrees of freedom. Usually α is taken as 0.05 for a 95 percent level of confidence, so $t_{n-2}(\alpha/2)$ is abbreviated by $t_{(n-2)}$ (Appendix A, Table 2).

For the revenue-message model mentioned earlier, $\hat{\sigma}_b = 0.076$ (see Figure 11.1). A 95 percent confidence interval for b is

$$b \pm 1.96\hat{\sigma}_b = 3.42 \pm 0.15 = 3.27 \text{ to } 3.57.$$

Likewise, in repeated samples of size n from the same normal population, the values of the intercept a as well as the slope b would be subject to random variation. The values of Y are normally distributed around a population mean value $\mu_{Y(x)}$ of Y for that X with an estimated standard deviation $\hat{\sigma}_{\hat{y}}$.

A *95 percent confidence interval for the line* is

$$\hat{y} \pm t_{(n-2)}\hat{\sigma}_{\hat{y}},$$

or approximately two standard errors above and below the line for large n.

The *95 percent prediction interval for a new observation* is

$$\hat{y} \pm t_{(n-2)}\hat{\sigma}_{(y-\hat{y})}.$$

Increasing the sample size will tend to narrow the confidence interval for a new observation only insofar as it reduces the confidence interval for the line. Even for an infinitely large sample, the width would not be zero. Thus a lower limit on the width is set by the fact that Y varies for a given value of X, and even complete knowledge of the population distribution for Y at a given value of X will not make possible exact prediction of individual values of Y from X.

The expressions for prediction variances and confidence limits in multiple regression models are very similar but more complex than those just shown. Explicit formulae can be found in Draper and Smith (1981), for example.

Figure 14.2 shows a plot of monthly toll revenue history, the predictions for 1980, and their 95 percent confidence limits, for the model based on the revenue-message data in the telecommunications example. The inner bands correspond to the confidence limits for each month individually. The outer bands correspond to the cumulative confidence limits. Thus, the toll revenue forecaster can be 95 percent certain that corresponding to a given message volume, the expected or true revenue would be found between the corresponding limits of the inner confidence interval.

If the forecaster wants to know the confidence interval for the sum of the monthly predictions, the outer confidence interval is used. The reason why the cumulative confidence limits are *not* simply the sums of the monthly confidence limits will be discussed in the section on confidence limits for time series.

A plot of predicted errors (Actual − Fitted values) with associated (95 percent) confidence intervals for the *regression errors* is shown in Figure 14.3. This plot can be used to identify large residuals that may correspond to potential outliers.

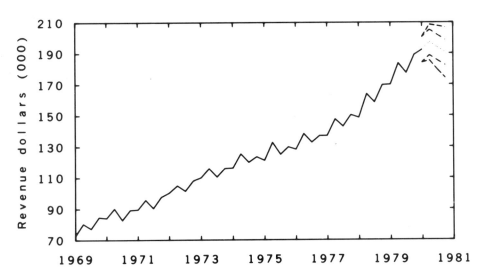

Figure 14.2 Ninety-five percent confidence intervals for the 1980 revenue forecasts and historical values from 1969–1979, from a monthly revenue–message model. Revenue predictions are shown as dotted line.

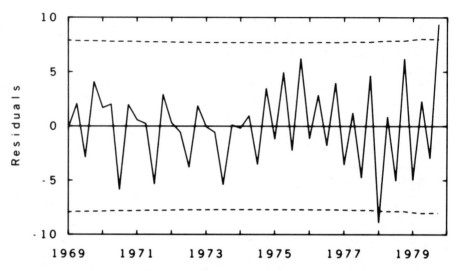

Figure 14.3 Prediction error plot with 95 percent confidence limits for the regression errors over the fit period 1969:1–1979:12 for the revenue–message model.

A Note of Caution!

Since X may take on any value within the range used in the regression, the confidence limits are relevant only over the range of the fit (sometimes called *interpolation,* because the selected value of X falls within the range of X's). A common application made by forecasters is to use the confidence limits for Y with an X value that is *outside* the range of the X's over which the regression is performed. (This is *extrapolation.*)

There are several dangers in extrapolating values based on values of X outside the regression interval. The first is mathematical. In the derivation of the confidence intervals, the further the values of X are away from their mean $\bar{x}$, the wider the confidence intervals will be. Thus the precision that one would like to have becomes increasingly more difficult to achieve.

A second pitfall is a practical one. For example, consider a problem that farmers in the Midwest could have in determining the proper amount of fertilizer to be used to increase the yield of crops per acre. Suppose that a statistician performed a regression analysis based on the application of from 100 to 700 pounds of fertilizer per acre. It is noted that the yield in terms of bushels per acre increases linearly.

The linear model based on these data would show that the more fertilizer used, the greater the yield. The problem that the model does not take into account is that too much fertilizer will "burn out" the crop. The model is inaccurate but the statistician may not realize it. Over the regression period the relationship between yield and fertilizer is linear. However, beyond the range of fertilizer used in the regression, the more nonlinear the series becomes (Figure 14.4). In practice, one may not have

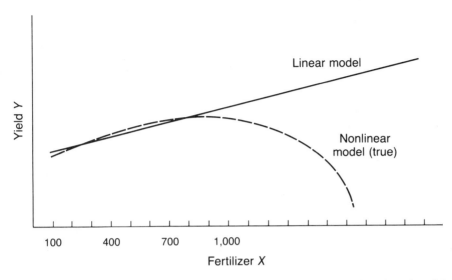

Figure 14.4   A pitfall of extrapolating values beyond the valid range of a selected model; beyond the range of observed data, the model may actually be invalid for reasons the model does not reveal.

models good enough to permit valid extrapolation beyond the range of the observed data. Whenever regression methods are used to assist in solving a problem, it is important to keep in mind the potential dangers of extrapolation. There may be no choice but to extrapolate, but the practical as well as mathematical problems involved should be fully recognized.

What If *X* Is Not Given?

In the treatment so far, the values for the independent variable are assumed to be accurate; i.e., there is no error in the value of X. As one might expect, in the usual forecasting situations the values of the independent variable are obtained from an independent forecasting organization or perhaps even from another regression model. This is especially true in econometric forecasting.

In such cases, the confidence intervals described earlier are conservative. Since there is also uncertainty in X, more realistic confidence intervals should be wider, but how much? It is difficult to state how large they could be since one now needs to know how the uncertainty about the forecast of X impacts the forecast variance for Y. A Monte Carlo simulation might be an appropriate technique for developing approximate confidence limits when X is not known precisely.

CONFIDENCE LIMITS FOR TIME SERIES

The confidence limits presented so far have been based on normal regression theory for simple linear regression. They are appropriate for the prediction of Y at a given point in time when time is the independent variable. The forecaster often deals with aggregated data and would like to know the confidence limits about an annual forecast, which is the sum of twelve monthly (or four quarterly) predictions from a monthly (or quarterly) model. To develop the appropriate confidence limits requires that the variance for the sum of the prediction errors be calculated. This can be derived by using the variance formula

$$\text{Var}(\Sigma\hat{\varepsilon}_i) = \Sigma Var(\hat{\varepsilon}_i) + 2 \sum_{i \neq j} \text{Cov}(\hat{\varepsilon}_i, \hat{\varepsilon}_j).$$

If the forecast errors have zero correlation—in particular, if they are independent of one another—the covariance term would equal zero and the variance of the sum would equal the sum of the prediction variances. The estimated standard error would be

$$\hat{\sigma}_{\hat{y}} = \left[\frac{\Sigma \text{Var } \hat{\varepsilon}_i}{n - 1} \right]^{1/2}.$$

The most common form of correlation in the forecast errors of time series models is positive autocorrelation. In this case, the covariance term is positive and the confidence limits derived by using the standard deviation in the above formula would be too small.

In the case of negative covariance, the confidence limits would be too large. Rather than deal with this complexity, most computer programs assume the covariance is zero. The forecaster should recognize that, in the typical case, the confidence limits are probably too conservative.

Relating Percent Errors to Confidence Intervals

Some executives may find a discussion of confidence intervals obtuse. In such cases, the forecaster may find greater acceptance of this technique if forecast confidence limits are expressed in terms of percentages. For example, a 95 percent confidence limit for a forecast might mean that the forecast will be within ± 15 percent of the actual numerical value. The percent error associated with any confidence limit may be calculated as follows:

$$\text{Percent error} = \frac{(\text{Forecast standard deviation})(t_\nu) \times 100}{\text{Predicted value}}$$

where t_ν is the tabulated value of the Student t-distribution for ν degrees of freedom.

This calculation provides the percent error for any particular period. Values can be calculated for all periods—for example, for each month of the year. The median percent error could be used in place of an arithmetic average error. A plot similar to Figure 14.5 can be generated to translate confidence limits to percent errors.

The confidence limits and percent errors calculated in Figure 14.5 are for monthly or quarterly errors. Under the assumption of random errors, the cumulative percent error will be less than the monthly or quarterly percent error since positive and negative residuals will cancel to some extent. As an approximate rule, the average monthly percent error can be divided by the square root of the number of months of the forecast to determine the cumulative percent error. For example, the annual percent error is calculated by dividing the average monthly percent error by $\sqrt{12}$ or the average quarterly percent error by $\sqrt{4}$ (or 2).

The formula for determining the percent error associated with given confidence limits can be transposed to calculate the confidence limits to be used to obtain a given percent error objective. Consider the situation in which accuracy objectives are provided for each time series. To determine standard error units for monthly predictions, the following formula can be used as an approximation:

$$\frac{\text{Confidence level}}{(t\text{-statistic})} = \frac{(\text{Percent error for the period})(\text{Predicted value})}{(\text{Forecast standard deviation})(100)}.$$

Figure 14.5 Relating confidence limits to percent errors.

In a given case, if the accuracy objective on a monthly basis were to be within 10 percent, the confidence level might only be 70 percent. To estimate the *t*-statistic for an annual forecast, the following formula would apply:

$$\frac{\text{Confidence level}}{(t\text{-statistic})} = \frac{(\text{Percent error for the year})(\text{Annual forecast})}{(\text{Forecast standard deviation})(100)(\sqrt{4} \text{ or } \sqrt{12})}.$$

The $\sqrt{4}$ is used for quarterly data and the $\sqrt{12}$ is used for monthly data. Quarterly data are often preferable because there is less "noise" in each observation. Tracking monthly data is difficult because of errors in recording, weather conditions, the higher volatility of the data, and similar short-term data problems.

A Forecasting Example

Consider the toll revenue–toll message forecasting model discussed earlier. Assume that a forecast of message volumes has been prepared (perhaps with a model relating it to employment growth) for one-year-ahead by quarters. Figure 14.6 shows the most likely forecast of message volumes. Alternative optimistic and pessimistic forecasts have also been provided based upon different assumptions of factors such as inflation rates, taxes, and fiscal and monetary policies.

In this example, the sum of the quarterly revenue forecasts for the most likely view is—let us just say—$773. The 95 percent cumulative confidence limits for the annual "most likely" or "best bet" forecast are $757 to $790. The annual confidence

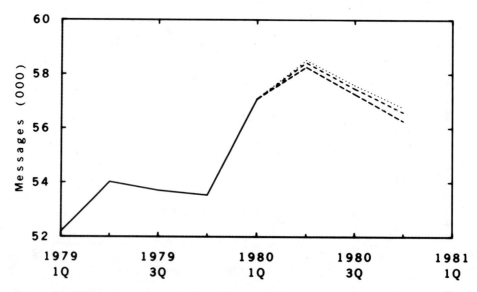

Figure 14.6   Three scenarios (optimistic, most likely, and pessimistic), for a one-year-ahead message forecast, by quarters.

limits are based on the assumption that the quarterly forecasts are uncorrelated. The confidence limits are based on the assumption that there is no error in the message volume forecasts.

Figure 14.7 shows another way to depict uncertainty in forecasting telephone revenues—namely, using the regression equation and the alternative message volume forecasts (shown in Figure 14.6) to generate range forecasts based on optimistic and pessimistic message volume forecasts. Although it may not be possible to determine objectively the associated chances of exceeding one of the alternative forecasts, the forecast user can decide on the level of risk he or she is willing to take. These *range forecasts* can be useful when decision makers are asked to commit themselves to given levels of revenues, expenses, and earnings for future periods. *Risk analysis* requires a grounding in probability concepts, which is beyond the scope of the present treatment (see, for example, Wheelwright and Makridakis, 1980, Chapter 13).

ROLE OF TRACKING

Forecasters track results not only to know where they are today relative to where they predicted they would be, but also to help make better forecasts. *Forecast tracking* consists of comparing recently published actuals against current forecasts and communicating the comparisons to higher management as appropriate. Clearly, it is necessary to monitor the assumptions on which the forecasts are based as well.

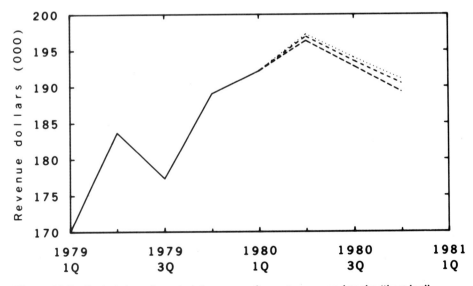

Figure 14.7 Optimistic and pessimistic revenue forecasts compared to the "best bet" view (based on scenario views of the message volumes).

Ongoing Communication with Management

The purpose of ongoing communications is to keep management informed about current levels of results and forecasting performance as well as to recommend changes in forecasts when appropriate. Normally, forecasters should prepare a set of standard reports and analyses of current results and forecast performances. They should also strive to limit such reports to the minimum number necessary, since managers can easily become buried in reports from subordinates. If there are too many reports, an important change may be missed among the routine reports.

Rather, management should have confidence that the forecaster will issue timely reports of exceptions when unusual or unforecasted events occur. The forecaster should take the initiative at such times and not wait for a request from management. When managerial confidence is lacking, forecasters may find themselves being asked to issue daily and weekly reports full of data signifying nothing. This can be a tremendous drain on the productivity of both a forecasting organization and management.

The forecaster and manager should establish a minimal number of report dates, probably one a month, as actuals are received, and the forecaster should have the responsibility for issuing exception reports whenever necessary. The reports must provide accurate, concise, and timely analyses of results together with probable forecast revisions, if appropriate. By identifying changing forecast conditions and immediately advising management to adjust policies to cope with changed conditions, a forecaster will go a long way toward preventing management from being surprised by changes about which nothing can be done.

There will be times when the forecaster does not yet wish to change a forecast, yet it is probable that a change will be required if a short-term trend continues. The existing forecast, when issued, probably had a 50 percent probability of overrun or underrun. Several months later, it may be apparent that the forecast is frequently underestimating results and that actual results may well exceed the forecast. If the overrun is not large, the forecaster and manager may decide only to change the probability of overrun from 50 percent to—say—70 percent. However, managers usually want to know and use the new "most likely" forecast. The management decision about whether or not to change the forecast will be based on the information supplied by the forecaster and the impact the change would have on company operations.

Monitoring Key Assumptions

It is usually worthwhile to look first outside the firm for changing conditions. Are the values for the independent variable(s) used in the forecasting models coming in as expected? Are the deviations from predicted values significant enough to cause concern? Why are the independent variables behaving as they are? The forecasts for the independent variables are key assumptions upon which the forecast of demand for the firm's goods or services are based. If these assumptions are not valid, a new forecast is required.

The larger a firm, the more likely it is that a communications breakdown will occur and that the forecaster will not be aware of marketing decisions or other internal policy decisions by various field and staff groups. Subsequent to the issuance of the latest forecast, the sales department may decide to stage a promotion for a given product; the accountant may become concerned about an increase in uncollectibles and recommend new deposit, credit, or collection practices; the research department may produce a new product that is competitive with an existing product; competitors may announce new offerings which appear superior to the firm's existing product line. Any or all of these kinds of changes can take place after the forecast has received management approval. If the impact of these changes is significant, the forecaster has the responsibility to advise management that exceptional events require a change in the forecast. By developing "pipelines" to key decision makers, the forecaster can minimize the frequency of forecast changes.

TOOLS FOR TRACKING FORECASTS

A number of methods for identifying and evaluating significant differences follow. They include the use of ladder charts, prediction-realization diagrams, monthly and cumulative confidence limit charts, and tracking signals.

Ladder Charts

A ladder chart is a simple yet powerful tool for monitoring forecast results. The ladder chart illustrated in Figure 14.8 is somewhat more detailed than those normally used. There are six items of information shown for each month of the year: average of the past five years; the past year's performance; the five-year low; the five-year high; the current year-to-date; and the monthly forecasts for the remainder of the current year.

The five-year average line usually provides the best indication of the seasonal pattern, assuming this pattern is not changing over time. By plotting the current year's monthly forecasts on a ladder chart, the forecaster can determine if the seasonal pattern in the forecast looks reasonable. In fact, this is a good check for reasonableness that can be done before submitting the forecast for approval.

The level of the forecast can be checked for reasonableness relative to the prior year (dashed line in Figure 14.8). The forecaster can determine whether or not the actuals are consistently overrunning or underrunning the forecast. In this example, the residuals are positive for three months and negative for three months. The greatest

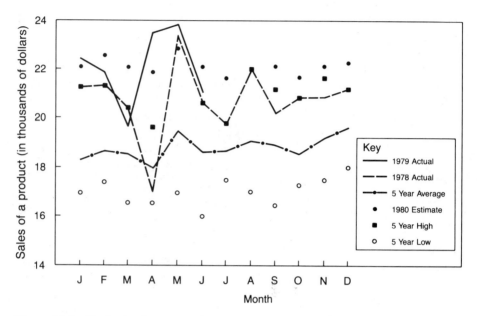

Figure 14.8   Monitoring forecast performance with the use of a ladder chart.

difference between actual and forecast values appears only in March and April, but here the deviations are of opposite signs: some additional research should be done to uncover the cause of the unusual March-April pattern. The forecasts for the remainder of the current year (1980) look reasonable, though some minor adjustments might be made. The ladder chart is one of the best tools for quickly identifying the need for major changes in forecasts.

Prediction-Realization Diagrams

Another useful approach to monitoring forecast accuracy is the prediction-realization diagram due to Theil (1958). This diagram indicates how well a model or forecaster has predicted turning points and also how well the magnitude of change has been predicted given that the proper direction of change has been forecast.

If the predicted values are indicated on the vertical axis and the actual values on the horizontal axis, perfect forecasts would be represented by a straight line with a 45-degree slope. This is called the "line of perfect forecasts" (Figure 14.9). In practice, the prediction-realization diagram is sometimes rotated so that the line of perfect forecasts is horizontal.

The diagram has six sections. Points falling in Sections II and V are a result of turning point errors. In Section V a positive change was predicted while the actual change was negative. In Section II a negative change was predicted and a positive

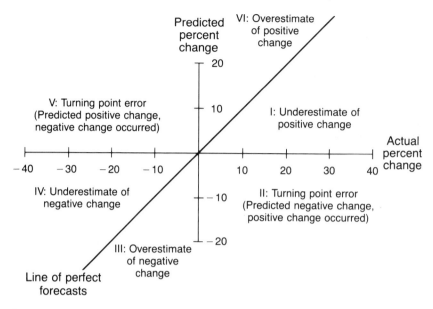

Figure 14.9 A prediction-realization diagram.

change occurred. The remaining sections involve predictions which were correct in sign but wrong in magnitude. Points above the line of perfect forecasts reflect actual changes that were less than predicted. Points below the line of perfect forecast represent actual changes that were greater than predicted.

The prediction-realization diagram can be used to record forecast results on an ongoing basis. Persistent overruns or underruns indicate the need to adjust the forecasts or to reestimate the model. In this case, a simple error pattern is evident and one can raise or lower the forecast based on the pattern and magnitude of the errors.

More importantly, the diagram will indicate turning point errors that may be due to misspecification or missing variables in the model. The forecaster may well be at a loss to decide how to modify the model forecasts. An analysis of other factors that occurred when the turning point error was realized may result in inclusion of a variable in the model that was missing from the initial specification.

Figure 14.10 illustrates a prediction-realization diagram for a model discussed in Chapter 13—main gain versus housing starts. The model is a regression of the annual change in main gain (over the same quarter the prior year) as a function of the annual changes in housing starts.

A simple method for the construction of *empirical confidence limits*, when no error distributions can be assumed, is described in Goodman and Williams (1971). The procedure is to go through the ordered data, making forecasts at each point in time. Then, the comparison of these forecasts with known actuals will yield an empirical distribution of forecasting errors. If the future errors are distributed like

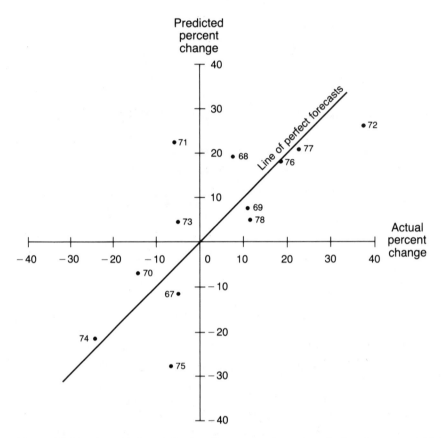

Figure 14.10   A prediction-realization diagram for the main gain–housing starts model.

the most recent past forecast errors, then the empirical distribution of these errors can be used to set confidence intervals for subsequent forecasts. In practice, the theoretical size and the empirical size of the intervals have been found to agree closely.

Confidence Limits on Forecast Errors

An early warning signal is a succession of overruns or underruns. This is evident when the forecast errors are plotted over time together with their confidence limits and the forecast errors continually lie above or below the zero line. Even though the individual forecast errors may lie well within the monthly confidence band, a plot of the cumulative sum of the errors may indicate that their sum is outside their confidence band. This danger signal is evident in Figures 14.11 and 14.12. It can be seen that the monthly errors lie well within the 95 percent confidence limits for

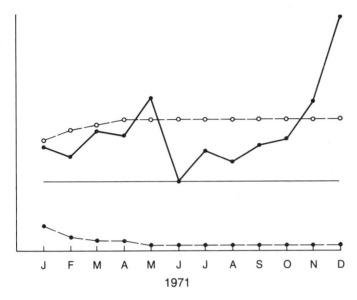

Figure 14.11 Monthly forecast errors and associated 95 percent confidence limits for a time series model.

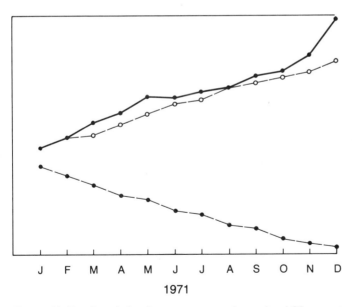

Figure 14.12 Cumulative forecast errors and associated 95 percent confidence limits for a time series model.

nine of the twelve months, with two of the three exceptions occurring in November and December. The forecast errors by themselves indicate that the monthly forecasts are reasonable. However, it is apparent that none of the errors are negative—certainly they do not form a random pattern.

The cumulative confidence limit plot confirms the problem with the forecast. The cumulative forecast errors are on or outside the confidence limits for all twelve months. This model is clearly underforecasting. Either the model has failed to capture a strong cyclical effect occurring in 1971 or the data are growing exponentially and the analyst has failed to make the proper transformation of the data in the modeling process. By using these two plots, the forecaster would probably recommend an upward revision in the forecast after several months. It certainly would not be necessary to wait until November to identify the problem.

A second monitoring danger signal is the appearance of an excessive number of forecast errors falling outside the confidence limits. For example, with 90 percent confidence limits, only 10 percent (approximately one month in a year) of the errors should be outside the confidence limits. Figure 14.13 shows a plot of the monthly forecast errors for a time series model. In this case, five of the twelve errors lie outside the 95 percent confidence limits. Clearly, this model is unacceptable as a predictor of monthly values. However, the error pattern is random and the annual forecasts from this model may be acceptable. Figure 14.14 shows the cumulative forecast errors and confidence limits. It is apparent that the annual forecast lies within the 95 percent confidence limits and is acceptable.

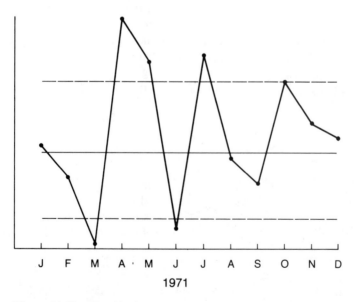

Figure 14.13 Monthly forecast errors and confidence limits for a time series model.

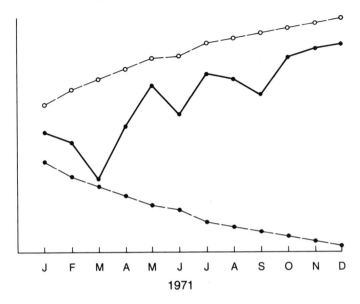

Figure 14.14   Cumulative forecast errors and 95 percent confidence limits for a time series model.

The conclusion that can be reached from monitoring the two sets of forecast errors is that neither model is wholly acceptable, nor can either be rejected. In one case, the monthly forecasts were good but the annual forecast was not. In the other case, the monthly forecasts were not good but the annual forecast was acceptable. Whether either model would be retained by the forecaster depends on the purpose for which the model was constructed. It is important to notice that by monitoring cumulative forecast errors, the forecaster was able to determine the need for forecast revision much earlier than if he or she were only monitoring monthly forecast errors. This is the kind of early notification of forecast revision that management expects from the forecaster.

Tracking Signals

The tracking signal, proposed by Trigg (1964), indicates the presence of nonrandom errors. The tracking signal is the ratio of two smoothed errors E_t and M_t. The numerator E_t is a simple exponential smooth of the errors e_t, and the denominator M_t is a simple exponential smooth of the absolute value of the errors. Thus

$$T_t = E_t/M_t;$$
$$E_t = \alpha e_t + (1 - \alpha)E_{t-1};$$
$$M_t = \alpha|e_t| + (1 - \alpha)M_{t-1};$$

and

$$e_t = y_t - F_t,$$

where e_t is the difference between the observed value y_t and the forecast F_t at period t. Trigg showed that when T_t exceeds 0.51 for $\alpha = 0.1$ or 0.74 for $\alpha = 0.2$, the errors are nonrandom at the 95 percent confidence level.

Tracking signals are useful when large numbers of items need to be monitored. This is often the case in inventory management systems. When the tracking signal for an item exceeds the threshold level, the forecaster's attention is drawn to the problem.

Table 14.1 illustrates the use of tracking signals for an adaptive smoothing model of seasonally adjusted airline data. The tracking signal correctly provides a warning at time period 15 after five consecutive periods where the actual exceeded the forecast. Period 11 has the largest error, but no warning is provided because the sign of the error became reversed. It is apparent that the model errors can increase substantially above prior experience, without a warning being signaled, as long as the errors change sign. Once a pattern of over- or underforecasting is evident, a warning is issued.

Table 14.1   Trigg's tracking signal ($\alpha = 0.1$).

Time period	Error	Smoothed error	Smoothed absolute error	Tracking signal (T_t)
1	−1.58			
2	2.54	−1.17	1.68	−0.70*
3	5.24	−0.53	2.04	−0.26
4	−0.51	−0.53	1.89	−0.28
5	0.59	−0.42	1.76	−0.24
6	2.26	−0.15	1.81	−0.08
7	1.49	0.01	1.78	0.01
8	1.31	0.14	1.73	0.08
9	0.43	0.17	1.60	0.11
10	−7.73	−0.62	2.21	−0.28
11	11.57	0.60	3.15	0.19
12	8.98	1.44	3.73	0.39
13	3.82	1.68	3.74	0.45
14	4.17	1.93	3.78	0.51
15	1.06	1.84	3.51	0.53[†]

Note: Example is taken from a seasonally adjusted simple adaptive
    smoothing model of airline data.
*Starting Value—Ignore.
[†]Exceeds 0.51—Warning.

TRACKING THE MODEL

Tracking by confidence limits may work well for regression and time series models. This technique is generally not available for the more complicated multivariate time series and econometric models discussed in *The Professional Forecaster*. For single-equation models the calculation of confidence limits assumes perfect forecasts of the independent variable(s). Of course, this leads to a dilemma in the forecasting mode. Nevertheless, the confidence limits express the expected variation due to the model, but it must be realized that the actual uncertainty may be greater because of errors in the forecasts for the independent variable(s).

If the forecaster is interested in an "after-the-fact" evaluation of the forecasting performance, the model can be rerun with actual values for the independent variables in the forecast period (these are known as *ex post* forecasts). The realistic forecast is made by using predictions for the independent variables and is referred to as the *ex ante* forecast.

In Figure 14.15, the annual error is divided into its component parts, the part due to the model itself and the part due to the imperfect forecasts of the independent variable(s). If the major contribution to the error is the model, perhaps a better model can be built. If the major contribution to the error is the poor forecasts for the

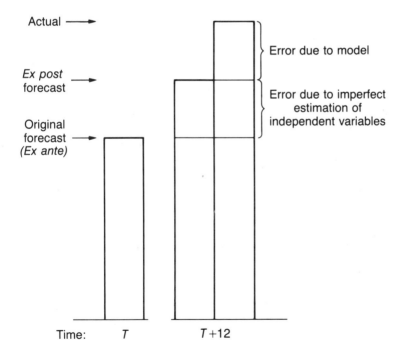

Figure 14.15   Forecast performance analysis for demand models.

the independent variables, the forecaster may want to seek better forecasts for these variables.

If good forecasts cannot be obtained, perhaps another variable can be substituted for which more accurate forecasts are obtainable. It is entirely possible that the original forecast is better than the *ex post* forecast because of compensating errors in the predictions of the independent variable(s). In this case, the forecaster has the right answer for the wrong reason. The forecaster should not place too much confidence in the model when this occurs.

The forecaster may also choose to compare residuals from the original model with those of the *ex post* model. If autocorrelated residuals, or some other residual pattern, exist in the original model but not in the latter, the model itself may be a good one. Once again, improved forecasts for the independent variable(s) are needed.

FORECAST TRACKING CHECKLIST

____ Are independent/exogenous and policy variables monitorable?

____ Are ladder charts used to highlight forecast deviations?

____ Are confidence limits developed about the forecast errors for time series models? Monthly or quarterly? Cumulative?

____ Is there a succession of overruns or underruns in the errors?

____ Are the monthly or quarterly forecast errors within the appropriate confidence limits?

____ Are the cumulative forecast errors within the confidence limits?

____ Has an *ex post* analysis been made on the accuracy of the model?

____ Was the major contribution to the forecast error due to forecasts of independent/exogenous variables? The model itself?

____ Can other independent/exogenous variables be used where better forecasts are obtainable?

____ Does the importance of the forecast warrant the expense of applying a Monte Carlo simulation for random sampling of errors?

____ Does the model "blow up" when extreme values are input for the independent/exogenous variables?

____ Was a sensitivity analysis performed under different scenarios?

____ Does the forecaster have a sound evaluation of the uncertainty that exists in the model's forecasts?

____ Is it helpful to talk to management in terms of percent errors rather than confidence limits?

In the forecasting environment, it is often necessary to extrapolate values beyond the range over which the regression was performed. Care must be exercised since nonlinear relationships may exist. It also becomes necessary to forecast values for the independent variables and this introduces additional errors in the forecast.

SUMMARY

In linear regression theory

- The predicted value of the dependent variable is the average value of Y for a given value of the independent variable(s) X.

- Confidence limits are generated to express the probability that the average value of Y will be within a specified range.

- Confidence limits about residuals provide a valuable tracking tool since they can be used to signal a need to revise a forecast.

- The tracking of results is essential to ensure the continuing relevance of the forecast. By properly tracking forecasts and assumptions, the forecaster can inform management when a forecast revision is required. It should not be necessary for management to inform the forecaster that something is wrong with the forecast.

- Tracking techniques include the use of ladder charts, prediction-realization diagrams, confidence limits about the forecasts and the residuals, and tracking signals that identify nonrandom error patterns.

- The tracking of results also helps the forecaster to better understand the models, their capabilities, and the uncertainty associated with the forecasts derived from them.

USEFUL READING

DRAPER, N. R., and H. SMITH (1981). *Applied Regression Analysis,* 2nd ed. New York, NY: John Wiley and Sons.

GOODMAN, M. L., and W. H. WILLIAMS (1971). A Simple Method for the Construction of Empirical Confidence Limits for Economic Forecasts. *Journal of the American Statistical Association* 66, 752–54.

PLATT, R. B. (1974). Statistical Measures of Forecast Accuracy, in *Methods and Techniques of Business Forecasting,* Butler et al., eds. Englewood Cliffs, NJ: Prentice-Hall.

THEIL, H. (1958). *Economic Forecasts and Policy.* Amsterdam: North Holland Publishing Co.

TRIGG, D. W. (1964). Monitoring a Forecasting System. *Operational Research Quarterly* 15, 272–74.

WALLIS, W. A., and H. V. ROBERTS (1966). *Statistics, A New Approach*. New York, NY: The Free Press.

WHEELWRIGHT, S. C., and S. MAKRIDAKIS (1980). *Forecasting Methods for Management.*, 3rd ed. New York, NY: John Wiley and Sons.

PROBLEMS

Developing Plausible Forecasts

1. Using several years (say five) of the quarterly main gain data (QTMG) provided in Appendix B, estimate the seasonal variation by following these steps:

   a. Arrange a table with headings.

Obs#	Qtr	QTMG	4-pt Mov Avg	Centered Mov Avg	QTMG as % of Mov Avg
(1)	(2)	(3)	(4)	(5)	(6)

   b. To eliminate the effect of quarterly variation within years, calculate a four-point moving average under column (4). Note that the first value in your calculation is centered between observation #2 and #3.

   c. Center the four-point moving average by calculating a two-point moving average under column (5). Where should the first value be placed? What does this column represent in terms of the time series decomposition $T \times C \times S \times I$?

   d. In column (6), determine the $S \times I$-component by dividing column (3) into column (5). How do you interpret the entries in column (6)?

   e. The irregular component I in column (6) can be removed by averaging the entries by quarter. As an alternative calculate the four quarterly medians and compare them with the four seasonal indices determined by averaging.

   f. Adjust the average quarterly seasonal components so that their total is 400. What is the interpretation of these indices?

   g. Suppose a first quarter forecast is given as 450,000. How could you seasonally adjust this observation?

2. By comparing the "average age" of the data in a 2-period moving average and single exponential smoothing model with smoothing constant α, it is shown in the text that

$$\alpha = 2/(n + 1)$$

Show that the same result can be obtained by equating the variance of S_t and the variance of the moving average M_t.

3. Confirm that the weight given past observations in the simple exponential smoothing model sum to unity, that is

$$(1 + \alpha) + \alpha(1 - \alpha) + \alpha(1 - \alpha)^2 + \cdots = 1 \text{ for } 0 < \alpha < 1.$$

4. Show that single exponential smoothing forecasts made at time t for horizons one and two periods ahead are the same.

5. Assume

$$Y_t = \mu + \epsilon_t$$

represents a model for demand that is constant over time. Let SS_E denote a sum of weighted squared errors, where

$$SS_E = \sum_{t=1}^{T} \alpha^{T-t} (Y_t - \mu)^2 \qquad 0 < \alpha < 1$$

so that the weights decrease geometrically with the age of the data.

   a. Show that SS_E is minimized with respect to μ at period T when

$$\hat{\mu}_T = \frac{1 - \alpha}{1 - \alpha^T} \sum_{t=1}^{T} \alpha^{T-t} Y_t.$$

   b. Reexpress $\hat{\mu}_T$ as a function of Y_t and
   c. Show that for T large, $\hat{\mu}_T$ is identical to a single exponential smoothing.

6. Assume a process where the mean (or expected value) changes linearly with time according to the model

$$Y_t = \beta_0 + \beta_1 t + \epsilon_t.$$

that is, the expected value at time t is a linear function of t

$$E(Y_t/t) = \beta_0 + \beta_1 t.$$

If single exponential smoothing were applied to the observations from this process, show that at time $t = T$, the first order exponentially smoothed statistic S_T will tend to lag behind $E(Y_t)$; thus

$$E(S_T) = E(Y_t) - \frac{1 - \alpha}{\alpha} \beta_1.$$

7. Repeat question 1 for the quarterly housing starts data (HOUS) in Appendix B. For part g use a forecast of 350.0.

8. Repeat question 1 for the quarterly index of consumer sentiment (MOOD) in Appendix B. How strong is the seasonal component? How stable is the irregular component? For part g use a forecast of 85.0.

9. For the U.S. nonfarm employment series NFRM in Appendix B, prepare a cycle forecast using the time series decomposition method. (Note: series is already seasonally adjusted.)

   a. Plot the series.

   b. Fit a trend line.

   c. Calculate and plot deviations from the trend.

   d. Prepare a table similar to Table 9.3 based on historical durations (begin the first cycle at the first trough). Given the limited number of cycles, calculate the median as well as the average durations.

   e. Project the series 8 quarters ahead using optimistic, pessimistic, and most likely scenarios.

   f. Describe your rationale for each scenario.

10. Regress quarterly main gain (QTMG) on quarterly housing starts (HOUS). Make plots of Y against X, residuals against fitted values, absolute residuals against fitted values, a normal Q-Q plot of the residuals, and a correlogram of the residuals. Interpret the results from these plots only. Is there a strong functional relationship? What is your intuition about the relationship between telephone gain and housing starts?

11. Repeat question 10 for the differences of order 4 of both time series. Contrast your answers with those from question 10. How would you best describe the relationship between telephone gain and housing starts in the absence of any additional explanatory variables?

12. Interpret the regression output from question 11.

13. Repeat question 10 by regressing the logarithms of the revenue data (REV) on the logarithms of the message volumes (MSG).

14. Interpret the regression output from question 13. Contrast your results with the revenue-message relationship discussed in Chapter 11. What

effect does a 10 percent increase in the message volumes have on the revenues?

15. Develop a correlation matrix of the following variables and compare your results with Table 11.1. The four time series are cube roots of revenues (REV), square roots of messages (MSG), square roots of business main telephone (BMT), and the nonfarm employment (NFRM).

16. Develop a correlation matrix of:

    a. Quarterly main gain (QTMG), quarterly housing starts (HOUS), quarterly index of industrial production (FRB), and quarterly money supply (M1).

    b. The difference of order 4 of the time series in part (a). Are the relationships stronger for the differenced or original data? How would you interpret and quantify these relationships?

17. Using the results from question 16(b), develop an order in which you would fit a relationship for quarterly main gain in terms of one or more of the other three independent variables. Why did you choose that order? Run the regressions and interpret your results. Is there a "best" model? What other variables would you suggest to "explain" telephone gain?

18. Regress the logarithms of the revenue data (REV) against the logarithms of the nonfarm employment data (NFRM). How well does the employment series explain revenues? Provide a rationale. Interpret the regression results using both the regression results and appropriate plots. Do a forecast performance test and summarize your results. (An [ex-post] forecast performance test is performed by doing regressions over "sliding windows" of data, and generating forecasts by using actual values for the independent variable over the "forecast" period.) Calculate percent errors for several one-year-ahead and two-year-ahead forecasts.

19. Repeat question 18 for the differences of order 12 of the business main telephone data (BMT) as the dependent variable and the differences of order 12 of the nonfarm employment data (NFRM) as the independent variable. Rerun your results using the differences of order 12 of the nonfarm employment less manufacturing employment (NFMA) as the independent variable. Is one model preferred and if so, provide a rationale.

20. Repeat question 18 after converting the data to:

    a. quarterly series

    b. annual series. What effect does aggregation appear to have on the · results?

21. Repeat question 19 after converting the data to:

    a. quarterly series—use differences of order 4.

    b. annual series—use first differences. What effect does aggregation appear to have on the results?

22. (Question 18 continued). Examine the correlogram of the residuals. Is first-order serial correlation present? If appropriate, make an adjustment based on one of the autocorrelation correction procedures.

23. Repeat question 22 using the results from question 19.

24. For the normal simple linear regression model, find the formula of the new observation forecast error when:

    a. The intercept α is known exactly and the slope β is estimated.

    b. The intercept is estimated and the slope is known exactly. What is the shape of the confidence bands?

25. (Question 13 continued). Assume the 1979 forecasts for September 1979 through December 1980 for MSG are 18,150 , 18,290 , 17,810 , 16,770 , 18,450 , 18,230 , 19,650 , 19,150 , 19,610 , 19,530 , 18,180 , 19,960 , 19,580 , 19,730 , 19,220 , 18,100 . Generate and plot the 95 percent confidence intervals for the forecast period. For this same model, what are the 95 percent confidence intervals for the intercept and slope, respectively?

26. (Question 25 continued). Assume an optimistic scenario 15 percent above forecasted levels and a pessimistic scenario 10 percent below forecasted levels. Plot the optimistic, "best bet", and pessimistic revenue forecasts associated with the message scenarios.

COMPUTER WORKSHOPS

Workshop 3—Linear Regression for Time Series

- Attempt to model the transformed data from Workshop 2 by taking fourth-order differences (twelfth-order differences for monthly data) of the dependent variable against time (straight line trend). Analyze the statistical measures produced from the regression run.

- At this point the residuals of the model represent primarily cyclical and irregular effects in the time series. Some of the cyclical portion of the model can be explained by one or more of your independent variables. Choose one or more series that you suspect would explain the cyclical component by comparing the deseasonalized and detrended series' time plots against the residual plot. An independent variable might be expected to explain the cyclical portion if it has a time-plot pattern similar to the residual plot.

- Rerun the model incorporating one or more independent variables. Generate the regression analysis and analyze the statistical measures and residuals again. Compare this residual plot to the previous one. Are you satisfied with your results? If not, try one or more different independent variables.

- Select the model that you feel best explains your dependent variable on the basis of logic (e.g. economic theory) and statistical analysis. Generate diagnostic plots such as a normal Q-Q plot of the residuals for the model.

Workshop 4—Residual Analysis and Autocorrelation for Time Series

- Analyze the residual plots produced in the previous workshop.

- Try another model if your residual analysis performed in the previous step revealed any violations of model assumptions. Repeat the residual output and residual analysis for your new model.

- Analyze the correlogram and calculation the Durbin-Watson statistic. Determine the extent of autocorrelation in the residuals.

- If possible, try a few of the autocorrelation correction procedures, such as Hildreth-Lu (H-L), Cochrane-Orcutt (C-O), Maximum Likelihood (M-L), or first differences of the dependent variable.

- Compare the available models. How widely did the coefficients range? What information can be obtained from the residual plots? What does the Durbin-Watson statistic tell you in each case? What method generates the best results and why?

- Identify any other data characteristics and/or patterns in your dependent variable, such as higher-order autocorrelation, additional cyclical pattern in the residuals, etc.

Workshop 5—Specialized Models

- Using the model from Workshop 4, introduce seasonal variables by generating a sequence of indicator variables (0–1). Since you are using indicator variables to account for seasonality, use the original dependent variable. Generate a regression analysis, residual plots, and appropriate diagnostics.

- Analyze the results of this model. Implement any previously learned procedures to enhance the model if necessary.

- Compare the model using indicator variables to account for seasonality with models using fourth-order differences or seasonally adjusted data. Are they comparable?

- If applicable, you may wish to experiment with lagged variables in your model.

- Also, you may wish to do some forecast testing of your model using a smaller subset of the data for model fitting and making comparisons in "future" time periods.

Workshop 6—Robust Techniques

- Develop several robust/resistant estimates for location and dispersion. How do they differ from the (nonrobust) classical OLS estimates? Were they instrumental in helping you pick out any potential outliers? If they were not instrumental, how could they have been used?

- Calculate robust correlations among your variables. Compare the robust correlations with the classical correlation matrix. Do they differ?

- Run your best regression model again using a robust option. Compare these results with your nonrobust model. Print the dependent variable, predicted values, residuals, and robust weights. Do the observations with weights less than 0.5 agree with those you identified as potential outliers?

- Run your best model again using another robust option (if available). Compare these results with your nonrobust model. Print the dependent variable, predicted values, residuals, and robust weights. Do the observations with weights less than 0.5 agree with those you identified as potential outliers?

- Compare all variations of your best model. What are the advantages of each variation? If one of the robust variations does a better job than the nonrobust variation, continue your analysis through residual and partial residual plots and any other techniques. Be prepared to discuss why you did/did not use a robust variation.

Part 4

The Econometric Approach to Forecasting

CHAPTER 15

An Introduction to Econometric Methods

This book has emphasized the use of regression and time series methods to represent relationships between variables for a variety of forecasting applications.

- The models presented so far have been single equation models, relating the variable of interest to one or more economic variables thought to cause or influence the former.

- Economic models can be created, more generally, by groupings of relationships or equations. Such groupings describe an econometric system if the model that results can be used to estimate and test economic theories.

This chapter presents techniques that are appropriate for systems of equations. The topics treated include:

- Specifying the equations of an econometric system.

- Estimating the system in reduced form by using OLS.

- The identification problem of estimating the system of structural equations.

- Estimating recursive systems by using OLS.

- Estimating simultaneous systems by using a two-stage least squares method.

SPECIFYING AN ECONOMETRIC SYSTEM

In previous chapters, all models were of the single equation form comprising a dependent variable and one or more independent or lagged variables. However, in many cases, one or more independent variables may be *jointly* determined with the dependent variable in an econometric *system of equations*. For example, quantity and price may be simultaneously determined. Price may not be fixed, but may instead be established on the basis of an expectation of the quantity that can be sold to yield the highest profit; if the quantity sold does not meet expectations, price is adjusted to yield the highest profit the marketplace will allow. Therefore, a separate equation is required to account for the behavior of price.

Econometrics is concerned with the empirical estimation and testing of economic models, with the quantification of relationships between economic variables. This requires a specification of a model in terms of mathematical equations. The variables in these equations need to be relevant to the economic problem and to be measurable as statistical data. With the application of appropriate statistical tools, the parameters in the econometric system can be estimated and tests of significance can be performed.

The *specification* of a regression model consists of a formulation of the regression equation(s), and of assertions about the right-hand side variables in those equations (regressors or explanatory variables), as well as error or disturbance terms. Specification of an econometric model requires proper consideration of economic theory, relevant variables, functional form, and lag structure. A *specification error* refers to an incorrect assertion about the form (linear, logarithmic) and the content (the variables that are selected) of a regression equation, or incorrect assumptions about the regressors and the disturbance term.

Econometric Assumptions

The present state of art of economic theory is such that there are few well known and well behaved utility functions that one can specify for use in estimating equations. As Phlips (1974, p. 93) suggests: "One therefore often proceeds otherwise, specifying directly the demand equations that seem appropriate for the problem at hand, and taking care to impose general restrictions which ensure their theoretical plausibility." These restrictions can include the sign and magnitude of coefficients and the lag structure.

As Phlips further notes:

> To identify a given relationship one has to take other possible relationships into account. To be able to identify a demand function with the help of statistical data, one has to realize that supply has simultaneously influenced the same data, for the simple reason that the observed prices are the results of the equalization of demand and supply.

The underlying assumptions behind an econometric system include these:

- Economic behavior can be described by a system of mathematical equations.
- The representation will capture the essential features of the economic relationships.
- Future values can be obtained for predictive purposes.

- As a policy tool, alternative economic scenarios can be developed by varying control variables.

Another basic assumption of an econometric model involves the specification of a disturbance or random error term. Relationships among economic variables will at best be only approximate, so the uncertainty inherent in the model is expressed through stochastic error terms (usually additive).

There are also two technical problems in constructing an econometric system of equations, which should be stressed.

- A mathematical problem of solving k equations in n unknowns ($k < n$).

- A statistical problem of estimating the parameters of an equation by using ordinary least squares (OLS).

In the practice of econometrics, several simplifying assumptions are generally made that must be kept in mind. The first is the *ceteris paribus* assumption, which states that all variables that are excluded from the model are held constant. Their mean effect is captured by the constant term of the regression equation and their variability is captured by determining the variance of the errors. This assumption is necessary but not generally realistic. However, omission of relevant explanatory variables results in biased and inconsistent parameter estimates (See Chapter 19).

A second general assumption is the *aggregation assumption,* which assumes that, for example, the aggregate income elasticity equals the individual income elasticity. This assummption requires that all individual income elasticities be equal and that the income distribution remain fixed. Obviously, there will always be differences between a model based on aggregate data and one based on individual data. The unavailability of data about individual incomes forces an analyst to use aggregate data.

The aggregation assumption is also made when per capita specifications are used. One hopes that the division of aggregate income by population yields a per capita income that is representative of the individual incomes of the members of the population. When there is a wide income distribution, the aggregate assumption can become a problem. In most cases, there is little an analyst can do, except to be aware of the problem, since data for individual incomes are generally not available.

Explanatory Variables

Since the purpose of the independent variables in the model is to "explain" the variation in the dependent variable, you should consider variables that measure price, income, market size, advertising, and habit. The price variable often enters the equation in the form of a price index. It can be deflated by a measure of overall changes in prices to yield "real" price.

The income variable can be personal (before tax) or disposable income, nominal or real income, or aggregate or per capita income. There are also instances where consumers appear more concerned with a stream of income over time than with income at a particular point in time. A house may be purchased on the basis of current income and expected future income. In other cases, consumers may not change consumption patterns immediately after changes in income but change them more slowly over time. The lag terms in models are often used to estimate this gradual or *distributed* response to changes in the level of the independent variables.

Defining the Variables

In simultaneous equation applications, those variables that are determined *within* the system are called *endogenous* variables. Those variables that are determined *outside* the system of equations are called *exogenous*. Variables related to government expenditures, taxes, and interest rates are often considered as exogenous. This is particularly true when the econometric system of equations is used to predict the demand for a firm's products as contrasted with a model of the entire U.S. economy.

A third kind of variable is called *predetermined* if it is statistically independent of current and future error terms in the model. Endogenous variables cannot be predetermined, though exogenous variables can be; and lagged endogenous variables can also be predetermined if the current error is independent of all past errors. Since its value in the current period is known (i.e., has already occurred), a predetermined variable is treated as an exogenous variable for all practical purposes.

A Classical Example

As an example, consider the classical *consumption function*

$$C_t = \alpha + \beta Y_t ,$$

which relates consumption C_t to national income Y_t in a simple economic system. The Keynesian *income-determination model* consists of a consumption function,

$$Y_t = C_t + I_t ,$$

and an income identity,

$$I_t = I ,$$

where I_t denotes investment (Pindyck and Rubinfeld, 1976, Chapter 10).

The inclusion of the additional equation, even though it is an identity, has complicated the model, since consumption C_t both determines and is determined by income. Investment is assumed to be an exogenous (or predetermined) variable, since its value is determined outside the system. Moreover, I_t and C_t are assumed to be statistically independent. Both Y_t and C_t are regarded as endogenous variables.

More realistically, investment I_t is likely to depend on C_t or Y_t; that is, it too should be an endogenous variable. This can be achieved by the following set of *structural equations:*

$$C_t = \beta_0 + \beta_1(Y_t - T_t) + \varepsilon_{1t} ,$$
$$I_t = \beta_2 Y_{t-1} + \beta_3 R_t + \varepsilon_{2t} ,$$

and

$$Y_t = C_t + I_t + G_t .$$

This simultaneous equation model includes an additional equation and some *a priori* restrictions—namely, $0 < \beta_1 < 1$, $\beta_2 > 0$, $\beta_3 < 0$. Here G_t denotes government expenditure on goods and services, T_t are taxes on income, and R_t is a government regulator, such as interest rates. In this representation, I_t becomes an endogenous variable; T_t, R_t, and G_t are exogenous variables; and Y_{t-1} is called a *lagged endogenous* variable. There is an equation for each endogenous variable.

Notice that this "classification into endogenous and exogenous is a relative one, depending on the nature and extent of the system being studied and the purpose for which the model is being built" (Johnston, 1972).

The above equations are referred to as structural equations in that they describe the *structure* or behavior of the economy of the nation or the economy of a business firm. Since endogenous variables exist on both the left-hand and right-hand sides of the equation, the independent variables, treated as fixed when applying OLS, are no longer fixed. In the demand model that follows this discussion, it will be seen that the endogenous variables on the right-hand side are often correlated with the error term. In this situation, the OLS estimators can be shown to be inconsistent; OLS is therefore inappropriate for estimating the equations.

Methods of estimation for econometric systems can be classified according to whether they are applied to each equation separately or to the system as a whole. The single-equation methods include OLS for recursive systems and two-stage least squares (2SLS). The 2SLS is by far the most widely used and will be discussed later in this section. However, full treatment of these methods is beyond the scope of this text, and the reader is therefore referred to any modern text in econometrics for this.

METHOD OF INDIRECT LEAST SQUARES (ILS)

The method of *indirect least squares* can in some cases be used to estimate parameters for simultaneous equations. The method is applied to the reduced form of the equations in which the endogenous variables are eliminated from the right-hand side of the structural equations through successive substitutions.

For example, refer back to the structural equations for C_t, I_t, and Y_t. Through successive substitutions a reduced form equation for C_t can be obtained as follows:

$$C_t = \beta_0 + \beta_1 Y_t - \beta_1 T_t + \varepsilon_1 t.$$

Eliminate endogenous variable Y_t by substitution from

$$Y_t = C_t + I_t + G_t$$
$$C_t = \beta_0 + \beta_1(C_t + I_t + G_t) - \beta_1 T_t + \varepsilon_{1t}$$
$$(1 - \beta_1)C_t = \beta_0 + \beta_1 I_t + \beta_1 G_t - \beta_1 T_t + \varepsilon_{1t}.$$

Eliminate endogenous variable I_t by substitution from

$$I_t = \beta_2 Y_t - {}_1 + \beta_3 R_t + \varepsilon_t$$
$$(1 - \beta_1)C_t = \beta_0 + \beta_1[\beta_2 Y_t - {}_1 + \beta_3 R_t + \varepsilon_{2t}] + \beta_1 G_t - \beta_1 T_t + \varepsilon_{1t}$$
$$(1 - \beta_1)C_t = \beta_0 + \beta_1\beta_2 Y_t - {}_1 + \beta_1\beta_3 R_t + \beta_1 G_t - \beta_1 T_t + \varepsilon_{1t} + \beta_1\varepsilon_{2t}.$$

Assume ε_{1t} and ε_{2t} are independent and let

$$\mu_t = \varepsilon_{1t} + \beta_1\varepsilon_{2t}.$$

Then

$$C_t = \frac{\beta_0}{(1 - \beta_1)} + \frac{\beta_1\beta_2}{(1 - \beta_1)} Y_{t-1} + \frac{\beta_1\beta_3}{(1 - \beta_1)} R_t + \frac{\beta_1}{(1 - \beta_1)} G_t -$$

$$\frac{\beta_1 T_t}{(1 - \beta_1)} + \frac{\mu_t}{(1 - \beta_1)}.$$

This is the *reduced form* equation for C_t which can be estimated by OLS. C_t is a function of exogenous variables and a predetermined variable, Y_{t-1}. More advanced estimation techniques, including Generalized Least Squares, can be applied when it cannot be assumed that ε_{1t} and ε_{2t} are independent.

IDENTIFICATION PROBLEMS

Identification problems hinge on whether or not the structural parameters can be uniquely determined. Three cases must be recognized:

- *Underidentification*, in which it is impossible to obtain estimates of some or all of the structural parameters.

- *Exact identification,* in which the structural parameters can be uniquely determined from reduced-form coefficients.

- *Overidentification,* in which nonuniqueness of results can occur.

In the last case, there is more than one solution for the structural coefficients, and the solutions are unlikely to be the same. In essence, a *reduced-form* system of equations (a solution of the system for the endogenous variables in terms of the *predetermined*—exogenous and lagged endogenous—variables and residuals) may be appropriate for a variety of different structural equations. This is clearly a problem, since the same data can yield a variety of structural equations. In the case of overidentification, the structural parameters can be solved directly by using the two-stage least squares (2SLS) estimation technique so long as appropriate restrictions are placed on the equations. These will be discussed under estimation procedures.

The most comprehensive (and mathematical) treatment of identification problems is given in Fisher (1966). Other treatments are given in Johnston (1972, Chapter 12) and in Wonnacott and Wonnacott (1979, Chapters 8 and 18), to which the interested reader should refer.

Specification Errors

All errors arising from a misspecification of an econometric system are called specification errors. *Specification errors* can result from:

- The omission of a relevant explanatory variable.

- Disregarding a qualitative change in one of the explanatory variables (e.g., quality of a product).

- The inclusion of an irrelevant explanatory variable.

- Incorrect definition of a variable.

- Incorrect specification of the manner in which the error term enters the equation.

- Incorrect time lags.

Most commonly, specification errors involve omitting relevant variables and including irrelevant variables, and incorrectly specifying the functional form of the relevant variables. For example, a consumer price index may be a relevant but omitted variable in the demand equation for a consumer good. Likewise, temperature may be an included but irrelevant variable in this case. Specification errors of this kind could lead to esimated coefficients that have undesirable statistical properties, such as biasedness (see for example, Fisher, 1966; Johnston, 1972; Pindyck and Rubinfeld, 1976).

Other forms of misspecification are also important. In demand modeling, for example, it is important to correctly define quantity, price, income, and the market variable. Incorrect use of a price variable, instead of using "relative price," has been known to produce misleading results. The incorrect specification of the error term in a model can lead to vastly different inferences. For example, an additive error term in a log-linear model corresponds to a multiplicative error, not to an additive error in the original domain of the dependent variable.

Incorrect specification of the time lag in a model with lag-dependent variables can result from misspecifying the length or form of the time lag. Time lag specification occurs in the estimation of distributed lag models.

Problems of simultaneity will be discussed in connection with a "Connects-Disconnects" case study based on telephone data. Also to be considered are the specification errors that arise when error variances are not constant and normality assumptions are not satisfed.

A Recursive System

The flowchart shown in Figure 15.1 represents a *sequential* or *recursive* econometric model for main telephone gain in a geographic area. Each individual regression is performed sequentially, starting with the first, until all the regressions have been run. The predictions from the previous equations are available as forecasts for the

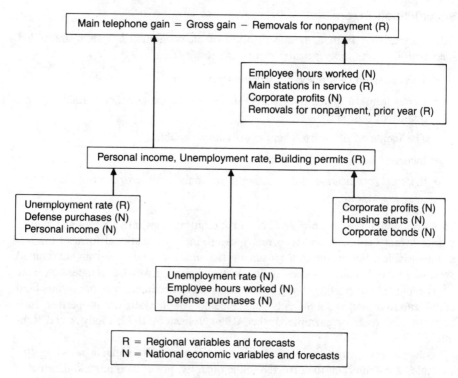

Figure 15.1 A sequential econometric model for main telephone gain in a region.

exogenous variables in later equations. In this example, the exogenous variables include regional, national, economic, and telephone data. This model would be referred to as an *econometric model* because it contains a set of related equations and it attempts to explain an economic system.

Consider a series of models to help predict the gain in main telephones in a particular region of the United States. Main telephones do not include extension sets. A typical residential customer would have one main telephone and one or more extension telephones. Main telephone gain is defined to be the total telephone gain less removals of telephones as a result of nonpayment of bills. Total telephone gain is considered to be a function of personal income in a region, its unemployment rate, and building permits issued in the region. Removals for nonpayment are considered to be a function of employee hours worked in the nation, main telephones in service (the potential number of telephones that could be terminated), national corporate profits, and the number of removals for nonpayment during the past year.

Each of the variables that determines gross gain is a function of other variables. Personal income is a function of the unemployment rate, national defense purchases, and national personal income. The regional unemployment rate is a function of the national unemployment rate, employee hours worked, and defense purchases. Regional building permits are assumed to be a function of U.S. corporate profits in 1958 dollars, national housing starts, and the interest rate on corporate bonds. The average yield on new issues of high-grade corporate bonds is the particular interest rate used.

The basic philosophy incorporated in this model is that the U.S. economy drives the nation and its various regions; therefore, the economic forecasts for the region are related to the economic forecasts for the United States. The demand for telephone service is then related to these forecasts of economic activity. The regression models define the linkages between the national economy and the region and, in turn, the regional economy and the demand for main telephone service.

The Simultaneity Problem

Unlike the example of a recursive system, there are situations in which multi-equation systems do not lend themselves to a satisfactory solution unless the *simultaneous* nature of the economic relations is understood. This involves understanding the mathematical completeness of the system, which requires that the model have as many independent equations as endogenous variables.

The simultaneity problem is illustrated by the way that an independent variable can be correlated with the error term; such correlation violates the OLS assumption.

Suppose that a demand model is built to forecast connections and disconnections of telephones. For connections, a model that includes income, price, disconnections, and an error term is given by

$$\text{Connections}_t = \alpha_0 + \alpha_1(\text{Income})_t + \alpha_2(\text{Price})_t + \alpha_3(\text{Disconnections})_t + \varepsilon_t .$$

The reason for incorporating disconnections is that there are many cases where the customer relocates within a geographical area. The customer's move results in the simultaneous issuance of a disconnection order at the old household location and a connection order at the new household location. Therefore, there would be no connection if there were no disconnection, and there would be no disconnection unless there were a connection. In other words, the move is one transaction as far as the customer is concerned and this transaction results in the simultaneous connection and disconnection of telephone service.

Next, it is hypothesized that disconnections are related to connections, unemployment, price, and an error term:

$$\text{Disconnections}_t = \beta_0 + \beta_1(\text{Connections})_t + \beta_2(\text{Unemployment})_t + \beta_3(\text{Price})_t + v_t.$$

The two preceding equations—one for connections and the other for disconnections—can be looked upon as a system, and an analyst can determine whether or not the independent variables are likely to be correlated with the error term. With all other factors (e.g., income, price) held constant, high values for the error term ε_t will be a result of high values for connections. However, from the disconnections model it can be seen that (unemployment and price held constant) high values of connections mean that there will be high values for disconnections. Therefore, disconnections will be high when ε_t is high and low when ε_t is low. It is in this manner that the exogenous variable in an equation can be correlated with the error term.

The correlation between the independent variable and the error term in an equation can occur even if there is no second equation. The fact that disconnections and connections are simultaneously or jointly determined makes simultaneity a problem: the connections model does not adequately describe the process when OLS is used to estimate the parameters, because of the presence of the disconnections variable. The problem that this kind of correlation presents is that the estimated coefficient for the disconnections variable in the first equation will be too high. The OLS procedure will give too much credit for the variation in connections versus disconnections and not enough credit to the random errors. This means that in making predictions of connections, too much weight will be given to the predictions of disconnections. Therefore, in a system of equations such as those just presented, it is necessary to think through the process involved to determine if any exogenous variables are jointly determined with the endogenous variable.

One way to determine how much *bias* in the forecast results from the simultaneity problem is to see if the same parameters can be estimated by OLS and 2SLS. If both methods yield estimates that are approximately the same, there is little evidence of simultaneity, and one should use OLS. If the parameter estimates differ significantly, then 2SLS should be used to estimate the parameters instead of OLS, because the particular independent variable is correlated with the error.

The method of comparing OLS and 2SLS estimates will also work if the number of equations is small and the number of parameters is small. For large systems with many unknowns, this method may be too costly.

In the example we have used, price, income, and the unemployment rate are considered exogenous: connections and disconnections of telephones do not determine a person's income level or employment status. Factors outside the control of the telecommunications industry determine these variables.

Price could be considered within a company's control, but it is extremely difficult to build a set of equations to describe pricing. Because of regulation in the telephone industry, for example, the price charged is a function of revenues, expenses, investment, government regulations, public utility commission approvals, and many other factors. This means that there is a long delay between the decision that prices need to be changed and the implementation of a new rate schedule. Therefore, price is generally considered exogenous in the telephone industry. In analyzing the agricultural business, where current supply and demand determine price, price would be considered endogenous.

Special techniques, such as the use of instrumental variables, can be used to solve the estimation problem where endogenous variables are correlated with the error term. An *instrumental variable* is one that is very highly related to the independent variable (disconnections, in the telephone example) but not correlated with the error term. It may be that by searching through reams of time series the analyst can find such a variable. However, it turns out that for relatively small models, an easier way is by means of 2SLS. To see how this is so, let us continue to use the telephone example.

A Two-Stage Least Squares Solution

The first step in the two-stage process is to find an instrumental variable D^* that is highly correlated with disconnections but not correlated with the error term. This can be accomplished by regressing the disconnections variable on all exogenous and predetermined variables in *both* equations.

Since the connections variable is also a *right-hand-side exogenous variable,* an instrumental variable C^* is constructed similarly. In the first stage of the two-stage least squares process, each *endogenous* variable that is on the *right-hand side* of the equality sign of any equation is regressed against all the exogenous and predetermined variables in the system (i.e., in all the equations that make up the system). (It should be apparent that 2SLS is not appropriate for systems comprising 100–200 equations: there would be a greater number of exogenous variables than observations, and the first-stage regressions could not be performed.)

The reason for using *all* exogenous and predetermined variables in the first stage is to have only one instrumental variable for each right-hand-side endogenous variable. In the example of disconnections, there are seven potential instrumental variables based on the possible combinations of price, income, and unemployment. The simplest procedure for deciding which one to use is to include all exogenous variables, letting the regression procedure determine the weights to be applied to each exogenous variable. If a particular exogenous variable has no relationship with disconnections, its coefficient will be very low and no harm will be done. The first-stage equation is only used to create instrumental variables, to solve the simultaneity problem. This equation is not used for forecasting. Therefore, primary interest lies in having a very *high R-squared value,* so that the instrumental variable is very much like the dependent variable.

The instrumental variable is a function of exogenous variables. Since the variables are exogenous, each is independent of the error term in a connection or disconnection model. Moreover, a linear combination of exogenous variables is also independent of the error series.

In the second stage of the 2SLS procedure, each equation is estimated by OLS. However, the instrumental variables created from the first stage replace the right-hand-side endogenous variables in the appropriate equations: therefore, it can be seen that the 2SLS procedure incorporates two stages of OLS estimation; the first stage involves the estimation of instrumental variables for each *right-hand-side endogenous variable;* the second stage is the estimation of the parameter values for each equation in which any right-hand-side endogenous variables have been replaced by their first-stage predictions.

If an instrumental variable from the first stage is not highly correlated with an endogenous variable, some other exogenous series will have to be found—if one believes that the problem of error correlation is severe.

The following requirements must be met in order to use the 2SLS methodology:

- There must be an equation for each endogenous variable.

- There must be at least as many exogenous and/or predetermined variables as there are endogenous variables, or there must be a greater number of the former.

- In *any* equation containing right-hand-side endogenous variables, there must be *at least as many exogenous* (and/or predetermined) variables in the *system of equations* that are *not included in that equation* as there are right-hand-side endogenous variables that *are included.*

To illustrate the reason for the last restriction, a simplified example should suffice. Consider again the connections-disconnections model, as follows:

$$\text{Connections}_t = \alpha_0 + \alpha_1(\text{Disconnections})_t + \alpha_2(\text{Price})_t + \varepsilon_t,$$

and

$$\text{Disconnections}_t = \beta_0 + \beta_1(\text{Connections})_t + \beta_2(\text{Price})_t + \nu_t.$$

In this model, the third requirement would mean that, for the connections equation, there must be at least one exogenous/predetermined variable in the system that is not also in the connections equation. Since "price" is common to both equations, this requirement is not met for either the connections or disconnections equation.

The first stage of the 2SLS process for this model involves a regression of disconnections on price, and then a second regression—of connections on price. In the second stage, the connections equation would look as follows:

$$\text{Connections}_t = \alpha_0 + \alpha_1(\text{Disconnections})_t{}^* + \alpha_2(\text{Price})_t + \varepsilon_t .$$

But

$$\text{Disconnections}_t{}^* = \hat{\delta}_1 + \hat{\delta}_2(\text{Price})_t$$

from the first stage of 2SLS. Therefore,

$$\text{Connections}_t = \alpha_0 + \alpha_1(\hat{\delta}_1 + \hat{\delta}_2\, \text{Price}_t) + \alpha_2(\text{Price})_t + \varepsilon_t .$$

The same variable cannot appear twice on the right-hand side of any equation. Nor can a linear combination of right-hand-side variables appear as an additional independent variable. This is what was described earlier as a problem of identification in econometrics, and it suggests an incorrectly specified model (Fisher, 1966).

In summary, it is possible for an independent variable to be correlated with the errors in an equation. This correlation has the effect of *overstating* the contribution of the independent variable and *understating* the variance of the errors when OLS procedures are used. The 2SLS methodology is an appropriate estimation method when faced with this problem for relatively small models. To establish the need for a simultaneous-equations solution, you can try both OLS and 2SLS estimation and compare the parameter estimates. If the estimates are essentially the same, you should use the simpler OLS estimation. If the parameter estimates differ significantly and the *instrumental variables are good,* use of the 2SLS estimation procedures is recommended.

ECONOMETRICS AND FORECASTING

Many econometric systems are often used for forecasting purposes. A variety of commercial timesharing vendors and academic institutions provide the business community with a plethora of economic forecasts from sophisticated, computerized econometric systems. These forecasts are an important asset to the decision maker in a rapidly changing economic environment.

While there is a widespread use of forecasts from econometric systems, there does not appear to be a universal acceptance that econometric systems produce consistently reliable and accurate forecasts. (See, for example, Armstrong, 1978; Granger and Newbold, 1977, Section 8.4.) There are often simpler approaches yielding more accurate projections. However, the role of econometrics in forecasting is to provide an economic rationale for the process along with a mechanism for projecting numerical "forecasts."

RELATIONSHIP OF ECONOMETRIC MODELS TO ARIMA TIME SERIES MODELS

There is sufficient literature to suggest that simpler, more parsimonious representations often possess better extrapolative properties than do large econometric systems. While the ARIMA time series models are based purely on historical patterns, they often provide less costly and more accurate forecasts. Thus forecasters must be aware of the pitfalls and advantages of any quantitative forecasting method before applying it in practice. It is often desirable, however, to use both econometric and time series approaches in a forecasting system. The predictions of each can often be subjectively combined into a useful and dependable forecast.

It is shown in Granger and Newbold (1977) that traditional econometric and modern time series (ARIMA) models are closely related. Both approaches can be interpreted as a system in which a number of inputs are entered into a "black box" that transfers the values to an output. When expressed in mathematical terms, the "black box" is a linear system that derives its name from systems engineering. The manner in which the parameters describing the system are estimated and interpreted represents the key difference between the two methodologies.

ECONOMETRIC SYSTEMS CHECKLIST

_____ (1) Are any "independent" variables determined jointly or simultaneously with the dependent variable?

_____ If the answer to 1 is yes, can OLS be applied to the reduced-form equations?

_____ If the answer to 1 is yes, can the equations be arranged so that they can be estimated sequentially or recursively?

_____ If the answer to 1 is yes, has a 2SLS solution been tried? How do the parameter estimates for right-hand-side endogenous variables compare for OLS versus 2SLS? Is a 2SLS solution warranted?

_____ If a 2SLS solution was attempted, are the first-stage instrumental variables adequate (how high is the R-squared value for each instrument)?

_____ If a 2SLS solution was attempted, is there an equation for each endogenous variable?

_____ For 2SLS, are there at least as many exogenous and/or predetermined variables as there are endogenous variables in the system of equations, or more?

_____ For 2SLS, in each equation containing right-hand-side endogenous variables, are there at least as many exogenous or predetermined variables in the system of equations that are not included in that equation as there are right-hand-side endogenous variables that are included in that equation?

SUMMARY

The description of economic behavior with systems of mathematical equations

- Has prompted forecasters to take considerable interest in the field of econometrics.
- Has led to the extensive use of econometric systems in forecasting and planning models.
- Has contributed to the study of how alternative economic assumptions affect policy making.

When confronted with econometric systems, the forecaster/analyst has several possible alternatives:

- Use OLS on reduced-form equations.
- Use OLS for recursive systems.
- Use 2SLS (or other specialized techniques) for estimating the structural equations of simultaneous-equations systems.

Since the forecaster is usually less concerned with the implications of the parameters of structural equations and more concerned with accurate forecasts, reduced-form equations may be perfectly satisfactory. Econometricians, in their policy recommendation role, are generally more concerned with what the structural equations imply. They are more likely to pursue 2SLS and other simultaneous-equation estimation methods even when reduced-form equations can be estimated.

The following Chapter is concerned with the steps for performing demand analysis studies.

USEFUL READING

ARMSTRONG, J. S. (1978). Forecasting with Econometric Methods; Folklore versus Fact. *Journal of Business* 51, 549–64.

FISHER, F. M. (1966). *The Identification Problem*. New York, NY: McGraw-Hill.

GRANGER, C. W. J., and P. NEWBOLD (1977). *Forecasting Economic Time Series*. New York, NY: Academic Press.

JOHNSTON, J. (1972). *Econometric Methods*. 2nd ed. New York, NY: McGraw-Hill.

PHLIPS, L. (1974). *Applied Consumption Analysis*. New York, NY: American Elsevier Publishing Co.

PINDYCK, R. S., and D. L. RUBINFELD (1976). *Econometric Models and Economic Forecasts*. New York, NY: McGraw-Hill.

WONNACOTT, R. J., and T. H. WONNACOTT (1979). *Econometrics,* 2nd edition. New York, NY: John Wiley and Sons.

CHAPTER 16

The Demand Analysis Process

This chapter presents a seven-step procedure for estimating elasticities in the demand analysis process. These steps are:

- Defining measures of demand.
- Identifying determinants of demand.
- Collecting data.
- Estimating model coefficients.
- Generating demand response functions.
- Producing forecasts.
- Tracking results.

DEMAND ANALYSIS AS A PROCESS

Historical demand data must be analyzed during periods when the causal factors have changed. For instance, to develop a demand model that assesses the impact a price change has had on demand for a product, the historical data must be analyzed during periods when the price has changed. Assuming that such data are available, the resulting model can be used to generate the price-demand curve that existed *during the historical or past period being analyzed*. If one assumes that the historical market structure will remain relatively stable into the future, it is reasonable to use this curve to estimate how demand will respond to *future* price changes.

If this assumption is unrealistic, the demand response predicted by the model should be modified by using testimonial data (i.e., surveys of consumers and/or market experts) and the judgment of the product/service manager about future demand or price. However, if historical price–demand data exist, a demand curve based on a model of these data is a useful starting point for estimating future price–demand relationships, regardless of the judgmental refinements that may later be required.

Demand analysis for a particular product or service can be divided into seven sequential steps. Each step includes a unique part of the analysis; however, execution of the steps is often an iterative process. A close correspondence between the demand analysis process and the general forecasting process should be noted (see the Flowchart).

Defining Measures of Demand

1. *Define one or more appropriate measures of demand.*

The most common measures for telephone *product* demand, for example, are in-service quantities and what is known as inward movement (i.e., sales). However, there is increasing need to model the total market size and the relative portion served by a particular product line. The most common measure of telephone *service* demand is usage. Examples would be total messages and the average length of a message. Quite often a useful surrogate for the demand for a group of products or services is its associated revenue divided by an appropriate price index. This ratio is an equivalent unit of demand that incorporates all of the internal cross-elasticities within a particular product line (e.g., PBX equipment) or a major service category (e.g., Message Toll Service).

Identifying Determinants of Demand

2. *Use economic theory and marketing knowledge to identify the most likely determinants of demand.*

Economists have long attempted to determine what causes people to behave as they do in the marketplace. Over the years, one aspect of this research has evolved into a theory of demand (Samuelson, 1978). *Demand* expresses the inverse relationship between price and quantity; it shows the maximum amount of money consumers are willing and able to pay for each additional unit of some commodity, or the maximum amount of the commodity they are willing and able to purchase at a given price. There may not be enough of the commodity available to satisfy the demand. Economists concern themselves not with a *single* item purchased by members of a group (a market) but rather with a *continuous flow* of purchases by that group. Therefore, demand is expressed in terms of the *amount desired* per day, per month, or per year.

There are a number of *determinants of demand*. Demand varies with tastes, total market size, average income, the distribution of income, the price of the good or service, and the prices of competing and complementary goods.

Some changes in taste are passing fads, such as the demand for hula hoops; others are more permanent, such as the demand for private automobiles rather than public transportation. Advertising is quite often intended to bring about a change in tastes. But whatever the causes, whenever tastes change, the demand for some goods increases, and the demand for others decreases.

Market Size

If a specific forecasting problem suggests that the size of the market should be modeled, suitable factors are population and the number of households.

All other things being equal, one would expect the demand for a good to increase in proportion to the growth in the total population or certain age groups within the population. Of course, these people must have the ability to pay for the good.

Income

The demand for a good generally increases as real income increases. When people are poor, food, clothing, and shelter account for most of their expenditures. As households become wealthier, more income is left over to be spent for additional items, such as durables (appliances and furnishings), housing improvements, and services. Also, it is important to consider real or constant dollar income when considering income as a determinant of demand. If inflation eats up all the increases in current dollar income, the household is no better off than it was before; there is no additional money available to purchase nonbasic goods or services.

Distribution of Income

Average household income may or may not be a very good measure of wealth, depending on the distribution of income. For example, in some population areas there are few rich people and many poor people; consequently one must consider the distribution of income as well as its average value when determining demand for an item.

Price

The Law of Demand states that demand for a good declines as the price of the good increases. Goods and services are desired to satisfy wants and needs, however, and since there are often alternative or competing goods available, a rise in the price of one good will cause some people to substitute other goods or services.

Goods or services can be considered as complementary or competitive commodities. *Complementary commodities* are used together to achieve a result. An increase in the price of one good will result in a decrease in the demand for its complement. For example, gasoline and automobiles are complementary. When the price of gasoline increased significantly, the demand for automobiles tended to decline—especially the demand for less fuel-efficient models.

There are also many goods or services that are *competing* to satisfy the same needs or desires. Consequently, a decrease in the price of one of these goods will cause a decrease in demand for its competitor.

The most important step in this stage is to develop a theoretically sound but not too restrictive framework, consistent with the data obtainable for analysis. In many cases, economic theory is inadequate or incomplete, thus complicating the specification problem.

Many aspects of this step are unique to each model; however, it is often useful to begin by partitioning the determinants of demand into controllable and noncontrollable groups. The determinants that are under management control are called decision variables or *marketing instruments* and include price, advertising, promotional campaigns, sales effort, distribution techniques, and so on.

The only marketing instrument whose influence on demand is strongly supported by economic theory is price. The *Law of Demand* states that an inverse relationship between demand and price will exist. However, the other marketing instruments, especially advertising and sales efforts, can logically be expected to influence demand in a positive way.

In most cases, the number of marketing instruments to be considered are severely limited by a lack of data. The prices of the product being modeled and potential cross-elastic product prices are the most common instruments for which historical data are available. However, with some work, reasonable historical indicators of advertising and sales efforts can occasionally be obtained.

If one or more of the marketing instruments did not change in value during the historical period, they can be immediately dropped from consideration. Although these instruments may be important determinants of demand, their influence cannot be measured through demand modeling if they did not change in value.

Once the marketing instruments have been identified, it is necessary to identify the noncontrollable determinants of demand. These determinants are called *environmental variables* and will usually determine the total market size and its fundamental growth rate. Quite often, one or two environmental variables can adequately explain most of the fundamental market movement. A few possible environmental variables are personal income, a business activity index, an unemployment rate, number of business establishments, and population. Some important but often unavailable environmental variables are competitive sales activity and prices. However, a surrogate for these influences can sometimes be developed.

As a start, you should include the most important four or five variables explicitly, listing other potentially useful variables for later consideration. Starting with a few variables avoids getting embroiled in serious statistical problems early in the analysis and allows for maximum flexibility of interpretation.

Collecting Data

3. *Collect historical data on demand and its likely determinants.*

Once the potential determinants of demand have been identified, you proceed to the data collection phase. Measurement always involves data, so you must be aware of data availability and limitations. The data can be collected in two basic formats. One is the time series format, in which demand quantities for a particular product/service in a particular geographical area are obtained for several successive periods of time (e.g., past months, quarters, or years). The other is the cross-sectional format, in which demand quantities for several similar products/services or a single product/service in several geographical areas are obtained for one historical period.

These formats can be combined when the primary objective is to estimate *average* response functions (e.g., price–demand curves) across all cross sections. The combined format is called a "pooled" data base and can sometimes yield more accurate estimates of a response curve than either of the separate formats can. However, if the demand model is to be used to make forecasts over time in the various cross sections (e.g., cities, states), it is usually best to develop separate demand models each of which uses a separate time series data base for each cross section. If the model is needed for an *aggregate* forecast over all cross sections, a time series data base aggregated over all cross sections will often be appropriate.

Since it is not always clear in advance which type of data will produce the best model, the data gathered for a demand analysis should have both times series and cross-sectional dimensions, and it should be easy to aggregate the data across either dimension.

Estimating Model Coefficients

4. *Use statistical estimation procedures to identify and validate the most likely structure for the demand model.*

After data collection has been completed, you must specify plausible ways in which the potential determinants of demand can be analytically related to demand. For instance, one plausible relationship might be to express the *level* of demand as a linear combination of relative price, or a business activity index, or the number of business establishments demanding some product, and variables that account for seasonal and/or exceptional influences.

Another plausible relationship might be to transform all variables (logarithmically) so that the percent changes in demand are expressed as a linear combination of the percent changes in the determinants. In general, each plausible model should contain measures of relative price, relative ability to purchase, and potential market size.

In addition, cross-elastic prices, advertising expenditures, sales effort measurements, and indicators of seasonal variation or variation owing to special events should be considered. Also, analytic structures that allow for dynamic (lagged variable) relationships (i.e., short-run versus long-run responses) should be considered (see, for example, Parsons and Schultz, 1976; Phlips, 1974; Pindyck and Rubinfeld, 1976).

Demand theory appears to give little guidance as to model form, other than to indicate the imposed constraints that lead to easily interpreted coefficients. An *additive* demand model would imply that the elasticities are *changing*. On the other hand, *constant* elasticities are implicit in a *multiplicative* or *log-linear* demand model.

In theory, signs of parameter values can be assigned that are based on the nature of the product or service. There is, however, little theoretical information that will help to establish the magnitude of the coefficients. In practice, empirical studies may verify the signs and relative sizes of the coefficients. Such studies must of course be based on detailed knowledge of the product or the services as well as clear understanding of the underlying market conditions.

The end result of the estimation and validation step is the selection of a statistically and economically sound demand model that most reasonably explains the historical patterns of demand. This final model is generally a single equation that expresses demand as a function of its determinants and their respective elasticity coefficients.

In practice, it is sometimes possible to select a model simply on the basis that it has been used for some closely related empirical study. Other times the selection may be based on implicit assumptions about elasticities. An analyst always looks for evidence that certain model forms are more defensible than others, however.

Alternatively, you may decide to take an orthodox approach and reject the data rather than the theoretically specified model. A preferable alternative would be to modify the theoretically specified model in accordance with the evidence displayed by the data.

Each potential model structure will constitute a hypothesis of market behavior. Each hypothesis can then be accepted or rejected after standard statistical tests have been made. This process is not as open ended as it may appear, since only a small number of logical model structures will apply in any particular situation.

To test alternative models, the response parameters (e.g., elasticities) in each model must be computed from the historical data by using statistical estimation procedures. The most common procedure is multiple regression analysis. It can produce accurate estimates of the response parameters, and provides a variety of statistical measures useful in comparing alternative models.

Generating Demand Response Functions

5. *Use the demand model to generate price–demand and other demand response relationships.*

The demand curves and related elasticity coefficients of the marketing instruments can often be computed directly from the model structure. However, in some cases, the demand curves can only be determined by inserting simulated values of the marketing instruments into the model and observing the resulting demand response.

In many cases these procedures will be limited to the generation of price–demand and environmental variable response functions. However, as historical data for other marketing instruments become available, their response curves can also be incorporated into the demand model.

Producing Forecasts

6. *Use the demand model to generate conditional demand forecasts.*

To forecast with a demand model, you must obtain reliable forecasts of the determinants of demand and enter these forecasts into the demand model. The model will then generate a *conditional* demand forecast. That is, it will produce a demand forecast that depends on the accuracy with which the determinants of demand are forecast.

The demand model therefore translates the problem of forecasting demand to the problem of forecasting the determinants of demand. Although this may appear to be a questionable tradeoff, it often turns out to be very sensible. Some governmental and private organizations specialize in developing reliable forecasts of the environmental variables included in typical demand models, so accurate data for these variables can be obtained without difficulty. Also, product/service managers should be able to forecast the future values of their marketing instruments with reasonable accuracy, so they are also a potential source of reliable data. Indeed, a strength of demand models is that they provide a *systematic* way to combine the best available information on future product/service demand.

The inherent strength of the conditional demand forecast is its ability to quantify all the assumptions in a demand forecast rigorously. The response assumptions (i.e., elasticity coefficients) are an integral and readily identifiable part of the model structure. The input assumptions are simply the values selected for the forecasted determinants of demand. Thus if the demand forecast does not materialize, the reasons for this can often be isolated and explained with a minimum of supplementary analysis.

The forecast provided by the demand model will often *not* be the final forecast. Purely judgmental adjustments may need to be made: this is most common when *new* products/services are introduced, which are expected to be cross elastic with the forecast of demand. In this case, the original demand model forecasts can serve as a basis to track and measure the accuracy of the judgmental estimates of cross-elastic response.

Tracking Results

7. Track model forecasts and actual product/service demand and use the differences between them to guide future refinements of the model and make preliminary elasticity estimates of new marketing instruments.

This last step in the demand analysis process is one of the most critical. A demand model is not a "one-time shot." Although it is a valid representation of past and current market structures, it may have diminishing validity in the future. By regularly comparing the model forecast against actual demand quantities, you can use the pattern of differences to determine when the model structure needs modification.

Equally important is the use of the differences between a forecast and an actual outcome to make preliminary estimates of the elasticity coefficients of new marketing instruments. In many cases, the demand model will not contain any information about a particular marketing instrument. However, if the value of that marketing instrument changes in the future, the simultaneous change between what has been predicted and actual performance can often be used to estimate the elasticity coefficient of the responsible instrument. Preliminary estimates of self and cross elasticities of a price change can be made through this "tracking" procedure.

The execution of these seven steps is fairly straightforward for a trained analyst. However, the development of a valid model requires a large amount of creativity and a reasonable amount of time. Once the data are collected, an experienced analyst should be able to construct and document a valid model in a reasonably short time. However, take into account the iterative nature of certain steps, especially those pertaining to the collecting of data and testing of alternative model structures, since these may require additional time.

SPECIAL PROBLEMS TO WATCH OUT FOR

It has been noted that a problem with measuring the demand curve (quantity versus price) is that all the determinants of demand and supply will always be changing. If there are enough sufficiently varying data, regression methods can assist in measuring the demand curve.

Regression done with ordinary least squares (OLS) works best when there is no correlation among the independent variables. If the independent variables are correlated, the coefficient estimates produced by OLS analysis may not be valid. In practice, all independent variables have some correlation and one problem is to determine whether the correlations among independent variables are sufficiently strong to invalidate the regression results. Regression analysis therefore does have limitations, especially when *multicollinearity* exists among independent variables.

When multicollinearity exists, in effect, the OLS procedure cannot be used to determine which of the independent variables "explains" the variation in the dependent variable. As a result of multicollinearity it is possible to have a significant F statistic for the overall regression and yet to find that none of the coefficients of the individual independent variables are significant. Also, the signs of the coefficients may disagree with what theory indicates should be the way the market should function. For example, the model may suggest that quantity demanded increases as price increases, or decreases as income increases. One may not believe this to be true. Collinearity problems will be treated again in the case study in the next chapter and in Chapter 19.

Other problems to consider are *specification errors,* such as the omission of relevant variables, the inclusion of inappropriate functional forms, and the inclusion of irrelevant variables. All these point to the importance of starting first with simple (parsimonious) specifications, so that potential and existing modeling problems can be understood thoroughly and handled appropriately.

There are other statistical questions that need to be considered for demand models. The significance of an included variable can be assessed by testing whether an estimated parameter for such a variable is significantly different from zero. The model should have overall significance as well, and no excluded variables should be able to make a significant change in the model when they are tested. A careful residual analysis should always be made to verify the validity of underlying assumptions about data distribution.

A CROSS-SECTIONAL DEMAND MODEL FOR RESIDENTIAL EXTENSION TELEPHONES

The following example illustrates the demand analysis and forecasting process. An analysis was performed to help identify the potential for increased sales of extension telephones within residences in 470 geographic areas. A requirement was that the model should incorporate local economic and demographic data in a formulation understandable and acceptable to local sales personnel responsible for stimulating demand. Areas with below-average development, as predicted by the model, would be candidates for future sales campaigns.

Variable Selection

After experimentation with a variety of possible independent variables, on theoretical and statistical considerations several were ultimately selected. Median family income, adjusted for cost-of-living differences among the geographic areas, was an obvious candidate. Of the total work force in each area, the percent engaged in white-collar employment was selected, since these employees are generally intensive users of telephones on the job, and tend to take their telephone habits home with them. Of all households, the percent in which more than one automobile was owned was selected as an indicator of the propensity to consume rather than to save income. A number of other variables could also have served this purpose.

The Model-Building Process

As a first step in building a model, a plotting was made of the percent of residential extension telephones (residential extensions per hundred main residential telephones) by area. It showed a lack of symmetry in areal distribution, particularly so where percentages of extension telephones were high.

Scatter diagrams were next plotted to investigate relationships between the dependent and independent variables. In Chapter 12, we noted that, in a multiple linear regression model, inclusion of partial residuals plots may be helpful, since they show the relationship between the dependent variable and each independent variable, given that all the variables have been entered into the model.

A regression model containing the three independent variables and the partial residual plots was examined. The partial residual plots associated with income, employment, and automobiles are shown in Figures 16.1, 16.2, and 16.3, respectively. In Figure 16.1 most of the points are concentrated in the $10,000–$18,000 range, with a relatively small number of high-leverage points above $20,000. Figures 16.2 and 16.3 show a more uniform distribution. In all three plots the relationships appear to be positive and linear.

Diagnostic checks for constancy of variance and normality in the residuals were next made, and these completed the residual analysis. Figure 16.4 compares residuals against the values that were predicted in the model described above, and Figure 16.5 shows the normal Q-Q plot of the residuals of this model; Figure 16.4 reveals an apparent problem of increasing residual variance, and most of the residuals associated with development above 85 percent are positive; the normal Q-Q plot in Figure 16.5 shows that the high positive residuals form a longer tail than is present in the normal curve.

In most cases, you could stop at this point, since the departures from the assumptions of the model are not too severe. However, it was decided to go further to see if a more constant residual variance as well as a more linear Q-Q plot (one closer to normality) could be obtained, and if a better partial residual plot against income could be obtained by transforming the variables. For example, a transformation of the dependent variable might improve the Q-Q plot.

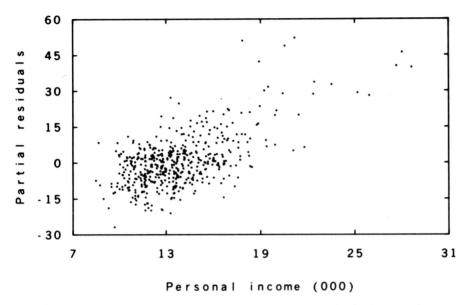

Figure 16.1 A plot of partial residuals against the income variable, for the extension telephone case-study.

Figure 16.2 A plot of partial residuals against the employment variable.

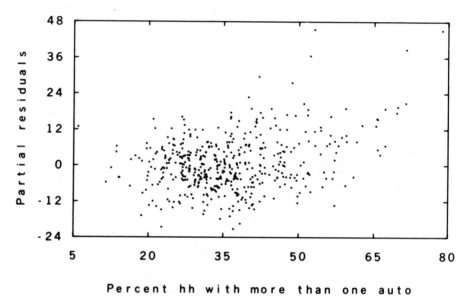

Figure 16.3   A plot of partial residuals against the automobile-ownership variable.

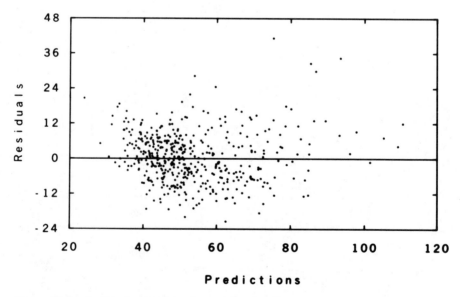

Figure 16.4   A plot of residuals against predicted values.

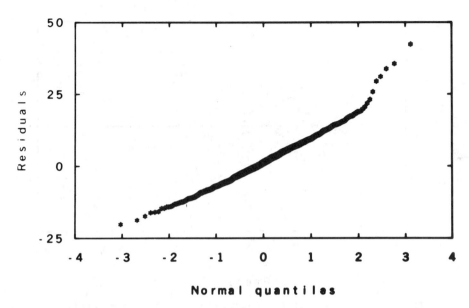

Figure 16.5   A normal Q-Q plot of the residuals.

Figure 16.6 shows a plot of the residuals against predictions for the model after a *logarithmic transformation* of the percentage development was taken. In this case, an obvious pattern of decreasing variance resulted, leading us to conclude that the logarithmic transformation is inappropriate.

Figure 16.7 shows a plot of the residuals aginst predictions for an alternative model in which a *square root transformation* has been applied to the dependent variable and a *logarithmic transformation* has been applied to the income variable. This is a two-step operation, the results of which are combined in the figure for convenience. (The logarithmic transformation was taken to obtain a linear relationship in the partial residual plot between the two time series.) Recall that the square root transformation is often helpful with data involving counts or percents. This plot is similar to Figure 16.4 but is an improvement, since Figure 16.7 shows a more uniform residual variance over the range of predictions. Also, the residuals are not as concentrated as the low end of the percent-of-development scale.

Figure 16.8 shows the Q-Q plot of the residuals of both models against the normal curve. A more linear pattern, and therefore a more normal pattern, exists. Figures 16.9, 16.10, and 16.11 show the partial residuals against (respectively) the logarithms of income, the percent of employment that is white-collar, and the percent of households with more than one automobile. Figure 16.9 is an improvement over Figure 16.1, since there are fewer high-leverage points far away from the bulk of the data. Figures 16.10 and 16.11 are slight improvements over 16.2 and 16.3, in that they appear to have a higher slope (and therefore a higher correlation) and fewer outliers. The refined model is an improvment over the original model.

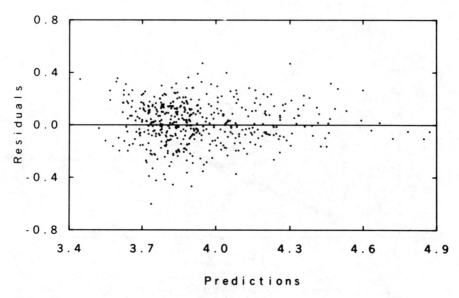

Figure 16.6 A plot of residuals against predictions after taking logarithms of the dependent variable.

In the early stages of development of the model for this case study, an analyst failed to notice that of the 473 geographical areas being examined, there were three areas for which no values (observations) were given in the dependent variable, yet there were values in the independent variables for these areas. The computer set the values for the missing observations equal to zero, by default. Later, a plot of residuals against the predictions offered by the final model (in which zeroes appeared as observed values for the three areas) demonstrated that the three residuals were in fact so large that they dominated all others and had the effect of lowering the R-squared statistic from 0.69 to 0.43. The analyst then made a Q-Q plot of the residuals against the normal curve, and it also made the appearance of the three outliers quite striking.

A Robust Alternative

Robust regression would offer some protection against outliers such as those just described, as is illustrated in Table 16.1. The left-hand part of the table shows that ordinary least squares (OLS) and robust regression analyses yield almost identical results, with no extreme values and approximately normal residuals. Comparison of the left-hand and right-hand sides show that the OLS results were distorted by the outliers, while the robust results were not. Recall that only three of the 473 observations were extreme, yet these three altered the income coefficient and the constant term significantly. This example should suggest to you that a difference between OLS and robust regression coefficients of approximately one standard deviation is cause to review the OLS model and the original data in much greater detail.

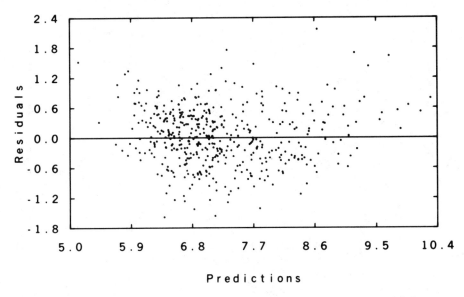

Figure 16.7   A plot of residuals against predictions after taking square roots of the dependent variable and logarithms of the income variable.

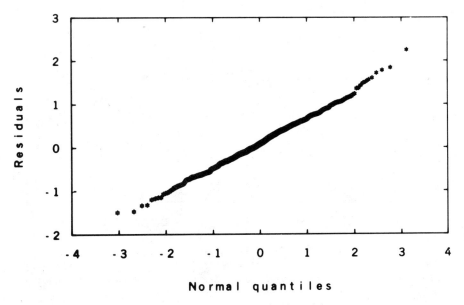

Figure 16.8   A Q-Q plot of the residuals for the refined model.

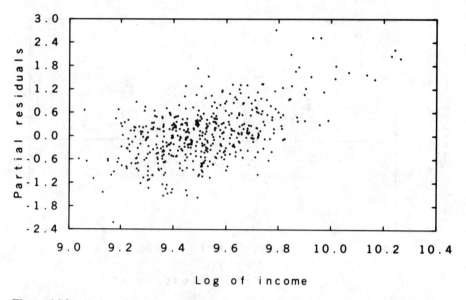

Figure 16.9 A plot of partial residuals against logarithms of the income variable for the refined model.

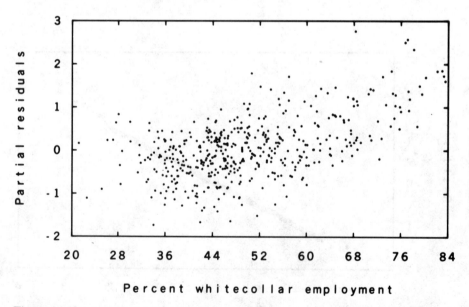

Figure 16.10 A plot of partial residuals against employment variable for the refined model.

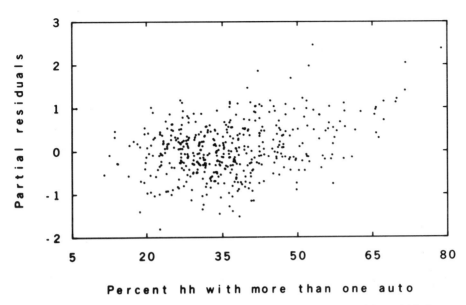

Figure 16.11   A plot of partial residuals against the automobile-ownership variable for the refined model.

One reason why demand analysis is often not used effectively is simply that data are inadequate. Historical data are needed to measure market responses to any decision a company's management makes. If these data have not been collected and maintained in a systematic manner, only a very limited form of demand analysis can be done. Because systematic collection of data is often not done, it is often difficult to obtain detailed historical data on individual product lines; then much effort has to be expended to obtain accurate data on a disaggregated basis.

SUMMARY

Demand analysis

- Is one of the most comprehensive methods for understanding and measuring the factors that influence demand.
- Is a widely used technique for developing estimates of historical price–demand relationships.
- Is sometimes called demand modeling since it produces a mathematical model that explains demand in terms of its causal factors.

Table 16.1 A comparison of OLS and robust regression results for the final model with and without the outliers.

Variable	No extreme outliers OLS		Robust	Three extreme outliers OLS		Robust
	Coefficient	Estimated standard deviation	Coefficient	Coefficient	Estimated standard deviation	Coefficient
Interest	−13.328	2.2627	−13.366	−9.6892	3.467	−13.366
Income	1.9275	0.2561	1.944	1.5500	0.392	1.944
White-collar employment	0.0319	0.0035	0.0308	0.0300	0.0057	0.0308
Households with more than one auto	0.0173	0.0037	0.0154	0.0171	0.0054	0.0155

▪ Is one important area where the anaytical methods discussed so far can be applied. Linear and log-linear regression methods are the primary statistical tools used to quantify relationships postulated by the theory of demand treated in this chapter.

A primary reason for building a demand model is that it enables you to interpret key regression coefficients. The forecasts produced from these models are of secondary significance; although good forecasting properties are a valuable attribute of any model. However, the inability of a demand model to produce reasonably accurate forecasts may reduce its overall credibility.

Some of the most important topics in demand modeling are:

▪ The data should be adjusted for outliers such as might result from unforeseen events (e.g., strikes) or missing observations.

▪ Replacement values for outliers should be estimated whenever possible.

▪ Relationships between the dependent and independent variables should be examined by means of scatter plots and partial residual plots.

▪ Transformations may be necessary to establish linear relationships between variables or to correct for increasing variability in the residuals of the model.

▪ It is important to use residual plots as a means of checking modeling assumptions.

USEFUL READING

BELSLEY, D. A., E. KUH, and R. E. WELSCH (1980). *Regression Diagnostics: Identifying Influential Data and Sources of Collinearity.* New York, NY: John Wiley and Sons.

DRAPER, N. R., and SMITH, H. (1981). *Applied Regression Analysis.* 2nd ed. New York, NY: John Wiley and Sons.

PARSONS, L. J., and R. SCHULTZ (1976). *Marketing Models and Econometric Research.* New York, NY: North-Holland Publishing Co.

PHLIPS, I. (1974). *Applied Consumption Analysis.* New York, NY: American Elsevier Publishing Co.

PINDYCK, R. S., and D. L. RUBINFELD (1976). *Econometric Models and Economic Forecasts.* New York, NY: McGraw-Hill.

SAMUELSON, P. (1978). *Economics,* 9th ed. New York, NY: McGraw-Hill.

CHAPTER 17

Estimating Demand Elasticities

Two important determinants of a firm's profitability—indeed its survival—are cost and the demand for its products or services. Demand must exist or be created if the firm is to survive. It must also be high enough at least to cover fixed costs. Because of its key role, all corporate planning activities require a careful analysis of demand over time.

Forecasters are also concerned with the relationship between quantity demanded and price and can play an important role in helping their firms make pricing decisions by estimating price elasticities for products and services with their models.

This chapter addresses:

- The definition of demand and supply curves.
- The definition of elasticity.
- Arc versus point elasticity.
- What determines price elasticity.
- Estimating elasticity with regression models.
- Constant elasticity models.
- Short- versus long-term price elasticity.

THE DEMAND CURVE

All of the determinants of demand referred to in Chapter 16 are acting simultaneously to establish the demand for a product. Because of this simultaneity, it is not possible to develop a simple theory of demand if all the variables are allowed to change at once.

To circumvent simultaneity, one can use a technique employed in all scientific research: assume that all but one of the determinants of demand are held constant. It is then possible to measure the effect of one independent variable, such as price, with all others held constant. A different determinant, such as income, can then be made to vary, and changes in the quantity of the product for which there is demand can be measured. This is simple in theory, but in the real world it is not possible to hold other determinants constant. Empirical verification of demand must take this into account.

The demand for a product will increase as the price of the product decreases, all other determinants held constant. As price falls, a product becomes cheaper relative to its substitutes, and thus it becomes easier for the product to compete for the consumer's dollar. The relationship, known as the *demand curve,* is plotted in Figure 17.1.

Movement along the Curve

When the quantity of a demanded product changes because of a change in price, this is referred to as *movement along the demand curve.*

When the entire curve shifts to the right or left because of a change of something other than price, it is referred to as a *shift in the demand curve.* The solid line in

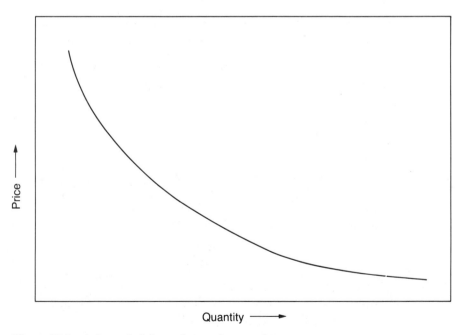

Figure 17.1   A theoretical demand curve for a product.

Figure 17.2 shows the original demand curve of Figure 17.1. A shift to the right, as shown by the dotted line, could result from an increase in income to a higher level, I_1. The curve could also shift as a result of an increase in the price of a competitive product, a favorable change in tastes, an increase in population, and a change in the distribution of income, for example.

Some groups of consumers, having certain product preferences, will be able to buy more of a product if their income increases as a result of an increase in government transfer payments or favorable changes in tax policy.

Demand theory recognizes that there are also certain goods that are considered to be less preferable by a consumer allocating an increased income. Examples of these goods are potatoes or frozen foods, which a consumer willingly substitutes with more expensive food, given the opportunity. An increase in income will result in a decrease in the quantity of these goods that is demanded.

Relationship to Supply

The demand curve is only one-half of the story. One must also be concerned with supply. Let us discuss briefly the notion of supply and its relationship to demand and price. Many of the forecasts from econometric models in the past several years

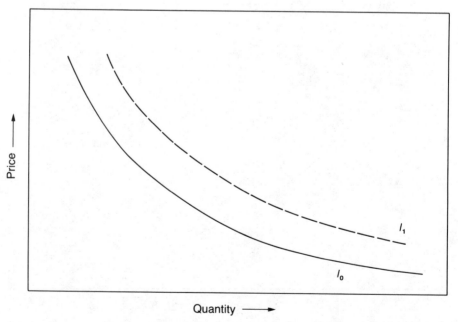

Figure 17.2   A shift in demand caused by a change other than price.

were incorrect because of a failure to correctly model the supply side of the equation and its impact on price.

Supply is the maximum amount of an item a producer or manufacturer is willing and able to sell (i.e., produce) at a given price, or it shows the minimum price a producer will accept to provide one additional unit of an item. It is stated in terms of quantity per unit of time (day, month, year).

The factors that impact supply include the goals of business firms, the state of technology, the price of a product, the prices of alternative products, and the costs of the factors of production.

It is rather obvious that the goal of a business firm is a critical consideration of supply. The objective of most companies is to maximize profits within certain constraints. However, some firms choose to market only products that result in high rates of return on invested capital, rather than to market a product for which there is a larger demand but a lower rate of return. Some firms do not want to take risks and have smaller production runs than could otherwise be achieved.

At any given time, what is produced and how it is produced is a function of the technology that currently exists. As knowledge expands, it often becomes possible to manufacture a product at costs that are substantially lower than in an earlier period. The invention of the transistor is a case in point. The mass production of the transistor and, later, large-scale integrated circuits made it possible to manufacture many electronic devices at substantially reduced costs. Electronic devices such as radios, calculators, and televisions now have a mass market instead of a select market because of technological changes and consequent lowered prices.

All other things being equal, the profitability of a higher-priced product exceeds that of a lower-priced product. In deciding what markets to enter, firms will seriously consider the price that they believe can be charged for the product. Production will be shifted to the highest-profit items to the extent feasible and these are often the higher-priced goods.

Changes in the factors of production also affect profitability. These factors include land, labor, and capital. A rise in the cost of one factor—say labor—may result in the lower profit for a product. The firm may choose to produce less of that product and shift to a different product that requires less labor per unit of output. Changes in the cost of one factor relative to others will also change the methods of production.

The relationship between the quantity of a good that is supplied and its price is referred to as the *supply curve*. An example of a supply curve is shown in Figure 17.3. The relationship is upward-trending. It is assumed that all determinants of supply other than the price of the good are held constant. The assumption that the supply curve is upward-sloping has a great deal of intuitive appeal. Generally, if a firm can obtain a higher price for its goods or services, it will be willing to supply more of these.

Movement along the supply curve means that the quantity a firm is willing to supply is measured by the price of the good or service. A shift in the supply curve means that, at any given price, the firm is willing to provide either more or less of

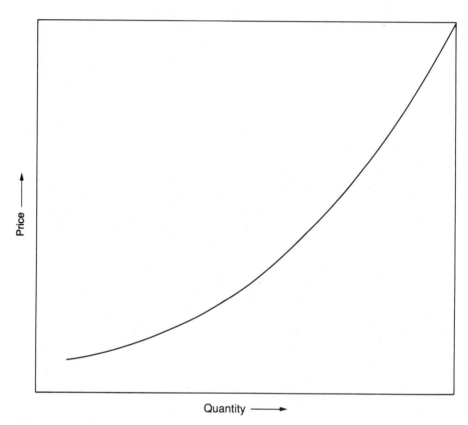

Figure 17.3 A theoretical supply curve.

the product. The shift is a result of a change in one or more of the determinants of supply other than the price of the product. For example, the curve for the product might shift to the left if the state of technology for that product is not advancing as rapidly as for another product. That is, it may be becoming more expensive to continue providing this product than to switch to another for which new technology has substantially reduced the costs of production.

Equilibrium Price

The market price for a product is determined by the *intersection* of the supply and demand curves. This can be seen in Figure 17.4. An illustrative example shows why this is the long-run equilibrium price. Suppose the quantity that is demanded as a function of time, Q_t^D, has the following relationship with price, P_t:

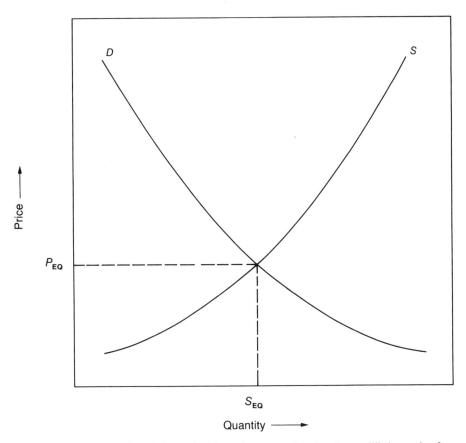

Figure 17.4 Intersection of demand and supply curves showing the equilibrium price for a product.

$$Q_t^D = 3.0 - P_t.$$

The quantity that is demanded at any time is given by a constant amount (3.0), less the current price. As price increases, the quantity demanded decreases.

Now, suppose the quantity that is supplied, as a function of time, has the equation

$$Q_t^S = 0.5 + 0.5P_{t-1}.$$

The quantity that is supplied at any time is given by a constant amount (0.5), plus one-half times last period's price. If last period's price went up, a firm will be willing to increase the quantity it supplies.

Further, assume there is no capability of storage or inventory and that all of the product that is supplied will be consumed in each period. This might be the case for an agricultural commodity, for example.

Assume that last period's price for an agricultural commodity was $1.33. The supply equation would then indicate that the quantity supplied next period would be 1.17 units. (Partial units are of no concern because the data could be in thousands of units.) The demand equation would indicate that at that level of supply ($Q^D = Q^S$), the price would be $1.83. The change in price is +$0.50. For several more iterations (periods), the change in price will alternate in sign and successively diminish to some arbitrarily small amount. At equilibrium, the price is $1.66, and equilibrium demand is 1.34 units.

Figure 17.5 shows the "cobweb" pattern that leads to an equilibrium price and quantity. Starting with an initial quantity of 1.17, the price will rise from $1.33 to $1.83 by progressing vertically up to the demand line. At that price, the quantity that is supplied in the next period will increase to 1.41 by progressing horizontally to the supply curve. With the quantity of supply at 1.41 units, the price must be dropped to $1.59 to sell all the product. The progression to the equilibrium price looks like a cobweb.

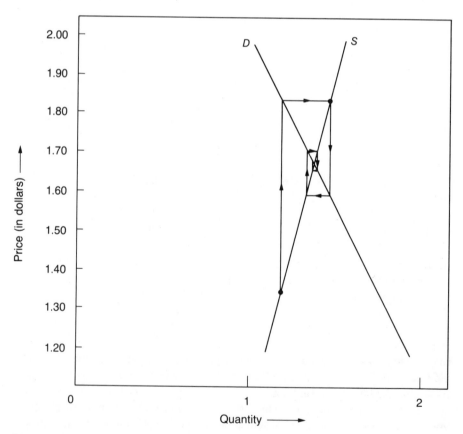

Figure 17.5   A cobweb pattern results from progression to an equilibrium price.

In many cases, the marketplace actually works this way. For agricultural products and cattle, the supply is generally fixed and must be sold. The price is based on available supply. Farmers and cattlemen do base their adjustments of future supplies on current prices. It may take a period of time, perhaps a year or two, before a new equilibrium price is established. In regulated industries, prices must be approved by governmental agencies after the presentation of a rate case. This means that prices tend to remain fixed for a relatively long time, and the quantity that is demanded of a good or service must change in response to the new price, to establish an equilibrium level.

In practice, there may be a market-period equilibrium (all inputs are fixed and consumers have no chance for adjustment), a short-run equilibrium (in which some adjustments are possible), and a long-run equilibrium (in which firms have had a chance to adjust all production factors and consumers have had a chance to change their consumption habits.)

PRICE ELASTICITY

The *demand function* describes the relationship between the quantity that is demanded of a good or service and all of the variables that determine demand. The *demand curve* is that part of the demand function that relates the price that is charged to the quantity that is demanded, *when all other variables are held constant*. While this curve is important, it fails to show how sensitive the quantity demanded is to price. The missing element is *elasticity,* and it explains the responsiveness of changes in demand to changes in prices or any of the other variables.

While the notion of elasticity can be used to interpret relationships between the dependent variable and any or all independent variables, primary attention is often given to price elasticity. *Price elasticity, E,* is defined as the percentage change in the quantity demanded, Q, as a result of a given percentage change in price, P:

$$E = \frac{\text{Percentage change in } Q}{\text{Percentage change in } P} = \frac{\Delta Q/Q}{\Delta P/P} .$$

An important condition in the definition of elasticity is that all factors influencing demand other than *own-price* (price of the item under consideration) are held constant while own-price is varied.

Consider message toll service, a telephone service, as an example. The price elasticity will be a negative number, since fewer messages Q will be placed at higher prices P, with all else held constant. Also note that it is a dimension-free number.

In Figure 17.6, consider the equilibrium position at the intersection of supply curve S_1 and the demand curve D at point E_1. If the supply curve is shifted up and to the left to S_2, the small price increase causes a substantial change in quantity

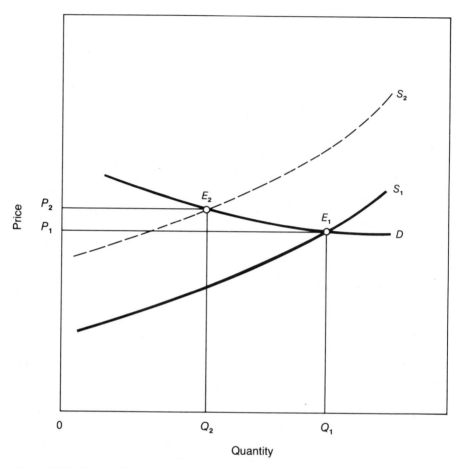

Figure 17.6   Intersecting supply and demand curves—the quantity demanded is *sensitive* to price changes.

demanded. In this case, demand is very sensitive to price. Figure 17.7 shows a different relationship between supply and demand. Again, equilibrium is reached at E_1, but when the supply curve moves from S_1 to S_2, the quantity that is demanded drops only a small amount from Q_1 to Q_2. (Of course, for these examples, the visual effect of a "large" or "small" amount would depend on the scaling that is chosen for the plots.) For actual applications, a quantitative measure of response is desired. A useful formula for actually measuring elasticity is the one that determines the *average elasticity* between points E_1 and E_2 on the demand curve:

$$E = \frac{\text{Change in } Q/\text{Average } Q}{\text{Change in } P/\text{Average } P} = \frac{\Delta Q / \tfrac{1}{2}(Q_1 + Q_2)}{\Delta P / \tfrac{1}{2}(P_1 + P_2)} = \frac{\Delta Q (P_1 + P_2)}{\Delta P (Q_1 + Q_2)}.$$

With this formula, the elasticity is the same whether the starting point is E_1 or E_2.

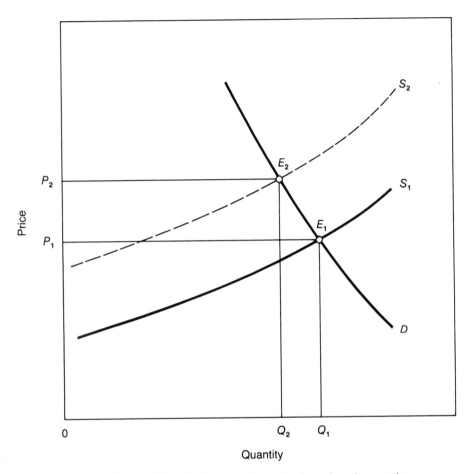

Figure 17.7 A different relationship between demand and supply—the quantity demanded is *insensitive* to price changes.

Arc Elasticity

Table 17.1 shows the data that go into the calculations of arc elasticity for three different hypothetical products. The elasticity for Product A equals the percent change in the quantity that is demanded (33 percent) divided by the percent change in price (-16.7 percent), or -2.0. For Products B and C, the elasticities are -1.0 and -0.5, respectively.

The demand for Product A is very responsive to price changes, since the elasticity exceeds unity in absolute value. This is referred to as an *elastic* product. Product B demonstrates *unitary elasticity*, since the percentage decrease in price equals the percentage increase in quantity demanded. Product C is referred to as *inelastic*, since the percent change in the quantity that is demanded is less than the percent change in price. These examples are all arc elasticities. *Arc elasticity* is a measure of the average elasticity over the range of the prices and quantities specified.

Table 17.1 Data for calculation of an arc elasticity.

Product description	Old amount	New amount	Change	Average	Change (percent)	E
PRODUCT A						
Price	$1.95	$1.65	− $.30	$1.80	− 16.7	Elastic
Quantity	10,000	14,000	+ 4,000	12,000	+ 33	
PRODUCT B						
Price	$1.80	$1.40	− $.40	$1.60	− 25	Unitary
Quantity	10,500	13,500	+ 3,000	12,000	+ 25	
PRODUCT C						
Price	$1.80	$1.20	− $.60	$1.50	− 40	Inelastic
Quantity	10,800	13,200	+ 2,400	12,000	+ 20	

Point Elasticity

A second measure of elasticity is point elasticity. *Point elasticity* is calculated at a specific point on the demand curve, as is illustrated in Figure 17.8. At point 1, the elasticity is calculated from the tangent (*T*) to the curve at point 1. Figure 17.9 shows that there are several possible arc elasticities (1–4, 1–5, 1–2, 1–3) for the demand curve, but only one point elasticity. If the arc in Figure 17.8 is successively shortened from *b'* to *b''*, the arc elasticity approaches the point elasticity.

A linear demand curve is shown in Figure 17.10. Except for a horizontal or vertical demand line, the point elasticity changes in value when calculated at different points on the demand curve. The percent change in quantity divided by the percent change in price is a constant, but the ratio *P/Q* will be different for each point on the line.

Determination of price elasticities is more than an academic exercise. Price elasticities tell how price changes affect total revenues. Depending upon the price elasticities, a price change will result in an increase in total revenues, no change, or a decrease in total revenues. If elasticity is unitary, total revenues are unchanged by price changes. If demand is elastic, total revenues decline if price is increased, because the quantity demanded drops by a greater percent than the price increases. For inelastic demand, total revenues rise when price increases and drop when price decreases.

Determinants of Price Elasticity

To attempt to explain the determinants of elasticity at a given time requires an understanding of economics, psychology, consumer preference, and many other things. Nevertheless, it is possible to make some general statements about what

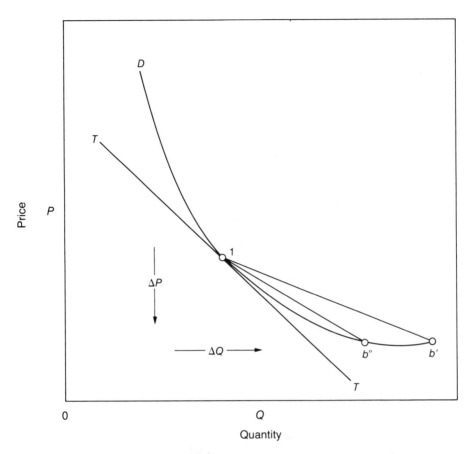

Figure 17.8   A point elasticity is calculated at a specific point on the demand curve.

determines demand and elasticity. The model-building process requires that you know what independent variables should be included in the model and have a feeling for their sizes and signs.

In general, price elasticity is determined by at least four factors:

- Whether or not the good is a necessity.
- The number and price of close substitutes.
- The proportion of the budget devoted to the item.
- The length of time the price change remains in effect.

If the product or service is a necessity, its demand will be inelastic. Consumers will pay any reasonable price for a necessity. Lack of substitutes for a product will also cause demand to be inelastic. If a good is both a necessity and without a

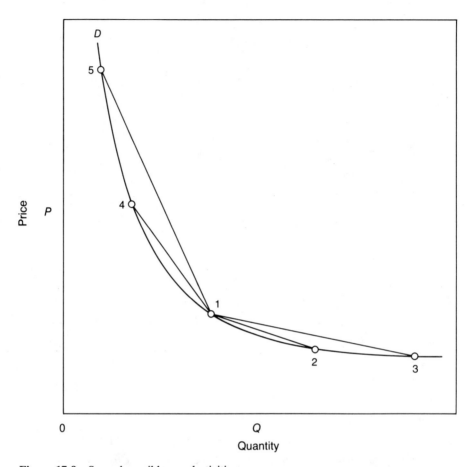

Figure 17.9   Several possible arc elasticities.

substitute, demand will tend to be very inelastic. If substitutes are available, consumers will switch their purchases to those substitutes that have not increased in
price. If the proportion of income spent for a good is small, price changes may not
have too great an impact on the demand for the good. If the proportion of the income
is large, price increases will cause postponements in demand or reductions in the
quantity demanded.

In the telephone industry, basic telephone service is considered to be a necessity
for most businesses and households. There are certainly some substitutes for telephone service, such as mail service or telegrams, but these services are often considered inferior to verbal communication. Further, the cost of telephone service is
not normally a major part of a family's income or a business's expense. For that
reason, the average household or business is likely to absorb increased telephone
costs so long as they are moderate.

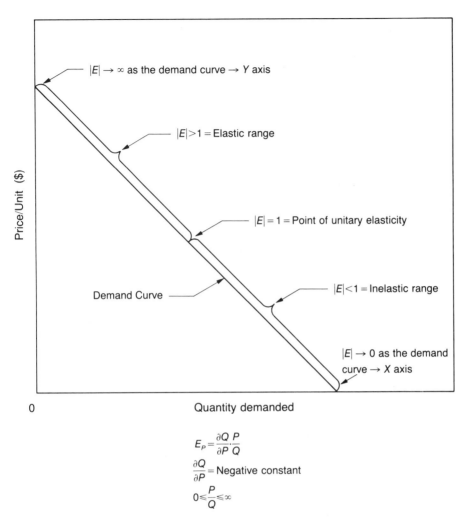

Figure 17.10   The linear demand curve.

"Vertical services," such as telephone extensions, premium sets, Touch-Tone, and Custom Calling may demonstrate a different demand pattern (Taylor, 1980). These items are not necessities, and price changes may cause significant reductions in the quantity demanded.

Finally, there is the amount of usage of a basic service that is generated by the customer—the number and length of calls. Some calls may be important enough that they will be made regardless of price changes. Other calls may be for convenience or casual purposes, and these calls can be postponed or eliminated. However, the determination of elasticity is even more complex in this area. Customers may shift their calling patterns and make telephone calls in the evening or on weekends when rates are less. They may change the number as well as the duration of calls, and they may dial the calls themselves instead of using an operator.

The longer a price change remains in effect, the more elastic the demand for a product. Consumers become aware of price changes and adjust their consumption habits to the new circumstances. "Elastic" as used here is a relative term. Demand becomes "more elastic" as time goes by; but it could still be inelastic—i.e., less than one.

Other factors influencing price elasticity are the frequency of purchases and the presence or absence of complements (e.g., automobiles and gasoline). Frequently purchased and relatively inexpensive products may be more inelastic than infrequently purchased expensive items.

Price Elasticity and Revenue

Price elasticities are used to show how price changes can affect total revenue. Since revenue equals unit price *times* quantity demanded, a price change can result in an increase, no change, or a decrease in total revenue (Figure 17.11).

Let us consider first the impact of own-price elasticity on revenue by means of an example, deferring the impact of cross-elasticity until later. Suppose a forecast for a service predicts $1000 in revenues for a particular future year. Assume the own-price elasticity is -0.2. Defining P = existing price, Q = forecast of demand at the existing price, and R = forecast of revenue at the existing price, then $R = P \cdot Q = \$1000$.

What will be the impact of a 10-percent price increase in the service under consideration, effective at the start of the future year? The new price is clearly just $1.10 \cdot P$, but quantity demanded would be somewhat less than before. With $E = -0.2$, a 10-percent price increase would result in approximately a 2-percent demand loss. Hence, the new demand will be approximately $0.98 \cdot Q$, and the revenue R' after the price change will be

$$R' = (1.1P)(0.98Q)$$
$$= 1.08 \, R.$$

Thus the 10-percent price increase will increase revenues by only about 8 percent. In general, the own-price elasticity effect will cause an X-percent price increase to yield less than an X-percent increase in revenues. The "reprice" value of a rate or price increase is the incremental revenue that would result if there were no demand reaction. It would be $100 in the example. The amount by which revenues fall short of the reprice value, $20 here, is called *revenue repression*. A revenue repression factor may be defined as the ratio of revenue repression to reprice value. In this case, it is 0.2.

An elasticity of -0.2 implies a minimum revenue repression factor of 0.2; e.g.,

Behavior of model	Unitary	Inelastic	Elastic
Price rise	Total revenue remains the same	Total revenue increases	Total revenue decreases
Price decline	Total revenue remains the same	Total revenue decreases	Total revenue increases
Gain versus loss	Gain = Loss	Gain>Loss	Gain<Loss

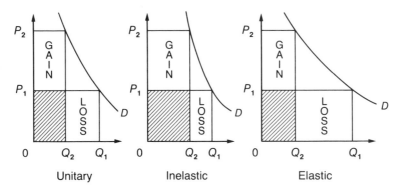

Figure 17.11   The relationship of price to revenue.

at least $20 for a price increase worth $100 on a reprice basis. The revenue repression factor often goes up with the magnitude of the price change.

To continue with the $1000 service example, suppose it has been determined that this service must yield $1100 to enable the company to earn its objective rate of return. A 10-percent rate increase will not be sufficient, owing to the revenue repression of $20 (revenue repression factor of 0.2). Evidently, to net $100 in incremental revenues, almost a 12.5-percent increase in price will actually be necessary. The reprice value ($1000 · 1.125) of such an increase is $1125. A repression of $25 (0.2 · $125) leaves a net of $1100.

Demand for a given good or service is frequently affected by prices of other goods and services as well as its own price. A cross-elasticity coefficient measures this interaction effect. The *cross-elasticity* measures the percentage change in the demand for good A as a result of a given percent change in the price of good B. If a good has a close substitute, a price increase for one will probably create increased demand for the other. When products are complementary (used together), a decrease in the price of one will lead to an increase in demand for both products. The cross-elasticity is positive for substitutes, and negative for complementary goods. As before, this is a dimensionless number, since it is defined in terms of percent changes.

As an example, let us use the price of WATS (Wide Area Telephone Service—a discounted long-distance offering based on a flat rate for specified hours of use; the elimination of the cost of itemizing individual calls permits a lower rate to be charged). One expects the price of WATS to affect MTS demand (Message Toll Service—the normal long-distance rates apply). An increase in WATS prices is expected to result in an increase in demand for MTS, resulting in a positive cross-elasticity. Thus MTS and WATS are examples of *substitute* services. Note, however, the asymmetry in the definition: the relationship between *MTS demand* and *WATS prices* is not necessarily the same as the corresponding relationship between *WATS demand* and *MTS prices*.

Consider now the relationship between demand for MTS and the price of basic local-telephone service. This would suggest that as the price of local service goes up, customers might be expected to cut back on toll calling, which is more discretionary. In this case local and MTS services are examples of *complementary services*, where the cross-elasticity is negative.

In summary, gaining knowledge of price elasticities, both own-price and cross-, for at least all of the major services and products of the business, is essential for intelligent and effective business forecasting and planning. While this is by no means an easy goal to achieve, it represents an area where much progress has been made in recent years and must continue to be made in the years to come.

OTHER DEMAND ELASTICITIES

Attention so far has been concentrated on price elasticity. However, there is an elasticity associated with each independent variable in the demand function. Income is another determinant of demand that also receives attention. For most goods and services, one would expect a positive relationship between demand and income. *Income elasticity* is the percent change in demand divided by the percent change in income. However, the elasticity is now positive instead of negative. If the demand for a good is income-inelastic, the increase in demand will not be proportional to the percent increase in income. As national income rises, for instance, a business firm will not experience a proportional growth in revenues, and its share of national income will decline.

Income elasticity is a two-edged sword. If the economy contracts and income declines, the revenues of an income-inelastic firm will shrink less than the revenues for an income-elastic firm. The firms whose goods are income-elastic are more concerned with anticipating the business cycle expansions and contractions.

EMPIRICAL ESTIMATION

The previous example has served to illustrate a very important principle: ignoring the impact of own-price elasticities in a rate- or price-planning process will lead to revenue shortfalls. Of course, compensating for this effect implies that the price elasticity coefficient must be estimated by one method or another. This quantification is frequently not an easy task.

If there has been at least one change in price, a manual calculation of elasticity can be performed. The change in quantity demanded that is owing to the price change will have to be subjectively estimated. After that, you should determine what the demand would have been had there been no price increase. This can be done by using actual data for the other determinants of demand, or by making a time series model where predictions are generated by using actuals up to the time of the price change. By whatever means seems most reasonable, you can subjectively determine what the quantity demanded would have been had there been no price increase. Since the actuals for past changes in price are available, the average elasticity can be calculated. If a price increase is expected in the future, the forecasts can be adjusted downward by using this manual elasticity calculation. Obviously, this is a rough estimate of elasticity and depends on the judgment of the analyst. However, the results can still be helpful to management and forecasters in predicting the impact of proposed price changes.

Using Regression Models

Since all of the independent variables in a demand function can change simultaneously, regression analysis is the primary tool for estimating elasticities. A model may take the form

$$Q_Y = Q(P_Y, I, P_X, A, B, \varepsilon, \ldots),$$

where the quantity demanded, Q_Y, is a function of the (deflated) price P_Y of the product, income I, the price P_X of a competing or complementary product, and other factors, which could include market potential, A, advertising, B, any of a number of other variables, and a random error term, ε.

In an application of demand models, either an additive or a multiplicative model may be appropriate in a given situation. Elasticities can be calculated from either model, but the calculation is different for the additive model than for the multiplicative model.

The *multiplicative* model has the simpler calculation and will be discussed first: this demand model has the form

$$Q_Y = \alpha P_Y^{\beta_1} I^{\beta_2} P_X^{\beta_3} A^{\beta_4} B^{\beta_5} e^{\varepsilon},$$

where e^{ε} is a *multiplicative* error term.

To estimate the coefficients by using ordinary least squares, it is convenient to take a logarithmic transformation ($\ln = \log_e$):

$$\ln Q_Y = \beta_0 + \beta_1 \ln P_Y + \beta_2 \ln I + \beta_3 \ln P_X + \beta_4 \ln A + \beta_5 \ln B + \varepsilon ,$$

where $\beta_0 = \ln \alpha$.

The point elasticity for price (the partial derivative of $\ln Q_Y$ with respect to $\ln P_Y$) is represented by the coefficient β_1 of the demand function.

The conclusion drawn from a *multiplicative* demand function is that the elasticities are given directly by the regression coefficients. This is a *constant elasticity* model: regardless of the location on the demand curve, the elasticity is the same. This may or may not be a realistic assumption, in practice.

With any regression model, it is useful to see how stable the coefficients are over different regression periods. If the purpose of the model is to identify elasticities, the coefficients must remain relatively stable in order to satisfy the requirement that they be accurately determined. Multicollinearity (Chapter 19) among independent variables often causes the coefficients to change significantly over different time periods.

The elasticities should also make sense. If it is believed that income is positively related to demand, the coefficients of income should be positive. The price coefficient should be negative. If this is not the case, the models may be improperly specified, or the wrong independent variables may be included in the model. More likely, the independent variables are multicollinear.

The calculation of elasticity is more detailed for an additive demand model than for the multiplicative model. In an *additive* demand model,

$$Q_Y = \beta_0 + \beta_1 P_Y + \beta_2 I + \beta_3 P_X + \beta_4 A + \beta_5 B + \varepsilon .$$

The point elasticity for price (the partial derivative of $\ln Q_Y$ with respect to $\ln P_Y$) is given by $\beta_1 P_Y / Q_Y$. This can be demonstrated by using a simplified model,

$$Q_t = a - bP_t.$$

Let

$$Q_{t-1} = a - bP_{t-1},$$

and subtract Q_{t-1} from Q_t; then

$$Q_t - Q_{t-1} = (a - bP_t) - (a - bP_{t-1}) = -b(P_t - P_{t-1}),$$

or

$$\Delta Q = -b\Delta P.$$

Thus,

$$b = -\frac{\Delta Q}{\Delta P}.$$

To obtain the elasticity, you multiply by P/Q and obtain

$$\frac{\Delta Q}{Q_Y} \Big/ \frac{\Delta P}{P_Y} = -bP_Y/Q_Y.$$

Therefore, the price elasticity varies at every point (Q_Y, P_Y) along the demand curve, since the ratio of P_Y to Q_Y is different for every point on the demand curve.

A Revenue Model

In a revenue model, the same variable (price) may appear on both sides of the equal sign. Statistical bias may be introduced; therefore, extra care is required. Suppose that revenues are related to price P and income I in a multiplicative model,

$$Q_Y = \alpha P^{-\beta_1} I^{\beta_2} e^{\varepsilon}.$$

Then the revenue R is

$$R = QP$$
$$= \alpha P^{(1-\beta_1)} I^{\beta_2} e^{\varepsilon},$$

and

$$\ln R = \ln \alpha + (1 - \beta_1)\ln P + \beta_2 \ln I + \varepsilon.$$

The point elasticity is the coefficient of $\ln P$, namely $(1 - \beta_1)$.

The elasticity range for a model of quantity demanded versus a model of revenues is shown in Table 17.2.

The price elasticity for a revenue model is one greater than the elasticity of the corresponding model for quantity demanded. Therefore, it is possible for the price elasticity of a revenue model to be positive.

Figure 17.12 shows three different elasticities. In the market period all inputs are fixed and demand is perfectly inelastic. In the short-run, there is some elasticity and the long-run elasticity may be perfectly elastic.

Long-Term Elasticity

The usual price elasticity referred to in demand models is a constant one-time elasticity. However, demand models that use lagged quantity as an independent variable allow for an increasing elasticity over time. Referred to as *dynamic* models, they are appropriate when a relatively long period of time passes before the restrictive effects have run their course. Consider a large computer system as an example. A large increase in rental rates may cause a customer to decide to replace the current system with a lower-priced competitive offering. However, it might take several years to replace the computer system, owing to the long planning, manufacturing, and installation intervals for such a large-scale project.

Consider a simplified demand for such a situation

$$\ln Q_t = a \ln Q_{t-1} - b \ln P_t.$$

The current-quarter (short–term) price elasticity is equal to $-b$. Assume that price is increased at time $t = 0$ and held constant thereafter. The *long-term elastic effect* of the price change can be determined as follows. At $T = t + 1$,

$$\ln Q_{t+1} = a \ln Q_t - b \ln P_{t+1}.$$

Since $\ln P_{t+1} = \ln P_t$,

$$\begin{aligned} \ln Q_{t+1} &= a(a \ln Q_{t-1} - b \log P_t) - b \ln P_t \\ &= a^2 \ln Q_{t-1} - b(1 + a)\ln P_t \end{aligned}$$

Similarly, at $T = t + 2$,

$$\ln Q_{t+2} = a \ln Q_{t+1} - b \ln P_{t+2}.$$

Table 17.2 Range of elasticity for a quantity model versus a revenue model.

Range	Quantity model	Revenue model
Elasticity	$-\infty < E < -1$	$-\infty < E < 0$
Unit elasticity	$E = -1$	$E = 0$
Inelasticity	$-1 < E < 0$	$0 < E < 1$

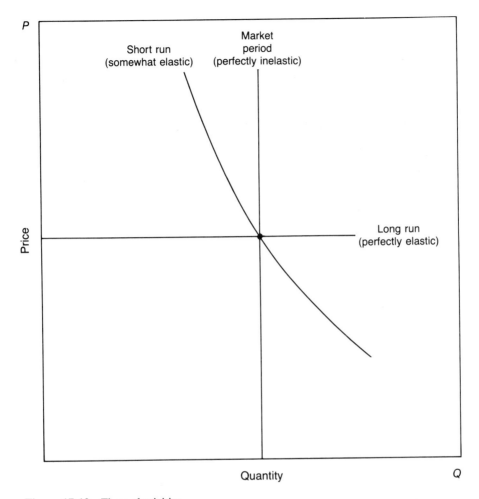

Figure 17.12 Three elasticities.

Since $\ln P_{t+2} = \ln P_t$,

$$\ln Q_{t=2} = a(a^2 \ln Q_{t-1} - b(1+a) \ln P_t) - b \ln P_t$$
$$= a^3 \ln Q_{t-1} - b(1 + a + a^2) \ln P_t.$$

If the process is continued, the elasticity at each time is given by

$t = 0$	$E = -b$
$t = 1$	$E = -b(1 + a)$
$t = 2$	$E = -b(1 + a + a^2)$

$$t = 3 \qquad E = -b(1 + a + a^2 + a^3)$$

$$\cdot \qquad\qquad \cdot$$
$$\cdot \qquad\qquad \cdot$$
$$\cdot \qquad\qquad \cdot$$

$$t = n \qquad E = -b(1 + a + a^2 + a^3 + \cdots + a^n).$$

For demand models that use a lagged dependent variable, the *long-run price elasticity* can be shown to equal *the short-run elasticity divided by (1 minus the coefficient of the lagged dependent variable)* (Pindyck and Rubinfeld, 1976).

In this case, as t approaches infinity, the long-term elasticity is given by $-b/(1 - a)$, since

$$\sum_{i=0}^{\infty} a^i = \frac{1}{1 - a}.$$

Figure 17.13 shows two different elasticity profiles based on different values for a and b. The closer a is to 1.0, the longer it takes to reach the long-term elasticity. It is also apparent that the elasticity approaches its long-term value asymptotically. After an initial rise, further increases in elasticity are relatively minor. For this reason, it is more practical to consider the amount of time that elapses until

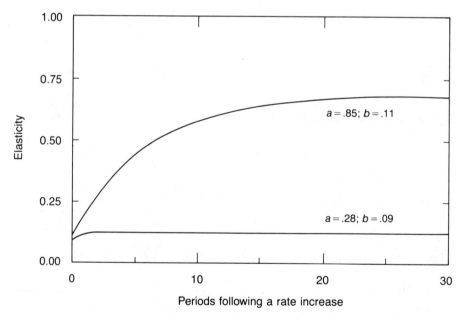

Figure 17.13 Two different elasticity profiles based on different values for a and b.

90 percent or 95 percent of the long-term effect is reached. For example, the time to reach 90 percent of the long-term effect is

$$\ln (0.10)/(\ln a - 1),$$

where a is the coefficient of the lagged dependent variable.

Long-term elasticity can be extremely important, since it can be considerably larger than current-period elasticity. For example, if $a = 0.75$ and $b = -0.3$, the long-term elasticity $= -0.3/(1 - 0.75) = -1.2$. What appears to be highly inelastic in the short term can be elastic in the long term. If this distinction is not recognized, a company may continue to raise prices in the belief that demand is inelastic, and constantly find revenue shortfalls one or two years in the future.

A DEMAND MODEL FOR TELEPHONE TOLL SERVICE

An extended example demonstrating the estimation of the price elasticity of telephone toll service illustrates the application of demand analysis to a business problem. Toll revenues generated through telephone use are a significant part of the revenue of telephone companies. The price elasticity of the service must be understood before an optimum pricing scheme can be established. The demand model should also be helpful in predicting future revenues.

Developing a Price Index

To measure price elasticity in the first of our case studies, it was necessary to develop a price index that, at any point in time, would measure the difference between price of a typical call and the price of that call in a given base period. The "basket," or distribution of calls used to develop the price index, will need to take into account the number of calls made between various locations, the time of day these are made, the extent of operator assistance, and the duration of the calls (conversation time). A *chain index* was used; such an index has a value of 1.0 in the base period; the basis for that period is the initial distribution of calls and the price per call. At the time of each price change, the percentage increase in prices, based on the *current distribution* of calls, is computed. The existing price index is then multiplied by the most recent percentage change in price. This form of the price index allows customers to change the distribution or pattern of calling over time in response to differential price changes (e.g., large increases in the price of operator-handled calls will encourage customers to place fewer operator-handled calls and more directly dialed calls).

Developing a Demand Model

The dependent variable that will be used in the regression is the revenue derived from the service divided by the price index. This yields a surrogate for "quantity" that has as its advantage that it measures other customer reactions to price changes than simple reduction in the number of calls. Since a customer can offset a price increase by reducing conversation time, by calling in discount periods, or by dialing calls directly instead of by using an operator, as well as by reducing the number of calls made, changes in revenues will be a more meaningful variable in the regression than changes in the number of calls.

Independent variables for consideration in the model are the number of telephones in service and personal income in constant dollars. Before it is included as a variable in the right-hand side of the formula for our model, the price index is deflated by dividing by the Consumer Price Index to yield a relative price index. Finally, as a measure of habit, the "quantity" in the prior period $(t-1)$ is included. An advertising variable could also be tried.

Six years of quarterly historical data are available for use.

Consider the tentative model that has been described:

$$\text{Quantity}_t = f(\text{Quantity}_{t-1}, \text{Price}_t, \text{Income}_t, \text{Telephones}_t).$$

A multiplicative model form (for constant elasticity) is considered; then logarithms are taken so that ordinary least-squares regression can be applied to estimate the parameters. (In the following formula, Q = quantity, P = price, I = income, and T = telephones; $\ln = \log_e$.) We have

$$\ln Q_t = \beta_0 + \beta_1 \ln Q_{t-1} + \beta_2 \ln P_t + \beta_3 \ln I_t + \beta_4 \ln T_t + \epsilon_t.$$

The coefficient of the price variable provides an estimate of the price elasticity of the service. Table 17.3 summarizes the results of the tentative model and Table 17.4 shows the correlation matrix of the variables. The model explains 90 percent of the variation about the mean of the "quantity" series. All of the independent variables except price are very highly correlated with the dependent variable; but the income, telephone, and lagged quantity variables are also highly correlated with each other. Plots of these series (Figures 17.14–17.16) show a strong linear trend and, as a consequence, a potential multicollinearity problem may exist.

Dealing with Multicollinearity

The OLS estimation procedure works best when there is zero correlation between pairs of independent variables. When two or more independent variables have similar linear trends, multicollinearity exists and it may be difficult to interpret individual parameter estimates. Chapter 19 discusses several approaches that may be tried to

Table 17.3 Summary of results for the demand model.

Variable (expressed in logarithms)	Coefficient	t Statistic
Constant	−2.93	−0.67
Lagged Quantity	−0.007	−0.03
Tels *(T)*	1.10	2.43
Income *(I)*	0.58	1.90
Price *(P)*	−0.29	−2.66
R^2:	0.90.	
Residual standard deviation:	0.032	

Table 17.4 The correlation matrix for the variables in the model.

1	Quantity *(Q)*	1.00				
2	Lagged *Q*	0.86	1.00			
3	Tels *(T)*	0.92	0.92†	1.00		
4	Income *(I)*	0.25	0.35	0.45	1.00	
5	Price *(P)*	0.90	0.87†	0.93†	0.47	1.00

†Indicates high correlation among independent variables. Variables are expressed in terms of logarithms.

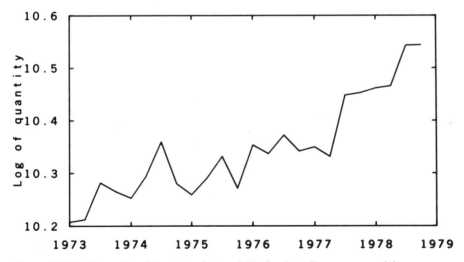

Figure 17.14 Time plot of the dependent variable for the toll revenues model—telephone toll revenues divided by the price index from first quarter 1973 through fourth quarter 1978.

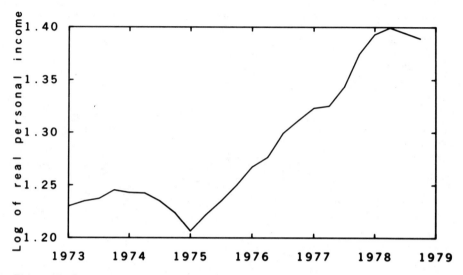

Figure 17.15   A time plot of personal income in constant dollars.

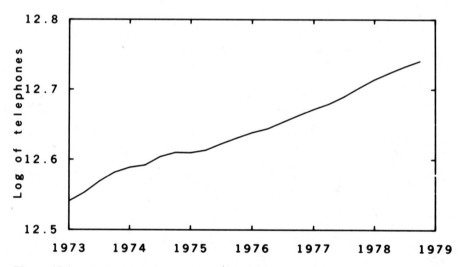

Figure 17.16   A time plot of the number of telephones in service.

deal with multicollinearity. For the present case study, the problem is confirmed when the regression analysis is reviewed. The t statistic for the *lagged quantity* Q_{t-1} indicates that the parameter is insignificant, even though there is a correlation of 0.86 between "quantity" Q_t and *lagged quantity* Q_{t-1}.

Residual Analysis

The correlogram of the residuals (Figure 17.17) of the model indicates a significant correlation at lags 2 and 4. Even though the quantity series is dominated by trend, a seasonal pattern exists in the residuals. To correct this problem, a seasonal adjustment of the series can be made prior to modeling; if the seasonal pattern is not changing over time, it may be appropriate to make use of dummy variables (dealt with in Chapter 18) to account for the seasonal pattern.

Improving the Model

In our case study, dummy variables were introduced to account for seasonality and one of the independent variables was pruned from the model to reduce the multicollinearity problem. Two alternative models were then possible—the first model excluded the telephone variable T_t and the second model excluded the habit variable (lagged quantity, Q_{t-1}). The regressions that result for both alternatives are summarized in Table 17.5. Both models have very high values for the R-squared statistic,

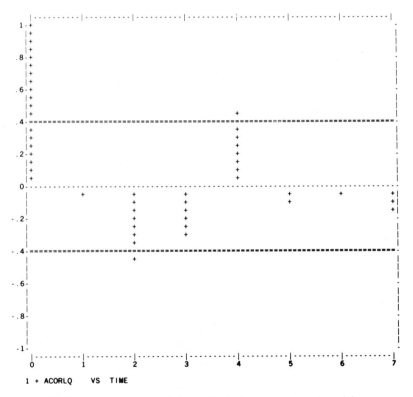

Figure 17.17 A correlogram of the residuals from the demand model.

Table 17.5 Summary of regression results for alternative models.

Variable (expressed in logarithms)	Model 1		Model 2	
	Coefficient	t statistic	Coefficient	t statistic
Constant	4.63	3.2	−1.65	−0.7
Lagged Quantity	0.55	3.6	—	—
Tels (T)	—	—	0.98	4.6
Income (I)	0.76	3.7	0.64	3.3
Price (P)	−0.22	−2.6	−0.27	−3.7
Dummy 1	0.020	1.2	−0.006	−0.5
Dummy 2	0.016	1.0	−0.007	−0.6
Dummy 3	0.072	4.3	0.04	3.3
R^2:	0.95		0.96	
Residual standard deviation:	0.025		0.023	
Durbin-Watson statistic:	NA		1.66	

significant values for the F statistic; and parameter estimates for lagged quantity, income, price, and telephones are all significant and of the expected sign. While only Dummy 3, the dummy variable introduced to represent the fourth quarter of each year, is individually significant, the incremental F test indicates that as a group the dummies are significant. For example, the mean squared error of Model 2 without the dummies is 10.43×10^{-4}, and with the dummies it is 5.01×10^{-4}. The incremental F test is computed as

$$F = \frac{(\text{Residual SS}_{old} - \text{Residual SS}_{new})/(\text{df}_{old} - \text{df}_{new})}{\text{Residual SS}_{new}/\text{df}_{new}}$$

$$= \frac{(10.43 - 5.01) \times 10^{-4}/(18 - 15)}{(5.01 \times 10^{-4})/15} = 5.4.$$

The incremental F statistic exceeds the critical value (3.29) for 3 and 15 degrees of freedom; this indicates that as a group the dummy variables are significant.

The Durbin-Watson statistic cannot be used to test for first-order residual auto-correlation in Model 1 because of the presence of the lagged dependent variable. The Durbin h statistic (see Chapter 12) can, however, be used as a test of this.

The Durbin h statistic is a large-sample statistic ($n > 30$); however, its value was so close to zero in the test that was made that the rejection of the hypothesis of first-order autocorrelation seems plausible.

The D-W statistic can be used for Model 2 and gives a value of 1.66 for 17 degrees of freedom, which is outside the range of positive autocorrelation (Appendix A, Table 5). Neither the h nor the D-W statistics will pick up the problem of serial correlation at lags other than one, and this indicates a need to plot the residual correlogram.

When correlograms of the residuals of each model were plotted, these confirmed a significant residual correlation at lag 2, with a value of approximately 0.40 for Model 1 and 0.48 for Model 2. An approximate test of significance is $2/\sqrt{n} = 2/\sqrt{24} \simeq 0.42$, where n is the number of observations—in this case 24 quarters. The residual autocorrelation at lag 2 is less than 0.42 in Model 1 but is greater than this in Model 2. A new independent variable might be found to explain this pattern.

For Model 2, residuals were plotted against the predicted values; this plot indicated a relatively large outlier at the fourth quarter of 1975. The second quarter of 1977 also showed a large negative residual. There were no obvious outliers in any of the variables that would suggest transcription errors within these time series.

A robust regression was performed to determine what impact these unexplained values had on the parameter estimates for Model 2. The price elasticity changed from -0.27 to -0.28 in the robust regression and the income elasticity dropped from 0.64 to 0.53: the relatively large residuals had not significantly changed the estimated price elasticity and had changed the income elasticity by less than one standard error. When a Q-Q plot was made, it did not indicate substantial deviations from normality.

Model Conclusion

While not perfect, the two models do provide an approximation of the price elasticity for telephone toll service. Model 1 estimates the elasticity to be $-0.22 \pm 2(.08)$ and Model 2 estimates it to be $-0.27 \pm 2(.07)$. The range of the price elasticity is -0.06 to -0.41 at the 95-percent confidence level. Once again, the problem of having only 24 observations for analysis results in rather imprecise estimates of the elasticity and argues against using 95-percent confidence limits; perhaps using 50-percent confidence limits would make more sense for this example. Using monthly rather than quarterly data would also improve the precision of the parameter estimates. Another alternative, pursued in Chapter 20, is the use of a *pooled* model: data for one geographic area are combined with data for adjacent areas to increase the degrees of freedom in a pooled regression model.

When Model 1 was compared with Model 2, both models indicated that a price elasticity of approximately -0.22 to -0.27 is the most likely value for a quarter in which price is changed. However, Model 1 is a dynamic model and indicates a long-term elasticity of $-0.22/(1 - 0.55) = -0.49$. This suggests that, all other variables held constant, the long-term response to a price change is about twice the short-term response. By conducting a controlled experiment, it would be possible to determine which model makes the best actual fit to empirically observed results.

The results of the first of our case studies should demonstrate that a high value for the R-squared statistic does not necessarily mean you have a good model. Problems of multicollinearity, serially correlated errors, and heteroscedasticity (not a problem here) could invalidate a model even if its R-squared statistic were high, and a high R-squared statistic does not necessarily mean that the model will forecast well; you must go beyond the R-squared statistic to develop worthwhile models.

Forecasting Results

Given the limited historical data, one-year-ahead forecasts were generated for 1977 and 1978; these indicated forecast misses of -3.4 percent and -6.2 percent for Model 1 and -1.2 percent and 1.6 percent for Model 2, respectively. In this example, Model 2 provided more accurate forecasts than the model incorporating a lagged dependent variable.

DEMAND ANALYSIS CHECKLIST

_____ Have the determinants of demand been identified (price, market potential, income . . .)?

_____ Have the determinants of supply been identified?

_____ Are there sufficient data to build a regression model?

_____ Do the data have sufficient variability to estimate elasticities?

_____ Is there a multicollinearity problem?

_____ Is the model to be used for forecasting or explanatory purposes?

_____ Is an additive or multiplicative model more appropriate?

_____ Does the estimated elasticity seem reasonable given the nature of the product (necessity, substitute's price)?

_____ Lacking adequate data for modeling, can a manual elasticity estimate be made?

SUMMARY

The determination of elasticities

- Is an important function essential for understanding business growth.
- Is important for predicting revenue growth as well as quantity growth.

Demand modeling is an analytical as well as a forecasting activity.

- The ideal demand model will identify elasticities and forecast well.
- Caution is warranted when trying to use demand models for forecasting purposes.
- It is rarely the case that a good demand model will automatically be a good forecasting model.

For estimating price elasticity, the forecaster can

- Use a demand analysis (theory of demand) framework to select the variables that should be included in the model.
- Select the appropriate model form (multiplicative or additive). The multiplicative model is the more frequently used of the two.
- Estimate the model by regression methods, provided that model assumptions have not been violated.
- Determine the elasticity directly in the case of the multiplicative model.
- Calculate a long-term elasticity if a lagged quantity is a variable in the model.

USEFUL READING

PINDYCK, R. S., and D. L. RUBINFELD, (1976). *Econometric Models and Economic Forecasts*. New York: McGraw-Hill, Inc.

TAYLOR, L. D. (1980). *Telecommunications Demand: A Survey and Critique*. Cambridge, MA.: Ballinger Press.

CHAPTER 18

Using Dummies and Lagged Variables

In Chapters 14–16, a theory of demand was developed in which a single dependent variable was regressed on a set of independent variables that were assumed to explain the dependent variable. The forecaster must often apply special treatments, because these variables create significant statistical problems. Solutions to these problems include:

- The use of indicator variables for qualitative factors, and for seasonal and outlier adjustment.

- The use of lagged variables to describe effects that unfold over time.

USE OF INDICATOR VARIABLES

Indicator variables, better known as *dummy variables,* are useful for extending the application of independent variables to representation of various special effects or factors, such as

- One-time or fixed-duration factors or effects, such as wars, strikes, and weather conditions.

- Significant differences in intercepts or slopes for different consumer attributes, such as sex, race, and so on.

- Discontinuities related to changes in qualitative factors.

- Seasonal variation.

- The effects of outliers.

- The need to let the intercept or slope coefficients vary over different cross sections or time periods. This subject will be treated along with the pooling of time series and cross-sectional data in Chapter 20.

Indicator Variables for Qualitative Factors

In addition to quantifiable variables of the type discussed in earlier chapters, the dependent variable may be influenced by variables that are essentially qualitative in nature. Changes in government or public policy, wars, strikes, and weather patterns are examples of factors that are either nonquantifiable or very difficult to quantify. However, the presence of such factors can influence consumer demand for products and services. Dummy or indicator variables may then be used to indicate the existence or absence of an attribute or condition.

For example, suppose that for any given income level, the sales S of a product to women exceed the sales of the same product to men. Also, suppose that the rate of change of sales relative to changes in income is the same for men and women. A dummy variable can be included in the sales equation to account for sex. Let $D = 0$ for sales to men and $D = 1$ for sales to women. Then

$$S_t = \alpha_0 + \alpha_1 D_t + \beta_1 (\text{Income})_t + \varepsilon_t.$$

For this example the base or control condition will be "male" $(D_t = 0)$. The prediction $\hat{S}$ of sales to men is therefore

$$\hat{S}_t = \hat{\alpha}_0 + \hat{\beta}_1 (\text{Income})_t, \qquad \text{for } D_t = 0,$$

and the prediction of sales to women is

$$\hat{S}_t = \hat{\alpha}_0 + \hat{\alpha}_1 + \hat{\beta}_1 (\text{Income})_t, \qquad \text{for } D_t = 1.$$

The coefficient $\hat{\alpha}_1$ is called the *differential intercept* coefficient. It indicates the amount by which sales to women exceed sales to men at a given level of income. The t test can be used to determine if $\hat{\alpha}_1$ is significantly different from zero. Figure 18.1 shows a plot of the two regression lines for the example just given.

Similarly, the mean sales of a product in one geographical area may show the *same* rate of change relative to an economic variable that the sales in another area show, yet total sales for each state may be *different*.

Models that combine both quantitative and qualitative variables, as both of the foregoing examples do, are called *analysis-of-covariance models*.

You must always be careful to introduce one less dummy variable than the number of categories represented by the qualitative variable. In the above case, the two categories (male, female) can be represented by one dummy variable.

Using Dummy Variables to Identify Different Slopes and Intercepts

In the above example, suppose you want to know whether the intercepts and slopes are different for women and men. This can be tested in a regression model of the form

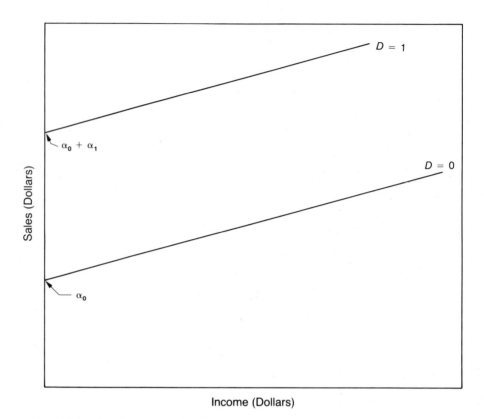

Figure 18.1 Plot of two regression lines.

$$S_t = \alpha_0 + \alpha_1 D_t + \beta_1(\text{Income})_t + \beta_2 D_t(\text{Income})_t + \varepsilon_t.$$

Then

$$\hat{S}_t(\text{Men}) = \hat{\alpha}_0 + \hat{\beta}_1(\text{Income})_t, \qquad \text{for } D_t = 0.$$

Likewise,

$$\hat{S}_t(\text{Women}) = (\hat{\alpha}_0 + \hat{\alpha}_1) + (\hat{\beta}_1 + \hat{\beta}_2)(\text{Income})_t, \qquad \text{for } D_t = 1.$$

The use of the dummy variable in the additive form allows you to identify differences in intercepts. The introduction of the dummy variable in the multiplicative form allows you to identify different slope coefficients. An example of the analysis-of-covariance approach will be discussed under pooling of cross-sectional and time series data in Chapter 20.

Using Dummy Variables to Measure Discontinuities

A change in a government policy or a change in a price may alter the trend of a revenues series. In the case of a price change, the preferable course of action is to develop a price index. Suppose that for any of a variety of reasons, such as lack of time or data, this is not possible. A dummy variable may be introduced into the model as follows. Let

$$Y_t = \beta_0 + \beta_1 X_t + \beta_2 D_t + \varepsilon_t, \qquad \text{where } D_t = 0 \text{ for } t < T^* \text{ and } D_t = 1 \text{ for } t \geq T^*.$$

T^* is the time of the policy or price change, and D_t is a dummy variable with a value of zero for all time less than T^* and a value of one for all time greater than or equal to T^*; X_t is an explanatory variable.

In this example, the predicted values of revenues are:

$$\hat{Y}_t = \hat{\beta}_0 + \hat{\beta}_1 X_t, \qquad \text{if } t < T^*,$$

and

$$\hat{Y}_t = (\hat{\beta}_0 + \hat{\beta}_2) + \hat{\beta}_1 X_t, \qquad \text{if } t \geq T^*.$$

Another situation that often occurs is one involving a "yes–no" or "on–off" possibility. For example, the demand for business telephones is very strongly affected by presidential and congressional elections. These are held in even-numbered years: storefront campaign offices and candidates' headquarters are established; there is a large increase in the demand for business main telephones in September and October; then in November, the telephones that were related to the election campaign are disconnected. In odd-numbered years, local political elections are held; local politicians do not have the financial resources to establish as many campaign offices. Consequently, the impact on telephone demand is not as great in odd-numbered years. Aside from this, one can be sure that elections occur in odd- and even-numbered years alike. Therefore, it is possible to use a dummy variable that assumes that half the telephone gain attributable to an election occurs in September, and half in October, and that it all disappears in November. In this case, for a given year, the important consideration in assessing election-influenced telephone gain is whether there is or is not an election. This is what is meant by a yes–no, on–off, or categorical variable. The variable does not continue to take on different values for an extended time and in that sense is not quantitative in nature.

Using Dummy Variables for Seasonal Adjustment

There are numerous studies in which the analyst may decide to use dummy variables to account for seasonality in quarterly data. In these a dummy variable is used for the second, third, and fourth quarters. The seasonal effect of the first quarter is then captured by the constant term in the regression equation

$$Y_t = \alpha_0 + \alpha_1 D_{1t} + \alpha_2 D_{2t} + \alpha_3 D_{3t} + \beta_1 X_{1t} + \beta_2 X_{2t} + \epsilon_t,$$

where $D_{1t} = 1$ for the second quarter, $D_{2t} = 1$ for the third quarter, and $D_{3t} = 1$ for the fourth quarter. For monthly data, eleven dummy variables would be used (February through December, for example), and then the January seasonality would be captured by the constant term in the regression equation.

It is possible that only one month or quarter has a significant seasonal pattern. However, this is not generally the case in forecasting demand or sales of telephones (for instance): usually *each* month or quarter has a unique seasonal pattern. Dummy variables may be of of limited usefulness if the season changes over time, since the dummy variable approach assumes a *constant* seasonal pattern.

A useful attribute of the X-11 and SABL seasonal adjustment programs (discussed in detail in *The Beginning Forecaster*) is that they may be used with data that do not show a constant seasonal pattern. And most series do seem to exhibit changing seasonality over time. The advantage of using dummy variables in a regression is that seasonality and trend-cycle can be estimated simultaneously, in a one-step process; otherwise, a two-step process would be necessary: (1) seasonal adjustment of data, and (2) performance of the regression. The ease of using seasonal adjustment programs on timeshared computers is minimizing the one-step advantage of the dummy variable approach. In the one-step process, the dummy variable provides an index of average seasonality and this can then be tested for significance by using the t test for an individual dummy variable or the incremental F test for a group of dummy variables.

Eliminating the Effects of Outliers

To illustrate the use of dummy variables to eliminate the effect of outliers, consider the following telephone application. There was a telephone company strike in April and May of 1968 and disconnections of telephone service because of nonpayment of telephone bills were not reported for those months. This distorted the 1968 annual totals, which were subsequently used in a model for predicting telephone gain. It was decided to incorporate a dummy variable into the model. The dummy variable, in this case, was a variable that can generally be set equal to zero for all observations except the unusual event or outlier. Thus, the values for the dummy variable were equal to zero for all years but 1968, when it had a value of one.

Because the dummy variable equalled zero for all periods except that in which the outlier appeared, the dummy variable explained the outlier perfectly. That is, the predicted value equalled the actual value for the outlier. Use of such a dummy variable tends to reduce the estimated standard deviation of the predicted errors artificially, because what is in fact a period of wide variation has been assigned a predicted error of zero. For this reason, it is recommended that dummy variables be used very sparingly for outlier correction. They tend to result in a model with a higher R-squared statistic than can perhaps be justified.

In the case of outliers caused by nonexistent values, it is usually preferable to estimate a replacement value based on the circumstances that existed at the time the outlier occurred.

You need to be especially cautious when dummy variables and lagged dependent variables occur in the same equation. For example, a dummy variable might be used to correct for a strike that could have a large negative impact on the quantity of a product sold. But it is then necessary to adjust the value for the subsequent period, or the value of the lagged dependent variable will drive next period's predicted value too low. A preferable alternative is to adjust the original series for the strike effect (if lagged dependent variables are included in the model).

You also need to understand that the presence of dummy variables for outlier adjustment will result in an artificially inflated value for the R-squared statistic: the model will appear to explain more of the variation than can be attributed to the independent variables. In some cases, the outliers may be a result of an inadequate demand theory (or supply constraints), and you need to be aware of this.

In some circumstances, robust regression techniques may offer a method for estimating regression coefficients so that the results are not distorted by a few outlying values. The variability in the data will not be understated and the very large residuals will readily indicate that the model, as presently specified, is incapable of explaining the unusual events.

On the other hand, residuals in a model in which dummy variables have been used for outliers suggest that unusual events are perfectly estimated. A robust regression alternative has considerable appeal from a forecasting viewpoint. Since it will not understate the variability in the data, there will be less of a tendency to expect a greater degree of accuracy in the forecast period than can be achieved over the fitted period.

At times it may be necessary to introduce dummy variables because it is almost impossible to estimate a replacement value for a missing or extreme data value: there may be too many unusual events occurring at the same time. For example, a company strike may have coincided with the introduction of wage–price controls or an oil embargo. It would be extremely difficult to determine the demand for a product or service had there been no strike, because too many other variables also changed.

Moreover, if you were to attempt to build a model to predict gasoline consumption, based on data that included the 1973–1974 period, you would likely incur problems. Since the period encompassed a fuel supply shortage, as a result of the Arab oil embargo, actual consumption in that period was a function of supply more than of demand. This situation did not exist in any of the historical data. It might be better to use a robust regression, leaving out the data for 1973–1974, or to use a dummy variable to account for that time period.

LAGGED VARIABLES

Many econometric formulations require the inclusion of lagged independent and dependent variables to incorporate the effects of a variable over time. The impact of a given economic factor may not manifest itself for several time periods in the future, or its effect may be distributed over several time periods. To incorporate these situations in econometric models, econometricians have devised various *distributed-lag schemes* (Dhrymes, 1972; Fisher, 1966; Pindyck and Rubinfeld, 1977).

Distributed Lags

Generally, a *distributed-lag scheme* involving only lagged explanatory variables takes the form

$$Y_t = \alpha + \beta_0 X_t + \beta_1 X_{t-1} + \cdots + \beta_k X_{t-k} + \varepsilon_t,$$

or, alternatively,

$$Y_t = \alpha + \beta(\omega_0 X_t + \omega_1 X_{t-1} + \cdots + \omega_k X_{t-k}) + \varepsilon_t,$$

where the order k is generally unknown. Since there may be quite a few regressor variables, this can lead to a variety of statistical problems, including multicollinearity and the imprecise estimation of lagged coefficients when k is large.

The weights ω_i are interpreted as the proportion of the total effect achieved in a given time interval (this is called the *lag effect*). The coefficient β is interpreted as the economic reaction of Y_t to a sustained unit change in X (this is called the *economic effect*).

The distributed-lag coefficients β_i in the first of the two equations above equal a fixed β multiplied by a variable lag weight ω_i. The long-run response of Y to a unit change in X is the sum of the lag coefficients

$$\sum_{i=0}^{k} \beta_i = \beta \sum_{i=0}^{k} \omega_i.$$

To circumvent some of the estimation problems that arise when an equation contains numerous regressor variables, certain simplifying assumptions must be made in practice. One such assumption made many years ago was that the coefficients should decrease over time. Thus the scheme proposed by Koyck (1954) is an exponentially decreasing sequence given by

$$\beta_j = (1 - \lambda)\lambda^j \qquad \text{for} \qquad 0 < \lambda < 1.$$

A model with such coefficients can be written as

$$Y_t = \alpha + \beta(X_t + \omega X_{t-1} + \omega^2 X_{t-2} + \cdots) + \varepsilon_t.$$

This implies an *infinite lag* with weights declining *geometrically* toward zero.

The model can be simplified by lagging Y_t by one period, multiplying by the weight ω, and subtracting the result from the equation for Y_t (as shown above). Then

$$Y_t - \omega Y_{t-1} = (\alpha - \alpha\omega) + \beta X_t + \beta(\omega X_{t-1} - \omega X_{t-1}) + \ldots + (\epsilon_t - \omega \epsilon_{t-1}).$$

Figure 18.2 illustrates the distribution of weights for various values of ω. This implies *a priori* knowledge of the proper weighting pattern.

The model may be further rewritten as

$$Y_t = \alpha(1 - \omega) + \omega Y_{t-1} + \beta X_t + (\varepsilon_t - \omega \varepsilon_{t-1}).$$

This can be fitted by OLS, by letting $\varepsilon_t^* = \varepsilon_t - \omega \varepsilon_{t-1}$ and assuming that the ε_t^*'s are uncorrelated. The simplifying assumption has made the model more tractable at the expense of considerable realism. Analyzing simplified structures may, however, pay off in increased insight into economic relationships and simplified economic interpretations.

Possible weighting schemes

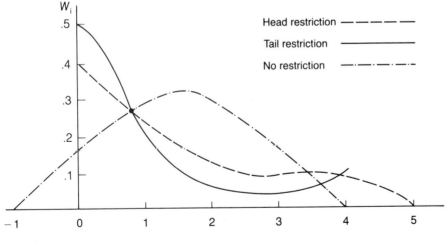

Head restriction $\blacklozenge$ $\omega_{-1} = 0$, ω_0 (Head) $< \omega_0$ (Tail, No)

Tail restriction $\blacklozenge$ $\omega_5 = 0$, Lag forced to zero, smooths tail

Figure 18.2 Distribution of weights for a Koyck scheme.

Partial Adjustment and Adaptive Expectations Models

Two other common formulations that also include lagged dependent variables are the *partial adjustment* model (for measuring habit persistence) and the *adaptive expectations* model (for measuring error-caused learning). The rationale behind the partial adjustment model is that inertia, high costs of change, or other factors restrict the immediate response of Y to a given change in X (Y would represent a consumer and X the product). In this case Y_t^* represents the optimum response and is given by

$$Y_t^* = \beta_0 + \beta_1 X_t + \varepsilon_t.$$

Economists suggest that in the current time period the consumer will move only part way from the initial position Y_{t-1} to the desired position Y_t^*, or

$$Y_t - Y_{t-1} = \delta(Y_t^* - Y_{t-1}) \qquad \text{for} \qquad 0 < \delta < 1.$$

This could also be the case when the availability of resources, or the costs of changing the level of production to a higher (or lower) level in response to a change in demand, prevents a manufacturer from making an immediate response.

The final form of the *partial adjustment model* is

$$Y_t = \beta_0 \delta + \beta_1 \delta X_t + (1 - \delta)Y_{t-1} + v_t, \text{ where } v_t = \delta \varepsilon_t.$$

This model is very similar to the Koyck model.

The assumption that only the current value of X_t is important in determining the optimum value of Y_t is subject to question, and has led to the *adaptive expectations model*. In this model, the observed value of Y_t is related to the expected value of X_t; that is,

$$Y_t = \beta_0 + \beta_1 X_t^* + \varepsilon_t,$$

where X_t^* is the expected value of X_t and is not observable. A further assumption is that the expectations are updated each period by a proportion of the difference between the actual value for X_t and the previous expected value for X_t. Thus

$$X_t^* - X_{t-1}^* = (1 - \lambda)(X_t - X_{t-1}^*) \qquad \text{for } 0 < \lambda < 1.$$

These equations have to be manipulated to eliminate nonobserved values. It can be shown that the final form of the adaptive expectations model is

$$Y_t = \beta_0(1 - \lambda) + \beta_1(1 - \lambda)X_t + \lambda Y_{t-1} + \mu_t,$$

where $\mu_t = \varepsilon - \lambda \varepsilon_{t-1}$ represents the error term. This model formulation is also of the Koyck form.

Almon Lags

Another approach that has received a considerable amount of attention in the econometric literature is the Almon lag scheme (see Almon, 1965). Rather than estimating all the β's in the model, the *Almon scheme* postulates that the β's can be approximated by a polynomial of a suitable (but unknown) degree. If the degree of the polynomial is much less than the order k of the model, this simplifies the statistical estimation problem. It is beyond the scope of this exposition to explore the ramifications of the Almon approach. In recent years the seriousness of the difficulties with this approach has somewhat diminished its usefulness in applications.

DUMMIES AND LAGGED VARIABLES CHECKLIST

_____ If quantitative data are not available, are dummy variables appropriate to represent

(a) One-time effects (e.g., strikes, etc.)?
(b) Fixed-duration effects (e.g., war–peace)?
(c) Discontinuities related to changes in qualitative factors?
(d) Seasonal variation?
(e) Differences in slopes or intercepts for different attributes (e.g., sex, race)?

_____ Can a replacement value be used in place of a dummy variable when outliers are present?

_____ Are dummy variables (for outliers treatment) and lagged dependent variables included in the same equation? (If so, carefully examine model predictions for the period following the outlier.)

_____ Does a robust regression offer a better alternative for treating outliers than dummy variables?

_____ Are lagged variables appropriate? Is response to a change in an independent variable distributed over time?

_____ If distributed lags of exogenous variables are called for, have you used Koyck or Almon lags to conserve degrees of freedom (if necessary)?

_____ Are irrelevant variables included in the model?

_____ Are relevant variables excluded from the model?

SUMMARY

The use of dummy variables and lagged variables offers additional flexibility to the econometrician.

- Dummy variables provide the capability to include qualitative factors or effects in the model.

- Lagged variables provide the opportunity to allow responses to some change to have distributions over time.

You need to exercise considerable care when using these variables because of potential forecasting problems and associated statistical problems.

USEFUL READING

ALMON, S. (1965). The Distributed Lag Between Capital Appropriations and Expenditures. *Econometrica* 30, 178–96.

DHRYMES, P. J. (1971). *Distributed Lags: Problems of Estimation and Formulation.* San Francisco, CA: Holden-Day.

FISHER, F. M. (1966). *The Identification Problem.* New York, NY: McGraw-Hill.

KOYCK, L. M. (1954). *Distributed Lags and Investment Analysis.* Amsterdam, Netherlands: North-Holland Publishing Co.

PINDYCK, R. S., and D. L. RUBINFELD (1976). *Econometric Models and Economic Forecasts.* New York, NY: McGraw-Hill.

CHAPTER **19**

Additional Specification Issues

This chapter discusses a number of specification issues arising in econometric forecasting applications. These include:

- The identification of heteroscedastic errors by means of residual plots and the Goldfeld-Quandt test.

- Transformations and weighted least squares estimation as solutions for heteroscedasticity.

- The Chow test for determining if a model is structurally stable over time.

- The identification of multicollinearity.

- Errors in the measurement of the independent variables.

HETEROSCEDASTICITY

Errors in the classical linear regression model that do not have constant variance are said to be *heteroscedastic*. In practice, this phenomenon usually manifests itself as an increasing variability in the residuals with increasing values of the independent variable(s).

Heteroscedasticity occurs frequently in cross-sectional analysis. The changes in the dependent and independent variables are likely to be of the same order of magnitude in time series models. However, in cross-sectional studies of sales of firms, for example, the sales of larger firms may be more variable than the sales of smaller firms. In cross-sectional studies of family income and expenditures, the spending of low-income families may be less variable than the spending of high-income families, since high-income families have more disposable income available for "spur-of-the-moment" spending, durable goods purchases, or savings.

The effect of heteroscedasticity is to place more emphasis on variables with greater variance. The problem that heteroscedasticity poses in studies such as these is that while the estimated regression coefficients are unbiased and consistent, they are not efficient and will not become efficient as the sample size increases (see Chapter 10); this leads to confidence intervals that are narrower than the correct ones. That is, if the variance is understated, the confidence intervals for the estimated regression coefficient are too narrow. Because of this, the confidence intervals will more often than appropriately *not* span zero, which causes one to overstate the significance of each variable in the model.

Heteroscedasticity cannot be detected by looking only at the results of a regression analysis. A plot of the residuals against the predicted values of the dependent variable or of one of the independent variables may indicate whether the residual variance is constant over all observations. Because the residual variance is a function of the distribution of the independent variables as well as the variance of the true error term, statistical tests can be performed to detect the presence of heteroscedasticity.

The Goldfeld-Quandt Test

The Goldfeld-Quandt test for heteroscedasticity (Goldfeld and Quandt, 1965) consists of the following steps:

- The data are sorted in order of ascending value for the independent variable thought to be related to the error variance.

- The middle observations, perhaps as many as 20 percent of them, are omitted and two separate regressions are performed for the two remaining data subsets. For small samples ($n < 30$), no observations need to be eliminated.

- For each regression, the sum of squares of the residuals is calculated.

- Assuming the errors are normally distributed and have zero autocorrelation, the ratio of the larger residual sum of squares to the smaller residual sum of squares is distributed as an F statistic with $(n - d - 2k)/2$ degrees of freedom in both the numerator and the denominator. The number of observations is n, d is the number of omitted values, and k is the number of independent variables.

- The null hypothesis is that there is no significant difference in variance between the two sums. When the computed F statistic is larger than the tabulated F value (Appendix A, Table 4), you reject the assumption that the error term has a constant variance.

If there is an indication of heteroscedasticity, solutions to this problem include overall maximum-likelihood estimation, weighted least squares, and the transformation of variables.

A Weighted Least-Squares Solution

Consider the simple linear regression model

$$Y_t = \beta_0 + \beta_1 X_t + \varepsilon_t$$

ruled by the usual assumptions. The parameters β_0 and β_1 are estimated by minimizing

$$\sum_{t=1}^{n} (Y_t - \beta_0 - \beta_1 X_t)^2.$$

When the error variance σ_t^2 can be assumed known but perhaps not constant, a weighted least-squares analysis is appropriate; the minimization is given by

$$\sum_{t=1}^{n} \frac{1}{\sigma_t^2} (Y_t - \beta_0 - \beta_1 X_t)^2.$$

Thus, the squared deviations are weighted by the known factor $1/\sigma_t^2$ before summing. General mathematical expressions for the weighted least-squares solution may be found in Wonnacott and Wonnacott (1979, Chapter 16). Except for a few simple cases, these expressions are rather complex.

It may be worthwhile to illustrate one situation in which heteroscedasticity can be easily solved. Suppose that the variance of the error term in the model increases in proportion to the square of the independent variable X_t, such that

$$\sigma_t^2 = k^2 X_t^2, \qquad \text{where } t = 1, 2, \ldots, n.$$

By transforming the model into

$$\frac{Y_t}{X_t} = \frac{\beta_0}{X_t} + \beta_1 + \frac{\varepsilon_t}{X_t},$$

it can be seen that the transformed error term has constant variance k^2, and an ordinary least-squares analysis can be applied to this transformed equation. It can be shown that a weighted least-squares analysis would yield the same solution. In general, the expression for σ_t^2 is unknown and may not be simple. Nevertheless, it may be fruitful to try a simple transformation, like the one above, as part of a preliminary exploration prior to specifying the model.

A TEST FOR STRUCTURAL STABILITY

Forecasters are concerned with the *structural stability* of their models over time. If the model is appropriate for the first part of the data, it is important to ask if it is still applicable for more recent data. The *Chow test* (Chow, 1960) is an F test that can be applied in these situations. The procedure is as follows:

- Combine all observations $(n_1 + n_2)$ and perform a regression over the entire time period. Calculate the sum of squared residuals (RSS_0) with $n_1 + n_2 - k$ degrees of freedom (k = number of parameters to be estimated, including the constant term).
- Perform two separate regressions over time periods T_1 and T_2 (not necessarily equal) and calculate the sum of squared residuals for each model (RSS_1 and RSS_2). The degrees of freedom are $n_1 - k$ and $n_2 - k$, respectively.
- Add the sums of squared residuals from the separate regressions ($RSS_1 + RSS_2$) and subtract this value from the sum of squared residuals of the complete model.
- Compute the F statistic:

$$F = \frac{\{RSS_0 - (RSS_1 + RSS_2)\}/k}{(RSS_1 + RSS_2)/(n_1 + n_2 - 2k)};$$

test this with k and $n_1 + n_2 - 2k$ degrees of freedom.
- If the value of F is significant, you reject the hypothesis that there is no significant difference between the two regressions and conclude that the entire model is structurally unstable.

MULTICOLLINEARITY

Multicollinearity is probably the most widely discussed and most easily misunderstood phenomenon in econometric model building. In its simplest form, *multicollinearity* arises whenever explanatory variables in a regression model are highly correlated. Multicollinearity is difficult to deal with, because it is almost invariably a problem of degree rather than kind. Multicollinearity results in bias, inconsistency, and inefficiency of estimators, which is undesirable, at least from a theoretical viewpoint. Practically, remedies must be found so that model assumptions can be made approximately true without completely destroying the statistical validity of the fit (Belsley et al., 1980).

Some of the practical effects of multicollinearity include imprecise estimation. While the concepts of bias, consistency, and inefficiency have very precise theoretical definitions, their effect on the inferences that are drawn from a model may be difficult to determine in every practical application. Problems of multicollinearity also encourage misspecification of a model if they are not carefully noted. The stability of coefficients can be severely affected, so that different segments or subsets of the data can give rise to vastly different results. This lack of sensitivity precludes the possibility of making sound interpretations of model coefficients.

The presence of multicollinearity can be tested in a variety of ways. Estimated coefficients will lack stability in a sensitivity analysis that makes use of different segments of the data. There will likely be low t values and a high F value in the regression analysis. Simple correlations between variables can be calculated, although these would not be conclusive. For more than two independent variables, partial correlations should be examined as well.

The Farrar-Glauber test (Farrar and Glauber, 1967; Johnston, 1972, Section 5.7) considers the R-squared statistic between each independent variable and the remaining independent variables in a specification. The test is based on the inspection of the F statistics constructed with each R-squared statistic and the appropriate degrees of freedom:

$$F_i = \frac{R_i^2/(k - 2)}{(1 - R_i^2)/(n - k + 1)}, \qquad \text{where } i = 2, \ldots, k,$$

and where R_i^2 is the coefficient of multiple determination between each X_i and the remaining $(k - 1)$ explanatory variables, and k is the number of explanatory variables. A significant value for F_i indicates that the variable X_i is not independent.

In time series analysis, collinearity may often be reduced by eliminating trend from each variable. In the example presented in Chapter 13, the product-moment correlations of the *differenced* data are shown below the diagonal in the following matrix. The entries above the diagonal represent a "robust" version of the ordinary correlations (see *The Beginning Forecaster,* Chapter 17).

		1	2	3
1	GAIN	1	0.32	0.47
2	HOUS	0.72	1	0.36
3	DFRB	0.57	0.42	1

The robust correlations are all somewhat lower, possibly due to outliers or a few influential data values. This can be compared to the matrix of correlations for the original (undifferenced) data:

	1	2	3
1	1	0.07	0.74
2	0.01	1	0.14
3	0.47	0.32	1

While there are some significant correlations among the differenced independent variables, they are probably not large enough to introduce serious multicollinearity problems. The forecaster should become cautious, however, when simple correlations exceed values from 0.8 to 0.9.

OMISSION OF A RELEVANT VARIABLE

In Chapter 15 it was mentioned that omitting a relevant explanatory variable results in biased and inconsistent estimators. For example, assume that a correctly specified model is given by the equation

$$Y_t = \beta_0 + \beta_1 X_{1t} + \beta_2 X_{2t} + \varepsilon_t$$

and that the incorrectly specified model that is estimated is:

$$Y_t = \beta_0 + \beta_1 X_{1t} + \mu_t.$$

From the second equation, β_1 is estimated using OLS as:

$$\hat{\beta}_1 = \Sigma(X_{1t} - \overline{X}_1)(Y_t - \overline{Y})/\Sigma(X_{1t} - \overline{X}_1)^2.$$

From the correctly specified model we know that

$$(Y_t - \overline{Y}) = \beta_1(X_{1t} - \overline{X}_1) + \beta_2(X_{2t} - \overline{X}_2) + (\varepsilon_t - \overline{\varepsilon}).$$

Therefore,

$$\hat{\beta}_1 = \Sigma(X_{1t} - \overline{X}_1)[\beta_1(X_{1t} - \overline{X}_1) + \beta_2(X_{2t} - \overline{X}_2)]/\Sigma(X_{1t} - \overline{X}_1)^2$$
$$= \beta_1 + \beta_2 \Sigma(X_{1t} - \overline{X}_1)(X_{2t} - \overline{X}_2)/\Sigma(X_{1t} - \overline{X}_1)^2.$$

Thus, $\hat{\beta}_1$ will be biased if the second term is not equal to zero. Since

$$\hat{\alpha} = \overline{Y} - \hat{\beta}_1 \overline{X},$$

it will also be biased unless the second term equals zero. The second term will only be zero if X_{1t} and X_{2t} are uncorrelated. Similarly, the variance of $\hat{\beta}_1$ from the misspecified model can be shown to be larger than for the correct model. There will be a tendency to accept the null hypothesis of no significant correlation more often than is warranted at a given level of significance.

ERRORS IN VARIABLES

The classical regression formulation does not include assumptions about any measurement error in the independent variables. The error term is usually associated with the dependent variable and the regressors are assumed to be fixed. When both the dependent and independent variables are subject to error, estimation methods need to be developed to overcome the limitation of OLS analysis. Among these techniques the *errors-in-variables* method is widely used by econometricians. Consider again the simple linear regression

$$Y_t = \beta_0 + \beta_1 X_t + \varepsilon_{1t},$$

where β_0 and β_1 are parameters to be estimated. If there is also an error term associated with $X_t (= X_t^* + \varepsilon_{2t})$, then the model becomes

$$Y_t = \beta_0 + \beta_1(X_t^* + \varepsilon_{2t}) + \varepsilon_{1t},$$

or

$$Y_t = \beta_0 + \beta_1 X_t^* + (\varepsilon_{1t} + \beta_1\varepsilon_{2t}).$$

The error term $(\varepsilon_{1t} + \beta_1\varepsilon_{2t})$ involves β_1 as well. These complications give rise to problems in estimating coefficients and in determining their statistical properties. A treatment of this subject may be found in Johnston (1972, Section 9.4).

Sensitivity Analysis

It is common practice to vary the values of the independent variables over a range of, say, plus or minus fifteen percent of the basic values in increments of five percent. For each simulation, the forecast values of the dependent variable are printed out. The procedure does not involve as much computer expense as the Monte Carlo simulation does. The analyst can decide to vary one or all of the independent variables.

The purposes of this kind of simulation are:

- You can determine how the model will perform with various values for the independent variables. In other words, how sensitive is the model? Will one or more variables cause wide fluctuations in the forecasts? Are the forecasts reasonable for extreme values of these variables? If the model is multiplicative and/or differenced, this may be the only practical way to determine how sensitive it is to changes.

- Producing various scenarios of the future allows you to estimate some subjective "confidence limits" about the forecast or simply to estimate a range of expected values for the forecast itself. In this manner, the forecaster can talk about the expected variation around the forecast, just as is done with simple regression and ARIMA models.

The difficulty in varying the predictions for the independent variables one at a time is the tremendous number of combinations and permutations that are possible. The forecast user becomes perplexed, since it is not quickly obvious which combinations should be considered seriously. A more desirable alternative is to develop three scenarios—*reasonably pessimistic, best bet,* and *reasonably optimistic.* A consistent set of forecasts can then be made for the independent variables for each scenario. For example, an optimistic scenario (improving economy) would have, as independent variables, higher income, a larger market potential, and lower unemployment.

With the above approach, the forecaster has minimized the time and expense required to express the uncertainty in the forecast and reduced the alternatives to a level that the user can cope with.

A SPECIFICATIONS-PROBLEMS CHECKLIST

_____ Do the residuals from the fitted model show a nonconstant or nonhomogeneous variance?

_____ Has the Chow test been performed to determine if the model is structurally stable over time?

_____ Is multicollinearity of the independent variables evident from

- Coefficients that lack stability when used in different segments of the data?

- Simple correlation among independent variables?

- One independent variable correlated with the remaining independent variables (Farrar-Glauber test)?

SUMMARY

In this chapter a number of potential modeling pitfalls have been identified. These include

- Specification errors that may manifest themselves in the form of heteroscedastic residuals.
- Structurally unstable models.
- A variety of problems resulting from collinearity in the independent variables.

The plotting and analysis of residual patterns is an essential element of modeling and will help you to identify some of these problems. Coefficients that have wrong signs or wrong magnitudes or that show significant changes when a model is updated or estimated for different segments of the data suggest multicollinearity problems. The solutions proposed will improve model performance in most instances.

USEFUL READING

BELSLEY, D. A., E. KUH, and R. E. WELSCH (1980). *Regression Diagnostics: Identifying Influential Data and Sources of Collinearity.* New York, NY: John Wiley and Sons.

CHOW, G. C. (1960). Tests of Equality Between Sets of Coefficients in Two Linear Regressions. *Econometrics* 28, 591–605.

DRAPER, N. R., and H. SMITH (1981). *Applied Regression Analysis,* 2nd ed. New York, NY: John Wiley and Sons.

FARRAR, D. E., and R. R. GLAUBER (1967). Multicollinearity in Regression Analysis: The Problem Revisited. *Review of Economics and Statistics* 49, 92–107.

GOLDFELD, S. M., and R. E. QUANDT (1965). Some Tests for Homoscedasticity. *Journal of the American Statistical Association* 60, 539–47.

JOHNSTON, J. (1972). *Econometric Methods,* 2nd ed. New York, NY: McGraw-Hill.

WONNACOTT, R. J., and T. H. WONNACOTT (1979). Econometrics. 2nd ed. New York, NY: John Wiley and Sons.

CHAPTER 20

Pooling of Cross-Sectional and Time Series Data

The regression models covered up to this point have involved the estimation of model parameters through use of either time series or cross-sectional approaches. In some cases, cross-sectional data are available over time. The analyst has the choice of building time series, cross-sectional models, or pooled models. This chapter addresses:

- The reasons why pooled models are considered.
- Some commonly used pooling methods for estimation.
- The steps in building pooled models.
- Considerations in selecting the pooling method for a forecasting problem.

WHY CONSIDER POOLING?

A *pooled model* includes observations for N cross sections over T time periods. For example, suppose you are interested in per capita electricity consumption for the United States and annual data are available for 50 states for ten years. You can build 50 time series models, ten cross-sectional models, or one pooled model. But what advantage does pooling offer?

There are several reasons why pooled models may be desirable:

- Pooling can increase the reliability of the parameter estimates by increasing the degrees of freedom and decreasing the standard errors of the parameter estimates. In the above example, each of the 50 state models will have only ten time series observations. A pooled model, if appropriate, will have 500 observations.

- Since cross sectional variation is normally substantially greater than time series variation, the estimates for a pooled model may be based on a wider range of variation in a potential independent variable than will exist for time series models.

- Pooling allows for the analysis of data in a unified model that considers both time and cross-sectional variation.

Several pooled models for demand analysis have indicated elasticities that are less in absolute value than those indicated by comparable time series or cross-sectional models. The reason for this, in the case of time series models, may be that data are increasing over time because of a factor not included in the model. This misspecification may not be apparent because of multicollinearity, and the effect may be to overstate the parameter estimates of the model.

In the case of cross sectional models, the reason may be attributable to slow consumer response to changes in income, or to habits of buying that are strong. However, a more basic reason may be the fact that for some data, the cross-sectional model has an inherent misspecification. Suppose that for a given data set, the constant term or slope should be allowed to vary for each state or location. This cannot be accomplished in a purely cross sectional model.

Pooling can be helpful in increasing the reliability of the parameter estimates by greatly increasing the number of observations in the model. An argument can be made that pooling methods should be used even when the model assumptions are not precisely met. You may be willing to accept parameter estimates that have a small bias but much less variance than those of time series or cross-sectional alternatives. However, if the structure of the relationships is substantially different over the cross sections, pooling is inappropriate.

If you examine the residuals of the pooled model related to one cross section (state, area) over time, a serial correlation problem may exist. Similarly, if you examine the residuals across all the cross sections at a point in time, heteroscedasticity may exist. It is also possible that the residuals from one cross section are correlated with the residuals from another cross section. Some relevant journal articles for the interested reader include Balestra and Nerlove (1966), Bass and Wittink (1975), Maddala (1971), Mundlak (1978), Swamy (1970), and Zellner (1962).

METHODS FOR ESTIMATION OF POOLED MODELS

The method used to build a pooled model depends on the underlying assumptions that are involved, and these are based on the characteristics of the data under investigation. Three generic classifications of methods are generally considered:

- Ordinary least squares (OLS).
- Ordinary least squares with dummy variables.
- Generalized least squares (GLS).

Pooling through Use of OLS

The OLS model has the form

$$Y_{it} = \alpha + \beta X_{it} + \varepsilon_{it}, \qquad \text{for } i = 1, 2, \ldots, N \text{ and } t = 1, 2, \ldots, T.$$

N represents the number of cross sections and T denotes the number of time periods. In this case, you can estimate T cross-sectional or N time series models. If both α and β are constant over time for all cross sections, more efficient parameter estimates can be obtained by combining all the data in one large pooled model, with N times T observations (500 in the case of the electricity consumption example).

When it is feasible to assume that the intercepts are fixed (not random) and equal for all cross sections, that the coefficients of the independent variables are fixed and equal for all cross sections, that autocorrelation and heteroscedasticity are *not* present, and there is *no cross correlation* among the residuals of the cross sections, then OLS is the method to be applied. The foregoing represent a rather restrictive set of assumptions that will generally not be satisfied. However, when these conditions exist, there is an opportunity to obtain more efficient (minimum variance) estimators, since the fewest number of parameters are estimated, leaving the largest number of degrees of freedom.

If autocorrelation is present, this can be corrected by transforming the data, by using autocorrelation correction techniques, such as the Cochrane-Orcutt or Hildreth-Lu techniques (Chapter 13). Then, OLS can be used on the transformed data.

When using cross section data, you should generally expect to find heteroscedasticity and adjust for it, when necessary, before pooling. Homoscedasticity is unlikely among cross sections and you should satisfy yourself that the condition truly does exist. In the example that follows, the assumptions of no autocorrelation and presence of homoscedasticity will be examined.

Other pooling methods are considered when conditions exist such that the normal OLS assumptions are not valid. Specifically, aggregation bias may result from combining the cross sections before estimation. The assumption of constant intercepts over the cross sections may not be realistic. In the electricity example, there may be some factors influencing demand that are peculiar to a given geographical region. By constraining the intercepts to be the same for all cross sections, significant bias may be introduced in the estimates of parameters.

The assumption in OLS analysis that there is no correlation between the residuals of the various cross sections may also not be valid. Cross correlation among cross sections can result if there are omitted variables that are common to all equations.

For example, it is frequently found that regions of the country respond in a similar fashion to changes in economic prosperity. These changes cannot always be explained with the independent variables at hand. Since state boundaries are somewhat arbitrary relative to regional economic influences, it may be the case that the residuals of individual state models will be correlated. Methods using generalized least squares estimation can be used when this kind of cross correlation is present.

The ability to generate estimators in situations where traditional OLS cannot generate these is the primary value of analysis of covariance and the generalized least squares method.

The Analysis of Covariance Model

A slightly more general model can result if dummy variables are used to allow for different intercepts for each cross section and/or different time period: such a model is

$$Y_{it} = \alpha + \beta X_{it} + \gamma_2 W_{2t} + \cdots + \gamma_N W_{Nt} + \delta_2 Z_{i2} + \cdots \delta_t Z_{it} + \varepsilon_{it} ,$$

where $W_{it} = 1$ for the ith cross section and zero elsewhere, and $Z_{it} = 1$ for the tth time period and zero elsewhere.

OLS models incorporating dummy variables of this form are referred to as *analysis-of-covariance models*. These models have the same form as those referred to in Chapter 18. When dummy variables are used, the intercept can be viewed as having as many as three components—a "national or regional average," a variation by cross section, and a variation over time. A limitation of the model is that while it allows the intercept coefficients to vary, the cause of the variation is not identified. Throughout the remainder of this chapter, only dummy variables for cross sections will be discussed. Note there are at most $(N - 1)$ dummy variables (e.g., 49 to allow for varying intercepts for the 50 states; the first state effect is captured by the constant α.) Some cross sections may have the same intercept, thereby reducing the number of dummy variables.

The form of the analysis-of-covariance model presented earlier allows for different intercepts for each cross section. A second form of the analysis-of-covariance model allows for different coefficients for one or more independent variables. For example, the price elasticity for consumption of electricity might be the same for all all regions, but the income elasticity might be different. (See Chapter 18 for the multiplicative dummy variable model.)

An important aspect of pooling is to determine the constraints that are appropriate for a given study; i.e., are constant or different intercepts appropriate? Can all slope coefficients or only some be considered constant?

As a practical matter, pooling does not yield the "best" estimators in the statistical sense of unbiasedness and minimum variance. A decision is required as to the degree of constraint that will be applied to the intercept and the coefficients of the equation. Since constraint may introduce bias in the estimators, it is important that the constraint be the minimum required, so that the estimators will have minimum mean squared errors. In the example that follows, we will show how to decide on the constraints to be applied, based on the data under study.

Generalized Least Squares Method

Explanations of the *generalized least squares* (GLS) estimation methods are treated in Johnston (1972, Section 6.3); Kmenta (1971, Chapter 12) and Maddala (1977, Section 14.2). The example that follows shows how cross correlation can be identified. A GLS computer program is used to correct for cross correlation in the residual series.

Another class of model allows for random intercepts and coefficients. The random coefficients and/or random intercepts models assume that an additional error term is required to account for a random variation that is specific to a given cross section. For example, if you were to build 50 models for electricity consumption—one for each state—the assumption of fixed (nonrandom) coefficients and intercepts is reasonable. If you were to select ten states randomly and build a pooled model to estimate electricity consumption for the nation, it might be appropriate to allow for an additional source of variation in the parameters resulting from the sampling process: a selection of ten different states might yield slightly different results. Since forecasters are not usually involved in randomly selecting forecast entities (areas, products, etc.), the random-effects models are not treated in this book.

STEPS IN BUILDING A POOLED MODEL

The considerations involved in building pooled models will be reviewed by extending the example presented in Chapter 17. Recall that the objective was to build a model to estimate the price elasticity of telephone toll service. With only six years of quarterly data available for the state being modeled, the estimated standard deviation of the price parameter was quite large. Since data are available for two additional states for the same time period, it may be possible to build a pooled model that is more efficient (one in which there is smaller parameter-variance).

As with all modeling efforts, this process will begin with an examination of the data. This leads to the specification of an appropriate model. Two alternative models were considered previously. Model 1 had a lagged dependent variable and Model 2 had a telephones-in-service variable in lieu of the lagged variable. With $ln = \log_e$,

Model 1: $ln\,Q_t = \alpha + \beta_0\,ln\,Q_{t-1} + \beta_1\,ln\,\text{Price} + \beta_2\,ln\,\text{Income} + \beta_3 D_1 + \beta_4 D_2 + \beta_5 D_3 + \varepsilon_t$.

Model 2: $ln\,Q_t = \alpha + \beta_0\,ln\,\text{Price} + \beta_1\,ln\,\text{Income} + \beta_2\,ln\,\text{Telephones} + \beta_3 D_3 + \varepsilon_t$.

In both models D_1, D_2, and D_3 were dummy variables to account for seasonality. (Do not confuse these dummy variables with those that are used to allow for different intercepts for each cross section.) In Model 2, only the fourth quarter seasonality was significantly different from the first quarter (captured by α). Thus, only the dummy variable D_3 was needed.

Recall that there was no autocorrelation for Model 1, but Model 2 did have autocorrelated residuals. The three states for which data are available are labeled A, B, and C. The previous modeling was done for state B alone. In addition to state B, we now want to review the data for states A and C, to determine if a pooled model is appropriate.

The steps to be followed are:

1. *Examine the data and specify an appropriate starting point for time series models for each cross section.*

Figure 20.1 shows a scatter plot of the logarithms of quantity against the logarithms of the number of telephones-in-service for each state. Notice that the range of the

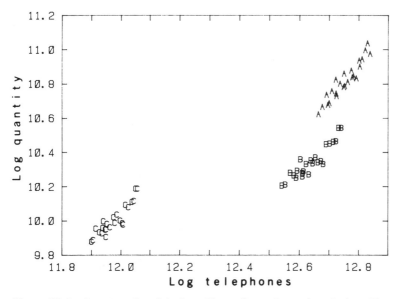

Figure 20.1   A scatter plot of the logarithms of quantity against the logarithms of number of telephones-in-service for each state.

independent variable has been increased with the addition of states A and C. This plot suggests that the same slope may be appropriate for all cross sections, but that the intercepts for each state are different. Plots of the logarithms of quantity against the remaining variables show similar relationships. The only variable for which both the slope and the intercept are constant for all cross sections is the lagged quantity variable. Based on the results so far, the OLS assumption of constant intercepts would be rejected for a simple linear regression model.

2. *Build N separate time series models* (e.g., for cross sections A, B, C).

3. *Develop the assumptions for the tentative pooled model.*
   a. *Analyze the coefficients for constancy across cross sections.*
   b. *Check for potential autocorrelation problems by looking at the Durbin-Watson statistic.*

   - Are the residuals *within* cross sections autocorrelated? If so,
   - Are the autocorrelation parameters equal over *all* cross sections?
   - Are the autocorrelation parameters equal over *some* cross sections?
   - Did you correct for autocorrelation?

   c. *Check for potential problems of heterosedasticity and mutual correlation.*

   - Are the residual covariances over some cross sections insignificant? If not, did you correct for mutual correlation?
   - Did you correct for heteroscedasticity?
   - Are the residual covariances cross sections insignificant? If not, did you correct for mutual correlation?

Tables 20.1 and 20.2 provide the model statistics and parameter estimates with their standard errors for Models 1 and 2, respectively. Most of the answers to the above questions can be obtained from these tables. First, a review of Table 20.1 for Model 1 indicates:

- The h statistics for the three cross sections (not shown) are insignificant, indicating that residual autocorrelation is not a problem.

- The estimated standard deviations of the residuals of the models (0.023, 0.025, 0.021) do not suggest problems of heteroscedasticity.

- The coefficients for cross sections B and C are very similar and are within two standard errors. The coefficients for cross section A appear different for lagged quantity, income, and the three dummies. The standard errors are so large that it is difficult to reject totally the assumption of constant coefficients. An F test will be introduced later to help make this decision.

- The intercepts for cross sections B and C are similar, but they appear different from A.

- Tests for cross correlation of residuals will be taken up later.

Table 20.1 Individual regressions for each cross section
for Model 1. (Standard errors are shown in parentheses.)

	Cross section		
Parameter	A	B	C
Intercept	1.78	4.64	3.96
Log of lagged quantity-coefficient	0.84	0.55	0.65
	(0.09)	(0.15)	(0.13)
Log of price	−0.12	−0.21	−0.24
	(0.09)	(0.08)	(0.08)
Log of income	0.35	0.76	0.94
	(0.18)	(0.20)	(0.24)
D_1	0.06	0.02	0.02
	(0.02)	(0.02)	(0.01)
D_2	0.09	0.02	0.02
	(0.02)	(0.02)	(0.01)
D_3	0.12	0.07	0.07
	(0.01)	(0.02)	(0.01)
R-squared statistic	0.97	0.95	0.95
Residual standard deviation (df = 16)	0.023	0.025	0.021

Note: The Durbin-Watson statistic is not applicable, since there is a
lagged dependent variable in the model.

Based on the information gathered so far for Model 1, the following assumptions
can be made for a tentative pooled model:

- Cross sections B and C are very similar and a pooled model for these cross
  sections could assume constant slopes and intercepts. If we attempt to include
  cross section A, at a minimum we should assume different intercepts. The
  probable difference in slope coefficients is a potential problem when including
  cross section A in the pooled model.

- Autocorrelation and heteroscedasticity are not present.

- You may want to pool only cross sections B and C.

A review of Table 20.2 for Model 2 indicates that:

- The Durbin-Watson statistics fall in the indeterminate region in each cross
  section. It may be desirable to correct for autocorrelation in a pooled model.

- The estimated standard deviations of the residuals of each model do not indicate
  heteroscedasticity.

- The intercepts are probably different.

Table 16.2 Individual regressions for each cross section, for Model 2. (Standard errors are shown in parentheses.)

Parameter	Cross section		
	A	B	C
Intercept	− 12.56	− 1.89	− 3.72
Log of telephones-coefficient	1.90	1.00	1.23
	(0.19)	(0.20)	(0.19)
Log of price	−0.21	−0.27	−0.33
	(0.09)	(0.07)	(0.07)
Log of income	0.02	0.63	0.78
	(0.21)	(0.19)	(0.23)
D_3	0.06	0.05	0.05
	(0.01)	(0.01)	(0.01)
R-squared statistic	0.97	0.96	0.96
Residual standard deviation (df = 19)	0.022	0.022	0.020
Durbin-Watson d statistic	1.33	1.65	1.52

- Tests for cross correlation will be considered later.
- The same considerations as for Model 1 are valid regarding pooling across some or all cross sections.

The OLS model with dummy variables for different intercepts, applied with correction for autocorrelation, is a tentative pooling model. For this example, all three states are pooled.

4. *Combine the data from separate cross sections and examine the combined data with the appropriate assumptions developed from step 3. Analyze the coefficients for constancy across cross sections.*

- Are the coefficients equal over all cross sections?
- Are the coefficients equal over some cross sections?
- Are the intercepts equal across all cross sections?
- Are the intercepts equal across some cross sections?
- Are the coefficients equal but the intercepts different for all or some cross sections.

5. *Decide on an appropriate pooling method.* The most desirable condition exists when the coefficients and intercepts are constant and the OLS method can be performed on the combined data. Using the assumptions that seem operative (autoregression, heteroscedasticity, constant/different intercepts,

constant/different slopes for some variables, all or some cross sections), select the pooling method.

For Model 1, the tentative pooled model will be an analysis-of-covariance model (different intercepts) with no corrections for autocorrelation or heteroscedasticity. In this example we will pool all three states.

For Model 2, the tentative pooled model will also be an analysis-of-covariance model (different intercepts) with corrections for autocorrelation but not for heteroscedasticity. All three states will be pooled.

The above pooled models with different intercepts can be compared to pooled models with a constant intercept to determine if separate intercepts are required (see Step 7).

6. *Estimate the pooled model.*

7. *Perform statistical (homogeneity) tests to determine if the pooling method is appropriate.* Recall that constraining intercepts or slopes to be constant over the cross sections may introduce bias in the parameter estimates: an F test can be applied to determine the appropriate set of constraints for the data under study. The test determines the increase in explanatory power (i.e., reduction in residual variance) of an equation when intercepts or slopes are left unconstrained:

$$F = \frac{\dfrac{\text{ESS}_{\text{more-restrictive model (mrm)}} - \text{ESS}_{\text{less-restrictive model (lrm)}}}{df_{\text{mrm}} - df_{\text{lrm}}}}{\dfrac{\text{ESS}_{\text{lrm}}}{df_{\text{lrm}}}}.$$

In the example we have been using, the less-restrictive model is one in which separate regressions are made for each cross section and the more-restrictive model is the combined OLS model. Therefore,

$$F = \frac{\dfrac{\text{ESS}_{\text{pooled (OLS)}} - \text{ESS}_{\text{SR}}}{df_{\text{OLS}} - df_{\text{SR}}}}{\dfrac{\text{ESS}_{\text{SR}}}{df_{\text{SR}}}}.$$

If the F statistic is not significant, then there is no evidence that the more restrictive model (all coefficients and intercepts the same) should be rejected. If the mean squared error statistics show significant differences, the more restrictive model assumptions are not valid and OLS is not appropriate. In this way, the F test can be used to help select the appropriate pooling method.

Similarly, the OLS model with dummy variables (analysis-of-covariance or COV model) is less restrictive than the OLS model, since the intercepts may be different for each cross section. Assume that OLS is not a valid estimation method. You can then use an F test to consider whether the analysis-of-covariance model should be applied.

$$F = \frac{\dfrac{\text{ESS}_{\text{COV}} - \text{ESS}_{\text{SR}}}{\text{df}_{\text{COV}} - \text{df}_{\text{SR}}}}{\dfrac{\text{ESS}_{\text{SR}}}{\text{df}_{\text{SR}}}};$$

ESS = estimated sum of squares, COV = covariance, SR = separate regressions, and df = degrees of freedom. If there is no significant difference in the mean squared errors, the covariance model may be used for pooling.

The F test may also be helpful in determining whether to use OLS or the co-variance method, assuming both techniques are appropriate when compared to separate regressions. If the ratio indicates a significant value for F, the less restrictive covariance model is generally selected, since the more restrictive OLS model has significantly higher residual variance. If you are willing to accept some bias, another test for determining if the unconstrained intercepts differ from one another is to calculate the simultaneous confidence intervals of the difference between all intercepts and see if zero lies within the interval. This will also point to cross sections that may be causing the problem.

For each of Models 1 and 2, we can use the F test to help decide what constraints to apply. The least restrictive model is the separate or individual regressions for each cross section (no pooling). The most-restrictive model is OLS with constant slopes and intercepts. A less-restrictive model is OLS with dummy variables (different intercepts).

Table 20.3 summarizes the F tests for the pooled models. The OLS assumptions are too restrictive in that both F statistics exceed the critical values. However, the bias in Model 1 is much less than that of Model 2. The assumption of different intercepts but constant slopes for all variables is not rejected in either case.

What impact does this result have for this study? Table 20.4 presents the estimated price elasticity and associated standard error for Model 1 for B alone and for the pooled model. Notice the large reduction in the estimated standard deviations of the price coefficient and, therefore, the smaller confidence intervals for the price elasticity.

   8. *Analyze residual plots to help verify the appropriate pooling method.*

- A correlogram of the residuals may be used to identify serial correlation in the pooled model. The constraints may introduce bias and autocorrelation.

- Plots of residuals against predictions for each time period or for the total model may be used to identify heteroscedasticity. In this regard, it is convenient to label the residuals from each cross section as shown in Figure 20.2 for Model

Table 20.3   A summary of the F tests for the pooled models.

F test	Model 1 (untransformed data)		Model 2 (data transformed for autocorrelation)	
	SSE	df	SSE	df
Sum of individual residuals (SR)	0.02537	48	0.02602	57
Pooled—OLS	0.05163	62	1.1711	67
Pooled—Analysis-of-covariance (COV)	0.03534	60	0.03471	65

Model 1

$$F_{(OLS,SR)} = \frac{(SSE_{OLS} - SSE_{SR})/(df_{OLS} - df_{SR})}{SSE_{SR}/df_{SR}} = \frac{(0.05163 - 0.02537)/(62 - 48)}{0.02537/48}$$

$$= 3.55;$$
$$F_{(14,48)} = 2.25.$$

$$F_{(COV,SR)} = \frac{(SSE_{OLS} - SSE_{SR})/(df_{COV} - df_{SR})}{SSE_{SR}/df_{SR}} = \frac{(0.03534 - 0.02537)/(60 - 48)}{0.02537/48}$$

$$= 1.57;$$
$$F_{(12,48)} = 2.41.$$

Model 2

$$F_{(OLS,SR)} = \frac{(1.1711 - 0.02602)/(67 - 57)}{0.02602/57} = \frac{0.11451}{0.000456}$$

$$= 251.11;$$
$$F_{(10,57)} = 2.63.$$

$$F_{(COV,SR)} = \frac{(0.03471 - 0.02602)/(65 - 57)}{0.02602/57} = \frac{0.001086}{0.000456}$$

$$= 2.38;$$
$$F_{(8,57)} = 3.02.$$

2. This plot suggests homoscedasticity (constant residual variance) and shows no problem areas.

Figure 20.3, on the other hand, shows a hypothetical situation where the residuals (while approximately constant in variance) are a problem for individual cross sections. Note the D residuals are all negative, the B residuals are zero or positive, the C residuals are generally positive, while the A and E residuals appear reasonable. In this case, the pooling has gone too far, since the cross sections are obviously

Table 20.4 Estimates of price elasticities, with their associated standard errors, for Model 1.

Parameter	Individual regression (State B)		Pooled (COV)	
	Coefficient	Estimated standard deviation	Coefficient	Estimated standard deviation
Constant	4.64	1.46	3.08	0.659
*Intercept B	—	—	−0.06	0.021
*Intercept C	—	—	0.23	0.053
Log of price	−0.21	0.084	−0.20 to 0.02	0.049
Log of income	0.76	0.203	0.61	0.112
Lagged Q	0.55	0.153	0.72	0.064
D_1	0.02	0.017	0.03	0.009
D_2	0.16	0.017	0.04	0.009
D_3	0.72	0.017	0.09	0.009

*Intercept for cross sections B or C equals *constant* plus the coefficients for the *intercept* B or C.

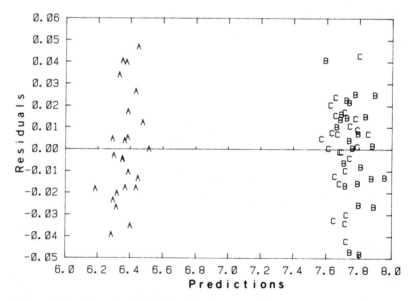

Figure 20.2 Plot of residuals from each cross section.

different in some aspect. If an additional variable in a multiple regression model would not solve this problem, pooling across all cross sections should be abandoned.

- The Q-Q plot of the residuals against the normal curve will indicate if the normality assumption is appropriate.

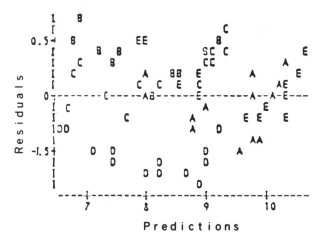

Figure 20.3   Plot of residuals for individual cross sections in a hypothetical situation.

- Cross correlograms indicate whether residuals of one cross section are correlated with the residuals of other cross sections.

The cross correlations for Model 2 between cross sections A and B and A and C
were insignificant. The cross correlogram in Figure 20.4 shows significant cross
correlation between the residuals of sections B and C at lag zero. This indicates the
need for generalized least squares estimation.

Table 20.5 summarizes the results for Model 2 for the individual regression for
cross section B corrected for autocorrelation; the pooled model with separate intercepts corrected for autocorrelation (COV); and the pooled model with separate intercepts corrected for autocorrelation and cross correlation (GLS). Notice the significant reduction in the estimated standard deviation of the price coefficient (0.076 to
0.058) with the final pooled model. In this instance, the correction for cross correlation did not improve the efficiency of the price parameter estimate. The greatest
improvement in efficiency results when the cross correlation between the residuals
of the cross sections is high and the independent variable (price in this case) in each
cross section has low correlation with the same variable in other cross sections (see
Kmenta, 1971, Chapter 12).

9. *Modify the pooling method as required on the basis of tests and information
obtained from the plots.*

10. *Stop when a satisfactory model is obtained.*

These steps were performed for the example using the pooling procedures of the
STATLIB software package—the programs used throughout this book to produce
the figures and examples. Figure 20.5 shows a flowchart containing the various
STATLIB pooling commands available to develop the pooled models.

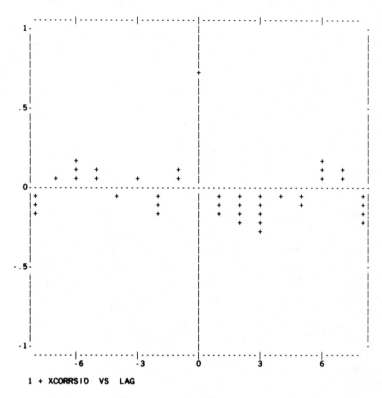

Figure 20.4 A cross correlogram between residuals for cross sections B and C.

Table 20.5 Estimates of price elasticities, with their associated standard errors, for Model 2 (corrected for autocorrelation).

Parameter	Individual Regression		Pooled (COV)		Pooled (GLS)	
	Coefficient	Estimated standard deviation	Coefficient	Estimated standard deviation	Coefficient	Estimated standard deviation
Constant	−1.83	2.593	−6.13	1.73	−7.79	1.792
*Intercept B	—	—	−0.26	0.015	−0.27	0.015
*Intercept C	—	—	−0.59	0.068	0.54	0.068
Log of price	−0.27	0.076	−0.27	0.052	−0.26	0.058
Log of income	0.64	0.202	0.44	0.153	0.23	0.145
Log of telephones	1.00	0.221	1.38	0.146	1.53	0.150
D_3	0.05	0.010	0.05	0.005	0.05	0.005

*Intercept for cross section B or C equals *constant* plus the coefficient for the intercept B or C.

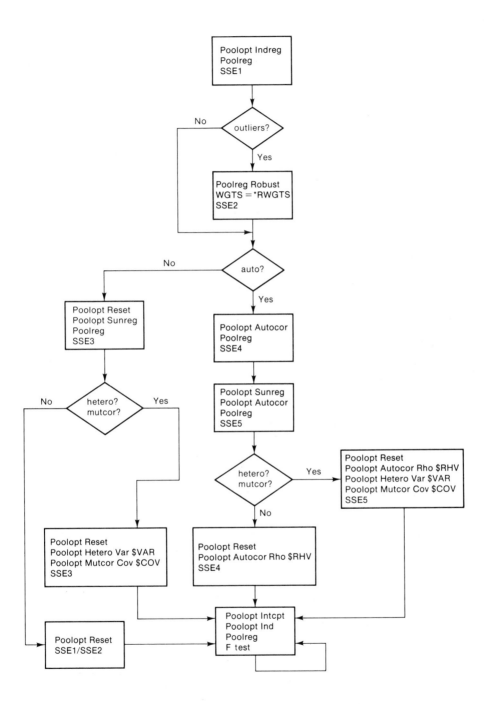

Figure 20.5 Flowchart depicting STATLIB pooling commands for developing pooled models.

POOLED MODELS CHECKLIST

_____ If both time series and cross-sectional data are available, can a "pooled" model be built to take advantage of the larger data set?

_____ Consider assumptions about each coefficient.

- Is each equal over all cross sections? That is, does $\beta_{i1} = \beta_{i2} = \cdots = \beta_{iN}$?
- If not, is each equal over some cross sections?
- Is it a fixed or random effect?

_____ Consider assumptions about the intercept:

- Is it equal over all cross sections? That is, does $\alpha_1 = \alpha_2 = \cdots = \alpha_N$?
- If not, is it equal over some cross sections?
- Is it a fixed or random effect?

_____ Consider assumptions about autocorrelation.

- Are the error terms within cross sections autocorrelated?
- If so, are the autocorrelation parameters equal over all cross sections?
- If not, are they equal over some cross sections?

_____ Consider assumptions about error variances.

- Are the error variances equal over all cross sections?
- Are they equal over some cross sections?
- Are they different on all cross sections?

_____ Are the error terms correlated over cross sections?

SUMMARY

The subject of pooling time series and cross-sectional data has received increasing attention from forecasters in recent years. Pooling

- Provides the potential for increasing the reliability of the parameter estimates by increasing the sample size and the range of variation of the independent variables.
- With a pooled OLS model, the assumption is that all intercepts and coefficients are the same across all cross sections.
- With the dummy variables for different intercepts (analysis-of-covariance) method, the assumption is that the coefficients are constant but that the inter-

cepts may be different in each cross section and over time. (A multiplicative analysis-of-covariance model also allows for some coefficients to be different for each cross section.)

USEFUL READING

BALESTRA, P., and M. NERLOVE (1966). Pooling Cross Section and Time Series Data in the Estimation of a Dynamic Model: The Demand for Natural Gas, *Econometrica* 34, 585–612.

BASS, F. M., and R. R. WITTINK (1975). Pooling Issues and Methods in Regression Analysis with Examples in Marketing Research. *Journal of Marketing Research* 12, 414–25.

JOHNSTON, J. (1972). *Econometric Methods*. Second Edition. New York, NY: McGraw-Hill.

KMENTA, J. (1971). *Elements of Econometrics*. New York, NY: MacMillan.

MADDALA, G. S. (1977). *Econometrics*. New York, NY: McGraw-Hill.

MADDALA, G. S. (1971). The Use of Variance Components Models in Pooling Cross Section and Time Series Data. *Econometrica* 39, 341–58.

MUNDLAK, Y. (1978). On the Pooling of Time Series and Cross Section Data. *Econometrica* 46, 69–85.

SWAMY, P. A. V. B. (1970). Efficient Inference in a Random Coefficient Regression Model. *Econometrica* 38, 311–23.

ZELLNER, A. (1962). An Efficient Method of Estimating Seemingly Unrelated Regressions and Tests for Aggregation Bias. *Journal of the American Statistical Association* 57, 348–68.

COMPUTER WORKSHOPS

Workshop 7—Data Display for Cross-Sectional Data

- Review the cross-sectional data available for analysis. Make sure you understand what each variable represents before proceeding.

- Review the printout of the contents of the data matrix. Examine each variable's observations and make sure you understand each definition (e.g., %, $, per household, etc.). Also examine the box plot of each variable. Check for data points that do not make sense and could possibly be outliers.

- Select a representative sample of independent variables and generate histograms and Q-Q plots. Examine the shape and characteristics of the distributions.

- Examine the relevant tables and charts for each variable's characteristics. This important data analysis will serve as your basis in following workshops.

Important Note: Save all pertinent output because your data analysis will recur through your case problems.

Workshop 8—Initial Data Analysis for Cross-Sectional Data

- Generate a correlation matrix. Examine this matrix and feel free to change any of the independent variables you selected in Workshop 6.

- Generate a scatter plot for the dependent variable versus each potential independent variable you selected.

- Analyze the scatter plots and determine the need for transforming variables. Generate the scatter plots mentioned above for the transformed data. Have you gained anything with your transformation?

- Generate descriptive statistics for all your variables.

- Review the scatter plots, box plots, and descriptive statistics.

- Examine them to determine which variables may be useful in modeling the dependent variable and look for potential outliers in the data.

- Consider what effect, if any, potential outliers may have on your model-building process. Adjust your data accordingly if outliers are a problem and perform the necessary data analysis on this adjusted data, including a new correlation matrix.

- Output your "best" data matrix (including transformed variables) to a file for permanent storage.

Workshop 9—Classical Linear Regression for Cross-Sectional Data

- Review your data analysis from previous workshops. Identify one independent variable as the "best" in explaining the dependent variable. Run a simple linear regression with this independent variable.

- Analyze the statistical measures. How well does your model predict the dependent variable? Repeat the above procedure with a different independent variable if you are dissatisfied with your results.

- Print the independent variable, the predicted values, and the residuals.

Produce a plot with the dependent variable on the vertical axis and the independent variable on the horizontal axis. Plot your residuals versus the independent variable.

- Analyze the statistical measures and check for violations of assumptions. How well does your model predict the dependent variable? Repeat the above sequence with a different independent variable if you are dissatisfied with your results.

- Develop the "best" regression model for the dependent variable versus any number of independent variables. Analyze the statistical measures and check all plots for violations of assumptions.

- Print and plot the dependent variable and predicted values. Obtain a Q-Q plot of the predicted values against the dependent variables. How do they compare?

Part 5

The Box-Jenkins
Approach to Forecasting

CHAPTER 21

Filtering Techniques for Forecasting

The fourth part of this book deals with a class of models that can produce forecasts based on a synthesis of historical patterns in data. The construction of these models

- Applies a single, unified theory to the description of a wide range of stationary and nonstationary (seasonal and trending) time series.

- Allows a linear representation of a stationary time series in terms of its own past values and a weighted sum of a current error term and lagged error terms.

- Provides a systematic procedure for forecasting a time series from its own current and past values.

This chapter introduces the concept of stationarity for time series and provides a description of the class of autoregressive moving-average (ARMA) models, which can be used with stationary time series. The next chapter introduces the Box-Jenkins strategy for fitting models to nonstationary as well as stationary time series data, and the remaining four chapters will treat the specifics of this modeling strategy for a wide variety of other kinds of time series.

FILTERING TECHNIQUES FOR TIME SERIES

Autoregressive moving-average (ARMA) models are a specialized but highly powerful class of *linear* filtering techniques by which a random input is "filtered" so that the output represents the observed or transformed time series. Filtering techniques, widely used in control engineering, have only in recent years found practical use in business forecasting. The general theory of linear filters (Whittle, 1963) is not new, since much of the original work was done by the renowned mathematicians Kolmogorov and Wiener in the 1930's for automatic control problems. The special kind of *linear* filter called the *autoregressive* (AR) model goes back a little further: AR models are generally considered to have been first used by Yule (1927). Another kind of filter, called the *moving-average* (MA) model, was introduced by Slutsky (1937). Autoregressive moving-average (ARMA) theory, in which these models are combined, was developed by Wold (1954).

A general *model-building strategy* for these models can be attributed to Professors G. E. P. Box and G. M. Jenkins; developed during the past three decades, their strategy is the result of their direct experience with forecasting problems in business, economic, and engineering environments. In Box and Jenkins (1976) they present a formally structured class of time series models that are sufficiently flexible to describe many practical situations. Known as *autoregressive integrated moving-average* (ARIMA) models, these are capable of describing various stationary *and* nonstationary (time-dependent) phenomena (unlike ARMA models, which require stationary data) in a statistical rather than in a deterministic manner. Other treatments of the *Box-Jenkins procedure* may be found in Anderson (1976), Granger and Newbold (1977), Hoff (1984), Mabert (1975), Makridakis and Wheelwright (1978), Nelson (1973), and Pankratz (1983).

WHY USE ARIMA MODELS?

In *The Beginning Forecaster,* it was shown how to analyze a trend/seasonal time series by constructing a two-way table. Although such a table requires the estimation of many coefficients (e.g., monthly and yearly means), the information that is obtained cannot be used effectively for predicting future values. Alternatively, regression analysis offered a means of fitting linear models in which functions of time (e.g., straight lines and polynomials) were independent variables: they often fit well over a limited range, yet often forecast poorly when extrapolated. Moreover, although regression models utilize external (economic and demographic) independent variables, forecasts of these must be added to a comprehensive, final forecast in order to obtain an effective prediction of future values. ARIMA models offer a way of circumventing some of these difficulties.

The ARIMA models have also proved to be excellent *short-term* forecasting models for a wide variety of time series. In a number of studies (see Granger and Newbold, 1977), forecasts from simple ARIMA models have frequently outperformed larger, more complex econometric systems for a number of economic series. Nevertheless, while it is possible to construct ARIMA models with only two years of monthly historical data, the best results are usually obtained when at least five to ten years of data are available—particularly if the series exhibits strong seasonality.

The drawback of ARIMA models is that, because they are univariate, they have very limited explanatory capability. The models are essentially sophisticated extrapolative devices that are of greatest use when it is expected that the underlying factors causing demand for products, services, revenues, etc., will behave in the future much in the same way as in the past. In the short term, this is often a reasonable expectation, however, because these factors tend to change slowly; data tend to show inertia in the short term.

A significant advantage of ARIMA models is that forecasts can be developed in a very short time. More time is spent obtaining and validating the data than in building the models. Therefore, a practitioner can often deliver significant results early in a project for which an ARIMA model is used. The forecaster should always consider ARIMA models as an important forecasting method whenever these models are relevant to the problem being studied.

CREATING A STATIONARY TIME SERIES

The autoregressive moving-average (ARMA) time series models are designed for *stationary* time series; that is, series whose basic statistical properties (e.g., means, variances, and covariances) remain constant over time. Thus, in order to build ARMA models, nonstationarity must first be identified and removed. Nonstationarity typically includes periodic variations and systematic changes in mean (trend) and variance.

The precise definition of stationarity is a complex one. Suffice it to say that for practical purposes, the data used in a random process are said to be *weakly stationary* if the first and second moments of the process are time-independent. This assumption implies, among other things, that the mean and variance of the data are constant and finite.

Another critical assumption in describing stationary time series comes as a result of the chronological order of the data. The difference between conventional regression methods and time series modeling of the sort possible with ARMA models is that independence of the observations cannot be assumed; in fact, in ARMA modeling it is the *mutual dependence* among observations that is of primary interest.

Identifying Nonstationarity

Generally, many kinds of nonstationarity are present in time series data. The simplest is known as *nonstationarity in the level of the mean* and occurs when the level of the mean changes or "drifts" over different segments of the data. A trending time series is a good example.

Nonstationarity can also occur as a result of a seasonal pattern in the data. A seasonal series cannot be considered stationary because the variation in the data is a function of the time of the year.

Another kind of nonstationarity is the result of increasing or decreasing variability of the data with time. Sales data may have a nonlinear trend or show increasing variability in the seasonal peaks and troughs over time.

Still another kind of nonstationarity can occur as a result of a drastic change in the level of some series. Examples of time series that change drastically are price or unemployment data. An unemployment rate is a series that tends to stay at a high or a low level, depending on economic conditions: the change is usually abrupt and time-dependent.

A combination of several or all of the above characteristics will usually be present in nonstationary real data. In reality, most time series are nonstationary.

Removing Nonstationarity through Differencing

In practice, many time series can be made stationary through differencing. Such a nonstationary series is termed *homogeneous*. Fortunately, many of the time series that arise in economics and business are of this type. Let us examine a typical homogeneous time series and see how it can be made stationary.

Consider the seasonally adjusted money supply series shown in Figure 21.1; this is the U.S. Treasury Department M1 Series. It shows nonstationary behavior in its level. This trend pattern is removed by taking difference of order 1 of the data. Figure 21.2 (a) shows the differenced series; it has an increase in level and an increasing variability with time.

Consider taking a second difference of order 1, shown in Figure 21.2(b); this gives rise to a series that now appears to have a constant mean, but continues to show an uneven variability over time. It is unlikely that further differencing is called for.

In most economic data it appears that differences should be taken, at most, twice. The number of times that the original series must be differenced before a stationary series results is termed the *order of homogeneity* of the series. As a first step, it is important to identify the *minimum* amount of differencing required to create a stationary series. "Overdifferencing" can rarely be compensated for by modeling.

In the case of the money supply data, it is not possible to obtain constancy of variance through differencing. It is better to take logarithms of the data first and then take first differences of the log-transformed data. (It is clear that the logarithms of the money supply data are nonstationary.) By taking first differences of the log-transformed data (growth rates), as shown in Figure 21.3, the resulting series appears stationary.

Another transformation that often works prior to differencing is the square-root transformation. The first differences of the square root of the money supply data did

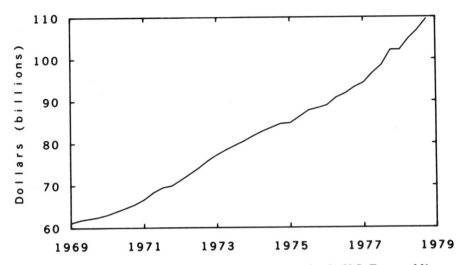

Figure 21.1 A time plot of seasonally adjusted money supply: the U.S. Treasury M1 Series, 1969–79.

Source: Board of governors of the Federal Reserve System.

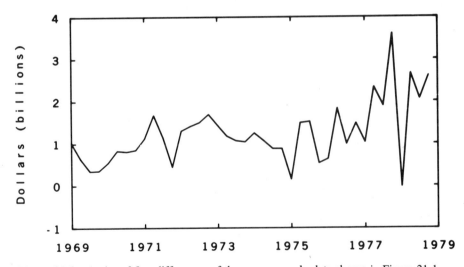

Figure 21.2 A plot of first differences of the money supply data shown in Figure 21.1.

not appear to be very different from the percent changes of the money supply. Thus it would appear to be more natural to work with the percent changes (growth rates) of the money supply series as the stationary series for modeling purposes.

There are situations in which differencing alone can change a nonstationary series to a reasonably stationary one. More general situations may require a trans-

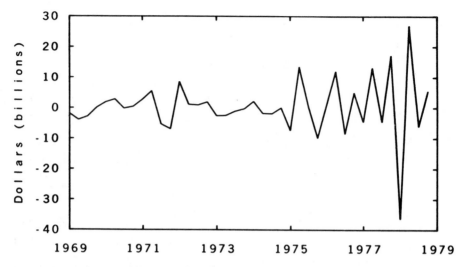

Figure 21.2(b)   A plot of the second differences of the money supply data shown in 21.1.

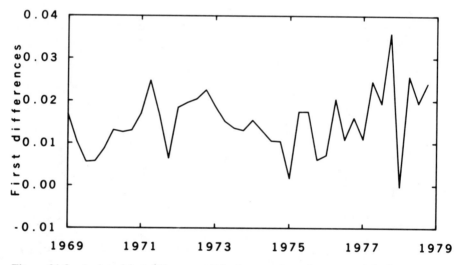

Figure 21.3   A plot of first differences of the log-transformed money supply data.

formation of the Box-Cox type prior to differencing (Granger and Newbold, 1976); this includes taking a square root transformation and a logarithmic transformation. The class of time series models discussed in the remainder of this book assumes that stationarity can be achieved essentially through differencing and transformations.

LINEAR MODELS FOR STATIONARY SERIES

Once a time series has been made stationary, it can be used with a linear filter in order to devise a forecast. Once an appropriate filter has been determined for the series, an *optimal* forecasting procedure follows directly from the theory.

The Linear Filter as a Black Box

The ARMA models are important because they are mathematically tractable; moreover, they are flexible enough to describe many time series. The role they play is equivalent to that of the linear differential equation in the study of deterministic systems, such as are encountered in control theory or physics.

Application of linear models is based on the idea that a time series in which successive values are highly dependent can also be thought of as having come from a process involving a series of independent errors or "shocks" $\{\varepsilon_t\}$. The general form of a (discrete) *linear process* is

$$Y_t = \alpha + \varepsilon_t + \psi_1\varepsilon_{t-1} + \cdots + \psi_n\varepsilon_{t-n} + \cdots,$$

where α and all ψ are fixed parameters and the $\{\varepsilon_t\}$ is a sequence of identically, independently distributed random errors with zero mean and constant variance. Thus the process is *linear* because Y_t is represented as a linear combination of current and past shocks. It is often referred to as a *black box* or filter because the model relates a random input to an output that is time-dependent. The input is filtered or "damped" by the equation so that what comes out of the equation has the characteristics that are wanted.

A linear process can be visualized as a *black box* in this manner (Figure 21.4): white noise—purely random error $\{\varepsilon_t\}$—is transformed to the observed series $\{Y_t\}$ by the operation of a linear filter; the filtering operation simply takes a weighted sum of previous shocks. The weights are known as ψ coefficients.

The concept of *white noise,* which we explained earlier, is of central importance to time series analysis, just as independent observational error is of central importance to classical statistical analysis. The reason is that the next value ε_t of white noise is *unpredictable* even if all previous values $\varepsilon_{t-1}, \varepsilon_{t-2}, \ldots$, and subsequent values $\varepsilon_{t+1}, \varepsilon_{t+2}, \ldots$, are known.

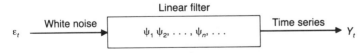

Figure 21.4 A black-box representation of the linear random process.

The ARMA Model as a Linear Filter

In many problems, such as those in which it is required that future values of a series be predicted, it is necessary to construct a *parametric model* for the time series. To be useful, the model should be physically meaningful and involve as few parameters as possible. A powerful parametric model that has been widely used in practice for describing empirical time series is the previously mentioned autoregressive moving-average (ARMA) model:

$$Y_t = \alpha + \emptyset_1 Y_{t-1} + \cdots + \emptyset_p Y_{t-p} + \varepsilon_t - \theta_1 \varepsilon_{t-1} - \cdots - \theta_q \varepsilon_{t-q} \, ,$$

where $p =$ the highest lag associated with the data, and $q =$ the highest lag associated with the error term.

Consider a time series $Y_t = \varepsilon_t, \ t = 0, \pm 1, \pm 2, \ldots$, where ε_t is independent of all other values $\varepsilon_{t-1}, \varepsilon_{t-2}, \ldots, \varepsilon_{t+1}, \varepsilon_{t+2}, \ldots$. This time series is *purely random*. If all ε_t are normally distributed, as well, the data are said to be *white noise*. The counts of radioactive decay from a long-lived sample and even the changes in the level of stock prices are examples of data that are stationary and can be regarded as white noise.

One simple *linear* random process is the moving average (MA) process. For example, the formula for a *first-order MA process* (MA(1)) is

$$Y_t = \alpha + \varepsilon_t - \theta_1 \varepsilon_{t-1} \, ,$$

where α and θ are parameters and σ_ε^2 is the variance of all ε_t .

An example of an MA(1) process with $\theta_1 = 0.25$ is given in Figure 21.5. In general, a qth-order MA process has the form

$$Y_t = \alpha + \varepsilon_t - \theta_1 \varepsilon_{t-1} - \theta_2 \varepsilon_{t-2} - \cdots - \theta_q \varepsilon_{t-q} \, ,$$

where the model is specified by the $q + 2$ parameters $\sigma_\varepsilon^2, \alpha, \theta_1, \ldots, \theta_q$. This model states that the values of Y_t consist of a moving average of the errors ε_t reaching back q periods. The coefficients (parameters) of the error terms are designated by θ's and the minus signs are introduced by convention. It is still assumed that the errors are independent, but the observed values of Y_t are dependent, being a weighted function of prior errors.

Another simple linear random process is the autoregressive (AR) process. The formula for a *first-order AR process* (AR(1), also known as a Markov process), is

$$Y_t = \alpha + \emptyset_1 Y_{t-1} + \varepsilon_t \, ,$$

where $\sigma_\varepsilon^2, \alpha$, and $\emptyset$, are parameters. This model states that the value Y_t of the process is given by $\emptyset_1$ times the previous value plus an error ε_t . Realizations of an AR(1) process with $\emptyset_1 = +0.9$ and -0.9 are shown in Figures 21.6 and 21.7, respectively.

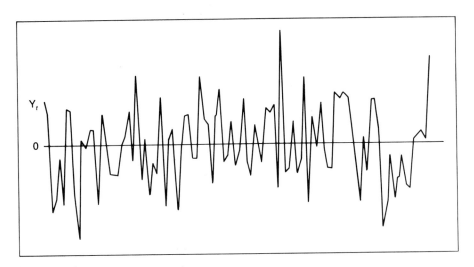

Figure 21.5   Realization of an MA(1) process ($\theta_1 = 0.25$).

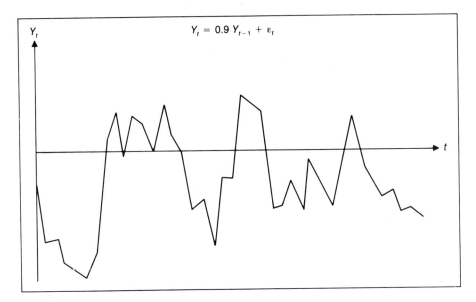

Figure 21.6   Realization of an AR(1) process ($\emptyset_1 = 0.9$).

In general, a pth-order AR process has the form

$$Y_t = \alpha + \emptyset_1 Y_{t-1} + \emptyset_2 Y_{t-2} + \cdots + \emptyset_p Y_{t-p} + \varepsilon_t .$$

The term autoregression that is used to describe such a process arises because an AR(p) model is much like a multiple linear-regression model. The essential

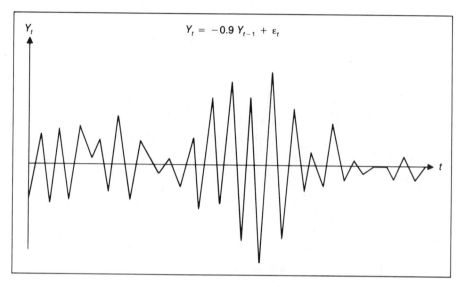

Figure 21.7 Realization of an AR(1) process ($\emptyset_1 = -0.9$).

difference is that Y_t is not regressed on independent variables but rather on lagged values of itself: hence the term *autoregression*. A realization of an AR(2) process, with $\emptyset_1 = +1.0$ and $\emptyset_2 = -0.5$, is shown in Figure 21.8.

It can be shown that any linear process can be written formally as a weighted sum of the current and all past *errors*. If that weighted sum has only a finite number of nonzero error terms, then the process is a moving average process. The linear process can also be expressed as a weighted sum of all past *observations* plus the current error term. If the number of nonzero terms in this expression is finite, then the process is autoregressive.

Thus, an MA process of finite order can be expressed as an AR process of infinite order, and an AR process of finite order can be expressed as an MA process of infinite order. This duality has led to the *principle of parsimony* in the Box-Jenkins methodology (discussed in the next chapter), in which it is advocated that the practitioner employ the smallest possible number of parameters for adequate representation of a model.

It may often be possible to describe a stationary time series with a model involving fewer parameters than either the MA or the AR process has by itself. Such a model will possess qualities of both autoregressive and moving average models: it is called an ARMA process. An ARMA(1,1) process has one prior observation term of lag 1 and one prior error term:

$$Y_t = \alpha + \emptyset_1 Y_{t-1} + \varepsilon_t - \theta_1 \varepsilon_{t-1} .$$

The general ARMA(p,q) process of autoregressive order p and moving-average order q has the form

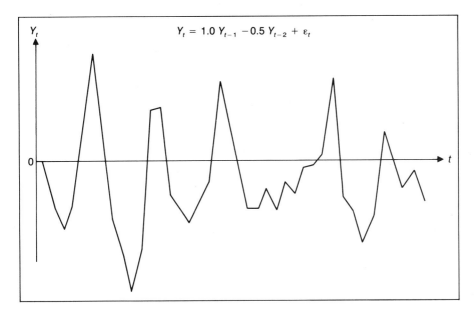

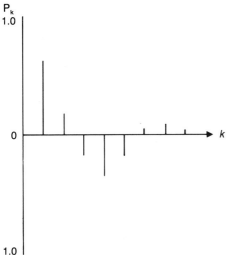

Figure 21.8   Realization and ACF process ($\emptyset_1 = 1.0$, $\emptyset_2 = -0.5$).

$$Y_t = \alpha + \emptyset_1 Y_{t-1} + \emptyset_2 Y_{t-2} + \cdots + \emptyset_p Y_{t-p} + \varepsilon_t - \theta_1 \varepsilon_{t-1} - \cdots - \theta_q \varepsilon_{t-q}.$$

In short, the ARMA process is a *linear random* process. It is linear if Y_t is a linear combination of lagged values of Y_t and ε_t. It is random if the errors (also called disturbances or shocks) are introduced into the system in the form of white noise. The random errors ε_t are assumed to be independent of each other and to be identically distributed with a mean of zero and a variance of σ_ε^2.

LINEAR MODELS FOR NONSTATIONARY SERIES

We noted earlier that most time series encountered in forecasting applications are not stationary. If a nonstationary time series can be made stationary by taking *d* differences (usually of order 0, 1, or 2), this gives an ARMA model for the *differenced* series; this is called an ARIMA model for the original series; hence the term *integrated* to suggest "undifferencing."

The *order* of an ARIMA model is given by the three letters *p*, *d*, and *q*. By convention, the order of the autoregressive component is *p*, the order of differencing needed to achieve stationarity is *d*, and the order of the moving-average part is *q*.

The ARIMA(*p,d,q*) model is the most general model considered here. It is also the most widely used model. Many times it is necessary to take differences to achieve stationarity, but the resulting series may require only an autoregressive (*p*) or a moving-average (*q*) component. These models will be called *autoregressive integrated* (ARI) or *integrated moving-average* (IMA) models. The term "integrated" is used when differencing is performed to achieve stationarity since the stationary series must be summed ("integrated") to recover the original data. The number of differencing is generally 1 or 2 in practice (Figure 21.9).

Many economic forecasting methods use exponentially weighted moving averages and they can be shown to be appropriate for a particular type of nonstationary process. Indeed, the stochastic model through which the exponentially weighted moving average produces an optimal forecast is a member of the class of ARIMA models: a range of ARIMA models exists to provide stationary and nonstationary treatments of the time series met in practice.

SUMMARY

The autoregressive integrated moving-average (ARIMA) models are capable of describing a wide variety of time series for forecasters. They form the framework for

- Expressing various forms of stationary and nonstationary behavior in time series.

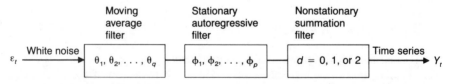

Figure 21.9   A block-diagram representation of an autoregressive integrated moving-average (ARIMA) model.

- A flexible modeling methodology.
- Producing optimal forecasts for a time series from its own current and past values.

USEFUL READING

ANDERSON, O. D. (1976). *Time Series Analysis and Forecasting—The Box-Jenkins Approach*. London, England: Butterworth.

BOX, G. E. P., and G. M. JENKINS (1976). *Time Series Analysis, Forecasting and Control, Revised Edition*. San Francisco, CA: Holden-Day.

GRANGER, C. W. J., and P. NEWBOLD (1977). *Forecasting Economic Time Series*. New York, NY: Academic Press.

HOFF, J. (1984). *A Practical Guide to Box-Jenkins Forecasting*. Belmont, CA: Lifetime Learning Publications.

MABERT, V. A. (1975). *An Introduction to Short-Term Forecasting Using the Box-Jenkins Methodology*. Production Planning and Control Monograph Series No. 2. Norcross, GA: American Institute of Industrial Engineers.

MAKRIDAKIS, S., and S. C. WHEELWRIGHT (1978). *Forecasting Methods and Applications*. New York, NY: John Wiley and Sons.

NELSON, C. R. (1973). *Applied Time-Series Analysis*. San Francisco, CA: Holden-Day.

PANKRATZ, A. (1983). *Forecasting with Univariate Box-Jenkins Models*. New York, NY: John Wiley and Sons.

SLUTSKY, E. (1937). The Summation of Random Causes as the Source of Cyclic Processes. *Econometrica* 5, 105–46.

WHITTLE, P. (1963). *Prediction and Regulation by Linear Least-Squares Methods*. London, England: English University Press.

WOLD, H. O. (1954). *A Study in the Analysis of Stationary Time Series*, 1st edition 1938. Uppsala, Sweden: Almquist and Wicksell.

YULE, G. U. (1927). On a Method of Investigating Periodicities in Disturbed Series, with Special Reference to Wolfer's Sunspot Numbers. *Philosophical Transactions* A 226, 267-98.

CHAPTER 22

The Box-Jenkins Model-Building Strategy

The previous chapter introduced a powerful class of time series models, known as ARIMA models, that have found extensive application in a number of areas.

The selection of ARIMA models or, indeed, of any sufficiently flexible, physically interpretable class of models for describing time series can be achieved through a three-stage iterative procedure. This procedure consists of

- Identification.

- Estimation.

- Diagnostic checking.

A THREE-STAGE PROCEDURE FOR SELECTION OF MODELS

A three-stage strategy for modeling a time series with ARIMA models was developed in the pioneering work of Box and Jenkins (1976).

- *Identification* consists of using the data and any other knowledge that will tentatively indicate if the time series can be described with a moving average model, an autoregressive model, or a mixed autoregressive moving-average model for a selection of the (p,d,q) values of the model.

- *Estimation* consists of using the data to make inferences about the parameters that will be needed for the tentatively identified model, and to estimate values of them.

- *Diagnostic checking* involves the examination of residuals from fitted models, which can result in either

- No indication of model inadequacy, or
- Model inadequacy, together with information on how the series may be better described.

Thus the residuals would be examined for any lack of randomness and, if the residuals are serially correlated, this information would be used to modify the model. The modified model would then be fitted and subjected to diagnostic checking again until an adequate model is obtained.

IDENTIFICATION TOOLS

In identification of an appropriate ARIMA model, the first thing to do is to transform and/or difference the data to produce stationarity, thereby reducing the model to one in the ARMA class. Then the ordinary and partial correlograms for the various patterns of differencing that are found in the adjusted data need to be displayed and compared to a basic catalog of theoretical patterns. These are taken up in Chapter 23.

The Ordinary Correlogram

The basic tools for identification are the autocorrelation function, designated ACF, and the partial autocorrelation function, designated PACF. The *ordinary* and *partial correlograms* are estimates of the ACF and PACF. For example, the ordinary correlogram is determined by correlating the previously adjusted or transformed series with versions of the series in which the units of time have been shifted. This yields a set of numbers, which can be plotted successively, corresponding to each time shift or *lag*. The ordinary or *auto*correlogram is simply a plot of the estimated autocorrelations.

Nonstationarity may be present if the values plotted in the correlogram do not diminish at large lags. When the original series or correlogram exhibits nonstationarity, successive differencing is carried out until the correlogram of the differenced series dies out reasonably rapidly. It is usually sufficient to look at the correlograms of the original series and of its first- and second-order differences.

The correlogram is a powerful tool for deciding whether the process shows pure autoregressive behavior or moving average behavior. The correlogram of a time series can be obtained by computing

$$r_j = c_j/c_0$$

for $j = 0, 1, 2, 3, \ldots, k$, where

$$c_j = \frac{1}{n} \sum_{t=1}^{n-j} [(y_t - \bar{y})(y_{t+j} - \bar{y})] ,$$

and

$$\bar{y} = \frac{1}{n} \sum_{t=1}^{n} y_t .$$

For large n, r_j is approximately normally distributed with a mean of $-1/n$ and variance of $1/n$. Thus approximate 95-percent confidence limits can be plotted at $\pm 1.96/\sqrt{n}$. Observed values of r_j that fall outside these limits are significantly different from zero at the 5-percent level. If the first 20 values of the correlogram are plotted, then you might expect one significant value even if the r_j's are random.

In practice, the number of r_j's calculated for a correlogram varies with the length of the series and the length of the seasonal cycle. Generally, for a 12-month seasonal series, about 36 to 60 monthly values are appropriate. No more than about $n/4$ to $n/3$ correlations should be calculated for a series of length n. Otherwise, there are not enough terms in the calculation for higher lags for any inferences to be meaningful. It is desirable that $n > 50$.

The Partial Correlogram

The *partial correlogram* complements the ordinary correlogram. Although more difficult to interpret, it measures the strength of the relationship between time periods in a series when dependence on intervening time periods has been removed. If the data in period t are highly related to period $t - k$, then the partial autocorrelogram would result in a large value (or "spike") at lag k.

If you assume that the model for the time series is purely autoregressive, an estimate of the order p can be obtained by successively fitting autoregressive models of orders one, two, three, four, and so on, to the series. The partial autocorrelation coefficient at lag k is an estimate of the *last parameter* ϕ_k in an autoregressive *model* of order k that is fitted to the series. If the order of the model is p, then all partial autocorrelations greater than p should be zero. By noting when the last significant lag in the partial autocorrelogram occurs, you can make an initial estimate of p.

The kth value R_k of a partial correlogram is given by the solution of the set of equations

$$r_j = \emptyset_1 r_{j-1} + \emptyset_2 r_{j-2} + \cdots + \emptyset_k r_{j-k} , \qquad \text{for } j = 1, 2, \ldots, k ,$$

and with $R_k = \emptyset_k$.

The variance of the kth partial correlogram coefficient, under the hypothesis that the process is of order $p < k$, is approximately $1/n$. If the PACF truncates (that is, if it has a value of zero after a certain number of lags), the process is AR, and the truncation point specifies the order p. A useful simple approximation is that the partial correlogram estimate R_k, $k > p$, is described approximately by a normal random variable with zero mean and variance $1/n$. Hence, if a series of R_k values beyond the pth lie within the 95-percent limits, $\pm 1.96/\sqrt{n}$, it may be reasonable to infer that the process is AR(p).

Some general guidelines for selecting appropriate ARMA models on the basis of ACF and PACF plots and through their interpretations, are covered next.

Interpreting Autocorrelation Functions

Extreme care must be taken in interpreting autocorrelation functions. The interpretation is complex and requires considerable experience. Attention should be directed to the *values* as well as the *patterns* of the autocorrelation coefficients. The ACF's of low-order ARMA models will be used later to help identify the model.

The theoretical autocorrelation function (ACF) of the pure MA(q) process truncates, being zero after lag q, while that for the pure AR(p) process is of infinite extent (Figure 22.1). MA processes are thus characterized by truncation of the ACF while AR processes are characterized by attenuation of the ACF.

In some situations it may not be clear whether the ACF truncates or attenuates. Hence it is useful to supplement the analysis by considering the partial autocorrelation function, PACF. For an AR process, the ACF attenuates and the PACF truncates; conversely, for an MA process, the PACF attenuates and the ACF truncates.

Autocorrelation Function (ACF)

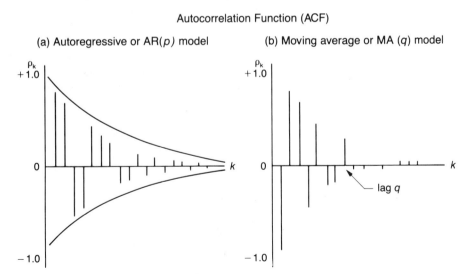

Figure 22.1   The autocorrelation function (ACF) of (a) a pure AR(p) model and (b) a pure MA(q) model.

The ACF of an AR process behaves like the PACF of an MA process and vice versa. If both the ACF and the PACF attenuate, then a mixed model is called for. This subject will be treated in more detail in Chapter 23.

PARAMETER ESTIMATION

The second stage of the model-building strategy is the estimation or fitting stage. ARMA models can be fitted by least squares. An iterative nonlinear least-squares procedure is used to obtain the parameter estimates

$$(\hat{\alpha}, \hat{\emptyset}, \hat{\theta},) = (\hat{\alpha}, \hat{\emptyset}_1, \ldots, \hat{\emptyset}_p, \hat{\theta}_1, \ldots, \hat{\theta}_q)$$

of an ARMA(p,q) model. The estimates minimize the sum of squares of errors; that is,

$$S(\alpha, \emptyset, \theta) = \sum_{t=1}^{n} \varepsilon_t^2 ,$$

given the form of the model and the data. Since the procedure is, in general, non-linear (because of the moving-average terms), initial values for the parameters must be estimated so that minimization can be started.

There are a variety of parameter-estimation methods available in the literature (see Box and Jenkins 1976, Chapter 7) to which an interested reader can refer for details. For low-order ARMA models there are software programs that can be used to plot certain data in the neighborhood of estimated parameters, so that the behavior of a model can be visualized. This can provide insight into the sensitivity with which various starting values produce various results, and hence, gives estimates of the precision of the coefficients. For higher-order models few general guidelines exist, except to direct the model builder towards a preference for the use of *parsimonious* models ("the fewer parameters the better"). Parsimony is a practical rather than a theoretical consideration. Experience with many kinds of data series has convinced us that parsimonious models are generally better forecasting models.

Once the parameters are estimated it is also important to determine a matrix of estimated variances and covariances of the coefficients. Based on large-sample theory, the standard deviations of the parameter estimates (usually referred to as standard errors) are obtained from this and used to determine if the parameters are significantly different from zero.

Under the hypothesis that a single parameter $\beta = \beta_0$, approximate tests may be derived from

$$\frac{\hat{\beta} - \beta}{s(\hat{\beta})} \sim N(0,1),$$

where $s(\hat{\beta})$ denotes the estimated standard deviation of $\hat{\beta}$. Usually, the hypothesis to be tested is formulated as: "Is β significantly different from zero?" Also, a 95-percent confidence interval for β is given by

$$\hat{\beta} - 1.96 \, s(\hat{\beta}) < \beta < \hat{\beta} + 1.96 \, s(\hat{\beta}) \, .$$

The variance σ_ε^2 of the error term in the model also needs to be estimated. An estimate of σ_ε^2 is $S(\hat{\alpha}, \hat{\theta}, \hat{\phi},)/n$, where S is the sum-of-squares function minimized for the $p+q+1$ parameters. In practice there appears to be little importance to modifying the denominator n to $n-p-q$, unless n is very small.

It must be remembered that the basic assumption of independence is violated when applying classical regression theory to time series; however, some comfort can be taken in the fact that most results are valid provided there are "enough" observations. In formal terms, the results are asymptotically valid.

DIAGNOSTIC CHECKING

The last stage of the model-building strategy involves diagnostic checking. Analytical techniques are used to detect inadequacies in the model and to suggest model revisions. It may be necessary to introduce new information into the model after this stage and to initiate another three-stage procedure for assessing the new model.

To ensure that the best forecasting model has been obtained it is important to examine the fitted residuals. If the model is ultimately selected for use as a forecasting tool, the performance of the model should also be monitored periodically during its use so that it can be updated when appropriate.

Diagnostic checking involves examining statistical properties of the residuals. Tests should be designed to detect departures from the assumptions on which the model is based and to indicate how further fitting and checking should be performed. When the model is adequate the residual series should be independently and randomly distributed about zero. Any dependence or nonrandomness would indicate the presence of information that could be exploited to improve the accuracy of the model.

There are three ways in which a fitted model can be checked for adequacy of fit.

- The model can be made intentionally more complex by *overfitting;* those parameters whose significance is in question can be tested statistically.

- A more technical test involves the testing of correlogram estimates individually or in an overall *chi-squared test.*

- A third check involves a *cumulative periodogram* test.

These three diagnostic tests will now be treated in greater detail.

Overfitting

When a tentatively identified model is to be enhanced, an additional parameter can be added to the model (this is the method of overfitting) and the hypothesis that the additional parameter is zero can be tested by a t test. Thus an AR(1) model could be tested by overfitting with an AR(2) model or an ARMA(1,1) model, for instance.

The estimate $\hat{\sigma}_\varepsilon^2$ of the square of the residual standard error can also be used for diagnostic checking. A plot of $\hat{\sigma}_\varepsilon^2$ (adjusted for degrees of freedom) against the number of additional parameters should decrease with improved fitting. When overfitting, the improvement, if any, in decreased $\hat{\sigma}_\varepsilon^2$ may be inconsequential.

A Chi-squared Test

Correlograms and partial correlograms are probably the most useful diagnostic tools available. If the residuals are not random these diagrams may suggest residual auto-correlations that can be further modeled.

A chi-squared test can be used to evaluate whether the overall correlogram of the residuals exhibits any systematic error. When the chi-squared statistic exceeds the threshold level, the residual series contains more structure than would be expected for a random series. The test statistic due to Box and Pierce (1970) and modified by Ljung and Box (1978) is given by the formula

$$Q = n(n + 2) \sum_{k=1}^{m} (n - k)^{-1} r_k^2 ,$$

where r_k ($k = 1, \ldots, m$) are residual autocorrelations, n is the number of observations used to fit the model, and m is usually taken to be 15 or 20. Then Q has an approximate chi-squared distribution with $(m - p - q)$ degrees of freedom. For an ARIMA(p,d,q) model, n is the number of terms in the differenced data. This is a general test of the hypothesis of model adequacy, in which a large observed value of Q points to inadequacy. Even if the statistic Q is not significant a review of the residual time series for unusual values is still appropriate.

It may also appear practical to examine individual values in the correlogram of the residuals relative to a set of confidence limits. Those values that fall outside the limits are examined further. Upon investigation, appropriate MA or AR terms can be included in the model.

Periodogram Analysis

In case of periodic nonrandom effects the cumulative periodogram can be an effective diagnostic tool. The test has its basis in "frequency domain" analysis of time series (Jenkins and Watts, 1968).

For the residual series $\{\varepsilon_t\}$ a *periodogram* $I(f_i)$ is defined by

$$I(f_i) = \frac{2}{n}\left[\left(\sum_{t=1}^{n} \hat{\varepsilon}_t \cos 2\pi f_i t\right)^2 + \left(\sum_{t=1}^{n} \hat{\varepsilon}_t \sin 2\pi f_i t\right)^2\right],$$

where $f_i = i/n, \ i = 0, 1, \ldots, n/2$ is the frequency. Large values of $I(f_i)$ are produced when a pattern with given frequency f_i in the residuals correlates highly with a sine or cosine wave at the same frequency. Then the *normalized cumulative periodogram* is defined by

$$C(f_j) = \frac{1}{ns^2}\sum_{i=1}^{j} I(f_i),$$

where s^2 is an estimate of σ_ε^2.

For a white-noise residual series, the plot of $C(f_j)$ against $f_j, \ j=0,1,\ldots,n/2$ would be scattered about a straight line joining the coordinates $(0,0)$ and $(0.5,1)$. Inadequacies in the fit to a model would show up as systematic deviations from this line. A standard statistical test, called the *Kolmogorov-Smirnov test,* uses the maximum vertical deviation of the plot from the straight line as the statistic for determining unsuspected periodicities in the data (Box and Jenkins 1976, Chapter 8).

SUMMARY

This chapter has covered the three-stage ARIMA modeling process; the three stages are

- Identification (or specification) of forecasting models by using data analysis tools (plotting of raw, differenced, and transformed data), correlograms, and partial correlograms, for the purpose of making *tentative guesses* at the order of the parameters in the ARMA model.

- Estimates of parameters for tentative models.

- Diagnostic checking, which is a critical step in looking for model *inadequacies* or for areas where *simplification* can take place.

The Box-Jenkins approach for ARIMA modeling provides the forecaster with a very powerful and flexible tool. It is an excellent method for forecasting a time series from its own current and past values, but it should not be applied blindly and automatically to all forecasting problems. Its complexity requires a fair amount of sophistication and judgment in its use. The results in terms of forecasting accuracy and understanding processes generating data can be significant in the hands of a skilled user.

USEFUL READING

ANDERSON, O. D. (1976). *Time Series Analysis and Forecasting—The Box-Jenkins Approach*. London, England: Butterworth.

BOX, G. E. P., and G. M. JENKINS (1976). *Time Series Analysis: Forecasting and Control, Revised Edition*. San Francisco, CA: Holden-Day.

BOX, G. E. P., and D. A. PIERCE (1970). Distribution of Residual Autocorrelations in Autoregressive Integrated Moving-Average Time-Series Models. *Journal of the American Statistical Association* 65, 1509–26.

JENKINS, G. M., and D. G. WATTS (1968). *Spectral Analysis and Its Applications*. San Francisco, CA: Holden-Day.

LJUNG, G. M., and G. E. P. BOX (1978). On a Measure of Fit in Time Series Models. *Biometrika* 65, 297–303.

NELSON, C. R. (1973). *Applied Time Series Analysis for Managerial Forecasting*. San Francisco, CA: Holden-Day.

CHAPTER 23

Identifying Regular ARIMA Models

This chapter describes the identification of *regular* ARIMA models. These models are appropriate for

- Nonseasonal time series.

- Seasonally adjusted series.

- Series with strong trend characteristics.

- Series that exhibit a random walk (like changes in stock prices).

Seasonal models are discussed in Chapter 25. In many cases time series are modeled best with a combination of regular and seasonal parameters.

EXPRESSING ARIMA MODELS IN COMPACT FORM

The ARIMA model, in its fullest generality, is cumbersome to write down. It relates a dependent variable to lagged terms of itself and to lagged error terms. Fortunately, there is a convenient notational device for expressing an operation in which a variable is lagged or shifted; it is known as a *backshift operator*. This notation makes the expression and manipulation of a model much simpler and more like an algebraic operation.

The Backshift Operator

The *backshift operator B* is a convenient notational device for expressing ARIMA models in a compact form. It is defined to be B "operating" on the index of Y_t so that BY_t produces Y_{t-1}, which is the value of Y_t shifted back in time by one unit (say one month). Hence $B^2Y_t = B(BY_t) = BY_{t-1} = Y_{t-2}$. The B^2 operation shifts the subscript of Y_t by two time units. Similarly, $B^kY_t = Y_{t-k}$.

In the B notation a first difference is simply

$$Y_t - Y_{t-1} = Y_t - BY_t = (1 - B)Y_t .$$

This looks like a polynomial in B "operating" on Y_t. The AR(1) model becomes

$$(1 - \emptyset_1 B)Y_t = \alpha + \varepsilon_t ,$$

where ε_t is white noise.

Notice that the first difference corresponds to the special AR(1) model in which $\emptyset_1 = 1$. The real advantage of using the B notation will become more evident when you want to write down expressions for multiplicative ARIMA models (Chapter 25). It is also convenient to suppress the constant term α in the model. This can be done by redefining Y_t to include α, so that Y_t henceforth is $(Y_t - \alpha)$. In practice, this is accomplished by modeling $Y_t - \overline{Y}$, where $\overline{Y}$ is the mean of the time series.

The AR(1) model can now be written as $(1 - \emptyset_1 B)Y_t = \varepsilon_t$. Dividing by $(1 - \emptyset_1 B)$ gives Y_t in terms of ε_t:

$$Y_t = \varepsilon_t/(1 - \emptyset_1 B).$$

If we expand the operator, so that

$$1/(1 - \emptyset_1 B) = 1 + \emptyset_1 B + \emptyset_1^2 B^2 + \cdots ,$$

it becomes clear that

$$Y_t = (1 + \emptyset_1 B + \emptyset_1 B^2 + \cdots)\varepsilon_t$$
$$= \varepsilon_t + \emptyset_1\varepsilon_{t-1} + \emptyset_1^2\varepsilon_{t-2} + \cdots .$$

Hence the AR(1) model is equivalent to an MA model of infinite order. Similarly, the MA(1) model $Y_t = (1 - \theta_1 B)\varepsilon_t$ can be regarded as an autoregressive model of infinite order.

The higher-order AR, MA, and ARMA models can be written as special cases of

$$(1 - \emptyset_1 B - \emptyset_2 B^2 - \cdots - \emptyset_p B^p)Y_t = (1 - \theta_1 B - \theta_2 B^2 - \cdots \theta_q B^q)\varepsilon_t .$$

The series Y_t is assumed to be mean-adjusted, so that the α term is suppressed in the above representation. If we write

$$Y_t = \frac{(1 - \theta_1 B - \theta_2 B^2 - \cdots - \theta_q B^q)}{(1 - \emptyset_1 B - \emptyset_2 B^2 - \cdots - \emptyset_p B^p)} \varepsilon_t$$

$$= H(B)\varepsilon_t \ ,$$

it is evident that Y_t is represented as the output from a linear filter whose input is a random series ε_t with zero mean and constant variance, and whose filter *transfer function* $H(B)$ is a ratio of two polynomials in the backshift operator B. The purpose of modeling linear models of the ARMA class is to identify and estimate $H(B)$ with as few parameters as possible *(parsimonious representation)*. Once this is done, the representation can be used for forecasting.

Regular ARIMA Models

Let $W_t = (1 - B)Y_t$, so that W_t represents the first difference of Y_t. An ARMA model for W_t is an ARIMA model for Y_t.

Assume that a series can be reduced to stationarity by differencing the series some finite number of times (possibly after removing any deterministic trend). The order of differencing is denoted by d. Then it is assumed that

$$W_t = (1 - B)^d Y_t$$

is stationary.

For a *regular* ARIMA(p,d,q) model, the general form is assumed to be

$$(1 - \emptyset_1 B - \emptyset_2 B^2 - \cdots - \emptyset_p B^p)(1 - B)^d Y_t = (1 - \theta_1 B - \theta_2 B^2$$
$$- \cdots - \theta_q B^q)\varepsilon_t \ ,$$

where the ε_t's are white noise—a sequence of identically distributed uncorrelated errors.

It is required that the roots of the two polynomial equations in B—namely,

$$\emptyset(B) = 0 \qquad \text{and} \qquad \theta(B) = 0$$

—all lie outside the unit circle. The first condition ensures the *stationarity* of W_t— that is, the statistical equilibrium about a fixed mean; the second one, known as the *invertibility* requirement, guarantees uniqueness of representation (the weights applied to the past history of W_t to generate forecasts die out).

This notation is frequently simplified to

$$\emptyset_p(B)(1 - B)^d Y_t = \theta_q(B)\varepsilon_t \ ,$$

where the AR(p) terms are given by the polynomial

$$\emptyset_p(B) = (1 - \emptyset_1 B - \emptyset_2 B_2 - \cdots - \emptyset_p B^p)$$

and the MA(q) terms are

$$\theta_q(B) = (1 - \theta_1 B - \theta_2 B^2 - \cdots - \theta_q B^q) \,.$$

Thus an ARIMA(1,1,1) model takes the form

$$(1 - \emptyset_1 B)(1 - B)Y_t = (1 - \theta_1 B)\varepsilon_t \,.$$

AUTOCORRELATIONS AND PARTIAL AUTOCORRELATIONS

As we indicated in the preceding chapter, the autocorrelation function (ACF) and the partial autocorrelation function (PACF) are the two principal tools used to characterize the structure of a theoretical ARMA model. The ACF and PACF have patterns that are useful for identifying the order and lag structure of an ARMA model.

The Moving Average Process

The moving average model MA(q), of order q, is given by

$$W_t = (1 - \theta_1 B - \theta_2 B^2 - \cdots - \theta_q B^q)\varepsilon_t \,,$$

where the current value W_t of the time series is assumed to be a linear combination of the current and previous error terms ε_t. In practice, these models are useful for describing events that are affected by random events such as strikes and policy decisions. Many economic and planning series exhibit behavior that can be reasonably described by a model containing MA components.

The theoretical autocorrelation function (ACF) of the pure moving average model, MA(q), *truncates* at lag q. After lag q the values of the ACF are zero. The PACF does not cut off, but *decays* to zero.

The ACF and PACF of an MA(1) model with positive θ are depicted in Figure 23.1(a). There is a single negative spike at the lag 1 in the ACF. There is a decaying pattern in the PACF. The ACF of an MA(1) process with negative θ (Figure 23.1(b))

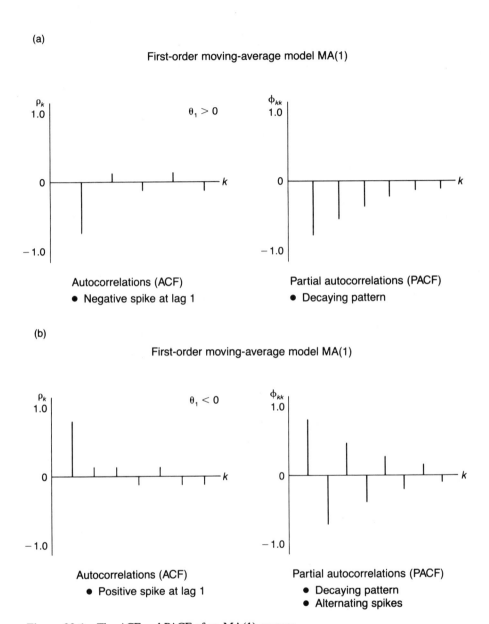

Figure 23.1 The ACF and PACF of an MA(1) process.

shows a single positive spike but the PACF shows a decaying pattern with spikes alternating above and below the zero line.

No restrictions on the size of θ are required for an MA process to be stationary. However, to avoid certain modeling problems an *invertibility* requirement needs to be imposed. This arises because, for an MA(1) model that has a coefficient of either θ or $1/\theta$, the ACF will be the same. An MA(1) model is said to be invertible if $|\theta_1| < 1$.

The multiplicity of a model is not the only thing that determines its invertibility or noninvertibility. Models are called *noninvertible* because it is impossible to estimate the errors ε_t. Since starting values ε_0, ε_{-1}, . . . are unknown, there will be errors in estimating the early ε_t's. With noninvertible models these errors grow instead of decay.

The Autoregressive Process

The autoregressive process AR(p) of order p is given by

$$(1 - \emptyset_1 B - \emptyset_2 B^2 \cdots - \emptyset_p B^p)W_t = \varepsilon_t \, ,$$

where the current value W_t is assumed to be a linear combination of previous values of the series and the current error ε_t. In contrast to an MA model, the AR model is like a multiple linear regression model in which the W_t is regressed on past values of itself; hence the term "autoregression."

For an AR(p) process the patterns in the ACF and PACF are reversed from what they are in the moving average process. The values in the ACF diminish to a tail or decay with increasing lags, and in the PACF values (possibly zero) occur from lag 1 through p and then they are zero *(truncate)* thereafter.

The ACF and PACF of an AR(1) process are depicted in Figure 23.2. There is a decaying pattern in the ACF; the decay is exponential if $\emptyset_1 < 1$ (part (b) of the figure). The PACF shows a single positive value at lag 1 if $0 < \emptyset_1 < 1$. The ACF of an AR(1) process with negative $\emptyset_1$ ($-1 < \emptyset_1 < 0$) shows a decaying exponential tail with values alternating above and below the zero line. The corresponding PACF has a single negative value at lag 1.

A somewhat more complicated process that occurs fairly often in practice is the AR(2) process. In this case there are two autoregressive coefficients $\emptyset_1$ and $\emptyset_2$. Figure 23.3 shows the ACF and PACF of an AR(2) model with $\emptyset_1 = 0.3$ and $\emptyset_2 = 0.5$. The values in the ACF diminish according to the formula

$$\rho_k = \emptyset_1 \rho_{k-1} + \emptyset_2 \rho_{k-2} \, .$$

The PACF shows positive values at lags 1 and 2 only. The PACF is very helpful because it suggests that the process is autoregressive and, more significantly, that it is second-order autoregressive.

If $\emptyset_1 = 1.2$ and $\emptyset_2 = -0.64$, the ACF and PACF have the following patterns, shown in Figure 23.4; the values in the ACF decay in a sinusoidal pattern; the PACF has a positive value at lag 1 and a negative value at lag 2.

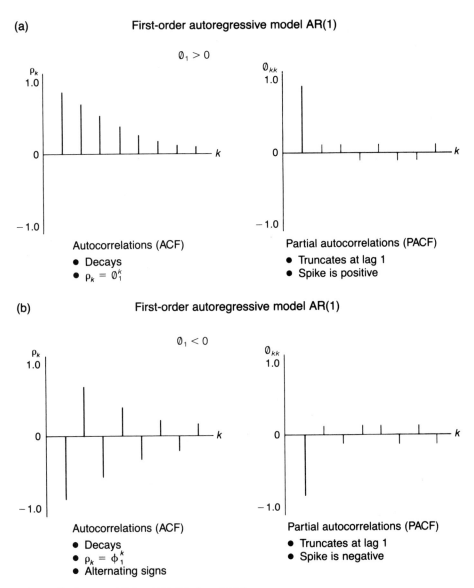

Figure 23.2   The ACF and PACF of an AR(1) process.

There are a number of possible patterns for AR(2) models. The allowable values for $\emptyset_1$ and $\emptyset_2$ in the stationary case are described by the triangular region

$$\emptyset_1 + \emptyset_2 < 1, \qquad \emptyset_2 - \emptyset_1 < 1, \qquad \text{and} \qquad -1 < \emptyset_2 < 1.$$

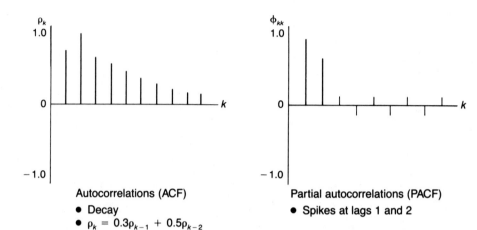

Second-order autoregressive model AR(2)
$\emptyset_1 = 0.3, \emptyset_2 = 0.5$

Autocorrelations (ACF)
- Decay
- $\rho_k = 0.3\rho_{k-1} + 0.5\rho_{k-2}$

Partial autocorrelations (PACF)
- Spikes at lags 1 and 2

Figure 23.3   The ACF and PACF of an AR(2) process with parameters $\emptyset_1 = 0.3$ and $\emptyset_2 = 0.5$.

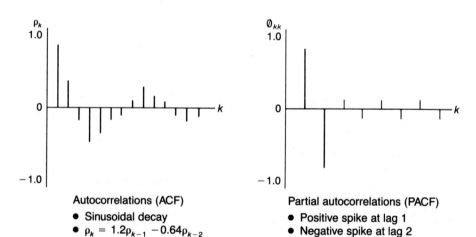

Second-order autoregressive model AR(2)
$\emptyset_1 = 1.2, \emptyset_2 = -0.64$

Autocorrelations (ACF)
- Sinusoidal decay
- $\rho_k = 1.2\rho_{k-1} - 0.64\rho_{k-2}$

Partial autocorrelations (PACF)
- Positive spike at lag 1
- Negative spike at lag 2

Figure 23.4   The ACF and PACF of an AR(2) process with parameters $\emptyset_1 = 1.2$ and $\emptyset_2 = -0.64$.

(a)

Autoregressive moving-average model
ARMA (1,1) $\emptyset_1 = 0.7$, $\theta_1 = -0.6$

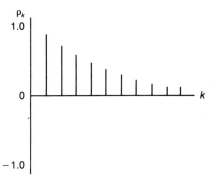

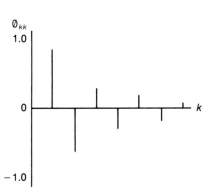

Autocorrelations
- Irregular 1st spike
- Decaying pattern after lag 1

$$\rho_k = \emptyset_1^k$$

Partial autocorrelations
- Decaying pattern
- Alternating spikes

(b)

Autoregressive moving-average model
ARMA (1,1) $\emptyset_1 = -0.7$, $\theta_1 = 0.6$

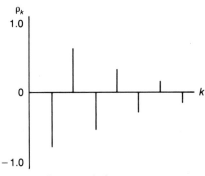

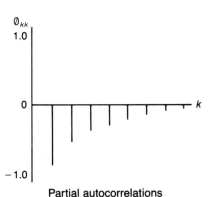

Autocorrelations
- Irregular 1st spike
- Decaying pattern after lag 1

$$\rho_k = \emptyset_1^k$$

Partial autocorrelations
- Decaying pattern

Figure 23.5 The ACF and PACF of an ARMA(1,1) process with parameters $\emptyset_1 = 0.7$ and $\theta_1 = -0.6$.

If $\emptyset_1^2 + 4\emptyset_2 > 0$, the ACF decreases exponentially with increasing lag. If $\emptyset_1^2 + 4\emptyset_2 < 0$, the ACF is a damped cosine wave.

ARMA Processes

The mixed autoregressive moving-average process, ARMA(p,q), contains p AR terms and q MA terms. It is given by

$$(1 - \emptyset_1 B - \emptyset_2 B^2 - \cdots - \emptyset_p B^p)W_t = (1 - \theta_1 B - \theta_2 B^2 - \cdots - \theta_q B^q)\varepsilon_t .$$

This model is useful in that stationary series may often be expressed more parsimoniously (with fewer parameters) in an ARMA model than in the pure AR or MA models.

The mixed ARMA model is a more difficult process to identify. Both p and q must be determined from the sample ACF's and PACF's. The ACF of an ARMA(p,q) process has an *irregular pattern* at lags 1 through q, then the tail diminishes according to the formula

$$\rho_k = \emptyset_1 \rho_{k-1} + \cdots + \emptyset_p \rho_{k-p} , \qquad k > q.$$

The PACF tail also diminishes. So the best way to identify an ARMA process initially is to look for a *decay* or *tail in both the ACF's and PACF's*.

The ACF and PACF of an ARMA(1,1) process with $\emptyset_1 = 0.7$ and $\theta_1 = -0.6$ is shown in Figure 23.5(a). The value at lag 1 in the ACF is high. The remaining values show an exponential decay. The PACF also shows a decay or tail.

The ACF and PACF of the same ARMA(1,1) process, but with the signs of $\emptyset_1$ and θ_1 reversed, would show alternating decaying values in the ACF (Figure 23.5(b)). In the PACF there would be a large negative value at lag 1 followed by an exponential decay in the remaining values.

When Are Correlogram Estimates Significant?

Just as there are for the ordinary correlation coefficient, there are approximate confidence limits for the correlogram that establish which correlogram estimates can reasonably be assumed to be zero. As a rough guide for determining whether or not theoretical autocorrelations are zero beyond lag q, Bartlett (1946) has shown that for a sample of size n the standard deviation of r_k is approximately

$$n^{-1/2}[1 + 2(r_1^2 + r_2^2 + \cdots + r_q^2)]^{1/2} \qquad \text{for } k > q.$$

Quenouille (1949) has shown that, for a pth-order autoregressive model, the standard errors of the partial autocorrelogram estimates $\hat{\phi}_{kk}$ are approximately $n^{-1/2}$ for $k > p$. Assuming normality for moderately large samples, as shown by Anderson (1942), the limits of plus or minus two standard deviations about zero should provide a reasonable guide in assessing whether or not the correlogram estimates are significantly different from zero.

EXAMPLES OF MODEL IDENTIFICATION

So far the theoretical forms of an ACF and PACF have been treated only for ARMA models. To learn how various time series models can be identified by correlograms, refer to Anderson (1976), Box and Jenkins (1976), Granger (1980), Granger and Newbold (1977), Hoff (1984), Mabert (1975), Makridakis and Wheelwright (1978), Nelson (1973), and Pindyck and Rubinfeld (1976).

Consider now some examples of time series and their associated correlograms. It is helpful to make some observations regarding the displays:

- A time plot is useful to establish what data adjustments and transformations may be needed. The appropriate amount of differencing should be performed to achieve stationarity, and the differenced data should be plotted.

- The ordinary correlogram should be inspected for pure AR or MA structure.

- It is helpful to inspect the partial correlogram to confirm or supplement the information derived from the ordinary correlogram.

- The inspection of the ordinary and partial correlograms together should suggest a preliminary model to be fitted in the first iteration of the model-building process. The most significant patterns in the correlograms should be documented for future reference.

At the early stages of modeling it is generally simpler to attempt to identify only the most obvious patterns. Once the parameter estimates are obtained for a tentative model, the correlogram of the residuals of the model should be inspected for any significant remaining patterns. With experience, it is possible to identify complex patterns relatively quickly. For the beginner, however, a careful consideration of a number of examples is recommended. Table 23.1 provides general guidance for selecting starting models.

The Index of Consumer Sentiment

The first example we will consider is the University of Michigan Survey Research Institute's quarterly index of consumer sentiment. The index of consumer sentiment

Table 23.1 Model identification for nonseasonal time series.

Partial autocorrelation function	Autocorrelation function	
	Decays	Truncates
Truncates	AR	Mixed (ARMA)
Decays	Mixed (ARMA)	MA

is published in the *Business Conditions Digest,* a monthly publication of the U.S. Department of Commerce. The data come from a survey that attempts to ascertain the anticipations and intentions of consumers. While they reflect only the respondent's anticipations (what they expect others to do) or expectations (what they plan to do), and not firm commitments, such information is nevertheless useful as a valuable aid to economic forecasting.

The quarterly index is shown in Figure 23.6; it is not stationary in level, so that a first difference must be taken. Figure 23.7 shows the differenced series, and Figure 23.8 shows the corresponding correlogram and partial correlogram. Both show significant spikes at lag 10, which does not suggest a regular ARIMA model. Possibly the spike is spurious, or a seasonal model is required. A starting model is

$$(1 - B)Y_t = \alpha + \varepsilon_t .$$

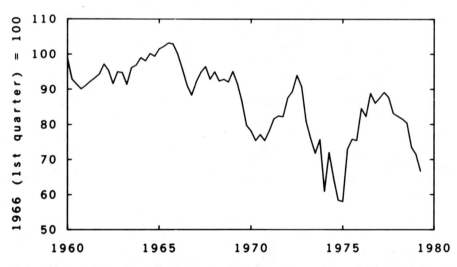

Figure 23.6 A time plot of the University of Michigan Survey Research Institute index of consumer sentiment (quarterly).
Source: University of Michigan, Survey Research Institute.

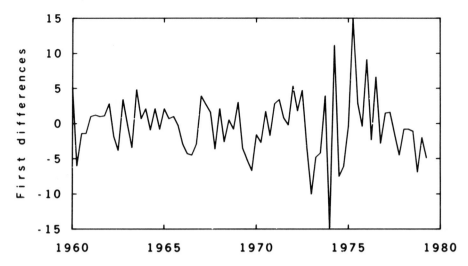

Figure 23.7   A time plot of first differences of the consumer-sentiment index series.

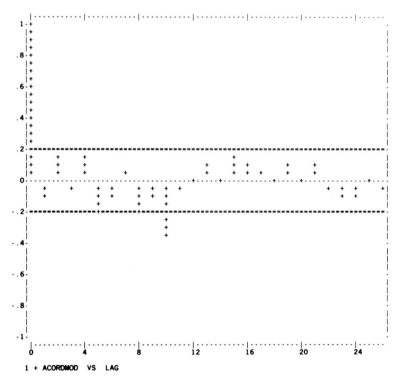

1 + ACORDMOD VS LAG

Figure 23.8(a)   The ordinary correlogram of first differences of the consumer sentiment index series.

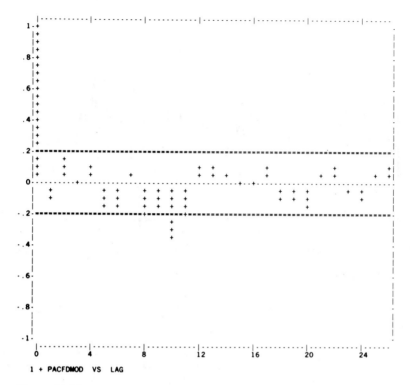

Figure 23.8(b) The partial correlogram of first differences of the consumer sentiment index series.

Seasonally Adjusted U.S. Money Supply

The seasonally adjusted U.S. money supply (M1) series, shown in Figure 21.1, is also not stationary, and it also requires a first difference. After differencing the series once, the plot still shows a slight trend and increasing variability (Figure 21.2(a)).

Since the original money supply series probably requires a variance-stabilizing transformation, logarithms may indeed give better results. The first differences of the log-transformed data (Figure 21.3) appear stationary. The correlograms (Figure 23.9) suggest the ARIMA(2,1,0) model because of the decay in the ordinary correlogram and the spike at lags 1 and 2 in the partial correlogram. Thus the starting model is an ARIMA(2,1,0) for the log-transformed money supply data.

Another possibility that could be tried on these data is to take a second difference of the original data. The time plot in Figure 21.2(b) depicts a time series with increasing variability. The correlograms in Figure 23.10 suggest an ARIMA(1,2,0) model. This is based on the pattern of alternating decay in the ordinary correlogram and the significant negative spike at lag 1 in the partial correlogram. Figure 23.11

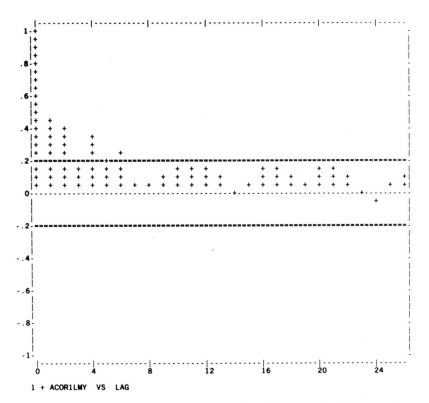

1 + ACOR1LMY VS LAG

Figure 23.9(a)   The ordinary correlogram of first differences of the log-transformed money supply series.

shows the ordinary correlogram of the residuals of this tentative model. The negative spike at lag 2 suggests the addition of a second order moving average parameter to the model. Thus this model could also be contemplated for the money supply data.

Although a forecast test would provide one of the most important criteria for model selection, we will forego making such a test: the first differences of the log-transformed series are closest to stationarity and it is likely that this order of differencing will provide the best results.

The FRB Index of Industrial Production

The FRB Index of Industrial Production is not stationary, since level and slope both change over time. Both the ordinary and partial correlograms of the raw quarterly data would suggest taking first differences.

The first differences of the FRB data do appear stationary. The ordinary correlogram in Figure 23.12(a) shows a significant spike at lag 1. The partial correlogram in Figure 23.12(b) shows alternating decay; these characteristics suggest an MA(1)

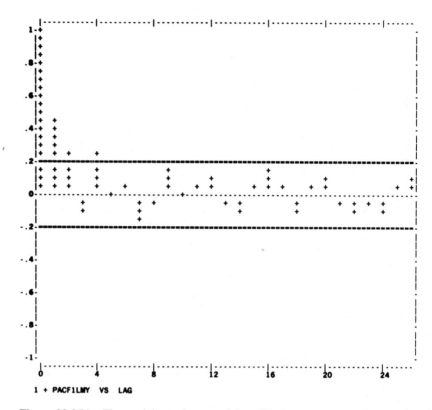

Figure 23.9(b)   The partial correlogram of first differences of the log-transformed money supply series.

model of the first differences of the quarterly series. We will return to this model in Chapter 26 as part of the case study for forecasting main telephone gain (see also Levenbach, 1980).

Granger (1980, p. 74) develops a model for the monthly FRB index (seasonally adjusted). His estimated model for the longer time period January, 1948 to October, 1974 is derived from an AR(1) model of the first differences:

$$(1 - B)Y_t = 0.4(1 - B)Y_{t-1} + \varepsilon_t .$$

SUMMARY

The identification of ARIMA models for nonseasonal data is accomplished primarily by analyzing correlograms and partial correlograms. To summarize the rules for identification:

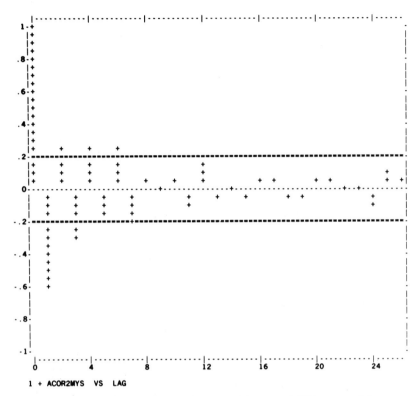

1 + ACOR2MYS VS LAG

Figure 23.10(a)   The ordinary correlogram of the second differences of the money supply series.

- If the correlogram "cuts off" at some point, say $k = q$, then the appropriate model is MA(q).

- If the partial correlogram cuts off at some point, say $k = p$, then the appropriate model is AR(p).

- If neither diagram cuts off at some point, but does decay gradually to zero, the appropriate model is ARMA(p', q') for some p', q'.

USEFUL READING

ANDERSON, O. D. (1976). *Time Series Analysis and Forecasting: The Box-Jenkins Approach*. London, England: Butterworth.

ANDERSON, R. L. (1942). Distribution of the Serial Correlation Coefficient. *Annals of Mathematical Statistics* 13, 1–13.

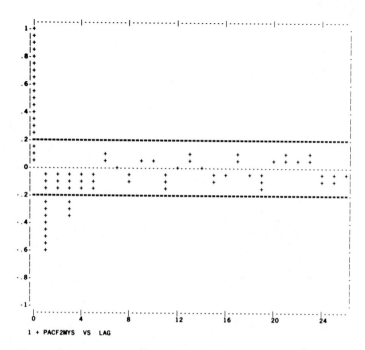

Figure 23.10(b) The partial correlogram of the second differences of the money supply series.

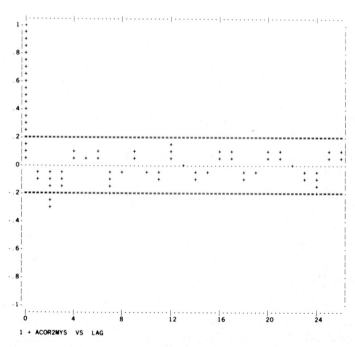

Figure 23.11(a) The ordinary correlogram of the residuals of a tentative (1,2,0) model for the seasonally adjusted U.S. money supply series.

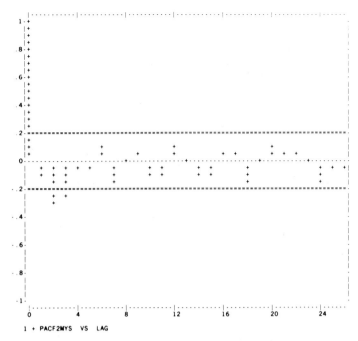

1 + PACF2MYS VS LAG

Figure 23.11(b)   The partial correlogram of the residuals of a tentative (1,2,0) model for the seasonally adjusted U.S. money supply series.

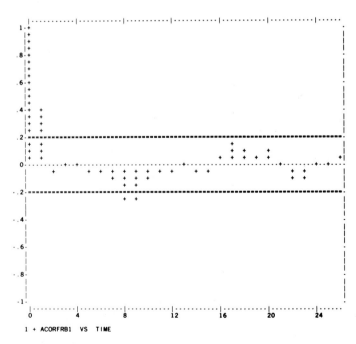

1 + ACORFRB1 VS TIME

Figure 23.12(a)   The ordinary correlogram of first differences of the FRB Index of Industrial Production.

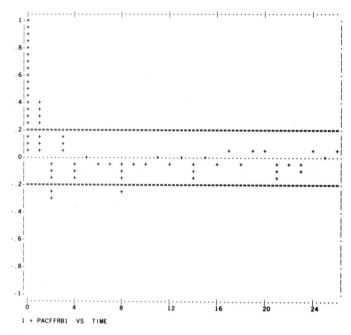

Figure 23.12(b) Partial correlogram of first differences of the FRB Index of Industrial Production.

BARTLETT, M. S. (1946). On the Theoretical Specification of Sampling Properties of Autocorrelated Time Series. *Journal of the Royal Statistical Society* B 8, 27–41.

BOX, G. E. P., and G. M. JENKINS (1976). *Time Series Analysis, Forecasting and Control, Revised Edition*. San Francisco, CA: Holden-Day.

GRANGER, C. W. J. (1980). *Forecasting in Business and Economics*. New York, NY: Academic Press.

GRANGER, C. W. J., and P. NEWBOLD (1976). *Forecasting Economic Time Series*. New York, NY: Academic Press.

HOFF, J. (1983). *A Practical Guide to Box-Jenkins Forecasting*. Belmont, CA: Lifetime Learning Publications.

LEVENBACH, H. (1980). A Comparative Study of Time Series Models for Forecasting Telephone Demand. *In* O. D. Anderson, ed. *Forecasting Public Utilities*. Amsterdam, Netherlands: North-Holland Publishing Co.

MABERT, V. A. (1975). *An Introduction to Short-Term Forecasting Using the Box-Jenkins Methodology*. Production Planning and Control Division Monograph No. 2. Norcross, GA: American Institute of Industrial Engineers.

MAKRIDAKIS, S., and S. C. WHEELWRIGHT (1978). *Forecasting Methods and Applications*. New York, NY: John Wiley and Sons.

NELSON, C. R. (1973). *Applied Time Series Analysis for Managerial Forecasting*. San Francisco, CA: Holden-Day.

PINDYCK, R. S., and D. L. RUBINFELD (1976). *Econometric Models and Economic Forecasts*. New York, NY: McGraw-Hill.

QUENOUILLE, M. H. (1949). Approximate Tests of Correlation in Time Series. *Journal of the Royal Statistical Society* B 11, 68–84.

Forecast Profiles and Confidence Limits

Once a tentative ARIMA model is identified and estimated, fore-casts can be computed. This chapter is concerned with

- Generating minimum mean square error (MSE) forecasts from the difference equation of an ARIMA model.
- Developing expressions for prediction variances and confidence limits for forecasts.
- Utilizing forecast errors as a way of monitoring forecasts.

FORECASTS AND FORECAST PROFILES

It is assumed that the number of observations used to fit any model is sufficiently large that errors in estimating the parameters will not seriously affect the forecasts: it is assumed the model is known exactly and that it will remain essentially unchanged for the period for which the forecast is being made. The variance of the forecast error is used to construct confidence limits for forecasts. Confidence limits are used in monitoring the forecast in the following ways:

- If a high proportion of the forecast errors begin to fall outside the appropriate limits, the values of the model coefficients may have changed or at least they should be reestimated. However, the new model might produce significantly different forecasts.

- If systematic patterns appear, the structure of the process may also have changed, and additional terms (or transformations) may be required in the model.

- A time plot of the *cumulative sum* of the forecast errors may indicate changes in the structure of the process as a result of changes in external factors.

ℓ-Step-Ahead Forecasts

By expressing an ARIMA model in terms of the backshift operator B and expanding it as a difference equation, a forecast profile can be obtained (Anderson, 1976; Box and Jenkins, 1976; and Nelson, 1973). For example, the AR(1) model

$$(1 - 0.5B)Y_t = 2.0 + \varepsilon_t,$$

can be expanded and rewritten as

$$Y_t = 0.5Y_{t-1} + 2.0 + \varepsilon_t.$$

Some observed data y_t and fitted errors (residuals) $\hat{e}_t$ from the model are given in Table 24.1.

To produce forecasts for future time periods, one first generates a one-step-ahead forecast to obtain an estimate of Y_{t+1}: the subscript t is replaced with $t + 1$ in the equation for Y_t. Since the errors are assumed to have zero mean and constant variance, the best estimate of future errors is zero. Thus, the formula for the one-step-ahead forecast will be

$$\hat{Y}_t(1) = 0.5Y_t + 2$$
$$= 5.0 .$$

The two- and three-step-ahead forecasts are derived through the following steps:

1. Replace t by $t + 2$ in $Y_t = 0.5Y_{t-1} + 2.0 + \varepsilon_t$: then

$$Y_{t+2} = 0.5Y_{t+1} + 2.0 + \varepsilon_{t+2}.$$

2. Use the estimated value of $\hat{Y}_t(1)$ in place of Y_{t+1}.

3. Assume $\hat{e}_{t+2} = 0$. Then the two-step-ahead and three-step-ahead forecasts are, respectively,

Table 24.1 Sample data for forecasting.

Time origin	Data y_t	Residuals $\hat{e}_t$
$t - 4$	10.0	-3.0
$t - 3$	4.0	2.0
$t - 2$	5.0	1.0
$t - 1$	8.0	0
t	6.0	2.0

$$\hat{Y}_t(2) = 0.5\hat{Y}_t(1) + 2.0 + \hat{\varepsilon}_{t+2}$$
$$= 4.5.$$

and

$$\hat{Y}_t(3) = 0.5\hat{Y}_t(2) + 2.0 + \hat{\varepsilon}_{t+3}$$
$$= 4.25.$$

Notice that the forecast of $Y_{t+\ell}$ with $\ell \geq 1$ is made from a *time origin*, designated t, for a *lead time*, designated ℓ. This forecast, denoted by $\hat{Y}_t(\ell)$, is said to be a *forecast at origin t, for lead time ℓ*. It is the *minimum mean square error (MSE) forecast* (Box and Jenkins, 1976). When $\hat{Y}_t(\ell)$ is regarded as a function of ℓ for a fixed t, it is referred to as the *forecast function* or *profile* for an origin t.

The forecast error for the lead time ℓ,

$$e_t(\ell) = Y_{t+\ell} - \hat{Y}_t(\ell),$$

has zero mean; thus the forecast is *unbiased*.

It is also important to note that any *linear* function of the forecasts $\hat{Y}_t(l)$ is a minimum MSE forecast of the corresponding linear combination of future values of the series. Hence, for monthly data, the best year-to-date forecast can be obtained by summing the corresponding 1, 2, . . . , l-step-ahead forecasts.

A *forecast function* or *profile* can be generated by plotting the l-step-ahead forecasts for a fixed time origin, $\ell = 1, 2, 3, \ldots$. It can be seen from Figure 24.1 that for this example there is a geometrical decay to a mean value; the mean equals the constant term divided by $(1 - \emptyset_1)$. In this case, the mean is 4.0. The equation for the l-step-ahead forecast $\hat{Y}_t(l)$ is then given as

$$\hat{Y}_t(l) = 4.0 + 0.5^l(Y_t - 4.0) .$$

In the same manner as for the AR(1) model, forecasts for the MA(1) model can be developed. Suppose the MA(1) model is given by

$$Y_t = 3.0 + \varepsilon_t - 0.5\varepsilon_{t-1}.$$

Once again t is replaced by $t + 1$ and all future errors are set to zero. Then $Y_{t+1} = 3.0 - 0.5\ \varepsilon_t$ and all Y_{t+i}'s $(i = 2, 3, \ldots)$ are equal to 3.0.

The forecast profile for an MA(1) model consists of one estimate based on last period's error, followed by the constant mean ($= 3.0$) for all future periods. This makes sense intuitively because the ACF of the MA(1) model has nonzero correlation only at lag 1, hence a "memory" of only one period.

The forecast profile for an MA(q) can be generalized rather easily. It consists of values at $l = 1, 2, \ldots, q$ that are determined by the past errors, and then equals the mean of the process for periods greater than q.

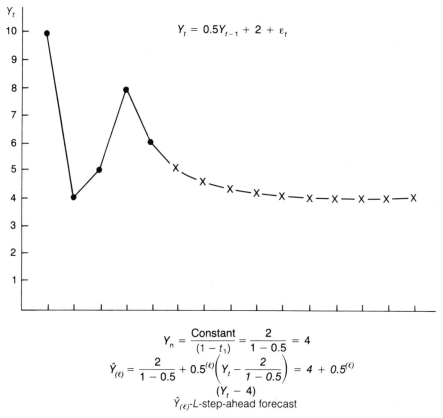

$$Y_n = \frac{\text{Constant}}{(1 - t_1)} = \frac{2}{1 - 0.5} = 4$$

$$\hat{Y}_{(\ell)} = \frac{2}{1 - 0.5} + 0.5^{(\ell)}\left(Y_t - \frac{2}{1 - 0.5}\right) = 4 + 0.5^{(\ell)}$$

$$(Y_t - 4)$$

$\hat{Y}_{(\ell)}$-L-step-ahead forecast

The forecast profile is an exponential decay to the mean ($= 4$) from the last observation.

Figure 24.1   Forecast profile of the AR(1) model.

A Forecast Profile for ARMA(1,q) Models

Consider an ARMA(1,1) model of the form

$$Y_t = 0.5Y_{t-1} + 2.0 + \varepsilon_t - 0.5\varepsilon_{t-1}.$$

By following the same procedure of replacing t by $t + 1$, assuming ε_{t+1}, ε_{t+2}, $\ldots = 0$, and using estimates $\hat{Y}_t(1)$, $\hat{Y}_t(2)$, $\ldots$, one can obtain successive forecasts.

The forecast profile for this model is as follows. The forecast for the first period is a function of last period's actual observation and last period's error. All future forecasts are based only on predicted values of Y_t. As in the AR(1) case, it shows a geometrical decay to the mean after the first forecast period.

For the forecast profile for ARMA(1,q) model, the forecasts of the first "q" periods will be a function of observations, estimated values, and errors. After "q" periods ahead, there will be a geometrical decay to the mean.

Forecast Profile for an IMA(1,1) Model

An example of an IMA(1,1) model is

$$Y_t = Y_{t-1} + 3.0 + \varepsilon_t - 0.5\varepsilon_{t-1} .$$

By following the procedure of replacing t by $t + 1$, assuming $\epsilon_{t+1}, \epsilon_{t+2}, \ldots$, $= 0$, and using estimates $\hat{Y}_t(1)$, $\hat{Y}_t(2)$, . . . , the forecasts are obtained.

The forecast profile for this model is a straight line after the one-period-ahead forecast. The slope of the line is equal to the constant α in the model. If $\alpha = 0$, the forecast profile is a horizontal line at the level given by $\hat{Y}_t(1)$.

Three Kinds of Trend Models

For time series with a linear trend, it is interesting to compare the characteristics of alternative forecasting models. Table 24.2 shows three alternative approaches to forecasting a trending series.

The first model uses "time" as an independent variable. As new observations are added, the forecasts produced by this model would not change, unless the model were to be reestimated. The slope and the intercept of the line of forecasts are constant.

Table 24.2   Three approaches to forecasting a trending time series.

Model type	Equation	Characteristics of updated forecasts	
		Intercept	Slope
Deterministic	$Y_t = \alpha + \beta t + \varepsilon_t$	Constant	Constant
ARIMA with deterministic trend constant	$(1 - B)Y_t = \alpha + \varepsilon_t$	Varies	Constant
ARIMA without deterministic trend constant	$(1 - B)^2 Y_t = \varepsilon_t$	Varies	Varies

The second model is an expansion of the first:

$$Y_t = Y_{t-1} + \alpha + \varepsilon_t .$$

This model has a slope α. The forecasts from this model are updated as new Y_t's become available. This has the effect of changing the intercept of the line of future forecasts but the slope remains constant.

The third model can be written as

$$Y_t = 2Y_{t-1} - Y_{t-2} + \varepsilon_t .$$

Both the slope and the intercept of the lines of updated forecasts will change as new observations become available. The trend can change direction with this model.

Unless there is reason to believe that a deterministic relationship exists (e.g., physical or theoretical reasons), autoregressive models are more adaptive or responsive to recent observations than straight-line models are. The choice of taking first differences with a trend constant or second differences without a trend constant should depend on the data. Since it is not helpful to overdifference a time series, second differences should be used only when first differences do not result in a stationary series.

A Comparison of an ARIMA(0,1,0) Model and a Straight-Line Model

It is of interest to see how the forecasts of an ARIMA(0,1,0) model differ from straight-line models using "time" as the independent variable. Consider a (seasonally adjusted) quarterly series that is generally increasing in trend. Moreover, the series contains business cycles with downturns in 1957–58, 1960–61, 1969–70, and 1974–75.

The correlogram of the data has a gradual decay that suggests a nonstationary series. The original data have a pattern of nonstationarity in trend. Therefore, first differences of the quarterly data were taken; a plot of the first differences shows a constant mean and no signs of increasing variability. The correlogram and partial correlogram of the first idfferences are shown in Figure 24.2.

There are no significant patterns in either diagram. Therefore an ARIMA(0,1,0) model of the seasonally adjusted quarterly data is appropriate:

$$Y_t - Y_{t-1} = \alpha + \varepsilon_t .$$

The first differences have a mean value that is 1.35 standard deviations from zero, so a deterministic trend constant is included; the fitted values are given by

$$\hat{Y}_t = Y_{t-1} + 332.0 .$$

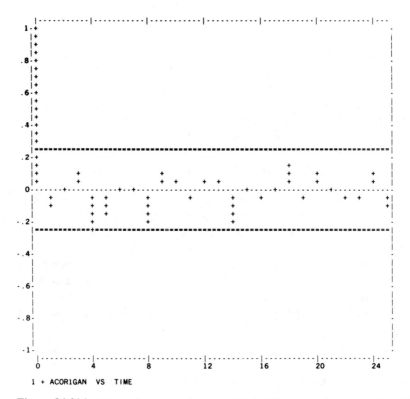

1 + ACOR1GAN VS TIME

Figure 24.2(a)   The ordinary correlogram of first differences of a seasonally adjusted quarterly time series.

This is perhaps one of the simplest time series models covered so far. Note that a one-period-ahead forecast would simply be the data value for the current quarter plus 332.0. All information prior to the last observation has no effect on the one-period-ahead forecast. Prior data were used to determine that the trend constant should be 332.0.

To compare the forecast profile of the ARIMA(0,1,0) model with a simple linear regression model with "time" as the independent variable, a straight-line model was fitted to the data:

$$\hat{Y}_t = 7165.2 + 60.8t \qquad t = 1, 2, \ldots .$$

You can see that the forecast profile of this model is a straight line with a slope = 60.8. Since "time" is always increasing, the forecasts are always increasing.

To compare the forecasts of the two models over the time periods 1970 and 1971, four regressions were performed, all starting in the first quarter of 1957. The first

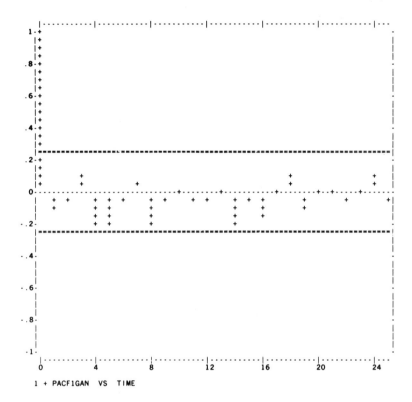

1 + PACF1GAN   VS   TIME

Figure 24.2(b)   The partial correlogram of first differences of a seasonally adjusted quarterly time series.

regression was performed through the fourth quarter of 1969, and then four quarterly forecasts for 1970 were generated. Subsequent regressions and forecasts were also generated by fitting through the second quarter of 1970, and then forecasting through the fourth quarter of 1970; fitting through the fourth quarter of 1970, and then forecasting the four quarters of 1971; and lastly, fitting through the second quarter of 1971, and then forecasting the remaining two quarters of 1971.

The effect of new data on the predictions of the two models can be seen in Figure 24.3, which shows the predictions of the two models for the four quarters of 1970. The predictions that the straight-line regression model gives are closer to the actuals for each of the four quarters when the regression period ends in the fourth quarter of 1969; and when two or more quarters of data are included and the third and fourth quarters of 1970 are predicted, once again the straight-line model predictions are close to the actual values.

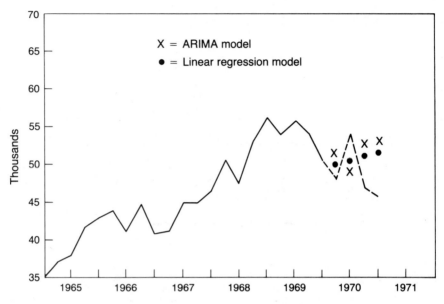

Figure 24.3 Comparison of forecasts generated by the ARIMA(0,1,0) model and the straight-line regression model for 1970.

When more data are added, the predictions made by the models for 1970 are as shown in the following chart:

| Period | Model | |
1970	ARIMA	Straight line
Quarter 3	+ 2756	+ 96
Quarter 4	+ 2807	+ 100

Clearly, the ARIMA model responds to the new data by a much greater amount than does the straight-line model. In fact, for this ARIMA model, the forecasts will equal the latest data value plus a constant. Notice that the second quarter of 1970 was unusually high; this distorted the forecasts for the remainder of 1970.

Next, two more quarters of actuals were added to the regression period and the four quarters of 1971 were predicted. Now the predictions of the straight-line model were once again superior to the ARIMA model.

The last regression with actuals through the second quarter of 1971 was done next. For this time, the plot of the data had started to show a sharp turn upward. The model forecasts showed changes in predictions for 1971 that were as follows:

Period 1971	Model	
	ARIMA	Straight line
Quarter 3	233	116
Quarter 4	11,449	118

Once again, the ARIMA model reacted much more quickly to changing conditions. Figure 24.4 shows that this time the ARIMA model was correct since the data were indeed continuing upward.

The forecast test just described is not done to claim either model as superior. Rather it shows how differently the ARIMA(0,1,0) model and straight-line regression models react to new data. There is almost no reaction in the forecasts of a straight-line model (versus time) when new data are introduced. However, ARIMA models are affected significantly by recent data. Which model should be selected will depend on the circumstances of the application.

If future demand in a given year is expected to be substantially above or below trend (say, for economic reasons), then the forecast of a straight-line model must be modified. A "turning point analysis" or a trend-cycle curve-fitting approach may be the best way of supplementing judgment about the cycle to a straight-line model (Wecker, 1979).

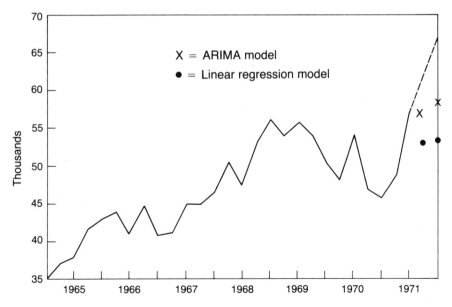

Figure 24.4 Comparison of forecasts generated by the ARIMA(0,1,0) model and the straight-line regression models for the second half of 1971.

If it is believed that the current short-term trend in the data will continue, an ARIMA model should be seriously considered. Univariate ARIMA models cannot predict turning points. If the economy is near a turning point, extreme care should be exercised in using the ARIMA models. Regression models with explanatory variables, econometric models, and transfer function models (see *The Professional Forecaster,* Chapters 23 and 24) offer other ways of modifying forecasts to take into account changes in the business cycle.

CONFIDENCE LIMITS FOR ARIMA MODELS

One of the goals of quantitative forecast modeling is to be able to make probability statements about the forecasts. This is normally accomplished by calculating forecast error variances with the assumption that the forecast errors are independent, identically distributed random variables.

To examine confidence limits for ARIMA models, let us first illustrate their use for the MA(2) model.

Confidence Limits for an MA(2) Model

Consider the following model:

$$Y_t = \varepsilon_t - 0.6\varepsilon_{t-1} - 0.4\varepsilon_{t-2} .$$

Future values are

$$Y_{t+1} = \varepsilon_{t+1} - 0.6\varepsilon_t - 0.4\varepsilon_{t-1} ,$$
$$Y_{t+2} = \varepsilon_{t+2} - 0.6\varepsilon_{t+1} - 0.4\varepsilon_t ,$$

and

$$Y_{t+3} = \varepsilon_{t+3} - 0.6\varepsilon_{t+2} - 0.4\varepsilon_{t+1} .$$

As time passes and the actual observations at times $t + 1$, $t + 2$, $t + 3$, . . . become available, there is a discrepancy between the one-step-ahead forecast and the observed value. For the one-step-ahead forecast, the forecast error will be the value of ε_{t+1}. If ε_{t+1} is not zero, the forecast will be off by the value of ε_{t+1}.

For the two-step-ahead forecast, the forecast error will equal

$$\varepsilon_{t+2} - 0.6\varepsilon_{t+1} .$$

The forecast error now is a result of the two unobserved errors (ε_{t+2}, ε_{t+1}).

For the three-step-ahead forecast, the forecast error is equal to

$$\varepsilon_{t+3} - 0.6\varepsilon_{t+2} - 0.4\varepsilon_{t+1} .$$

For forecasting purposes it is assumed that ε_{t+3}, ε_{t+2}, and ε_{t+1} will be equal to their expected values (zero). In actuality, they will differ from zero by some amount that cannot be known at the time of the forecast. For all forecasts longer than three steps ahead, the forecast error will be the result of three unknown future errors that are assumed to be zero but will actually be somewhat different from zero.

It is of interest to relate the variance of the l-step-ahead forecast to the variance var(Y_t) of the series. For the example of the MA(2) model we have been using,

$$\text{var}(Y_t) = (1 + 0.36 + 0.16)\sigma_\varepsilon^2$$
$$= 1.52\sigma_\varepsilon^2 .$$

Thus the variance of series is 1.52 times the variance of the error term (Box and Jenkins (1976, Chapter 3)). The variance of the one-step-ahead forecast is σ_ε^2—the variance of the error. This is less than the variance of the series—just determined to be $1.52\sigma_\varepsilon^2$. Consequently, you would expect to have less variability in the one-step-ahead forecast than in the series as a whole.

The two-step-ahead forecast error is equal to $\varepsilon_{t+2} - 0.6\varepsilon_{t+1}$. With the assumption that the ε_t's are independent of each other and have a constant variance σ_ε^2, the variance of the two-step-ahead forecast error is equal to $1.36\sigma_\varepsilon^2$. That is, the variance of the two-step-ahead forecast is still less than the variance of the series. Therefore, the model estimates future observations in a smaller range than just the variance of the series. The variance of the three-step-ahead forecast error is $1.52\sigma_\varepsilon^2$—the variance of the series: once three or more periods are forecast with the MA(2) model, the variance of the l-step-ahead forecast equals the variance of the series.

All forecasts beyond the three steps ahead into the future for Y_t will give the mean of Y_t, or zero in this case. To summarize, for the MA(2) model, the best forecast of the distant future is the mean of the process. The variability about that mean (the variance of the forecast) can be estimated from the available data.

This can be visualized in Figure 24.5. The actual observations are connected by a solid line. The dotted line represents the forecasts for one, two, three, and four steps ahead. The confidence limits expand from the one-step-ahead to the three-step-ahead forecast. The variance of the forecast error equals the variance of the series for all forecasts three or more periods into the future.

Let s_ε be an estimate of σ_ε, the standard deviation of the white noise process. Then the first three approximate $1 - \eta$ confidence limits are, respectively,

$$\hat{Y}(1) \pm U_{\eta/2}s_\varepsilon$$
$$\hat{Y}(2) \pm U_{\eta/2}(1 + \theta_1^2)^{1/2}s_\varepsilon;$$

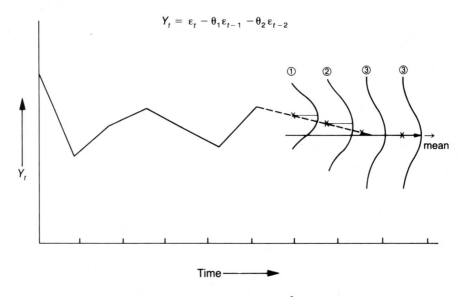

$$Y_t = \varepsilon_t - \theta_1 \varepsilon_{t-1} - \theta_2 \varepsilon_{t-2}$$

Time ⟶

① One-step-ahead forecast variance $= \sigma_\varepsilon^2$
② Two-step-ahead forecast variance $= (1 + \theta_1^2)\, \sigma_\varepsilon^2$
③ Three-step-ahead forecast variance $= (1 + \theta_1^2 + \theta_2^2)\, \sigma_\varepsilon^2$

Figure 24.5   Forecasts generated by the MA(2) model with associated confidence limits.

and

$$\hat{Y}(3) \pm U_{\eta/2}(1 + \theta_1^2 + \theta_2^2)^{1/2} s_\varepsilon;$$

in each, $U_{\eta/2}$ is the deviation exceeded by a proportion $\eta/2$ of the standard normal distribution (Appendix A, Table 1). Here $\hat{Y}(3)$ is the mean, which was assumed to be zero. From here on out, the confidence limits (and the forecast) remain the same for the MA(2) model.

The following conclusions are reached for the MA(2) model:

- The confidence limits expand up to the three-step-ahead forecast.

- The confidence limits become constant after the three-step-ahead forecast.

Forecast Error and Forecast Variance for ARIMA Models

Consider the general form of the model given by

$$\emptyset_p(B)(1 - B)^d Y_t = \theta_q(B)\varepsilon_t .$$

This can be expanded as

$$(1 - \emptyset_1 B - \emptyset_2 B^2 - \cdots - \emptyset_{p+d} B^{p+d}) Y_t = (1 - \theta_1 B - \cdots - \theta_q B^q)\varepsilon_t .$$

An observation at time $t + l$ generated by this process can be written as

$$Y_{t+l} = \emptyset_1 Y_{t+l-1} + \cdots + \emptyset_{p+d} Y_{t+l-p-d} + \varepsilon_{t+l} - \theta_1 \varepsilon_{t+l-1} - \cdots - \theta_q \varepsilon_{t+l-q} .$$

Alternatively, Y_{t+l} can be written as an *infinite weighted sum* of current and previous errors ε_j :

$$Y_{t+l} = \varepsilon_{t+l} + \psi_1 \varepsilon_{t+l-1} + \psi_2 \varepsilon_{t+l-2} + \cdots + \psi_l \varepsilon_t + \psi_{l+1} \varepsilon_{t-1} + \cdots .$$

Consider the l-step-ahead forecast, $\hat{Y}_t(l) = \hat{Y}_{t+l}$, which is to be a linear combination of current Y_t, previous observations $Y_{t-1}, Y_{t-2}, \ldots$, and errors $\varepsilon_{t-1}, \varepsilon_{t-2}, \ldots$. It can also be written as a linear combination of current and previous errors $\varepsilon_t, \varepsilon_{t-1}, \ldots$; thus

$$\hat{Y}_t(l) = \psi_l^* \varepsilon_t + \psi_{l+1}^* \varepsilon_{t-1} + \psi_{l+2}^* \varepsilon_{t-2} + \cdots ,$$

where the ψ_j^* are to be determined. An important result in ARIMA time series theory is that the mean square error of the forecast is minimized when $\psi_{l+j}^* = \psi_{l+j}$ (Box and Jenkins, 1976).

The variance of the forecast error $e_t(l)$ is given by

$$\text{var}(Y_{t+l} - \hat{Y}_t(l)) = (1 + \psi_1^2 + \psi_2^2 + \cdots + \psi_{l-1}^2)\sigma_\varepsilon^2 .$$

These estimates of variance are based on the assumption that the ψ_l are correct. That is, the error in estimating parameters is assumed to be negligible relative to the successive one-step-ahead prediction error.

Consider the simple AR(1) model as an example. The forecast errors are

$$e_t(1) = Y_{t+1} - \hat{Y}_t(1) = \varepsilon_{t+1} ;$$
$$e_t(2) = Y_{t+2} - \hat{Y}_t(2) = \emptyset_1 \varepsilon_{t+1} + \varepsilon_{t+2} ;$$
$$e_t(l) = Y_{t+l} - \hat{Y}_t(l) = \sum_{j=0}^{l-1} \emptyset_1^j \varepsilon_{t+l-j}.$$

The variance of the forecast error is

$$\text{var}(e_t(l)) = \sigma_\varepsilon^2 \sum_{j=0}^{l-1} \emptyset_1^{2j}.$$
$$= \sigma_\varepsilon^2 (1 - \emptyset_1^{2l})/(1 - \emptyset_1^2).$$

For a stationary AR(1) model, with $-1 < \emptyset_1 < 1$, the variance increases to a constant value $\sigma_\varepsilon^2/(1 - \emptyset_1^2)$ as l tends to infinity. For nonstationary models, on the other hand, the forecast variances will increase without bound with increasing values of l.

An important property of forecast errors, worth noting here, is that while errors in one-step-ahead forecasts are uncorrelated, the errors for forecasts with longer lead times are in general correlated. It is worth remembering in practice that there are two kinds of correlations to be considered:

- The correlation between forecast errors $e_t(l)$ and $e_{t-j}(l)$ made at the *same* lead time l from *different* time origins t and $t - j$.

- The correlation between forecast errors $e_t(l)$ and $e_t(l + j)$, made at *different* lead times from the *same* origin t.

General expressions for these correlations are given in Box and Jenkins (1976).

Confidence Limits for ARIMA Models

The general procedure for calculating confidence limits for ARIMA models follows the same pattern as the derivation of confidence limits for the MA(2) model. First, an expression for the l-step-ahead forecast error $e_t(l) = Y_{t+l} - \hat{Y}_t(l)$ is written down. Next the variance of the forecast error is expressed in terms of σ_ε^2 and the ψ weights, which are computed from the estimated θ's and $\emptyset$'s.

Let s_ε^2 denote an estimate of the variance σ_ε^2. Then approximate $1 - \eta$ confidence limits $Y_t^+(l)$ and $Y_t^-(l)$ for Y_{t+l} are given by

$$Y_{t+l}(\pm) = \hat{Y}_t(l) \pm U_{\eta/2} \left[1 + \sum_{j=1}^{l-1} \psi_j^2 \right]^{1/2} s_\varepsilon,$$

where $U_{\eta/2}$ is the deviation exceeded by a proportion $\eta/2$ of the standard normal distribution.

For a simple linear regression model, the confidence limits about the regression line expand in both directions away from the mean value of the independent variable. For a stationary ARIMA model, the concern is not so much with the value of the "independent" variables. The confidence limits for the forecasts of a stationary series will initially expand but will become constant. From this point on, they stay the same for all values into the future.

For a nonstationary ARIMA model, the confidence limits will continue to expand into the future. This is similar to the pattern displayed by the confidence limits of simple linear regression models as the independent variable takes values further away from its mean.

ARIMA FORECASTING CHECKLIST

_____ Has a model been forecast-tested over a sufficient period of time (e.g., several business cycles) to determine its forecasting capabilities?

_____ Is the model parsimonious? Or instead, have you created an overly complex model?

_____ Will a relatively simpler model with perhaps a higher chi-squared statistic perform as well?

_____ Have you performed a forecast test for any alternative models, too?

_____ How rapidly does the model respond to new data?

_____ Does the model predict turning points well (or, at all)?

SUMMARY

This chapter has

- Demonstrated the possibility of generating forecasts from ARIMA models.

- Shown examples of forecast profiles for several simple model types.

- Compared a specific ARIMA model and a simple straight-line regression model to see how responsive each is to new data. It was evident that the ARIMA model's forecasts were greatly influenced by actual current data observations. This was shown to be advantageous during certain time periods but disadvantageous in others.

- Emphasized the importance of understanding models and their limitations so that the forecaster can select the appropriate model for the application at hand.

USEFUL READING

ANDERSON, O. D. (1976). *Time Series Analysis and Forecasting, The Box-Jenkins Approach*. London, England: Butterworth.

BOX, G. E. P., and G. M. JENKINS (1976). *Time Series Analysis, Forecasting and Control, Revised Edition*. San Francisco, CA: Holden-Day.

NELSON, C. R. (1973). *Applied Time Series Analysis for Managerial Forecasting*. San Francisco, CA: Holden-Day.

WECKER, W. E. (1979). Predicting the Turning Points of a Time Series. *Journal of Business* 52, 35–50.

CHAPTER 25

Forecasting Seasonal Time Series

Seasonal ARIMA models are used for time series in which a seasonal pattern is present. This chapter deals with

- The extension of regular ARIMA models to include the modeling of seasonal patterns.

- The identification of an appropriate seasonal ARIMA model through use of correlograms and partial correlograms.

- The Holt-Winters approach to seasonal forecasting and its relationship to the ARIMA models.

WHY BUILD SEASONAL MODELS?

Many of the economic series that are available in publications and computerized data banks are seasonally adjusted. These data are used in models for forecasting trend-cycle and in cases where seasonal patterns would otherwise mask the information of interest to the forecaster. Regular ARIMA models (discussed in Chapter 23) and econometric regression models are appropriate for these situations. Since seasonal variation is seldom unchanging, seasonal adjustment procedures usually leave some seasonal pattern in the data. Time plots and correlograms, along with the ANOVA (analysis of variance) table and low-resolution displays (discussed in *The Beginning Forecaster*), can provide adequate indication of the relative importance of a seasonal pattern in data.

Often it is desirable to forecast seasonal series that are unadjusted for seasonality. In airline traffic design, for example, average traffic during the months of the year when total traffic is greatest is of central importance. Obviously, monthly traffic data rather than the seasonally adjusted traffic data are required.

Sometimes seasonality shifts with time. For example, changes in school openings and closings during the year can affect a variety of time series, such as energy demand. If the seasonal change persists, models based on unadjusted data rather than seasonally adjusted data are likely to be more flexible and useful. If changing seasonality is expected, it is therefore better to take account of it through the development of a properly specified ARIMA model.

SEASONAL ARIMA MODELING

For time series that contain a seasonal periodic component that repeats every s observations, a supplement to the nonseasonal ARIMA model can be applied. For a seasonal time series with period s, $s = 4$ for quarterly data and 12 for monthly data. In a manner very similar to the regular ARIMA process, *seasonal* ARIMA (P,D,Q) models can be created for seasonal data (to differentiate between the two kinds, it is customary to use capital P, D, and Q when designating the parameters of the seasonal models).

Seasonal Differencing

When strong seasonal fluctuations exist, a seasonal difference of order D may be required to achieve stationarity. This creates a new series:

$$W_t = (1 - B^s)^D Y_t$$
$$= (1 - B^{12})Y_t,$$

for (as an example) $D = 1$ and seasonal period $s = 12$.

The need for seasonal differencing is evident from a plot of the raw data or from the correlogram. In an example of the monthly main-telephone gain data it is apparent that the data are highly seasonal. The correlogram plotted in Figure 25.1 shows there is a repetitive pattern with spikes at months 12, 24, and 36. In fact, all spikes 12 lags apart have comparable magnitudes; there is no significant decay towards zero.

The period of these data is 12 months. The differences of order 12 of the original data would produce a correlogram that is free of the repetitive spikes. Rather, it would show a pattern that may be described by a regular ARIMA model.

Combining Seasonal and Regular Models

Since models in which seasonal and regular parameters are combined can become unwieldy, the Box and Jenkins modeling strategy recommends that these models

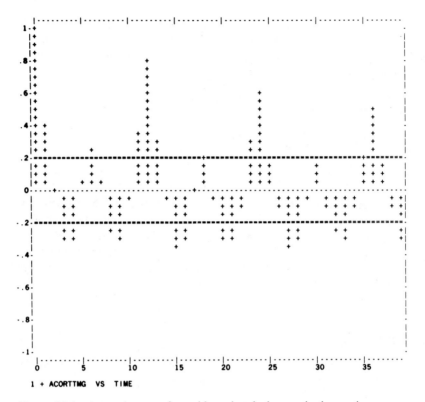

Figure 25.1 A correlogram of monthly main-telephone gain time series.

should be parsimonious. By this is meant that the number of parameters in the model should be kept to a minimum; always try to keep the model simple!

For time series models seasonality is introduced into the model *multiplicatively*. While this is arbitrary, it may be intuitively understood by considering that if a month—say January—is related to the December preceding it and to the previous January, then it is also related to the December thirteen months previous.

It seems reasonable to expect that for monthly data one January would be similar to previous Januarys, and that the remaining monthly subseries would also be related in a similar manner. If the backshift operator B^s is used to denote a relationship between points s time periods apart, a *seasonal ARIMA* model then takes the general form

$$\Phi_P(B^s)(1 - B^s)^D Y_t = \Theta_Q(B^s)a_t,$$

where B^s is the seasonal backshift operator, and where

$$\Phi_P(B^s) = (1 - \emptyset_s B^s - \emptyset_{2s} B^{2s} - \cdots - \emptyset_{Ps} B^{Ps})$$

and

$$\Theta_Q(B^s) = (1 - \Theta_s B^s - \Theta_{2s} B^{2s} - \cdots - \Theta_{Qs} B^{Qs}) .$$

Generally $s = 12$ or 4 and P, D, Q have values of 0, 1, or 2.

Notice that a_t need not be an uncorrelated, white-noise process. Indeed, a_t is assumed to be a *nonseasonal* process.

General multiplicative models incorporating both regular and seasonal components can be used for describing a typical twelve-month seasonal series with increasing trend.

To remove the linear trend from such a series requires at least one first difference. This operation is expressed by $(1 - B)^d Y_t$, where $d = 0, 1, 2$ in practice. The resultant series would still show strong seasonality with perhaps some residual trend. This may call for taking a difference of order 12 for the residual series. Year-over-year differences often give rise to stationary data (free from the seasonal pattern). Thus

$$(1 - B^{12})(1 - B)Y_t = Y_t - Y_{t-1} - Y_{t-12} + Y_{t-13} .$$

Notice that the order in which the differencing operators are applied is immaterial and that the operation of successive differencing is *multiplicative* in nature.

The combined operation suggests that if the residual series resembles a series of random numbers or "white noise," then a model of the original data could have the form

$$Y_t = Y_{t-1} + Y_{t-12} - Y_{t-13} + \varepsilon_t .$$

The forecast is then the sum of the values for the previous year's month (Y_{t-12}) and the increase in the values of the previous months $(Y_{t-1} - Y_{t-13})$. This is a special case of an autoregressive model in which past values have been given a constant weight of plus or minus one. It also shows that weights given to Y_{t-1} and Y_{t-13} are equal but have opposite signs.

It occurs relatively frequently in practice that both seasonality and trend are present in data. Hence an AR(13) model of the form

$$Y_t = \alpha + \emptyset_1 Y_{t-1} + \emptyset_2 Y_{t-12} + \emptyset_3 Y_{t-13} + \varepsilon_t$$

can be used to interpret the underlying structure. If the coefficients at lags 1 and 13 are approximately equal and of opposite sign and $\emptyset_2$ equals approximately 1, then the multiplicative model

$$(1 - \emptyset_1 B)(1 - B^{12})Y_t = \alpha + \varepsilon_t$$

is a good starting point for modeling such series parsimoniously.

The Multiplicative ARIMA Model

The regular and seasonal components can be combined into a general multiplicative ARIMA model of the form

$$\emptyset_p(B)\,\Phi_P(B^s)(1 - B)^d(1 - B^s)^D Y_t = \theta_q(B)\Theta_Q(B^s)\varepsilon_t \,,$$

where the operators are defined as before.

The regular and seasonal autoregressive components, differences, and moving average components are multiplied together in the general model. Fortunately, in most practical examples, most parameters are 0 and the resulting models are often quite simple.

A useful notation to describe the orders of the various components in the multiplicative model is given by

$$(p,d,q) \times (P,D,Q)^s$$

and corresponds to the orders of the regular and seasonal factors, respectively.

By representing a time series in terms of a multiplicative model it is often possible to reduce the number of parameters to be estimated. It also aids in the interpretation of the model structure.

Of course, the forecasting performance of these different representations of seemingly similar model structures should always be evaluated and the models that pass diagnostic checking and have the best performance should be retained.

Consider a monthly seasonal model that has a seasonal difference and also regular and seasonal first-order autoregressive parameters. Thus

$$(p,d,q) \times (P,D,Q)^s = (1,0,0) \times (1,1,0)^{12} \,.$$

This can also be expressed in terms of the backshift operator as

$$(1 - \emptyset_1 B)(1 - \emptyset_{12} B^{12})(1 - B^{12})Y_t = \alpha + \varepsilon_t \,.$$

Expanding the left-hand side gives

$$(1 - \emptyset_{12}B^{12} - \emptyset_1 B + \emptyset_1\emptyset_{12}BB^{12})(1 - B^{12})Y_t = \alpha + \varepsilon_t \,.$$

or

$$(1 - \emptyset_{12}B^{12} - \emptyset_1 B + \emptyset_1\emptyset_{12}B^{13} - B^{12} + \emptyset_{12}B^{24} + \emptyset_1 B^{13} - \emptyset_1\emptyset_{12}B^{25})Y_t = \alpha + \varepsilon_t \,.$$

In terms of the variable Y_t,

$$Y_t = \alpha + \emptyset_1 Y_{t-1} + (1 + \emptyset_{12})Y_{t-12} - \emptyset_1(1 + \emptyset_{12})Y_{t-13} - \emptyset_{12}Y_{t-24}$$
$$+ \emptyset_1 \emptyset_{12} Y_{t-25} + \varepsilon_t .$$

As a multiple linear regression, this AR(25) model has six parameters to be estimated. Expression as a multiplicative model, however, requires only three parameters. A distinct advantage of the multiplicative ARIMA model is that it can be used to represent a wide variety of time series with a minimum number of parameters in an easily interpretable manner. (Parsimony, again!)

Identifying Seasonal ARIMA Models

As with regular ARIMA models, seasonal ARIMA models can be classified as autoregressive and moving average. The seasonal MA process is analogous to the regular MA process. However, the ACF (autocorrelation function) of a pure seasonal MA process has a *single value at the period of the seasonality*. The PACF (partial autocorrelation function) shows a *decaying pattern at multiples of 12* if the seasonality has a 12-month period. This differs from a regular MA process of order 12 where there could be significant values at lags 1 *through* 12 in the ACF. If there is a *single dominant value* at 12, then this indicates a *seasonal* MA process.

In practice, it is possible to find significant spikes at other unusual lags of—say—5 or 9 in the correlogram of a residual series. Generally, these are spurious and may not suggest a secondary seasonal pattern. Their removal through a lag structure generally has little impact on forecasts generated from such a model. It is important, however, to isolate and interpret seasonal lags corresponding to realistic periodicities.

The seasonal AR process is also analogous to the regular AR process. However, the pattern of decay that is evident in the ACF is noticed at multiples of the period. For example, the ACF of a first-order seasonal (monthly) AR process has a decaying pattern in the values at multiples of 12. The PACF has a single value at lag 12. It is worth noting that pure monthly seasonal models look like 12 independent series, so that the ACF and PACF are approximately zero, except at multiples of 12.

The ACF of a particular, simple combined regular and seasonal moving average process is depicted in Figure 25.2. Upon expanding the factors in the model it becomes apparent that the current error as well as errors 1, 12, and 13 periods back in time affect Y_t. The pattern that results in the ACF is a large value at lags 1 and 12 and smaller values at lags 11 and 13.

As a general rule there will be smaller values at lag 12 plus or minus each regular moving average parameter. For example, if the process was regular MA(2), there would be smaller values at lags 10, 11, 13, and 14.

The easiest way to identify the order of combined MA processes is to introduce first a seasonal moving average parameter in the model. The order of the regular MA parameter will then be apparent from the correlogram of the residuals.

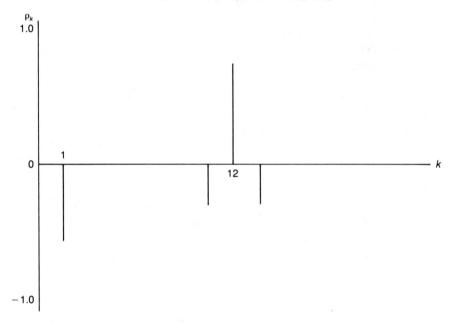

AUTOCORRELATIONS OF COMBINED SEASONAL & REGULAR
MOVING-AVERAGE MODEL

$$Y_t = (1 - \theta_1 B^1)(1 - \theta_{12} B^{12}) \varepsilon_t$$
$$Y_t = \varepsilon_t - \theta_1 \varepsilon_{t-1} - \theta_{12} \varepsilon_{t-12} + \theta_1 \theta_{12} \varepsilon_{t-13}$$

Figure 25.2   An ACF of a combined regular and seasonal MA model.

Another process that occurs in practice is the combination of regular and seasonal autoregressive components. Figure 25.3 shows the ACF of a particular regular AR(1) and a seasonal AR(12) process. A pattern in which the values reach a peak at multiples of 12 is noticeable, as are buildups to and decays from that peak at the other lags.

There are a large variety of patterns that can emerge in the modeling process. The Box-Jenkins approach is so general that it is impossible to catalog all possibilities. So it is essential to follow an iterative procedure in developing successful forecasting models.

AN ARIMA MODEL FOR PREDICTING REVENUES

Let us examine a case study to illustrate the use of ARIMA models. The case study will result in a forecast of telephone toll revenues for a geographic area. The data have been adjusted for rate changes and data recording errors.

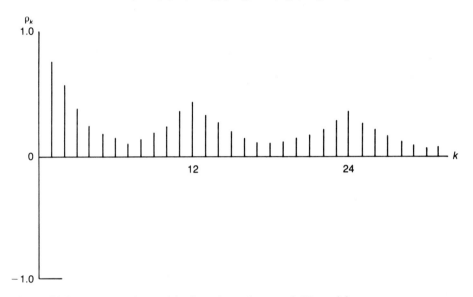

AUTOCORRELATION OF COMBINED SEASONAL & REGULAR
AUTOREGRESSIVE MODEL

$$(1 - \emptyset_1 B)(1 - \emptyset_{12} B^{12}) Y_t = \epsilon_t$$
$$Y_t = \emptyset_1 Y_{t-1} + \emptyset_{12} Y_{t-12} - \emptyset_1 \emptyset_{12} Y_{t-13} + \epsilon_t$$

Figure 25.3 An ACF of a combined regular and seasonal AR model.

Preliminary Analysis

Plots of the raw data, of differences of order 1, of 12, and of both 1 and 12 are shown in Figures 25.4, 25.5, 25.6, and 25.7, respectively. An ANOVA decomposition suggests that the variation due to trend, seasonality, and irregularity accounts for 91.6 percent, 7.4 percent, and 1.0 percent, respectively, of the total variation about the mean. Figure 25.4 illustrates the overall trend and also shows increasing dispersion in the seasonal variation. This pattern is reenforced in the first differences of the data (Figure 25.5). The differences of order 12 show a cyclical pattern (Figure 25.6). The combination of differences of order 1 and 12 finally appear somewhat stationary (Figure 25.7). This is designated Series C.

The increasing dispersion in the data was considerably reduced by taking logarithms before differencing. A stationary series (Series D) is obtained by taking differences of order 1 and 12 after making the logarithmic transformation (compare Figures 25.7 and 25.8). For analysis purposes it is sufficient to model the differenced data (of order 1 and 12 together) with and without the logarithmic transformation. For the purposes of exposition models will also be built for the differenced data (of orders 1 and 12, separately). Series A and B data are first differences on the original and transformed data, respectively.

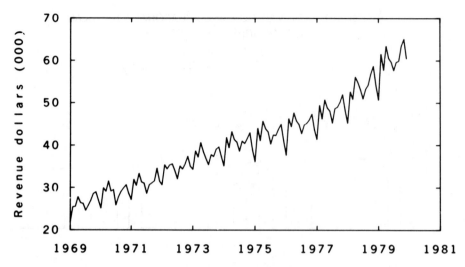

Figure 25.4   A time plot of monthly telephone toll revenues.

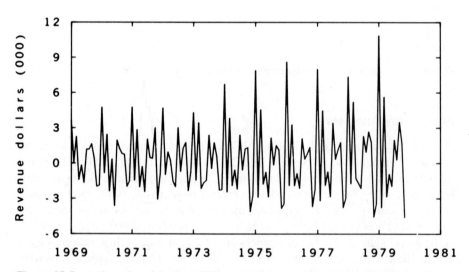

Figure 25.5   A time plot of the first differences of the revenue series (called Series A).

Identification

Figure 25.9 shows the ordinary and partial correlograms of Series C. Figure 25.10 shows the same correlograms for Series D. As expected, the patterns are very similar and suggest the same model. The single, negative spike at lag 1 in the ordinary correlogram suggests a first-order moving-average model. This is confirmed by the

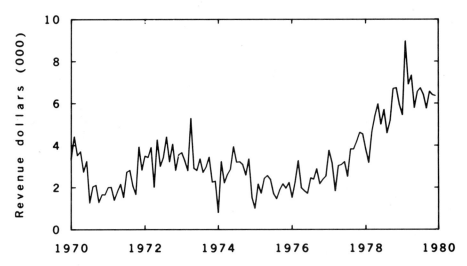

Figure 25.6 A time plot of the differences of order 12 of the revenue series.

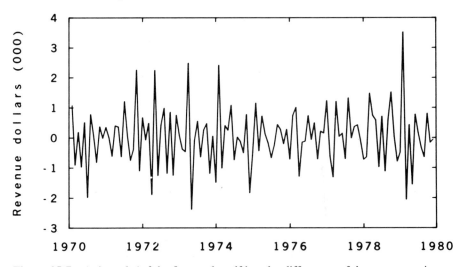

Figure 25.7 A time plot of the first- and twelfth-order differences of the revenue series (called Series C).

decaying pattern in the partial correlogram. The need for moving average parameters frequently occurs with data that have been differenced. Often, a seasonal moving-average parameter is required when a seasonal difference is taken, this is evident by the negative spike at lag 12 in the ordinary correlogram. The $(0,1,1) \times (0,1,1)^{12}$ model was built for both series; when the residuals from these models were examined they showed no significant spikes or patterns in the correlograms.

Figure 25.11 shows the ordinary and partial correlograms of Series A. The corresponding correlograms for Series B are almost identical. The ordinary correl-

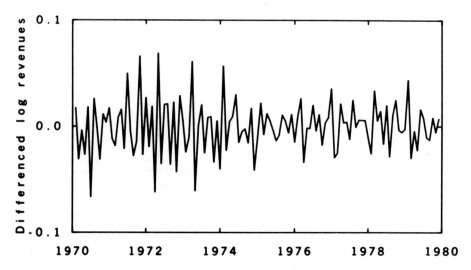

Figure 25.8 A time plot of the first- and twelfth-order differences of the log-transformed revenue series (called Series D).

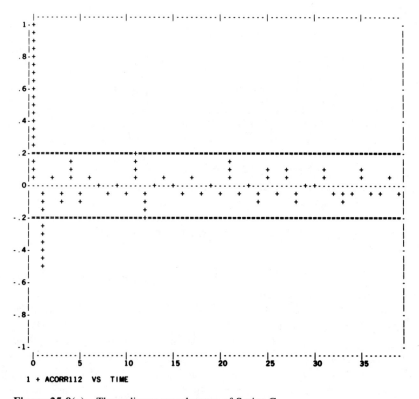

1 + ACORR112 VS TIME

Figure 25.9(a) The ordinary correlogram of Series C.

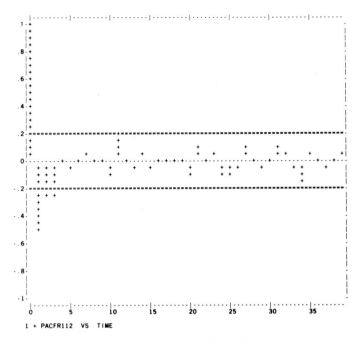

1 + PACFR112 VS TIME

Figure 25.9(b)   Partial correlogram of Series C.

ogram suggests a seasonal autoregressive model because of the decaying pattern of spikes at lags 12, 24, and 36 (also 6, 18, 30, and similar patterns of lags separated by 12). This is confirmed by the spike in the partial correlogram at lag 12.

The suggested model (seasonal autoregressive) was fitted to the data and the correlograms of the residuals were plotted (Figure 25.12). The negative spike at lag 1 in the ordinary correlogram and the decaying pattern in the partial correlogram indicates the need to add a first-order regular moving average parameter to the model. After this was done, resultant correlograms of the residuals showed no significant spikes or patterns.

Estimation and Diagnostic Checking

The following models were built:

Series	ARIMA model for revenues or transformed revenues
A	$(0,1,1) \times (1,0,0)^{12}$
B	$(0,1,1) \times (1,0,0)^{12}$
C	$(0,1,1) \times (0,1,1)^{12}$
D	$(0,1,1) \times (0,1,1)^{12}$

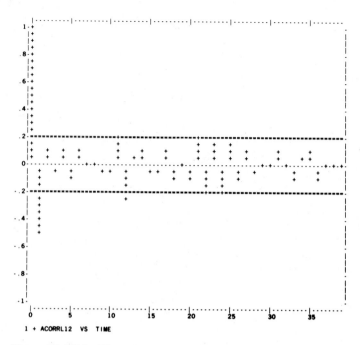

Figure 25.10(a)   The ordinary correlogram of Series D.

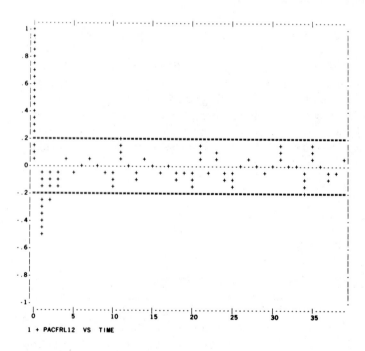

448   **Figure 25.10(b)**   The partial correlogram of Series D.

For each of these models, Table 25.1 shows the estimated parameter values, the associated 95-percent confidence limits, how many standard deviations the mean of the residuals is away from zero, the chi-squared test statistic, and the covariance of the parameter estimates.

The chi-squared test statistics for randomness in the residuals are all less than the tabulated values for the appropriate degrees of freedom. Therefore, there is no evidence suggesting that the residuals did not arise from a white noise process in all four cases.

Models C, D, and B need to have only two parameters estimated. The estimated parameters do not span zero, so they appear significant in all cases. The mean of the residuals in Model C are 0.9 standard deviations from zero and thus it appears reasonable to exclude a deterministic trend constant. For Model D, A and B there is clearly no need for a deterministic trend constant. The confidence limits for the DTC in Model A span zero indicating the parameter can be deleted.

In Model A, the estimate of the seasonal autoregressive parameter (SAR-12) exceeds unity, which suggests nonstationarity. However, taking a difference of order 12, instead, would give Model C. In Model B, the estimate of the seasonal autoregressive pattern is less than but close to unity. This may also point the need to take a difference of order 12, instead.

The estimated covariances for the parameter estimates in all models suggest that the parameter estimates are not highly correlated.

Forecast Test Results

Forecast tests were performed for all four models. Four one-year-ahead forecasts (1975–78) were generated. Table 25.2 shows the results of the tests. Model D had the best results (when measured in terms of average absolute percent of forecast error) followed by Models B and C. Model A should not be used since it is nonstationary. The best results were obtained by using the stationary series generated from the combination of differences of orders 1 and 12. Model B needs to be carefully monitored, if used on an ongoing basis, since the estimated seasonal autoregressive parameter is close to unity.

SEASONAL EXPONENTIAL SMOOTHING

Exponential smoothing procedures have their most common application in routine sales forecasting, where forecasts of future sales of a large number of products might be required. The single or linear/quadratic models are inappropriate for seasonal

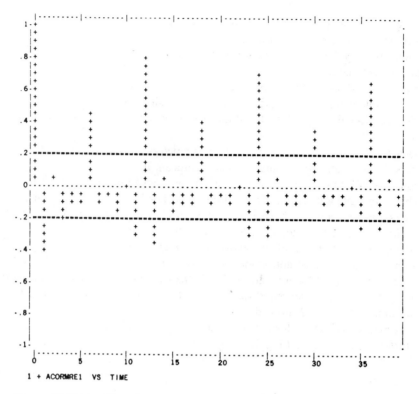

Figure 25.11(a)   The ordinary correlogram of Series A.

data. A three-parameter Winters model is frequently used for the great majority of series that exhibit seasonal patterns. The three parameters are α, β and γ, where:

- α smooths randomness.
- β smooths seasonality.
- γ smooths trend.

Holt (1957) and Winters (1960) developed a low-cost exponential smoothing method to forecast trend-seasonal patterns.

Winters's multiplicative trend-seasonal model is appropriate for time series in which the height of the seasonal pattern is proportional to the average level of the series. The seasonal index I_t is calculated from

$$I_t = \beta \frac{Y_t}{S_t} + (1 - \beta)I_{t-s},$$

where s is the length of the season, and β is a constant between 0 and 1. The current observed seasonal variation is determined from the current value of the series Y_t

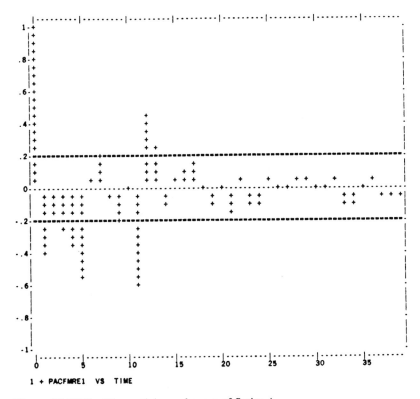

Figure 25.11(b)   The partial correlogram of Series A.

divided by the current single smoothed value for the series S_t. This index is used in the equation

$$S_t = \alpha \frac{Y_t}{I_{t-s}} + (1 - \alpha)(S_{t-1} + T_{t-1}) \, ,$$

where α is a smoothing constant between 0 and 1, to adjust the data for randomness A trend term given by T_t is

$$T_t = \gamma(S_t - S_{t-1}) + (1 - \gamma)T_{t-1} \, ,$$

where γ is a smoothing constant between 0 and 1.

The trend forecast is $(S_t + mT_t)$ and seasonality is introduced with the multiplicative seasonal factor I_{t-s+m}. The forecast based on Winters's method is computed as

$$S_{t+m} = (S_t + mT_t)I_{t-s+m}, \qquad \text{for } m = 1, 2, \ldots, s \, .$$

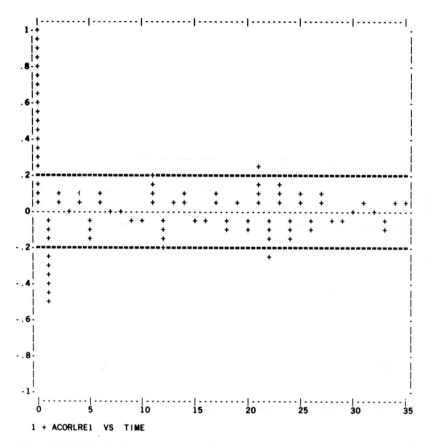

Figure 25.12(a) Ordinary and partial correlograms of the residuals.

The procedure is developed heuristically and requires three smoothing constants as well as initial values for the smoothed statistics. Several approaches are proposed in the literature (Bowerman and O'Connell, 1979; and Montgomery and Johnson, 1976); however, the smoothing concept is similar to the one performed in the single exponential smoothing method (see Chapter 8).

The selection of the smoothing parameters α, β, and γ is generally an iterative, *ad hoc* process. The criteria generally used in selection of α, β, and γ is the minimization of the mean square error (MSE), although the mean percent of error (bias) and mean absolute percent of error are also utilized. In an application using airline data (Box and Jenkins, 1976, series G), a variety of Winters-type models were estimated. The impact of inadequate starting values were found in two of the models. For values of α less than 0.2 to 0.3, the initial estimates were very poor and severely distorted comparisons based on average absolute error or MSE. It is interesting to note that over the preceding five years, the highest individual monthly

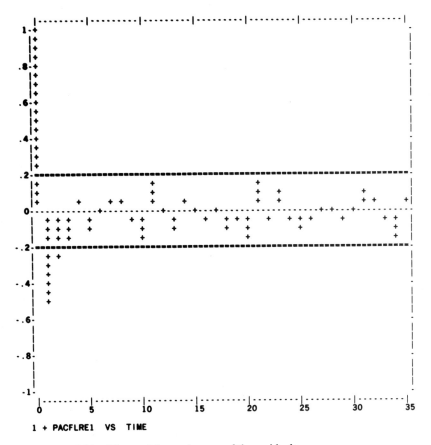

Figure 25.12(b)   The partial correlogram of the residuals.

error (average) for Model 1 ($\hat{\alpha} = 0.1$, $\hat{\beta} = 0.2$, $\hat{\delta} = 0.5$) is 2.6 percent and for Model 2 ($\hat{\alpha} = 0.2$, $\hat{\beta} = 0.2$, $\hat{\delta} = 0.5$) is 2.7 percent. Figure 25.13 compares box plots of the monthly errors over the preceding five years for the two models. The relative similarity in model performance, once starting values have stabilized, is not apparent by looking only at the MSE.

By holding two parameters constant and varying the third it became apparent that increasing β improved the monthly percentage error. While the fine-tuning was not completed, Model 3, with $\hat{\alpha} = 0.4$, $\hat{\beta} = 0.5$, and $\hat{\gamma} = 0.4$, produced the best model statistics and minimum monthly errors over the past five years. The smoothing constants in this model are often larger in magnitude than those of the simpler smoothing models. Figure 25.14 shows a box plot of these errors. It is apparent that a seasonal pattern still exists in the errors.

A basic change in the process of generating a time series requires a change in parameter values. An adaptive smoothing modification can be tried, or one can select

Table 25.1 Model statistics for Series A through D.

Model	Parameter	Lower confidence limit	Value	Upper confidence limit	Standard deviation*	Chi-squared statistic	Parameter variance-covariance		
A	RMA-1	0.41	0.57	0.73	0.85	28.5 (48df)	1.0		
	SMA-12	0.02	0.23	0.44			−0.15	1.0	
B	RMA-1	0.38	0.55	0.71	0.64	31.3 (48df)	1.0		
	SMA-12	0.17	0.36	0.55			−0.16	1.0	
C	SAR-12	0.95	1.02	1.08	0.02	26.7 (47df)	1.0		
	RMA-1	0.45	0.61	0.76			−0.26	1.0	
	DTC	−0.04	0.02	0.08			−0.04	−0.01	1.0
D	SAR-12	0.87	0.93	0.99	0.31	29.5 (48df)	1.0		
	RMA-1	0.44	0.59	0.75			−0.03	1.0	

*Number of standard deviations by which the mean of the residuals differs from zero.
DTC = Deterministic Trend Constant

Table 25.2 Forecast test results for Models A through D (in percent).

	Model A	Model B	Model C	Model D
One-year-ahead results				
1975	−1.04	−0.94	−1.31	−1.52
1976	0.87	0.56	0.22	−0.21
1977	2.38	2.20	2.21	1.82
1978	1.71	1.72	2.34	1.76
Average absolute error	1.50	1.36	1.52	1.33
Two-year-ahead results				
1976	−0.89	−0.83	−2.17	−3.24
1977	4.64	3.62	2.89	1.76
1978	7.90	7.36	7.35	6.39
Average absolute error	4.48	3.94	4.14	3.80

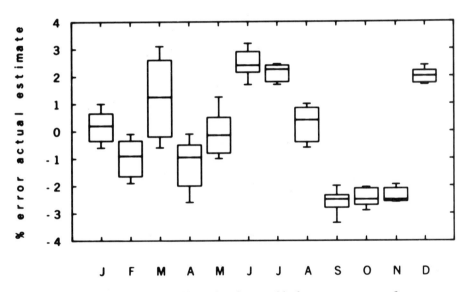

Figure 25.13(a)   A comparison of box plots for monthly forecast errors over five years for airline Model 1 ($\hat{\alpha} = 0.1$, $\hat{\beta} = 0.2$, $\hat{\delta} = 0.5$).

parameter values in the 0.1-to-0.2 range and allow the forecasts to change gradually. A major drawback of this approach is the large number of possible combinations of parameter values that need to be tested.

Other examples may be found in Bowerman and O'Connell (1979, Chapter 7), Makridakis and Wheelwright (1980, Chapter 4), Montgomery and Johnson (1976), and Sullivan and Claycombe (1977, Chapter 5). In fact, the last of these references provides a listing of FORTRAN programs for making forecasts with a number of techniques including the Winters method of exponential smoothing.

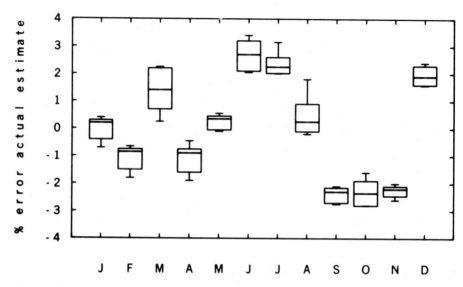

Figure 25.13(b)   A comparison of box plots for monthly forecast errors over five years for airline Model 2 ($\hat{\alpha} = 0.2$, $\hat{\beta} = 0.2$, $\hat{\delta} = 0.5$).

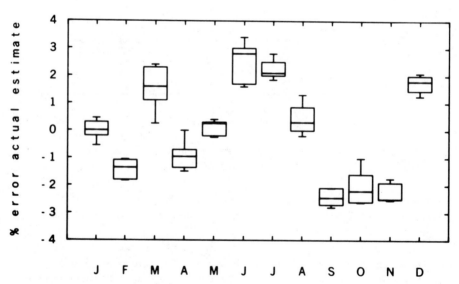

Figure 25.14   A comparison of box plots of the monthly forecast errors for airline Model 3 ($\hat{\alpha} = 0.4$, $\hat{\beta} = 0.5$, $\hat{\delta} = 0.4$).

Exponential smoothing methods are intuitively reasonable procedures whose optimality properties can be related to ARIMA processes. Indeed, if the Winters *additive* seasonal predictor is to produce optimal forecasts, it can be shown that the time series must be generated by a five-parameter ARIMA model, whose coefficients are all functions of the three Winters smoothing constants (Granger and Newbold, 1977, Chapter 5).

It is also possible to represent seasonality by combinations of sine and cosine trigometric functions (Harrison, 1965), or even seasonal dummy variables. However, these approaches

- Tend to increase greatly the number of parameters in the model.

- Can induce or leave undisturbed higher order seasonal autocorrelation.

- Imply (in the case of dummy variables) a different error structure than would be adopted when using the Box-Jenkins approach (Thomas and Wallis, 1971).

ARIMA MODELING CHECKLIST

_____ Is the series stationary?

_____ Examine the correlation matrix. There should *not* be a high degree of correlation between parameter estimates (e.g., over 0.9).

_____ Have all the model parameters (i.e., terms) been included in the model as required?

_____ Have the parameter estimates and their standard errors been examined? The confidence interval for each parameter (including the trend constant if there is one) should not span zero, but should be either positive or negative. If the confidence interval does include zero and the interval is basically symmetric about zero, then consideration should be given to eliminating the parameter.

_____ If a regular autoregressive or seasonal autoregressive term is included in the model, the parameter estimates should not be close to 1.0 (e.g., over 0.90 or 0.95). If either is close to 1.0, a regular or seasonal difference should be tried in the model and a forecast test performed to determine which—the differenced model or the autoregressive model—is better.

_____ Do the sum of squares of the errors and the standard error of the residuals become smaller as fits of the model improve?

_____ Does the chi-squared statistic fall below the critical value for the associated degrees of freedom? If so, this indicates white noise. (*Note:* a quick, conservative check for white noise is to see if the model has a chi-squared statistic below the number of degrees of freedom.)

_____ Are there significant patterns in the correlograms of the residuals? Review the ordinary and partial correlograms for any remaining pattern in the residuals. Give primary emphasis to patterns in the correlogram. (*Notes:* (1) The confidence limits on the correlogram and partial correlogram are approximately 95 percent. Hence, 1 spike in 20 would be expected to be outside the confidence limits owing to randomness alone. (2) Decaying spikes in the correlogram, which by visual inspection appear to originate at 1.0, indicate a regular autoregressive process, decaying spikes which originate at a lower level indicate a mixed autoregressive moving-average model.)

——— Has a deterministic trend constant been estimated? It is suggested that a deterministic trend constant not be added until the very last. Then if the mean of the residuals of the final model is more than one standard deviation from zero, put a trend constant in the model and test it for significance. (There may be times when one doesn't want the model to put a trend in the forecasts.)

——— Are you watchful of "overdifferencing"? Be alert to the requirement that moving average parameters corresponding to the differencing that has been taken must achieve stationarity. For example, first differences may induce the need for a moving average parameter of order 1. Differencing of order 4 may induce the need for a seasonal moving average parameter in quarterly series. A check of the correlogram helps here. "Overdifferencing" may be apparent if regular and seasonal moving-average parameter estimates are very close to unity.

——— There are some combinations of parameters that are unlikely to result within the same model. If these combinations are present reevaluate the previous analysis of

- Seasonal differences and seasonal autoregressive parameters.

- Seasonal autoregressive and seasonal moving average parameters.

- Seasonal moving average parameters at other than lags 4 or 12 (or multiples of 4 and 12) for quarterly and monthly series, respectively.

SUMMARY

This chapter has dealt with building forecasting models for seasonal data.

- Regular ARIMA models can be enlarged to include seasonal data by building a multiplicative ARIMA model.

- Seasonal exponential smoothing can be used as an intuitively reasonable, low-cost alternative for short-term forecasting with scarce data.

USEFUL READING

BOWERMAN, B. L., and R. T. O'CONNELL (1979). *Time Series and Forecasting*. North Scituate, MA: Duxbury Press.

BOX, G. E. P., and G. M. JENKINS (1976). *Time Series Analysis, Forecasting and Control, Revised Edition*. San Francisco, CA: Holden-Day.

HARRISON, P. J. (1965). Short-term Forecasting. *Applied Statistics* 14, 102–39.

HOLT, C. C. (1957). *Forecasting Trends and Seasonals by Exponentially Weighted Moving Averages*. Pittsburgh, PA: Carnegie Institute of Technology.

MONTGOMERY, D. C., and L. A. JOHNSON (1976). *Forecasting and Time Series Analysis*. New York, NY; McGraw-Hill.

SULLIVAN, W. G., and W. W. CLAYCOMBE (1977). *Fundamentals of Forecasting*. Reston, VA: Reston Publishing Company.

THOMAS, J. J., and K. F. WALLIS (1971). Seasonal Variation in Regression Analysis. *Journal of the Royal Statistical Society* A. 134, 57–72.

WHEELWRIGHT, S. C., and S. MAKRIDAKIS (1980). *Forecasting Methods for Management, 3rd edition*. New York, NY: John Wiley and Sons.

WINTERS, P. R. (1960). Forecasting Sales by Exponentially Weighted Moving Averages. *Management Science* 6, 324–42.

CHAPTER 26

Modeling Univariate ARIMA Time Series: Expanded Examples

This chapter presents a variety of univariate ARIMA models for the series presented throughout the book. In particular,

- A univariate ARIMA model will be derived for the main-telephone gain data as a prelude to developing an explanatory model in terms of the FRB Index of Industrial Production and U.S. housing starts.

- Univariate ARIMA models will be derived for the U.S. housing starts series and the FRB Index of Industrial Production series.

- A univariate ARIMA model will also be derived for nonfarm employment, a series used in the telecommunications forecasting example in Chapter 1, and utilized further in *The Professional Forecaster,* Chapter 24 in a transfer function model for telephone toll revenues.

AN ARIMA MODEL FOR MAIN TELEPHONE GAIN

In Chapter 15 the main-telephone gain series was modeled by using a multiple linear regression approach. In this chapter, an ARIMA model will be built for the same time series. In *The Professional Forecaster,* Chapter 24 a combined transfer function and noise model is developed relating main telephone gain to U.S. housing starts and the FRB Index of Industrial Production.

Obtaining Stationarity

A time plot of the main gain data, as a quarterly time series from the first quarter of 1959 to the fourth quarter of 1978, is shown in Figure 26.1. The data show

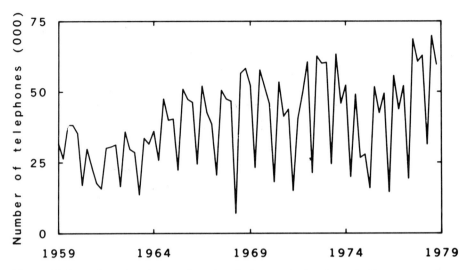

Figure 26.1   A time plot of quarterly main-telephone gain data from the first quarter of 1959 to the fourth quarter of 1978.

increasing volatility in the seasonal pattern over time. An ANOVA decomposition of this series indicated that trend, seasonal, and irregular variation accounted for 7.3 percent, 81.3 percent, and 11.4 percent, respectively of the variation about the mean. The quarters in 1968 and 1971 in which labor strikes occurred are quite evident (low values), although the 1971 strike is not as pronounced as the 1968 strike. However, when comparable quarters of prior and following years are considered, it does appear that the third quarter of 1971 is low.

At this point it is necessary to adjust the original strike data to more reasonable levels. The intervention modeling approach (presented in *The Professional Forecaster,* Chapter 23) provides one way of establishing replacement values. To demonstrate the effect that the strike outliers have on the estimation of model parameters, univariate models will be developed for the unadjusted series and a strike-adjusted version of the series. In addition to impacting the parameter estimates, outliers can affect model forecasts dramatically *if* they occur in the most recent data *and* are part of the calculation of the forecasts.

In this example, the same model structure results (in terms of the order of the autoregressive and moving average parameters) when either version of the time series is used. This is not always the case. Even though the order of the models is identical, the model coefficients are different. Since identical model structures apply, the model identification steps will be covered only for the adjusted series.

The ordinary correlogram of the series shown in Figure 26.2 takes a long time to decay, indicating a need for seasonal differencing (differences of order 4).

Figure 26.3(a) shows the ordinary correlogram of the differences of order 4 of the series. It dies out and becomes insignificant relatively quickly, suggesting that the data are stationary.

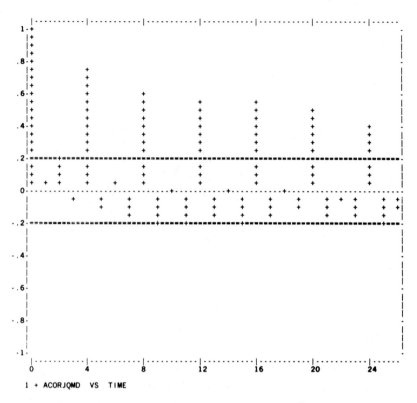

1 + ACORJQMD VS TIME

Figure 26.2 Plot of the ordinary correlogram of the data shown in Figure 26.1.

Identification of ARMA Models

The identification of a tentative ARIMA model requires the ordinary correlogram and the partial correlogram for the differences of order 4 in the main gain data. The decay in the correlogram (Figure 26.3(a)) suggests a regular autoregressive process. In the partial correlogram (Figure 26.3(b)), the significant positive value at lag 1 confirms an autoregressive model and indicates that the order of the model is equal to 1.

The tentative $(1,0,0) \times (0,1,0)^4$ model was estimated and the residual ordinary correlogram has a negative spike at lag 4 which suggests the need for a seasonal moving average parameter. The pattern of negative spikes at lags 4, 8, and 12 in the partial correlogram (not shown) confirms the need for a seasonal moving average parameter. The starting model, Model A, in $(p, d, q) \times (P,D,Q)^5$ notation, is $(1,0,0) \times (0,1,1)^4$.

Parameter Estimation and Diagnostic Checking

Table 26.1 shows that the parameter estimates of the two models fitted to the adjusted and unadjusted data are all significant, i.e., the confidence intervals do not span 0.

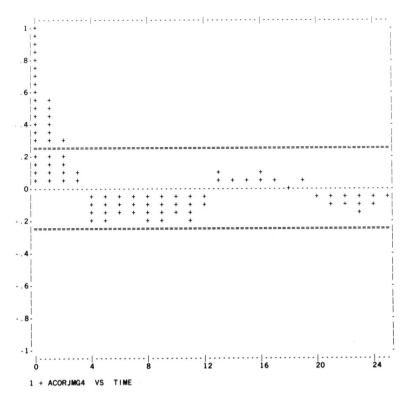

1 + ACORJMG4   VS   TIME

Figure 26.3(a)   Plots of the ordinary correlogram of the fourth-order differences of the data shown in Figure 26.1.

The estimated parameters in each model are not highly correlated (the estimated variance-covariance matrix is not shown). The mean value of the residuals is 1.4 standard deviations from 0. The analyst has the option of whether or not to include a deterministic trend constant in the model. Omitting a trend constant usually results in a model that is more responsive to new observations. Since the main gain series is volatile, it was decided not to include a trend constant.

The residual correlograms did not show any significant values or patterns. The sample chi-squared statistic ($= 2.67$) is less than the theoretical value ($= 12.59$) for white noise for six degrees of freedom at the 5-percent level (Appendix A, Table 3). There is no evidence to reject the null hypothesis of random residuals. Diagnostic checking has shown that no modifications in the initial models are called for.

Forecast Test Results

Forecast tests were performed for the two models and the results are shown in Table 26.2. Five one-year-ahead forecasts and four two-year-ahead forecasts were generated. In terms of the average absolute percent error, the model based on the adjusted data had slightly more accurate one-year-ahead forecasts but was somewhat

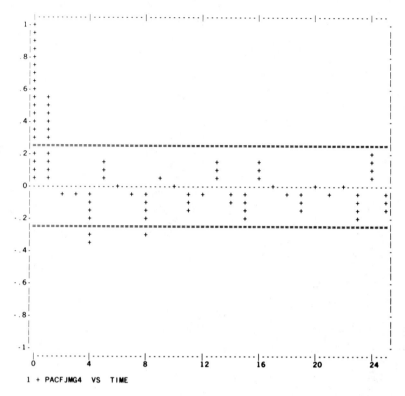

1 + PACFJMG4 VS TIME

Figure 26.3(b) Plot of the partial correlogram of the fourth-order differences of the data shown in Figure 26.1.

inferior for two-year-ahead forecasts. If the outliers occurred in the most current periods, the forecasts from the (unadjusted) model would have been distorted.

In a similar context, Levenbach (1980) studied a number of time series models for main telephone gain by using a methodology due to Priestley (1971). The quarterly series used in that paper differed from the study in this chapter in two respects:

- The timespans used for fitting and evaluating one- and two-year-ahead forecasts were not the same.
- The definition of "strike adjustment" in the data was different.

Consequently, model specifications differ somewhat. However, these differences did not turn out to be significant for forecasting purposes. Clearly, similar model specifications are possible and should not cause too much concern for the practicing forecaster.

AN ARIMA MODEL FOR HOUSING STARTS

The Federal Reserve Board Index of Industrial Production series and U.S. housing starts series were used in multiple linear regression models for quarterly main gain

Table 26.1 Summary of univariate models fitted to main-telephone gain data.

Model type	Estimated model, and (standard errors)	Residual variance ($\times 10^8$)
Seasonal differences (unadjusted series)	$(1 - 0.66B)(1 - B^4)\text{GAIN} = (1 - 0.58B^4)\varepsilon_t$ (± 0.09) $\quad\quad\quad\quad\quad\quad$ (± 0.10)	46.4
Seasonal differences (adjusted series)	$(1 - 0.74B)(1 - B^4)\text{GAIN*} = (1 - 0.51B^4)\varepsilon_t$ (± 0.08) $\quad\quad\quad\quad\quad\quad$ (± 0.10)	33.8

Table 26.2 Forecast test results for two models for the main-telephone gain data.

Model type	Average absolute percent error	
	One year ahead	Two years ahead
Seasonal differences (unadjusted series)	9.7	22.5
Seasonal differences (adjusted series)	9.5	24.0

in Chapter 12. Univariate ARIMA models will be developed now to predict future values for these series.

The quarterly housing starts series is noticeably seasonal, and this was confirmed by the significant value at lag 4 in the correlogram (Figure 26.4). The series was assumed to be stationary and a model with regular and seasonal autoregressive parameters was tried. The pattern in the ordinary correlogram at low order lags is similar to that described in Figure 25.3. The residual correlogram shown in Figure 26.5 indicates a decaying pattern (autoregressive) at lags 1–3 and a significant negative spike at lag 4. A regular autoregressive parameter (second order) was added to account for the remaining autoregressive decay. A seasonal moving average parameter was included to care for the spike at lag 4. At this time the spike at lag 10 was not addressed. The model was estimated and the residual correlogram indicated a significant positive spike at lag 2; the spike at lag 10 was no longer significant. Before attempting to enlarge the model, the estimated parameters were reviewed. The model equation (with standard errors shown below) was

$$(1 - 1.14B + 0.29B^2)(1 - 0.96B^4)\,\text{Hous} = (1 - 0.42B^4)\varepsilon_t.$$
$$(\pm 0.11) \quad (\pm 0.11) \quad\quad (\pm 0.02) \quad\quad\quad\quad (\pm 0.14)$$

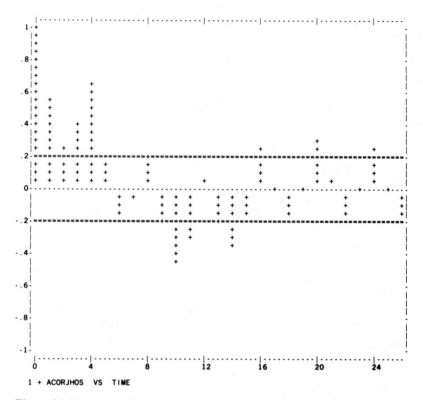

Figure 26.4(a)   Plot of the ordinary correlogram of the housing starts data.

The very large value for the seasonal autoregressive parameter (= 0.96) indicated that the model was very close to being nonstationary. This suggests taking seasonal differences prior to modeling.

Figure 26.6 shows the resulting ordinary correlogram and partial correlogram of the differenced series; now the sinusoidal decay in the correlogram (Figure 26.6(a)) indicated an autoregressive process of an order greater than 1. The significant spikes up to lag 3 in the partial correlogram (Figure 26.6(b)) suggested that the order of the process should be 3. If this were to be too high, however, the higher-order parameters would be insignificant when the model is estimated. A negative spike at lag 4 in the residual correlogram and a pattern of decay for negative spikes at lags 4, 8, etc., in the residual partial correlogram indicated the need for a seasonal moving average parameter of order 1. This model was estimated, and the correlogram of the resulting residuals showed no further patterns. However, the second-order autoregressive term was not significant and was deleted in the final model. The residual chi-squared statistic (= 2.35) is less than the tabulated value (= 9.49) for four degrees of freedom.

Since the autoregressive parameters in the previous model suggested a rather complex model, and the second-order term was insignificant, consideration was

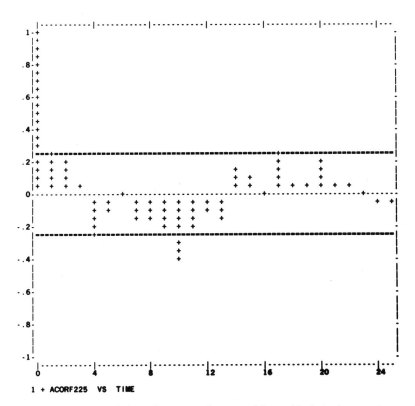

Figure 26.5 Plot of the ordinary correlogram of the residuals in the tentative model of the housing starts.

given to reducing the regression period and modeling the more recent observations to see if a simpler model would result. The time period was shortened to cover the 1965–1978 period. In this case, a regular autoregressive model of order 2 was sufficient. This reduced the order of the autoregressive model by one, however the residual variance increased.

Table 26.3 summarizes the housing starts models and Table 26.4 compares the forecast test results. The regular autoregressive model of order 3 provided improved forecasts.

AN ARIMA MODEL FOR THE FRB INDEX OF INDUSTRIAL PRODUCTION

Figures 26.7 and 26.8 show the quarterly FRB Index of Industrial Production and its correlogram. The series is the sum of a number of components with different seasonalities and is generally reported on a seasonally adjusted basis so there is no significant seasonal pattern in the correlogram. The slow decay in the correlogram

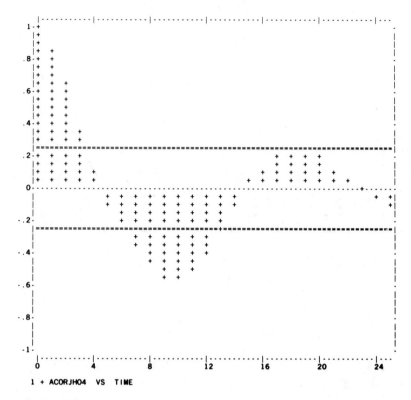

Figure 26.6(a)   Plot of the ordinary correlogram of the differences of order 4 of the housing starts.

indicated the need for taking differences of order 1. Figure 26.9 shows the correlogram and partial correlogram of these first differences of the series. The large positive spike in the correlogram (Figure 26.9(a)) at lag 1 and the alternating decay in the partial correlogram (Figure 26.9(b)) indicated the need for a regular moving average parameter of order 1. This model was estimated, and there was no significant pattern in the correlogram of the residuals.

AN ARIMA MODEL FOR NONFARM EMPLOYMENT

In *The Professional Forecaster,* Chapter 24 a transfer function model is developed relating telephone toll revenues to nonfarm employment. Transfer function modeling begins by building a univariate ARIMA model for the independent (input) series. Such a model is now used to generate nonfarm employment forecasts.

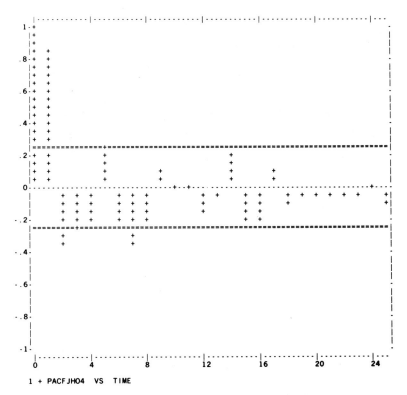

1 + PACF JHO4   VS   TIME

Figure 26.6(b)   Plot of the partial correlogram of the differences of order 4 of the housing starts.

Table 26.3   Summary of univariate models for U.S. housing starts data.

Model type (years)	Estimated model, and (standard errors)	Residual variance ($\times 10^8$)
Seasonal differences (1959–1978)	$(1 - 1.12B + 0.28B^3)(1 - B^4)\text{HOUS} = (1 - 0.76\,B^4)\varepsilon_t$ $(\pm 0.07)\ (\pm 0.07)$ (± 0.10)	1306
Seasonal differences (1965–1978)*	$(1 - 1.21B + 0.32B^2)(1 - B^4)\text{HOUS} = (1 - 0.85B^4)\varepsilon_t$ $(\pm 0.13)\ (\pm 0.13)$ (± 0.05)	1571

*A model of the same order but based on data from 1959–1978 had an estimated residual variance of 1254.

Table 26.4 Forecast test results for two models of U.S. housing starts data.

Model type	Average absolute percent error	
	One year ahead	Two years ahead
$(1 - \phi_1 B - \phi_3 B^3)(1 - B^4)Y_t = (1 - \theta_4 B^4)\varepsilon_t$	21.1	59.0
$(1 - \phi_1 B - \phi_2 B^2)(1 - B^4)Y_t = (1 - \theta_4 B^4)\varepsilon_t$	31.2	81.4

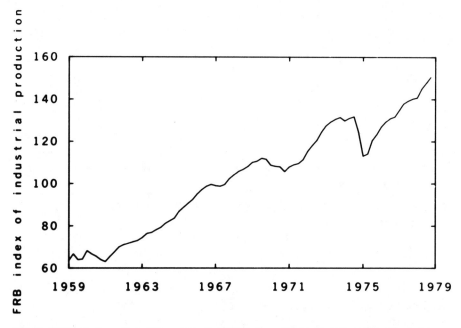

Figure 26.7 A time plot of the quarterly FRB Index of Industrial Production from the first quarter of 1959 to the fourth quarter of 1978. *Source:* Board of Governors of the Federal Reserve System.

Obtaining Stationarity

Figure 26.10 shows the monthly nonfarm employment series and Figure 26.11 shows the ordinary correlogram of the data. The gradual decay in the correlogram indicated the need for regular differences of order 1. The ordinary correlogram of the first-differenced series showed a gradual decay at multiples of lag 12; this indicated the need for taking differences of order 12 as well, to obtain a stationary series.

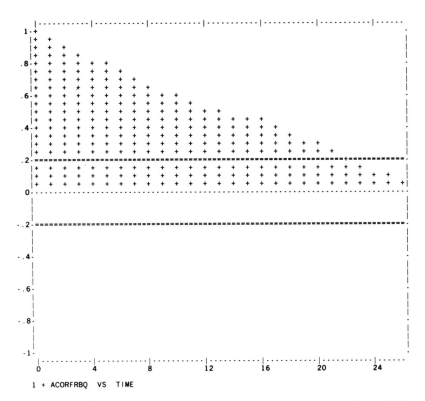

Figure 26.8   Plot of the ordinary correlogram of the data shown in Figure 26.7.

Plots of the correlograms for the differenced nonfarm employment data are shown in Figure 26.12. The correlogram in Figure 26.12(a) decays quickly, indicating a stationary series.

Identification

In Figure 26.12(a) the sinusoidal decay in the correlogram at low-order lags suggested a regular autoregressive model of order greater than 1. The negative spikes at lags 12 and 24 in the correlogram (Figure 26.12(a)) indicated a seasonal moving average model of order 2. The spike at lag 2 in the partial correlogram (Figure 26.12(b)) indicated that the order of the regular autoregressive process should be 2. The decay of negative spikes at lags 12, 24, and 36 in the partial correlogram confirmed that seasonal moving average parameters would be required.

Parameter Estimation and Diagnostic Checking

The final model for nonfarm employment (NFRM) was estimated and took the following form (standard errors are shown beneath the formula for the model):

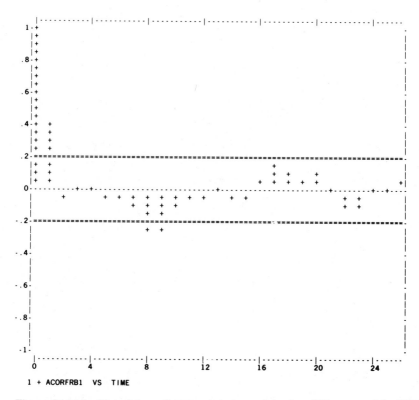

Figure 26.9(a)   Plot of the ordinary correlogram of the first differences of the FRB Index of Industrial Production.

$$(1 - 1.116B + 0.236B^2)(1 - B)(1 - B^{12})\,\text{NFRM} = (1 - 0.591B^{12} - 0.314B^{24})\varepsilon_t \,.$$
$$(\pm\,0.090)\quad(\pm\,0.090)\qquad\qquad\qquad\qquad(\pm\,0.085)\quad(\pm\,0.084)$$

In comparison with the standard errors, all the estimates of the model parameters are significant. Moreover, the parameter estimates are not highly correlated. The mean of the residuals is not significantly different from zero, and the chi-squared statistic ($= 2.18$) is less than the theoretical value ($= 31.4$) for 20 degrees of freedom. There were no significant patterns in the residual correlograms.

Forecast Test Results

The model predicts future values with an average absolute one-year-ahead forecast error of 0.77 percent and a two-year-ahead error of 2.79 percent. A similar model using the *logarithms* of nonfarm employment was tested, and the forecast test results were almost identical to those of the untransformed series.

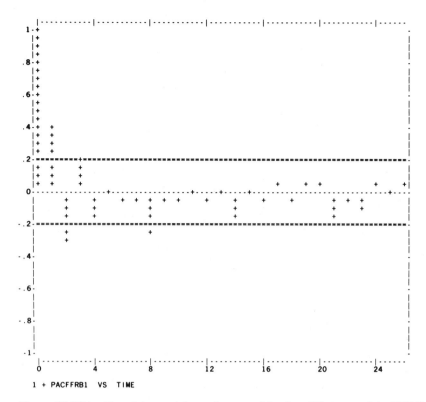

1 + PACFFRB1 VS TIME

Figure 26.9(b) Plot of the partial correlogram of the first differences of the FRB Index of Industrial Production.

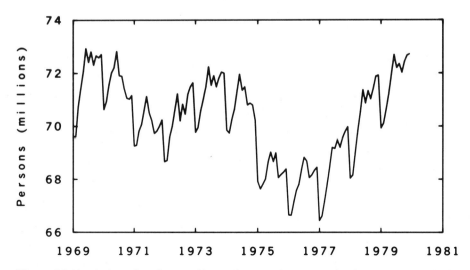

Figure 26.10 A time plot of a monthly nonfarm employment series from January 1969 to December 1979.

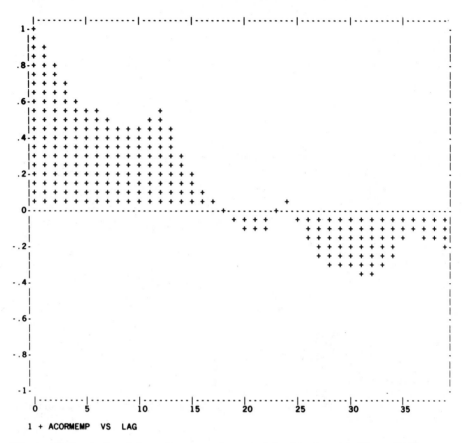

Figure 26.11 A plot of the ordinary correlogram of the data shown in Figure 26.10.

OTHER STUDIES

Numerous studies exist in the literature on univariate ARIMA modeling. In addition to the examples found in the textbooks dealing with the Box-Jenkins modeling strategy, several published studies related to the ones in this chapter include Bhat-tacharyya (1974), Box et al. (1967), Brubacher and Wilson (1976), Chatfield and Prothero (1973), Jensen (1979), Thompson and Tiao (1971), and Tomasek (1972).

SUMMARY

This chapter provided an illustration of the identification stage for a number of univariate models of three time series.

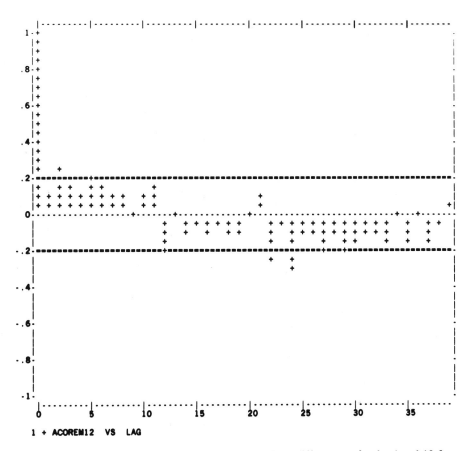

Figure 26.12(a) Plot of the ordinary correlogram of the differences of order 1 and 12 for the nonfarm employment data.

- A univariate model for *quarterly* main-telephone gain.
- Univariate ARIMA models for U.S. housing starts and the FRB Index of Industrial Production to be related to main telephone gain.
- A univariate model for a *monthly* nonfarm employment series.

The modeling exercise demonstrated that several tentative models can be entertained for any given series. Diagnostic checks for stationarity, invertibility, significance of coefficients, white noise residuals, and heteroscedasticity may eliminate some of the models from further consideration. Forecasters must use judgment and establish their criteria for selecting the most appropriate model for a given application.

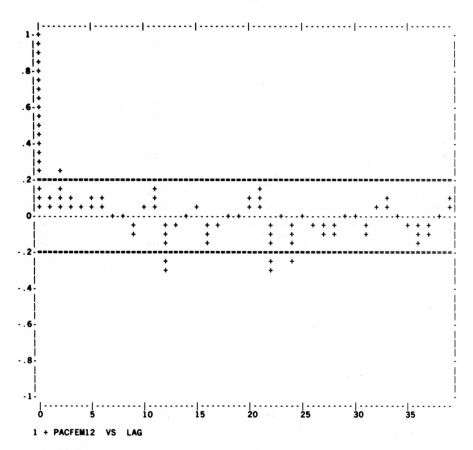

Figure 26.12(b) Plot of the partial correlogram of the differences of order 1 and 12 for the nonfarm employment data.

USEFUL READING

BHATTACHARYYA, M. N. (1974). Forecasting the Demand for Telephones in Australia. *Applied Statistics* 23, 1–10.

BOX, G. E. P., G. M. JENKINS, and D. W. BACON (1967). Models for Forecasting Seasonal and Nonseasonal Time Series. *In* B. Harris, ed. *Advanced Seminar on Spectral Analysis*. New York, NY: John Wiley and Sons.

BRUBACHER, S., and G. T. WILSON (1976). Interpolating Time Series with Application to the Estimation of Holiday Effects on Electricity Demand. *Applied Statistics* 25, 107–16.

CHATFIELD, C., and D. L. PROTHERO (1973). Box-Jenkins Seasonal Forecasting: Problems in a Case Study. *Journal of the Royal Statistical Society* A 136, 295–315.

JENSEN, D. (1979). General Telephone of the Northwest: A Forecasting Case Study. *Journal of Contemporary Business* 8, 19–34.

LEVENBACH, H. (1980). A Comparative Study of Time Series Models for Forecasting Telephone Demand. *In* O. D. Anderson, ed., *Forecasting Public Utilities*. Amsterdam, Netherlands: North-Holland Publishing Co.

PRIESTLEY, M. B. (1971). Fitting Relationships between Time Series. *Bulletin of the International Statistical Institute* 44, 295–324.

THOMPSON, H. E., and G. C. TIAO (1971). An Analysis of Telephone Data: A Case Study of Forecasting Seasonal Time Series. *Bell Journal of Economics and Management Science* 2, 514–41.

TOMASEK, O. (1972). Statistical Forecasting of Telephone Time Series. *ITU Telecommunications Journal* 39, 1–7.

PROBLEMS

1. Using a table of random numbers or a computer-generated set of pseudo-random numbers (about 50), construct a time plot and ordinary correlogram of:

   a. The sequence of random numbers.

   b. An AR(1) model with $\emptyset_1 = 0.7$.

   c. An AR(1) model with $\emptyset_1 = -0.4$. Compare with (a).

   d. An MA(1) model $\theta_1 = 0.7$.

   e. An MA(1) model with $\emptyset_1 = 0.4$. Compare with (c).

   f. An ARMA(1,1) model with $\emptyset_1 = 0.7$ and $\theta_1 = -0.7$.

   g. An ARMA(1,1) model with $\emptyset_1 = 0.7$ and $\theta_1 = 0.4$.

   Compare with (e).

2. Using a table of random numbers or a computer-generated set of random numbers (about 50), construct a time plot and ordinary correlogram of:

   a. An AR(2) model with $\emptyset_1 = 1.0$, $\emptyset_2 = -0.75$. What is the general pattern of the correlogram?

   b. An AR(2) model with $\emptyset_1 = 0.4$, $\emptyset_2 = 0.5$. What is the general pattern of the correlogram?

   c. An MA(2) model with $\theta_1 = -0.7$, $\theta_2 = 0.2$.

   Compare with problems 1(d) and 1(f).

d.   An MA(2) model with $\theta_1 = 0.4$, $\theta_2 = 0.2$. Compare with problems 1(e) and 1(g).

3.   Show that an MA(1) model is equivalent to single exponential smoothing.

4.   The theoretical autocorrelation functions (ACF) of the five models cited in problems 1 and 2 are:

AR(1):

$$\rho_k = \emptyset_1^k \qquad k \geqslant 1$$

AR(2):

$$\rho_1 = \emptyset_1/(1 - \emptyset_2)$$
$$\rho_k = \emptyset_1\rho_{k-1} + \emptyset_2\rho_{k-2} \qquad k \geqslant 2$$

MA(1):

$$\rho_1 = -\ \theta_1/(1 + \theta_1^2)$$
$$\rho_k = 0 \qquad k \geqslant 2$$

MA(2):

$$\rho_1 = -\theta_1(1 - \theta_2)/(1 + \theta_1^2 + \theta_2^2)$$
$$\rho_2 = -\theta_2/(1 + \theta_1^2 + \theta_2^2)$$
$$\rho_k = 0 \qquad k \geqslant 3$$

ARMA(1,):

$$\rho_1 = (1 - \theta_1\emptyset_1)(\emptyset_1 - \theta_1)/(1 + \theta_1^2 - 2\emptyset_1\theta_1)$$
$$\rho_k = \rho_{k-1}\emptyset_1 \qquad k \geqslant 2$$

Plot the ACF's for the models cited in problems 1 and 2. Compare with the corresponding empirical correlograms.

5.   Consider the quarterly index of consumer sentiment (MOOD) data in Appendix B. Divide the data into 2 equal parts, and plot the correlograms of the first differences in each case. Is there evidence of a significant spike at lag 10 as in Figure 23.8(a)?

6.   Consider the quarterly U.S. money supply (M1) data in Appendix B. Divide the data into 2 equal parts, take logarithms and plot the correlograms of the first and second differences in each case. If feasible, also display the corre-

sponding partial correlgrams. What starting models do each of these correlogram plots suggest?

7. Consider the quarterly index of industrial production (FRB) in Appendix B.
    Divide the data into 2 equal parts, take first differences and plot the ordinary
    and partial correlograms in each case. What starting models do you suggest?

8. Suppose the model for problem 7 is an ARIMA $(1,1,0)$ model:

    $$(1 - B)FRB_t = 0.4(1 - B)FRB_{t-1} + \epsilon_t.$$

    a. Express the model as an AR(2) model.
    b. Determine the forecasts for the 4 quarters of 1979.
    c. Assume this model was obtained with data accounting through the
        fourth quarter of 1976. Determine the forecasts for 1977 and 1978.
        Compare the forecasts with the FRB actuals in Appendix B.

9. Consider an AR(2) model developed for second differenced data of the form:

    $$(1 - B)^2 Y_t = 0.4(1 - B)^2 Y_{t-1} + 0.5(1 - B)^2 Y_{t-2} + \epsilon_t.$$

    a. Express the model as an AR(4) model.
    b. Suppose the mean is 0.5 and the last 4 data values are $Y_{50} = 100$,
        $Y_{49} = 86$, $Y_{48} = 95$, and $Y_{47} = 105$. Develop forecasts for periods
        51–55.

10. Suppose the model for problem 7 is an ARIMA$(0,1,1)$ model:

    $$(1 - B)FRB_t = 1.8 + 0.4 \epsilon_{t-1} + \epsilon_t.$$

    a. Determine the forecasts for the 4 quarters of 1979, assuming that
        the residual error for 1978:4 is $+1.5$.
    b. Assume this model was obtained with the data accounting through
        the fourth quarter of 1976.

        Assuming the residual error for 1976:4 is $+4.0$, determine the
        forecasts for 1977 and 1978. Compare the forecasts with the FRB
        actuals in Appendix B.

11. Shows that the forecast equations for an ARIMA $(2,1,0)$ are:

    $$\hat{Y}_t(1) = (1 + \emptyset_1)Y_t + (\emptyset_2 - \emptyset_1)Y_{t-1} - \emptyset_2 Y_{t-2}$$
    $$\hat{Y}_t(a) = (1 + \emptyset_1)\hat{Y}_t(1) + (\emptyset_2 - \emptyset_1)Y_t - \emptyset_2 Y_{t-1}$$
    $$\hat{Y}_t(3) = (1 + \emptyset_1)\hat{Y}_t(2) + (\emptyset_2 - \emptyset_1)\hat{Y}_t(1) - \emptyset_2 Y_t$$
    $$\hat{Y}_t(l) = (1 + \emptyset_1)\hat{Y}_t(l-1) + (\emptyset_2 - \emptyset_1)\hat{Y}_t(l-2) - \emptyset_2 \hat{Y}_t(l-3) \quad l = 4,5, \ldots$$

12. Show that the forecast equations for an ARIMA (1,2,0) are:

$$\hat{Y}_t(1) = (2 + \emptyset_1)Y_t - (1 + 2\emptyset_1)Y_{t-1} + \emptyset_1 Y_{t-2}$$

$$\hat{Y}_t(2) = (2 + \emptyset_1)\hat{Y}_t(1) - (1 + 2\emptyset_1)Y_t + \emptyset_1 Y_{t-1}$$

$$\hat{Y}_t(3) = (2 + \emptyset_1)\hat{Y}_t(2) - (1 + 2\emptyset_1)\hat{Y}_t(1) + \emptyset_1 Y_t$$

$$\hat{Y}_t(l) = (2 + \emptyset_1)\hat{Y}_t(l-1) - (1 + 2\emptyset_1)\hat{Y}_t(l-2) + \emptyset_1\hat{Y}_t(l-3) \quad l = 4,5, \ldots$$

13. Suppose the model for the quarterly U.S. money supply (M1) data in Appendix B is an ARIMA (2,1,0) model with coefficients $\emptyset_1 = 0.5$ and $\emptyset_2 = 0.3$.

   a. Develop forecasts for the 4 quarters of 1979.

   b. Assume this same model was obtained with the data accounting through the fourth quarter of 1976. Obtain forecasts for 1977 and 1978 and compare the forecasts with the M1 actuals.

14. Suppose the model for the quarterly U.S. money supply (M1) data in Appendix B is an ARIMA (1,2,0) model with $\emptyset_1 = -0.6$.

   a. Develop forecasts for the 4 quarters of 1979.

   b. Assume this same model was obtained with the data accounting through the fourth quarter of 1976. Obtain forecasts for 1977 and 1978 and compare the forecasts with the M1 actuals.

COMPUTER WORKSHOPS

Workshop 10—Building Univariate ARIMA Models

- Review the analysis of the data in Workshop 2—Basic Time Series. Analysis. Employ the appropriate differencing operation and transformations to make a stationary time series.

- Obtain an ordinary and partial correlogram of the stationary series. Determine an appropriate starting model by analysis of the correlogram patterns.

- Build the model and obtain the correlograms (ordinary and partial) of the residuals. Perform diagnostic checks on the residuals and modify the model as required. Use the modeling checklist.

- Run an (ex-post) forecast test by successively deleting several periods of current data and analyzing the forecast errors. Summarize over several periods. Check the stability of the coefficients.

- Write out the final model in (p,d,q) notation, along with parameter estimates and estimated standard deviations. How can the final model be improved?

- Prepare a statement summarizing the assumptions that went into the model, along with its strengths and weaknesses. What recommendations can you make as to the best uses of the model?

Workshop 11—Building Seasonal ARIMA Models

- Consider a seasonal time series (quarterly or monthly) and perform the appropriate differencing operations so as to achieve stationarity.

- Obtain an ordinary and partial correlogram of the stationary series. Is it appropriate to use a seasonal autoregressive term, rather than a seasonal difference in your model? Determine the appropriate starting model or models.

- Build the model and obtain the correlograms (both ordinary and partial) of the residuals. Modify the model as necessary and perform the diagnostic checks for randomness.

- Write out the model in $(p,d,q) \times (P,D,Q)s$ notation. Display the estimated coefficients and corresponding standard errors. What other deficiencies does your model have that you cannot account for?

- Perform a forecast test on your model and summarize its (ex-post) performance over a number of different periods. Examine the stability of the estimated coefficients.

Part 6

Principles of
Forecast Management

CHAPTER 27

Managing The Forecasting Function

The success of a forecasting organization depends upon the extent to which traditional management philosophies and practices are applied to an unconventional business discipline. For the purposes of this discussion, the forecasting organization will be considered to be an in-company staff that is part of a larger company. To clarify the distinction between managers of forecasters and other managers within the business who are using the forecast the "other managers" will be referred to as "clients."

Specific managerial approaches for strengthening forecasting organizations can result from

- Setting goals for the organization.
- Establishing standards of performance.
- Measuring performance.
- Implementing new methods.
- Making optimum use of outside consulting opinion.

MANAGEMENT BY RESULTS

Managers are concerned with making decisions in the presence of *uncertainty* about the future. In many regards the future seems increasingly unstable: this is reflected in increasing prices, costs, and availability of goods; in inflation; in concern about environmental issues; and in demographic patterns. Consequently, bad decision making is becoming increasingly costly, not only in economic terms but also to society. The managers of the nation's social and economic systems should therefore

485

be increasingly concerned with improved planning and forecasting as a *management* activity (Jenkins, 1979; Wheelwright and Makridakis, 1980); Makridakis and Wheelwright, 1982).

The first step in improving the effectiveness of a forecasting staff is to develop a management plan that includes six key components:

- A statement of the purpose of the forecasting organization.
- A definition of major areas of responsibility.
- Long-term objectives for each area of the forecaster's responsibility.
- Indicators of performance.
- Short-term goals.
- Measurement of performance relative to the goals.

The first of these six components—the statement of purpose—is best kept concise. It can be a one-sentence statement. While this is simple in concept, forecasters and their managers can spend many hours wrestling with the purpose of their jobs. Since the forecaster is an advisor to management, a purpose might be "to provide the best possible advice to the client about the future demand for the company's products and services." For managers of independent forecasting companies (i.e., consulting firms), this statement may need to be expanded to include the need to generate new projects in addition to continuing (or follow-up) projects, so that an independent firm will remain financially viable.

The *areas of responsibility* may include revenue forecasting, expense forecasting, product or service forecasting; or other areas, such as forecast evaluation, measurement, monitoring, and presentation; or managerial responsibilities, such as forecaster appraisal and development.

The *objectives* for these areas of responsibility should be sufficiently general to have long-term significance and ought to indicate the striving for improvement that will make each an objective rather than simply a description. Some examples might be: "to improve the accuracy of . . . ," "to improve managerial and technical skills," "to improve the credibility of the forecasting organization," and "to insure the continuing relevance of . . . ."

Developing meaningful *indicators of performance* can be the source of much debate among staff members. Experience will cause you to reject some indicators and replace them with others more relevant. However, until this is done it will not be possible to state explicitly that the forecasting organization is achieving its objectives. The key to success is to make the areas of responsibility, indicators, and goals all job-relevant. An emphasis on joint manager-forecaster goal setting and communications will increase the probability that the organizational goals will be internalized by the members of the organization.

Emphasis should be placed on developing meaningful indicators of performance that can be directly applied to an organization engaged in forecasting in a business environment. Of course, modification of the recommendations can be made to more closely approximate the forecasting requirements of specific firms or organizations.

ESTABLISHING FORECASTING STANDARDS OF PERFORMANCE

How can a forecast manager tell a good forecast from a bad forecast at the time it is presented for approval? This is one of the most perplexing problems that forecast managers face in the normal course of events. Certainly, after the forecast time period has elapsed, anyone can look back and determine how closely the forecast predicted actual results; but this is after the fact—what in football is called "Monday morning quarterbacking." The manager wants to be confident that the forecast is reasonable at the time it is prepared.

What is needed is a *process* that, if followed, will increase the likelihood of good forecasting performance. In other words, it is necessary to establish standards of performance for forecasters that will increase the probability of improved forecast accuracy. A checklist that can be used by both forecasters and forecast managers to measure a specific forecast relative to some established standards is included at the end of this chapter, and its use is recommended.

Setting Down Basic Facts

The checklist is general in nature and covers the essential elements that must be a part of an effective forecasting process. It begins with the establishment of basic facts concerning past trends and forecasts. To be satisfied that these facts have been adequately researched, a forecast manager should expect to see tables and plots of historical data. The data should be adjusted to account for changes in geographic boundaries or other factors that would distort analyses and forecasts. If appropriate, the data should be seasonally adjusted to give a better representation of trend-cycle. Outliers or other unusual data values should be explained and replaced, if this is warranted. It is useful to indicate the National Bureau of Economic Research reference dates for peaks and troughs of business cycles. This provides the manager with an indication of the extent to which a client's data series are impacted by the national business cycles. Knowing this relationship will be helpful when the manager reviews the assumptions about the future state of the economy and assesses how these assumptions are reflected in the forecast.

Tables and plots of annual percentage changes provide an indication of the volatility of a series and are useful later in checking the reasonableness of the forecast compared to history. If possible, ratios should be developed between the forecast series and other stable data series that are based on company or regional performance. These ratios should be shown in tables or plots. Once again, these ratios provide reasonableness checks. If some major change is expected in the forecast period, these ratios should help identify the change.

Whenever possible, there should be at least a decade of data available for the manager's review. It may not be necessary to show this much history when presenting the forecast to the clients; but it will be necessary to have this much data available to analyze the impact of business cycles. If possible, data back to the 1957–58 recession should be available since, with the exception of 1980–82, that was the last major recession. However, in many forecasting circumstances, data this old may no longer be relevant.

There should also be available a record of forecasts and actual performance for at least the past three years. This will allow the manager to know how well the organization has done in the past and to gauge the possible reaction of the clients to changes in the forecast. It will also be possible to determine from these data if any or all of the forecasters on the staff have a tendency to be too optimistic or too pessimistic over time.

Causes of Change

The next segment of the checklist deals with the causes of changes in past demand trends or levels. The first step is to identify the trend in the data. Regression analysis is an excellent tool for this. A regression against time, as a starting point, will provide a visual indication as to whether the trend is linear or nonlinear. There should be a plot of the series and its fitted trend on a scale of sufficient breadth to clearly identify deviations from trend. The reasons for the deviations should then be identified and explained in writing. These explanations need to be specific. Was there unusual construction activity? Was there a change in corporate policy or prices? Did the deviation correspond to a regional or national economic pattern? What was the source of the explanation—the forecaster, or someone else? Finally, how certain is the forecaster that the reason or explanation stated is correct? Documentation of history is an important step that can serve as reference material for all future forecasts and forecasters. It is particularly helpful to a new forecaster and improves productivity.

Causes of Differences

The next segment of the checklist is concerned with the reasons for the differences between previous forecasts and actual results. This form of results analysis is useful for uncovering problem areas, for identifying the need for new or improved methods, and for determining the quality of the prior forecasts. At this time, however, the manager is merely looking for a pattern of overforecasting or underforecasting. The key to identifying the reasons for forecast deviations is to have written records of basic assumptions, which should be reviewed. These assumptions should then be tested for specificity against the standards shown on the checklist.

Accompanying each assumption should be a rationale indicating why the assumption is necessary. The source of the assumption should be identified and the degree of confidence in the assumption should be stated. The source might be the forecaster, company economists, industry analysts, government publications, or newspaper clippings and journal articles. The forecaster may be absolutely certain that the assumption will prove correct. On the other hand, the forecaster may indicate that it was necessary to make the assumption, but that considerable doubt existed as to whether or not the future would be as assumed.

Factors Affecting Future Demand

The next segment of the checklist is concerned with the factors likely to affect future demand and, therefore, the forecast. Assumptions will have to be made about factors such as income, habit, price of a company's product, price of competing goods, and market potential. In addition, the manager should check to see that there is a logical time integration between historical actuals and the short- and long-term forecasts. Also, there should be a logical time integration between related forecast items, such as forecasts of economic conditions, revenues, and expenses.

At this time, the manager can ascertain that the forecasting methodologies used represent the best methods available at the time.

The purpose of the checklist is to establish standards for the forecasting organization: both the forecaster and the forecast manager can use the checklist in the preparation and subsequent review of the forecast. By establishing meaningful forecasting standards, forecast evaluation can be greatly simplified. The philosophy of forecast evaluation is one in which primary emphasis is placed on the process rather than the numbers. If a proper forecasting process has been meticulously followed by the forecaster, the end result will be as good a forecast as can be developed. If that result does not come about, then the manager needs to train the forecaster better or to select a different person to make the forecast.

Within limits, it is very difficult for a manager to "fine-tune" the numbers presented with any degree of confidence that the changes are appropriate. However, the manager can carefully review the forecast assumptions for reasonableness. The assumptions are the heart of the forecast, and considerable probing of these assumptions can satisfy the manager as to their appropriateness for the forecast period. The manager can also review the technical soundness of the analysis and be satisfied that no errors were made. Having performed these forecast evaluations, the manager can discriminate between a good forecast and a bad one at the time he or she is asked to approve it.

The continued development of checklists such as the one that follows will go a long way towards improving the quality of a forecast.

FORECAST MANAGEMENT CHECKLIST

Step 1: SETTING DOWN BASIC FACTS ABOUT PAST TRENDS AND
FORECASTS

_____ Are historical tables and plots available?

_____ Are base-adjusted data available? (A "constant base" is what is wanted: for examples, have historical revenues been adjusted to today's price; have data been adjusted for mergers, acquisitions, etc.?)

_____ Are seasonally adjusted data available?

_____ Have outliers been explained? (As discussed in the treatment of ARIMA modeling, they may significantly affect the forecasts).

_____ Have NBER cyclical reference dates been overlaid?

_____ Are percentage changes shown in tables and plots?

_____ Have forecast-versus-actual comparisons been made for one or more forecast periods?

Step 2: DETERMINING CAUSES OF CHANGE IN PAST DEMAND TRENDS

_____ Is a trend identified?

_____ Is it linear or nonlinear?

_____ Are there plots of data and fitted trends?

_____ Is the scale of sufficient breadth to see deviations?

_____ Have the deviations been explained in writing?

_____ Are explanations about causes specific?

_____ Has the source of explanations been identified?

_____ Is the degree of certainty about the explanation noted?

Step 3: DETERMINING CAUSES OF DIFFERENCES BETWEEN PRE-VIOUS FORECASTS AND ACTUAL DATA

_____ Are differences explained?

_____ Are there any patterns to the explanations?

_____ Are there basic assumptions that can be reviewed?

Step 4: DETERMINING FACTORS LIKELY TO AFFECT FUTURE DEMAND

_____ Do assumptions relate to the future?

_____ Do assumptions indicate direction of impact?

_____ Do assumptions indicate the amount or rate of impact, the timing of the impact, and the duration of the impact on demand?

_____ Are there rationale statements for each assumption?

_____ Are the sources for a rationale statement identified?

Step 5: MAKING THE FORECAST FOR FUTURE PERIODS

_____ Time integration: are long-term and short-term forecasts and history all shown on one chart? Are the transitions reasonable?

_____ Item integration: are ratios of related items shown as well as their history through the long-term forecast?

_____ Functional integration: are related forecasts identified and relationships quantified? (For example, are revenue and product forecasts consistent?)

_____ Have multiple methods been used for key items and have results been compared?

_____ Has the impact on the user of the forecast been considered?

SUMMARY

A basic grounding in management is essential for anyone assuming control of a forecasting organization. The "management by objectives" or "management by results" framework is recommended for implementation in a forecasting organization. This chapter has provided ideas on approaches that can be helpful in implementing such a plan.

The availability of time-shared computers has brought many sophisticated forecasting methodologies out of the theoretical environment of the classroom into the business world. However, as is true in most areas of endeavor, business organizations must have managers with the foresight to try new approaches and management skills in order to set goals, establish standards, and measure performance before they can profit from the new knowledge. Without proper management, considerable resources can be expended with little commensurate payback. This invariably leads to frustration and abandonment of the effort.

The ideas presented here, and the checklists that summarize them, provide managers with a framework to increase the professionalism of their organization, improve forecast accuracy, and strengthen user acceptance of their forecast products.

USEFUL READING

CLEARY, J. P. and H. LEVENBACH (1982). *The Professional Forecaster.* Belmont, CA: Lifetime Learning Publications.

JENKINS, G. M. (1979). *Practical Experiences with Modelling and Forecasting Time Series*. Jersey, Channel Islands: Gwilyn Jenkins and Partners Ltd.

LEVENBACH, H., and J. P. CLEARY (1981). *The Beginning Forecaster.* Belmont, CA: Lifetime Learning Publications.

MAKRIDAKIS, S. and S. C. WHEELWRIGHT, editors (1982). *Handbook of Forecasting— A Manager's Guide*. New York, NY: John Wiley and Sons.

WHEELWRIGHT, S. C., and S. MAKRIDAKIS (1980). *Forecasting Methods for Management*. New York, NY: John Wiley and Sons.

COMPUTER WORKSHOP

Workshop 12—Model Building Case Presentation

Guidelines

- Limit presentation for your case group to the time allowed by the instructors.

- All members of the team *must participate equally* in the presentation. Logically divide the presentation into parts and assign parts to members of the group for presentation.

- Plan your efforts step-by-step, drawing on the combined experience present among you.

- Be specific in laying out your tactics and strategy.

- Note on paper each step that you plan to follow.

Strategy

- Be prepared to discuss your study with the appropriate audience (a *management audience,* not your peers, or a *technical audience,* possibly your peers).

- Emphasis should be placed on the steps you have taken and what conclusions can be drawn from the analysis.

- Use back-up details to make a point, if necessary. Do not burden the audience with irrelevant details. However, details should be readily available, in case of a question from the audience.

- Be professional, clear, and concise in your choice of words and visuals.

- An *effective* picture or graphic is much better than a table of numbers or statistics. Take this into consideration when presenting your study.

Appendixes
Bibliography
Index

Appendix A

Table 1 Standardized Normal Distribution

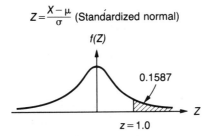

$$Z = \frac{X - \mu}{\sigma} \text{ (Standardized normal)}$$

z	.00	.01	.02	.03	.04	.05	.06	.07	.08	.09
0.0	.5000	.4960	.4920	.4880	.4840	.4801	.4761	.4721	.4681	.4641
0.1	.4602	.4562	.4522	.4483	.4443	.4404	.4364	.4325	.4286	.4247
0.2	.4207	.4168	.4129	.4090	.4052	.4013	.3974	.3936	.3897	.3859
0.3	.3821	.3783	.3745	.3707	.3669	.3632	.3594	.3557	.3520	.3483
0.4	.3446	.3409	.3372	.3336	.3300	.3264	.3228	.3192	.3156	.3121
0.5	.3085	.3050	.3015	.2981	.2946	.2912	.2877	.2843	.2810	.2776
0.6	.2743	.2709	.2676	.2643	.2611	.2578	.2546	.2514	.2483	.2451
0.7	.2420	.2389	.2358	.2327	.2296	.2266	.2236	.2206	.2177	.2148
0.8	.2119	.2090	.2061	.2033	.2005	.1977	.1949	.1922	.1894	.1867
0.9	.1841	.1814	.1788	.1762	.1736	.1711	.1685	.1660	.1635	.1611
1.0	.1587	.1562	.1539	.1515	.1492	.1469	.1446	.1423	.1401	.1379
1.1	.1357	.1335	.1314	.1292	.1271	.1251	.1230	.1210	.1190	.1170
1.2	.1151	.1131	.1112	.1093	.1075	.1056	.1038	.1020	.1003	.0985
1.3	.0968	.0951	.0934	.0918	.0901	.0885	.0869	.0853	.0838	.0823
1.4	.0808	.0793	.0778	.0764	.0749	.0735	.0721	.0708	.0694	.0681
1.5	.0668	.0655	.0643	.0630	.0618	.0606	.0594	.0582	.0571	.0559
1.6	.0548	.0537	.0526	.0516	.0505	.0495	.0485	.0475	.0465	.0455
1.7	.0446	.0436	.0427	.0418	.0409	.0401	.0392	.0384	.0375	.0367
1.8	.0359	.0351	.0344	.0336	.0329	.0322	.0314	.0307	.0301	.0294
1.9	.0287	.0281	.0274	.0268	.0262	.0256	.0250	.0244	.0239	.0233
2.0	.0228	.0222	.0217	.0212	.0207	.0202	.0197	.0192	.0188	.0183
2.1	.0179	.0174	.0170	.0166	.0162	.0158	.0154	.0150	.0146	.0143
2.2	.0139	.0136	.0132	.0129	.0125	.0122	.0119	.0116	.0113	.0110
2.3	.0107	.0104	.0102	.0099	.0096	.0094	.0091	.0089	.0087	.0084
2.4	.0082	.0080	.0078	.0075	.0073	.0071	.0069	.0068	.0066	.0064
2.5	.0062	.0060	.0059	.0057	.0055	.0054	.0052	.0051	.0049	.0048
2.6	.0047	.0045	.0044	.0043	.0041	.0040	.0039	.0038	.0037	.0036
2.7	.0035	.0034	.0033	.0032	.0031	.0030	.0029	.0028	.0027	.0026
2.8	.0026	.0025	.0024	.0023	.0023	.0022	.0021	.0021	.0020	.0019
2.9	.0019	.0018	.0018	.0017	.0016	.0016	.0015	.0015	.0014	.0014
3.0	.0013	.0013	.0013	.0012	.0012	.0011	.0011	.0011	.0010	.0010

Source: Based on *Biometrika Tables for Statisticians,* Vol. 1, 3rd ed. (1966), with the permission of the *Biometrika* trustees.

Note: The table plots the cumulative probability $Z > z$.

Table 2 Percentiles of the *t*-Distribution

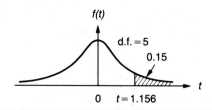

Degrees of freedom	Probability of a value at least as large as the table entry					
	0.15	0.1	0.05	0.025	0.01	0.005
1	1.963	3.078	6.314	12.706	31.821	63.657
2	1.386	1.886	2.920	4.303	6.965	9.925
3	1.250	1.638	2.353	3.182	4.541	5.841
4	1.190	1.533	2.132	2.776	3.747	4.604
5	1.156	1.476	2.015	2.571	3.365	4.032
6	1.134	1.440	1.943	2.447	3.143	3.707
7	1.119	1.415	1.895	2.365	2.998	3.499
8	1.108	1.397	1.860	2.306	2.896	3.355
9	1.100	1.383	1.833	2.262	2.821	3.250
10	1.093	1.372	1.812	2.228	2.764	3.169
11	1.088	1.363	1.796	2.201	2.718	3.106
12	1.083	1.356	1.782	2.179	2.681	3.055
13	1.079	1.350	1.771	2.160	2.650	3.012
14	1.076	1.345	1.761	2.145	2.624	2.977
15	1.074	1.341	1.753	2.131	2.602	2.947
16	1.071	1.337	1.746	2.120	2.583	2.921
17	1.069	1.333	1.740	2.110	2.567	2.898
18	1.067	1.330	1.734	2.101	2.552	2.878
19	1.066	1.328	1.729	2.093	2.539	2.861
20	1.064	1.325	1.725	2.086	2.528	2.845
21	1.063	1.323	1.721	2.080	2.518	2.831
22	1.061	1.321	1.717	2.074	2.508	2.819
23	1.060	1.319	1.714	2.069	2.500	2.807
24	1.059	1.318	1.711	2.064	2.492	2.797
25	1.058	1.316	1.708	2.060	2.485	2.787
26	1.058	1.315	1.706	2.056	2.479	2.779
27	1.057	1.314	1.703	2.052	2.473	2.771
28	1.056	1.313	1.701	2.048	2.467	2.763
29	1.055	1.311	1.699	2.045	2.462	2.756
30	1.055	1.310	1.697	2.042	2.457	2.750
(Normal) ∞	1.036	1.282	1.645	1.960	2.326	2.576

Source: Abridged from Table IV in Sir Ronald A. Fisher, *Statistical Methods for Research Workers,* 14th ed. (copyright © 1970 by University of Adelaide, a Division of Macmillan Publishing Co., Inc.) with the permission of the publisher and the late Sir Ronald Fisher's Literary Executor.

Table 3   Percentiles of the Chi-Squared Distribution

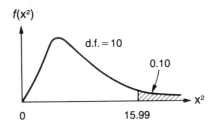

Degrees of freedom	Probability of a value at least as large as the table entry								
	0.90	0.75	0.50	0.25	0.10	0.05	0.025	0.01	0.005
1	0.0158	0.102	0.455	1.323	2.71	3.84	5.02	6.63	7.88
2	0.211	0.575	1.386	2.77	4.61	5.99	7.38	9.21	10.60
3	0.584	1.213	2.37	4.11	6.25	7.81	9.35	11.34	12.84
4	1.064	1.923	3.36	5.39	7.78	9.49	11.14	13.28	14.86
5	1.610	2.67	4.35	6.63	9.24	11.07	12.83	15.09	16.75
6	2.20	3.45	5.35	7.84	10.64	12.59	14.45	16.81	18.55
7	2.83	4.25	6.35	9.04	12.02	14.07	16.01	18.48	20.3
8	3.49	5.07	7.34	10.22	13.36	15.51	17.53	20.1	22.0
9	4.17	5.90	8.34	11.39	14.68	16.92	19.02	21.7	23.6
10	4.87	6.74	9.34	12.55	(15.99)	18.31	20.5	23.2	25.2
11	5.58	7.58	10.34	13.70	17.28	19.68	21.9	24.7	26.8
12	6.30	8.44	11.34	14.85	18.55	21.0	23.3	26.2	28.3
13	7.04	9.30	12.34	15.98	19.81	22.4	24.7	27.7	29.8
14	7.79	10.17	13.34	17.12	12.1	23.7	26.1	29.1	31.3
15	8.55	11.04	14.34	18.25	22.3	25.0	27.5	30.6	32.8
16	9.31	11.91	15.34	19.37	23.5	26.3	28.8	32.0	34.3
17	10.09	12.79	16.34	20.5	24.8	27.6	30.2	33.4	35.7
18	10.86	13.68	17.34	21.6	26.0	28.9	31.5	34.8	37.2
19	11.65	14.56	18.34	22.7	27.2	30.1	32.9	36.2	38.6
20	12.44	15.45	19.34	23.8	28.4	31.4	34.2	37.6	40.0

Source: Based on *Biometrika Tables for Statisticians*, Vol. 1, 3rd ed. (1966), with the permission of the *Biometrika* trustees.

Table 4   F-Distribution, 5 Percent Significance

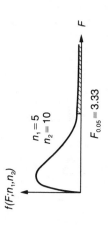

$f(F;n_1,n_2)$

$n_1 = 5$
$n_2 = 10$

$F_{0.05} = 3.33$

Degrees of freedom for numerator

	1	2	3	4	5	6	7	8	9	10	12	15	20	24	30	40	60	120	∞
1	161	200	216	225	230	234	237	239	241	242	244	246	248	249	250	251	252	253	254
2	18.5	19.0	19.2	19.2	19.3	19.3	19.4	19.4	19.4	19.4	19.4	19.4	19.5	19.5	19.5	19.5	19.5	19.5	19.5
3	10.1	9.55	9.28	9.12	9.01	8.94	8.89	8.85	8.81	8.79	8.74	8.70	8.66	8.64	8.62	8.59	8.57	8.55	8.53
4	7.71	6.94	6.59	6.39	6.26	6.16	6.09	6.04	6.00	5.96	5.91	5.86	5.80	5.77	5.75	5.72	5.69	5.66	5.63
5	6.61	5.79	5.41	5.19	5.05	4.95	4.88	4.82	4.77	4.74	4.68	4.62	4.56	4.53	4.50	4.46	4.43	4.40	4.37
6	5.99	5.14	4.76	4.53	4.39	4.28	4.21	4.15	4.10	4.06	4.00	3.94	3.87	3.84	3.81	3.77	3.74	3.70	3.67
7	5.59	4.74	4.35	4.12	3.97	3.87	3.79	3.73	3.68	3.64	3.57	3.51	3.44	3.41	3.38	3.34	3.30	3.27	3.23
8	5.32	4.46	4.07	3.84	3.69	3.58	3.50	3.44	3.39	3.35	3.28	3.22	3.15	3.12	3.08	3.04	3.01	2.97	2.93
9	5.12	4.26	3.86	3.63	3.48	3.37	3.29	3.23	3.18	3.14	3.07	3.01	2.94	2.90	2.86	2.83	2.79	2.75	2.71
10	4.96	4.10	3.71	3.48	3.33	3.22	3.14	3.07	3.02	2.98	2.91	2.85	2.77	2.74	2.70	2.66	2.62	2.58	2.54
11	4.84	3.98	3.59	3.36	3.20	3.09	3.01	2.95	2.90	2.85	2.79	2.72	2.65	2.61	2.57	2.53	2.49	2.45	2.40
12	4.75	3.89	3.49	3.26	3.11	3.00	2.91	2.85	2.80	2.75	2.69	2.62	2.54	2.51	2.47	2.43	2.38	2.34	2.30
13	4.67	3.81	3.41	3.18	3.03	2.92	2.83	2.77	2.71	2.67	2.60	2.53	2.46	2.42	2.38	2.34	2.30	2.25	2.21
14	4.60	3.74	3.34	3.11	2.96	2.85	2.76	2.70	2.65	2.60	2.53	2.46	2.39	2.35	2.31	2.27	2.22	2.18	2.13
15	4.54	3.68	3.29	3.06	2.90	2.79	2.71	2.64	2.59	2.54	2.48	2.40	2.33	2.29	2.25	2.20	2.16	2.11	2.07

Table 4 (*continued*)

								Degrees of freedom for numerator										
	1	2	3	4	5	6	7	8	9	10	12	15	20	24	30	40	60	120	∞
16	4.49	3.63	3.24	3.01	2.85	2.74	2.66	2.59	2.54	2.49	2.42	2.35	2.28	2.24	2.19	2.15	2.11	2.06	2.01
17	4.45	3.59	3.20	2.96	2.81	2.70	2.61	2.55	2.48	2.45	2.38	2.31	2.23	2.19	2.15	2.10	2.06	2.01	1.96
18	4.41	3.55	3.16	2.93	2.77	2.66	2.58	2.51	2.46	2.41	2.34	2.27	2.19	2.15	2.11	2.06	2.02	1.97	1.92
19	4.38	3.52	3.13	2.90	2.74	2.63	2.54	2.48	2.42	2.39	2.31	2.23	2.16	2.11	2.07	2.03	1.98	1.93	1.88
20	4.35	3.49	3.10	2.87	2.71	2.60	2.51	2.45	2.39	2.35	2.28	2.20	2.12	2.08	2.04	1.99	1.95	1.90	1.84
21	4.32	3.47	3.07	2.84	2.68	2.57	2.49	2.42	2.37	2.32	2.25	2.18	2.10	2.05	2.01	1.96	1.92	1.87	1.81
22	4.30	3.44	3.05	2.82	2.66	2.55	2.46	2.40	2.34	2.30	2.23	2.15	2.07	2.03	1.98	1.94	1.89	1.84	1.78
23	4.28	3.42	3.03	2.80	2.64	2.53	2.44	2.37	2.32	2.27	2.20	2.13	2.05	2.01	1.96	1.91	1.86	1.81	1.76
24	4.26	3.40	3.01	2.78	2.62	2.51	2.42	2.36	2.30	2.25	2.18	2.11	2.03	1.98	1.94	1.89	1.84	1.79	1.73
25	4.24	3.39	2.99	2.76	2.60	2.49	2.40	2.34	2.28	2.24	2.16	2.09	2.01	1.96	1.92	1.87	1.82	1.77	1.71
30	4.17	3.32	2.92	2.69	2.53	2.42	2.33	2.27	2.21	2.16	2.09	2.01	1.93	1.89	1.84	1.79	1.74	1.68	1.62
40	4.08	3.23	2.84	2.61	2.45	2.34	2.25	2.18	2.12	2.08	2.00	1.92	1.84	1.79	1.74	1.69	1.64	1.58	1.51
60	4.00	3.15	2.76	2.53	2.37	2.25	2.17	2.10	2.04	1.99	1.92	1.84	1.75	1.70	1.65	1.59	1.53	1.47	1.39
120	3.92	3.07	2.68	2.45	2.29	2.18	2.09	2.02	1.96	1.91	1.83	1.75	1.66	1.61	1.55	1.50	1.43	1.35	1.25
∞	3.84	3.00	2.60	2.37	2.21	2.10	2.01	1.94	1.88	1.83	1.75	1.67	1.57	1.52	1.46	1.39	1.32	1.22	1.00

Source: Reproduced with the permission of the Biometrika Trustees from M. Merrington and C. M. Thompson, "Tables of percentage points of the inverted beta (F) distribution," *Biometrika* 33(1943), 73.

Table 5   The Durbin-Watson Test Statistic d: 5 Percent Significance of d_l and d_μ

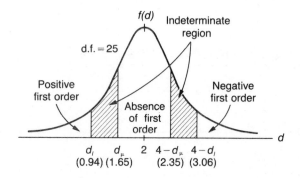

Degree of freedom	k = 1		k = 2		k = 3		k = 4		k = 5	
n	d_l	d_μ	d_l	d_μ	d_l	d_μ	d_l	d_μ	d_l	d_μ
15	0.95	1.23	0.83	1.40	0.71	1.61	0.59	1.84	0.48	2.09
16	0.98	1.24	0.86	1.40	0.75	1.59	0.64	1.80	0.53	2.03
17	1.01	1.25	0.90	1.40	0.79	1.58	0.68	1.77	0.57	1.98
18	1.03	1.26	0.93	1.40	0.82	1.56	0.72	1.74	0.62	1.93
19	1.06	1.28	0.96	1.41	0.86	1.55	0.76	1.73	0.66	1.90
20	1.08	1.28	0.99	1.41	0.89	1.55	0.79	1.72	0.70	1.87
21	1.10	1.30	1.01	1.41	0.92	1.54	0.83	1.69	0.73	1.84
22	1.12	1.31	1.04	1.42	0.95	1.54	0.86	1.68	0.77	1.82
23	1.14	1.32	1.06	1.42	0.97	1.54	0.89	1.67	0.80	1.80
24	1.16	1.33	1.08	1.43	1.00	1.54	0.91	1.66	0.83	1.79
25	1.18	1.34	1.10	1.43	1.02	1.54	(0.94)	(1.65)	0.86	1.77
26	1.19	1.35	1.12	1.44	1.04	1.54	0.96	1.65	0.88	1.76
27	1.21	1.36	1.13	1.44	1.06	1.54	0.99	1.64	0.91	1.75
28	1.22	1.37	1.15	1.45	1.08	1.54	1.01	1.64	0.93	1.74
29	1.24	1.38	1.17	1.45	1.10	1.54	1.03	1.63	0.96	1.73
30	1.25	1.38	1.18	1.46	1.12	1.54	1.05	1.63	0.98	1.73
31	1.26	1.39	1.20	1.47	1.13	1.55	1.07	1.63	1.00	1.72
32	1.27	1.40	1.21	1.47	1.15	1.55	1.08	1.63	1.02	1.71
33	1.28	1.41	1.22	1.48	1.16	1.55	1.10	1.63	1.04	1.71
34	1.29	1.41	1.24	1.48	1.17	1.55	1.12	1.63	1.06	1.70
35	1.30	1.42	1.25	1.48	1.19	1.55	1.13	1.63	1.07	1.70
36	1.31	1.43	1.26	1.49	1.20	1.56	1.15	1.63	1.09	1.70
37	1.32	1.43	1.27	1.49	1.21	1.56	1.16	1.62	1.10	1.70
38	1.33	1.44	1.28	1.50	1.23	1.56	1.17	1.62	1.12	1.70
39	1.34	1.44	1.29	1.50	1.24	1.56	1.19	1.63	1.13	1.69
40	1.35	1.45	1.30	1.51	1.25	1.57	1.20	1.63	1.15	1.69
45	1.39	1.48	1.34	1.53	1.30	1.58	1.25	1.63	1.21	1.69
50	1.42	1.50	1.38	1.54	1.34	1.59	1.30	1.64	1.26	1.69

Table 5   *(continued)*

Degree of freedom, n	k = 1		k = 2		k = 3		k = 4		k = 5	
	d_l	d_μ	d_l	d_μ	d_l	d_μ	d_l	d_μ	d_l	d_μ
55	1.45	1.52	1.41	1.56	1.37	1.60	1.33	1.64	1.30	1.69
60	1.47	1.54	1.44	1.57	1.40	1.61	1.37	1.65	1.33	1.69
65	1.49	1.55	1.46	1.59	1.43	1.63	1.40	1.66	1.36	1.69
70	1.51	1.57	1.48	1.60	1.45	1.63	1.42	1.66	1.39	1.70
75	1.53	1.58	1.50	1.61	1.47	1.64	1.45	1.67	1.42	1.70
80	1.54	1.59	1.52	1.63	1.49	1.65	1.47	1.67	1.44	1.70
85	1.56	1.60	1.53	1.63	1.51	1.66	1.49	1.68	1.46	1.71
90	1.57	1.61	1.55	1.64	1.53	1.66	1.50	1.69	1.48	1.71
95	1.58	1.62	1.56	1.65	1.54	1.67	1.52	1.69	1.50	1.71
100	1.59	1.63	1.57	1.65	1.55	1.67	1.53	1.70	1.51	1.72

Source: Reprinted with permission from J. Durbin and G. S. Watson, "Testing for Serial Correlation in Least Squares Regression: II" *Biometrika* 38(1951), 159–77.

Appendix B

Time series data used for examples in the text

	Toll revenue volumes for the telecommunications example (REV) for a given region					
	1969	1970	1971	1972	1973	1974
1	21821.	25157.	27163.	30653.	34306.	35120.
2	25490.	29910.	31927.	35349.	38617.	41843.
3	25565.	29082.	30484.	34388.	37187.	39401.
4	27819.	31526.	33327.	35342.	40623.	43236.
5	26427.	29165.	31325.	35585.	38490.	41350.
6	26259.	29508.	31036.	34040.	36847.	40786.
7	24614.	25886.	28622.	32044.	35398.	38596.
8	25792.	27840.	30660.	35063.	37774.	40991.
9	26970.	29082.	31147.	34365.	37335.	40425.
10	28605.	29900.	31572.	35634.	39074.	41656.
11	28987.	30651.	34576.	37389.	39642.	42991.
12	27023.	28678.	31502.	35060.	37362.	38881.
SUM	315372.	346385.	373341.	414912.	452655.	485276.

	1975	1976	1977	1978	1979	
1	36133.	37656.	41423.	45238.	50687.	
2	44003.	46263.	49410.	52583.	61547.	
3	41120.	44386.	46222.	50869.	57783.	
4	45671.	47650.	50690.	56078.	63420.	
5	43914.	45748.	48829.	54799.	60589.	
6	43167.	44886.	48112.	53109.	59672.	
7	40303.	42753.	45271.	50974.	57707.	
8	42452.	44843.	48678.	53265.	59672.	
9	42320.	45203.	49029.	54213.	59973.	
10	43825.	45995.	50191.	56892.	63458.	
11	44955.	47341.	51961.	58695.	65100.	
12	41121.	43658.	48199.	54142.	60500.	
SUM	508984.	536382.	578015.	640857.	720108.	

Monthly message volumes for the telecommunications example
(MSG) for a given region

	1969	1970	1971	1972	1973	1974
1	7600.	8391.	8775.	9851.	11003.	11638.
2	7630.	8244.	9079.	10268.	10988.	11575.
3	8131.	9388.	10017.	10893.	11874.	12456.
4	8104.	8946.	9719.	10285.	11609.	12437.
5	8207.	9102.	9638.	10858.	11986.	12807.
6	8577.	9594.	10343.	11408.	12067.	12651.
7	8150.	8946.	9404.	10159.	11242.	12101.
8	8583.	9333.	10175.	11321.	12393.	12855.
9	8662.	9491.	10205.	10993.	11845.	12685.
10	8862.	9340.	9916.	11293.	12311.	12973.
11	8175.	8961.	10003.	10946.	11885.	11955.
12	8444.	9084.	9583.	10510.	11307.	11739.
SUM	99125.	108820.	116857.	128785.	140510.	147872.

	1975	1976	1977	1978	1979
1	12330.	12572.	13621.	15299.	17092.
2	12029.	12857.	13681.	15195.	16894.
3	12972.	13882.	15172.	16782.	18210.
4	12759.	13531.	14285.	15552.	17746.
5	12810.	13375.	14561.	16364.	18176.
6	13286.	14110.	15277.	16939.	18100.
7	12488.	12869.	13828.	15115.	16853.
8	13054.	13897.	15402.	17052.	18498.
9	13162.	13997.	15257.	16777.	
10	13266.	13690.	15032.	16928.	
11	12044.	13474.	14700.	16498.	
12	12377.	13171.	14190.	15539.	
SUM	152577.	161425.	175006.	194040.	141569.

Number of business telephones for the telecommunications example
(BMT) for a given region

	1970	1971	1972	1973	1974	1975
1	491,195	502,336	504,071	511,665	518,522	517,100
2	493,068	503,013	503,785	512,555	518,797	516,520
3	495,482	504,042	505,736	513,653	519,290	516,136
4	498,042	505,292	507,537	514,959	520,869	515,213
5	499,660	504,720	507,267	514,576	519,606	513,040
6	499,004	504,378	506,704	515,345	520,006	512,909
7	499,602	503,571	507,436	515,712	519,274	512,306
8	500,065	503,158	508,378	517,240	520,072	512,918
9	502,858	505,757	510,861	519,132	521,234	514,679
10	502,468	504,828	511,251	519,159	520,631	514,246
11	502,589	503,905	510,768	518,610	519,474	513,864
12	502,504	503,434	510,505	518,296	517,935	512,591
SUM	5,986,540	6,048,433	6,094,300	6,190,904	6,235,709	6,171,521

	1976	1977	1978	1979
1	512,615	512,286	515,163	520,438
2	512,553	512,363	515,423	521,051
3	512,702	512,626	516,766	522,419
4	513,165	513,296	517,439	523,345
5	510,701	511,400	515,357	521,849
6	510,229	511,621	515,885	522,547
7	510,610	511,656	516,345	522,333
8	510,771	512,889	517,708	523,943
9	512,981	514,907	520,203	526,622
10	513,713	515,563	521,043	526,921
11	512,950	515,422	520,522	526,194
12	512,042	514,829	519,938	525,297
SUM	6,145,032	6,158,857	6,211,791	6,282,958

	Nonfarm employment for the telecommunications example (NFRM) for a given region					
	1970	1971	1972	1973	1974	1975
1	7063	6926	6866	6977	6985	6792
2	7092	6929	6871	6995	6974	6763
3	7157	6982	6960	7059	7024	6782
4	7202	7007	7000	7102	7064	6801
5	7221	7059	7062	7149	7130	6865
6	7282	7112	7122	7224	7196	6903
7	7191	7050	7020	7154	7135	6866
8	7189	7022	7083	7191	7149	6900
9	7140	6973	7045	7148	7080	6806
10	7106	6982	7120	7181	7087	6818
11	7102	7000	7149	7204	7080	6827
12	7116	7024	7164	7200	7022	6839
SUM	85861	84066	84462	85584	84926	81962

	1976	1977	1978	1979		
1	6666	6645	6804	6993		
2	6665	6662	6816	7011		
3	6715	6718	6903	7065		
4	6758	6781	6984	7122		
5	6781	6847	7055	7196		
6	6837	6920	7137	7269		
7	6883	6916	7086	7220		
8	6868	6948	7133	7235		
9	6806	6920	7102	7202		
10	6816	6957	7142	7243		
11	6834	6980	7188	7267		
12	6845	6998	7192	7272		
SUM	81474	82292	84542	86095		

	Nonfarm less manufacturing employment for the telecommunications example NFMA, for a given region					
	1970	1971	1972	1973	1974	1975
1	5275	5282	5295	5393	5413	5365
2	5279	5279	5285	5391	5393	5344
3	5336	5326	5361	5443	5436	5365
4	5403	5365	5406	5495	5479	5393
5	5439	5418	5465	5534	5540	5457
6	5489	5465	5507	5589	5588	5483
7	5463	5457	5469	5558	5570	5474
8	5429	5397	5472	5560	5558	5478
9	5380	5335	5420	5506	5486	5362
10	5400	5350	5491	5541	5511	5374
11	5411	5368	5516	5562	5525	5387
12	5427	5421	5548	5586	5531	5417
SUM	64731	64463	65235	66157	66031	64897

	1976	1977	1978	1979
1	5267	5231	5365	5527
2	5252	5237	5370	5528
3	5286	5276	5437	5575
4	5325	5332	5514	5631
5	5340	5389	5578	5696
6	5382	5442	5636	5748
7	5458	5472	5624	5727
8	5418	5475	5636	5730
9	5342	5436	5603	5686
10	5358	5468	5641	5725
11	5375	5490	5673	5758
12	5406	5527	5693	5777
SUM	64207	64776	66768	68109

Quarterly Main Telephone Gain (QTMG)

	YEAR 1954	1955	1956	1957	1958	1959	1960	1961	1962	1963	1964	1965	1966
1	249679.	358564.	423229.	377986.	164807.	317226.	353447.	177644.	313381.	285708.	361548.	404286.	462908.
2	204516.	236151.	300893.	241968.	123983.	264067.	170885.	157912.	166104.	136829.	258118.	223398.	244708.
3	294982.	382640.	392587.	295255.	308345.	383382.	298119.	301541.	359254.	336509.	475483.	509525.	507942.
4	424727.	500542.	452339.	337936.	359827.	383118.	234686.	305968.	296630.	316041.	400456.	473682.	438942.
SUM	1173904.	1477897.	1569048.	1253145.	956962.	1347793.	1057107.	943065.	1135369.	1075087.	1495605.	1610891.	1654500.

	YEAR 1967	1968	1969	1970	1971	1972	1973	1974	1975	1976	1977	1978
1	386302.	467437.	522283.	457594.	438612.	606276.	604273.	523096.	278828.	494632.	520828.	628897.
2	206038.	249421.	232433.	182076.	151339.	214223.	245344.	200434.	160309.	146937.	193675.	314386.
3	505738.	541052.	577507.	521684.	587128.	601458.	633181.	491069.	517081.	557075.	686848.	698346.
4	474880.	608599.	517563.	426037.	506291.	574168.	459256.	267300.	425497.	438487.	607449.	596196.
SUM	1552958.	1866509.	1849786.	1587391.	1683370.	1996125.	1942054.	1481899.	1381715.	1637131.	2008800.	2237825.

Quarterly U.S. Housing Starts (HOUS)

Year	1	2	3	4
1959	322.9	451.0	422.7	320.3
1960	267.2	376.0	341.5	267.4
1961	248.7	375.2	379.1	310.0
1962	274.5	439.8	398.5	350.0
1963	293.4	491.1	439.0	379.6
1964	328.3	457.1	398.7	344.8
1965	282.5	453.7	392.0	344.7
1966	273.7	391.5	290.1	209.6
1967	212.0	371.1	374.6	333.9
1968	291.7	440.8	410.7	364.3
1969	323.5	461.8	379.4	302.0
1970	255.4	388.6	400.4	389.2
1971	380.7	593.4	572.6	505.5
1972	505.2	660.5	638.1	552.7
1973	484.6	641.6	548.2	370.8
1974	318.7	456.1	336.0	226.9
1975	191.0	324.3	348.5	296.6
1976	280.8	439.3	434.3	382.9
1977	367.4	581.1	561.5	476.4
1978	302.2	511.3	459.8	387.0
1979	269.2	486.9	455.0	381.3

Source: U.S. Department of Commerce, Bureau of Census.

Quarterly Index of Industrial Production (FRB)

YEAR	1953	1954	1955	1956	1957	1958	1959	1960	1961	1962	1963	1964	1965
1	54.9667	51.4333	55.8000	60.7000	62.9000	56.3667	63.6333	68.2000	63.0667	71.0667	74.5000	79.3333	86.9000
2	55.7000	51.2333	58.1667	60.4667	62.1000	55.4000	66.7000	66.7000	65.5667	71.7667	76.4667	81.2000	88.9000
3	55.6333	51.4667	59.0667	60.1333	62.3333	58.3333	64.0000	65.6000	67.6667	72.5000	76.9667	82.5000	90.7667
4	53.1000	52.9000	60.5000	62.3000	59.7333	60.9667	64.2667	64.0000	70.0333	73.1000	78.2667	83.7000	92.6333
SUM	219.4000	207.0333	233.5334	243.6000	247.0666	231.0667	258.6000	264.5000	266.3334	288.4334	306.2001	326.7333	359.2000

YEAR	1966	1967	1968	1969	1970	1971	1972	1973	1974	1975	1976	1977	1978
1	95.2333	99.1000	104.2333	110.1667	108.9000	108.0333	115.4667	127.5333	129.8333	113.2000	127.0333	134.8000	140.8000
2	97.2667	98.7667	105.9000	110.7000	108.3333	109.0667	118.1667	129.3333	131.0333	114.2333	129.3667	138.0000	145.1000
3	98.7667	99.6667	106.9000	112.1333	108.1000	109.6667	120.6000	130.6333	131.7667	120.5000	130.9333	139.3000	147.9000
4	99.7000	102.4333	108.2667	111.7000	105.8000	111.5000	124.5333	131.4333	124.5667	123.3667	131.7333	140.3000	150.7000
SUM	390.9667	399.9667	425.3000	444.7000	431.1333	438.2667	478.7667	518.9332	517.2000	471.3000	519.0666	552.4000	584.5000

Source: Board of Governors of the Federal Reserve System

Quarterly Index of Consumer Confidence (MOOD)

YEAR	1953	1954	1955	1956	1957	1958	1959	1960	1961	1962	1963	1964	1965
1	90.7000	82.0000	93.1000	99.0000	96.6000	78.5000	93.1000	98.9000	91.1000	97.2000	94.8000	99.0000	101.5000
2	87.3000	82.9000	99.1000	98.2000	92.9000	80.9000	95.3000	92.9000	92.3000	95.4000	91.4000	98.1000	102.2000
3	84.1000	84.9000	99.4000	99.2000	88.6000	85.9000	94.5000	91.5000	93.3000	91.6000	96.2000	100.2000	103.2000
4	80.8000	87.0000	99.7000	100.2000	83.7000	90.8000	93.8000	90.1000	94.4000	95.0000	96.9000	99.4000	102.9000
SUM	342.9000	336.8000	391.3000	396.6000	361.8000	336.1000	376.7000	373.4000	371.1000	379.2000	379.3000	396.7000	409.8000

YEAR	1966	1967	1968	1969	1970	1971	1972	1973	1974	1975	1976	1977	1978
1	100.0000	92.2000	95.0000	95.1000	78.1000	78.2000	87.5000	80.8000	60.9000	58.0000	84.5000	87.5000	82.3000
2	95.7000	94.9000	92.4000	91.6000	75.4000	81.6000	89.3000	76.0000	72.0000	72.9000	82.2000	89.1000	81.5000
3	91.2000	96.5000	92.9000	86.4000	77.1000	82.4000	94.0000	71.8000	64.5000	75.8000	88.8000	87.6000	80.4000
4	88.3000	92.9000	92.1000	79.7000	75.4000	82.2000	90.8000	75.7000	58.4000	75.4000	86.0000	83.1000	73.5000
SUM	375.2000	376.5000	372.4000	352.8000	306.0000	324.4000	361.6000	304.3000	255.8000	282.1000	341.5000	347.3000	317.7000

Source: University of Michigan, Survey Research Institute

Quarterly U.S. Money Supply (M1)—Seasonally adjusted

| | *YEAR* | | | | | | | | | | | | |
	1953	1954	1955	1956	1957	1958	1959	1960	1961	1962	1963	1964	1965
1	382.700	387.300	400.500	406.700	410.600	408.200	427.800	429.000	434.500	447.500	455.500	472.000	493.500
2	385.300	388.200	402.900	407.800	410.800	412.900	431.400	428.300	438.100	449.500	460.000	476.500	497.400
3	385.900	391.900	404.600	407.900	410.900	417.000	433.600	431.800	440.600	448.600	464.400	484.300	503.100
4	386.200	395.900	405.300	409.800	408.700	422.100	430.900	432.700	444.900	451.300	469.200	490.200	511.500
SUM	1540.100	1563.300	1613.300	1632.200	1641.000	1660.200	1723.700	1721.800	1758.100	1796.900	1849.100	1923.000	2005.500

| | *YEAR* | | | | | | | | | | | | |
	1966	1967	1968	1969	1970	1971	1972	1973	1974	1975	1976	1977	1978
1	520.000	531.500	567.300	612.200	631.100	667.200	712.800	773.100	818.500	848.300	890.200	943.500	1021.600
2	526.400	539.200	578.300	618.500	639.400	683.900	726.900	784.900	829.200	863.200	908.500	966.900	1048.200
3	525.800	551.600	590.000	622.000	647.500	695.300	741.900	795.600	838.000	878.400	918.400	985.800	1068.800
4	526.400	559.800	602.000	625.600	656.000	699.800	758.800	806.000	846.800	883.800	933.200	1021.800	1094.900
SUM	2098.600	2182.100	2337.600	2478.300	2574.000	2746.200	2940.400	3159.600	3332.500	3473.700	3650.300	3918.000	4233.500

Source: Board of Governors of the Federal Reserve System

Bibliography

[numbers in brackets refer to page numbers in this book]

ABRAHAMS, B., and J. LEDOLTER (1983). *Statistical Methods For Forecasting*. New York, NY: John Wiley and Sons.

AFIFI, A. A., and S. P. AZEN (1979). *Statistical Analysis—A Computer Oriented Approach*, 2nd ed. New York, NY: Academic Press. [97]

ALMON, S. (1965). The Distributed Lag Between Capital Appropriations and Expenditures. *Econometrica* 33, 178–96. [343]

ANDERSON, O. D. (1976). *Time Series Analysis and Forecasting, The Box-Jenkins Approach*. London, England: Butterworth. [378, 409, 421]

ANDERSON, R. L. (1942). Distribution of the Serial Correlation Coefficient. *Annals of Mathematical Statistics* 13, 1–13. [409]

ANDREWS, D. F., P. J. BICKEL, F. R. HAMPEL, P. J. HUBER, W. H. ROGERS, and J. W. TUKEY (1972). *Robust Estimates of Location: Survey and Advances*. Princeton, NJ: Princeton University Press. [84, 91, 172]

ARMSTRONG, J. S. (1978). Forecasting with Econometric Methods: Folklore versus Fact. *Journal of Business* 51, 549–64. [15, 280]

ARMSTRONG, J. S. (1978). *Long-Range Forecasting: From Crystal Ball to Computer*. New York, NY: John Wiley and Sons. [15]

This book concentrates on methods for long-range forecasting that are applicable to all areas of social, behavioral, and management sciences.

ARMSTRONG, J. S., and M. C. GROHMAN (1972). A Comparative Study of Methods for Long-Range Forecasting. *Management Science* 19, 211–21.

ARTLE, R., and C. AVEROUS (1973). The Telephone System as a Public Good: Static and Dynamic Aspects. *The Bell Journal of Economics and Management Science* 4, 89–100.

ASCHER, W. (1978). *Forecasting—An Appraisal for Policy Makers and Planners*. Baltimore, MD. The John Hopkins University Press.

Intended for users of forecasting in both the public and private sectors. Examines long-range forecasting accuracy in the areas of population, economy, energy, transportation, and technology.

ASCHER, W., and W. H. OVERHOLT (1983). *Strategic Planning and Forecasting*. New York: John Wiley and Sons.

BALESTRA, P., and M. NERLOVE (1966). Pooling Cross Section and Time Series Data in the Estimation of a Dynamic Model: The Demand for Natural Gas. *Econometrica* 31, 585–612. [355]

BARR, A. J., J. H. GOODNIGHT, J. P. SALL, and J. T. HELWIG (1976). *A User's Guide to SAS 76,* Raleigh, NC: SAS Institute, Inc.

BARTLETT, M. S. (1935). Some Aspects of the Time-Correlation Problem in Regard to Tests of Significance. *Journal of the Royal Statistical Society* B 98, 536–43.

BARTLETT, M. S. (1946). On the Theoretical Specifications of the Sampling Properties of Autocorrelated Time Series. *Journal of the Royal Statistical Society* B 8, 27–41. [408]

BASS, F. M., and R. R. WITTINK (1975). Pooling Issues and Methods in Regression Analysis with Examples in Marketing Research. *Journal of Marketing Research* 12, 414–25. [355]

BAUMOL, W. J. (1972). *Economic Theory and Operations Analysis.* Englewood Cliffs, NJ: Prentice-Hall.

BECKER, R. A. and J. M. CHAMBERS (1977). GR-Z: A System of Graphical Subroutines for Data Analysis. *Proceedings of Computer Science and Statistics, Tenth Annual Symposium on the Interface.* National Bureau of Standards Special Publication 503, 409–15. [61]

BELL, D. (1976). *The Coming of Post-Industrial Society—A Venture in Social Forecasting.* New York, NY: Basic Books.

For students and researchers interested in social forecasting.

BELSLEY, D. A., E. KUH, and R. E. WELSCH (1980). *Regression Diagnostics.* New York, NY: John Wiley and Sons. [191, 349]

BHATTACHARYYA, M. N. (1974). Forecasting the Demand for Telephones in Australia. *Applied Statistics* 23, 1–10. [474]

Estimates an ARIMA model over the period from July 1962 through June 1971, in which the dependent variable is the 12-month percentage change in the number of new telephones installed and the independent variable is the 12-month percentage change in the connection charge plus annual rental.

BLOOMFIELD, P. (1976). *Fourier Analysis of Time Series—An Introduction.* New York, NY: John Wiley and Sons.

Treats time series forecasting methodologies of increasing complexity, including harmonic regression, the fast Fourier transform, complex demodulation, and spectrum analysis.

BOWERMAN, B. L., and R. T. O'CONNELL (1979). *Time Series and Forecasting.* North Scituate, MA: Duxbury Press. [113, 119, 452, 455]

A textbook for applied courses in time series and forecasting. Part II discusses the forecasting of time series described by trend and irregular components. The exponential smoothing approach to forecasting such time series is discussed there.

BOX, G. E. P. (1953). Non-Normality and Tests on Variances. *Biometrika* 40, 318–35. [90]

BOX, G. E. P. (1966). Use and Abuse of Regression. *Technometrics* 8, 625–29.

BOX, G. E. P., and D. R. COX (1964). An Analysis of Transformations. *Journal of the Royal Statistical Society* B 26, 211–52. [205].

BOX, G. E. P., and G. M. JENKINS (1976). *Time Series Analysis—Forecasting and Control, Revised Edition*. San Francisco, CA: Holden-Day. [117, 378, 394, 397, 409, 421, 431, 434, 452]

BOX, G. E. P., G. M. JENKINS, and D. W. BACON (1967). Models for Forecasting Seasonal and Nonseasonal Time Series. *In* B. Harris, ed. *Advanced Seminar on Spectral Analysis*. New York, NY: John Wiley and Sons. [474]

BOX, G. E. P., and D. A. PIERCE (1970). Distribution of Residual Autocorrelations in Autoregressive Integrated Moving-Average Time-Series Models. *Journal of the American Statistical Association* 65, 1509–26. [396]

BOX, G. E. P., and G. C. TIAO (1975). Intervention Analysis with Applications to Economic and Environmental Problems. *Journal of the American Statistical Association* 70, 70–79.

BRELSFORD, W. M., and D. A. RELLES (1981). *STATLIB—A Statistical Computing Library*. Englewood Cliffs, NJ: Prentice-Hall.

BRILLINGER, D. R. (1981). *Time Series—Data Analysis and Theory*. Expanded edition. San Francisco, CA: Holden-Day.

Deals with theoretical aspects of time series forecasting useful for graduate level courses and as reference source for researchers.

BROWN, R. G. (1959). *Statistical Forecasting for Inventory Control*. New York, NY: McGraw-Hill. [113]

BROWN, R. G. (1963). *Smoothing, Forecasting, and Prediction of Discrete Time Series*. Englewood Cliffs, NJ: Prentice Hall. [113, 117, 119]

BRUBACHER, S., and G. T. WILSON (1976). Interpolating Time Series with Applications to the Estimation of Holiday Effects on Electricity Demand. *Applied Statistics* 25, 107–16. [474]

BUTLER, W. F., R. A. KAVESH, and R. B. PLATT, eds. (1974). *Methods and Techniques of Business Forecasting*. Englewood Cliffs, NJ: Prentice-Hall. [41]

Compilation of papers in business forecasting with emphasis on microeconomic forecasting in government, industry, and academia.

CENTER for the STUDY of SOCIAL POLICY (1975). *Handbook of Forecasting Techniques*. Menlo Park, CA: Stanford Research Institute; Reproduced by the National Technical Information Service, Springfield, VA, 1975; also a two-part supplement, 1977.

Report discusses twelve methods of forecasting suitable for long-range forecasting. A supplement (in 2 parts, 1977) contains brief evaluations of seventy-three forecasting techniques. [83]

CHAMBERS, J. M., W. S. CLEVELAND, B. KLEINER, and P. A. TUKEY (1983). *Graphical Methods for Data Analysis*. Boston, MA: Duxbury Press. [83]

CHAMBERS, J. C., S. K. MULLICK, and D. D. SMITH (1971). How to Choose the Right Forecasting Technique. *Harvard Business Review* 49, 45–74.

CHAMBERS, J. C., S. K. MULLICK, and D. D. SMITH (1974). *An Executive's Guide to Forecasting*. New York, NY: John Wiley and Sons. [20, 30, 33]

A nontechnical description of forecasting aimed at practitioners who are concerned with how different forecasting techniques can be used.

CHATFIELD, C. (1980). *The Analysis of Time Series: An Introduction, 2nd Ed.* New York, NY: Chapman and Hall.

An introductory book intended to bridge the gap between theory and practice in time series analysis.

CHATFIELD, C. (1978). Adaptive Filtering: A Critical Assessment, *Journal of Operational Research Society,* 29, 891–96.

CHATFIELD, C. (1978). The Holt-Winters Forecasting Procedure. Applied Statistics 27, 264–79.

CHATFIELD, C., and D. L. PROTHERO (1973). Box-Jenkins Seasonal Forecasting: Problems in a Case Study. *Journal of the Royal Statistical Society* A 136, 295–336. [476]

CHATTERJEE, S., and B. PRICE (1977). *Regression Analysis by Example.* New York, NY: John Wiley and Sons. [191, 192]

Emphasizes informal data analysis techniques for exploring interrelationships among a given set of variables for developing regression equations.

CLEARY, J. P., and H. LEVENBACH (1982). *The Professional Forecaster.* Belmont, CA: Lifetime Learning Publications. [255, 430, 460, 461, 468]

CLEVELAND, W. S., D. M. DUNN, and I. J. TERPENNING (1978). *The SABL Seasonal Analysis Package—Statistical and Graphical Procedures.* Computing Information Service, Bell Laboratories, 600 Mountain Ave., Murray Hill, NJ 07974.

CLEVELAND, W. S., D. M. DUNN, and I. J. TERPENNING (1979). SABL—A Resistant Seasonal Adjustment Procedure with Graphical Methods for Interpretation and Diagnosis, in *Seasonal Analysis of Economic Time Series,* A. Zellner, ed. Washington, DC: U.S. Government Printing Office.

CLEVELAND, W. S., and S. J. DEVLIN (1980). Calendar Effects in Monthly Time Series; Detection by Spectrum. *Journal of the American Statistical Association* 75, 489–96.

CLEVELAND, W. S., and G. C. TIAO (1976). Decomposition of Seasonal Time Series: A Model for the Census X-11 Program. *Journal of the American Statistical Association* 71, 581–87.

COCHRANE, D., and G. N. ORCUTT (1949). Application of Least Squares to Relationships Containing Autocorrelated Error Terms. *Journal of the American Statistical Association* 44, 32–61. [229]

COHEN, M. (1976). Surveys and Forecasting, in *Methods and Techniques of Business Forecasting,* W. F. Butler, R. A. Kavesh, and R. B. Platt, eds. Englewood Cliffs, NJ: Prentice-Hall.

CONFERENCE BOARD (1978). *Sales Forecasting*. New York, NY: The Conference Board. [26]

COOPER, R. L. (1972). The Predictive Performance of Quarterly Econometric Models of the United States. *In* B. Hickman, ed., *Econometric Models of Cyclical Behavior,* 2. Conference on Research in Income and Wealth 36, New York, NY: Columbia University Press.

CYRIAX, G. R. (1981). *World Index of Economic Forecasts*. Westmead, Farnborough, England: Gower Publishing Co.

DAGUM, E. B. (1976). Seasonal Factor Forecasts from ARIMA Models. *Proceedings of the International Statistical Institute, 40th Session, Warsaw, 1975*. Warsaw: International Statistical Institute, 206–19. [135]

DAGUM, E. B. (1978). Modeling, Forecasting, and Seasonally Adjusting Economic Time Series with the X-11 ARIMA Method. *The Statistician* 27, 203–16. [135]

DAMSLETH, E., and B. H. SOLLIE (1980). Forecasting the Demand for New Telephone Main Stations in Norway by Using ARIMA Models. *In* O. D. Anderson, ed., *Forecasting Public Utilities*. Amsterdam, Netherlands: North-Holland Publishing Company.

DANIEL, C., and F. S. WOOD (1977). *Fitting Equations to Data*. New York, NY: John Wiley and Sons.

DANIELS, L. M. (1980). *Business Forecasting for the 1980's—and Beyond*. Baker Library, Reference List, No. 31, Boston, MA: Harvard Business School.

This bibliography concentrates on forecasting books, services, and a few articles published since 1972. Most of the books are briefly annotated.

DAUTEN, C. A. and L. M. VALENTINE (1978). *Business Cycles and Forecasting,* 5th ed., Cincinnati, OH: Southwestern.

A text dealing with business fluctuations, forecasting economic activity and sales, and proposals for achieving economic growth and stability.

DAVIS, B. E., G. J. CACCAPPOLO, and M. A. CHAUDRY (1973). An Econometric Planning Model for American Telephone and Telegraph Company. *The Bell Journal of Economics and Management Science* 4, 29–56.

DEVLIN, S., R. GNANADESIKAN, and J. R. KETTENRING (1975). Robust Estimation and Outlier Detection with Correlation Coefficients. *Biometrika* 62, 531–45. [191]

DHRYMES, P. J. (1971). *Distributed Lags; Problems of Formulation and Estimation,* San Francisco, CA: Holden-Day. [340]

DIXON, W. J., and M. B. BROWN (1979). *BMDP-79 Biomedical Computer Programs P-Series*. Los Angeles, CA: University of California Press. [75, 97]

DOBELL, A. R., L. D. TAYLOR, L. WAVERMAN, T. H. LIU, and M. D. G. COPELAND (1972). Telephone Communications in Canada: Demand Production, and Investment Decisions. *The Bell Journal of Economics and Management Science* 3, 175–219.

DRAPER, N. R., and H. SMITH (1981). *Applied Regression Analysis, 2nd ed*. New York, NY: John Wiley and Sons. [168, 173, 177, 191, 192, 235, 239]

DUNN, D. M., W. H. WILLIAMS, and W. A. SPIVEY (1971). Analysis and Prediction of Telephone Demand in Local Geographical Areas. *The Bell Journal of Economics and Management Science* 2, 561–76.

Paper focuses on forecasting inward and outward movement of business and residence main stations in three Michigan cities over the period 1954–1968 by using monthly models including simple trend-seasonal-irregular time series decomposition and adaptive exponential smoothing with and without exogenous variables.

DURBIN, J. (1970). Testing for Serial Correlation in Least Squares Regression When Some of the Regressors are Lagged Dependent Variables, *Econometrica* 38, 410–21.

DURBIN, J., and G. S. WATSON (1950). Testing for Serial Correlation in Least Squares Regression: I. *Biometrika* 37, 409–28. [182, 223]

DURBIN, J., and G. S. WATSON (1951). Testing for Serial Correlation in Least Squares Regression: II. *Biometrika* 38, 159–78. [182, 223]

DURBIN, J., and G. S. WATSON (1971). Testing for Serial Correlation in Least Squares Regression III. *Biometrika* 58, 1–19.

EBY, F. H., Jr. and W. J. O'NEILL (1977). *The Management of Sales Forecasting.* Lexington, MA: Lexington Books, D. C. Heath.

Provides the sales forecaster with an understanding of both the general management of the forecasting operation and of specific forecasting procedures.

ECKSTEIN, O., E. W. GREEN, and A. SINAI (1974). The Data Resources Model: Uses, Structure, and Analysis of the U.S. Economy. *International Economic Review* 15, 595–615.

ENRICK, N. L. (1979). *Market and Sales Forecasting—A Quantitative Approach.* Huntington, NY: Krieger Publishing Co.

ERICKSON, B. H., and T. A. NOSANCHUK (1977). *Understanding Data.* Toronto, Canada: McGraw-Hill-Ryerson Ltd. [57, 83]

EVERITT, B. S. (1978). *Graphical Techniques for Multivariate Data.* New York, NY: North-Holland Publishing Co.

EZEKIEL, M., and K. A. FOX (1959). *Methods of Correlation and Regression Analysis.* New York, NY: John Wiley and Sons. [211]

FAIR, R. C. (1970). *A Short-Run Forecasting Model of the U.S. Economy.* Lexington, MA: D. C. Heath.

FARRAR, D. E., and R. R. GLAUBER (1967). Multicollinearity in Regression Analysis: The Problem Revisited. *Review of Economics and Statistics* 49, 92–107. [349]

FELS, R., and C. E. HINSHAW (1968). *Forecasting and Recognizing Business Cycle Turning Points.* National Bureau of Economic Research. New York, NY: Columbia University Press.

Two papers dealing with the problem of recognizing peaks and troughs in business cycles.

FILDES, R. (1979). Quantitative Forecasting—The State of the Art: Extrapolative Models. *Journal of the Operational Research Society* 30, 691–710.

FILDES R., and D. WOOD, eds. (1978). *Forecasting and Planning*. Farnborough, England: Saxon House.

A collection of readings dealing with the application of advanced forecasting techniques in practice.

FILDES, R., D. DEWS, and S. HOWELL, editors (1981). *A Bibliography of Business and Economic Forecasting*. Westmead, Farnborough, England: Gower Publishing Co.

More than 4000 items are indexed, mostly articles from forty journals over the period 1971–1978.

FIRTH, M. (1977). *Forecasting Methods in Business and Management*. London, England: Edward Arnold Ltd.

Describes the applicability, usefulness, and limitations of a range of formal forecasting techniques for general managers. Aimed at students heading for management careers in forecasting as well as practicing managers interested in recent developments in forecasting.

FISHER, F. M. (1966). *The Identification Problem*. New York, NY: McGraw-Hill. [273, 279, 340]

FISHER, R. A. (1960). *The Design of Experiments*. 7th ed. Edinburgh, Scotland: Oliver and Boyd.

FULLER, W. A. (1976). *Introduction to Statistical Time Series*. New York, NY: John Wiley and Sons.

GEURTS, M. D., and I. B. IBRAHIM (1975). Comparing the Box-Jenkins Approach with the Exponentially Smoothed Forecasting Model Application to Hawaii Tourists. *Journal of Marketing Research,* 182–88.

GILCHRIST, W. (1976). *Statistical Forecasting*. New York, NY: John Wiley and Sons.

The author describes a number of forecasting methods including, linear trend models, growth curves, adaptive methods, and other extensions.

GEURTS, M. D., and I. B. IBRAHIM (1975). Comparing the Box-Jenkins Approach with the Exponentially Smoothed Forecasting Model Application to Hawaii Tourists, *Journal of Marketing Research* 12, 182–88. [34]

GILCHRIST, W. (1976). *Statistical Forecasting*. New York, NY: John Wiley and Sons.

The author describes a number of forecasting methods, including linear trend models, growth curves, adaptive methods, and other extensions.

GLASS, G. V., V. L. WILLSON, and J. M. GOTTMAN (1975). *Design and Analysis of Time Series Experiments*. Boulder, CO: Colorado Associated University Press.

GNANADESIKAN, R. (1977). *Methods for Statistical Data Analysis of Multivariate Observations,* New York, NY: John Wiley and Sons.

GOLDFELD, S. M., and R. E. QUANDT (1965). Some Tests for Homoscedasticity. *Journal of the American Statistical Association* 60, 539–47. [346]

GOODMAN, M. L. (1974). A New Look at Higher-order Exponential Smoothing for Forecasting. *Operations Research* 22, 880–88.

GOODMAN, M. L., and W. H. WILLIAMS (1971). A Simple Method for the Construction of Empirical Confidence Limits for Economic Forecasts. *Journal of the American Statistical Association* 66, 752–54. [249]

GRAFF, P. (1977). *Die Wirtshaftsprognose*. Tubingen, West Germany: J. C. B. Mohr.

Describes the analysis and utilization of long-term trends for forecasting. In German.

GRANGER, C. W. J. (1980). *Forecasting in Business and Economics*. New York, NY: Academic Press. [409, 414]

GRANGER, C. W. J., and O. MORGENSTERN (1970). *Predictability of Stock Market Prices*. Lexington, MA: D. C. Heath.

GRANGER, C. W. J., and P. NEWBOLD (1977). *Forecasting Economic Time Series*. New York, NY: Academic Press. [34, 280, 378, 409, 457]

Treats the analysis of economic data from the perspective of time series (ARIMA) methods and classical econometrics.

GRANGER, C. W. J., and P. NEWBOLD (1976). Forecasting Transformed Series. *Journal of the Royal Statistical Society* B 38, 189–203. [382]

GREGG, J. V., C. H. HASSELL, and J. T. RICHARDSON (1964). *Mathematical Trend Curves: An Aid to Forecasting*. ICI Monograph No. 1. Edinburgh, Scotland: Oliver and Boyd.

GROFF, G. K. (1973). Empirical Comparison of Models for Short-range Forecasting. *Management Science* 20, 22–31. [34]

GROSS, C. W., and R. T. PETERSON (1976). *Business Forecasting*. Boston, MA: Houghton Mifflin Company.

An introduction to business forecasting, with emphasis on forecasting at the firm and industry level, as opposed to aggregate economic forecasting.

HAITOVSKY, Y., and G. I. TREYZ (1972). Forecasts With Quarterly Macroeconometric Models, Equation Adjustments, and Benchmark Predictions: The U.S. Experience. *Review of Economic Statistics* 54, 317–25.

HAITOVSKY, Y., G. I. TREYZ, and V. SU (1974). *Forecasts with Quarterly Macroeconometric Models*. New York, NY: National Bureau of Economic Research.

Examines macroeconomic forecasting models in order to analyze the magnitude and source of errors in the resulting forecast.

HANNAN, E. J. (1970). *Multiple Time Series*. New York, NY: John Wiley and Sons.

HARRISON, P. J. (1965). Short-term Forecasting. *Applied Statistics* 14, 102–39. [113]

HARRISON, P. J., and C. F. STEVENS (1971). A Bayesian Approach to Short-term Forecasting. *Operational Research Quarterly* 22, 341–62.

HARRISON, P. J., and O. L. DAVIES (1964). The Use of Cumulative Sum (Cusum) Techniques for the Control of Routine Forecasts of Product Demand. *Operations Research* 12, 325–33.

HARRISON, P. J., and C. F. STEVENS (1976). Bayesian Forecasting (with discussion). *Journal of the Royal Statistical Society* B 38, 205–407.

HARTWIG, F., and B. E. DEARING (1979). *Exploratory Data Analysis*. Sage University Paper on Quantitative Applications in the Social Sciences, 07-016. Beverly Hills, CA: Sage Publications. [57, 83]

HELMER, R. A., and J. K. JOHANSSON (1977). An Exposition of the Box-Jenkins Transfer Function Analysis with Application to the Advertising-Sales Relationship. *Journal of Marketing Research* 14, 227–39.

HICKMAN, B. G. (1975). *Econometric Models of Cyclical Behavior.* New York, NY: Columbia University Press.

HILDRETH, G., and J. Y. LU (1960). *Demand Relations with Autocorrelated Disturbances*. Agricultural Experiment Station, Technical Bulletin 276. Lansing, MI: Michigan State University. [229]

HIRSCH, A. A. (1973). The B. E. A. Quarterly Model As a Forecasting Instrument. *Survey of Current Business* 53, 24–38.

HOADLEY, W. E. (1974). Reporting Forecasts to Management and the Use of Forecasts as a Management Tool, in *Methods and Techniques of Business Forecasting*, Butler et al., eds. Englewood Cliffs, NJ: Prentice-Hall.

HOAGLIN, D. C., F. MOSTELLER, and J. W. TUKEY, editors (1983). *Understanding Robust and Exploratory Data Analysis*. New York, NY: John Wiley and Sons. [57, 68]

HOCKING, R. R. (1976). The Analysis and Selection of Variables in Linear Regression. *Biometrics* 32, 1–49.

Problems of subset selection and variable analysis in linear regression are reviewed. The discussion covers the underlying theory, computational techniques, and selection criteria.

HOERL, A. E., and R. W. KENNARD (1970). Ridge Regression: Biased Estimation for Nonorthogonal Problems. *Technometrics* 12, 55–67.

An historical paper on ridge regression.

HOFF, J. (1984). *A Practical Guide to Box–Jenkins Forecasting*. Belmont, CA: Lifetime Learning Publications. [378, 409]

HOLT, C. C. (1957). *Forecasting Trends and Seasonals by Exponentially Weighted Moving Averages*. O.N.R. Memorandum No. 52. Pittsburgh, PA: Carnegie Institute of Technology. [113, 119, 450]

HOTELLING, H. (1927). Differential Equations Subject to Error and Population Estimates. *Journal of the American Statistical Association*, 22, 283–314.

HUBER, P. J. (1964). Robust Estimation of a Location Parameter. *Annals of Mathematical Statistics* 35, 73–101. [92]

HUBER, P. J. (1973). Robust Regression: Asymptotics, Conjectures, and Monte Carlo. *Annals of Statistics* 1, 799–821. [92]

INTRILIGATOR, M. D. (1978). *Econometric Models, Techniques, and Applications*. Englewood Cliffs, NJ: Prentice-Hall. [15]

JENKINS, G. M. (1979). *Practical Experience with Modeling and Forecasting Time Series*. Jersey, Channel Islands: GJ&P (Overseas) Ltd. [155, 486]

JENKINS, G. M., and D. G. WATTS (1968). *Spectral Analysis and its Applications*. San Francisco, CA: Holden-Day. [396]

JENSEN, D. (1979). General Telephone of the Northwest: A Forecasting Case Study. *Journal of Contemporary Business* 8, 19–34. [474]

JOHNSTON, J. (1972). *Econometric Methods,* 2nd edition, New York, NY: McGraw-Hill. [224, 271, 273, 349, 351, 358]

JONES, H. and B. C. TWISS (1978). *Forecasting Technology for Planning Decisions*. New York, NY: MacMillan.

A two-part book on the practice and methodology of forecasting for corporate planning.

KALLEK, S. (1978). An Overview of the Objectives and Framework of Seasonal Adjustment, in *Seasonal Analysis of Economic Time Series*, A. Zellner, ed. Washington, DC: U.S. Government Printing Office. [133]

KENDALL, M. (1975). *Multivariate Analysis, second edition*. London, England: Charles Griffin and Company, Ltd.

Describes the full range of multivariate statistical techniques, including regression analysis, with an orientation to applications.

KENDALL, M. (1976). *Time Series*. 2nd ed. London, England: Charles Griffin and Company.

KLEIN, L. R. (1971). *An Essay on the Theory of Economic Prediction*. Chicago, IL: Markham.

KLEIN, L. R. (1971). Forecasting and Policy Evaluation Using Large Scale Econometric Models: The State of the Art. *In* M. D. Intriligator, ed., *Frontiers of Quantitative Economics*. Amsterdam, Netherlands: North-Holland Publishing Company.

KLEIN, L. R., and R. M. YOUNG (1980). *An Introduction to Econometric Forecasting and Forecasting Models*. Lexington, MA: D. C. Heath and Co.

Monograph presents non-technical introduction to the Wharton quarterly forecasting model.

KMENTA, J. (1971). *Elements of Econometrics*. New York, NY: MacMillan Publishing Co. [358, 367]

KOLMOGOROV, A. N. (1941). Interpolation and Extrapolation of Stationary Random Sequences. Bulletin Moscow University. *URRS. Ser. Math. 5.*

KOYCK, L. M. (1954). *Distributed Lags and Investment Analysis*. Amsterdam, Netherlands: North-Holland Publishing Co. [340]

LARSEN, W. A., and S. J. McCLEARY (1972). The Use of Partial Residual Plots in Regression Analysis. *Technometrics* 14, 781–90. [216]

LEUTHOLD, R. M., A. J. MACCORMICK, A. SCHMITZ, and D. G. WATTS (1970). Forecasting Daily Hog Prices and Quantities: A Study of Alternative Forecasting Techniques. *Journal of the American Statistical Association* 65, 90–107.

LEVENBACH, H. (1980). A Comparative Study of Time Series Models for Forecasting

Telephone Demand. *In* O. D. Anderson, ed., *Forecasting Public Utilities*. Amsterdam, Netherlands: North-Holland Publishing Co. [414, 464]

LEVENBACH, H., and J. P. CLEARY (1981). *The Beginning Forecaster.* Belmont, CA: Lifetime Learning Publications. [109, 151, 159, 349, 429, 436]

LEVENBACH, H., and B. E. REUTER (1976). Forecasting Trending Time Series with Relative Growth Rate Models. *Technometrics* 18, 261–72.

LEVENBACH, H., W. M. BRELSFORD, and J. P. CLEARY (1983). *A STATLIB PRIMER. The Forecasting Process Through Statistical Computing*. Belmont, CA: Lifetime Learning Publications. [75, 97]

LEWIS, C. E. (1975). *Demand Analysis and Inventory Control*. Lexington, MA: Saxon House/Lexington Books.

Book contains a variety of short-term forecasting techniques, including adaptive filtering for use in production planning and control systems.

LING, R. F., and H. V. ROBERTS (1980). *User's Manual for IDA*. Palo Alto, CA: The Scientific Press. [75]

LINSTONE, H. A., and D. SAHAL, eds. (1976). *Technological Substitution—Forecasting Techniques and Applications*. New York, NY: American Elsevier.

LINSTONE, H. A., and M. TUROFF, eds. (1975). *The Delphi Method*. Reading, MA: Addison-Wesley.

LITTLECHILD, S. C. (1975). Two-part Tariffs and Consumption Externalities. *The Bell Journal of Economics* 6, 661–670.

LIU, L. (1980). Analysis of Time Series with Calendar Effects. *Management Science* 26, 106–12.

LJUNG, G. M., and G. E. P. BOX (1976). *A Modification of the Overall χ^2 Test for Lack of Fit in Time Series Models*. Technical Report 477, Department of Statistics. Madison, WI: University of Wisconsin.

LJUNG, G. M., and G. E. P. BOX (1978). On a Measure of Fit in Time Series Models. *Biometrika* 65, 297–303. [396]

McCARTHY, M. D. (1972). *The Wharton Quarterly Econometric Forecasting Model (Mark III)*. Phildadelphia, PA: University of Pennsylvania.

McGILL, R. J., J. W. TUKEY, and W. A. LARSEN (1978). Variations of Box Plots. *The American Statistician* 32, 12–16. [86, 87]

McLAUGHLIN, R. L. (1975). A New Five-Phase Economic Forecasting System. *The Journal of Business Economics*. 49–60.

McLAUGHLIN, R. L. (1979). Organizational Forecasting: Its Achievements and Limitations. *In* S. Makridakis and S. C. Wheelwright, eds., *Forecasting*, New York, NY: North-Holland Publishing Co.

McLAUGHLIN, R. L. (1962). *Time Series Forecasting*. Marketing Research Techniques Series, No. 6, Chicago, IL: American Marketing Association.

McNEES, S. K. (1975). An Evaluation of Economic Forecasts. *New England Economic Review 4,* 3–39.

McNEIL, D. R. (1977). *Interactive Data Analysis.* New York, NY: John Wiley and Sons [57, 75, 83, 97]

MABERT, V. A. (1975). *An Introduction to Short-term Forecasting Using the Box-Jenkins Methodology.* Production Planning and Control Monograph Series No. 2. Atlanta, GA: American Institute of Industrial Engineers. [378, 409]

MACAULEY, F. R. (1930). *The Smoothing of Time Series.* Cambridge, MA: National Bureau of Economic Research. [132]

MAGLIARO, A., and C. L. JAIN (1983). *An Executive's Guide to Econometric Forecasting.* Flushing, NY: Graceway Publishing Co.

MADDALA, G. S. (1971). The Use of Variance Components Models in Pooling Cross Section and Time Series Data. *Econometrica* 39, 341–58. [355]

MADDALA, G. S. (1977). *Econometrics.* New York, NY: McGraw-Hill. [358]

MAKRIDAKIS, S., and M. HIBON (1979). The Accuracy of Forecasting: An Empirical Investigation (with Discussion). *Journal of the Royal Statistical Association* A 142, 97–145. [34]

MAKRIDAKIS, S., and S. C. WHEELWRIGHT (1977). Adaptive Filtering: An Integrated Autoregressive/Moving Average Filter for Time Series Forecasting. *Operational Research Quarterly* 28, 425–37.

MAKRIDAKIS, S., and S. C. WHEELWRIGHT (1977). Forecasting: Issues and Challenges for Marketing Management, *Journal of Marketing,* 24–38.

MAKRIDAKIS, S., and S. C. WHEELWRIGHT (1978). *Interactive Forecasting—Univariate and Multivariate Methods.* San Francisco, CA: Holden-Day. [15, 75, 113, 119, 378, 409]

A basic description of a wide range of both univariate and multivariate time series and regression forecasting methodologies. Has practical use as a user's manual for the SIBYL/RUNNER interactive forecasting computer programs.

MAKRIDAKIS, S., and S. C. WHEELWRIGHT, and V. E. McGEE (1983). *Forecasting—Methods and Applications.* Santa Barbara, CA: Wiley-Hamilton.

A comprehensive text describing the fundamentals of a wide range of forecasting methodologies, including numerous examples and sample problems.

MAKRIDAKIS, S., and S. C. WHEELWRIGHT, eds. (1979). *Forecasting.* New York, NY: North-Holland Publishing Co.

A special issue of *Management Science* dealing with current forecasting methodologies for both practitioners and researchers.

MAKRIDAKIS, S., and S. C. WHEELWRIGHT, editors (1982). *Handbook of Forecasting—A Manager's Guide.* New York, NY: John Wiley and Sons. [34, 486]

Outlines management requirements for forecast techniques for preparing forecasts, discussion of important issues in forecasting applications, and managing the forecasting function.

MALLOWS, C. L. (1979). Robust Methods—Some Examples of Their Use. *The American Statistician* 33, 179–84. [90]

MARTINO, J. P. (1972). *Technological Forecasting for Decision making*. New York, NY: American Elsevier.

MARTINO, J. P. (1972). *An Introduction to Technological Forecasting*. London, England: Gordon and Breach Science Publishers.

MASS, N. J. (1975). *Economic Cycles: An Analysis of Underlying Causes*. Cambridge, MA: Write-Allen Press.

Describes a series of system dynamics models (of the Forrester-type) used to explore the basic factors underlying short-term and long-term cyclical movements in the economy.

MEHRA, R. K. (1979). Kalman Filters and Their Applications to Forecasting. *In* S. Makridakis and S. C. Wheelwright, eds., *Forecasting*. New York, NY: North-Holland Publishing Co.

A survey of Kalman filtering techniques and their applications to forecasting. Includes a case study on forecasting of stock earnings for 49 U.S. companies, as well as numerous references.

MICHAEL, G. C. (1979). *Sales Forecasting*. American Marketing Association Monograph Series No. 10. Chicago, IL: American Marketing Association.

Oriented to business decision-makers who have a need of forecasts, and would like to be more comfortable in choosing the most effective forecasting technique. A Forecasting Decision Matrix is provided as a useful tool in comparing major forecasting techniques.

MILNE, T. E. (1975). *Business Forecasting—A Managerial Approach*. London, England: Longman Group Ltd.

Aimed at the nontechnical or managerial reader interested in practical aspects of forecasting. Covers a wide range of approaches including subjective methods.

MONTGOMERY, D. C., and L. A. JOHNSON (1976). *Forecasting and Time Series Analysis*. New York, NY: McGraw-Hill Book Co. [111, 112, 113, 119, 452, 455]

Covers the full range of short-term forecasting methods, including exponential smoothing methods, the Box-Jenkins approach, and Bayesian forecasting. Computer programs for several exponential smoothing methods are included.

MOORE, G. H. (1975). The Analysis of Economic Indicators. *Scientific American* 232 (January), 17–23.

A general account on the use of economic indicators.

MOORE, G. H., and J. SHISKIN (1972). *Early Warning Signals for the Economy in Statistics*. J. M. Tanur et al., eds. San Francisco, CA: Holden-Day. [140]

MOORE, R. W. (1978). *Introduction to the Use of Computer Packages for Statistical Analyses*. Englewood Cliffs, NJ: Prentice-Hall.

MOSTELLER, F., and J. W. TUKEY (1977). *Data Analysis and Regression*. Reading, MA: Addison-Wesley Publishing Co. [109, 163, 165, 192, 193]

MULLER, M. E. (1980). Aspects of Statistical Computing: What Packages for the 1980's Ought to Do. *American Statistician* 34, 159–68.

MUNDLAK, Y. (1978). On the Pooling of Time Series and Cross Section Data. *Eonometrica* 46, 69–85. [355]

NAYLOR, T. H., T. G. SEAKS, and D. W. WICHERN (1972). Box-Jenkins Methods: An Alternative Approach to Econometric Models. *International Statistical Review* 40, 123–37.

NELSON, C. R. (1972). The Prediction Performance of the FRB-MIT-PENN Model of the U.S. Economy, *American Economic Review* 62, 902–17.

NELSON, C. R. (1973). *Applied Time Series Analysis for Managerial Forecasting*. San Franciso, CA: Holden-Day. [378, 409, 421]

NEWBOLD, P. (1979). Time-Series Model Building and Forecasting: A Survey. *In* S. Makridakis and S. C. Wheelwright, eds., *Forecasting*. New York, NY: North-Holland Publishing Company.

Reviews Box Jenkins methodology, surveys important developments since 1970, and indicates the range of applications of the procedures in practical forecasting problems.

NEWBOLD, P., and C. W. J. GRANGER (1974). Experience with Forecasting Univariate Time Series and the Combination of Forecasts. *Journal of the Royal Statistical Society* A 137, 131–46. [34]

NEWBOLD, P., and G. V. REED (1979). The Implication For Economic Forecasting of Time Series Model Building Methods. *In* O. D. Anderson, ed., *Forecasting,* New York, NY: North-Holland Publishing Company.

NIE, N. H., C. H. HALL, J. G. JENKINS, K. STEINBRENNER, and D. H. BENT (1975). *SPSS: Statistical Package for the Social Sciences,* 2nd ed. New York, NY: McGraw-Hill Book Co. [75, 97]

NIE, N. H., C. H. HALL, M. N. FRANKLIN, J. G. JENKINS, K. J. SOURS, M. J. NORUSIS, and V. BEADLE (1980). *SCSS: A User's Guide to the SCSS Conversational System.* New York, NY: McGraw-Hill Book Co. [75]

O'DONOVAN, T. M. (1983). *Short Term Forecasting, An Introduction to the Box-Jenkins Approach.* New York, NY: John Wiley and Sons.

OLIVER, F. R. (1964). Methods for Estimating the Logistic Growth Function. *Applied Statistics* 13, 57–66.

PACK, D. J. (1977). Revealing Time Series Interrelationships. *Decision Sciences* 8, 377–402.

PANKRATZ, A. (1983). *Forecasting with Univariate Box-Jenkins Models.* New York, NY: John Wiley and Sons. [378]

PARKER, G. G. C., and E. L. SEGURA (1971). How to Get a Better Forecast, *Harvard Business Review,* 99–109.

PARSONS, L. J., and R. SCHULTZ (1976). *Marketing Models and Econometric Research.* New York, NY: North-Holland Publishing Co. [288]

PHLIPS, L. (1974). *Applied Consumption Analysis*. New York, NY: American Elsevier. [268, 288]

PIERCE, D. A. (1980). A Survey of Recent Developments in Seasonal Adjustment. *The American Statistician* 34, 125–34.

PINDYCK, R. S., and D. L. RUBINFELD (1976). *Econometric Models and Economic Forecasts*. New York, NY: McGraw-Hill. [270, 273, 288, 324, 340, 409]

Treats single- and multiple-equation models and time series models in detail.

PLATT, R. B. (1974). Statistical Measures of Forecast Accuracy, in *Methods and Techniques of Business Forecasting*, Butler et al., eds. Englewood Cliffs, NJ: Prentice-Hall.

PLOSSER, C. I. (1979). Short-Term Forecasting and Seasonal Adjustment. *Journal of the American Statistical Association* 74, 15–24. [135]

POPKIN, J., ed. (1977). *Analysis of Inflation: 1965–1974*. Cambridge, MA: Ballinger Publishing Company for NBER.

PRIESTLEY, M. B. (1971). Fitting Relationships between Time Series. *Bulletin of the International Statistical Institute* 44, 295–324. [464]

PROTHERO, D. L., and K. F. WALLIS (1976). Modelling Macroeconomic Time Series (with Discussion). *Journal of the Royal Statistical Society* A 139, 468–86.

QUENOUILLE, M. H. (1949). Approximate Tests of Correlation in Time Series. *Journal of the Royal Statistical Society* B 11, 68–84. [409]

QUENOUILLE, M. H. (1957). *The Analysis of Multiple Time Series*. London, England: Griffin.

RAO, C. R. (1973). *Linear Statistical Inference and Its Applications*. New York, NY: John Wiley and Sons. [177]

RAO, P., and R. L. MILLER (1977). *Applied Econometrics*. Belmont, CA: Wadsworth Publishing Co.

RAO, V. R. and J. E. COX, Jr. (1978). *Sales Forecasting Methods: A Survey of Recent Developments*. Cambridge, MA: Marketing Science Institute.

Review of sales forecasting literature, with particular focus on recent methodological developments. Also contains a semi-annotated bibliography of articles and books on sales forecasting.

REID, D. J. (1971). Forecasting in Action: A Comparison of Forecasting Techniques in Economic Time Series. *Proceedings, Joint Conference of the Operations Research Society*, Long-Range Planning and Forecasting. [34]

RENTON, G. A., ed. (1975). *Modelling the Economy*. London, England: Heinemann Educational Books.

ROHLFS, J. (1974). A Theory of Interdependent Demand for a Communications Service. *The Bell Journal of Economics and Management Science*. 5, 16–37.

ROBERTS, H. V. (1974). *Conversational Statistics*. Hewlett-Packard University Business Series. Palo Alto, CA: The Scientific Press. [202]

RYAN, T. A., B. L. JOINER, and B. F. RYAN (1976). *Minitab Student Handbook*. North Scituate, MA: Duxbury Press. [75, 97]

SAMUELSON, P. (1978). *Economics*, 9th ed. New York, NY: McGraw-Hill. [284]

SAS (1980). *SAS/ETS User's Guide, Econometric and Time Series Library*. Cary, N.C.: SAS Institute, Inc. [75, 97]

SEARLE, S. R. (1977). *Linear Models*. New York, NY: John Wiley and Sons.

SEBER, G. F. (1977). *Linear Regression Analysis*. New York, NY: John Wiley and Sons. [177]

SHISKIN, J. (1957). *Electronic Computers and Business Indicators*. Cambridge, MA: National Bureau of Economic Research. Occasional Paper 57.

SHISKIN, J., and H. EISENPRESS (1957). Seasonal Adjustments by Electronic Computer Methods. *Journal of the American Statistical Association* 52, 415–49.

SHISKIN, J., and C. H. LAMPART (1976). Indicator Forecasting, in *Methods and Techniques of Business Forecasting*, W. F. Butler, R. A. Ravesh, and R. B. Platt, eds. Englewood Cliffs, NJ: Prentice-Hall.

A detailed account on the use of indicators in economic forecasting.

SHISKIN, J., and G. H. MOORE (1967). *Indicators of Business Expansions and Contractions*. Cambridge, MA: National Bureau of Economic Research. [140, 148]

SHISKIN, J., A. H. YOUNG, and J. C. MUSGRAVE (1967). *The X-11 Variant of Census Method II Seasonal Adjustment Program*. Technical Paper No. 15, U.S. Department of Commerce, Bureau of the Census. Washington, DC: U.S. Government Printing Office. [133]

SILK, L. S., and M. L. CURLEY (1970). *Business Forecasting—With a Guide to Sources of Business Data*. New York, NY: Random House. [147]

SLUTSKY, E. (1937). The Summation of Random Causes as the Source of Cyclic Processes. *Econometrica* 5, 105–46. [378]

SOBEK, R. S. (1973). A Manager's Primer on Forecasting. *Harvard Business Review* 5, 1–9. [140]

SQUIRE, L. (1973). Some Aspects of Optimal Pricing for Telecommunications. *The Bell Journal of Economics and Management Science* 4, 515–25.

STEKLER, H. O. (1970). *Economic Forecasting*. New York, NY: Praeger.

STRALKOWSKI, C. M., R. E. DEVOR, and S. M. WU (1974). Charts for the Interpretation and Estimation of the Second-Order Moving Average and Mixed First-Order Autoregressive-Moving Average Models. *Technometrics* 16.

SULLIVAN, W. G., and W. W. CLAYCOMBE (1977). *Fundamentals of Forecasting*. Reston, VI: Reston Publishing Company. [15, 122–123, 455]

Enables the nonstatistical reader to apply popular forecasting techniques. Includes listings of computer programs that implement some of the simpler methodologies covered in the text.

SWAMY, P. A. V. B. (1970). Efficient Inference in a Random Coefficient Regression Model. *Econometrica* 38, 311–23. [355]

TAYLOR, L. D. (1975). The Demand for Electricity: A Survey. *The Bell Journal of Economics* 6, 74–110.

TAYLOR, L. D. (1980). *Telecommunications Demand: A Survey and Critique*. Cambridge, MA: Ballinger Press. [315]

THEIL, H. (1958). *Economic Forecasts and Policy*. Amsterdam, Netherlands: North-Holland Publishing Company.

THEIL, H. (1966). *Applied Economic Forecasting*. Amsterdam, Netherlands: North-Holland Publishing Company.

THOMAS, J. J., and K. F. WALLIS (1971). Seasonal Variation in Regression Analysis. *Journal of the Royal Statistical Society* A 134, 57–72.

THOMOPOULOS, N. T. (1980). *Applied Forecasting Methods*, Englewood Cliffs, NJ: Prentice-Hall.

An introductory book on forecasting (primarily time series analysis) for practitioners and students in business administration, management science, and industrial engineering.

THOMPSON, H. E., and G. C. TIAO (1971). An Analysis of Telephone Data: A Case Study of Forecasting Seasonal Time Series. *The Bell Journal of Economics and Management Science* 2, 515–41. [474]

Develops ARIMA models for forecasting monthly telephone inward and outward movements in Wisconsin for the period from January 1951 through October 1966.

TOMASEK, O. (1972). Statistical Forecasting of Telephone Time Series. *Telecommunications Journal* 39, 1–7. [474]

Develops ARIIMA models for forecasting monthly inward movement of telephone main stations in Montreal over the period 1961–70.

TRIGG, D. W. (1964). Monitoring a Forecasting System. *Operational Research Quarterly* 15, 271–74. [253]

TRIGG, D. W., and A. G. LEACH (1967). Exponential Smoothing with Adaptive Response Rate. *Operational Research Quarterly* 18, 53–59. [113]

TUKEY, J. W. (1977). *Exploratory Data Analysis*. Reading, MA: Addison-Wesley Publishing Co. [57, 83, 86, 88, 109]

VELLEMAN, P. F., and D. C. HOAGLIN (1981). *Applications, Basics, and Computing for Exploratory Data Analysis*. Boston, MA: Duxbury Press. [57, 75, 83, 97]

VELLEMAN, P. F., J. SEAMAN, and J. E. ALLEN (1977). *Evaluating Package Regression Routines*. Technical Reprint 877/008-010. Ithaca, NY: New York State School of Industrial and Labor Relations, Cornell University.

VON RABENAU, B., and K. STAHL (1974). Dynamic Aspects of Public Goods: A Further Analysis of the Telephone System. *The Bell Journal of Economics and Management Science* 5, 651–69.

WALL, K. D., A. J. PRESTON, J. W. BRAY, and M. H. PESTON (1975). Estimates of a Simple Control Model of the UK Economy. *In* G. A. Reaton, ed., *Modelling the Economy*. London, England: Heinemann.

WALLIS, W. A., and H. V. ROBERTS (1966). *Statistics, A New Approach*. New York, NY: The Free Press. [235]

WALSH, J. E. (1962). *Handbook of Nonparametric Statistics*. Princeton, NJ: Van Nostrand Co. [202]

WECKER, W. E. (1979). Predicting the Turning Points of a Time Series, *Journal of Business* 52, 35–50. [429]

WELLENIUS, B. (1970). A Method for Forecasting the Demand for Urban Residential Telephone Connections. *Telecommunication Journal* 37.

Develops a model for forecasting the residential demand for telephones in Santiago, Chile as a function of income.

WHEELWRIGHT, S. C., and D. G. CLARKE (1976). Corporate Forecasting: Promise and Reality, *Harvard Business Review* 54, 40–64.

WHEELWRIGHT, S. C., and S. MAKRIDAKIS (1980). *Forecasting Methods for Management, 3rd ed.* New York, NY: John Wiley and Sons. [15, 20, 22, 30, 34, 113, 245, 486]

For the practitioner who seeks to better understand the wide range of forecasting methods and their advantages and disadvantages.

WHITTLE, P. (1963). *Prediction and Regulation by Linear Least-Squares Methods*. London, England: English Universities Press. [378]

WINTERS, P. R. (1960). Forecasting Sales by Exponentially Weighted Moving Averages. *Management Science* 6, 324–42. [113, 119, 450]

WOLD, H. (1954). *A Study in the Analysis of Stationary Time Series*. (First edition, 1938). Uppsala, Sweden: Almquist and Wiksell. [378]

WONNACOTT, R. J., and T. H. WONNACOTT (1979). *Econometrics, second edition*. New York, NY: John Wiley and Sons. [273, 347]

WOOD, D., and R. FILDES (1976). *Forecasting for Business*. New York, NY: Longman.

Aimed for the practicing manager and student of forecasting interested in the tools and framework necessary to produce a good forecast without becoming a statistician/econometrician.

YOUNGER, M. S. (1979). *Handbook for Linear Regression*. North Scituate, MA: Duxbury Press.

YULE, G. U. (1926). Why Do We Sometimes Get Nonsense Correlations Between Time Series? A Study In Sampling and The Nature of Time Series. *Journal of the Royal Statistical Society* B 89, 1–64.

YULE, G. U. (1927). On a Method of Investigating Periodicities in Disturbed Series, with

Special Reference to Wolfer's Sunspot Numbers. *Philosophical Transactions* A 226, 267–98. [378]

ZELLNER, A. (1962). An Efficient Method of Estimating Seemingly Unrelated Regressions and Tests for Aggregation Bias. *Journal of the American Statistical Association* 57, 348–68. [201]

ZELLNER, A., and F. PALM (1974). Time Series Analysis and Simultaneous Equation Econometric Models. *Journal of Econometrics* 2, 17–54. [355]

Index

About the Authors

Hans Levenbach (Ph.D. in Statistics, University of Toronto) is President of Core Analytics, Inc., in New Jersey. Formerly Division Manager of the Analytical Support Center for AT & T, he has been intimately involved in forecasting research for many years. He has published and lectured extensively on the subject.

James P. Cleary is Division Controller of Marketing/Sales for AT & T Information Systems. He has served as Division Manager of Revenue Management and Forecasting for the New York Telephone Company, and he developed and taught forecasting training courses at the Bell System Center for Technical Education in Illinois. Mr. Cleary holds a B.S. in Electrical Engineering from Rensselaer Polytechnical Institute and an M.B.A. from Hofstra University.

Also Available from Lifetime Learning Publications

A Practical Guide to BOX-JENKINS Forecasting
by John C. Hoff, Ph.D.

This book presents the popular Box-Jenkins method of time series forecasting in terms that the statistical layman can understand. Emphasis is placed on applications of the Box-Jenkins method, not on theory. The author offers numerous practical examples and graphics, employs a self-teaching approach, and points out common problems. Also includes information on the use of existing computer software to implement the method and emphasizes model building throughout. 316 pages • 6½ x 9¼″ • hardbound • $30.00

A STATLIB Primer
The Forecasting Process Through Statistical Computing
by Hans Levenbach, Ph.D., William M. Brelsford, Ph.D., and James P. Cleary, M.B.A.

A handbook for practicing forecasters using AT&T's STATLIB package of statistical computer programs. Designed to accompany *The Beginning Forecaster* and *The Professional Forecaster*. 180 pages • 6½ x 9¼″ • paperback • $16.95

Computer-Aided Multivariate Analysis
by A. A. Afifi, Ph.D., and Virginia Clark, Ph.D., both UCLA

This handbook is for investigators who are doing multivariate analyses with their data and who need to fully understand the results. It uses real-life data and strongly emphasizes the use of standard computer packages. The authors discuss in detail issues of data entry, data screening, data reduction, and data analysis. They stress practical techniques and include numerous graphics and detailed applied examples. No sophisticated mathematics are required to understand the explanations. 360 pages • 6½ x 9¼″ • hardbound • $32.00

The Beginning Forecaster
The Forecasting Process Through Data Analysis
by Hans Levenbach, Ph.D., and James P. Cleary, M.B.A.

Describes reliable, computer-based forecasting methods as practiced in leading American corporations. Emphasis is placed on establishing a *process* for effective forecasting; selecting appropriate techniques; *analyzing data* before building models; using *robust/resistant methods*; performing *residual analysis*. Integrated coverage with practice and review materials prepares forecasters for professional practice. 372 pages • 6½ x 9¼″ • hardbound • $31.50

The Professional Forecaster
The Forecasting Process Through Data Analysis
by James P. Cleary, M.B.A., and Hans Levenbach, Ph.D.

Describes advanced techniques of statistical forecasting, emphasizing *data analysis* and powerful computer-based techniques. Important features include: the forecasting *process* rather than disconnected techniques; computer-graphical methods for analyzing, summarizing, and displaying data; selecting appropriate forecasting and analytical techniques; how to evaluate and present forecasts; management of the forecasting process. Some of the newest techniques included are based on pioneering developments at Bell Laboratories and Bell Operating Companies. 402 pages • 6½ x 9¼″ • hardbound • $31.50

Order your free 15-day trial copy today!

Please send me the books I have indicated. I'll return any books I don't want within the 15-day trial period without further obligation. For those I keep, I'll pay the amounts shown plus my local sales tax and a small charge for postage and handling. Offer valid in U.S. and Canada only.

___ Save Money. Enclosed is my check or money order. Publisher pays postage and handling. Same return privileges, full refund guaranteed. (Residents of CA, KY, MA, MI, NC, NJ, NY, and WA please add sales tax.)

___ Credit Cards.
Charge my ___ VISA ___ MasterCard ___ American Express

Card # _____ Exp.Date _____

___ Bill me.

Sign here: Your order cannot be processed without your signature.

Signature _____

___ A PRACTICAL GUIDE TO BOX-JENKINS FORECASTING (0-534-02719-9) @ $30.00

___ A STATLIB PRIMER (0-534-97936-X) @ $16.50

___ COMPUTER-AIDED MULTIVARIATE ANALYSIS (0-534-02786-5) @ $32.00

___ THE BEGINNING FORECASTER (0-534-97975-0) @ $31.50

___ THE PROFESSIONAL FORECASTER (0-534-97960-2) @ $31.50

___ THE MODERN FORECASTER (0-534-03361-X) @ $31.50

NOTE: Prices are subject to change without notice. If your order totals $100 or more, please attach a company purchase order or enclose at least 25% partial payment.

Detach and mail to:

Lifetime Learning Publications • 10 Davis Drive • Belmont, CA 94002

(415) 595-2350 Ext. 219